# KARL MARX
# FREDERICK ENGELS
## COLLECTED WORKS
### VOLUME
9

# KARL MARX
# FREDERICK ENGELS

## COLLECTED
## WORKS

LAWRENCE & WISHART

LONDON

# KARL MARX
# FREDERICK ENGELS

## Volume
## 9

**MARX AND ENGELS: 1849**

1977

LAWRENCE & WISHART

LONDON

This volume has been prepared jointly by Lawrence & Wishart Ltd., London, International Publishers Co. Inc., New York, and Progress Publishers, Moscow, in collaboration with the Institute of Marxism-Leninism, Moscow.

Editorial commissions:
GREAT BRITAIN: Jack Cohen, Maurice Cornforth, Maurice Dobb, E. J. Hobsbawm, James Klugmann, Margaret Mynatt.
USA: James S. Allen, Philip S. Foner, Dirk J. Struik, William W. Weinstone.
USSR: for Progress Publishers—N. P. Karmanova, V. N. Sedikh, M. K. Shcheglova, Y. V. Yeremin; for the Institute of Marxism-Leninism—P. N. Fedoseyev, L. I. Golman, A. I. Malysh, M. P. Mchedlov, A. G. Yegorov, V. Y. Zevin.

ISBN 0 85315 354 X

*Printed in the Union of Soviet Socialist Republics*

# Contents

## KARL MARX AND FREDERICK ENGELS
### ARTICLES FROM THE *NEUE RHEINISCHE ZEITUNG*
March 6-May 19, 1849

*March*

### March-April

*April*

## May

KARL MARX AND FREDERICK ENGELS

ARTICLES AND STATEMENTS

May-July 1849

## APPENDICES

## NOTES AND INDEXES

## ILLUSTRATIONS

TRANSLATORS:

JACK COHEN: Articles 70-73

CLEMENS DUTT: Articles 1, 5, 8, 9, 12-14, 18, 19, 23-25, 29-31, 36, 39, 41, 48, 53, 54, 65, 74, 80, 85, 88, 92, 98, 99, 102-05, 107, 108, 110-12, 115, 120-22, 124, 129-36, 140, 142-45; Appendices 2, 3, 5, 6, 8-11, 13-18, 21-25

MICHAEL HUDSON: Articles 34, 35, 37, 38, 40, 42-47, 49, 50, 82, 84, 86, 87, 89-91, 93-97, 100, 101

DOROTHY JAESCHKE: Articles 106, 109, 113, 114, 116-19, 123, 125, 126, 128

HUGH RODWELL: Articles 51, 52, 55, 57-60

BARBARA RUHEMANN: Articles 20-22, 26-28, 32, 33, 62-64, 66-69, 75-79, 81

SALO RYAZANSKAYA: Articles 61, 83, 127, 138, 139, 141; Appendix 12

BARRIE SELMAN: Articles 2-4, 6

CHRISTOPHER UPWARD: Articles 137, 146; Appendices 1, 4, 7, 19, 20

JOAN and TREVOR WALMSLEY: Articles 7, 10, 11, 15-17

# Preface

Volume 9 of the *Collected Works* of Karl Marx and Frederick Engels is the last in the group of three volumes which show the activities of the founders of scientific communism during the revolutionary years 1848 and 1849. It covers the period from March 6, 1849 to August 1849.

Like volumes 7 and 8, this volume consists in the main of articles written by Marx and Engels for the *Neue Rheinische Zeitung,* an organ of German and European democracy, and in particular of its revolutionary proletarian wing. It was during the last stage of the revolution, when the objective preconditions for uniting the proletariat and creating a proletarian mass party began to take shape, that the proletarian trend of the paper edited by Marx and Engels became especially pronounced. During this period the *Neue Rheinische Zeitung* played an increasingly important role as the legal centre which directed the activity of the Communist League members and inspired the revolutionary actions of the proletarian masses.

Marx's and Engels' strategy and tactics during the revolution were based on their materialist conception of the dialectic of social change and on the theoretical generalisation of the experience gained by the masses in the struggle. Their activities in that period, as in the earlier stages of the revolution, demonstrated the organic unity of revolutionary theory and practice. In the circumstances that arose in the spring of 1849, they brought a new element into their tactics: still seeking to rally all revolutionary forces against the advancing counter-revolution, they tried to promote an independent political line for the working class, and to differentiate it from the general

democratic movement by creating a political proletarian mass
organisation.

The distinctive features of the spring and summer of 1849 were
the rearguard actions fought by the revolutionary forces and the
increasing attacks made by the counter-revolutionaries on the
people's democratic achievements. The reactionary ruling circles in
Austria, Prussia and Tsarist Russia were seeking to revive the Holy
Alliance in order to crush the revolutionary movement with the help
of the French monarchists and the British bourgeois and aristocratic
oligarchy. At the same time the people everywhere continued to
defend their political and social rights. Proletarian and democratic
organisations became increasingly active in spite of police persecutions. A national liberation struggle was waged in Hungary and
many parts of Italy. Peasants' uprisings took place in Slovakia, Galicia
and the Bukovina. A new clash between proletarian and petty-
bourgeois democrats on the one hand and the counter-revolutionary
bourgeoisie on the other was imminent in France. All this led Marx
and Engels to expect that a new revolutionary surge would soon take
place in Europe, Germany included (see, for instance, this volume,
p. 57).

They pinned their hopes on the French proletariat taking the
revolutionary initiative, for they thought it would be able to repel any
attack by international counter-revolution. They expected the
working class to play a major part in the next stage of the
bourgeois-democratic revolution and that this would make it possible
to extend and consolidate democratic achievements vital to the
proletariat, and to carry the revolutionary process further and
transform it into a proletarian revolution. Writing about the workers
of the Rhine Province Engels observed that "the present movement
is only the prologue to another movement a thousand times more
serious, in which the issue will concern their own, the workers', most
vital interests" (see this volume, p. 449). Thus the course of events in
1848 and 1849 helped them shape their ideas about the relations of
the bourgeois-democratic and proletarian stages of the revolution.
These ideas form part of the Marxist theory of "permanent
revolution", which Marx and Engels were to formulate more
explicitly and fully later on the basis of analysing the lessons of these
events.

Despite the increasingly counter-revolutionary climate in Germany, the militant spirit and revolutionary optimism of their articles
in the *Neue Rheinische Zeitung* continued unabated. The paper
constantly called upon the masses to remain vigilant and to fight on
against the counter-revolution.

It was the altered balance of class forces in the spring of 1849, the treachery of the liberal bourgeoisie, which became more and more evident, and the vacillation of the petty-bourgeois democrats, which led Marx, Engels and their comrades in the Communist League to do everything they could to ensure the ideological and political independence of the proletariat, and its leading role in the revolutionary struggle. They took practical steps to create a working-class political party embracing the whole of Germany, whose core was to be the Communist League—a task which Marx and Engels had put forward already at the beginning of the revolution. They took into account the fact that the months of revolutionary struggle had brought about changes in the political consciousness of the most advanced section of the German workers, that the German workers were beginning to free themselves from the influence of petty-bourgeois ideas and that the labour movement was overcoming its limitations and disunity. Events were destroying the narrow framework of the craft guilds and turning them towards politics. The Workers' Fraternity and other German workers' organisations were becoming politically active. There was a tendency to unite the workers' associations and to set up a single German workers' organisation with social as well as political aims. Marx and Engels were eager to play their part in forming this German workers' organisation. They did all they could to strengthen the Cologne Workers' Association, to establish contacts between it and other workers' associations and to call a Workers' Congress of the whole of Germany (see this volume, pp. 502-03).

On April 14, 1849, Marx, Engels and their associates, supported by the most class-conscious section of the workers, resigned from the Rhenish District Committee of Democrats in order to set up a new and "closer union of the workers' associations" consisting of like-minded people (see this volume, p. 282). Soon afterwards the Cologne Workers' Association under their leadership decided to establish relations with the union of German workers' associations and to withdraw from the Union of the Democratic Associations of the Rhine Province (see this volume, p. 494). However, according to Marx and Engels the ideological, political and organisational separation from the petty-bourgeois democrats did not mean that the working class should refuse to take part in concerted actions with members of the democratic movement. On the contrary, they constantly stressed that all progressive forces must unite more closely in the struggle against the counter-revolution. But they considered that in the given situation united action could not be achieved within the framework of a single organisation.

Marx's work *Wage Labour and Capital*, which is published in this volume, played an important part in preparing the German workers ideologically for setting up an independent political party. The work is based on lectures given by Marx at the German Workers' Society in Brussels in December 1847. He had been prevented from publishing it at the time by the outbreak of the February revolution in France. It was printed in the *Neue Rheinische Zeitung* in April 1849 as a series of leading articles. In these articles Marx emphasised in particular the class nature of the objectives set forth in the newspaper. In his short preface to the series Marx wrote: "Now, after our readers have seen the class struggle develop in colossal political forms in 1848, the time has come to deal more closely with the economic relations themselves on which the existence of the bourgeoisie and its class rule, as well as the slavery of the workers, are founded" (see this volume, p. 198).

*Wage Labour and Capital* shows how far economic theory had been worked out by Marx at the end of the 1840s.

In this work Marx examines the nature of the production relations in bourgeois society, which are based on the exploitation of wage labour. He points out that capital and wage labour are mutually interdependent, and on the other hand he emphasises the antagonistic nature of these relations and the radical opposition between the interests of capitalists and workers. He shows that capital comes into being only at a definite stage of social development, and that capitalist society is therefore a historical, transient phenomenon. Bourgeois economists for the most part defined "capital" as a sum of material objects and resources, or accumulated labour. In contrast to this superficial view Marx maintained that the transformation of material objects or accumulated labour into capital presupposes definite social relations. Marx writes—and this has become a classical definition of *capital* in Marxist political economy: "*Capital*, also, is a social relation of production. It is a *bourgeois production relation*, a production relation of bourgeois society" (see this volume, p. 212).

*Wage Labour and Capital* marks an important step in making clear the economic basis of capitalist exploitation. By means of vivid examples Marx shows that the value produced by the worker exceeds the value of the means of subsistence which he receives in the form of wages, and that this excess is the source of the capitalist's profit. After examining various aspects of the problem of wages, Marx states an important law, namely that even under the most favourable circumstances for the worker the relative share of wages in the social product falls compared with the share appropriated by the capitalist. Profit and wages stand in inverse proportion to one another. Marx concludes that the growth of capital and the development of the productive forces in bourgeois society were bound to lead to the increasing exploitation of the wage-workers.

So long as the capitalist mode of production continues, the working class cannot free itself from the oppressive system of wage labour. Marx stressed that as social wealth and the productivity of labour increase in bourgeois society, the proletariat forges for itself "the golden chains by which the bourgeoisie drags it in its train" (see this volume, p. 221).

*Wage Labour and Capital* was written at a time when Marxist political economy had not yet arrived at its mature scientific formulation. In this work Marx still uses the terms "labour as a commodity", "value of labour" and "price of labour", which he took over from the English classical economists, though he gave these terms a new meaning. In 1891, when Engels prepared this work for a mass edition, he changed throughout the term "labour as a commodity" to "labour power as a commodity" etc. All these changes are given in footnotes in this volume. In the Preface to Volume II of *Capital*, Engels wrote that in working out the theory of surplus value in the 1850s Marx showed that "it is not labour which has a value. As an activity which creates value it can no more have any special value than gravity can have any special weight, heat any special temperature, electricity any special strength of current. It is not labour which is bought and sold as a commodity, but labour *power*. As soon as labour power becomes a commodity, its value is determined by the labour embodied in this commodity as a social product. This value is equal to the labour socially necessary for the production and reproduction of this commodity" (Karl Marx, *Capital*, Vol. II, Moscow, 1974, pp. 18-19).

*Wage Labour and Capital* marks an important stage in the working out of a proletarian political economy. And at the same time it exhibits to a marked degree Marx's talent for popularising and explaining complicated economic problems to workers in a language which they can understand. The work greatly helped to spread the ideas of scientific communism among the working class.

*Wage Labour and Capital* as well as other articles and reports on current political questions written by Marx and Engels for the *Neue Rheinische Zeitung* provided material for political discussions in the workers' associations and helped to make the German workers class conscious. The importance of the paper as a centre which united the forces of the revolutionary proletariat and explained and propagated the programme and tactical principles of the Communist League, was constantly growing. But the victory of the counter-revolution, and the fact that the *Neue Rheinische Zeitung* was forced to

cease publication and Marx and Engels were compelled to leave
Prussia cut short their intensive activity and prevented them from
putting into practice their plan for creating a workers' mass
party.

Marx and Engels expected the liberation struggle of the oppressed
nationalities to play a significant role in the revolutionary strategy of
the proletariat. They stressed the importance of Poland's liberation
for the European democratic movement and constantly returned to
the history of Poland's partition and subjugation by the Prussian
monarchy, the Austrian Empire and Russian Tsarism (see the article
"Posen"). They warmly welcomed the national liberation movements
of the Italian and Hungarian peoples. The renewed military
operations of the Piedmontese against Austria in the spring of 1849
were regarded by the *Neue Rheinische Zeitung* as a new indication
that the revolution was continuing to develop and as a serious blow at
the Habsburg monarchy which was now obliged to wage a war on
two fronts, against both Hungary and Italy.

Engels analysed the military campaign in Northern Italy in the
articles "The War in Italy and Hungary" and "The Defeat of the
Piedmontese" and in a series of reports printed under the heading
"From the Theatre of War" in the section "Italy". These articles,
which express the author's sympathy for the Italian people and call
upon them to throw off the Austrian yoke, contain many shrewd
observations on the specific features of revolutionary national
liberation wars and the conditions required for winning them. In his
article "The Defeat of the Piedmontese" Engels writes: "A nation
that wants to conquer its independence cannot restrict itself to the
*ordinary* methods of warfare" (see this volume, p. 171). In order to
gain victory it has to turn the war into a genuinely revolutionary
war supported by the masses of the people.

The reason for the reverse suffered by the Piedmontese army was,
according to Engels, above all the policies of the liberal and monarchical groups in Piedmont, which were strongly opposed to the
transformation of the war into a truly popular war, for they were
afraid that this might lead to a revolutionary upsurge and thus
undermine their own rule. "There is only one means to counter the
treachery and cowardice of the Government: revolution," Engels
pointed out (see this volume, p. 151). The defeat of the Piedmontese
put the last revolutionary strongholds in Italy, the republics of
Venice and Rome, in a very difficult position. Only a European, and
above all a French, revolutionary outbreak could, as Engels wrote,
save the situation.

Hungary was another centre where, in the opinion of Marx and Engels, a revolutionary conflagration might start which could spread to the whole of Europe. The Hungarian liberation struggle entered a new phase at that time. The heroic people's army, directed by Kossuth's revolutionary government, defied the armed forces of the Habsburg monarchy. In the spring of 1849 the Hungarian troops started their successful counter-offensive.

Marx and Engels watched the developments in the Hungarian revolutionary war closely and with great sympathy. In February 1849, at Marx's request, Engels began to write military and political surveys of the Hungarian events. Most of them were published under the heading "From the Theatre of War" in the section "Hungary" of the *Neue Rheinische Zeitung*. The first articles of this series are published in Volume 8 of this edition; the remainder form a significant part of this volume. Engels' article "Hungary", which generalises and partly sums up his analysis of the Hungarian revolutionary struggle, was published in the last issue of the *Neue Rheinische Zeitung* on May 19, 1849 (see this volume, pp. 455-63).

This series reveals Engels' remarkable talent in military matters. On the basis of Austrian Army Bulletins and reports printed in official Austrian and in German conservative and liberal newspapers, which as a rule were pro-Austrian—that is, on the basis of sources containing very tendentious and contradictory information—Engels, by critically sifting and comparing facts, was able to give a realistic account of the military operations. Closely following the course of events, he created a true and exact, though not a detailed (from the sources available to him this was quite impossible) picture showing the main features of the war. Moreover, many of these surveys (for instance "The Military Reports of the *Kölnische Zeitung*") contained sharp polemical remarks directed at the enemies of the Hungarian revolution, and also exposed the lies disseminated by the German chauvinistic newspapers. Engels' military reports, masterpieces which passionately defended the just cause of embattled Hungary, did much to spread the truth about the Hungarian national liberation struggle in Germany.

Even when the Austrian counter-revolutionary army, which had occupied a substantial part of Hungary, was still conducting offensive operations and the German conservative press was triumphantly announcing that Austria's final victory was imminent, Engels, assessing the military situation with great acuity, observed that the Hungarian revolutionary forces had sufficient resources not only for defence but also for launching a decisive counter-offensive. This prediction, like many others made by Engels in the military sphere, proved true. The April counter-offensive of the Hungarian army, as Engels noted in several of his articles, clearly revealed the genuinely revolutionary and popular nature not only of the war the Hungarians were waging, but also of their way of conducting military operations. Mobilisation of all national forces to repulse the invaders, energy and mobility, well-concerted action of the regular troops and the widespread guerilla movement, and the fact that the enemy was attacked not only at the front but also in the rear— these were the positive features mentioned by Engels in his analysis of the Hungarian campaign. "The entire might of all the 36 million Austrians has been frustrated and the victorious army which in Welden's words 'amazed half Europe' has been balked by the daring and enthusiasm of a small nation of barely five million people," he wrote in the article "Hungarian Victories". "The imperial forces are learning once again in Hungary the lesson they were taught at Jemappes and Fleurus 50 years ago: it is unwise to make war on revolution" (see this volume, p. 349).

When comparing the Austrian and Hungarian military systems Engels emphasised that the former exemplified the clumsiness, the mechanical drill and the stereotyped tactics peculiar to the armed forces of the feudal absolute monarchies, whereas the Hungarians demonstrated the mobility, initiative and tactical versatility, as well as the ability to take quick resolute decisions and to engage in daring manoeuvres, which are characteristic of a popular army welded together in the fire of a revolution. In his article "War in Hungary" Engels wrote, "The Magyars, though inadequately drilled and armed, oppose everywhere the most subtle calculation, the most masterly use of the terrain, the clearest overall view of the situation and the most daring and swift execution to the indolent and mindless but well-drilled mass of the Austrian armies. Superiority in genius is here doing battle with superiority in numbers, weapons and arms drill" (see this volume, p. 232). In its morale, in unity of the front and rear and support from the masses of the people, the Hungarian army far surpassed its enemy. Engels had a high opinion of the political and military leaders of the Hungarian revolution, of Kossuth and his associates, of the volunteers from Austria and especially of Polish commanders, like Bem and Dembiński, who chose to take part in the revolutionary war.

Engels considered that the strength of the Hungarian revolution stemmed from the progressive social and political transformation which had been carried out in the country, i.e. the abolition of many hitherto existing feudal institutions, the introduction of agrarian reforms and the deposition of the Habsburg dynasty. "The

Hungarians' first measure was to carry out a social revolution in their country, to abolish feudalism," Engels wrote in the article "Hungary" (see this volume, p. 463). Hungary, he said, showed once again that the national liberation movement acquired both strength and stability when together with the fight for independence there was the radical elimination of all feudal relics from the social and political structure.

The abolition of feudal obligations and the other measures which the leaders of the Hungarian revolution carried through in the interest of the peasantry, said Engels, not only ensured that the Hungarian peasants supported the revolution and played an active part in it, but also aroused sympathy for the Magyar struggle among the peasantry in various Slav areas of the Austrian Empire, in particular among the Slovaks, the Poles of Galicia and the Western Ukrainians in the Bukovina. At the end of April 1849 Engels wrote: "Fresh support for the Magyars, which just now, on the eve of their probable victory, is of the greatest significance, is *the Polish peasant rising* which is about to break out in Galicia" (see this volume, p. 345). In another report he observed that the Slovaks joined the Hungarians, after the latter had "abolished the feudal burdens of the Slovak peasants and made a number of concessions with regard to language and nationality" (see this volume, p. 390).

One of the most important indications of the growing anti-feudal struggle in the Slav areas of Austria was the peasant movement among the Ukrainians in the Bukovina which was led by Lucian Kobylica. Engels welcomed the struggle of the peasants against the nobility in this "most remote corner of the united monarchy" as a symptom of an impending peasant war throughout the Habsburg Empire, and noted the ties which existed between the peasant leaders and the Hungarian revolutionaries (see this volume, p. 289).

The successes of the Hungarian revolutionary army weakened the hold of the Austrian ruling circles on the subjugated Slav nationalities (Czechs, Croats, Serbs of the Voivodina etc.) in the Austrian Empire. By lies and false promises the Habsburgs had been trying to set one nationality against the other so as to use them as tools in the fight against the revolutionary movements in Hungary and Italy. Engels hoped that the further development of the Hungarian war would lead to changes in the national movements of these peoples and that the pro-Austrian elements would be pushed aside and the progressive forces would prevail, thus transforming these movements from reserve armies of the Austrian counter-revolution and of Tsarism into allies of revolutionary Hungary and of the European revolution as a whole. In his articles he cited facts to demonstrate that the Czechs and Southern Slavs did indeed have revolutionary leanings, sympathised with the Magyars and were growing more and more dissatisfied with the military despotism of the Austrian ruling classes and their bureaucratic and centralising tendencies. It was in this light that the people in the Slav areas regarded the Constitution which was imposed on the "united and indivisible Austrian monarchy" by Francis Joseph on March 4, 1849, and in which the earlier promises of autonomy were cynically flouted. In his brilliant denunciatory article "Military Dictatorship in Austria" (which has reached us in manuscript) Engels wrote in this connection: "The wrath previously felt only by the Germans and Magyars at the Austrian habit of gaining victory by cowardly acts of treachery, and after the victory surpassing in barbarity the most brutal bandits, this wrath was now shared by the Slavs as well. They were ensnared by the prospect of a 'Slav Austria', they were made use of to win victory in Italy and Hungary, and by way of thanks they are now being subjected again to the old Metternich whip" (see this volume, p. 105). In a number of articles, particularly in "From the Theatre of War.—The Confused Situation in Serbia" (see pp. 144-47) Engels quotes newspaper reports about an imminent revolutionary uprising in Bohemia which had prompted the Government to declare a state of siege in Prague; about the declining prestige of the Right-wing Czech leaders and the growing influence of the supporters of a Czech-German-Hungarian revolutionary alliance; and about the tendency observed in members of the Croatian and Serbian national movements to establish closer relations with the Magyars.

But at the same time Engels criticised the Right wing of the Serbian, Croatian and Slavonian movements which was still intent on union with the Habsburgs and on creating an autonomous Slav state within the framework of the Austrian Empire, although the Austrian ruling clique had thrown off its mask and had openly shown its hostility to Slav national interests (see this volume, pp. 307-10). The national movement of the Southern Slavs did not manage at the time to shake off the domination of these Right-wing sections, which were accomplices of the Austrian counter-revolution. This was partly the fault of the Hungarian leaders, who refused to recognise the national demands of the Serbs and other Slavs incorporated in Hungary under the administrative division in force at the time. Almost to the end of the revolution, the Hungarian Government pursued a national policy based mainly on the principle of Magyarisation and underestimation of the national aspirations of the other nationalities. Only on July 28, 1849, when the Hungarian revolutionary Government was about to fall, did it officially proclaim equality of rights for all the nationalities inhabiting the country.

Marx and Engels considered that the consolidation of the European reactionary forces and the attempts to form an Austro-Russian-Prussian counter-revolutionary alliance spelt danger not only to the Hungarian but also the European revolution. They considered that the impending armed intervention by Tsarist Russia in Hungary was fraught with grave danger (see for example "The Third Party in the Alliance", "The Tsar and His Subordinate Knyazes" etc.). Engels' hopes were never realised that the Hungarian revolutionary army would extend its operations into Austria, and that a fresh revolutionary conflagration would occur in Austria itself before Tsarist troops could come to the aid of the Habsburg monarchy. Owing to the defeat of the revolutionary and democratic forces in the other countries, the Hungarian national liberation movement, despite the successes it achieved in the spring of 1849, could not withstand the onslaught of the joint forces of the counter-revolution, and in the beginning of August 1849 the Hungarian revolution was crushed.

Marx and Engels pressed for an intensification of the struggle for a united democratic German republic brought about by a democratic transformation of the existing backward and divided petty states. They strongly opposed plans for the unification of Germany "from above", dominated by junker Prussia or feudal Austria, and were against the Prussianisation of Germany.

The main obstacle to the progressive development of Germany was, in their view, the counter-revolutionary Hohenzollern monarchy in Prussia, the bulwark of the most conservative sections—the aristocracy, the bureaucracy and the military—of the old society, which endeavoured to stifle the revolution completely and to re-establish the pre-revolutionary absolutist regime in a slightly refurbished form and masked by the "granted" Constitution. The Neue Rheinische Zeitung exposed the counter-revolutionary schemes of the Prussian ruling clique and the reactionary court camarilla in a number of articles, for example, "Government Provocations" and "The Counter-Revolutionary Plans in Berlin". Predicting the further course of development in Prussia, Engels wrote that one of the ultimate aims of the Prussian reactionaries was to set up a dictatorship of the sabre and to revise the limited Constitution of December 5, 1848, so as to make it even more conservative. Their intention was "by new dictated measures to get rid of the troublesome fetters which even the martial-law Charter of December 5 still imposed on our counter-revolution" (see this volume, p. 370).

The anti-democratic Bills introduced by the Brandenburg-Manteuffel Government in Prussia and designed to abolish freedom of assembly and association and freedom of the press and restore the former Prussian patriarchal laws were sharply attacked in Marx's articles "Three New Bills", "The Hohenzollern General Plan of Reform" and "The Hohenzollern Press Bill". Not a single case of coercion and arbitrary police rule escaped exposure in the *Neue Rheinische Zeitung* (see "Dissolution of the Second Chamber", "Longing for a State of Siege", "Counter-Revolutionary Offensive and Victory of the Revolution", "The New Martial-Law Charter" etc.).

The Prussian kings and their myrmidons were branded by Marx and Engels as hangmen of the liberation movement not only in Prussia but in the whole of Germany. Marx called them "*the royal terrorists*" who "are in practice brutal, disdainful and mean, in theory cowardly, secretive and deceitful, and in both respects *disreputable*" (see this volume, p. 453). He emphasised that to pursue a counter-revolutionary policy directed against the people was well-established tradition in the house of Hohenzollern. And about Frederick William II, he wrote in the article "The Deeds of the Hohenzollern Dynasty": "It is well known that in 1792 he entered into a coalition with Austria and England to suppress the glorious French Revolution and invaded France" (see this volume, p. 419). The history of rise of this Prussian dynasty, which became firmly established by means of plunder, treachery and violence, is narrated by Marx with biting sarcasm.

In a number of articles published in this volume — "Draft Address of the Second Chamber", "The Debate on the Address in Berlin", "Sitting of the Second Chamber in Berlin, April 13", "The Debate on the Law on Posters" — Engels deals with the proceedings in the Second Chamber of the Prussian Diet which was convoked on the basis of the "granted" Constitution of December 5, 1848, after the Prussian coup d'état. He exposes the attempts of the Government to consolidate the counter-revolutionary regime by means of the Diet, and then proceeds to criticise the members of the Left opposition, i.e. the liberals and democrats. Engels is indignant because the opposition, including the extreme Left, fail to defend the democratic rights of the people and "moderate their claims to the same extent as those of the Right increase theirs", thus revealing their lack of political principles and their compliant attitude (see this volume, p. 136). For they think that it is possible by parliamentary and con-

stitutional methods to achieve that which in the existing situation
can only be achieved by revolutionary means, by the use of arms.
"Instead of adopting an extra-parliamentary position in the
parliament, the only honourable one in such a Chamber, they make
one concession after another to parliamentary expediency; instead
of ignoring the constitutional point of view as far as possible, they
actually seek an opportunity of coquetting with it for the sake of
peace" (p. 136). The wavering and indecision of the Left wing in the
German Assembly at Frankfurt were also unreservedly condemned
by Marx and Engels (see Marx's articles "The March Association"
and "The Frankfurt March Association and the *Neue Rheinische
Zeitung*"). They saw it as dangerous collusion with the counter-
revolution.

Along with their criticism of the constitutional delusions of the
bourgeois and petty-bourgeois democrats, Marx and Engels outlined
the principles of truly revolutionary parliamentary tactics. The
democratic forces should use parliaments—even those composed
mainly of reactionary deputies—to expose the intrigues of the ruling
circles and to mobilise the people against them. They should
combine parliamentary forms of struggle with extensive non-
parliamentary mass action, for the latter is the main thing in the fight
against counter-revolutionary attacks and in the defence of the
people's democratic achievements. And they should recognise that
the decisive role in this struggle belongs to the proletariat, a class
which, as Engels said, "by its very position ... is revolutionary" and is
the main danger to the counter-revolutionary order (see this volume,
p. 326).

The events which followed very quickly confirmed Marx's and
Engels' opinion of the groundlessness of constitutional illusions. The
Prussian Government, which deemed that oppositional views were
being too strongly expressed in the Second Chamber of the Prussian
Diet, summarily dissolved it on April 27, 1849.

The bourgeois-democratic revolution in Germany now entered its
final phase, which was marked by mass action in defence of the
imperial Constitution drawn up by the Frankfurt National Assembly
and rejected by the King of Prussia and the counter-revolutionary
governments of the other German states.

According to Marx and Engels, the imperial Constitution could
not as such provide a programme or a banner for the proletariat and
the revolutionary democrats. As to the question of German
unification, the Constitution not only reflected the readiness of the
liberal, Prussophile majority of the Frankfurt National Assembly to
resort to compromise but also retained the monarchical form of

government. Marx and Engels had been warning for a long time that the anti-revolutionary policy of compromise pursued by the liberals in the National Assembly would end ingloriously, with the dissolution of the Assembly by the counter-revolutionary forces as soon as they felt that they no longer needed it as a protection against the pressure of the popular movement. "On the monument to be erected at the site of its wretched activity," said the article "Vienna and Frankfurt", "the wayfarer will read: 'Perished through its own fault, through cowardice, professorial stupidity and chronic meanness, amid in part the revengeful derision, and in part the complete indifference of the people'" (see this volume, p. 48). In the articles "A Prussian Kick for the Frankfurt Assembly" and "A New Prussian Kick for the Frankfurt Assembly" Marx and Engels depicted the complete political helplessness of the liberals and moderate democrats in the Frankfurt Parliament and their inability to repulse the reaction and to defend their own creation, the imperial Constitution.

Although Marx and Engels clearly understood the limitations of this Constitution, they emphasised the revolutionary nature of the popular movement that came to its defence. The defence of the Constitution was in fact a fight to preserve the still surviving achievements of the revolution, for though the Constitution was couched in extremely moderate terms, it nevertheless proclaimed a number of civil liberties and paved the way to overcoming the country's political fragmentation. Engels wrote: "The people regard every step, however small, towards the unification of Germany as a step towards abolition of the petty sovereigns and liberation from the oppressive burden of taxation" (see this volume, p. 378). In a series of articles ("News from Southern Germany", "The Prussian Army and the Revolutionary Uprising of the People", "The Approaching Revolution", "The Uprising in Elberfeld and Düsseldorf", "The Uprising in the Berg Country", "Elberfeld" etc.) the editors of the Neue Rheinische Zeitung greeted those who had fought, weapons in hand, in Saxony, the Rhine Province and South-West Germany, spoke of their fighting spirit and examined the democrats' chances of victory, and at the same time they denounced the murderous action of the punitive expeditions and the treachery of the moderate bourgeoisie. The fact that the armies in the Palatinate and Baden went over to the insurgents was in their eyes a reassuring sign, of great significance for the prospects of the revolution (see this volume, p. 399).

Marx and Engels hoped that the campaign for the imperial Constitution would develop into a national uprising, which, spreading through the whole of Germany, would merge with the

Hungarian revolution, the national liberation struggle of the Italian people and the revolutionary action of the French proletariat, to form one mighty stream. Although Marx and Engels did not agree with the political principles and tactics of the petty-bourgeois leaders of the movement in defence of the Constitution, they supported it with all the means at their disposal. Engels and other members of the Communist League took part in the Elberfeld uprising, and later fought in the insurgent army of Baden and the Palatinate against the counter-revolutionary troops.

But the German petty-bourgeois leaders proved incapable of solving revolutionary tasks. Marx and Engels tried in vain to persuade them to act more resolutely and in particular to induce the Left-wing deputies of the National Assembly to summon the revolutionary army of Baden and the Palatinate to Frankfurt, and thus to transfer the main battlefield to the centre of Germany. The uprisings in defence of the imperial Constitution lacked central direction, were isolated from one another and remained localised. They were brutally put down by the counter-revolutionary troops. The last centres of the movement in Baden and the Palatinate were suppressed in July 1849.

The Prussian Government had wanted for a long time to find a suitable opportunity to settle accounts with the *Neue Rheinische Zeitung*. During the May uprisings of 1849 the angry voice of the newspaper was particularly irksome to the powers that be. As the Chartist *Democratic Review* wrote, the newspaper proclaimed "in every line 'war to the knife' against his Prussian kingship, and all the oppressors and betrayers of the German people" (see this volume, p. 513).

In order to put an end to the *Neue Rheinische Zeitung*, the Government took advantage of Marx not being a Prussian citizen to expel him from Prussia, and began reprisals against the other editors. The last issue of the paper, printed in red, appeared on May 19, 1849. In it Marx summed up the newspaper's relentless fight for the revolutionary cause. He stressed the paper's role as harbinger of the militant consolidation of the revolutionary forces, defender of working-class interests and herald of the principles of proletarian internationalism (see the article "The Summary Suppression of the *Neue Rheinische Zeitung*"). He reminded his readers of the newspaper's solidarity with those who fought in the proletarian uprising in Paris and, addressing the men behind the police persecution, said: "*Was not the essence of the June revolution the essence of our paper?*" (see this volume, p. 453). The *Neue Rheinische Zeitung* had defended the democratic and national interests of the German people with equal fortitude and consistency. Marx proudly wrote, "We have saved the revolutionary honour of our country" (see this volume, p. 454).

The address to the workers of Cologne concludes thus: "In bidding you farewell the editors of the *Neue Rheinische Zeitung* thank you for the sympathy you have shown them. Their last word everywhere and always will be: *emancipation of the working class!*" (see this volume, p. 467).

After the suppression of the *Neue Rheinische Zeitung,* Marx and Engels used every opportunity to write for the surviving democratic press in the same revolutionary spirit. Several of their articles and statements published in this volume were written for the German democratic papers which were still able to appear.

In his article "The Revolutionary Uprising in the Palatinate and Baden" Engels answered the attempts of the German conservative press to blacken the revolutionaries fighting there. After refuting false accusations, Engels pointed out that the revolutionary struggle in South-West Germany was a component part of the European revolutionary movement. "The Palatinate and Baden," he wrote, "will stand on the side of freedom against slavery, of revolution against counter-revolution, of the people against the sovereigns, of revolutionary France, Hungary and Germany against absolutist Russia, Austria, Prussia and Bavaria" (see this volume, p. 476).

The sketch "Repudiation", written by Engels after the end of the military campaign in Baden and the Palatinate, was aimed at several petty-bourgeois German emigrants in Switzerland who tried to cast aspersions on one of the proletarian units of the insurgent army, a unit in which Engels himself had fought.

Marx's article "The 13th of June", which can also be found in this section, is of special importance. It discusses the political crisis in France which was bound up with the opposition of the Mountain—a petty-bourgeois party—against the Government and President Louis Bonaparte, who in violation of the Constitution had sent an army to Italy to crush the Roman Republic. The leaders of the Mountain, refusing more resolute measures at this crucial moment, called upon the masses to take part in an unarmed demonstration. Marx, who was in Paris at the time, saw the demonstrators being dispersed by troops.

Anticipating in this article the detailed analysis of these events which he was to give in *The Class Struggles in France,* Marx showed that the fiasco of the "parliamentary uprising" was the logical outcome of the French petty-bourgeois democrats' inconsistencies, which could be traced right back to the anti-proletarianism which the leaders, for instance Ledru-Rollin, had displayed during the rising of the Paris workers in June 1848. "... June 13, 1849 is only the retaliation for June 1848. On that occasion the proletariat was deserted by the 'Mountain', this time the 'Mountain' was deserted by the proletariat" (see this volume, pp. 478-79). Marx regarded the events of June 13, 1849 as a severe blow to the European revolutionary movement as a whole. The defeat suffered by the French petty-bourgeois democrats helped consolidate the political monopoly of the conservative, monarchist forces in France and, in the last analysis, it paved the way for the counter-revolutionary Bonapartist coup d'état of December 2, 1851.

The Appendices in this volume contain documents illustrating Marx's and Engels' participation in the work of various democratic and proletarian organisations. These give an idea of how Marx and Engels directed the activities of the Cologne Workers' Association, and of how their associates fought sectarian and splitting elements. This section also contains material about the Congress of the Workers' Associations of the Rhineland called in connection with the planned Congress of all the German Workers' Associations—to which Marx and Engels attached great importance, since it marked a new stage in the creation of a mass proletarian party. Also included are documents relating to the persecution of Marx and Engels by the Prussian authorities, and to the legal proceedings against the *Neue Rheinische Zeitung* and its editors, as well as comments of the workers' and democratic press in Germany and England on the closing down of the *Neue Rheinische Zeitung* and Marx's expulsion from Prussia. The police inspector's notification of Marx's expulsion from Paris in the summer of 1849 shows that the harassment of Marx continued and that this time it was organised by the French bourgeois government. All these documents throw light on the situation in which Marx and Engels worked during the last months of the revolution.

Nearly all revolutionary movements in Europe were defeated in the summer of 1849. The reasons which led to this defeat were pretty thoroughly examined by Marx and Engels in many of the articles published in volumes 7 to 9 of this edition. Again and again they had warned that unless the revolutionary forces succeeded in bringing about a radical change in the course of events, the swing over of a considerable section of the European bourgeoisie to the counter-revolutionary camp and the vacillation of the petty-bourgeois democrats would be fatal to the bourgeois-democratic revolution. In 1848-49 the bulk of the people, including the workers, had not yet reached a sufficient degree of political independence and ideological maturity to enable them ultimately to change the direction of social development in favour of the revolution.

However owing to the intrinsic laws governing revolutionary processes in general, as Marx and Engels observed later, the events of 1848 and 1849 influenced the historical process not only in this particular revolutionary period, but also at subsequent stages. The revolutions of 1848 and 1849 left unsolved a number of social and political tasks which remained, however, on the agenda of history. These revolutions, moreover, brought about significant changes in the social consciousness of various classes of society.

The years 1848 and 1849 were of special importance for the future development of Marxism. They confirmed the correctness and viability of its main conclusions and provided material for its further enrichment. On the other hand, none of the doctrinaire and sectarian trends in the revolutionary movement was able to stand the test of revolutionary reality, and the collapse of their illusions, antiquated traditions and utopian doctrines was one of the positive results of the revolution. The defeat of the revolutionary movement could shake neither the methodological basis of the Marxist theory, nor the political ideas and the strategic and tactical principles which Marx and Engels had put forward. For they were truly scientific conclusions drawn from progressive social processes which were actually taking place and which, though at that time they manifested themselves merely as tendencies of social development, later increasingly succeeded in forcing their way into history. Lenin was perfectly justified in saying that "the tactics of Marx in 1848 were *correct* ... they and only they really provided reliable, firm and unforgettable lessons for the proletariat" (Lenin, *Collected Works*, Vol. 15, p. 47).

The strategy and tactics worked out by Marx and Engels in 1848 and 1849 is an invaluable asset of the revolutionary labour movement of many countries. Many times has recourse been made—and it will continue to be made—to the lessons of that period.

\* \* \*

This volume contains not only the writings of Marx and Engels which were published in Volume 6 of the Russian and German editions of their *Collected Works*, but also many articles and documents discovered as a result of research carried out in the USSR and the GDR during the last few years. A total of 102 articles and reports, amounting to nearly one half of this volume, were only recently published as part of Volume 43 of the Second Russian Edition of the *Works* of Marx and Engels.

Of the 146 articles forming the main section of the volume, 140 appear in English for the first time and this is noted on each occasion at the end of the translation. Only *Wage Labour and Capital*, "The Deeds of the Hohenzollern Dynasty", "Counter-Revolutionary Offensive and Victory of the Revolution", "The Summary Suppression of the *Neue Rheinische Zeitung*", "Hungary" and "To the Workers of Cologne" have been previously published in English. Apart from a passage which appeared in the *Democratic Review*, the Appendices consist entirely of material not previously published in English. All the texts have been translated from the German except where otherwise stated.

Since it has not always been possible to determine whether a given article was written by Marx or by Engels, the author's name at the end of the article appears only where it has been definitely established which one of them wrote the article in question.

The titles of the articles are taken, wherever possible, from the tables of contents printed in the *Neue Rheinische Zeitung*. Those supplied by the editors of the present edition are in square brackets. If a periodical from which Marx and Engels quote is not available, references to other publications in which the material in question was also published are given in footnotes and also in the index of quoted and mentioned literature.

The volume was compiled and the preface and notes written by Velta Pospelova and edited by Lev Golman (Institute of Marxism-Leninism of the CC CPSU). The name index, the index of quoted and mentioned literature and the index of periodicals were prepared by Irina Shikanyan with the help of Evgenia Dakhina and Natalia Lapitskaya. For the reader's convenience, there is a glossary of geographical names which, in addition to the form generally used in the German press of the time, gives their modern equivalents. The glossary was prepared by Yury Vasin and the subject index by Vladimir Sazonov (Institute of Marxism-Leninism of the CC CPSU).

The translations were made by Jack Cohen, Clemens Dutt, Michael Hudson, Dorothy Jaeschke, Hugh Rodwell, Barbara Ruhemann, Barrie Selman, Christopher Upward and Joan and Trevor Walmsley (Lawrence and Wishart) and Salo Ryazanskaya

(Progress Publishers) and edited by Richard Abraham, Maurice
Cornforth, Sheila Lynd, Margaret Mynatt (Lawrence and Wishart),
Salo Ryazanskaya, Margarita Lopukhina, Vladimir Pavlov and Maria
Shcheglova (Progress Publishers) and Norire Ter-Akopyan, scien-
tific editor (Institute of Marxism-Leninism of the CC CPSU).

The volume was prepared for the press by the editor Margarita
Lopukhina and the assistant editor Natalia Kim (Progress Publishers).

# KARL MARX
## and
# FREDERICK ENGELS

## ARTICLES FROM
## THE *NEUE RHEINISCHE ZEITUNG*

### March 6-May 19, 1849

1

Vierteljähriger Abonnementspreis in Köln 1 Thlr.
7½ Sgr., bei allen preußischen Postanstalten 1 Thlr.
17 Sgr. — Im Auslande wende man sich, in Bezug auf die betreffenden Postzeitungen in Landes an
S. Thomas, 71 Gutheron-Street, Strand, in Paris
an B. Thomas, 38 Rue Vivienne, und an L. Hartot, 3 Rue Jean Jacques Rousseau.

Inferionen werden mit 18 Pf. die Petitzeile oder
deren Raum berechnet
Auslands, Annahme und Abgabe frankierter Briefe
gratis.
Nur frankierte Briefe werden angenommen.
Expedition Unter Hutmacher Nro 17.

# Neue
# Rheinische Zeitung
## Organ der Demokratie.

№ 239.   Köln, Mittwoch, den 7. März.   1849.

## THE STATE OF TRADE[1]

*Cologne*, March 6. *An Englishman is never more unhappy than when he does not know what to do with his money.* Therein lies the secret of all grandiose speculations, all profit-making enterprises, but it is also the secret of all bankruptcies, all financial crises and commercial depressions.

In 1840, 1841 and subsequent years, it was the new Asian markets, besides the customary commerce with the European continent, which claimed a special share of English export trade. Manufacturers and exporters had every reason to greet Sir Henry Pottinger[2] on the Manchester stock exchange with loud cheers. But the good times quickly passed. Canton, Bombay and Calcutta soon overflowed with unsalable goods, and capital, which no longer found any outlet in that direction, for a change once more sought application inside the country; it was poured into railway construction and so opened up a field for speculation in which the latter was soon rampant to a quite unprecedented extent.

According to a conservative estimate, the total sum invested in the enterprises could be put at 600 million and it would perhaps have gone still higher if the failure of the potato harvest in England, Ireland and many regions of the Continent, and further the high price of cotton, and as a result of both the reduced sale of manufactured goods, as well as, finally, the excessive railway speculation, had not caused the Bank of England on October 16, 1845 to raise the bank rate by one-half per cent.

In view of the superstitious fear in which the Britisher holds the omnipotence of his bank, this slight rise in the bank rate or, in other words, this lack of confidence on the part of the bank directors, at

once affected the existing level of activity, so that a general mood of
dejection set in, and the apparent prosperity was immediately followed by the restriction of credit and numerous bankruptcies. Consequently one of those great commercial crises, like those of 1825 and
1836, would have immediately developed if the repeal of the Corn
Laws[3] that followed soon afterwards had not suddenly come to the
aid of the falling confidence, and once more stimulated the spirits
of the entrepreneurs.

For the commercial world expected so much from the immediate
consequences of this great measure that it found it easy to forget
about the tribulations which had just overtaken it. The settlement of
the Oregon conflict which promised a continuation of the hitherto
extremely flourishing trade with America, and the British victories in
the Punjab[4] which ensured peace in Hindustan, played their part, of
course, in a revival of spirits. And although the bad harvest of 1845
was followed by a similar one in 1846, although everywhere the
reserves of former times had to be drawn upon and a credit for
business purposes involved paying 12-15 per cent, despite all this, all
the spinning mills of Lancashire and Yorkshire were set in continual
motion as though crop failures, railway speculations and glutted
markets had now suddenly become mere trifles which could be
coped with in a trice.

This happy state of affairs, however, was not destined to last long,
for whereas in September 1847 Dr. Bowring at the Brussels Free
Trade Congress was still expounding with such highly comical
eloquence the marvellous consequences of the repeal of the Corn
Laws,[a] it was already noticed in London that even the "all-powerful
measures of Sir Robert Peel" were no longer able to save the country
from the catastrophe which had so long been feared. One had to
submit to fate and the London firms which, like Read Irving and Co.,
owned landed property worth almost one million pounds on
Mauritius, were the first to start a series of bankruptcies—because of
the shattered state of affairs in that part of the English col-
onies—they collapsed, taking with them in their fall numerous
smaller East-Indian and West-Indian firms.

At the same time the big wigs of the factory districts realised that
they had been mistaken about the consequences of the repeal of the
Corn Laws. Business with all parts of the world was at a standstill and

---

[a] See Engels, "The Economic Congress" and "The Free Trade Congress at
Brussels" and Marx, "Speech on the Question of Free Trade" (present edition, Vol. 6,
pp. 274-78, 282-90 and 450-65).— *Ed.*

panic spread simultaneously in the City of London and in the stock exchanges of Liverpool, Manchester, Leeds etc.

Consequently, the crisis of October 1845, which had been delayed by various events, finally broke out in September 1847. Confidence was at an end. Courage had run out. The Bank of England abandoned the banks inside the country; these banks withheld credit from traders and manufacturers. Bankers and exporters restricted their business with the Continent, the continental trader, in his turn, put pressure on the manufacturer who owed him money; the manufacturer, of course, reimbursed himself at the expense of the wholesaler, and the latter fell back on the *boutiquier*.[a] Each one of them hit out at the others and gradually the distress due to the trade crisis affected the whole world, from the giants of the City of London down to the smallest German shopkeeper.

This was *before* February 24, 1848! England experienced the worst days in the last four months of 1847. There was a clean sweep of the railway speculators; between August 10 and October 15, twenty of the leading London firms trading in colonial merchandise, with a capital of £5 million, and paying dividends of about 50 per cent, went bankrupt; and in the factory districts the distress reached its peak when in Manchester on November 15, only 78 out of 175 spinning mills were working full-time, and 11,000 workers were out of work.

So ended the year 1847. It was reserved for the Continent to experience during 1848 the after-effects of this English crisis—after-effects that on this occasion were, of course, all the more perceptible because the political transformations did not exactly help to make good the consequences of this extraordinary English occurrence.

We now come to the most interesting moment in the recent history of commerce, namely, the influence which the revolutions had on commercial activity.

The tables of English export trade provide us with the best illustration of this because, in view of the dominant position of England in world trade, the contents of these tables are nothing but an expression in figures of the political and commercial situation or, more correctly, the expression in figures of the ability to pay of the various nations.

Therefore, when we see that exports in April 1848 fell by £1,467,117, and in May by £1,122,009, and that total exports in

---

[a] Retail salesman.— *Ed.*

1847 amounted to £51,005,798, and in 1848 to only £46,407,939, conclusions very unfavourable to the revolutions could, it is true, be drawn from this and such an idea could be arrived at all the more easily because exports in January and February 1848, i.e. immediately before the outbreak of revolution, were actually £294,763 higher than in 1847.

Nevertheless, such a view would be completely erroneous. Because, firstly, the increased exports in January and February, i.e. precisely in the two months separating the peak of the crisis from the revolution, are easily explained by the fact that the Americans, in return for their enormous deliveries of grain to England at that time, took more British manufactured goods than ever before and thus at least for a short while prevented the falling off that would otherwise have arisen. But, in addition, English trade history provides most striking proof that exports do not diminish immediately after a crisis, but only when sufficient time has passed for the crisis to spread also to the Continent.

The increased export of the first two months of 1848, therefore, should by no means mislead us, and we can turn without misgivings to a consideration of the total decline during the whole year.

This decline, as we have already mentioned, compared with 1847 amounted to £4,597,859—certainly a considerable decrease, which in the hands of the reactionaries, who behave in politics like yapping curs and in trade like old women, became an argument against the revolution, one that is only too effectively used towards the uninformed.

But there is nothing easier than to refute the fallacious assertions of the party of reaction, for one has only to look up the tables of exports for the past 30 years to demonstrate that the decrease in exports in 1848, brought about by the combined influence of a trade crisis and a revolution, bears no comparison with the decline in exports of previous years.

After the trade crisis of 1825, in which year total exports amounted to £38,870,851, exports dropped to £31,536,724 in 1826. Thus there was a decrease of £7,334,127. After the crisis of 1836, when exports amounted to £53,368,572, exports dropped to £42,070,744 in 1837. The decrease, therefore, was £11,297,828. Nothing can be more striking than that!

Hence after two trade crises, which, it is true, were caused exclusively by the over-production of manufactured goods but in their extent cannot at all be compared with the crisis just ended, the drop in exports was double that of 1848, a year which was preceded by a glut in the Asian markets, two bad harvests, and speculation on a scale never seen before in the world, and a year when every corner of old Europe was shaken by revolutions!

In truth, trade got off easily in 1848! The revolutions contributed to the fact that now and then trade stagnated, that sales became difficult and dangerous, and that many persons collapsed under the burden of their obligations. During the past year, however, under Louis Philippe, the same difficulties would have been met with in Paris in discounting a miserable 20,000 or 30,000 francs as under the republic. In Southern Germany, on the Rhine, in Hamburg and in Berlin, with or without the revolution we would have had our bankruptcies; and business in Italy would have been depressed just as much under Pius as under the heroes of Milan, Rome and Palermo.[5]

It is just as ludicrous, therefore, to ascribe the revival of trade to the temporary victories of the counter-revolution. The French are not paying 25 per cent more for wool at the London wool auctions because some of Louis Philippe's Ministers are again in power,—no, they are having to pay more because they need the wool, and they need more of it, their demand is growing, precisely because in the last years of Louis Philippe's rule it had greatly decreased. Such a fluctuation of demand can be observed throughout the history of commerce.

And the English are once more working a full day in all the mines, foundries, spinning mills, and in all their ports, not because a certain Prince Windischgrätz orders the summary shooting of the Viennese people,—no, they are at work because the markets of Canton, New York and St. Petersburg wish to be supplied with manufactures, because California is opening up a new market which the speculators regard as inexhaustible, because the bad harvests of 1845 and 1846 were followed by two good harvests in 1847 and 1848, because the English have given up railway speculation, because money has returned to its customary channels, and the English will go on working ... until there is a new trade crisis.

Above all, we must not forget that it was by no means the monarchical countries that in recent years were the chief source of employment for English industry. The country which has almost continuously placed the most colossal orders for English goods and whose demand at the present time, too, is able to empty the markets of Manchester, Leeds, Halifax, Nottingham, Rochdale, and all the great emporia of modern industry, and which can enliven the ocean with its ships—is a republican country, the United States of North America. And it is just now that these states are prospering most of all, when all the monarchical states of the world are collapsing.

If, however, in the recent period a few branches of *German* industry have to some extent improved their position, they owe it solely to the *English* period of prosperity.[a] From the whole of the history of commerce the Germans should know that they have no commercial history of their own, that they have to suffer for English crises, while in periods of over-production in England, a minute percentage is all that falls to their lot. But they have nothing to thank their Christian-Germanic governments for except accelerated bankruptcy.

Written on March 6, 1849

First published in the *Neue Rheinische Zeitung* No. 239, March 7, 1849

Printed according to the newspaper

Published in English for the first time

---

[a] This word is in English in the original.— *Ed.*

# FROM THE THEATRE OF WAR [6]

Yesterday's news of Magyar victories[a] has been followed today by an Austrian assurance of victory. The *Österreichischer Correspondent* reports from Olmütz:

"The following telegraphic dispatch has just reached Olmütz: Field Marshal Prince *Windischgrätz* defeated the insurgents at Kapolna [7] on February 26 and 27. The enemy fled in two directions. An entire battalion was taken prisoner."

The commentary to this report may be found in the following lines, which have also been corroborated from other quarters:

"In Vienna the news of the imperial victory was known on March 2 only as a stock exchange rumour: *the letters which arrived by the post from Pest on that day were not released.*"

It can be seen that the news of the imperial victory bears all the marks of a Windischgrätz triumph: the letters which are supposed to confirm it are *withheld by the post-office* in Vienna. This is the first time that the Vienna Government has had to resort to such methods. The victory must have been a brilliant one indeed!

Still no news from Transylvania about the battle on the 15th between Bem and Puchner.[8] The latest reports stop at the 14th but indicate that a Magyar victory is likely the following day. An issue of the *Lithographierte Correspondenz* from Vienna writes:

"At last we again have received letters direct from Hermannstadt up to the 14th, they are however anything but reassuring.

"Lieutenant-Field Marshal Puchner is *evidently still not strong enough* to take the offensive against the fanatical bands of the Szeklers [9] and the hordes of Bem. There seems to be some reluctance, for political reasons, to employ Russian aid to the extent that the sorry state of the Grand Duchy demands. The commercial letters from

---

[a] See Engels, "Magyar Victory" (present edition, Vol. 8, pp. 477-80).— *Ed.*

Hermannstadt and Kronstadt sound very miserable. From Temesvar it was reported to Hermannstadt that *the Serbs have refused to come to the aid of Transylvania.*This is also evident from the irresolute movements of generals Rukavina, Gläser and Todorovich."

The Austrians have suffered a fresh defeat at the hands of Kossuth, not on the battlefield but at the shopkeepers' counters and the portable stands of the Jewish pedlars. Kossuth saw that the imperial authorities were compelled to redeem his one- and two-gulden notes and immediately arranged the production of 15- and 30-kreutzer notes.[10] Windischgrätz, outraged at this high treason against the royal imperial exchequer, has now issued the following proclamation[a]:

"The rebels, who have fled to Debreczin, tireless in confusing even further the already severely disrupted conditions of the country, have, in addition to the bank-notes already issued without right or authority, produced 30- and 15-kreutzer notes which are already beginning to circulate. These notes are mainly coming into the hands of the poorer classes of artisans and country people who, almost entirely lacking a livelihood, are already hard-pressed, and should be particularly preserved from harm. For the time being, therefore, and until an order is issued concerning the Hungarian banknotes as well, I declare these completely illegal notes for 30 and 15 kreutzers null and void, and prohibit their acceptance both at public cash-offices and in private exchange."

As if Herr Windischgrätz could prevent the circulation of the Magyar banknotes as long as Austria is unable to issue any ready money and especially small coins!

According to Austrian reports, Görgey, whom the *Constitutionelles Blatt aus Böhmen* calls a man "with no talent for generalship" (!!),[b] is said to have resigned the command. We need not point out how absurd such rumours are. In the meantime we present the following report from the Austrian *Lloyd* on the latest operations of this skilful partisan in the Zips[c]:

"Until the 18th of last month Lieutenant-Field Marshal Ramberg, who commanded the two brigades of royal imperial troops under General Götz and Prince Jablonowsky in the Zips areas, was continuously engaged in skirmishes with Görgey's insurgent forces. [...] For Görgey had sent his baggage trains with a small escort from Kaschau, an area from which royal imperial troops had withdrawn, to the Theiss in the direction of Debreczin, and in order to protect this transport he used all his forces to halt the troops pursuing him, and therefore retained scarcely two squadrons of hussars in Kaschau. After his rearguard had been forced back from Wallendorf

---

[a] Windischgrätz's proclamation was first published in the *Pesther Zeitung* and then reprinted in the evening supplement to the *Wiener Zeitung* No. 51, February 28, 1849, and in *Der Lloyd* No. 101 (evening edition), February 28, 1849.— *Ed.*

[b] "Pest, 25. Febr.", *Constitutionelles Blatt aus Böhmen* No. 52, March 2, 1849.— *Ed.*

[c] The following is the quotation from "Käsmark, 23. Februar" published in *Der Lloyd* No. 104 (morning edition), March 2, 1849.— *Ed.*

to Margitfalva—when the royal imperial fusiliers captured five cannon (!)—he concentrated his main strength on this road, which, forming a narrow defile in the valley of the River Hernad, severely impeded the advance of the royal imperial troops. On the road to Eperies the smaller corps of Hungarians withdrew hastily, fearing to be cut off on the mountain road by the former garrison of Kaschau. [...] The *infantry* of the Hungarians is generally appalling, not only because it is neither trained nor disciplined—for these shortcomings would be to some extent compensated for *in battle by the phisical agility peculiar to the Magyars and their proven scorn for death*—but chiefly because their *officers* are incompetent and cowardly, *collected from all corners of the world,* and inspire no confidence in their men. [...] On the other hand, the *hussars,* whose officers, although mostly promoted NCOs, are ignorant, but at least courageous men, retain their inherent bravery; here in the mountains they could not often be used, but they frequently dismounted from their horses to cover the cannon and encourage the others; on outpost duty they are reckless in their daring and cause the royal imperial troops a good deal of trouble. [...]

"The engagements between the insurgents and the royal imperial troops were limited in this area to skirmishes and artillery salvoes; as the battalions drew nearer the insurgents retired; on the 19th, they assembled in Kaschau and then tried to reach the Theiss by forced marches in order either to effect a meeting with Dembiński or to *flee* to Debreczin. (!) [...]

"The town of Kaschau was illuminated to greet the insurgents, and received Görgey with a torchlight parade, thus saving itself from a levy such as was imposed on Eperies. Now the evil guests have fled, and on the 19th of last month Eperies was re-occupied by the royal imperial troops; and Kaschau, the day before yesterday.[a] In the village of Petrovian between Eperies and Kaschau, where the peasants had captured several hussars and taken them over the mountains to the royal imperial troops, the rebels had the local magistrate and a juryman shot as a punishment. We, the Zipsers, got off with a black eye; only the towns and villages on the Kaschau mountain road incurred severe damage during the various skirmishes. The earlier-mentioned attack by the imperial Major Kiesewetter was made on the town of Neudorf to punish it for its treachery, and it is now occupied by four companies of the Slovak *Landsturm* under Štúr, which naturally cannot be compared with the pleasantness of an occupation by the imperial troops. **We are all however disturbed by the presence of a rebel force under the insurgent Colonel Aulich in Lublau, which by all appearances intends to operate in the rear of the imperial army,** for men are claiming to have seen hussars first in one place, then in another; meanwhile, to our consolation, General Vogl has advanced from Galicia with 4,000 men via Bartfeld, and he will probably drive these hordes out of the border mountains before long (?)."

As a counterpart of this we present the following report from Agram of the *Constitutionelles Blatt aus Böhmen* on the South-Slav complications:

"*Agram,* February 25. In its latest issue, the *Napredak* [Напредак] discusses the causes of the state of siege which was imposed on Karlowitz; it endorses the view that the activities of the Central Committee[11] gave rise to this military measure. The *Napredak* excuses the Patriarch[b] by whose order the state of war was proclaimed in Karlowitz; the above newspaper further reports that at present the Patriarch is ruling

---

[a] On February 21, 1849.—*Ed.*
[b] Rajachich.—*Ed.*

alone, while the Odbor (Central Committee) has relinquished its duties and refrains from intervening publicly in the administration of the voivodeship. The differences between Rajachich and Stratimirovich are—judging by this newspaper—by no means eliminated yet. This is also averred by a member of the Serb constitutional commission recently arrived here, who hardly described things in the Voivodina as being at their best. From the information supplied by this member I am able to report the following to you on the situation there. *The majority of the people is for Stratimirovich,* only Syrmien and the Peterwardein borders [12] are opposed to him, there Radosavljevich, who was elected regimental commander and confirmed by the Patriarch, has totally paralysed the efforts of Stratimirovich. The Patriarch is reported to have been appointed civil governor, and—which sounds rather strange—also military head of the voivodeship. It has been confirmed that Rajachich *has been having repeated conflicts with the commanding officer at Temesvar,* with whom he used always to be on friendly terms. The latter is said to be working with all his energy to bring the Banat border under his control, and *to restore the old military authority there.* In fact several senior officers have apparently banded together whose endeavours are *aimed solely at everywhere placing obstacles in the path of the Serbs.* Rukavina and Todorovich are said to be at the head of this anti-Serb coterie. The latter is said to have lost the sympathies of all through his gruff, offensive conduct and his exaggeratedly 'black-and-yellow'[a] sentiments; his intolerance of everything that does not carry the royal imperial *port d'epée* apparently goes so far that he intended to grant the Serb national officers only corporals' pay.—The Serb constitutional commission recently commenced its work; the first result of its deliberations is an electoral law for the Voivodina, the draft of which is already completed."[b]

The "united monarchy" (*Gesamtmonarchie*) still has a number of strange experiences in store if the pan-Slavist uproar [13] that is now fermenting throughout Slav Austria breaks out some day!

Written by Engels about March 6, 1849

First published in the *Neue Rheinische Zeitung* No. 239, March 7, 1849

Printed according to the newspaper

Published in English for the first time

---

[a] The Austrian imperial colours.— *Ed.*

[b] "Agram, February 25", *Constitutionelles Blatt aus Böhmen* No. 51 (supplement), March 1, 1849.— *Ed.*

# THE MILITARY REPORTS
## OF THE *KÖLNISCHE ZEITUNG*

The *Kölnische Zeitung* celebrated yesterday a day of rejoicing, unfortunately subdued by a measure of moral indignation. The cause of its rejoicing was the telegraphic dispatch from Olmütz reporting the alleged victory of Windischgrätz; the moral indignation had naturally been caused by nobody else but us, with our observations about the greater or lesser credibility of the Magyar reports. What! This deplorable paper, the *Neue Rheinische Zeitung*, presumes to maintain that the *Kölnische Zeitung* "has not yet proved the Magyar reports guilty of a *single case* of exaggeration", but that the *Neue Rheinische Zeitung* itself has "critically ascertained the credibility of these reports"! And then three exclamation marks, each more wrathful and indignant than the last.

Let us leave unruffled the holy zeal with which our neighbouring journalist fights for Truth, Justice and Windischgrätz. Let us be content for today—as the news from Hungary is very meagre—with "critically ascertaining" the "credibility" of yesterday's report in the *Kölnische Zeitung*.

The *Kölnische Zeitung* commences with an important mien:

"Today we are in a position to give *more definite news* from the two theatres of war." Namely this: "Today we undergo the same experience with regard to the long Magyar victory-report in the *Breslauer Zeitung* as we so frequently had with regard to these reports: once again we must confirm that it has been nothing but a *ridiculous exaggeration.* The alleged *defeat* of Windischgrätz turns out to be a *victory* for the same; and there is *not a word of truth in the reported capture of Hermannstadt* by Bem."[a]

---

[a] Here and below Engels quotes the article "From the Theatre of War" published in the *Kölnische Zeitung* No. 56, March 7, 1849.— *Ed.*

That sounds grand enough. At a single stroke two fat "exaggerations" in the Magyar report have thus been supposedly discovered—we beg your pardon, communicated by our neighbouring journalist to his readers at second hand from Austrian newspapers. But let us now look at the matter in detail.

Firstly, the famous Olmütz telegraphic dispatch is reproduced and set up as an authority beyond all doubt. But why, we ask, does the triumphant Cologne newspaper not find it fitting to carry a news item that places this dispatch in a very strange light? On the same day that the Vienna Government distributed in Vienna the news of Windischgrätz' alleged victory, it *stopped all letters and newspapers from Pest at the post-office*. Probably in joy at the mighty victory of the armed forces of the fatherland. The *Kölnische Zeitung* must have read this news, as we did, in at least half a dozen East-German newspapers. But in order not to disturb the joy of its readers at the victory of "German arms", it does the same as the Austrian Government and withholds this piece of news. That is a sample of the way the *Kölnische Zeitung* "critically ascertains" the "credibility" of the Austrian victory dispatches.

But there is more to come. The Magyars are supposed to have been defeated at Kapolna. This is "significant".

"Kapolna is after all to the east of Gyöngyös; the Hungarians were thus in full *backward* movement."

When one is in "backward movement", reasons the worthy Cologne paper, one cannot but be defeated! Our neighbouring journalist has at last cast a glance at the map and discovered that the Magyars must have been defeated at Kapolna because "Kapolna is after all to the east of Gyöngyös"! Yes, very "significant" indeed! Further:

"The *Schlesische Zeitung*, whose reporter incidentally knows nothing about the recent battle, has *in this connection* (!) been informed from Vienna: 'The Hungarians have withdrawn again on all sides, Prince Windischgrätz will cross the Theiss and march on *Debreczin*. The big battle must be fought shortly, or (!) Debreczin will be lost, the Rump Parliament[14] dissolved and consequently the whole insurrection at an end.'[a]"

"Prince Windischgrätz *will* cross the Theiss and march on Debreczin." Prince Windischgrätz says so, and it is the duty of every respectable citizen to believe him implicitly. "Prince Windischgrätz *will*"! It is now, thank heavens, nearly six weeks since "Prince

---

[a] "Wien, 2. März", *Schlesische Zeitung* No. 53 (first supplement), March 4, 1849.— *Ed.*

Windischgrätz *will* cross the Theiss" and "*march* on Debreczin", and he is still in the same place. If, however, like our neighbouring journalist, one knows how to distinguish between "more definite news" and "ridiculous exaggerations", the entire Hungarian war has come to an end with the assurance of "Prince Windischgrätz" that he "*will* cross the Theiss" and "*march* on Debreczin". "Debreczin is lost, the Rump Parliament dissolved and consequently the whole insurrection at an end." The matter is settled in the twinkling of an eye. Our neighbouring journalist, who has "crossed" the Theiss and conquered Debreczin so many times already, according to whom more Magyars have already been killed than all Hungary has inhabitants, and who was already rejoicing four weeks ago: "The war in Hungary is coming to an end"—this same journalist has suddenly been re-electrified after a lengthy period of dejection, and is again shouting, "The war is coming to an end, *parturiunt montes*[a]" etc., and these are no "ridiculous exaggerations" but "more definite news"!

In this manner of making the Austrians win victories, the *Constitutionelles Blatt aus Böhmen* is a dangerous rival to the *Kölnische Zeitung*. For instance it reports today from Pest:

"A reverse inflicted on the royal imperial troops in Transylvania through infamous treachery *is, on the other hand, compensated for by the fact that Komorn is at present being heavily attacked*,[15] and a bombardment has already taken place."[b]

"So much for the main theatre of war. With this *renewed* Austrian *offensive* the Hungarian war has entered its *second stage* here."

How many "stages" our neighbour cares to make the Hungarian war enter is of little consequence. More interesting would be an answer to the question: how many "stages" has the reporting of the *Kölnische Zeitung on* the Hungarian war entered?

We pointed out right at the beginning of the war, even before the Austrians were in Pest, that the real battle-ground only begins beyond Pest, between the Theiss and the Danube, and that the scene of the final decision will be on the Theiss itself, or perhaps even on the far side of it. Even then we stated that the special proficiency of the Magyars in war, that the particular shortcomings of the Austrians, the difficulty of ensuring supplies and the whole nature of the terrain refer the Magyars to this area.[c] On various occasions, and

---

[a] A reference to "Parturiunt montes, nascetur ridiculus mus." (Mountains will be in labour, the birth will be a single laughable little mouse.) Horace, *Ars Poetica*, 139.— *Ed.*

[b] "Wien, 28. Febr.", *Constitutionelles Blatt aus Böhmen* No. 52 (second supplement), March 2, 1849.— *Ed.*

[c] See Engels, "The Struggle in Hungary" (present edition, Vol. 8, pp. 290-94).— *Ed.*

as recently as a few days ago, we have pointed out that all the "backward movements" of the Hungarians towards the Theiss do not determine anything whatsoever, because it is the Theiss that is their natural line of defence, behind which, for the present, they are fairly unassailable. We repeat: the further Prince Windischgrätz advances, the more difficult will his position become, the weaker his army, and the greater the Magyars' chances of victory. Moreover, the longer the decisive moment is postponed, the more time the Magyars have to arm, organise and reinforce their recently created army, while the position of the imperial forces is deteriorating rather than improving.

Supposing, then, that the Magyar report of the defeat of the Austrians were really false, their "victory" would anyway be restricted to insignificant skirmishes with the Magyar rearguard, whose job it was to cover the retreat of the main army in the direction of the Theiss and Hernad. A commanding officer like Dembiński will not accept a decisive battle *before* a river when he can fight much better *beyond* the river, unless he is ·*perfectly sure* of the outcome.

But as stated: hitherto there is no news, and neither the Magyar report nor the telegraphic dispatch have been confirmed in any way. The Vienna letters and newspapers have not reached us, the Breslau papers have likewise failed to arrive because there is no Monday issue, the Berlin papers have nothing new to tell, the Leipzig and Prague papers, which present the news one day later, only contain letters from Pest of the 27th which are still in ignorance of the battle which began on the 26th, and—a remarkable thing indeed—they do not print the Olmütz victory dispatch either.

Now to continue:

"We *lack* further news from Transylvania."

This news, that there is no news, is certainly very "definite"! An excellent fashion in which to repudiate the "ridiculous exaggerations" of the Magyars!

"The *Breslauer Zeitung*, which is by no means impartial" (a naive remark from the mouth of our Magyarophobe neighbour!), "is *surely* depicting the position of the Austrians *too gloomily*, for though it was *certainly very precarious* earlier on, it has *after all* improved recently."

"Surely, after all"! "It has *after all* improved!" "*Surely* depicting *too* gloomily"! Remarkably "more definite" news, in which nothing is "definite" except the tearful admission that the position of the Austrians was "*certainly very precarious earlier on*"!

"The story of the storming of Hermannstadt is a Magyar invention; for this is supposed to have occurred on February 15, and yet the Vienna *Lloyd* contains in its columns a letter from Hermannstadt of February 16 whose writer knows nothing of the alleged storming, but on the contrary etc."

And this letter from Hermannstadt, which is said to be dated the 16th, contains nothing whatsoever about the fate of the defeated Puchner, who rallied his troops again on the 12th outside Hermannstadt, contains nothing of the position of Bem advancing via Mühlbach, but merely drivels on about the raids of the Szeklers, about the few days left to hold out until "the victorious royal imperial troops, approaching ever nearer and nearer and closing in from all sides" (from whence?) eliminate the danger and so on. In short, this letter actually says nothing but what has long been known, and bears all the signs of a document fabricated in Vienna itself. Why are there then no official or semi-official reports available, if private newspapers have news from Hermannstadt of the 16th? And in a fictitious document like this the *Kölnische Zeitung* places its implicit trust! By means of information like this it "critically ascertains" the "ridiculous exaggerations" of the Magyar reports!

In addition, the *Kölnische Zeitung* contains some ludicrous snatches of gossip about the amateur theatres of the officers in Komorn, about the alleged dismissal of Görgey, about the "intentions" of Nugent etc., concluding, as usual, with "*a series of noteworthy judgments from the Austrian press on the intervention of the Russians*". When the gentlemen themselves lose their powers of judgment, this series of noteworthy judgments presents itself at the right moment for reproduction by anyone who cares to do so.

Such are the gentlemen of the *Kölnische Zeitung*. Too cowardly to indulge in any sort of polemic, which would be bound utterly to expose their hollowness, ignorance and empty-headedness, this literary lumpenproletariat seeks to vent its anger at all the blows it receives on the small Magyar people fighting against a force vastly superior to it. What does it matter to the *Kölnische Zeitung* that this heroic people of five million led, moreover, by officers who were nothing but traitors, is forced to defend itself against the entire might of Austria and Russia, against whole fanaticised nations, that it has taken on an unequal struggle compared with which the French revolutionary war was child's play. First it abused them as "cowards", "braggarts" etc., and when these cowards eventually put the whole of mighty Austria to flight, when they forced it humbly to beseech the Russians for aid, like a tiny sixth-rate country, against the few million Magyars, when 20,000 Russians then placed their weight in the scales in favour of Austria, this honourable little paper was unable to restrain its jubilation. And even now, as soon as there comes the slightest piece of news favourable to the imperial murderers, joy reigns in the columns of the *Kölnische Zeitung,* and it exults at the victory of the side enjoying the most crushing superiority, gloats over the desperate struggle of a small nation of heroic courage against two of the biggest powers of Europe!

When censorship still existed, in 1831, no German newspaper dared to cheer the Russians as they drew ever tighter circles around Warsaw.[16] Then all was sympathy for Poland, and those who did not agree at least kept quiet. But today we have freedom of the press, and the *Kölnische Zeitung* may unimpeded throw all its despicable drivel in the face of the Magyars in the most brutal fashion.

Written by Engels on March 7, 1849          Printed according to the newspaper

First published in the *Neue Rheinische*          Published in English for the first
*Zeitung* No. 240, March 8, 1849          time

# [THE 26th AUSTRIAN ARMY BULLETIN]

Just now, when the above article had already been written, we have received the following 26th Bulletin, in which the gallant Windischgrätz at last gives us an explanation of his brilliant victory at Kapolna announced by telegraph[a]:

"From Gyöngyös, Field Marshal Windischgrätz gave Lieutenant-Field Marshal Schlick the command to leave Petervasara on February 26 and join the main army by way of Verpeleth, in order to attack the insurgents with combined forces. The corps of Lieutenant-Field Marshal Wrbna and that of Lieutenant-Field Marshal Schwarzenberg encountered the enemy outside Kapolna on February 26. At first the latter showed the intention of threatening our left flank by occupying a wooded height with two battalions. He was, however, driven from there by a bayonet attack. Then, he attempted to pierce our centre with his cavalry, but was repulsed there too, and retired at all points towards Kapolna and Kaal. The fall of darkness put an end to the day's fighting. Early on the 27th Field Marshal Windischgrätz ordered the attack to be continued, having heard of the delayed arrival of Lieutenant-Field Marshal Schlick, who had been held up by the enemy's occupation of the narrow defile of Sirok and only succeeded in taking it after a stubborn fight. He pushed back the enemy as far as Verpeleth, where the latter gained a footing, and only surrendered this place after fierce fighting. The enemy again attempted to take Kapolna and made two attacks with numerous heavy guns; which were, however, unsuccessful. After the fighting had gone on all day, the insurgents withdrew and took up a position at Maklar. During the capture of Kapolna the Zanini battalion defending the church was taken prisoner. The casualties on the enemy side were 200-300 killed and 900-1,000 captured; those of the royal imperial troops were slighter, although the exact figures are not yet available."

It may be seen from this Bulletin:
1) That on the 26th, as the Magyar "exaggeration" *quite correctly* observes, the *Hungarians had indeed got the better of Windischgrätz.* For

---

[a] "26. Armee-Bulletin. Vom 3. März."—*Ed.*

were it true, as the Bulletin claims, that the imperial forces had been victorious on the 26th, on the following day, having been reinforced by the Schlick-Schulzig corps, they would have been in a position to inflict a severe defeat on the Magyars.

2) That Windischgrätz' "*victory*" is limited to an extremely insignificant skirmish, as the small number of casualties on the Magyar side proves. In two days of battle, 300 killed! As for the captured battalion, that means little.

There are still aristocratic traitors among the officers of the Hungarian army, who are only waiting for an opportunity to position their troops in such a way that they can be captured with due decency. The death-defying bravery of the Magyar soldiers even favours such treachery.

3) That the imperial forces should know the casualties of the *Hungarians* so exactly, whereas they have not yet established *their own*, is likewise highly "significant".

4) Finally: as far as the definite gains of the imperial forces are concerned, these are limited to *exactly one mile*[a] *of captured terrain*. The Hungarians engaged in battle at Kapolna and Verpeleth, and are now at Maklar, which lies one mile to the east. Erlau, about the same distance to the north of Maklar, is obviously also still in the possession of the Magyars, supporting their right flank; otherwise the Bulletin would have trumpeted out the recapture of this important town with due exultation.

5) *Summa Summarum*: After achieving the purpose of their expedition before the gates of Pest, the Hungarians have withdrawn, without engaging in any decisive battle on terrain that is less favourable to them. They have only fought insofar as it was necessary in order to cover their retreat to the Theiss and Hernad and to keep the imperial forces at a respectable distance. This object *has been fully attained.*

The whole tone of the Bulletin, and the fact that the imperial troops, according to their own report, have only advanced one mile, prove this. The result of the Hungarian advance to within six miles of Pest, quite apart from the moral impression, is this: Görgey is reunited with the main army, the comitats between the Hernad, Theiss and the Carpathians have been cleared of Austrians. The Magyars can lean their right wing on the Carpathians and establish direct contact with the Galician revolutionaries[17]; they have forced

---

[a] In this and other articles we have used "mile" when Engels uses the German word *Meile*. At that time *Meile* was a linear measure of different length in different German states, but it can be regarded as roughly $4^1/_2$ miles.— *Ed.*

Schlick away from his base of operations (Galicia), and thus compelled the Austrians to alter their entire plan of campaign.

Let the *Kölnische Zeitung*, which as we know has news of the 16th from Transylvania, tell us, though, why the Bulletin says nothing of the events that occurred around Hermannstadt up to the 16th.

Written by Engels on March 7, 1849

First published in the *Neue Rheinische Zeitung* No. 240, March 8, 1849

Printed according to the newspaper

Published in English for the first time

# THE ENGLISH SOLDIER'S OATH
## OF ALLEGIANCE

*Cologne*, March 7. The *Neue Preussische Zeitung* in great triumph publishes the English army oath of allegiance[a] and rejoices immeasurably at the discovery that the English soldier swears loyalty only to the Queen[b] but not to the Constitution. Should we then in Prussia, in the youngest constitutional state, should we, *contrary* to the example of the oldest constitutional country, compel our soldiers to swear allegiance to the Constitution?

But the *Neue Preussische Zeitung* forgets to inform the readers how the English soldier stands in relation to civil laws.

As a matter of course, the British soldier, for *all* offences which are not *mere offences against discipline*, is tried by the ordinary courts, the county courts, petty sessions, quarter sessions[18] or assize courts, and in all conflicts with other citizens he is treated *simply* as a *citizen*.

But that is not all. In England every citizen, whether an official, a soldier or whatever he is, is responsible before the law for all his actions and cannot plead as an excuse that the action in question was ordered by his superior. For example, a revolt occurs. Troops are called in. Legal demands to disperse are or are not issued. The people do not disperse. A civilian official (always a justice of the peace or an urban *elected* official) gives permission for the army to intervene, or does not do so. The soldiers open fire, there are deaths. The findings of an inquest on those killed come before a coroner's jury which establishes the facts in each case. If the jury decides that the intervention of the armed forces was not justified by the

---

[a] Published under the heading "Berliner Zuschauer", *Neue Preussische Zeitung* No. 54, March 6, 1849.— *Ed.*

[b] Victoria.— *Ed.*

circumstances, it brings in a verdict of *premeditated murder* against all the participants, including therefore the *civilian official* who gave permission for the intervention of the troops, the *officer* who gave the order to fire, and *all the soldiers who actually opened fire.*

If the civilian official did not give permission for intervention, the consequence is merely that he does not figure in the verdict. Matters remain unaltered as far as the officers and soldiers are concerned.

This verdict of premeditated murder is a formal indictment, on the basis of which criminal proceedings are instituted before the regular courts with their juries.

The English soldier, therefore, is by no means regarded by the law as a machine that has no will of its own and must obey without argument any order given it, but as a "free agent",[a] a man possessing free will, who at all times must know what he is doing and who bears responsibility for all his actions. English judges would give a stern reply to an accused soldier if he defended himself by saying that he had been ordered to fire and that he had had to "obey orders"!

In Prussia things are quite different. In Prussia the soldier declares that his immediate superior gave him the order to fire, and this frees him from all punishment. In Prussia, and likewise in France, the official is assured of complete impunity for every violation of the law when he can prove that the order for it had come from his proper superior in the proper hierarchical way.

The *Neue Preussische Zeitung* will probably take our word for it that we do not hold the view that the brief formula of an oath can alter a man and turn a black-and-white[b] Guards lieutenant into an enthusiast for "constitutional freedom".

In the last twelve months, the gentlemen who are "with God for King and Fatherland"[c] have themselves, through their own praiseworthy kith and kin, gained the most pleasant experience of the significance of the oath. We are not at all against the *Neue Preussische Zeitung* making the army swear allegiance to the king, the Dalai Lama or the man in the moon, so long as "My glorious army",[19] in the way which has been described above, *is put in exactly the same position in relation to the laws as the army in England.*

Written on March 7, 1849

First published in the *Neue Rheinische Zeitung* No. 241, March 9, 1849

Printed according to the newspaper

Published in English for the first time

---

[a] These words are in English in the original.— *Ed.*
[b] The colours of the Prussian monarchy.— *Ed.*
[c] From the motto of the *Neue Preussische Zeitung.*— *Ed.*

24

# FROM THE THEATRE OF WAR

Yesterday we already presented an extract from the last (26th) Army Bulletin published in the Vienna *Lithographierte Correspondenz.*[a] Today we have the complete text of the Bulletin before us.[b]

However hard Windischgrätz endeavours to give the action at Kapolna the character of a major battle, however violently he flings about bayonet-charges, cavalry attacks and bombardments—he is soundly defeated in his aim by the figures he himself gives of the dead and captured. 200-300 killed on the Magyar side in a major two-day battle in which "we had to deal with the *main force* of the enemy at all points"! It can be seen that the Magyars for their part threw no more than a few corps into the fighting which, as we said already yesterday, were at the most intended to cover the retreat of the main army and keep the Austrians at a respectable distance. For a battle between two large armies, particularly one lasting two days, results in far greater losses than a few hundred men.

But Windischgrätz exaggerates even more ridiculously when he speaks of the *"numerical superiority"* of the Magyars. The war in Hungary would have been over long ago if the small Magyar nation could even achieve *"numerical" equality* with the imperial troops—but numerical superiority! The superiority of 5 million over 31 million!!

One report goes as far as to maintain that 27,000 Austrians defeated twice as many Magyars at Kapolna! But this report is, in addition, so remarkably skilfully and credibly written that it relates in the same breath that, having retired to Erlau, the Magyars were met there by *Götz.* It is known, however, that Götz is wandering around some 30 miles away in the area of Kaschau and Eperies, and now he is suddenly supposed to have marched all the way to Erlau!

---

[a] See this volume, pp. 19-21.— *Ed.*

[b] "Wien, 3. März", *Der Lloyd* No. 107 (evening edition), March 3, 1849; "Wien, 3. März", Augsburg *Allgemeine Zeitung* No. 65, March 6, 1849.— *Ed.*

Otherwise the Bulletin contains nothing new, and we can safely put it aside.

Now to Transylvania. Here it is true that Bem has not taken Hermannstadt, and that for very simple reasons. After absorbing the 4,000 strong column from Hungary, he marched along the Maros in order *to join up with the Szekler Landsturm*.[20] While he was advancing from Mühlbach by way of Mediasch, the Szeklers from the opposite direction came to meet him and took Schässburg with 7,000 men on the 16th. The garrison and a part of the civic militia escaped to Hermannstadt; Bem pursued them and is now once again in the vicinity of this town, as a letter of the 18th from Hermannstadt relates. According to one report it is said to have already been evacuated by Puchner.

From this it is evident that Bem has executed another of those victorious advances across Transylvania in which he has already greatly distinguished himself several times. His connections with the intrepid Szeklers, who live close by the Moldavian border, after being momentarily threatened by Puchner and the Russians, have been restored; Sachsenland[21] is in extreme peril, he *"now has the keys of Sachsenland in his hands"*.

The Saxons moreover complain of the lack of good leadership from above, and of the Romanians' lack of courage. The latter are said to be displaying extreme cowardice. One report says[a]:

"The only trouble is the lack of good leadership from above and the lack of courage and endurance on the part of the Wallachian troops. All the unsuccessful engagements have hitherto been lost through the fault of the Wallachians. At Salzburg the regular Wallachian army threw itself flat on its belly at the first cannon shot, and at Kronstadt the Russians had to form up behind the Wallachians to prevent them from running away. But if the battle is won, they are always the foremost and cruellest in looting, and spare neither the enemy nor their wounded comrades lying on the battlefield."

This shows what gangs of brigands the royal imperial regime is employing to maintain its authority. Moreover, the *Siebenbürger Bote* is awaiting the following royal imperial reinforcements:

"According to reports received the corps heading for Transylvania under generals Gläser, Todorovich and Mengen is said to comprise the following troops: 8 battalions of infantry, Leiningen, Rukavina, men from Peterwardein,[22] Romanians, Illyrians, and German-Banat Borderers; 5 squadrons of Uhlans, 300 mounted Serbs, 80 Serezhans; one Congreve battery, one mounted foot-battery, two ordinary foot-batteries, 5 Serbian cannon. A total of 15,000 men."[b]

---

[a] Engels quotes from the *Kölnische Zeitung* No. 57 (special supplement), March 8, 1849.— *Ed.*

[b] "Nachrichten vom Kriegsschauplatz", *Der Siebenbürger Bote* No. 22, February 19, 1849.— *Ed.*

The Transylvanian Flemings[23] will have to pray many a Lords Prayer before these alleged 15,000 men get through. Unfortunately Damjanich and Vetter on the Lower Maros are still giving them more than enough to do, accordingly they are leaving Transylvania to the Russians.

From the Banat theatre of war, little news.[24] The Serbs boast of the following heroic deeds:

"Theresiopel has been taken by the Serbs, and on the 25th it is reported from the Sava that a skirmish has occurred at Futtak between the Syrmien provincial battalion and the Magyar garrison of Neusatz as a result of which the former town was reduced to ashes by the Magyars."

The truth or otherwise of this we leave as a matter for conjecture. At the same time we hear that the great hero Nugent, whom we have assumed to have long since reached the Lower Theiss or the area of Peterwardein, has still not even crossed the Danube, but *is only now* "thinking of crossing" this river "near Mohacs"!!

And while he is amusing himself with these thoughts the Magyars are taking the greatest liberties in his close vicinity, in the Tolna comitat, on the *right* bank of the Danube, at the rear of Ofen. Here, in a region which was—how many times—"cleaned up" by the royal imperial troops, the long-lost Perczel suddenly turns up as a guerilla leader and sets the whole area in motion. Just listen:

"In Battaszek an imperial officer was taken prisoner as a result of this agitation, in Paks an imperial courier was stopped and his escort of two men disarmed. In Dombovar district all cattle belonging to Prince Esterházy were slaughtered. In Laczhaza, too, just as the market was being held, 50 insurgents appeared from Duna Vecse and Solt with their lead-studded whips and seized all the cattle driven there for sale."

That was today's news. The victory of Windischgrätz reduced to a pointless and ineffectual attack, Bem's operations in Transylvania as skilful as they are successful, the Serbs in the Banat still standing on the banks of the Maros at a loss what to do, Nugent still unable to cross the Danube and move into the Banat, the area between the Drava and the Danube preparing to revolt against the imperial authorities—that is the résumé of the position of the warring parties according to the latest reports.

Written by Engels on March 8, 1849

First published in the *Neue Rheinische Zeitung* No. 241, March 9, 1849

Printed according to the newspaper

Published in English for the first time

# THE 27th BULLETIN.—MILITARY REPORTS

We have today a new Austrian Bulletin. Before we examine it more closely, however, we should like to return briefly to the battle at Kapolna and to mention some observations taken from the pro-Metternich Augsburg *Allgemeine Zeitung*[a] which, coming from *that* newspaper, are altogether highly "indicative". This paper, which usually supports so enthusiastically the black-and-yellow[b] cause, comes out with the following complaints:

"As is the case with most of the army's communiqués from Hungary, in the communiqué dealing with Kapolna (see below) we unfortunately find that very important points are again missing: one learns nothing about the strength of the respective combating armies, the previous movements of the enemy, the divisions comprising the enemy's forces, the names of their leaders, not even the name of their commander-in-chief. And yet the report otherwise contains many details which are to some extent trivial."

And it goes on to say:

"It is equally remarkable that the Bulletin dealing with the battle at Kapolna also talks of the enemy's numerical superiority, although the combined forces of Windischgrätz and Schlick were involved in the fighting there. The Field Marshal can hardly have fewer than 100,000 to 120,000 men under his command in Hungary. It is true that they are widely dispersed throughout the country, and Windischgrätz has to try to encircle the enemy in a wide arc with his various army corps. But neither can the Magyars operate with their combined forces from *one* central point; Komorn, Peterwardein, Szegedin etc. are still holding out, and there is still fighting in the Banat, in Transylvania and on the Theiss. We have searched *in vain* through the Vienna, Agram and Temesvar newspapers for information on the questions which thrust themselves upon one in this context."

---

[a] The following quotation is from the article "Oesterreich" published in the Augsburg *Allgemeine Zeitung* No. 65, March 6, 1849.— *Ed.*

[b] The Austrian imperial colours.— *Ed.*

Such doubts expressed by the Augsburg *Allgemeine* martial-law paper make any further comment from us superfluous. Now to turn to the 27th Army Bulletin[a]:

"On February 26 and 27 the head of the column of the advancing main army under His Highness Field Marshal Prince zu Windischgrätz attacked the rebels from behind the Tarna between Kapolna and Kaal and drove them back. The columns of Lieutenant-Field Marshal Schlick, which had advanced towards Verpeleth and Erlau, had taken the enemy in the flank and, as a result of this successful move, threatened his line of retreat towards Miskolcz and Tokaj. On February 28 the Field Marshal advanced all along the line and on that day moved his headquarters to Maklar, just after the enemy had left it and retreated towards Mezö-Kövesd.

"Quickly following the hurried retreat of the enemy the cuirassier regiment of Prince Karl of Prussia came upon the rearguard of the enemy which was concentrated near Mezö-Kövesd, a fierce cavalry battle took place, this being supported by the Wyss and Montenuovo brigades which were moving forward. In this first battle Major Prince Holstein and two officers were wounded. On March 1 the Field Marshal undertook large-scale reconnaissance along the whole line across the whole of the plain, which stretches from Mezö-Kövesd via István to the Theiss, however this did not produce the desired results because of the heavy fog and the snow.

"In the meantime the corps of Lieutenant-Field Marshal Schlick was operating on the right flank of the enemy, who was thus obliged in the course of that day to evacuate Mezö-Kövesd and retreat via Szemere and Eger Farmos towards Poroszlo. The Deym brigade, from the corps under the command of Lieutenant-Field Marshal Schlick, occupied Mezö-Kövesd.

"About midday, when the fog had lifted somewhat, the reconnoitring vanguard reported that the enemy had moved off in the direction of the Theiss and his crossing-point at Tisza-Füred. The Field Marshal at once dispatched three brigades along the enemy's line of retreat, and his rearguard was contacted at Szemere.

"At Eger Farmos the enemy tried once more to offer resistance but was thrown back, and in the evening the place was occupied by our victorious troops. At the same time the Field Marshal had dispatched a brigade of the first army corps, under the command of Major-General Zeisberg, from Besenyö along the road to Poroszlo, and on the morning of March 2, the date of the last report from the headquarters at Maklar, the whole army was advancing towards the Theiss."

As was to be expected, the Magyars have once more withdrawn beyond the Theiss. We have said it a hundred times: it would have been irresponsible and reckless of them if they had engaged in a decisive battle on the right bank of the Theiss without being *quite sure* of victory. The superior strength of the Austrians was still too great, a fact which is borne out by the above report from the Augsburg *Allgemeine Zeitung*. The Austrians were able to concentrate their main forces, whilst the Magyars had had to leave a strong reserve force behind, in particular a large part of their young troops at Debreczin, and generally beyond the Theiss. They have demonstrated to the Austrians that they are dealing neither with "cowards"

---

[a] "27. Armee-Bulletin. Vom 5. März."—*Ed.*

nor with a motley "rabble", and they did *well* to retreat once more beyond the Theiss after having achieved their aim.

Just how much respect Herr Windischgrätz now has for the Hungarian army is clear from all his operations. On February 28 he occupies Maklar, i.e. advances by only *one hour*. On March 1 he has reached Mezö-Kövesd, i.e. he is yet again one mile further on. There he does not attempt anything like a general attack but merely "large-scale reconnaissance"!! We notice that after his immense victory at Kapolna Windischgrätz pursued the Magyars with such vigour that after two or three miles he had *already lost trace of them* and had to reconnoitre to establish where they were!

Meanwhile Schlick was operating "on the right flank of the enemy"—and his great achievement, as a result of this, was that the "enemy" retreated to the very point to which he would have had to retreat *without* this splendid manoeuvre, namely to Tisza-Füred, his main crossing-point on the Theiss. All in all, Schlick, in his flanking movement, which incidentally looks highly peculiar on the map, has apparently treated the withdrawing Magyar army with just as much respect as Windischgrätz has at the front. In short, on March 2 the headquarters of the courageous Windischgrätz was still at Maklar, i.e. exactly *one* mile further on from the position held by Windischgrätz on the morning of February 26, six days before his great two-day victory!

From this position, on March 2, the whole army was "advancing towards the Theiss". We know that this is the third time that the imperial troops are "advancing towards the Theiss", and presumably they will have the same success this time that they had previously, and that will mean stopping at the Theiss and having to confine themselves to casting longing glances over to the unattainable Debreczin heath.

From the north we hear:

"The division of Lieutenant-Field Marshal *Ramberg* had already pushed its vanguard from Kaschau along the road which forks at Hidas-Nemethy, leading to *Tokaj* on the left and *Miskolcz* on the right."

In plain language: the above-mentioned division has pushed forward its vanguard exactly *four miles,* and this along a road where no large enemy forces are roaming about, but at most enemy guerillas, Kossuth hussars. Immense progress, achieved with remarkable bravery!

The Bulletin goes on to tell of several battles before Komorn,[25] which are more evidence of the courage of the Komorn garrison than of progress on the part of the Austrians. The reader will recall that as early as January the *Kölnische Zeitung* had the Komorn garrison hoisting the white flag at least ten times. And the alleged "initial bombardment" of Komorn, which was said already to have taken place, is now shown to have meant that, not the Austrians were firing bombs at Komorn, but on the contrary the Komorn garrison fired shells at the Austrians. The Bulletin says:

"At Komorn several battles occurred on the right bank of the Danube between the insurgents and the troops of the Lederer brigade—thus, as early as February 17, the garrison at Komorn made a sortie with nine companies, two guns, and half a squadron of hussars, and protected by brisk cannon-fire launched an attack from the bridgehead upon the left flank of the detachment occupying O-Szöny, under the command of Major Kellner of the Khevenhüller infantry. Major Kellner attacked the insurgents and drove them back, killing seventeen of them.—The garrison attempted a similar sortie on February 24, this time with two battalions of infantry, half a squadron of hussars and three guns. The enemy opened fire briskly on the position of Major Kellner, who was occupying O-Szöny with the second Khevenhüller battalion, half a squadron of Fiquelmont dragoons and half a battery of twelve-pounders. Forty shells hit the place causing fires in five points, as a result of which several houses were burned to the ground. Thanks to Major Kellner's expedient measures and the determination of his troops it was possible to check the fire. When, later, the offensive was begun, actively supported by a division under Captain Schmutz's command from the same regiment, which was dispatched with two cannon to the enemy's right flank, the insurgents, who lost fifty men, were driven back within the range of the garrison's cannon by the brave battalion, which thus managed to repulse this sortie as well.—Now Lieutenant-Field Marshal Simunich's division has arrived there on the left bank of the Danube. The Veigl brigade, which is part of it, is stationed on the left bank of the Waag. The Sossay brigade, which already arrived in N. Tany several days ago, is occupying the island of Schütt, and at Gönyö they are busy trying to construct a pontoon bridge in order to link up the two banks of the Danube for the besieging troops. As the battering train from Leopoldstadt has arrived* at Komorn the bombardment of the fortress will begin within the next few days."

Finally we learn the following, something which, printed in a royal imperial *Army* Bulletin, must astonish us:

"According to official reports from Cracow, which are dated March 3, 600 Cossacks are occupying the Russian border on their own territory from Michalovice to the Weichsel and from there to the Pilica. Cracow, which according to other reports was said to have been bombarded and even occupied by the Russians, was quiet, although numerous emissaries and gun-runners were bent on disturbing the peace. Lieutenant-Field Marshal Legeditsch there was perfectly prepared for any eventuality."

So *Cracow* is now also part of the theatre of war. When the official royal imperial bulletins start declaring this themselves, one is obliged to draw strange conclusions!

So much for the official news. From the unofficial sources we report the following:

The Karlowitz *Napredak* reports from the Banat:

"Subotica (Theresiopel) has been taken by the Serbs. The battle was fierce. The troops consisted of detachments from Todorovich's forces and a section of the Serbian auxiliary corps under the command of Kničanin. The Serbs lost 144 men, the number of Magyar dead is not yet known. The Magyars have suffered their most significant defeat here." [a]

From Transylvania only one report from Malkowsky has come in, telling of the curious operations at Bistritz. As we have already examined this [b] we do not need to touch on it again today. The only thing of interest to us is the following naive aphorism, which appeared in the Augsburg *Allgemeine Zeitung,* referring to the Germans' surprise at the arrival of the Russians:

"The Austrian army wishes, of course, to wage this battle without outside aid, but the *Austrian and Russian armies are old comrades in war and have fought side by side countless times on German battlefields. This is something those people apparently wish to forget who talk in such exaggerated terms of Russian support"*!!?[c]

Finally, for the amusement of our readers, we include the letter written by the Vladika[d] of Montenegro to the Serbian leader Kničanin, to accompany the decoration sent to him:

"To the illustrious Mr. Stephan Kničanin,

"Oh pride of our nation! You have totally justified the reputation of the heroes of Dushan and Karageorge. I, and every true Serb, owe you the deepest gratitude. Your noble spirit prompted you to sacrifice yourself for your nation and to hasten to the aid of your suffering comrades. For these reasons I shall always love you and hold you in great esteem, and in deepest gratitude for your untiring efforts I am sending you this likeness of the immortal Obilich. It will most fittingly adorn the breast of the victor of Tomasevec and the deliverer of Pancsova. Receive it then, heroic young scion of heroic forefathers, receive it with the same sincerity and delight with which, accompanied by fraternal greetings, it is sent.

Cetinje, January 28 (February 9), 1849

Vladika of Montenegro, *P. Petrovic Njegoš,* m.p."[e]

Moreover, just how close to the verge of bankruptcy Kossuth has brought the Austrians is evident from the following "proclamation":

"Since the news that Hungarian banknotes in Austria were to be withdrawn from circulation and confiscated has reached wide sections of the public, we wish to reassure

---

[a] This passage was also published in the newspaper *Constitutionelles Blatt aus Böhmen* No. 55, March 6, 1849.—*Ed.*

[b] See Engels, "From the Hungarian Theatre of War" and "Magyar Victory" (present edition, Vol. 8, pp. 471-73 and 477-80).—*Ed.*

[c] "Pesth, 26. Febr.", Augsburg *Allgemeine Zeitung* No. 65, March 6, 1849.—*Ed.*

[d] Ruler and metropolitan.—*Ed.*

[e] "Von der Save, 26. Febr.", *Der Lloyd* No. 107 (evening edition), March 3, 1849. m.p.—abbreviation of "manu propria"—with one's own hand.—*Ed.*

the public and to announce *that withdrawal or confiscation of Hungarian banknotes does not apply to private transactions in Hungary.* Ofen, March 2, 1849. Royal imperial army general headquarters."[a]

To sum up: At most Windischgrätz will reach the Theiss, the Serbs are at the Maros, Malkowsky is outside Bistritz.—All of them are just as far as they were four weeks ago. This is the "second stage" that, according to yesterday's *Kölnische Zeitung*,[b] the Hungarian war has entered.

Written by Engels about March 9, 1849

First published in the *Neue Rheinische Zeitung* No. 242, March 10, 1849

Printed according to the newspaper

Published in English for the first time

---

[a] "Ofen, 2. März", *Der Lloyd* No. 109 (evening edition), March 5, 1849.—*Ed.*
[b] *Kölnische Zeitung* No. 56, March 7, 1849. See also this volume, p. 15.—*Ed.*

# RUGE

*Cologne*, March 9. The *Deutsche Allgemeine Zeitung* contains the following statement of its old contributor Arnold Ruge, the Pomeranian personality and Saxon thinker.

"*Berlin*, March 5. The present members of the Central Committee of German Democrats,[26] d'Ester, Reichenbach and Hexamer, announce a new democratic newspaper entitled *Allgemeine demokratische Zeitung*,[a] which will be '*in reality*' an organ of the party in Berlin. This announcement could arouse the suspicion that the newspapers *Reform* and *Zeitungs-Halle* are *not really* organs of the party, and in the introduction to the announcement it is even fairly clearly indicated that both of them have been *suppressed*. The passage where the Central Committee proclaims and accepts the *suspension* by Wrangel as being *definitive suppression*, reads word for word as follows: 'The severe trials which the Democratic Party in recent months has had to endure in all parts of Germany have convinced it both of the necessity for a strong organisation, and of *the need for it to be represented in the press by definite organs belonging to the party*. Through their sabre regime the rulers have succeeded in *many places*' (the 'sabre regime' however exists only in *Berlin*!) 'in *suppressing* democratic organs of the press, *because* the **individuals concerned** *were unable to make such great sacrifices as would render these violent measures ineffective*.' Because of the sabre regime, everyone thinks only of *Berlin* when he reads of the 'many places'. Even democracy *as a whole* could have made these measures 'ineffective' only by abolishing the sabre, for Wrangel made both Berlin and the Berlin postal service inaccessible to the democratic organs of the press. Let the Central Committee name the means, or the 'sacrifices', by which in our situation *it* would have been able to make this violence ineffective. Even in Wrangel's opinion, however, the *Reform* and the *Zeitungs-Halle* have *not* been '*suppressed*'. However, according to my experience, democrats who have received the circular of the Central Committee, understand it to mean that the *Reform* and the *Zeitungs-Halle* would cease to appear and would be replaced by the *Allgemeine demokratische Zeitung*. I feel compelled to clear up this misunderstanding. *The 'Reform' has not been definitively closed down and, as soon as the state of siege in Berlin has been lifted, it will continue to be published in Berlin*, and indeed as a *real* organ of the Democratic Party, one which by

---

[a] This paper was never published.— *Ed.*

virtue of the definite decisions of the Lefts of the dissolved National Assembly[27] and of the former Central Committee of German Democrats no less '*belongs*' to the party than the new newspaper imposed from above by two members of the present Central Committee (d'Ester and Hexamer).

The Editorial Board of the *Reform*
Arnold Ruge"

Author's postscript: "*I* request all the highly respected editorial boards of German newspapers to publish this *our* statement[a] in their columns."

To our great satisfaction, we learn from this memorable statement that the *ci-devant* Frankfurt "editor of the rationale of events"[28] and at present book publisher—undoubtedly "as such"—declares that he is by no means satisfied with the *imposition* of a new democratic newspaper "in Berlin", a newspaper which is supposed to be "in reality" an organ of the "party in Berlin".

Herr Arnold Ruge, Frankfurt "editor of the rationale of events" and Berlin editor of the *Reform*, maintains "as such" that it was *also* the organ of the "party in Berlin"; by a decision of the "former" Central Committee of Democrats, the *Reform had been* (*elle avait été*, as the French say) "an organ belonging to the party". True, the "former" Central Committee no longer exists "in reality". Nevertheless the newly arising *Reform* can still be a "real" organ of the defunct Central Committee and of the superseded Left of the "dissolved" National Assembly.

Herr Arnold Ruge may certainly attack the newly imposed Berlin *Allgemeine demokratische Zeitung*, a rival in the publishing sphere; outside Berlin there will undoubtedly be fewer competitors for the honorary title of an organ of the "party in Berlin". We were at least never under any misapprehension regarding the *Reform* as the "real" organ of the "party in Berlin"; we are capable also of fully appreciating patriot Ruge's conquest over himself in connection with the above-mentioned "sacrifices". But in any case, it remains a most curious contradiction. The worthy printshop proprietor Ruge takes his stand on the *basis of legality* in order to maintain that his own newspaper, the *Reform,* is the "real" (patently *sans garantie du gouvernement*[b]) organ of the party. On the other hand, the philosopher Ruge takes his stand on the basis of revolt against the "real" democratic Central Committee in order "really" to be able to make further "sacrifices" in his sense of the word (that of a publisher).

A fact that might help to solve this contradiction is given below:

---

[a] "Erklärung der Redaction der *Reform*", *Deutsche Allgemeine Zeitung* No. 67 (supplement), March 8, 1849.— *Ed.*

[b] Without government guarantee.— *Ed.*

The democratic Central Committee told Ruge that it was prepared to appoint the *Reform* as its *Moniteur*[a] on condition that Ruge would refrain from all argumentation and writing.

Written on March 9, 1849

First published in the *Neue Rheinische Zeitung* No. 242, March 10, 1849

Printed according to the newspaper

Published in English for the first time

---

[a] Official organ of the French Government.— *Ed.*

# THE MARCH ASSOCIATION

*Cologne*, March 10. The Frankfurt so-called "March Association"[29] of the Frankfurt so-called "Imperial Assembly"[30] has had the insolence to send *us* the following lithographed letter:

"The March Association has decided to compile a list of all newspapers which have given us space in their columns and to distribute it to all associations with which we are connected in order that with the assistance of these associations the newspapers indicated will be given preference in being supplied with any relevant *announcements.*

"In informing you herewith of this list, we believe it is unnecessary to draw your attention to the importance of the paid '*announcements*' of a newspaper as a source of income for the whole enterprise.

"Further, the Central March Association has decided to recommend the associations to favour with their support the *Teutsches Volksblatt,* a democratic-constitutional newspaper appearing in *Würzburg,* edited by Dr. Eisenmann, in view of the fact that this newspaper is under the threat of succumbing to the competition of anti-democratic newspapers, and the editor has stated that he is not in a position to make further sacrifices over and above those he has already made.

Frankfurt, end of February 1849.

*The Managing Committee of the Central March Association*"

In the enclosed list of newspapers which "have given space in their columns to the March Association" and to which the supporters of the "March Association" should give preference in supplying "relevant announcements", one finds also the *Neue Rheinische Zeitung*, which, in addition, is given the honour of an asterisk.

We hereby announce to all the left-handed and the extreme left-handed members[31] of this so-called "March Association" of the *ci-devant* "Imperial Assembly" that the *Neue Rheinische Zeitung* has never consented to become the organ of a parliamentary party, least of all of a party of the comical Frankfurt imperial club, that our newspaper has never given space in its columns to the so-called

"March Association" of this club, and that in general the *Neue Rheinische Zeitung* has no knowledge of any "March Association". If, therefore, the "March Association" in its lithographed report to those newspapers which have really given it space in their columns designates our newspaper as one of its organs, this is simply calumny against the *Neue Rheinische Zeitung* and absurd boasting on the part of the "March Association". No doubt the patriotic upright men of the "March Association" will know how to reconcile this with their "conscience".

The reference of the "March Association" to our newspaper becomes still more ill-mannered owing to the "decision" of the Association to recommend the "democratic-constitutional" newspaper (the Germanic periodical: *Teutsches Volksblatt*) of "Dr. Eisenmann". Who would not be touched by the sad fate of the great "Germanic" primeval martyr Eisenmann? What upright man will not feel it as a blow that "Dr." Eisenmann, who sold his prison reminiscences to the "democratic-constitutional" King of Bavaria[a] for 12,000 guldens, cannot make "further sacrifices" and is under the threat of succumbing to the publishing "competition" of the ordinary newspapers that are not imposed and that are against the "March Association"? We leave it to the patriots to calculate into what deep neglect the *Teutsches Volksblatt* must have fallen if Eisenmann, the martyr with 12,000 guldens and deputy with a 5-taler salary, has to appeal for public "support". In any case, things must have gone badly, very badly, with the "democratic-constitutional" Eisenmanns if they produce a fictitious begging letter from the *Neue Rheinische Zeitung*, the only newspaper in Germany which has always attacked the "shameless, mean beggars" from among the patriots and imperial-beggarly assemblies.

To the dirty remark of the profit-greedy competition-goaded patriots about "the importance of the *paid* announcements of a newspaper as a *source of income for the whole* enterprise", we, of course, do not reply. The *Neue Rheinische Zeitung* has always differed from the patriots not only generally but also in that it has never regarded political movements as a territory for swindlers or a source of income.

Written by Marx on March 10, 1849     Printed according to the newspaper

First published in the *Neue Rheinische*    ·    Published in English for the first
*Zeitung* No. 243, March 11, 1849     time

---

[a] Maximilian II.— *Ed.*

# FROM THE THEATRE OF WAR

There is no news at all from the theatre of war today. The only interesting item concerning the most recent Austrian war operations is another article today in the Augsburg *Allgemeine Zeitung*, the martial-law paper, which proves above all how low our contemporary journalists have sunk. The *Kölnische Zeitung* is full of enthusiasm for Windischgrätz and goes no further than expressing regret that he is a poor writer of German—as if his intentionally inept style were not ten times more adept than the language of the most profoundly conceived leading articles of the *Kölnische Zeitung*! If Windischgrätz is "confused" and "obscure" in his reports that is only because he has intentionally made them confused and obscure, whether it be to conceal defeats or to make insignificant "advantages", which the Magyars granted him of their own accord, appear to be outstanding victories. But the *Kölnische Zeitung* is not so stupid as it looks. It finds Windischgrätz's reports contradictory or obscure and confused. And what does it conclude from that? Not that Windischgrätz is a bad commander-in-chief but rather a bad—stylist!

Whether the *Kölnische Zeitung* is in the pay of Austria we do not know. But we do know that the *Augsburger Zeitung* is in Austria's pay. And yet the *Augsburger Zeitung* is a thousand times more honest than the *Kölnische Zeitung*.

Compare, for instance, yesterday's article in that steadfast newspaper[a] with the following lines taken from the Augsburg paper, whose lack of principles is well known:

---

[a] A reference to the article "Ungarn" in the supplement to the *Kölnische Zeitung* No. 59, March 10, 1849.— *Ed.*

"The complications in the Hungarian revolutionary war are *unfortunately continuously growing.* Until a few days ago, when he moved his headquarters to Gyöngyös, Field Marshal Prince Windischgrätz remained on the defensive with the main body of the army, whilst the rebels were able to throw all their forces against the weakest points of our line, harass our detached units and often expose them to considerable danger. Whilst the rest of the army stands still, the Serbs, instead of operating concentrically with it, are conquering the Voivodina for themselves and somewhat more besides. Exposed to the bold operations of Bem in the strategically completely neglected Transylvania, Puchner has in his final moment of extreme need to seek Russian help in order to protect the Saxon towns, which alone in Transylvania have remained loyal to the Emperor, and all the victories of the ageing warrior, all the valour of his troops will not suffice to expel the rebel chief, who hour by hour can call upon the spare units of insurgents in Hungary as reinforcements, from the borderlands of that unfortunate country." [a]

The extent to which the Magyar reports boil down to nothing more than "ridiculous exaggerations" is shown by the following fact. The Magyars announced that they had captured Erbach, the Austrians prudently kept quiet about the matter. Now the *Deutsche Zeitung* in Frankfurt writes on March 6:

"Count Erbach, who, accompanied by only one dragoon, had been sent by General Schlick to Field Marshal Windischgrätz, was attacked by a unit of Magyar insurgents and taken prisoner. He was taken off to Debreczin and has written several letters here from there. He has been treated very well, numerous old comrades received him warmly, and his letters are apt to give us a more favourable idea of the Magyars' activity than one usually deduces from indirect reports." [b]

The remaining news from Hungary is summarised in the following report from Vienna, which the *Deutsche Allgemeine Zeitung* publishes:

"The leaders of the Jewish community in Pest had gone to the camp of the Field Marshal to complain that payment of the arrears of the toleration tax [32] amounting to 110,000 florins had been demanded in cash in twenty-florin coins, and that all Hungarian Jewish communities had been made collectively responsible for treasonable crimes of individuals. The Prince dismissed the complaints in very ungracious terms, and particularly strong words are said to have fallen about delegates Fischhof and Goldmark.—The army, which has been brought up to a strength of 700,000 men and has been put on a war footing, costs so much that one could easily be accused of exaggerating when working out the figure; but it certainly costs far more than can be afforded on the basis of the resources of the country without resorting to extraordinary efforts. And only the peasants, who have been released from the personal obligations and land taxes, appear to be in a healthy state, all other classes without exception being sick and infirm. Having new taxes imposed on him would make an illusion of the letters patent of September 7, 1848 [33] as far as the peasant is concerned, consequently for the time being the only expedients left are loans and, according to the signs so far, to an even greater extent paper money. The big bankers

---

[a] This paragraph is taken from the article "Wien (näheres über die Schlacht bei Kapolna)" published in the Augsburg *Allgemeine Zeitung* No. 66, March 7, 1849.— *Ed.*

[b] "Graf Erbach", *Deutsche Zeitung* No. 66, March 7, 1849.— *Ed.*

are constantly buying gold and silver, in the former particular preference being given to ring ducats and gold sovereigns. The Hungarian banknote crisis has by no means rendered this paper worthless, on the contrary, transactions are said to have been completed in Vienna and Pressburg yesterday in 5-florin and 100-florin notes at 86 and 90. That is why an announcement in Pest (see below) had a soothing effect and revived trading in agricultural products, which was transacted almost exclusively in Hungarian banknotes; since no check has, as yet, been carried through on the banknotes already issued this leaves, so to speak, a loophole open for Kossuth's banknote production. This much seems certain: there must be sound reasons for Prince Windischgrätz to show such forbearance and restraint in Hungary in contrast to the procedure adopted in the Austrian provinces."[a]

Incidentally, it is now even more widely acknowledged than ever that the noble Windischgrätz is hand in glove with the Magyar aristocrats such as the Josikas, the Széchenyis, the Esterházys. These are the "sound reasons" that he has. And just a fortnight ago the *Kölnische Zeitung* was looking for the "higher nobility" in the Debreczin camp. *Voilà ce qui s'appelle des savants sérieux!*[b]

From the new royal imperial model state, which goes under the name of Serbska Voivodina, we hear the following news:

"*Semlin*, February 24. At a general meeting held at Temesvar on the 15th of this month the internal administration of the Serbian Voivodina was organised in the following way: administrator and president of the Voivodina: Patriarch Josef Rajachich; vice-presidents: Joseph Rudics, Basil Fogarassy and Stretko Michailovich; heads of sections: 1. matters concerning the church: S. Kačanski, abbot, with four advisers; 2. ecclesiastical affairs and education: Eugen Gjurkovich with four advisers; 3. diplomatic affairs: Jacob Zivanovich with four advisers; 4. political questions: Marcus Popovich with five advisers; 5. economic and financial matters: Johann Šuplikac with five advisers; 6. administration of the law: Thodor Radosavljević with three advisers.—National secretary and director of the administrative office Johann Stankovich; secretary of the Voivodina Alex Stojacković.—Supreme Court: chairman Carl Latinovich; vice-president Joseph Mathich with twelve members. Economic and financial department: chairman Georg Warsan; Joseph Iovanovich, treasurer; Franz, vice-controller; Kolarovich, keeper of accounts with four advisers. First national commissioner Michael[c] Krestić. Agents Kosta Iovanovich, Svetozazhulitich.

"From this impartial election one can see that the Serbian deputies, worthy representatives of their constituents, having eliminated every trace of national hatred and religious differences—for Rudics, Fogarassy, Stein, Stminger and Wachtler are not Serbs and are adherents of the Catholic faith—bore strictly in mind only the elected people's qualifications to hold the offices entrusted to them, and that they are intent on establishing equality of status of every nationality in the Voivodina. In addition to the heads of the sections mentioned, the deputies of every Serb community have also been summoned to Kikinda, where '*sub Praesidio Patriarchae*'[d] they are laying

---

[a] "Wien, 5. März", *Deutsche Allgemeine Zeitung* No. 68, March 9, 1849.— *Ed.*
[b] These are people called real scholars (Paul de Kock, *L'amant de la lune*).— *Ed.*
[c] The name is given incorrectly in the newspaper; it should be "Nicolá".— *Ed.*
[d] Under the chairmanship of the Patriarch.— *Ed.*

the foundation of the constitution of the Serbian Voivodina and outlining its basic rights, and they will present this for approval to the Austrian Government" (*Lloyd*).[a]

"*Agram.* To our great astonishment we have read a report from Constantinople in a Belgrade newspaper published in Serbian[b] according to which the Austrian internuncio,[c] Count Stürmer, had a conference with the Porte Minister for External Affairs[d] on February 7 and asked him: 'What position does the Porte intend to adopt should the Austrian Slavs rise in revolt against the imperial Government?' The answer was that the Porte would remain neutral. However the question raises much more far-reaching considerations in our minds than the answer does. Is it possible that the masses of Russian troops in the Danube principalities are also connected with a similar question of the royal imperial Government?"[e]

Written by Engels on March 10, 1849

First published in the supplement to the *Neue Rheinische Zeitung* No. 243, March 11, 1849

Printed according to the newspaper

Published in English for the first time

[a] "Semlin, 24. Februar", *Der Lloyd* No. 107 (evening edition), March 3, 1849.— *Ed.*
[b] *Serbske Novine* (Србске Новине).— *Ed.*
[c] Title of the Austrian diplomatic representatives in Istanbul from 1678 to 1856.— *Ed.*
[d] Ali Mehemet Paşa.— *Ed.*
[e] *Constitutionelles Blatt aus Böhmen* No. 55, March 6, 1849.— *Ed.*

# THE MODEL REPUBLIC[34]

*Berne*, March 10. Just as Belgium is hailed by the constitutional bourgeoisie and ideologists as the "model state"[a] so is Switzerland the ideal of the republican bourgeoisie and ideologists. Switzerland is not ruled by a king, there is no nobility, taxes are moderate, the country enjoys a state of profound peace;—the only things that people find to grumble about are matters that have been disposed of, such as Jesuits and separatist [Sonderbund[35]] activities. Why, only recently a radical newspaper, the *Neue Deutsche*, was envying Switzerland its peace and contentment. It grieves us to have to destroy this idyllic view of the happiness and well-being of the Swiss people, and to have to point out ugly blemishes "in that most faithful mirror, which reflects freedom". Let us first of all review a few public meetings. On March 5 at Schönbühl in the canton of Berne a so-called communist meeting took place, which was very well attended by workers. The subjects under discussion were the poor-law administration and the emigration question. The descriptions given by the speakers of the conditions of the working people in Switzerland demonstrated the need for speedy and drastic remedies; however, the way in which this was discussed betrayed a great degree of helplessness and showed that, despite all the republican institutions, the proletariat still has very little understanding of its own position and the means of achieving its own salvation.

---

[a] Cf. Marx, "The 'Model State' of Belgium" (present edition, Vol. 7, pp. 333-36).— *Ed.*

The conservatives succeeded in exploiting the social movement for their own ends. The most vehement attacks were directed against the radical Government of Berne and in particular against those in charge of finance, and the defenders of the existing Government were only partially successful in justifying it. A *revision of the Constitution*[36] was decided upon as a remedy, but several speakers declared that they would follow a legal course only temporarily and tentatively. As a revision of the Constitution is the means by which the conservatives and in particular the patricians of Berne are seeking to oust the present Government, their plan to rouse the proletariat against the Government has for the time being been successful. This truly Jesuit tendency was even more evident at the meeting of the central committee of the Society for Emigration of the Berne canton, which was recently held at the Klösterli at Berne. Delegates from 25 superior bailiwicks, approximately 1,000 people, met to discuss every possible way of solving the emigration problem to the advantage of many thousands of unemployed and hungry citizens. As the Great Council,[a] on hearing the report of the government official Schneider, had not pursued the matter with the necessary energy and dedication, here too a revision of the Constitution was proposed without taking into consideration the fact that any attempt to oust the present radical Government would simply make possible the return of the people supporting the old system.

For this purpose a petition is to be circulated in all bailiwicks, and as soon as the 8,000 signatures required under the Constitution have been obtained, the necessary steps will be taken for resolving this problem. As the emigration question is being argued out and discussed everywhere because of the daily increase in unemployment and the growing scarcity of food, particularly in the Bernese Alps, it is not unlikely that the required number of signatures will be obtained, and that means that the present government will then have a big obstacle placed in its way.

In St. Gallen too the working-class movement is making progress.

"Whilst," according to the *Wächter*, "the *Arbeiter* undertakes theoretical experiments in social communism, they have started to put it into practice in the Gasterland under the presidency of Hofstitter; they intend to reduce the rate of interest to 2 per cent etc."

In fact where the radicals are now in power, they ought to take care not to repulse the workers through their indifference. The

---

[a] Supreme body of cantonal administration.— *Ed.*

Swiss proletariat is still largely what one describes as lumpenproletariat, prepared to sell themselves to anyone who will make
extravagant *promises*. The clergy and the aristocrats do not of course
remind the starving people of the times when the peasant was forced
to pay tithes to the parish and the lord of the manor; they only ask,
what is the present government doing for you? And the most loyal
supporters of the Government are unable to reply. If the proletariat
in Switzerland were strong enough and sufficiently advanced to
form an independent party then opposition to the present radicalism
would certainly be justified; under the present circumstances,
however, every stand that is taken against the radical politicians
amounts to a concession towards the conservatives.

The radicals should be generally much more go-ahead and active.
It is not enough to attack reactionary personalities and to make
indiscreet jokes about religion; the party whose main concern is
foreign policy [*Auslandspartei*] should oppose the neutralist politicians with the same energy that Herr Ochsenbein and company
displayed towards the Jesuits and separatists. It is more dangerous to
delay at this stage than it was before. The question of the
re-enlistment treaties,[37] which is being resolved by nine-tenths of the
Swiss people in opposition to the cowardly and doctrinaire
interpretation of the Federal Council, provides the radicals with a
weapon capable of quickly putting an end to the present wretched
state of things. The report from the political department (Furrer),
which was presented to the Swiss Federal Council[a] and dealt with the
subject of the re-enlistments, and which is being hailed by most
newspapers, especially the *Neue Zürcher Zeitung*, as the *ne plus ultra*[b]
of political wisdom, allows us an insight into the small shopkeeper
mentality that pervades the Federal Council, which lets a few pennies
and the principles of civil law guide it in its foreign policy making:

"Where," asks Furrer, "are we to get the money to pay compensation? It is
absolutely impossible for us to pay anything like a substantial portion of this sum from
the Federal Treasury.———This sum would therefore have to be provided by the
cantons. However, if one considers the circumstances calmly and dispassionately and
refuses to allow oneself to be carried away by blind enthusiasm, then one will see that
getting this money together is also an impossibility, especially as far as the future is
concerned, even if one grants that the present can exert such an inspiring influence."

And elsewhere:

"A large nation which cannot even muster a few regiments will hardly be capable
of maintaining independence and political freedom for any length of time."

---

[a] On February 20, 1849.— *Ed.*

[b] The uttermost point attainable, the summit of achievement, acme.— *Ed.*

The Italian republics will no doubt one day express their thanks in the appropriate manner to the neighbouring Swiss republic for this official declaration on the part of its highest-ranking functionary. The *Neue Zürcher Zeitung*, the semi-official organ of the Federal President, had declared that the decision that the ending of the existing re-enlistment treaties is a matter coming under the jurisdiction of the cantons, was taken unanimously by the Federal Council. That is incorrect. The Italian Franscini was not present and the man of "permanent revolution", Druey, had intended to make proposals to the Federal Assembly according to which "the re-enlistment treaties should be abolished when the position in Italy and Switzerland demanded it". He moved, moreover, that enlistment in the Neapolitan regiments be stopped until the matter had been resolved, and that is the main point.

Herr Ochsenbein, the Napoleon of the separatist wars, seeks to introduce not only the Prussian Lohbauer[38] but also the Prussian uniform. However, this laudable intention is being frustrated thanks to the question of cost.

The offer made by some Frenchmen to set up a casino in Switzerland caused great moral indignation among the virtuous republicans. The casino tenants in Germany must have been frightened by the decision of the venerable National Assembly in Frankfurt, otherwise they would not place the gentlemen governing the separatist cantons in the difficult position of having to choose between great financial advantage and traditional morality. The Great Council at Lucerne has also turned down by 79 votes to 67 a proposal to that effect made by a Herr Bias; the section of the people's association there has also sent a petition to the Federal authorities expressing the same sentiments; consequently the entrepreneurs addressed their requests to Schwyz (Stand) and St. Gallen (Rapperswyl), without seeing their wishes fulfilled however. Those gentlemen will now no doubt have to put up with the energy of the tenant of the casino at Homburg, who stated that his casino would endure longer than all Frankfurt parliaments.

The Great Council,[a] which resumed sitting a few days ago, and which still allows itself to be presided over by Herr von Tillier, despite the fact that he is suspected of high treason, is discussing, article by article, the employment regulations, from which we can find nothing to remark on here except the stipulation that political refugees may follow any occupation without further proof of

---

[a] Of the canton of Berne.— *Ed.*

reciprocity. Moreover, the Department of the Interior has proposed that a sum of 8,000 frs. be earmarked for science, the arts etc.

Written by Engels on March 10, 1849

Printed according to the newspaper

First published in the *Neue Rheinische Zeitung* No. 246, March 15, 1849

Published in English for the first time

# VIENNA AND FRANKFURT

*Cologne*, March 12. It was on the 15th of this month that the Imperial Diet in Kremsier intended to begin its consideration of the draft Constitution completed by the commission. The royal imperial brutes of summary jurisdiction then considered that the moment had come to thrust on the Imperial Diet the Constitution "by the grace of God", which had been lying ready for a long time, and to put an end to the whole Kremsier comedy of popular representation that had until then been tolerated.[39]

The whole imposition manoeuvre had already been worked out in the summer of last year between the anointed and unanointed counter-revolutionaries in Schönbrunn-Vienna, Potsdam-Berlin, London (where Metternich, as the master-spider of the Holy Alliance, sits at the centre of the web slowly spun around the peoples rising in revolt for their freedom), and Paris. That it was first of all put into operation by the Potsdam King[a] was due solely to the situation in Prussia which allowed such a step to be taken earlier than in Austria.[40]

In November, official Austria hurled the blood-stained head of Robert Blum at the feet of the deputies in St. Paul's Church.[b] A few days before this, the fine twin-pair of Imperial Commissioners, Welcker-Mosle, had returned from Windischgrätz's antechamber and from gourmandising in Olmütz covered with such disgrace that anyone else but the worthy Welcker-Mosle would have put a bullet through his brain rather than have dared to look anyone on earth in

---

[a] Frederick William IV.— *Ed.*
[b] The reference is to the Frankfurt National Assembly (see p. 36).— *Ed.*

the face. Instead of that, this diplomatic twin-pair even bragged about their roundabout travels.[41]

The majority of the National Assembly was "*satisfait*" just as the French Chamber under Louis Philippe declared itself "*satisfait*" even when faced with the vilest actions and the most striking proofs of corruption.

The blood of the murdered Robert Blum has indeed stained the faces of the deputies in St. Paul's Church. Their cheeks certainly reddened, not however because of shame or fury and an outburst of deepest indignation, but with the colour of pleasure and satisfaction. It is true, fresh Imperial Commissioners were sent to Austria. But the only result they achieved was to redouble the contempt with which the Austrian side had already treated the so-called National Assembly representatives and the Germany they had betrayed.

"*Mocht nix, 's is olles Aans!*"[a]—this was and is the motto of these gentlemen.

It will be recalled that shortly before the arbitrary acts of the Prussian Government Bassermann, Simson and, of course, the "noble" Herr Gagern etc. were in Berlin as Imperial Commissioners.[42]

And once again there are Imperial Commissioners in Austria, in Olmütz, while there, just as in Berlin, the Imperial Diet is being dispersed and a Constitution "by the grace of God" imposed on the people by means of Croats, Serezhans, Huzuls[43] etc.

Wherever freedom of the people is to be destroyed, Commissioners of the so-called Central Authority make their appearance like expectant vultures. Their sense of smell has always proved correct.

Now at last the Frankfurt frog-pond should realise that its turn will soon come. It itself will be punished for all its sins. On the monument to be erected at the site of its wretched activity the wayfarer will read: "Perished through its own fault, through cowardice, professorial stupidity and chronic meanness, amid in part the revengeful derision, and in part the complete indifference of the people."

Yet even now some of these miserable wretches dare to boast of the "fundamental rights" emanating from the Frankfurt factory[44] and are proud of them as though they were a great achievement. With the garrulity of washerwomen, they chattered about "fundamental *rights*" like scholastics in the Middle Ages, while the "*fundamental power*" of the Holy Alliance and its accomplices became ever more strongly organised and scoffed louder and louder at the chatter of the professors and philistines about fundamental rights. The former

---

[a] It does not matter, it is all one (Vienna dialect).— *Ed.*

affixed their "fundamental *rights*" to a scrap of paper, whereas the latter, the men of the counter-revolution, inscribed their "fundamental *power*" on keenly sharpened swords, guns and Slav redcoats.[45]

As soon as the German people in any part of the Germanic fatherlands made use or seemed to want to make use of their original fundamental right, that of revolt against feudal or philistine-constitutional tyranny, Frankfurt with the utmost haste sent "imperial troops" in order to punish the people and make them submissive by billeting troops, by plunder, massacres and military excesses of all kinds, and in order to maintain the tools of the counter-revolution in good condition, that is to say, to fatten them well at the expense of the people and its "fundamental rights" and to fortify them for further heroic deeds.

In such cases the Frankfurt gentlemen always had the necessary power, since they borrowed it from the ranks of the above-mentioned "fundamental power" of our gracious sovereigns.

Consequently, it is not surprising that the Frankfurt frog-pond has to maintain an impotent silence and look on helplessly whenever the anointed gentlemen proclaim *their* "fundamental rights", even if the fundamental rights of the gentlemen "by the grace of God" are aimed directly against it.

Hence also it will and must calmly witness that the Austrian Tamerlane[a] has now dictated 13 fundamental rights to his beloved "subjects" among whom is a considerable number of Germans by the grace of God and Sophia, and simultaneously with this coup he has once again dealt a rough slap in the face to the Frankfurt heroes. And that according to law and justice!

Written on March 12, 1849

First published in the *Neue Rheinische Zeitung* No. 244, March 13, 1849

Printed according to the newspaper

Published in English for the first time ·

---

[a] Emperor Francis Joseph I.— *Ed.*

# [THREE NEW BILLS]

*Cologne*, March 12. The Prussian monarchical power considers the time has come at last to unfold its full glory. The "unweakened" Crown, by the grace of God,[46] has today imposed on us three new Bills—on *associations* and *meetings*, on *posters*, and on the *press*—in which the Chambers are invited to burden us with a compact phalanx of the most delightful September-type laws.[47]

Tomorrow we shall publish the texts of these Bills with their preambles insofar as they have reached us. We shall return—more than once—to these magnificent Prussian products.[a] Today we give only a brief summary of them!

I. *The law on associations.*

"All meetings must be notified 24 hours in advance."

Thus, hastily convened meetings in response to suddenly occurring important events are banned, and it is just such meetings that are most important of all. Everyone must be allowed access, consequently it is forbidden to charge an entrance fee to cover the costs of the meeting. At meetings of associations a quarter of the space must be left for non-members of the association, so that the associations will be compelled to obtain larger and more expensive premises and so that paid agents of the police will be able to disrupt all discussion by noise, uproar and rowdy behaviour, and make every meeting impossible. And if all this should not yield the desired result, it is left open to "representatives of the police department" on any pretext to "immediately dissolve" any meeting in the same way as the

---

[a] See this volume, pp. 65-69, 125-32, 320-29.— *Ed.*

supreme head of the "police department", His Majesty our most gracious king, "immediately dissolved" the Agreement Assembly.[48] As soon as the police declare a meeting dissolved, all those present must leave at once unless they wish to share the fate of the Berlin paladins of agreement, i.e. if they do not want to be driven from the hall by bayonets.

True, the associations do not have to obtain any "preliminary permission", but instead they have to comply with such a mass of preliminary announcements and formalities for the local authorities that for that reason alone their activity becomes almost impossible. Public out-door meetings, processions etc., etc., on the other hand, definitely *require* preliminary police permission. Finally, in order to put an end to the wearing of red ribbons, rosettes and caps, the law further revives the old regulations for persecuting persons wearing black-red-and-gold[a] badges.

Such is the "right of association and assembly" that a year ago the truth-loving Hohenzollern, who keeps his word, guaranteed us with trembling lips!

II. *The law on posters.* All posters of a political nature, except for invitations to attend legal, *permitted* meetings (thus once again all meetings are only most graciously "*permitted*") are *forbidden.* Consequently, in troubled times the executive committees of the associations are not even allowed by posters to request the people to *keep calm,* in order that not a single victim will escape the heroic soldiery! Further: the *sale* or *free distribution* of printed matter in public places is also forbidden, unless one has a special *licence, which can be withdrawn at any moment!* In other words: the Prussian monarchical power wishes to present us with an *improved edition* of the law on *crieurs publics,* which in the worst times of Louis Philippe's bourgeois despotism was wrung from the terrified Chamber of Deputies in France.[49]

And what is the motive given for this law? It is that posters and newspaper-sellers obstruct street traffic, and that posters spoil the appearance of many public buildings!

III. *The law on the press.* But all that is nothing compared with the charming proposals by which it is intended to gag the press. It is known that in general since 1830 the benefaction of the Hohenzollern to the people consisted merely in ennobling the Prussian fatherly patriarchalism by combining it with the modern artful enslavement after the manner of Louis Philippe. Flogging has been retained and penal servitude added to it; censorship has continued

---

[a] The colours of the movement for the unification of Germany.— *Ed.*

and at the same time the full flower of the September legislation has been bestowed on us. In a word, we have simultaneously been given the benefit of all the advantages of feudal servitude, bureaucratic police administration and modern bourgeois *legal* brutality. And this is what is called "the world-famous liberalism of Frederick William IV".

The new Hohenzollern press Bill, after a long series of complicated formal definitions, favours us with a matchless fusion of: 1. the Code Napoléon, 2. the French September laws, 3. and chiefly the laudable *Prussian Law*.[50]

Para. 9 is borrowed from the Code [Napoléon]: In those provinces where the Prussian Law is in force an attempt, an incitement to commit a crime, even if successful, was hitherto less severely punished than the crime itself. In these areas a provision of the Code [Napoléon] is now introduced by which incitement to commit a crime, when successful, is regarded as equivalent to the crime itself.

Para. 10. The French September legislation states: Anyone who attacks *property* and the *family*, the foundations on which civil society is based, or incites citizens to *hatred or contempt for one another*, is liable to be punished by imprisonment for up to two years.

Compare the loi du 9 Sept. 1835, Article 8:

"Toute attaque contre la propriété ... toute provocation à la haine entre les diverses classes de la société sera punie" etc.[a]

The only difference is that the Prussian version: to incite *citizens* in general to hatred etc. for one another is much more ludicrous.

All the subsequent paragraphs of the Bill have been drawn up solely in order once more to confer on the Rhine Province the same magnificent features of the Prussian Law which we had enjoyed to the full for 33 years and of which we were deprived shortly after March 18.[51] Among other things, the following new crimes, totally unknown to our own Rhenish legislation, are to be thrust on us.

1. The arousing of *hatred and contempt towards institutions of the state or its government* by means of actual falsehoods or of facts that cannot be legally proven.

2. "Utterances" about a *legally existing* religious society (under the imposed Constitution[52] even Turks and pagans are legally existing religious societies!), which are calculated (!) to spread hatred and contempt for it.

---

[a] "Any attack on property ... any attempt to foment hatred between the various classes of society will be punished" etc. (*Collection complète des lois, décrets* ... par J. B. Duvergier; à Paris 1836; tome trente-cinquième, année 1835.)—*Ed.*

These two new crimes introduce among us a) the old-Prussian "*arousing of discontent*" and b) the old-Prussian concept of *insulting religion*, and are punished by *imprisonment* for up to two years.

3. *Lèse-majesté* and, in particular, *want of reverence (!!)* for
a) the king (!)
b) the queen (!!)
c) the heir to the throne (!!!)
d) any other member of the royal house (!!!!)
e) the supreme head of a German state (!!!!!),
is punished by imprisonment of from one month to *five years!*

4. The edifying provision that the assertion even of facts that can be proved to be true is to be punished as insult if it demonstrates the *intention to insult!*

5. Insult
1) *to either of the Chambers,*
2) to one of their members,
3) to a *state authority* (the Code does not recognise any insult to corporations as such),
4) to an official or member of the armed forces. All this is "*in connection* with their official function" and is punished by imprisonment of up to 9 months.

6. *Insult or calumny in private life.* The Code Napoléon recognises only *publicly uttered* or disseminated insults or calumnies. The new Bill, on the other hand, intends *to subject to the control of the police and Public Prosecutor's office and/or make punishable all utterances made in private conversation, in the home, in the bosom of the family, in private letters, i.e. it intends to organise the vilest, most universal espionage.* The military despotism of the all-powerful French empire respected at least the freedom of private conversation; it remained — at any rate in its legislation — outside the threshold of the private dwelling. Prussian paternal constitutional supervision and punishment reaches into the inmost sanctum of the private dwelling, into the most secret refuge of family life, which even the barbarians regarded as inviolable. Yet the same law, three Articles earlier, punishes all attacks against the family by two years' imprisonment!

Such are the new "achievements" which it is intended to bestow on us. Three of the cruellest laws mutually supplementing one another in order to attain the acme of cruelty and perfidy which is quite unprecedented — such is the price for lifting the state of siege in Berlin over which the "unweakened" Crown wants to strike a bargain with the Chambers!

The intention is obvious. The press Bill, at least, does not impose anything very new on the old provinces. The Prussian Law was already bad enough. The main anger of the embodiment of the divine grace is turned against *us Rhinelanders. They want to reimpose on us the very same infamous Prussian Law* which we have hardly got rid of, the removal of which, while we are still chained to Prussia, has at last enabled us to breathe somewhat more freely.

The wishes of the King by the grace of God are clearly stated through the mouthpiece of his servant Manteuffel in the preamble to this charming document: the King desires *"the establishment of a legal system that is as uniform as possible"* — i. e. he desires the elimination of the hated French law and the universal introduction of the disgraceful Prussian Law. Further the King desires "to fill the gap" which was caused "in the greater part of the *Rhine Province"* (just listen!) by the abolition of "the penal law on *lèse-majesté* in consequence of the decree of *April 15, 1848*"!

This means that the new penal law is intended to deprive us Rhinelanders of the only thing left to us of the results of the so-called revolution of 1848: *The undiminished validity of our own system of law.*

It is intended that we shall become *Prussians* at all costs, Prussians after the heart's desire of his All-gracious Majesty, with the Prussian Law, arrogant nobility, tyranny of officialdom, rule by the sabre, flogging, censorship and obedience to orders. These legislative proposals are only the very beginning. We have before us the plan of the counter-revolution, and our readers will be amazed at the plans that are being envisaged. We do not doubt that the gentlemen in Berlin will once again be strangely disappointed in the inhabitants of the Rhine Province.

We shall return again and again to these disgraceful Bills, on account of which alone *the Ministers* must be put *into the dock.* But there is something we must already say today: if the Chamber adopts anything looking even remotely similar to these Bills, *then it is the duty of the Rhenish deputies immediately to resign from the Chamber, which by such decisions seeks to throw their electors back into the patriarchal barbarism of the old-Prussian legislation.*

Written by Marx on March 12, 1849

First published in the special supplement to the *Neue Rheinische Zeitung* No. 244, March 13, 1849

Printed according to the newspaper

Published in English for the first time

# GOVERNMENT PROVOCATIONS

*Cologne,* March 12. The high anointed and unanointed lords want to revenge themselves for their sufferings in March 1848 by redoubled joy in March 1849. To this end they have moved heaven and earth so that on the various anniversary dates of the March events in the German fatherlands disturbances will take place in as many parts of Germany as possible thus offering the counter-revolutionaries new opportunities for acts of violence. For weeks past, therefore, the constitutional and aristocratic newspapers have daily concocted stories about enormous preparations for March insurrections, about repeated incursions of republican volunteer bands across the French and Swiss frontiers — in Switzerland there are about 15 $^1/_2$ German republicans; and on each occasion alarm has been aroused in the breasts of worthy philistines by hot air from "reliable sources", "indubitable indications", and "authentic reports". But the jokers endowed with divine grace sit calmly behind the scenes, rejoicing at the effects of their reports *à la* Santa Claus which are being systematically spread by the whole of the servile press, and they smile in a superior manner when the stupid philistines take these calculated cries of alarm *au sérieux.*

In this respect, Baden, i.e. Bekk, had to open the ball. Thereupon the hireling journalists began at once to repeat faithfully this whole litany about incursions, putsches and other foolishness. Then Württemberg and Bavaria had to hasten to perform similar services. Huckstering, venal Frankfurt, which has sold itself, this arrogant and worthless imperial city could not and did not want its "daily press" to lag behind. Hessians also, both the blind and the sighted,[a] as well as

---

[a] "Blinder Hesse" (blind Hessian) denotes a weak-sighted or weak-minded person.— *Ed.*

the Stüve-dominated Hanoverians, and the Brunswick makers of long sausages, and all the other hosts of passion martyrs among the imperial peoples of Germany—they all had to play the same tune. This was performed best of all by most worthy Wrangel-Manteuffel. Four hundred false passports for German refugees in Besançon were prepared, and in addition orders on how to behave and emissaries were dispatched to all corners of the black-and-white territory[a] in order to raise the loudest possible hullabaloo in the press and by oral propaganda about the approaching republican March insurrectionists.

However, many of those Christian-Germanic organs of the press, taking no notice of the very wily directives, made much too loud a noise at the very beginning. They then attempted to correct this mistake by a still stronger beating of drums and still more shameless lies.

Of course, Herr *Hansemann*, too, immediately and most willingly gave his support to this vociferous company in his new newspaper.[b] While apparently belonging to the opposition in the First Chamber, he makes up for this delusive appearance by printing in his newspaper, as a loyal shield-bearer of Manteuffel-Brandenburg, the most absurd information and correspondents' reports about the threatening March insurrections. We shall give only *one* example. He prints the following fabrication from Cologne as the very latest news:

"For some days we have been living—so to speak—in a state of complete anarchy. One has only to go into the streets to find that even *in broad daylight* there are *crowds of workers* strolling about, partly begging, partly robbing; the ale-houses and tobacco shops in particular are subject to numerous attacks. Matters have gone so far that for several days our town hall had to be guarded by a large force of soldiers. At night *no one can feel safe in the streets*. The worst feature in all this is that the mood of the workers is being artificially stimulated so as to bring about a full-scale insurrection on March 18."

Here in Cologne it suffices to reprint this article to expose all its perfidiousness and absurdity.

What could be seen here in broad daylight, and to an increased extent at night, were incessant bloody *fights between troops of different branches of the armed forces*. The intention, it seems, is to drown interpellations about "My glorious army"[53] by calumnies *against the workers*.

The governments are openly preparing for coups d'état which are

[a] Prussia.—*Ed.*
[b] *Constitutionelle Zeitung.*—*Ed.*

intended to complete the counter-revolution. Consequently, the people would be fully justified in preparing for an insurrection. But it knows perfectly well that the complicated situation in France, and especially in Hungary and Italy, will inevitably in the near future provide an opportunity for a rising. It will not therefore allow itself to be decoyed into a clumsily laid trap.

Written on March 12, 1849                 Printed according to the newspaper

First published in the *Neue Rheinische*      Published in English for the first
*Zeitung* No. 245, March 14, 1849            time

# AN AUSTRIAN REPORT
## PUBLISHED IN THE AUGSBURG *ALLGEMEINE ZEITUNG*

There are no direct reports. The post from Vienna, which was due yesterday, failed to arrive even in Breslau and Berlin, and the post expected for today is missing once again together with all postal deliveries from Berlin. We are therefore printing today several extracts from an article published in the Augsburg *Allgemeine Zeitung* which is well suited to cast a good deal of light on the black-and-yellow[a] bragging in which certain German newspapers indulge[b]:

"After the slight resistance which the imperial troops encountered as they proceeded through Hungary as far as Pest, the news of the two-day battle at Kapolna, which ended *without a decisive result* after fierce fighting, came as a considerable surprise. This was the first important battle with the insurgents, who for the first time brought their regular troops into action, men whose *acknowledged bravery*, under the leadership of a skilful commander like Perczel, was further increased by the *fanaticism of the hussars*. The battle proved that with more training and discipline the Magyars are *fighting with a courage and contempt for death* which has characterised this nationality for centuries. Yet, apart from demonstrating this, the battle *did not alter* matters *in any other way*, for, according to reports of March 2, the insurgents moved from Maklar to Mezö-Kövesd on February 28 and went back on the road from there to Poroszlo and Tisza-Füred, *in orderly line* but with the intention of crossing the Theiss; their rearguard fought with imperial troops at Kövesd and then later at two other places, in order to cover their retreat. Prince Windischgrätz brought his headquarters forward as far as Mezö-Kövesd and dispatched General Zeisberg to Tisza-Füred via Besenyö in order, if possible, to cut off the insurgents' retreat across the bridge there; should this manoeuvre prove successful then their leader, General Dembiński, would have to engage his troops in a second general battle in order to force the crossing of the

---

[a] The Austrian imperial colours.— *Ed.*

[b] There follows a quotation from "Wien, 5. März", published in Augsburg *Allgemeine Zeitung* No. 68, March 9, 1849.— *Ed.*

Theiss; otherwise they could cross the river without any trouble, join forces with the corps of insurgents which was constantly engaged in skirmishes with the imperial Ottinger brigade at Szolnok, and once more offer resistance to the Field Marshal. Anyone who puts together in his mind the present bitter clashes with the hints in the November edition of the Kossuth newspaper, and has read Kossuth's warnings that a retreat on the part of the Hungarian army into the interior of the country, were it to occur, should not be regarded as flight but rather as a strategic plan, anyone who has read his proclamation to the peasants telling them to arm themselves in the rear of the imperial troops, to cut off all supplies and to ambush individual units, and anyone who has read his instructions on conducting guerilla warfare etc., will understand the reasons for the speedy retreat to Pest and for the striking circumstance that Prince Windischgrätz was faced with a force of only 24,000 insurgents under Görgey. The insurgents had abatises and entrenchments built at Pressburg, Wieselburg and Raab, anticipating that these defensive measures would induce the imperial army to procure a fairly large artillery park and the necessary horses for it, and that they themselves would gain time to bring up their recruits from the Slav comitats in the area of the Theiss, to obtain the rifles ordered from Belgium and to train their army. The insurgents retreated as far as Pest almost without striking a blow because they intended to raise a *Landsturm* in the rear of the imperial troops and to weaken their strength by means of the garrisons left behind at Pressburg, Oedenburg and Raab and of the besieging troops at Komorn."

The Augsburg *Allgemeine Zeitung* then proceeds to a naturally one-sided, Austrian review of the war, and then goes on:

"In the meantime 8 brigades of imperial troops had joined forces at Rimaszombat and advanced on the insurgents—50,000 men with 120 cannon—who had joined forces at Mezö-Kövesd and Kapolna. Prince Windischgrätz brought several cavalry regiments from Pest to Gyöngyös and took charge of approximately 40,000 imperial troops and, as we are told, 140 cannon for the attack on the insurgents, who had taken up an advantageous position. The hussars fought stubbornly and recklessly, and it was they who for some time held the victory of the imperial army in the balance; the regular infantry, which consisted of barely 8,000 men, fought with courage and tenacity; the men of the army reserve held good for longer than usual but were soon however abandoned by their inexperienced and cowardly officers; the Italian Zanini battalion, which had deserted, was captured by the imperial troops at Kapolna; and the result was that the regular insurgents who continued fighting were no longer a match for the on-rushing columns of imperial troops and had thereupon only to cover the retreat of the whole insurgent force, thus preventing a rout. Just how much such troops can achieve when led by skilful and courageous officers is shown by the Hungarian infantry in Italy which incontestably belongs to the most courageous section of the Austrian army; it is a great pity that in their delusion they are fighting here for an insurrection which causes more harm in Hungary the longer it lasts. Baron Jellachich has gone to Temesvar to assume supreme command over the imperial and Serbian troops; his authority and energy will succeed in restraining the Serbs, who wish to regard the districts occupied with the assistance of the imperial army as their own property, and will succeed in containing their arbitrary behaviour. The Serbs under Kničanin are positioned outside Szegedin, two successive attacks have been repulsed by the Magyars who are weaker in number. In Transylvania Bem appears to have recovered and to be advancing on Hermannstadt, Lieutenant-Field Marshal Gläser, however, is said to be approaching him, in which case his corps could not escape being taken prisoner"(!).

As to other news items, the following is worth mentioning:

"*Pesth*, March 3. The Solt district has received an order from Debreczin stating that all men between 18 and 30 years of age are to take up arms and march against the Raizen.[54]

"Several Honved[55] officers, who had promised never again to fight against the imperial troops and were released from the fortress of Esseg, are said to be engaged in organising a popular uprising " (*Lloyd*).[a]

Written by Engels on March 13, 1849

First published in the *Neue Rheinische Zeitung* No. 245, March 14, 1849

Printed according to the newspaper

Published in English for the first time

---

[a] "Pesth, 3. März", *Der Lloyd* No. 110 (morning edition), March 6, 1849.— *Ed.*

# [FROM THE THEATRE OF WAR]

Once more the post from Berlin, which has just arrived and which was due yesterday evening, does not contain any letters or papers from Vienna. Nor were they received in Breslau. March 8 is the last date for which we have direct news from Vienna, and that contains *nothing more than rumours* from the Hungarian theatre of war. According to an issue of the *Lithographierte Correspondenz*, Windischgrätz has crossed the Theiss with his troops at Tisza-Füred. According to the *Allgemeine Zeitung* he was totally beaten straight after that in a great battle.

All the reports from Transylvania agree on the point that Bem and the Szeklers[56] control the whole country, with the exception of Kronstadt and Hermannstadt. Schässburg is still occupied by the Szeklers. Bem is said to have been summoned to the main army at Debreczin and another audacious Pole, Budinski, to have assumed his command in Transylvania. Just what is true in all these rumours one cannot say. However, the total silence on the part of all the official newspapers does not bode well for the fortunes of the royal imperial forces.

Reports have been confirmed that Perczel has neither been captured nor gone to Switzerland, but that *he is stirring up the population of the Tolna comitat in the rear of the imperial troops*. He had just time enough in Pest to pay a few polite visits and escaped to Tolna just as the military authorities began to search for him.

Whilst the people is thus rising in the Austrians' rear in the *South-West* the same is occurring in the *North-West*. Reports from various sides indicate that here, where Görgey was able for so long to hold up three whole army corps, once again a corps of 10,000-12,000 men is operating against the Slovak mountain towns and has completely destroyed the Czech, Moravian and Slovak volunteer corps under Štúr and Hurban. The leader of the Magyar-Slovak corps (for most of the Slovaks sympathise with the Magyars, and in these regions, which are inhabited almost entirely by Slovaks and Germans, it is quite impossible to raise an army corps without Slovaks) is said to be a certain *Clouth*. Individual refugees arriving at Miava on the Moravian border have passed this information on to the Slovanská-Lípa[57] at Prague.

The following item, taken from the *Siebenbürger Bote*, is likewise entertaining. It is a sample of the "ridiculous exaggerations" of the imperial forces in Transylvania, and it is now going the rounds in all the German papers. Whilst the imperial troops were retreating with all haste to Pest and Losoncz, the *Siebenbürger Bote*, whose military reports are acknowledged as having "an official character", had them achieve the following glorious victories:

"*Hermannstadt*, February 22. On the evening of the day before yesterday we received the news that from February 10 to 12 the combined troops of Lieutenant-Field Marshal Schlick and Schulzig had fought a murderous battle against the Hungarian rebels and *taken Grosswardein*. It was reported that *the whole battle-line from Debreczin to Grosswardein was strewn with the innumerable corpses of those who had fallen in battle, which were piled up in heaps.* The same news arrived here the day after from three other places"(!!!).[a]

Written by Engels about March 14, 1849        Printed according to the newspaper

First published in the second supplement        Published in English for the first
to the *Neue Rheinische Zeitung* No. 245,        time
March 14, 1849

---

[a] "Hermannstadt, 22. Februar", *Der Siebenbürger Bote* No. 24, February 23, 1849.— *Ed.*

# [AUSTRIAN DEFEATS]

The latest newspapers and letters have just arrived from Vienna and Bohemia. The official silence continues. On the other hand it is evident from unofficial reports:

1) that the imperial troops have been *beaten* at Szolnok. Instead of crossing the Theiss at Poroszlo, a section of the main Hungarian army set off down the Theiss, and, having joined forces with other Magyar mobile columns, attacked the royal imperial troops stationed outside Szolnok from the rear. At the same time the Magyars who were positioned on the right bank of the Theiss pressed forward over the river. The imperial troops were completely beaten, the railway from Szolnok to Abony was destroyed and the whole area occupied by the Magyars. Szolnok has therefore been snatched from the imperial troops *for a second time;*

2) that things do not look very bright for the imperial troops both at their centre and on their left flank: on March 5 *a huge number of cannon, Congreve batteries and waggon teams* from Kapolna *arrived in Pest* and were transported to the fortress of Ofen. And the great commander Windischgrätz—he is said to be *slightly wounded—has moved his headquarters back to Ofen.* He has transferred command to Lieutenant-Field Marshal Schlick, ordering him to advance across the Theiss without any further delay, to storm Debreczin and put an end to the affair!

In brief: The imperial forces have been beaten at Szolnok once more and dislodged from the town; Windischgrätz has gone back to Ofen and his artillery and waggon train have followed him; thus the imperial forces must also have been beaten there.

One defeat of the Austrians is certain, a second one probable—*Finis Hungariae!*

Written by Engels about March 14, 1849

Printed according to the newspaper

First published in the second supplement
to the *Neue Rheinische Zeitung* No. 245,
March 14, 1849

Published in English for the first
time

# THE HOHENZOLLERN GENERAL PLAN
## OF REFORM

*Cologne,* March 14. "The *exceptional* states of siege will be lifted as soon as the *general* state of siege has been imposed on the entire kingdom by laws and has become part of our constitutional customs. The series of these 'firm' laws will begin with *September legislation on associations and the press.*"

These are the words we used to accompany the publication of the speech from the throne (No. 234 of the *Neue Rheinische Zeitung*[a]). And what is the content of the first parliamentary act of the Government? It comes before the Chambers and declares:

"We shall deliver you from the state of siege. In exchange you will impose permanent martial law on meetings, associations and the press."

We cannot for a moment conceal the fact that from the outset the parliamentary Left by its timid behaviour has made it easier for the Government to go over to the offensive.

We shall compare *en détail* the splendid three Bills with the September laws, with the pre-March Bill on criminal legislation, and with the Prussian Law.[58] But first of all we inform our readers of the *general plan of the old-Prussian reformers,* to which our special supplement[b] the day before yesterday already drew attention.

On the very same day on which the unofficial Berlin newspapers published the three splendid Bills, the *Neue Preussische Zeitung,* that *Moniteur* of Brandenburg providence, published an "*Opinion on the Essential Tasks of the Present Assembly of the So-called Representation of*

---

[a] See article "Speech from the Throne" (present edition, Vol. 8, pp. 445-50).— *Ed.*
[b] See this volume, pp. 50-54.— *Ed.*

*the People*."[a] The Hohenzollern dynasty and its Brandenburg Government are of too "*noble*" a lineage to be hypocritical at moments when the sun of "power" shines on the unweakened Crown.[59] At such moments the royal heart knows no restraint and humiliates the plebeian masses by a rough, unceremonious expression of its most intimate desires and thoughts. It has pleased fate—the fact cannot be concealed—, heartless fate, more than once by a peculiar turn of events to bring to naught prophecies, threats and desires which "our good King", Frederick William IV (the ingenious *Frederick William IV*, who in putting on the crown used precisely the same words as Napoleon had when assuming the iron crown of Lombardy)[60] uttered at moments of triumphant power, moments of "divine intoxication", as *Goethe* says.[b] But it is well known that iron destiny rules even over the gods. In any case, for a royal heart, just as for a woman's heart, and for every heart, it remains an intoxicating supreme delight to give full vent without hindrance to one's most intimate thoughts, and to attune the world if only by a speech, by a document, to the desires of one's own heart.

Hence the outpouring of the *Neue Preussische Zeitung*, which is more or less that of the royal heart, is in itself of great psychological interest; on the other hand, it lets the people know what is expected of them, what if necessary will be *obtained by force* from them—of course, in their own well-understood interest.

The *Neue Preussische Zeitung* (No. 59, supplement), in order to facilitate a survey of the *Hohenzollern general plan of reform*, has arranged it *under headings*, which in any case is a commendable condescension towards the public. Was it not at liberty to report the royal decisions in apocalyptic form in the manner of the Revelations of St. John? Let us keep to the headings!

The "essential tasks of the present assembly of the so-called representation of the people" are sub-divided as follows:

1) *Purging the Chamber from political criminals. A Jove principium.*[c] The first law for a Chamber which should act in accordance with the wishes of the royal heart, is to transform itself in accordance with the wishes of the royal heart. For the time being, its composition is still a product of disrespectful universal suffrage, even if it is indirect suffrage.

And what does the royal heart demand?

---

[a] "Votum über die wesentlichen Aufgaben der jetzt versammelten sogenannten Volksvertretung", *Neue Preussische Zeitung* No. 59 (supplement), March 11, 1849.— *Ed.*

[b] J. W. Goethe, "Westöstlicher Diwan".— *Ed.*

[c] A divine principle—from Virgil's *Bucolica.*— *Ed.*

The present representation of the people, the *Neue Preussische Zeitung* divulges, is disfigured by "a *blemish*" which makes it unworthy and incapable of "being in its entirety an embodiment of *Prussian* honour, *Prussian* loyalty and love of the Fatherland". This is a nuisance of which it must rid itself, in order to be "righteous" in the eyes of His Majesty.

"This blemish, this nuisance, consists in the fact that its membership includes persons who took part in the criminal actions of the parliamentary faction headed by *Unruh,* particularly in the *factional decision on refusal to pay taxes."*

"The Government," it goes on to say, "owing to its own regrettable *weakness* or from *distrust* of the *judiciary,* which indeed is *to a large exent infected with revolutionary sentiments,* did not put those men *on trial.* To make up for this *omission,* this *mistake,* is the task of the *Chambers;* to press for this is particularly the *duty of all judges* and *lawyers* who are members of the Chambers, if only *to preserve the vanishing honour of their profession.* A motion therefore *must* be put to the *Government*—and it should be one of the *first* actions after the Chamber has been constituted—that the Minister of Justice should now institute a court investigation and punishment of these criminals. *Such an expurgation is the first and most urgent requirement for the successful progress of the deliberations."*

It is the dearest wish of the King to see punishment meted out to the tax-refusing evil-doers and desecrators unto the third generation.[a] The royal Government was too *weak* to fulfil this wish. The royal-Prussian people was so *shameless,* so obstinate that it once more elected evil-doers and sinners as its representatives in open revolt against the Emperor's heart. It is now up to the *Chambers* to *compel* the royal Government to carry out the most personal intentions of His Majesty. On bended knees, they must beg the Ministry to allow them to expel from their midst all infected elements who are in a higher sense *not presentable at court.* And, above all, the theologians and Pharisees, the "judges and lawyers", have to save their "profession", whose "honour" began to vanish from the moment Manteuffel began to harbour the suspicion, of course without foundation, that the Prussian Themis might remain blind to the clear hints of the Crown. But how can a judiciary save its honour in the eyes of the people, for which every fancy of the embodiment of divine grace would not be a law, which would not obey implicitly the orders of the King himself?

It is well known that in all religions penitence, sacrifice, and if possible self-sacrifice, are the real essence of divine worship, of the cult. The so-called representation of the people, in order to prove that it is a representation of the royal heart—and the royal heart is the vital, individualised incarnation of the real heart of the

___

[a] Exodus 20:5.— *Ed.*

people—the "so-called" representation of the people must therefore above all sacrifice *itself, that is itself as an emanation of the sovereignty of the people,* on the steps of the throne.

It must cast out all members who are obnoxious to His Majesty and deliver them to prison and the executioner as an expiatory offering of the religion of absolute monarchy. In that way it will atone, firstly, for the crime of its *original sin,* the sin of having been brought into existence by popular sovereignty. At the same time it will expiate a crime-laden past which is defamatory of royalty and therefore blasphemous. It will purify itself to become a true expression of the fullness of royal power. From a "*so-called*" popular representation it will become a *real* popular representation—in the higher, royal Prussian sense. The King is the *real* Prussian people. The real Prussian people—which must in no way be confused, after the bad foreign custom, with the superficial *number* of inhabitants of the state—therefore elects representatives solely in order that the royal wishes shall be re-echoed to the King as the people's wishes and in this way the most secret demands of his sovereign heart achieve a reality both prosaic and generally accepted in the form of public legislative proposals and decisions of the Chamber.

Consequently, we expect from the Berlin Chambers that they will commence their cult of the King by *self-sacrifice*, by casting out the sinners *who refuse payment of taxes.*

The *Neue Preussische Zeitung* does not conceal that even then the Chamber will still not be righteous in the eyes of His Majesty. The other part of the sacrifice, however, cannot be performed by the Chamber as a corporation. It remains dependent on the active consciousness of sin and the self-crucifixion of the individual members concerned.

"It is true that such a purge," says the *Neue Preussische Zeitung* with a sigh, "would not expel all *those* members whom, because of their antecedents in politics and statesmanship, it would be desirable to see removed for so long as they fail to *realise* and *repent* their *share* in the misfortune of the Fatherland and to *take a vow publicly pledging* themselves to check to the best of their ability the crimes[a] for which in part they were personally to blame. Nevertheless, it stands to reason that there can be no question of expelling from the Chambers on *legal* grounds all those persons who have served the revolution, who in particular between *March 18 and November 8* as highly placed officials have been *used up in this service*" (genuine Prussian grammar). "It would however be desirable that their *own consciousness* should cause them to absent themselves, unless they turn over a *new leaf* in the way indicated above. Also, in connection with this" (supreme) "wish, in all fairness distinctions make themselves felt, for example, *between Rhenish traders,* who should become pillars of the state

---

[a] In the *Neue Preussische Zeitung*: "Verderben" (ruin) and not "Verbrechen" (crimes).— *Ed.*

overnight, and men of the *old-Prussian*" (feudal) "families, whose honourable names have from of old been most closely bound up with the history of our royal house and of the *original heart-lands*" (is *Silesia* also an original heart-land?) "of the monarchy."

We told the "*Rhenish traders*" about this long ago. It is only with *dégoût*[a] that the feudal house of Hohenzollern chose this bourgeois canaille as a lowly tool and it waits impatiently for the moment when it can get rid of them with kicks in a radical fashion. *Hansemann! Camphausen! Kühlwetter!* On your knees! Clothed in a penitent's shroud in front of the royal palace, in full view of the people, with ashes strewn on your crime-laden heads, vow and publicly testify that in the most profound remorse you repent having for a moment dared with bourgeois-constitutional intrigues to prepare the counter-revolution, the accomplishment of which befits only "My glorious army"[61] and—you skinflints, haggling serfs, pedantic traders in fats,[62] cunning railway speculators—having not only saved the throne, but having even boasted of this salvation in high-flown woe-begone phrases. On your knees! Don the penitent's shroud! Or get you to a monastery!

And as regards the "*men of the old-Prussian families*", *nobly-born* and *favoured by predestination* off-shoots of the *chosen* people, we expect in the near future to read in the *Staats-Anzeiger* obituary notices of these, of an *Arnim, Auerswald, Bonin, Pfuel*. Only if they go voluntarily to their death can we believe in their repentance. From a *Rhenish trader* such as *Hansemann*, such greatness of soul is not to be expected. Hansemann is a Voltairean of the most objectionable sort, superficial, and above all, hard-hearted in money matters.

Vanish therefore from the Chambers, leave the stage, you living monuments of March 18, of royal tribulations, humiliations, inconsistencies and weaknesses! Withdraw from the Chambers, or condemn yourselves to be the scapegoats for March 18!

The Chambers themselves, however, will present the tax-refusers to the royal throne as a hecatomb of their purification and expiation and thus make themselves worthy of fulfilling the further "tasks" dictated by the King to "the so-called representation of the people".

(Continuation follows)[b]

Written by Marx on March 14, 1849          Printed according to the newspaper

First published in the *Neue Rheinische Zeitung* No. 246, March 15, 1849          Published in English for the first time

---

[a] Distaste.— *Ed.*
[b] See this volume, pp. 125-32.— *Ed.*

# THE CENSORSHIP

*Cologne*, March 14. The German daily press is certainly the flabbiest, sleepiest and most cowardly institution under the sun! The greatest infamies can be perpetrated before its very eyes, even directed against itself, and it will remain silent and conceal everything; if the facts had not become known by *accident*, one would never have learnt through the *press* what splendid March violets have been brought into being by divine grace in some places.

Last autumn citizen and communist Drigalski[63] tried to re-introduce censorship in Düsseldorf, on the pretext of the state of siege.[a] The attempt succeeded for two days; but the storm it aroused in public opinion compelled the sabre-bearing gentlemen immediately to abandon their yearning for censorship.

But what does the situation look like in the old provinces?[64]

*For three months censorship has existed in all its glory in two different districts,* but the entire old-Prussian press calmly passes over this scandalous encroachment on its rights!

Just listen to this:

*Rosenberg*, in Silesia, March 7. No. 19 of the *Rosenberg-Kreuzburger Telegraph* publishes the following statement at the top of the page.

"We ask the readers of our newspaper not to blame us for the delay in the appearance of this issue and its incompleteness, but to take into account that we are still under the state of siege and that the *Telegraph*—which *has* recently *been under the censorship* of the local royal district president, Herr Sack, who has been elected as a deputy to the Second Chamber—after his departure to Berlin *has now been placed under direct military censorship.*

*"The editorial board."*

---

[a] See Marx, "Drigalski—Legislator, Citizen and Communist" (present edition, Vol. 8, pp. 75-80).— *Ed.*

Furthermore:

Unrestrained *censorship has* likewise *been in existence* in *Erfurt since November 25.* The press there was at first censored by Herr *F. W. Huthsteiner,* now a police inspector, ex-editor of the *Barmer Zeitung* that had at one time been liberal under the censorship. Huthsteiner was ostensibly a liberal or democrat, later a subordinate of Duncker and a permanent Prussian policeman. Although this respectable gentleman even deleted articles from the unfortunate Berlin *National-Zeitung* (!), his official activity was nevertheless considered to be insufficiently Prussian and he was replaced by an *officer.* Therefore *military censorship* exists in Erfurt as well.

But that is not all: censorship is introduced also for newspapers and other publications printed abroad, i.e. outside the area under the state of siege. The *Erfurter Adressblatt* of February 7 contains the following announcement:

"On orders from the royal Commandant's office here, the Erfurt public is warned, on pain of **'appropriate police punishment'** and **'immediate arrest'**, against the *distribution* or bill posting of materials printed outside the town *which cast suspicion on government measures or launch malicious attacks against them*, and thereby have the effect of *alienating the minds* of the population from the existing constitutional *government*, or which tend to *provoke* animosity against specific classes of the population and, consequently, *unrest and friction in our town.*

Erfurt, February 5, 1849.

*The Municipal Administration, Police Department."*

The restoration of censorship, and the replacement of ordinary by military censorship, are surely things which closely concern the press. Yet the press of neighbouring places—the press of Breslau, Berlin, Leipzig—accept all that as if it were a matter of course! In fact the German press is still the old "*good press*".

But we ask our somnolent deputies in Berlin: will they still fail to move that the Ministers be promptly brought to trial?

Written on March 14, 1849        Printed according to the newspaper

First published in the *Neue Rheinische*     Published in English for the first
*Zeitung* No. 246, March 15, 1849      time

# FROM THE THEATRE OF WAR

There is little to add to the reports published this morning. The reports on the battle at Szolnok are extremely vague; but it seems that the Karger imperial brigade stationed there was attacked by the Magyars from the rear at Abony and driven to the opposite (left) bank of the Theiss, which is wholly in Magyar hands. If this is so, the brigade is lost and not a man can escape being killed or taken prisoner. Three battalions were sent from Pest to Abony; but they were too late, of course. Just as they were leaving by train, the defeated General Zeisberg arrived in Pest from Szolnok. He had to go by carriage as far as Abony, since the railway was already destroyed.

In Budapest new fortifications are being erected.

"The blockhouses at the two bridgeheads of the suspension bridge," writes the *Constitutionelles Blatt aus Böhmen*, "should be completed shortly and offer a firm bulwark against attacks, not easy to take.

"In spite of the announcement that there can be no question of calling in or confiscating Hungarian notes in private circulation in Hungary, there is a heavy surcharge on the purchase of Austrian banknotes with Hungarian paper money, and the latter's rate of exchange is likely to fall day by day, since the merchants here have to make many more payments of considerable sums to the other patrimonial dominions, in particular to Vienna, than they will be receiving from there. The Israelites of the capital have been given renewed orders to pay the instalments on the notorious arrears of the toleration-tax redemption in silver pieces of twenty, but the community has been granted an extension of a fortnight, or of 18 days, according to another report." [a]

From the comitat of *Tolna* we learn from the same paper:

"The Tolna county is again *in full rebellion*, despite its declarations of allegiance. The speeches which Moriz Perczel recently made at public meetings there sowed bad

---

[a] "Pest, 5. März", *Constitutionelles Blatt aus Böhmen* No. 59, March 10, 1849.— *Ed.*

seed, and the military authority was informed too late when he stayed incognito at his father's baronial estate a few days ago. Only his carriage and his innocent valet fell into the hands of the imperial troops."[a]

Nor do things look too brilliant for the imperial arms in the *south.* Let us quote once more the *Constitutionelles Blatt aus Böhmen*:

"As regards the capture of Alt-Arad a considerable snag has been encountered. General Todorovich wanted to leave his whole corps behind as garrison, but some of the officers regarded three battalions as sufficient for the purpose. So it happened that, when the main body of the Serbs moved into their camp, the defeated Magyars returned across the Maros, and as a result two battalions were driven out and one was partly captured, partly cut down."[b]

When the imperial troops took Esseg, they expected that the garrison would rush to join the imperial army, but of the four companies of former regular troops of the imperial army *not one man* and of all the Honveds[65] only *16 men* were recruited.

The following news comes from Croatia, on which "independence" has been imposed. The *Agramer Zeitung* writes:

"We hear from a reliable source that the Ministry of Trade intends in the near future to begin the regulation of the River Sava upstream to Sissek and then the building of a railway from Sissek to Agram and thence to Karlstadt and Steinbrück."[c]

Quite in order. Let the Royal and Imperial Government make rivers navigable there, build railways, bring commerce and industry into the country, and it will discover for how much longer it will then be able to rely on its Croats. No sooner will the Croat exchange the red-coat[66] for the frock-coat, than his enthusiasm for the martial-law emperor[d] will automatically cease.

Ban[e] Jellachich has told the Banal Council that he has granted an amnesty to the pro-Magyar Croats—including the six party leaders[67]—who fled to Hungary and were banned when they did not return after being asked three times.

Lastly, it is reported from the Turkish border that

"there is a great deal of activity in Turkey. In Bosnia large bodies of troops are being armed and concentrated at Travnik. Although scouts report that threats against

---

[a] "Pest, 6. März", *Constitutionelles Blatt aus Böhmen* No. 59, March 10, 1849.— *Ed.*

[b] "Von der Drave, 27. Feb.", *Constitutionelles Blatt aus Böhmen* No. 56 (first supplement), March 7, 1849.— *Ed.*

[c] The passage is quoted from the *Constitutionelles Blatt aus Böhmen* No. 59, March 10, 1849.— *Ed.*

[d] Francis Joseph.— *Ed.*

[e] Ban or Banus—Viceroy or Governor.— *Ed.*

the borderers[68] are sometimes heard being uttered, it is more likely that these preparations are connected with the political intrigue Palmerston is hatching in Constantinople regarding the Danube provinces with no lesser an aim than to drive the Russians from Moldavia and Wallachia and so uncover the Austrian flank to the east. Austria can expect a strong Note with regard to the 10,000 Russian troops protecting Transylvania."[a]

| | |
|---|---|
| Written by Engels about March 14, 1849 | Printed according to the newspaper |
| First published in the *Neue Rheinische Zeitung* No. 246, March 15, 1849 | Published in English for the first time |

---

[a] "Von der Drave, 27. Feb.", *Constitutionelles Blatt aus Böhmen* No. 56 (first supplement), March 7, 1849.— *Ed.*

# [FROM THE THEATRE OF WAR]

Today there is no news from the theatre of war, except for the Magyar report of the *Breslauer Zeitung*. It shows that the Austrians were indeed decisively defeated in the battle of Szolnok and forced to retreat towards Pest. *Kecskemét* is said to be again occupied by the Magyars. The Serezhan Colonel Albert Jellačić, Major Prince Holstein and even the royal imperial General Ottinger are said to have been killed.

The Magyar report claims that Stuhlweissenburg (on the right bank of the Danube, towards Vienna) is occupied by Magyars, and that in consequence of the Magyars' latest advances Prince Lobkowitz has gone to Debreczin to offer them *mediation proposals*. *More details tomorrow.*

Written by Engels on March 15, 1849

First published in the second supplement to the *Neue Rheinische Zeitung* No. 246, March 15, 1849

Printed according to the newspaper

Published in English for the first time

# FROM THE THEATRE OF WAR

Today's *Breslauer Zeitung* carries two Magyar reports, of March 6 and 7, which this time are for once written in a somewhat confused manner.[69] One gets from them a sense of the immense impression which the sudden hasty retreat of the Austrians made in Pest, and the thousand rumours it produced in which facts are mixed up with exaggerations.

At *Mezö-Kövesd,* one mile[a] beyond Maklar and two beyond Kapolna, a great battle is said to have taken place on March 3, in which Dembiński *totally defeated the imperial troops* by the masterly use of the terrain and skilful tactical manoeuvres. Their losses are given as 7,000 men and 60 cannon.

It is quite certain that the Hungarians have by no means retreated across the Theiss, as was trumpeted abroad by Austrian papers, but that on this side of the Theiss something must have happened that looks like a defeat of the imperial troops (even if the above particulars should prove exaggerated). Windischgrätz does not retreat without good reason.

That the imperial troops were also defeated at *Szolnok* and that their army corps which was drawn up there has been taken prisoner, as we surmised, is confirmed by the Magyar report of March 6:

"Yesterday morning at 7 a.m. the imperial army received another decisive blow. For the 5,000-strong Grammont brigade in Szolnok on the Theiss was surrounded by a Hungarian army which had crossed the Theiss at Czibakháza, and was taken prisoner along with Lieutenant-Field Marshal *Grammont* after a terrible carnage.

---

[a] See footnote on p. 20.— *Ed.*

General *Ottinger* of the cavalry there received a fatal wound from which he died yesterday in Ofen."[a]

Moreover, the Hungarians did not stop there. According to the Magyar report they advanced to *Szégléd* and there on the 5th, in bloody fighting, *defeated the imperial troops* (probably those three supporting battalions which were brought from Pest by Zeisberg). They have also re-occupied Kecskemét, a very important town between the Theiss and the Danube. In consequence of these defeats Jellachich is said to have followed Prince Windischgrätz and also *to have left Pest.* It is said that the fortifications around Pest are being demolished by the imperial troops themselves; so they do not want to defend Pest itself but merely to dominate it by the cannons from Ofen. The fortress of Ofen is being amply provisioned, but even from here guns of large calibre are being removed, which suggests that a very prolonged defence is not contemplated.

Thus far the reports of the Magyar correspondent which sound *probable*. The following appears less probable:

Görgey is said to be advancing towards Raab with an army corps and to be about to cut off the retreat of the imperial troops—whether this advance is occurring north or south of the Danube is not stated.

The Magyars are said to have crossed the Danube below Pest and to have occupied *Stuhlweissenburg* (in the rear of Pest) to cut off the retreat by way of the Fleischhackerstrasse.

What truth there is in these two rumours cannot be determined. But at any rate they seem exaggerated.

The Magyar correspondent reports further from the Hungarian camp:

"Travellers from Debreczin relate that on a motion by Kossuth the Hungarian National Assembly has decreed that a *Landsturm* is to be raised to support the regular army. Most of the deputies have been instructed to organise the *Landsturm* in their capacity of government commissioners. This extraordinary measure appears to have been taken following the news of the Russian intervention in Transylvania. The same travellers also relate that Minister of Police Ladislaus Madarász has resigned from the Provisional Government in Debreczin." [70]

From Vienna it is further reported on the 9th:

"The news I gave in my communication of yesterday about the battle at Szolnok is confirmed. *The Hungarians have gained a brilliant victory,* and they very nearly seized the headquarters. Prince Windischgrätz himself is seriously wounded in one arm. *Nothing at all is yet known* of the Zeisberg brigade but it is said *to have been completely wiped out.* The Karger brigade *was driven into the Theiss and only a few escaped.* General

---

[a] The passages quoted here and below are taken from a report published in the *Kölnische Zeitung* No. 63 (second edition), March 15, 1849.— *Ed.*

Karger himself owes his escape exclusively to the devotion of three dragoons, who together with him fought their way through. In short, *the defeat of the Austrians was general*, and even the enemy acknowledges that the leaders of the Hungarian army have demonstrated extraordinary strategic genius. In addition to the names recently given to you, generals Duchatel (probably meaning Duhamel), a Frenchman, Guyon (an Englishman), and Prince Czartoryski (son of Adam Czartoryski) deserve to be commended; they stood courageously by the side of General Dembiński, who was in supreme command."

Kossuth has *appointed* the Serbian leader *Stratimirovich Ban of Croatia and voivode of Serbia,* a choice which has found general approval since both Serbs and Croats hold this handsome and brave young man in high esteem.

"*Postscript.* 3 p.m. A traveller coming from Pest, who left the city on the 9th (?), reports that at the time of his departure the city was *full of excitement;* in *Ofen extensive defence measures* were being taken and both cities were teaming with a multitude of soldiers; the Magyars, on the other hand, *were hourly expecting their compatriots to march in,* and in many places the national enthusiasm gave vent to fiery exclamations, in spite of the great number of soldiers who, however, had other things to attend to."

Others write also from Vienna:

"The *tactics of Prince Windischgrätz* towards the fiery Magyars and Poles are the object of much disapproval by the army itself, which appears to be demoralised by them. The many generals commanding the Hungarians are receiving more and more reinforcements, and there is *no prospect of an early end* without treachery on one side or notable reinforcements on the other."[a]

Windischgrätz has, moreover, declared that *unless he receives reinforcements of* **50,000 men** *he cannot cope with the Magyars!!*

Let the *Kölnische Zeitung* now say what "stage" the Hungarian war has entered with these new Magyar victories and with this statement of Windischgrätz.[b]

| | |
|---|---|
| Written by Engels on March 15, 1849 | Printed according to the newspaper |
| First published in the *Neue Rheinische Zeitung* No. 247, March 16, 1849 | Published in English for the first time |

---

[a] "Wien, 10. März", *Deutsche Allgemeine Zeitung* No. 73, March 14, 1849.— *Ed.*
[b] See this volume, pp. 15 and 32.— *Ed.*

# THE MILLIARD

*Cologne*, March 15. Already soon after the February revolution there was a shortage of money in Paris. *Respect de la propriété*[a] was proclaimed universally and the poor petty bourgeois thought that this applied to them. The Provisional Government[71] was all the more willing to show its *respect de la propriété*, since the bank at once lent it 50 million without interest. The Provisional Government consisted mainly of petty bourgeois of the *National* and was misled by the *magnanimity* of the bank. The 50 million were soon exhausted. Meanwhile the shareholders and owners of the banknotes had time to make the best use of *respect de la propriété* by withdrawing all their gold from the bank. The petty bourgeois, who for their part also wished to take advantage of *respect de la propriété*, went to their banker in order to have their bills of exchange—which had been drawn against their *propriété*, i.e. against their industrial enterprises, *boutiques*[b] or factories—discounted. The bankers put forward the excuse of lack of money and refused to discount the bills. The petty bourgeois then went to other bankers in order to have their bills endorsed by their bankers and discounted in the bank; the bankers refused their endorsement. *Respect de la propriété!* It was therefore precisely the bankers who were the first to violate *respect de la propriété*, although they themselves knew very well how to exploit it. Then a general complaint arose that credit, *confiance*[c] had been lost. On the other hand, the petty bourgeois still did not abandon their

---

[a] Respect for property.— *Ed.*

[b] Shops.— *Ed.*

[c] Confidence.— *Ed.*

*respect de la propriété*; they thought that if "calm and order" were re-established, confidence also would return and then, their *propriété* serving as cover, their bills would surely be discounted. It is common knowledge that after the June battle,[72] when calm and order had been restored, all *propriété* came into the pockets of the bankers, as a result of judicial concordats, and that the petty bourgeois only understood the meaning of "respect", when their "property" had gone. Obviously, it was the workers who suffered most as a result of the financial crisis brought about by the big bourgeoisie. Just at the time when the Provisional Government, in order to solve its own difficulties, invented the notorious 45-centime tax,[73] a poster signed by workers appeared on the walls. It began with the words: *avez-vous besoin d'argent?* (do you need money?) and it contained a direct proposal to demand the return of the milliard granted to the *émigrés* in 1825 as compensation. Who were those *émigrés?* They were the very same people who had incited and supported from abroad the war against France and who had then returned to France in the company of foreigners. Who were to be found among the *émigrés* who benefited from the compensation? The Duke of Orleans, i.e. the King who had recently been driven out,[a] and the legitimists,[74] i.e. the followers of the King who had been driven out long ago.[b] The Constituent Assembly and the Convention had decreed the confiscation of the property of the *émigré* traitors; the kings and *émigrés* who had returned after both restorations[75] awarded the compensation to themselves and their friends. The kings were again driven out, the decisions of the Constituent Assembly and the Convention regained their full validity, and what could be more natural than that the compensation should again benefit the people. The poster which thus set out the demand for the return of the milliard was read by the workers with general jubilation; they stood round it in thousands and discussed its content in their own way. This continued for a whole day; the next day the poster had vanished from the walls. Recognising the serious danger threatening them, the legitimists and Orleanists[76] had paid large sums to hire persons for the special purpose of destroying all traces of the poster during the night. At that time there was a passion for new organisational plans. Everyone was thinking only of how to invent a new system and to introduce it at once into the "state", in spite of all existing conditions. The Provisional Government hit on the unfortunate idea of inventing the 45-centime tax to be imposed on the peasants. The

---

[a] Louis Philippe I.— *Ed.*
[b] Charles X.— *Ed.*

workers thought that the 45 centimes would have the same effect as
the milliard: a tax on landed property—and they abandoned the
plan regarding the milliard. The *Journal des Débats*, as also the stupid
*National*, strengthened them in this opinion, and in their leading
articles they argued that real capital was the "earth", original landed
property, and that the Provisional Government had every right to
levy this tax in favour of the workers. When the tax actually began to
be levied, the peasants raised a terrible outcry against the urban
workers. "What?" said the peasants, "we are worse off than the
workers. We have to borrow capital at high rates of interest in order
to cultivate our land and to be able to feed our families, and, besides
the taxes and interest paid to the capitalists, are we also to pay for the
upkeep of the workers?"

The peasants turned away from the revolution because, instead
of promoting their interests, it was detrimental to their interests.
The workers realised how cunning a tax the reactionary party
had suggested and only now the meaning of *respect de la propriété*
became clear to them as well: the difference between formal and
actual property became evident; it turned out that bourgeois
capital had, so to speak, separated the land from the earth, that
the formal owner of the land had become a vassal of the capitalist,
and that the tax fell only on the indebted vassal. And when, in addition, the real owner of the land made the poor peasants even more
conscious of his power, by withdrawing credit, by levying a distress
etc., then the revolution became even more hateful to them. The
legitimists, who as big landowners possessed great influence in
the countryside, exploited this situation, and the intrigues of the
royalists on behalf of Henry V then began. In these distressing
circumstances for the revolution, May 15 [77] arrived. Barbès' demand
for the milliard, although advanced in a different form, struck the
people once again like a flash of lightning and set them on fire. Even
the June battle could not stamp out this thought of the milliard and
now that the trial of Barbès has begun in Bourges, [78] this idea has
increasingly gripped the peasants. To demand from the legitimists,
who were their landlords and blood-suckers, the return of the
milliard which they, the peasants, had raised—that was a more
attractive bait than Napoleon. The agitation for the repayment of the
milliard has already spread throughout France and if it were put
forward for decision by universal suffrage, more votes would be cast
for it than for Napoleon. The demand for the milliard is the first
revolutionary measure to draw the peasants into the revolution. The
petitions coming from all parts and the tone in which they are
composed prove that this revolutionary measure has already struck

deep roots. In Cluny people demand not only the return of the milliard, but also the 3 per cent interest which it had yielded since 1825. From the start of the trial in Bourges these petitions have piled up in such a way that the judges in Bourges as well as the entire reactionary party begin to feel uneasy. Agey, Ancey, Malain, St. Vibald, Vittaux and numerous other communes have today again sent petitions to the Chamber through their parliamentary representatives. Under the headline "*Rappel du milliard*",[a] the newspapers day by day print the names of fresh communes giving their adherence to this magnificent measure. Soon on all the walls, in all the communes, it will be possible to read: "*Rappel du milliard*", and if the forthcoming elections[b] are held under this slogan, we shall be interested to see what the capitalists, whether they are called legitimists, Orleanists or bourgeois, can counterpose to this milliard in order to push aside the democratic candidates who intend to enter the new Chamber with the dowry of this milliard in order to use it for the benefit of the peasants and workers. But that is still not all. Louis Napoleon has been promising the peasants everywhere not only the return of the money paid under the 45-centime tax, but a reduction of taxation in general. The petitions generally put forward the demand that the greater part of the milliard be used for this purpose. As for the legal reasons for the return of the milliard, these have already been stated immediately after the July revolution in 1830. At that time paying out the money still remaining from the milliard was suddenly discontinued. If what had already been paid out was not demanded back at that time, it was only because Louis Philippe himself and his family had received a very large part of this money.

Since it is impossible for the counter-revolutionary party to dispute the justice of this measure, it contents itself for the time being with calling attention to the difficulty of implementing it. The difficulty is said to lie in discovering the persons who have received more or less large sums from the compensation granted. But nothing could be easier. Let us begin with the large sums. At the head of the list is the Duke of Orleans (later Louis Philippe) and his sister, Madame Adelaide, with 50 million, and one had only to take these 50 million from the countless estates which the National Assembly recently restored to the royal family.

Prince de Condé received 30 million, and who inherited this sum?

---

[a] Return of the milliard.— *Ed.*

[b] This refers to the elections to the Legislative Assembly which were held on May 13, 1849.— *Ed.*

The Duke d'Aumale and Madame de Feuchères. A good beginning, therefore, could be made with this! The royal family owns huge forests and estates in France, and the peasants are already beginning to calculate how much they have lost by the fact that these millions were not returned to them already in 1830.

Written on March 15, 1849

First published in the *Neue Rheinische Zeitung* No. 247, March 16, 1849

Printed according to the newspaper

Published in English for the first time

# THE FRANKFURT MARCH ASSOCIATION
## AND THE *NEUE RHEINISCHE ZEITUNG*

*Cologne,* March 15. We are returning once more to the unfortunate March Association,[a] this fitting offspring of the "March revolution". We are being reproached "with harming the cause of freedom" since we undermine the March Association. But did we not
already in December 1848, to the horror of the *Kölnische Zeitung,*
denounce the March Association as the *unconscious tool of counter-
revolution?*[79] Did we not, therefore, already long ago communicate to
the "March Association" our opinion of the "March Association"?
Were the March Association an organisation of a revolutionary
party, were it even only a logical sound fruit of the *March revolt,* we
would put up with such ineptitude as its *speculation with announcements* undoubtedly was. In the first place the March Association
displays no activity unless perhaps the issuing of addresses ranks as
such; further, the March Association is an optimistic simpleton
between the constitutionalists (whom we regard as worse supporters
of reaction than the club of the Knight von Radowitz[80]) and some
really worthy democrats who have allowed their sight to be clouded
by nebulous ideas of imperial conciliation. The majority in that
central commercial association[b] will always be governed by the
indecision peculiar to it; the Association will perhaps stimulate discontent among the people, but at the decisive moment it will betray
them and subsequently bemoan its error. Well, may the commercial
association fare well! Its sensitivity in other respects does not move
us, and freedom of the press seems still to be understood by these

---

[a] See this volume, pp. 36-37.— *Ed.*

[b] A pun (*Kommerz*=commerce, *März*=March) referring to the leading forces of
the Central March Association.— *Ed.*

liberal people merely as their personal achievement. Herr Eisenmann, for example, openly declared himself a constitutionalist for all time and an opponent of republicanism at the very same meeting of the March Association where the *Neue Rheinische Zeitung* was mentioned as a model of "true German disunity". Thus, it is being demanded of us that, out of a doltish desire for unification, we should support the newspaper of a man who, whatever else he may be the devil only knows, is at any rate a German national-minded dolt. For the sake of decency we would "take along with us" these gentlemen as far as they like, if it were not that their task in Frankfurt is to be "irremovable". There are thinking friends of history[81] among these gentlemen. It can hardly have escaped their notice that not merely in Germany but everywhere and at all times, in spite of all March Associations, the Feuillants[82] invariably had to be got out of the way before the outbreak of the real revolution. What use is it to the adherents of the social republic if the very same Vogt, who blustered "above all" against Bonaparte in the manner of the beer drinkers of a small university,[a] will become an unsuccessful imperial Barrot of a Bonaparte of the German empire?[83]

Written by Marx on March 15, 1849                    Printed according to the newspaper

First published in the *Neue Rheinische*                Published in English for the first
*Zeitung* No. 248, March 17, 1849                      time

---

[a] In Giessen.— *Ed.*

# [DRAFT ADDRESS OF THE SECOND CHAMBER]

*Cologne*, March 16. Below we give for the information of our readers the *draft Address of the Second Chamber*,[84] a pale, servile copy of the speech from the throne.[a] Its author is the notorious knight of the red land,[b] valiant (!) von *Vincke.*

The Commission that drafted the Address

"gratefully *recognises*" (Old-Testament style) "the establishment" of "legal order through the Constitution of December 5 of last year".[85]

The Commission even *expresses* this gratitude in the name of the "*Prussian people*". And why should, according to the Commission, the people be thankful for the December Constitution imposed by the sabre? Because it is "imbued with a longing for the *restoration* of *public legal order*". Unfortunate knight Vincke! He has had to prove that he is the champion of the "*legal basis*", which is his speciality. But how is it possible to recognise the "legal basis" when confronted with the Brandenburg Government which shattered this very basis of legality by tearing up the laws of April 6 and 8, 1848 [86]? Nothing is simpler! The Government has imposed a *new* legal basis, *martial law* and simultaneously the *Charter*, the Code and philosophy of *martial law*—the Constitution of December 5. First the Government abolishes "public legal order". Then the Government proclaims some other "public legal order", the first that comes to hand, e. g. a Croatian one, a legal basis of *quelconque*.[c] Then the Commission for drafting the Address in the name of the Prussian people, and Vincke

---

[a] See present edition, Vol. 8, pp. 445-50.— *Ed.*
[b] Westphalia.— *Ed.*
[c] Any kind.— *Ed.*

in the name of the Prussian Commission for drafting the Address, have nothing more urgent to do than to welcome the restoration of *some sort* (any sort, no matter what) of "public legal order"! The legal basis is dead! Long live the legal basis! If, tomorrow, the Prussian Government is overthrown, if a Comité du salut public[87] is proclaimed in Berlin, then among the first to offer congratulations and invite guests to the wedding there will undoubtedly be a "champion of the legal basis", some Vincke or other, who in moving tones will recognise the "restoration of" *some sort* of "public legal order".

The Address Commission and the dead ride fast.[a] First of all, "gratitude" (according to the prescription of the *Neue Preussische Zeitung*) for the coup d'état of December 5! Then the martial-law Constitution as the "henceforth valid fundamental law of the Prussian state"! Finally, the vow to carry out the "*revision* wholly inspired by reverence and loyalty towards Your Royal Majesty", i.e. a *revision in the sense desired by the donor.* In this way, it is to be hoped, we shall be led back to the period even *prior* to the United Diet[88]!

As for *Berlin's "state of siege"*, the Address Commission will be governed exclusively by the platitude that "true freedom cannot exist *without law and order*". People know the battle-cry of "*law and order!*" from the events in Warsaw.[89] If only Prussia could exist without money or obtain money without these importunate parliamentary chatterers! As for the states of siege sporadically occurring "outside the city of Berlin", the Address Commission considers it appropriate "to await a further report from Your Royal Majesty's Government". Meanwhile Erfurt and the districts of Silesia where a state of siege has been declared are left out in the cold. Vincke is *satisfait* as long as the Erfurt and Rosenberg military censorships[b] do not "cross out" his draft Address. There is no danger of that!

Vincke then makes a promise in the name of the Address Commission, and the commission makes a promise in the name of the Second Chamber, and the Second Chamber makes a promise in the name of the people to fulfil "by strenuous effort" and as satisfactorily as possible the tasks which the royal Prussian Government has entrusted to the "so-called representation of the people". Good luck!

"We too recognise with joy that the Prussian army has proved its military renown during the days of struggle and its loyalty in the course of severe trials."

---

[a] "The dead ride fast" from G. A. Bürger, *Lenore.—Ed.*
[b] See this volume, pp. 70-71.—*Ed.*

The Danish campaign of the Imperial Court of Law![90] The battles at Miloslavl and Wreschen! The victories in Anhalt, in Mainz, in Frankfurt am Main![91] More than this! Vincke joyfully recognises the loyalty with which "My glorious army" hounded Vincke's predecessor and used the official documents of the old National Assembly as fuel for the stove. Vincke has every reason to rejoice. Without the "loyalty" of the "Prussian army in the course of severe trials", our Vincke would never have had the opportunity to immortalise himself by this draft Address which he himself drew up. Moreover, we may point out incidentally that in this matter, too, the Address Commission copies in schoolboy fashion the provisions in the Hohenzollern general plan of reform[a] as given by the *Neue Preussische Zeitung*.

And the *German question?*

"Prussia" will shrink from "no sacrifice" in order to seize Little Germany,[b] by means other than those with which Frederick the Great seized Silesia. In regard to "conquests", modern Prussia subscribes to the principle of "peaceful" progress. Moreover, the Address Commission "hopes" that "all the German governments will come to an *understanding* with the German National Assembly". *We* hope that the German governments will not pay much attention to this imperial training-college for teachers.

The Address Commission further expresses the wish that there be "no disturbance of the peace" as a result of "the termination of the armistice by the Danish King". Vincke knows very well that this Danish termination of the armistice is not meant to be taken more seriously than the Prussian-Danish war itself.[92] The Prussian troops act as imperial troops in Schleswig-Holstein, the Schleswig-Holstein troops act as imperial troops in South Germany, the former here and the latter there declaring martial law!

Condolences for the death of Prince Waldemar, and assurances of readiness for self-sacrifice, by means of which von Bodelschwingh, Riedel, von Seckendorf, Arnim, Harkort, Count Renard, Camphausen, Vincke, Grün and suchlike rabble stoop to the role of Prussian Lycurguses and Solons; piety, respect for the law, public spirit, justice, providence, the hearts of the kings and the future of Prussia, "and with it the future of Germany",—all that is served up as a dessert by the Address Commission through the good offices of von Vincke!

---

[a] See Marx, "The Hohenzollern General Plan of Reform" (this volume, pp. 65-69).— *Ed.*

[b] i.e. the whole of Germany apart from Austria.— *Ed.*

*Idiocy* must have rights of citizenship in a national assembly and in a nation which a von Vincke, by means of such a miserable botchwork produced in the name of a commission, in the name of a Chamber, and in the name of the people itself, can dare to turn into the laughing-stock of the European gallery.

Written by Engels on March 16, 1849

First published in the special supplement to the *Neue Rheinische Zeitung* No. 247, March 16, 1849

Printed according to the newspaper

Published in English for the first time

# [FROM THE THEATRE OF WAR]

Our correspondence and newspapers from Vienna and Prague have again failed to arrive today. Nor do the Breslau, Leipzig and other papers carry a word from the Austrians on the military operations. The Magyar correspondent of the *Breslauer Zeitung*, on the other hand, writes of new fighting in the area of Szegléd, of great masses of wounded who were brought to Pest, and of preparations for retreat. But it does not yet report anything decisive either.

What is most striking about the Austrian silence is that nothing is reported from *anywhere*. Formerly, there was always some little corner from which the imperial side could report some small advantage. But now this also has ceased. The Magyars appear suddenly to be developing a quite unexpected energy at all points, placing the most unforeseen obstacles in the way of the advance of the 250,000 imperial troops.

Since February 16 or 17, that is for four weeks, there has been no news from Transylvania. Not a word of the advance towards Tokaj of the troops of Götz, Ramberg and Jablonowsky. Not a word of Nugent's operations in Syrmien. Not a syllable about the deeds of Rukavina, Todorovich and Gläser in the Banat. If we learn a word here or there, we learn it through unofficial, vague rumours.

In short, the silence of the official reports is becoming more and more uncanny, and the contents of the unofficial reports are becoming more and more menacing for Austria. On the latter a few details tomorrow.

According to a report in the *Allgemeine Oder-Zeitung*, the Austrians are preparing to allow *the Russians to march into Cracow*, as well as into Transylvania.

Written by Engels on March 16, 1849

First published in the special supplement to the *Neue Rheinische Zeitung* No. 247, March 16, 1849

Printed according to the newspaper

Published in English for the first time

# FROM THE THEATRE OF WAR

Now, following the résumé published in today's special supplement,[a] here are the detailed reports from the Hungarian theatre of war.

First concerning the operations *at Pest.* The fighting appears to be concentrated in the area of Szegléd, accordingly both the Hungarian and the royal imperial forces must have moved significantly south. At any rate we no longer hear of any fighting in the area of Erlau, Kapolna or Mezö-Kövesd. Jellachich is therefore said to have also moved off to Szegléd. It is confirmed that Windischgrätz, vexed by his ill successes, has moved his headquarters back to Ofen and has thus withdrawn from active command. That he has been wounded is, however, disputed. The great defeated general is now drawing all troops by any means available to himself, even from the Komorn siege corps and from Cracow, so as somehow to maintain his position.—With regard to the latest military operations the Magyar correspondent of the *Breslauer Zeitung* of March 9 writes:

"Yesterday a battle must have taken place in the direction of Szolnok for very many waggons full of wounded were brought in during the night. The fact that still no Bulletin has been issued and also that, on the orders of the military command, the entire front of the Donauzeile facing the fortifications of the Pest bridgehead had suddenly to be cleared and is being occupied by the military, points to a new defeat. For this last measure can only have been taken for the purpose of covering a hasty retreat. Moreover, the higher officers of the Ofen fortress garrison have today sent their wives away. Direct news is entirely lacking, since no traveller from the lower areas is allowed to approach Pest. Another battle is expected today, unless the heavy rain which is falling continually prevents it. If the battle is fought nevertheless, the retreat will involve heavy losses for the defeated side, for the roads there turn into deep mud whenever it rains, making it altogether unthinkable to bring away the guns and baggage. In Pest meat has risen in price by 2 kreutzers per pound because *a Hungarian raiding corps drove away a large consignment of oxen from Gödöllö, three hours from here.*

---

[a] See this volume, p. 90.— *Ed.*

From *Debreczin* we learn that the Hungarian Government has accused of high treason and deposed Johann Hám, the Lord Primate of Hungary, and two other high prelates, who remained in Pest. The clever and liberal Hungarian historian, Horvath Mihaly, formerly Canon, later Bishop of Chanad, has bec 1 appointed Lord Primate" (this is also confirmed from another source). "When last night many spectators gathered at the bringing in of the wounded, they were dispersed by a strong patrol sent out for the purpose. Incidentally, all hospitals and barracks are so overcrowded with wounded that newcomers had to be laid on the stairs and in the forecourts."

Moreover, that the imperial cause is in a very peculiar way can also be deduced from a proclamation of Prince Windischgrätz from Ofen headquarters, dated March 8,[a] prohibiting all direct or indirect intercourse with the rebels and the inhabitants of the areas occupied by them for the duration of the state of siege. Similarly, all trading links are disrupted. Anyone acting against these prohibitions is to be dealt with under martial law, as well as all who aid and abet them in any way. The goods, however, are confiscated and sold for the benefit of the state treasury.

In the rear of the imperial armies things look equally jolly. What stage these gentlemen at Komorn have reached and what illusions they endeavour to spread is shown by the following communication of the government *Lloyd* from Pressburg:

"While the main army under Field Marshal Windischgrätz, tireless in the pursuit of the enemy, is already active on the other side of the Theiss (!), the second army corps is operating at Komorn, where, according to reliable reports, a great offensive will begin on the 15th of this month (!). For this purpose *many* (!) steamboats with *very many* howitzers of *every* calibre and with *fourfold* powder supplies have been dispatched there from Vienna, Ofen and Esseg. On our bank of the Danube several tugboats, equipped with cannon and bombs in the manner of warships, are tied up, intended to serve as the main transport of the reserve. It will probably take but a few rocket-throwing exercises to bring the Komorn garrison to its senses and lead to the surrender of the fortress and the re-opening of the waterway between Vienna, here and Pest."[b]

The same article which began with these absurd boasts goes straight on to admit that the Slovak peasants do not want to have anything to do with the royal imperial occupation. For besides other arrests,

"last week 12 peasants from nearby Slovak villages accused of concealment of arms with evil intent, were placed under arrest, brought here, and sentenced to two, three or four years' imprisonment depending on their crime".

---

[a] The proclamation was published in the article "Pest, 9. März" in *Der Lloyd* No. 121 (evening edition), March 12, 1849, and also in the *Wiener Zeitung* No. 61, March 13, 1849.— *Ed.*

[b] "Pressburg, 9. März", *Der Lloyd* No. 119 (evening edition), March 10, 1849. Below the same article is quoted.— *Ed.*

The Slovaks, -who have been vainly incited to rebellion several times already, are so loyal to the Magyars that only 1,400 men out of 2 to 3 million could be recruited for Austria. Read the following report from Leutschau (Zips), which also confirms that the imperial troops are still where they were when Görgey moved to the Theiss:

"*Leutschau*, March 1. The Slovak *Landsturm* consists up to now of 15 companies of 90 men each. Three companies form the Leutschau garrison, five that of Eperies; the rest are moving to Kaschau. Yesterday, General Ramberg imposed a war-tax of 20,000 florins on this town. More than 500 people have fled from Eperies for fear of Görgey, many of them as far as Pest."

From the *south* we hear only that *Szegedin is still in the hands of 40,000 Magyars*, and that 30,000 Serbs are standing by ready to take the town.

Finally, we have received several reports from Transylvania, but which, strangely, still do not go beyond February 16 or 17. According to one of them (a Saxon report), Bem is supposed to be dangerously ill as a result of a wound in his hand; another report, about the Szeklers[93] taking Schässburg, is interesting because of the details which it gives of the strength of the Szeklers at a single point. On February 16, about 8,000 men and 12 cannon from Mediasch, 5,000 men and five cannon from Udvarhely and 3,000 men from Maros-Vásárhely advanced simultaneously on Schässburg. These fighting forces caused the brave Austro-Russian troops under Major von der Heydt and the virtuous civic militia of the town to withdraw without a fight to Hermannstadt and to leave wives, children and property to the mercy of the Szekler robber bands. These are said to have immediately imposed a war-contribution of 30,000 florins on the town:

"a much greater sum would be exacted from the administrative localities. The enemy was looking for lead and tin, as much as could be raised; he even fetched up the cartridges which had been sunk in the wells and dried the powder in the sun to make it usable again." [a]

Finally we quote the following interesting report from *Cracow*. This shows how completely preconcerted is the plot between Russia and Austria.

"*Cracow*, March 12. The royal imperial General *Legeditsch*, in command here, yesterday had Prince Stanislaw Jablonowski summoned before him and informed him quite abruptly that the municipal authority should make an application to the

---

[a] "Hermannstadt, 15. Febr.", *Deutsche Allgemeine Zeitung* No. 74 (supplement), March 15, 1849.— *Ed.*

administration asking *the Russian troops standing on the border to enter Cracow to maintain calm, since he* (Legeditsch) *would have to march off to Hungary with all Austrian forces.* The Prince, however, replied to the royal imperial General that the *people of Cracow would certainly not make such a request* and should the town be completely denuded of troops, the citizenry would guarantee to maintain law and order.

"It will be remembered that General Puchner in Transylvania, before the entry of the Russian troops, made a similar indirect demand to the towns of Kronstadt and Hermannstadt that they should call for Russian aid."

Finally, on the question of the Hungarian banknotes, the despotism of the sabre had to yield to the *necessitas rerum*,[a] the absence of credit of the royal imperial state. Part of the Kossuth notes have already been called in, despite the weeping and gnashing of teeth of the Pest petty bourgeoisie.

"In fact Field Marshal Windischgrätz on the 9th of this month issued an announcement in Pest by which Hungarian 100-florin and 5-florin notes were banned from acceptance at public counters. This announcement produced great consternation there and all transactions are at this moment completely disrupted."[b]

The Pest Fair, which is anyway sparsely attended, is therefore unlikely to be held at all. The Hungarian one- and two-florin notes will hardly have any other fate.

Written by Engels on March 16, 1849

First published in the *Neue Rheinische Zeitung* No. 248, March 17, 1849

Printed according to the newspaper

Published in English for the first time

---

[a] Force of circumstances.— *Ed.*

[b] "Wien, 12. März", *Kölnische Zeitung* No. 64 (special supplement), March 16, 1849.— *Ed.*

# FROM THE THEATRE OF WAR

As the Vienna mail has again failed to arrive, we are again without any direct news from Hungary. What has reached us via Prague and Augsburg contains very little that is new.

The Augsburg *Allgemeine Zeitung* carries a report from Pest of the 8th to the effect that Szolnok is again occupied by imperial troops.[a] Later reports, as we shall see, sound quite different. The *Allgemeine Zeitung*, incidentally, admits that the imperial troops have suffered "a considerable defeat" at Szolnok, in which "of two companies barely 40 men were saved". Concerning the fighting, the same paper reports from *Abony* near Szolnok:

"After the day of Kapolna we advanced as far as Kövesd, and then to Poroszlo. As the cavalry was unable to operate there because of the marshy nature of the ground, we received orders to go to Szolnok. We arrived just in time to put an end to the fighting which 15,000 Hungarians with 40 cannon had begun against two brigades and which cost us dear, for the Karger brigade was driven out of Szolnok. At the moment reinforcements are arriving from Pest and we shall oppose them with 15,000 men and 36 to 40 cannon, but we do not doubt that they will withdraw when they see a significant deployment of strength. The bravery of our troops is very commendable. *Szolnok got into Hungarian hands yesterday, it is true*, but by tonight we shall surely have it back again." [b]

What we are to think of these boasts about the re-taking of Szolnok is evident from a report from Pest, printed in the *Constitutionelles Blatt aus Böhmen* which says:

"The Ban did indeed start from Pest yesterday, and that at 4 a.m. Unfortunately we know nothing at all about the events in the theatre of war in our immediate

---

[a] "Pesth, 8. März", Augsburg *Allgemeine Zeitung* No. 72, March 13, 1849.— *Ed.*

[b] "Abony bei Szolnok, 6. März", Augsburg *Allgemeine Zeitung* No. 72, March 13, 1849.— *Ed.*

neighbourhood, between Szegléd and Abony, it is said. The local secret agitators tell marvels about the strength of the rebel army, nay even that it takes six hours to cross their camp. Of course these rumours are obviously much exaggerated, but it cannot be denied that along the Szolnok route *a considerable insurgent army* has now already for the second time *advanced closer to the capital than is desirable.* The anxiety of the loyally-inclined is even more increased by the doubtless necessary *measures to safeguard the communications* between the fortress of Ofen and the New Edifice, the new and only citadel of Pest. Yesterday afternoon *embrasures* were made in this construction, in great haste, and the inhabitants of the houses in the neighbourhood received strict orders to hold themselves in such *readiness to march* that they would be able to leave their quarters with bag and baggage *within six hours* of receiving notice. Moreover, the buildings, workshops etc. of the company which is building the suspension bridge, situated next to the blockhouses of the suspension bridge, were yesterday hastily demolished on both banks of the Danube. Hence a *gloomy mood* prevails among the few local loyalists, while the opposing party finds it difficult to hide its secret joy."[a]

How things are going in general for the imperial side is evident even from the fact that Windischgrätz has strictly prohibited all traffic and commerce with the areas occupied by the Magyars so as to cut off their connections. All individuals trafficking there are to be arrested and their goods confiscated. Extraordinary police measures against aliens have also been ordered for the approaching Pest Fair.

There is still not the slightest news from the left wing of the main army (Schlick). The Augsburg *Allgemeine Zeitung* claims, it is true, that he has already been standing 8 hours from Debreczin and that it was not yet known whether he had gone back again.[b] But this is a most impudent lie; Maklar, where the imperial armies were standing according to their own reports, is fully 15 German miles[c] from Debreczin, and the Theiss, with its milewide belt of swamps, lies between, 10 miles from Debreczin. In the absence of facts the *Constitutionelles Blatt aus Böhmen* boasts as follows[d]:

"We confidently expect (!) good results from the operations of Lieutenant-Field Marshal Count Schlick, and in general we may claim with pride (!) that Count Schlick has proved a most excellent general, especially in his plight after the skirmish at Tokaj!"

The *Constitutionelles Blatt aus Böhmen* also confirms that the Magyars have occupied the southern part of the Pest comitat at *Kecskemét.* They have even advanced to the Danube and are in contact with the insurgents on the opposite bank (the Tolna comitat):

---

[a] "Pest, 9. März", *Constitutionelles Blatt aus Böhmen* No. 61, March 13, 1849.— *Ed.*

[b] "Pesth, 8. März", Augsburg *Allgemeine Zeitung* No. 72, March 13, 1849.— *Ed.*

[c] See footnote on p. 20.— *Ed.*

[d] This and the following quotations are taken from two items "Pest, 8. März" published in the *Constitutionelles Blatt aus Böhmen* No. 60 (second supplement), March 12, 1849.— *Ed.*

"One of the main centres of insurgent activity is Kalocsa; they are stirring up the entire neighbourhood, particularly the Tolna comitat, on the other side of the Danube. There the rebels are so bold that they sink every ship that passes on the Danube. The peasants of Földvar and Duna Vecse are distinguishing themselves particularly in this respect. They have not the smallest fear of the royal imperial troops, imagining that 12,000 Honveds are at Kalocsa. They are constantly being made more fanatical by posters from Debreczin."

It follows from this that along the whole stretch from Duna Vecse to Tolna (9 to 10 miles as the crow flies) both banks of the Danube are in the Magyars' hands and shipping is greatly threatened.

The following report shows how the war is being conducted in this area and how little prospect the clumsy Austrians have of coping with these elusive bands of rebels.

"The detachment of troops which left a few days ago for Duna Földvar (Tolna comitat) by steamer to suppress the latest revolt has never come face to face with the enemy. Although the tugboat was shot at on landing, the mutineers dispersed like chaff in the wind even before the troops had disembarked. A true guerilla war! The Simunich brigade, according to a rumour, is said to be entering a fortified camp near the Bicske estate of Count Kasimir Batthyány, four hours drive from Ofen, to maintain the security and continuity of the new order of things beyond the Danube."

From Transylvania not a word.
From the Banat

"it is *expected* that simultaneously with the arrival of the Ban[a] (in the campaign against Szolnok) the long line of the Austro-Serb troops which extends from Baja to Temesvar *will* now be set in motion" (*Constitutionelles Blatt aus Böhmen*).

Indeed! Now at last we learn that the famous division Lieutenant-Field Marshal Gläser formed from the troops of Rukavina, Todorovich and other generals, greeted with so many newspaper fanfares, which was to conquer Transylvania and Grosswardein, has not even stood its ground on the Maros but has retreated to Temesvar! Magyar reports indeed told us this long ago, but they were not to be believed, of course!

And in another article in the same paper we read:

"Until yesterday (March 7) neither Szegedin nor Theresiopel (Subotica) were captured, in the neighbourhood of which, as I have already reported, the Serbs won a brilliant victory and literally made hay of the Magyars, and a Magyar corps has advanced in this direction. This is related by travellers who have come from these areas today."[b]

But thereby hangs a tale. The Serbs are to the highest degree dissatisfied with their chiefs. Patriarch Rajachich is making himself

---

[a] Jellachich.— Ed.
[b] "Von der Drave, 8. März", *Constitutionelles Blatt aus Böhmen* No. 61, March 13, 1849.— Ed.

daily more unpopular by outlawing Stratimirovich, by his intervention against the National Committee,[94] which he has now disbanded, reconstituted and moved to Becskerek, and by other arbitrary measures. Stratimirovich has disappeared and seems to have gone over to the Magyars. Rukavina and Todorovich are Serbs, it is true, but above all royal imperial generals, who know no other nationality than the Austrian. Moreover, considerable tension exists between the regular troops and the Serb frontier guards and volunteers.

"The Serbs complain of a shortage of cavalry, and, what is more, the imperial troops are in no hurry to leap to the aid of the Rascians,[95] a designation which has become popular again among the military" (*Constitutionelles Blatt aus Böhmen*).[a]

In short, since Stratimirovich has gone, the Serbs have become obstinate and what is more are *negotiating with the Magyars*, as even the Vienna papers report. What effect Kossuth's appointment of Stratimirovich as Ban and voivode will have remains to be seen.

Another blow for the Austrians is being prepared here by the *recall of the Turkish Serbs from Hungary*. The *Constitutionelles Blatt aus Böhmen* reports on this:

"By a princely decree from Belgrade the Serbs who are fighting on Austrian soil are recalled. Whether Kničanin's corps is included is not known, since the order is couched in too general terms. Our Serbs interpret this measure with suspicion, claiming to know that the Olmütz Court[b] has worked for this decree through diplomatic channels. Others see in it purely a matter of organisation and conscription, while we are inclined to connect it with the Turkish armament measures. Certainly, the Serbian irregulars knew nothing better than looting, killing and burning; they were the dregs of Serbia. Their rapacity was quite indiscriminate. They dragged their booty across the Sava by the cartload, and, wherever these hordes broke in, the complaint went up from all sides: Heaven preserve us from these friends, we can cope with our enemies."[c]

The same paper writes in another article on this affair:

"Another untoward circumstance which fills us with gloomy forebodings is the recall of the troops of the Serb Principality from the Voivodina. We are unable to penetrate the secret of this policy. It is said that The Porte, England and France have demanded the recall of these troops. We do not believe this, at any rate they had no right to do so; for the troops who came to our aid from the principality were not regular troops of whom the local government can dispose as it pleases, they are volunteers who came to take part in the liberation struggle of their compatriots. The Serbs, however, had a right to take part in this struggle, for Serbia is a constitutional

---

[a] "Agram, 5. März", *Constitutionelles Blatt aus Böhmen* No. 60, March 11, 1849.— *Ed.*

[b] The Austrian Court fled to Olmütz (Olomouc) during the Vienna uprising in October 1848.— *Ed.*

[c] "Von der Drave, 8. März", *Constitutionelles Blatt aus Böhmen* No. 61, March 13, 1849.— *Ed.*

country, its people are free people. There is no end to the South-Slav troubles, indeed they are increasing with every passing day."[a]

The following announcement by the Patriarch, dated Gross-Kikinda, February 24, shows moreover that the plundering by the Serbs must be very bad:

"As looting is on the increase by both the auxiliaries and even our regulars, I feel compelled to order: 1) Nobody shall dare to purchase any cattle or other effects taken as booty. 2) In case of violation the purchaser will lose both the booty he has bought and the purchase money handed over. 3) All objects taken as booty will be confiscated wherever found and the matter reported to me through the appropriate authority."[b]

But what angers the Serbs most, who are, after all, waging a national struggle, is the action taken in the interest of *Germanisation* by the noble Banus Jellachich, who as Ban is at the same time chief of the Military Border district.[96] The *Constitutionelles Blatt aus Böhmen* received the following report from the Sava dated March 1:

"Ban Jellachich has become the chief talk of the day; his latest action is cloaked in the darkness of secrecy, and the Southern Slavs do not regard him without suspicion. His order to the Patriarch announcing that the *German language* is to be re-introduced in the local Military Border district, was very badly received here. Indeed, Ban Jellachich has not grasped the implications of this pronouncement. The Serbs kindled the national war solely to rid themselves of the rule of an alien nation, to save from destruction their literature (!), their art (!), their songs, all their national treasures, to which they cling with loyal hearts; the Serbs will not readily obey this order. Whatever may have induced the highly respected Ban to issue it, we do not doubt for a moment that the Patriarch will reject it."

Clearly, the noble, gallant Ban is playing a most contemptible role. Sent for a time to Pest, under suspicion, he served the Government to cover all its acts that were unpalatable to the Slavs with his name and position. The noble personage, once having entered into relations with the Austrians, has irrevocably broken with the Magyars. Now, too late, he realises that despite his Slav cunning he has been ignominiously duped by the imperial side and cannot even refuse to sign such a disgraceful declaration as his recent one about his alleged quarrel with Windischgrätz. It serves him right.

Peterwardein is surrounded. The garrison is said to have taken all its officers prisoner as disloyal and traitorous.

We have learned more details about the battle in Slovakia against the Czechoslovak volunteers. The fighting took place at Turan on the Waag (at the foot of the Jablunka Pass, already once before so

---

[a] "Von der Save, 1. März", *Constitutionelles Blatt aus Böhmen* No. 60 (second supplement), March 12, 1849.— *Ed.*

[b] "Semlin, 4. März", *Constitutionelles Blatt aus Böhmen* No. 61, March 13, 1849.— *Ed.*

ominous for Messrs. Štúr and Hurban). The Magyar-Slovak corps, 12,000 strong, which was victorious here, is occupying the High Carpathians and is said to be under the command of Klapka and Aulich.

The Austrian Government is said to have disavowed Puchner's invitation to the Russians to enter Transylvania and insists on their withdrawal as soon as 15,000 Banat troops have arrived in Transylvania as reinforcements. But since the Serbs refuse to march, the Russian corps will surely stay for the time being.

The following is reported in Pest from Debreczin, according to the *Constitutionelles Blatt aus Böhmen*:

> A deputy is said to have proposed that the National Assembly should recognise the Emperor Francis Joseph as the legitimate King of Hungary. Nyáry was the first to support this pacification proposal, and even Kossuth made a brilliant speech in favour of the proposal which was then unanimously adopted.[a]

A letter from Pest the next day adds:

> "The news from Debreczin reported yesterday appears to find confirmation, and the National Assembly is indeed said to have recognised the Emperor Francis Joseph as legitimate King of Hungary. This recognition rests, however, on the Pragmatic Sanction, and the demands which Kossuth's party piles up on this basis we still remember from the last Imperial Diet but one.[97] According to reports received it has also been explicitly added that this step had been induced above all by the wish to prove to the European monarchies, especially to the great powers in the immediate neighbourhood, that there was not the least intention to found a united, big, perhaps even red, Sarmato-Magyar republic. This would therefore seem not to be a step towards actual pacification."[b]

If the Magyars have really taken this decision, such a manoeuvre would basically have little significance. If they are victorious and stand before Vienna, the "legitimate King of Hungary" will soon come to his end.

Moreover, in another letter from the Drava we read:

> "In and around Debreczin everything looks extraordinarily martial and warlike. An imperial officer who was discharged under bond because he did not want to fight against his brothers gave us information from which we single out the following as remarkable. 'Kossuth's army,' he said, 'must amount to about 100,000 men and the artillery to 400 (?) cannon. Rockets of a unique kind are being made. A regular infantry is also available and seven old-style hussar regiments, besides which seven more hussar regiments have been formed, the Kossuth-, Mészáros-, Batthyány-, Madarász-, Hunyadi-hussars etc. There is much drilling and for up to six miles from Debreczin the villages are very strongly fortified, and it would be a great mistake to think of victory over these rebels as easy and rapid'; so far the statements of our

---

[a] "Pest, 8. März", *Constitutionelles Blatt aus Böhmen* No. 60 (second supplement), March 12, 1849.— *Ed.*

[b] "Pest, 9. März", *Constitutionelles Blatt aus Böhmen* No. 61, March 13, 1849.— *Ed.*

informant. As far as our knowledge of the movements on the Theiss goes, we believe that our operations have to be carried out with all seriousness and caution, since skilful manoeuvres will here be necessary, and the troops in Hungary, at least at this present decisive moment, still appear to us *insufficient.* I do not want to be accused of pessimism. We see among the rebels much energy and among the masses in and around Romania[a] a veritable fanaticism; hence we regret the delay in recruitment in the northern provinces, since this hampers the Government in fighting the Magyars."[b]

With this report, which should make our neighbouring journalist[c] rejoice, we conclude for today, still waiting for *finem Hungariae.*

Written by Engels about March 17, 1849

First published in the *Neue Rheinische Zeitung* No. 249, March 18, 1849

Printed according to the newspaper

Published in English for the first time

---

[a] An allusion to Transylvania.— *Ed.*

[b] "Von der Drave, 8. März", *Constitutionelles Blatt aus Böhmen* No. 61, March 13, 1849.— *Ed.*

[c] An ironic reference to the journalist who wrote about the war in Hungary for the *Kölnische Zeitung* (see this volume, pp. 13-18).— *Ed.*

# [MILITARY DICTATORSHIP IN AUSTRIA][98]

*Cologne,* March 17. The year 1848 was the year of disappointment with revolutionary memories, illusions and other phrases. In 1848 the insurgent people of half Europe let themselves be put off with phrases, colourful rags, addresses and processions; and it was quite consistent that the revolution of 1848 should end in universal counter-revolutionary and military dictatorship.

The revolution of 1848 however had at least the result that it not only completely enlightened the people everywhere about the previous phrases, but that it also started a conflagration in the old Europe which all the Cavaignacs and Windischgrätzes in the world will be unable to stamp out.

1849 is the year of disillusion with the omnipotence of military dictatorship.

The military dictatorship comes to grief above all owing to two things: firstly, its inability to solve any of the complications; secondly, its costliness. It collapses as soon as it has to organise or as soon as it has to find regular sources of finance.

The first example of this collapse of military dictatorship is afforded by the "time-honoured" Imperial State of Austria, which could only save its existence by the most violent and extreme rule of the sabre. At the present moment Austria is perishing because of rule by the sabre.

When the revolution was quelled in Vienna with the help of the Slavs, when Pest was captured by the Slav-Austrian army,[99] when the heroes of martial law believed they could easily deal with the remainder of the Magyar revolution, and that within a fortnight they would re-establish the entire old predatory state from the Ticino and Po to the Dnieper and the Carpathians, the Olmütz camarilla quickly prepared a plan. It was intended, as soon as the sabre dictatorship had been introduced throughout Hungary, to dissolve

The first page of Engels' article "Military Dictatorship in Austria"

the Kremsier Imperial Diet, which had been useful previously on account of the Slavs, to cast aside the Slavs as a worn-out tool, to impose *pro forma* a Constitution which would never be implemented, and to restore the old Metternich system by the old method, the enslavement of one nation by another.

The defeats of the imperial robber bands at the Theiss delayed the execution of this benevolent project. The Slavs were still needed on the battlefield.

But the rumour of the imminent imposition of this plan spread. The Imperial Diet became apprehensive. The Slav Club[100] became daily more dangerous for the Ministers. Agreement was reached that on March 15 the draft Constitution should be adopted in its entirety, thus forestalling the imposition of a Constitution. No other course remained for the camarilla but to risk a desperate coup, to steal a march on the Imperial Diet, and *prematurely,* and in spite of the Slavs, to disperse the Imperial Diet and impose the so-called Constitution.[101]

This martial-law Charter burst like a bomb among the medley of Austrian peoples. The wrath previously felt only by the Germans and Magyars at the Austrian habit of gaining victory by cowardly acts of treachery, and after the victory to surpass in barbarity the most brutal bandits, this wrath was now shared by the Slavs as well. They were ensnared by the prospect of a "Slav Austria", they were made use of to win victory in Italy and Hungary, and by way of thanks they are now being subjected again to the old Metternich whip. Instead of a "Slav Austria" they are being given a so-called "equality of rights of nations", which denotes here an *equal lack of rights* of all nations in face of the all-powerful camarilla of the higher nobility, which has no nationality at all. Instead of the much vaunted "freedoms", they are being given bayonets, an Imperial Diet whose majority consists of Slavs is being dispersed by cudgel blows, and the holy cradle of pan-Slavism, Prague, is threatened with a state of siege.[a]

That is all the benefit the Austrian Slavs, and particularly the Czechs, have derived from allying themselves with the camarilla in order to achieve their national separatist[102] aims instead of joining the German and Magyar revolutions. The Germans and Magyars often enough warned them of what they would gain as a result; but they have chosen this. A province which, on the pretext of wanting to achieve a *special* freedom for itself, joins in a conspiracy with the counter-revolution against freedom for the whole country, deserves

---

[a] After this paragraph Engels deleted the following words: "The Czechs who form the vanguard of the Austrian Slavs, are the...."—*Ed.*

nothing better than that finally it, too, should be cheated by the counter-revolution and cast aside.

Little is yet known of the effect of the new counter-revolutionary coup d'état on the Slavs. No news has yet come from the south or from Galicia. The Moravians are a people too demoralised and enfeebled to be likely to regard the matter otherwise than with fatuous indifference. The Czechs, on the other hand, the spokesmen of the Austrian Slavs and the ones most insultingly swindled, have already expressed their feelings. Their rage knows no bounds. They have been so greatly disappointed that public opinion in Prague has been completely revolutionised. The heads of the Slav alliance with the camarilla, the previous idols of the Czechomaniacs, people such as the *Palackys, Strobachs, Brauners,* are the object of general imprecation. The German-Bohemian deputies were greeted at the railway station in Prague with loud, jubilant cries. Indeed, *Borrosch* the Germanophil, whose house in Prague had only shortly before been demolished, made a *truly triumphant entry into the capital city of pan-Slavism.* The Czech students carried him shoulder high from the railway station, innumerable cries of "hurrah" for the *German Lefts* in the Imperial Diet were uttered, and the assembled people of Prague sang "Was ist des Deutschen Vaterland".[a]

Now the Czechs, too, want to elect deputies to Frankfurt, now when it is too late. But the Austrian Government will probably reply by issuing a decree recalling all the Austrian deputies sitting in St. Paul's Church.[103]

These pronouncements by the Czechs will exert a decisive influence on the way the other Austrian Slavs will react to the martial-law Charter. In spite of all seeming concessions, the Croats and especially the Serbs will grasp the real reason for the imperial gift, and the Galician peasants will pull wry faces when they learn that they must now after all pay compensation for the feudal burdens.

The enthusiasm for Austria and the Emperor, not only of the Slav enthusiasts for nationalism and freedom, but of the Slav peasants as well, will come to an end through this coup d'état. Within fourteen days Austria will be unable to rely to the slightest degree on the Slavs, any more than it can on the Germans and Italians; Austria has now nothing else to depend on than its 600,000 soldiers and—Russia.

It is this coup d'état, which is intended to establish irrevocably the unity and indivisibility of the whole predatory state, that will give the

---

[a] "What is the Fatherland of a German" from Ernst Moritz Arndt's poem "Der Teutschen Vaterland" (music by Gustav Reichardt).— *Ed.*

impulse for the overthrow of the Austrian monarchy, and perhaps for European wars and revolutions.

In Hungary, the army has for the second time been thrown back from the Theiss, and the strength of the Magyar revolution is daily growing more formidable; the Serbs are negotiating with the Magyars, and perhaps—even according to Austrian reports—have already gone over to them; in Croatia, dissatisfaction is daily increasing; Vienna is a volcano which can hardly be kept under by 30,000 bayonets; Italy is on the threshold of war, which at this moment has perhaps already broken out, a war in which Radetzky's demoralised bands will find opponents quite different from those of last year; the financial position is daily growing worse, each month bringing a deficit of more than five million guldens; and in addition there is now the break with the Slavs, who have had a gauntlet flung in their face at a time when they were still urgently needed, precisely as if it were desired to provoke Jellachich to lead his Croats and borderers with drums beating into the Magyar camp!

That is too much for the old Austria. Only the intervention of Russia could save it, and the intervention of Russia, one more step farther than hitherto, means inevitably—a *European war.*

Such is the pass to which Austria has been brought by the military dictatorship; it has been brought to the verge of collapse, to the most complete dissolution, to the brink of bankruptcy.

The sabre can terrorise, but its power goes no further than that. The terrorism exercised by the sabre is the stupidest and most brainless of all. But the fact that a revolution has been put down by grape-shot does not mean that anything has been accomplished; it is easy to proclaim and put into effect a state of siege, but to *emerge from it* again, that is after all the chief thing, and that requires more than just a moustache.

Precisely to come out of the exceptional state of siege, to come out of the provisional regime, and in order to "*put an end to the revolution*", the aristocratic wielders of the sabre have imposed the Constitution. And precisely this Constitution is the cause that the Austrian revolution is *only now really beginning.*

"God save Emperor Francis!"[a]

Written by Engels on March 17, 1849

First published in: Marx and Engels, *Works,* Second Russian Edition, Vol. 43, Moscow 1976

Printed according to the manuscript

Published in English for the first time

[a] L. L. Haschka, National and State Anthem of Austria. Music by Joseph Haydn.—*Ed.*

# [THE 18th OF MARCH]

*Cologne*, March 18. We confess to our readers that we do not know how to write any leading article for today. The March revolution in Berlin, that feeble echo of the revolution in Vienna,[104] never aroused our enthusiasm. On March 19, 1848, Berlin sang: "*In Jesus is my trust!*"[a] We advise the worthy Berliners this time to say on March 18: "*In Wrangel is my trust!*"

The anniversary the *Neue Rheinische Zeitung* will celebrate will be that of *June 25.*[105]

And what will the *Kölnische Zeitung* do, that is to say, the "Cologne bourgeoisie"?

On March 22, 1848, the chief reproach of the *Kölnische Zeitung* against Herr von "Arnim" was that he had *banned* the *Rheinische Zeitung*. At that time Camphausen was not yet a Minister. We mention this for clarification.

We still remember the happy time when *Camphausen* collaborated with us in Cologne.[106] The attitude of Camphausen to us in the past and our present attitude to him—therein lies the *secret of the March revolution of 1848.*

Written by Marx on March 18, 1849

First published in the *Neue Rheinische Zeitung* No. 249 (second edition), March 18, 1849

Printed according to the newspaper

Published in English for the first time

---

[a] Initial words of the song "Jesus meine Zuversicht!"—*Ed.*

# [THE *NEUE PREUSSISCHE ZEITUNG* ON THE OCCASION OF THE 18th OF MARCH]

*Cologne,* March 18. The organ of *Frederick William IV,* the *Neue Preussische Zeitung,* writes as follows on the occasion of March 18, 1849:

**"Double woe, however, to the people that solemnly commemorates its revolution; to sin is human, but to take pride in the sin and to celebrate one's crime is of the devil."** [a]

In a feature article of the same issue, the newspaper calls the struggle on March 18 and 19 a **"bloody farce"**! That is the fitting reward "to My people" [107] for having made *half* a revolution.

Further, the newspaper reports that a few days ago Wrangel went to *"inspect"* Friedrichshain. [108]

We shall await what Herr Wrangel will **"inspect"** on March 18, 1850.

| | |
|---|---|
| Written by Marx on March 18, 1849 | Printed according to the newspaper |
| First published in the *Neue Rheinische Zeitung* No. 249 (second edition), March 18, 1849 | Published in English for the first time |

---

[a] *Neue Preussische Zeitung* No. 64, March 17, 1849.— *Ed.*

110

## [FROM THE THEATRE OF WAR]

The Vienna papers are missing again tonight. Frankly, we cannot explain this limitless muddle, which is becoming worse every day.

We have received news from Pest via Breslau up to the 11th of March. No official word from the theatre of war; but Magyar and Austrian reports, though not official, are in the main in *complete* agreement.

It is becoming more and more evident every day that for the last fortnight the imperial troops have suffered one defeat after another. At least half the royal imperial Austrian generals have proved to be sheer dolts and Windischgrätz, though no less incompetent, is now throwing them out of the command. *Zeisberg* has completely disappeared, *Karger* and *Deym,* who compromised themselves at Szolnok, are the subject of an enquiry; *Wrbna,* who according to Magyar reports was chiefly to blame for the defeat of the Austrians at Mezö-Kövesd, is also said to be involved in an enquiry, and, as all reports indicate, has "fallen into disgrace" and "likely to be pensioned off".

The nature of the so-called victory at Kapolna is revealed in the following report of the Vienna *Lithographierte Correspondenz:*

"According to the report of the Kapolna notary, who had to arrange for the burial of the fallen in the battle there, the number of dead on the Hungarian side was *1,500 and on the imperial side 4,000.*"[a]

Moreover, it is evident from Austrian reports that *Schlick* attended *a war council in Ofen* and that he is to take over the command of the Northern Army, Ban *Jellachich* that of the Southern Army, and that

---

[a] The report was reprinted under the heading: "Wien, 14. März" in the Augsburg *Allgemeine Zeitung* No. 76, March 17, 1849 and in *Kölnische Zeitung* No. 66 (second edition), March 18, 1849.— *Ed.*

Field Marshal *Windischgrätz* will remain in Ofen. It seems that people are not completely satisfied that the twin capitals[109] will be maintained.

The following reports of the Magyar correspondent of the *Breslauer Zeitung* show what impression Windischgrätz's latest measures regarding the Hungarian banknotes[110] have made in Pest:

"Commercial circles in Pest wanted to hold a meeting to consult about this measure, but Prince Windischgrätz would not allow it. The excitement in Pest was so great that the Prince found himself compelled to send 40,000 guldens in small Austrian banknotes to pay the workers' wages.—The Pest Commercial Bank also wanted to issue a circular saying that it would accept Hungarian notes as before, but Windischgrätz prohibited the Bank from accepting these notes. The Josephi Fair now being held in Pest is as good as non-existent because of the confusion over the banknotes, and in the end it is the Austrian merchants who are most hit by this, since they can neither sell nor collect outstanding amounts."

New evidence of the quite extraordinary measures which the imperial army finds itself compelled to introduce simply to retain the positions it now holds, is to be found in a decree of Windischgrätz from Ofen on March 10, which subjects the nobility and the citizens and also the cities and villages which join the rebellion to military requisitions without claim to compensation; next those sections of the nobility and the citizens which proved inactive in the imperial cause are required to bear the cost of provisioning the army; but in this case receipts will be issued and the claim to compensation is reserved. The faithful and loyal inhabitants have a special claim to full compensation; those who cause damage will incur sequestration of property.

The Magyar correspondent reports from the comitats of Tolna and Baranya:

"Yesterday the Mohacs mail was returned; Mohacs and Fünfkirchen were occupied by the Hungarians. The Hungarian General Perczel has marched with 10,000 men into Pentele on the Ofen bank of the Danube. Pentele is about 8 miles distant from Ofen. 400 imperial soldiers were driven out of Földvar on the Danube by the village peasants. On the Pest side operations proceed slowly and it appears that the main force of the Hungarians is crossing over to the Ofen bank of the Danube. The Hungarians seem very anxious to save Pest from bombardment, and must therefore direct their main offensive against Ofen, and when that is taken, Pest will fall automatically."

Reports that *Fünfkirchen* is in the hands of the Magyars and that a strong Magyar corps is marching to the right bank of the Danube certainly require confirmation.

The following (Austrian) report comes from Komorn:

"Six thousand sixty-pound bombs have been brought up for the bombardment of Komorn; communication trenches are being dug around the fortress and water is run into them so as to flood the subterranean buildings of the fortress (!). The garrison consists of 10 battalions. The inhabitants must hand over food mostly for nothing, since they cannot give change for the Kossuth 100-florin notes with which the men pay."[a]

"Communication trenches" by means of which "subterranean buildings are flooded" have hitherto been unknown and must be an entirely new royal imperial Austrian invention, rather like the famous balloons which were to bombard Venice.

The following report comes from Transylvania; it must surely be very painful to the neighbouring journalist who is such a Russophil:

"News has arrived in a roundabout way from Transylvania which brings us up to the 4th of the month. The cities of Kronstadt and Hermannstadt have to *produce a sum of 1,000 florins per day for the billeting of Russian troops*, about which they have complained to the general in command. Bem is still at Mediasch and Puchner is limited to his previous forces. *Without significant Russian support* (?) or a diversion from the Banat (!) the pacification of unhappy Transylvania is unthinkable."[b]

A diversion from the Banat! As if the Serbs had not been refusing for six weeks to leave their homeland to save the haggling Flemish Jews in the Transylvanian Sachsenland![111] And even if they wanted to, as if 40,000 Magyars on the Maros did not give them more than enough to do!

According to the *Ost-Deutsche Post*,[c] Dembiński is said to have resigned because of a dissension with Görgey, and Görgey is supposed to have become Commander-in-Chief on the Theiss. This news, which must have been sent from Pest on the 10th at the latest, appears to be a pure martial-law rumour, and is not even remotely confirmed by anyone. We give it only for the sake of completeness.

Written by Engels on March 17, 1849

First published in the *Neue Rheinische Zeitung* No. 249 (second edition), March 18, 1849

Printed according to the newspaper

Published in English for the first time

---

[a] This report was first published in the *Breslauer Zeitung* and then under the dateline "Wien, 14. März" reprinted in the *Kölnische Zeitung* No. 66 (second edition), March 18, 1849.— *Ed.*

[b] Ibid.— *Ed.*

[c] "Wien, 12. März", *Ost-Deutsche Post* No. 45, March 13, 1849.— *Ed.*

# MILITARY REPORTS FROM HUNGARY

*Cologne,* March 19. At last a Bulletin again, the 28th. But we search this document, printed in the *Wiener Zeitung* of March 15, in vain for reports from the Theiss, the main theatre of war; in vain we ask where Jablonowsky, Götz and their associates have gone; it is precisely on the most important events that the official Bulletin maintains a silence which speaks very loudly. On the other hand, it reports the following mighty advances of the imperial troops:

1) From *Transylvania*:

"To put an end to the devastating action of the enemy, who threatens to reduce the Saxon districts to complete ruin by the most oppressive requisitioning of money and victuals, and also to gain the line of the Kokel and thence to advance further towards Maros-Vásárhely and to link up with the corps of Lieutenant-Field Marshal von Malkowsky, who has advanced to Bistritz, the Commanding General, Lieutenant-Field Marshal Puchner, ordered the van der Null brigade to advance to Stolzenburg on the 28th of last month, to Markt-Schelken on March 1, to Arbegin and Frauendorf on the 2nd, to which it was followed on the 3rd by the main corps consisting of the two brigades of Stutterheim and Kalliani. After the first brigades had fought a victorious vanguard skirmish on March 2, the next day—when all three brigades had come together—the enemy was gradually driven back from all three positions which the insurgents had occupied (before Kopisch, at the inn of Grossprobsdorf and at Mediasch), with a loss of 300 dead and wounded and 85 prisoners. The insurgents withdrew in great haste to Maros-Vásárhely, whither they were pursued by a cavalry division,[112] an infantry battalion and two guns under Lieutenant-Colonel Bussek after the occupation of Mediasch. Since preparations are now being made for the occupation of Maros-Vásárhely communication with the Malkowsky corps and Colonel Urban as well as with the Bukovina will be restored."

Even if all this were true it proves merely that the imperial forces, evidently *reinforced by the Russians,* have taken Mediasch, while Bem was prevented by his wound from taking command. Thereby the imperial forces have gained a few miles of terrain. If the Bulletin boasts of the fact that preparations are being made for the occupation of Maros-Vásárhely and the to-be-expected restoration of communications with Malkowsky's corps in the Bukovina, it must be taken into consideration that Puchner is in Mediasch and Malkowsky at most in Bistritz, and that between these two places there lie 20 to 25 miles of high mountain country, so the boast of preparing to establish communications will mean about as much as if the Italians were to claim that by giving notice to the Piedmontese armistice[113] they had made preparations for "establishing communications" with the Magyars.

Incidentally, that Bem is seriously ill and that the Szeklers (for good reasons) have imposed really substantial contributions on the Saxon philistines as reward for their black-and-yellow[a] enthusiasm is proved by the following communication[b]:

"*Hermannstadt*, February 26. Bem, who is ill, drove to Maros-Vásárhely on the 23rd; his arm is in a very dangerous condition as a result of the amputation of a finger.—Schässburg has had to pay a contribution of 30,000 florins C.M.[114] and recently another 100,000 florins C.M. have been demanded from it and the administrative localities.—All the newspapers have mentioned the 195,000 men of the Romanian *Landsturm*; I can assure you that this figure exists merely on paper."

2) The Bulletin reports about *Komorn*:

"According to reports of the siege command of Komorn the pontoon bridge between Acs and Gönyö is completed and the closer encirclement of Komorn is thereby accomplished. On the 11th of this month the garrison of the Waag bridgehead made a sortie against Hetény, which was, however, beaten back by the Veigl brigade."

Duroc explained to Napoleon that Komorn was "impregnable". Short of betrayal, therefore, the imperial forces will not get in, and the Magyars have already taken strong measures to protect themselves against treason.

3) From the *Banat*:

"After the entire left bank of the Maros from the Transylvanian border to the Theiss was cleared of the enemy in February by the operations of the imperial Austro-Serbian army corps and the troops under Lieutenant-Field Marshal Baron Rukavina, Commanding General in the Banat, and secured by a well-planned arrangement of our troops in combination with the two fortresses of Arad and Temesvar, *it seemed no longer necessary for the Serb auxiliary corps to remain* in the Banat and in the Bacska comitat, and General Todorovich *was in a position* to comply with the wish expressed earlier by the Princely Serb Government, by allowing this brave auxiliary corps to go home to its peaceful occupation. At the beginning of this month the auxiliary corps returned to Belgrade in two steamboats along the Theiss and

---

[a] The Austrian imperial colours.— *Ed.*
[b] *Constitutionelles Blatt aus Böhmen* No. 62, March 14, 1849.— *Ed.*

Danube. On March 1 General Todorovich had his headquarters at Turkish Kanizsa on the Theiss, three hours from Szegedin and Theresiopel, in the direction of which the vanguard troops were moved forward on both banks of the Theiss into the immediate neighbourhood of these towns."

Really! The Serb auxiliary corps was no longer necessary! And what, then, has become of the mighty expedition to Transylvania and Grosswardein, which the last Bulletin but two announced with so much pomp?[a] After the left bank of the Maros has been cleared, the imperial troops suddenly confine themselves to the defensive, instead of marching on! But there are reasons for this, for which we must not, of course, ask the royal imperial bulletins. On the other hand, the organ of the Slavs, the *Constitutionelles Blatt aus Böhmen*, is enlightening us on this point. This paper carries a letter *from the Sava*, of March 9[b]:

"With every day dissensions increase among us, with every day our situation becomes more oppressive, and we are learning by experience that in this great struggle of the nations we *have helped to stage* the uncommonly instructive fable *of the squeezed lemon.* We have not yet recovered from the shock produced by the last order of Ban Jellachich introducing the German language; we have not yet forgotten the profound grief which stirred within us when we heard that all volunteer forces from the Serb principality might return home, and blow after blow new misfortunes are rained upon us. And now Prince Windischgrätz has issued an order to Patriarch Rajachich and General Todorovich to *dissolve all national departments* which have existed in the Voivodina since its conquest, and likewise *to abolish all garrisons except the imperial garrisons*, and to restore the *old army commands* and regiments to their former powers. This order of the Field Marshal caused much suspicion and dissatisfaction, and everyone was anxiously waiting for the reply of the Patriarch which, when it appeared, cheered the gloomy faces and gave room for hope. It said: 'So long as I am the administrator of these lands, I shall and will not admit this dissolution; this must not and cannot be. If you, however, insist on your order, I shall dissolve everything, but I cannot be held responsible for what the nation will say to that.' No less satisfactory was the reply of General Todorovich. *A most disagreeable impression* has been made by the news of the dissolution of the Kremsier Imperial Diet and the Constitution which has been imposed.[115]"

And when the Bulletin reports on the siege of Peterwardein as follows:

"Master of Ordnance[116] Count Nugent himself is engaged in the negotiations about the surrender of the important fortress of Peterwardein, where among the majority of the troops and of the population such a strong inclination to return to their duties has shown itself that this gives us great hope that we shall again see the royal imperial colours decorate this important military point in a few days, as they do the fortress of Esseg",

---

[a] See this volume, p. 62.— *Ed.*
[b] *Constitutionelles Blatt aus Böhmen* No. 62 (second supplement), March 14, 1849.— *Ed.*

the *Constitutionelles Blatt aus Böhmen* replies with the following South-Slav *Miserere*:

"*From the Drava*, March 9. Nugent has moved his headquarters from Dalja to Čerević in Syrmien, but Dalja must remain occupied since it could serve as a base for a sudden raid. Incidentally, the fact that troop detachments are frequently ordered to two different places and then it turns out that these contradictory orders were given in most pressing circumstances, indicates to some extent how insufficient our armed forces are.

"At Theresiopel in the Bacska comitat the Magyar troops mentioned yesterday were opposed only by three battalions and they had to yield to too great a superior force.

"In the operations against Peterwardein we are advancing rapidly. Consignments of siege guns leave Esseg daily in this direction, so *there is not a word of truth in the babble about the imminent surrender of the fortress.* Everything rests on sanguine illusions, although what has not yet happened will beyond doubt (!) happen, perhaps (!!) soon (!!!). The Austrian Serbs, who are much disgusted at the recall of their brothers from the other side of the border, do not even approve of the imperial troops operating against Peterwardein, for they regard this fortress as their own property and claim that their own national troops should take it. In the light of Stratimirovich's reservations, this reflects a certain mood which is now becoming articulate among the masses and the middle classes in the form of an admission that one wants to see whether Magyars, Swabians or Serbs will rule here. And here too we see that the particularist interests have the upper hand, and that there seems to be more concern for their attainment than for the preservation of the federal empire."[a]

It is quite evident that thunderclouds are gathering in the Serbian Voivodina for the foundering Austrian united monarchy, and that we were right to point out some time ago how little the camarilla can still rely on the Serbs.[b] But the following lines show that this does not refer to the Serbs alone, but that *all the Southern Slavs* share the same discontent with the renewed Austrian perfidy:

"Some Agram papers of the 9th already publish the imposed Constitution and reports on the dissolution of the Imperial Diet. We searched these papers in vain for effusions of joy; on the contrary, the *Slavenski jug* of the 10th expresses unconcealed resentment, and the *Südslavische Zeitung* of the 9th contains a few lines deploring this event."[c]

The official *Wiener Zeitung* moreover contains the following from Agram:

"For several days mobile national guards have been arriving, having arbitrarily left their posts on the cordon, alleging that they have received neither pay nor bread for some weeks. Whether this is really so, and if it is so, whose fault it is, we do not know; but in any case we must regret the return of our guards, who, against all expectations, devoted themselves eagerly to the cordon service, since the distrust aroused in the guardsmen by any withholding of their pay can have incalculably bad consequences. In any case it would be desirable for the worthy Banal Council[117] to discover the

---

[a] *Constitutionelles Blatt aus Böhmen* No. 63, March 15, 1849.— *Ed.*
[b] See this volume, pp. 97-98.— *Ed.*
[c] "Pest, 10. März", *Constitutionelles Blatt aus Böhmen* No. 62, March 14, 1849.— *Ed.*

reasons for this unauthorised return of the guards, make them public, and finally punish the guilty severely."[a]

All danger to the Magyars from the Slav south has consequently been eliminated, particularly since Kničanin, the most popular Serbian leader after Stratimirovich, has likewise returned to his fatherland, Turkish Serbia.

4) The Bulletin suddenly admits in the most naive way that, as the Magyar correspondence quite correctly reported, the Hungarian guerillas have again advanced to the Danube in the rear of the Austrians:

"The communication by water along the Danube has only been interrupted by bands of armed *Landsturm* brought together by hostile fanatics in the area of Kalocsa, Pataj and Solt, who wanted to stir up the right bank of the Danube at Paks and Földvar previously completely pacified. Suitable reinforcements which the garrison of Fünfkirchen has received from Slavonia, under Colonel Reiche, an expedition which three days ago went in 15 tugboats to the disturbed areas of both banks of the Danube on order from His Highness Field Marshal Prince Windischgrätz, and the operations of those troops of the army corps of Master of Ordnance Count Nugent which had been stationed at Szekszard and Mohacs and were commanded by Colonel Baron Lederer, will already have put a stop to these vain enterprises of dispersed enemy hordes and *made* the threatened areas permanently *safe.*"

"Will have made safe"! The royal imperial bulletins' habit of never reporting genuinely completed actions but only actions still to be accomplished, is becoming all too repetitive. If Welden does not give up this habit it will probably become impossible even for the *Kölnische Zeitung* to defend his bulletins.

In short: that the peasants *have* rebelled is a *fact*, and that the Austrians *will* pacify them is a *futurity.*

This is all the Bulletin reports. Fortunately, the silence of this official document does not prevent our receiving other news from the Theiss. A report asserts that Szolnok has again been evacuated by the Magyars. That this is a lie is proved by the silence of the Austrian Bulletin. On the contrary, the imperial troops are in a very difficult position there. The *Constitutionelles Blatt aus Böhmen* wails from Pest on March 10:

"If only the hundredth part of the verbal bulletins of the Magyars is to be believed we shall have the Hungarians in Pest-Ofen on March 15 at the latest. For my part I still rely confidently on the victory of the imperial arms. According to a fairly reliable source the Austrian army was still in Abony yesterday; but according to the reports of the local malcontents the imperial troops have withdrawn far beyond Szegléd and the Hungarians took this place at the point of the bayonet. Today the decisive battle is to be fought. May the God of Victory be with the imperial flag. I do not see ghosts and I

---

[a] *Wiener Zeitung* No. 62, March 14, 1849.—*Ed.*

do not believe in premonitions, but my heart will beat more calmly when the 15th of March has gone happily by. On that date, according to my blind faith, the last spark of danger for Pest-Ofen will be extinguished. The Hungarians are said to be firmly determined to celebrate this day with a mighty deed of arms."[a]

So there is still danger for Budapest! The Vienna *Lithographierte Correspondenz* writes, moreover:

"On the other hand, the reports on the stubborn resistance with which the royal imperial army is meeting corroborate each other. The latter has been increased to 148,000 men, it is true; but only a third of this number is used in military operations. The courage and daring of the Hungarian hussars is reported to be excellent and in particular the Wallmoden cuirassier regiment has suffered heavily from them. The inhospitable nature of the region in which the royal imperial troops are now encamped also contributes to making the campaign more difficult."

*Maklar,* according to authentic news the most remote village occupied by the imperial troops, was *burnt down* by them because there five waggons of ammunition have been played into the hands of the Magyars. The alleged culprits, five in number, were executed without ceremony. Such is the civilised conduct of the war by which the noble Windischgrätz seeks to ensure the victory which has hitherto eluded his colours. He also issued the following proclamation, the essential contents of which we indicated yesterday[b]:

*Pest.* "Hereby the following is decreed:

"1) All requisitioning will from now on be borne by the nobility and citizens who have taken part in the rebellion in Hungary without claim to any compensation or indemnification.

"2) All cities and villages which join the rebellion or which allow themselves to be misled into joining the *Landsturm* under any pretext whatever also come into this category.

"3) The heads of any comitat, district, town and village, as well as all public officials and landowners who leave their posts or residences at the approach of the royal imperial troops and thereby not only make the provisioning of the army more difficult but also lead to the oppression of the poor and innocent classes of the population, will immediately have their entire property, movable or immovable, conscribed and sequestered, and the produce and cattle found will at once be used to provision the royal imperial troops. Individuals and officials causing any damage to the imperial treasury with evil intent, who make loyal subjects of His Majesty the object of persecution or, given the opportunity, fail to prevent this to the best of their ability, come into the same category.

"4) Whatever else may be required for the provisioning of the royal imperial troops will be collected from that section of the more prosperous noblemen and citizens which has proved inactive in the sacred and just cause of His Majesty our most gracious Emperor and King.[c] These requisitions are, however, exacted against receipt and their claim to indemnification is reserved.

---

[a] *Constitutionelles Blatt aus Böhmen* No. 62, March 14, 1849.— *Ed.*
[b] See this volume, p. 111.— *Ed.*
[c] Francis Joseph I.— *Ed.*

"5) The peasants are obliged, it is true, to deliver immediately and without opposition any objects of requisition which are demanded by the royal imperial troop commanders, but complete compensation is guaranteed them from the properties of the above-mentioned categories 1, 2 and 3.

"6) In particular all those who have suffered or will suffer damage at the hands of the rebels for showing firm loyalty to His Majesty have a claim to complete. compensation.

"7) Should the compensation from the properties of the three mentioned categories guaranteed under paragraphs 5 and 6 be insufficient, the damages to those concerned will be conscientiously assessed by impartial commissions, and apportioned to the comitat or the whole land according to circumstances on fair principles.

Headquarters, Ofen, March 10, 1849.

> Alfred, Prince zu Windischgrätz,
> Royal Imperial Field Marshal."[a]

The fusillades are also beginning again. Thus the *Breslauer Zeitung* writes:

"According to reports of the 13th from Pest the Major of the perjured Zanini infantry regiment, who was taken prisoner at Kapolna, has been shot under martial law."

We hope Kossuth will not fail to take proper revenge for this foul murder.

These measures, combined with the stubborn silence of "Prince" Windischgrätz, prove more clearly than anything how brilliantly the all-mighty royal imperial army is faring on the Theiss and how soon "the war in Hungary will come to an end".

Finally we have from the Carpathians the following brief note which only proves how little progress the imperial forces are making there and how much the inhabitants of the Zips dislike the Slovak so-called *Landsturm*, which consists of mere riff-raff. The mass of the Slovak people, as we have often said already, support the Magyars. The article reads:

"*Kaschau*, March 3. Field Marshal Ramberg has issued a proclamation by virtue of which the population is ordered to regard the Slovak *Landsturm* with the same respect as the imperial troops. At the same time the leader of the *Landsturm* is authorised in accordance with the proclamation issued by Prince Windischgrätz on January 1 of this year *to raze to the ground* any place that dares to attack them.—Tomorrow Hurban, Štúr and other elected (!) trusted representatives (!) of the Slovak people are going to Olmütz to present to the Emperor the just wishes and grievances (!) of their people."[b]

---

[a] "Pest", *Constitutionelles Blatt aus Böhmen* No. 62 (second supplement), March 14, 1849.— *Ed.*

[b] "Kaschau, 3. März", *Constitutionelles Blatt aus Böhmen* No. 63, March 15, 1849. The date of Windischgrätz's proclamation as given by the newspaper is not accurate. It was signed on December 26, 1848.— *Ed.*

Messrs. Štúr and Hurban are such good "trusted representatives" of the Slovaks that they have already been chased over the Jablunka Pass to Moravia several times by these selfsame Slovaks!

Lastly we draw attention to a proclamation of Windischgrätz of the 11th,[a] in which he demonstrates how little the cause of the insurgents is a national cause since among 100 prisoners one meets at least 60 individuals of different nationality.

*Quod erat demonstrandum!* The Magyars have always had it cast in their teeth that their struggle was *not* a fight for liberty but a *national* struggle! Indeed! Nobody is so clever as an Austrian Field Marshal! In the same proclamation *the hard-pressed Windischgrätz calls for volunteer corps against the Magyars.*

A fine opportunity for our colleagues, the gentlemen of the *Kölnische Zeitung!*

Written by Engels on March 19, 1849

First published in the *Neue Rheinische Zeitung* No. 250, March 20, 1849

Printed according to the newspaper

Published in English for the first time

---

[a] "An die Bewohner Ungarns. Vom 11. März", *Wiener Zeitung* No. 64 (evening supplement), March 15, 1849.— Ed.

# FROM THE THEATRE OF WAR

Striking evidence of the fortunes of the imperial cause is given by the following report from Vienna:

"The claim made by several newspapers that *the situation in Hungary has taken a serious turn* has been *officially denied.* Yet the public firmly believes this to be so."

Consequently, the day after the publication of an official bulletin,[a] Welden still has to make a point of assuring the people that the situation in Hungary has not "taken a serious turn"! As though such a fact were not itself quite enough!

In addition, the following martial-law gossip has been disseminated in Vienna:

"The army operating in *Hungary* is occupying the following positions: *Tokaj* is occupied by Götz's brigade, *Miskolcz* by Jablonowsky's brigade; Lieutenant-Field Marshal Schlick's army corps is at *Erlau;* and the bulk of the army is concentrated between this area and *Szolnok;* the Ban has his headquarters at *Szegléd,* the Prince Field Marshal at *Ofen.*"

It is very difficult to deny that Schlick is at Erlau and Jellachich at Szegléd, for already a week ago they were occupying these positions which are situated far in the rear. But it is obviously untrue that Jablonowsky is in Miskolcz and especially that Götz is in Tokaj. The authors of yesterday's Bulletin must surely have known this.

The *Breslauer Zeitung* contains the following report from Hungary, which on this occasion, exceptionally, we must regard as very dubious, and at least *the first half* as nothing but gossip circulating in Pest:

"The *Rascians*[118] have *again been routed by the Hungarians* at Theresiopel. As a result, the imperial commandant of the Temesvar fortress, General Rukavina, has

---

[a] i.e. the 28th Army Bulletin. See this volume, pp. 113-20.— *Ed.*

sent a courier to Windischgrätz at Pest requesting immediate assistance, as otherwise he would have to surrender. *The Hungarian General Görgey has raised the siege of the Komorn fortress, which was already being bombarded by the imperial Lieutenant-Field Marshal Simunich. Simunich has retreated towards Leopoldstadt, leaving behind a great quantity of baggage.* Lieutenant-Field Marshal Count *Schlick,* to whom Windischgrätz entrusted the conduct of the retreat, *arrived in Pest* yesterday. In private conversation, Schlick expressed the greatest admiration for *Dembiński.*—Because of the new, extremely tight blockade, we are without reliable information on the present position of the Hungarian army, but the continuing return flow of guns and ammunition clearly indicates that the Hungarians are advancing. Yesterday, a *Hungarian patrol* entered *Promontor,* an hour and a half from Ofen, causing the greatest alarm in the Ofen fortress. Most of the Viennese wholesalers who are in Pest for the Josephi Fair currently in progress, have had their goods packed and sent back to Vienna."

Through the Austrian correspondent we have received the following reports from Transylvania. We are printing these, too, only with the greatest reservations, for they are excessively biased in favour of the Austrian side.

"*Kronstadt,* February 22. The local Saxon magistrate, who initially approached General Lüders for Russian help, seems already now not to be very happy about having done so. The Russians here have indeed acted in a rather extraordinary manner. There are reports of things occurring which, if they were confirmed, *would indeed make the speedy removal of the Russian auxiliary troops desirable.* In Kronstadt a sort of income tax has been levied on the inhabitants for the maintenance of the Russian troops; while we previously thought that this burden would on no account be imposed upon us.— *There is talk of large Turkish armies arriving here after marching through Wallachia; more Russian troops are also expected here.*"

"*Hermannstadt,* February 26. Diverse rumours are circulating here about *Bem,* proof that there is no precise information about his movements. Today it was said here that Bem had died as a result of the amputation he had undergone (!), which I do not yet believe. What is true is that he is short of munitions. As (!) he is expecting reinforcements and munitions from Hungary via Klausenburg, he is directing his force towards Maros-Vásárhely; for (!) even though Colonel Urban is operating with only four battalions of regulars, Bem is much more afraid of this hero than of all the corps commanders together with the Russian Cossacks. After spending two weeks here in inactivity, the troops were today beginning to move. At this moment two brigades are on the march, one towards Schässburg, the other towards Blasendorf via Mediasch. The Romanian Prefect A. Sever, who was posted in Resinari with 400 *Landsturm* men, has also received orders to march towards Blasendorf. Assistance from the Banat has still not arrived; on the other hand, there is talk of more Russian troops on their way here. I give the less credence to this as reports from the neighbouring country all agree that *large Turkish forces are moving towards Wallachia.*"

Written by Engels about March 20, 1849

First published in the *Neue Rheinische Zeitung* No. 251, March 21, 1849

Printed according to the newspaper

Published in English for the first time

# FROM THE THEATRE OF WAR

Since the failure of the second attempt of the imperial forces to cross the Theiss, military operations have again come to a halt. Windischgrätz is in Ofen, ostensibly to settle administrative matters; Schlick and Jellachich have held a council of war with him, at which the plan of operations was substantially changed. Schlick remains in command of the army of the North; Jellachich, having vainly sought for months to effect a crossing of the Theiss at Szolnok, will now give this up altogether and move southwards to Theresiopel, to unite his forces with the Serbs and border troops stationed at Szegedin, and will probably try to capture Szegedin, in order then to cross the Theiss there and operate on its left bank against Debreczin. The Magyars will know how to give him an appropriate welcome. It is questionable whether he will succeed in persuading the Serbian *Landsturm,* which constitutes the bulk of the troops stationed there, to join his army.

In the Banat of Temesvar, all is quiet. The Serbs, whose awareness of Austria's perfidy, by which they were duped, is growing daily, are not attacking anywhere. But without them, the imperial troops stationed there can do nothing. The *Südslavische Zeitung* reports from there:

"At Alt-Arad, the insurgents have once again concentrated a considerable body of troops under the command of the insurgent General Damjanich (previously a captain in the Rukavina regiment), General Vetter (previously a major in the Don Miguel regiment) and Colonel Gaal (a pensioned-off royal imperial Lieutenant-Colonel), who is leading the siege of the fortress."[a]

---

[a] *Constitutionelles Blatt aus Böhmen* No. 65, March 17, 1849.— *Ed.*

The insurrection in the comitats of Tolna and Baranya is becoming daily more threatening. All available troops have been sent there. It is worth noting that the Baranya comitat, the core of the insurrection, is for the most part populated by *Slavs*, Serbs and Slavonians.

In Transylvania, a French officer is said to have assumed command during Bem's illness. The operations at Szolnok are also said to have been directed by a Frenchman named Duchatel.

We shall return in more detail[a] to the Slav "troubles", which are taking an ever more edifying turn.

Written by Engels about March 21, 1849

First published in the *Neue Rheinische Zeitung* No. 252, March 22, 1849

Printed according to the newspaper

Published in English for the first time

---

[a] See this volume, pp. 133 and 162.— *Ed.*

# THE HOHENZOLLERN PRESS BILL

[*Neue Rheinische Zeitung* No. 252, March 22, 1849]

*Cologne,* March 21. In accordance with our promise[a] we return to the Hohenzollern plans to reform the freedom of the press and the right of association, plans which owe their inspiration to the state of siege. Today, a comparison with the previous plans for penal legislation, which were already *rejected* by the Rhenish Diet[119] under the aegis of the Camphausen opposition, will suffice to show what glorious "achievements" the *Rhinelanders* owe to the March uprising in Berlin, and what fresh features of the Prussian Law's love of violence have been bestowed on *Rhenish* legislation[120] by the "unweakened" Crown of the Grand Duke in Berlin.[b]

Two years ago at the United Diet, which as one remembers was brought into being by royal patent,[121] the junker Thadden-Triglaff from the Pomeranian Mancha entered the lists on behalf of freedom of the press. This associate of the Westphalian "valiant" young knight Vincke wielded his lance:

"Yes, public, but really public, proceedings for the gentlemen of the press: "*Freedom of the press, and along with it the gallows!*"[122]

The Bills which the November Government[c] seeks to impose represent the re-emergence of these old pre-March patented efforts. The "strong Crown of Prussia" exclaims in reply to the hated provisions of the *Code pénal,* and to the acquittal verdicts of Rhenish juries against tax refusers and agitators:

---

[a] See this volume, p. 69.— *Ed.*
[b] Frederick William IV.— *Ed.*
[c] i.e. the Brandenburg-Manteuffel Government which carried out the coup d'état in Prussia.— *Ed.*

"Yes, public, but really public, proceedings:

"*Freedom of the press, and along with it the gallows, the gallows of the Prussian Law!*"

The provisions of the *Code pénal* entirely ignore the easily offended susceptibility of the feelings of His Hohenzollern Majesty. In spite of the property qualification and infiltration by the police, it is not possible to find Rhenish jurymen who would punish the unspeakable crime of *lèse-majesté* with anything more than the 5-franc fine for insult to a "private person". The imperial despotism had too high an opinion of itself to state that its majesty could be "insulted", but the Christian-Germanic Father-of-the-people consciousness which understandably can in no way bear comparison with the lofty eminence of Napoleonic pride, feels a "deep-seated need" to re-establish the protection of its old-Prussian dignity in its Rhenish Grand Duchy. The "strong" Crown does not *dare* to abolish the Rhenish legal system, but it grafts on it the much more promising shoot of the legal concepts of the Prussian Law and exclaims:

"*Public, really public proceedings, and along with them the gallows of the Prussian Law!*"

As regards the "public proceedings" which for the time being are to be imposed on the Rhenish Code para. 22 of the Bill states:

"The police authorities are entitled to confiscate any publication intended for distribution **wherever found**, *even if it has already begun to be issued*, insofar as ... its content provides the basis for a crime or offence which *can* be *administratively* the subject of prosecution."

The police is entitled to confiscate newspapers displeasing to it in the post and in offices even if they have "*already begun to be issued*", that is to say, when the "preventive measures" of the police "as such" are supposed to cease and the matter "legally" comes within the competence of the courts. The police possesses this right of confiscation in all cases where the "content" of publications, newspapers etc. "provides the basis for a crime or offence" which can be "*the subject of prosecution*" "administratively", i.e. by the police, that is to say, where the police wishes to indulge its Uckermark [123] hankerings to play the role of the Public Prosecutor's office and considers it necessary to justify this inclination by the extremely odd plea of some kind of "crime or offence" or other circumstances which "can be the subject of *prosecution*". Finally, the police can confiscate all such printed matter, *c'est-à-dire* all that it suits the lord and his holy Hermandad [124] to confiscate, *wherever found*, that is to say, it can invade private houses and the secrets of family life, and where there are no grounds for protecting property by means of the state of siege and the Croats, under the power afforded by constitutional legality the private property of law-abiding citizens can be plundered by the police. The Bill, moreover, speaks of all publications "intended" for distribution, "*even if*" their issue has already begun; this presupposes "as a matter of course" the right of confiscation where the distribution has *not yet* begun, which *cannot yet be the basis* for any "crime or offence", and thus extends police robbery to the private possession of objects which are not legally "liable to prosecution". The French September laws,[125] the sabre-rattling censorship of Cavaignac's military dictatorship, and even the Bills on penal legislation put before the old Provincial Diets and Committees "to the displeasure of His Majesty", at least respected private property that "still gives no grounds for crime or offence". The press Bill based on the March achievements in Berlin, on the other hand, organises a public police vendetta against private property and the possessions of citizens and in the name of Christian-Germanic police morality violently drags into public view personal matters that have nothing whatever to do with penal law.

"*Public, really public proceedings, and along with them the gallows of the Prussian Law!*"

The improvement of these public proceedings goes hand in hand with improving the provisions of the Prussian Law.

The desired enactment concerning *lèse-majesté* is "constituted" in para. 12 in the following way:

"Anyone who by word, writing, printing or signs, by pictorial or other representation, *violates respect for the King* will be punished by imprisonment of from two months to *five years.*"

If the Rhenish subjects do not know what degree of "respect" is demanded from them by their Hohenzollern Grand Duke, who was foisted on them by the haggling over nations at Vienna,[126] they can look up the preamble to the Berlin penal law.

Up to now, the highest sentence that could be imposed by the Prussian Law[127] for *lèse-majesté* was *two years,* and for *violation of respect one year,* of imprisonment or detention in a fortress (Prussian Law [*Allgemeines Landrecht*], II. 20. paras. 199, 200).

These provisions, however, do not seem to have been an adequate safeguard for the august feelings of the "strong Crown of Prussia". Already in the "Bill concerning penal law for the Prussian states" submitted to the United Commissions[128] of 1847, "utterances in words or writing, or by pictures etc., which *intentionally* violate the *honour* of the King (para. 101), are punishable by *six months' to five years'* penal labour". On the other hand, however, "utterances and actions which, although *not* to be regarded in themselves *as insults to the King*, nevertheless violate *due respect to him* (para. 102), are punishable by imprisonment of from six weeks *to one year.*" In the official preamble to this Bill it is stated that while it is true that the Saxon Diet (in connection with a similar Bill of 1843) had proposed that "violation of respect" should be more narrowly defined by the addition of the word "intentional" in order to prevent utterances and actions being brought under the law "in which there was not the remotest *intention* to violate respect for the King", nevertheless such an addition must be rejected by the Government because it "would *blur* the distinction between *lèse-majesté* and violation of respect" and because *"intentional"* violations of "respect" must be regarded as "*lèse-majesté*".

From these reasons, which are still paramount in regard to the concepts used in the press law which is about to be imposed on us, it follows that "violation of respect", which at the present time like *lèse-majesté* is punished by two months' to *five years'* imprisonment, consists precisely in *"unintentional"* *lèse-majesté.*

At the same time the "preamble" informs us that the maximum length of punishment for "violation of respect" was at that time fixed at one year solely because of a motion by the Rhenish Diet.

The benefit of the "March achievements" for the Rhinelanders is obvious. The first attempts to adapt the *Code pénal* to the Prussian Law foisted on the Rhinelanders the new crimes of *lèse-majesté* punishable by two years' imprisonment and "violation of respect" punishable by one year's imprisonment.[129] In the Bills put forward in 1843 and 1847, the value of *lèse-majesté* was increased to five years, whereas, on the motion of the *Rhenish Diet*, violation of respect had to retain its valuation of one year. By the achievements of the March revolt under the state of siege, punishment for "violation of respect" (even if unintentional) is also increased to five years' imprisonment and by once again introducing new crimes the Rhenish Code of Law is brought closer to the old-Prussian Law.

*"Freedom of the press, public proceedings under the state of siege, and along with them the gallows!"*

[*Neue Rheinische Zeitung* No. 253, March 23, 1849]

**Cologne, March 22.**

"There was all the more reason why the provisions concerning *lèse-majesté* could not be omitted," states Manteuffel's preamble to para. 12 of the Bill, "because in the greater part of the *Rhine Province* the penal laws on *lèse-majesté* had been *made invalid* by the ordinance of April 15, 1848, and since then this *gap* has not been filled."

The Manteuffel preamble states that this part of the Hohenzollern legislation on the press, which surpasses even the old-Prussian Law and His Majesty's revelation in the Bills on penal legislation of 1843 and 1847, appeared essential chiefly with reference to the *Rhine Province.* The ordinances of April 15, 1848,[a] i.e. the promises which the "Crown that had fallen into the dust" (see the *Neue Preussische Zeitung* of the 20th of this month) condescended to make under the pressure of the March uprising, have "rendered invalid" in the Rhine Province the laboriously imposed adjustment made in the spirit of the Prussian Law and restored the *Code pénal* in its original defective purity. But in order fittingly to fill this "*gap*" due to the March achievements and simultaneously to testify to the progressive capacity for expanding the Hohenzollern Majesty's value the "strong" November Government proposes for the Rhinelanders not the old pre-March provisions of the Prussian Law,—no, it proposes a new declaration of respect for the King envisaging a punishment more than double that of all previous penal law projects. *Le roi est mort, vive le roi!*[b] Prior to March 1848, the still "unweakened" dignity of the Father of the people was valued in the Prussian Law at one year's imprisonment; in March 1849 the cost of disrespect to the Crown which had "fallen into the dust" has risen to five years' imprisonment. Prior to March 1848, the Rhenish law was supplemented only by the patriarchal additional provisions of the Prussian Law; in March 1849 the Manteuffel November achievements have been imposed on it:

"*Freedom of the press, sabre-rattling censorship, and along with them the gallows!*"

The "gap" in Rhenish legislation, however, reveals still further depths. Para. 12 of the Berlin press reform continues with the following additions:

"*The same punishment*' (from two months' to *five years'* imprisonment) "is incurred by anyone who in the way indicated above" (by word, writing or *signs*, by pictorial or *other* representation) "*insults the Queen.* Anyone who in the same way insults *the successor to the throne* (?) or *any other member of the royal house* ... will be punished by imprisonment of from one month to *three years.*"

As already mentioned, the old-Prussian Law punished insult even to the "supreme head of the state" with only two years' imprisonment. The advance made by the Bill on the press, which lays down

---

[a] "Verordnung über die Herstellung des Rheinischen Zivilgesetzbuchs in Betreff der Schliessung der Ehe..."; "Verordnung, betreffend das Verfahren bei politischen und Pressvergehen in der Rheinprovinz und die Wiederherstellung des Rheinischen Strafrechts und Strafverfahrens bei politischen und Amtsverbrechen."— *Ed.*

[b] The King is dead, long live the King!— *Ed.*

the term of imprisonment for insult to persons of lower rank—five years for the Queen, three years for the successor to the throne (?) and "other" members of the "royal house"—is very obvious.

Rhenish legislation no more recognises insult to the Queen etc. than it does insult to the "supreme head of the state". Rhenish newspapers hitherto were able with impunity to print stories about "hopes of the court for an unexpected event", which at times can, however, for medical reasons, amount to impugning the honour of the person involved.

Finally, the ex-patented Bill on penal legislation of the United Commissions ranked insult to the "Queen" as inferior to insult to the "supreme head of the state", by threatening it (para. 103) with three years' imprisonment instead of five years. And as regards equal punishment for insults to the "Queen" and insults to other members of the royal family, the 1847 preamble states that the Rhenish, Silesian, Saxon and Pomeranian Diets had already wanted a distinction to be made between these persons but that the Government could not put this lamentable "casuistry" into effect.

The strong Manteuffel Government did not consider the "casuistry" of the old Rhenish, Silesian and Saxon Diets beneath its dignity. Was not the successful von der Heydt also among the patented casuists of that period? The Manteuffel-von der Heydt press Bill "establishes" the casuistic distinction between the Queen and other members of the royal house; but it does it in accordance with the progressive development of the sovereign's dignity in general in the post-March period. The old Rhenish, Silesian and Pomeranian Diets demanded that a distinction be made between the Queen and other members of the royal family so that the equal punishment of three years' imprisonment for insulting the latter would be reduced. The strong Manteuffel-von der Heydt Government accepts the distinction, not in order to make this reduction but to raise the punishment for insulting the Queen to the newly increased level of punishment for insulting the "supreme head of the state".

That the concepts of majesty show a similar capacity for development is proved by the provision appended to the same paragraph, according to which insults to any "*German head of state*" and likewise insults to the "successor to the throne" are punished by three years' imprisonment.

According to Rhenish law, insults to other "heads of state" are punished like insults to private persons (a fine of 5 francs), and that only on the *demand of the person insulted* and not because his public character is the concern of penal law. Under the Bill on penal legislation which had already been rejected by the Rhenish Diet in

1843 thus incurring "the displeasure of His Majesty", and which was again put forward in 1847, insults to foreign rulers and "their spouses" incurred punishment of from two months' imprisonment to two years' penal labour. The Prussian Diet moved the entire deletion of this provision and the Westphalian opposition of junkers from the backwoods declared the original level of punishment too high. Finally the Manteuffel-von der Heydt Government filled the serious post-March gaps in the Rhenish legislation by increasing to three years the two years' term of punishment which the Westphalians elected on a property qualification were opposing, and by taking up the cudgels on behalf of the Pomeranian Don Quixote of the United Diet:

"*Freedom of the press, really public proceedings, and along with them the gallows!*"

In the plans for press reform inspired by His Majesty, para. 19 has furthermore a noteworthy amusing feature:

"Anyone guilty of insulting 1. either of the two Chambers ("as such"), 2. a member of either Chamber during the *course* of its sittings, 3. *any other* political *organisation,* an official authority, or an official ... by word, writing, printing, signs, by pictorial or other representation, will be punished by up to nine months' imprisonment."

While Manteuffel-von der Heydt are using bayonets to disperse "political organisations", Agreement Assemblies and Chambers, the Rhinelanders are having a botchwork of new crimes for "the protection of these Assemblies" inserted in their *Code pénal* to fill up its "gaps". From the divine-royal source of grace, the Manteuffel-von der Heydt Government is foisting on the country a national Constitution in order to introduce into the Rhenish Code of Law a *new, hitherto unknown crime* in the shape of "insult to the Chambers":

"*Freedom of the press, public proceedings, and along with them the gallows!*"

Let the Rhinelanders take care before it is too late. The history of previous attempts to adapt the Rhenish Code of Law to the Prussian Law, and the Hohenzollern *further elaboration* of the March promises, will tell them what they have to expect from the achievements made on the other side of the Rhine.

The aim of the martial-law attacks against the *Code pénal* hitherto has been nothing less than the complete incorporation of the Rhine territories in the old-Prussian provinces, an incorporation which was not complete so long as the Rhine Province was not wholly subjected to the cudgel of the Prussian Law. The new Bill, however, under the pretext of filling the "gaps" in the Rhinelanders' own legislation by means of the benefits of the Prussian Law, perfects also the Prussian Law for the old provinces as regards its "gap" of excessive mildness.

Miserable as the present Chamber is, nevertheless we do not expect it to accept these Bills. But in that case we do expect that there will be *imposed* on us also the Hohenzollern gallows for the press, and that is precisely what we wish.

Written by Marx on March 21-22, 1849

First published in the *Neue Rheinische Zeitung* Nos. 252 and 253, March 22 and 23, 1849

Printed according to the newspaper

Published in English for the first time

# FROM THE THEATRE OF WAR

The news from the theatre of war is not very noteworthy today. Jellachich has *returned to Pest*, after having been defeated, according to the Magyar report, by the Hungarians at Jasz-Bereny. One thousand wounded are said to have already arrived at Ofen. Schlick, too, is still in Ofen. The Magyar report continually declares that Görgey has invaded Slovakia with 30,000 men and occupied the hill towns (though for the time being we are regarding this as a Pest extravagance).

In the Földvar region, there were 2,000 Honveds[130] and 6,000 peasant insurgents. The ships sent there with the troops returned, however, already on the following day, without having accomplished anything. Mounted bands of rebels are swarming right up to the outskirts of Pest (*Constitutionelles Blatt aus Böhmen*[a]).

The Austrian Minister Schwarzenberg and the ex-Finance Minister Kübeck are said to be in Pest, to settle the affair of the Hungarian banknotes. (Magyar report.)

The report of a victory of the Serbs at Theresiopel and of the capture of this town has now been transformed into *news of their defeat* and the admission that the Magyars have now *occupied* in addition to Szegedin *Theresiopel* as well. Great agitation reigns in Syrmien, as among all the Southern Slavs.

Written by Engels on March 22, 1849

First published in the supplement to the *Neue Rheinische Zeitung* No. 253, March 23, 1849

Printed according to the newspaper

Published in English for the first time

---

[a] "Pest, 13. März", *Constitutionelles Blatt aus Böhmen* No. 65 (supplement), March 17, 1849.— *Ed.*

# [FROM THE THEATRE OF WAR]

According to letters of the 6th of March from the Moldavian border, the Russians stationed in Transylvania have not merely been reinforced by 8,000 men, but another Russian corps is standing on the border of the Bukovina, awaiting the order to move into the Bukovina. *Bem has assembled considerable reinforcements and is threatening Hermannstadt for the third time.* Malkowsky's corps (commanded by Urban) has had to *retreat*—to the border of the Bukovina, and *once again to surrender the town of Bistritz to the Hungarians.*

Written by Engels about March 23, 1849

Printed according to the newspaper

First published in the *Neue Rheinische Zeitung* No. 254, March 24, 1849

Published in English for the first time

# THE DEBATE ON THE ADDRESS IN BERLIN

*Cologne*, March 25. We must confess to our readers that it is only with reluctance that we can resolve to take a closer look at the debates of the so-called Second Chamber[131] in Berlin. The debates of the dissolved Agreement Assembly,[132] meaningless and dull as they were, nevertheless had the interest of being topical. The debates dealt with things which had no influence on the fate of Europe, and with laws which from the outset had no prospect of endurance, but they did deal with matters of immediate interest to us, and they provided a faithful mirror of the mounting reaction in Prussia. The debates of the present Chamber, on the other hand, serve no other purpose than that of legalising the already completed counter-revolution. They do not deal with the present time—that has been excluded by the ban on interpellations—they deal with the past, with the temporary interregnum lasting from December 5 to February 26,[133] and if the Chamber does not unconditionally recognise this interregnum it will be dispersed and once again its activity will have been in vain.

And people are supposed to take an interest in such deliberations, at a time when the revolution and the counter-revolution are fighting it out arms in hand in Hungary and Italy, when the Russians are stationed on the Eastern frontier and France is preparing for a new world-shaking revolution!

The debate on the Address is altogether one of the dreariest that we remember ever having read. The whole debate turned, of course, merely on recognition or non-recognition of the imposed so-called Constitution.[134] And what does it matter whether this Chamber, which was elected in circumstances of a state of siege and the crushing effect of a successfully carried out counter-revolution, which deliberates in a corner of Berlin under the state of siege, and which dare not utter a word of dissent if it does not want to be dissolved—what does it matter whether such an Assembly recognised this document or not? As if recognition or non-recognition would make the slightest difference to the course of the European revolution, which will reduce to dust all the imposed and not-imposed constitutions now in force!

The sole feature of interest in the whole debate is the puerile arrogance of the Right and the cowardly collapse of the Left.

The royalist gentlemen are incorrigible. As soon as their affairs are temporarily again in better shape thanks to the aid of the obedient soldiery, they imagine themselves back in the promised land and adopt a tone whose impudence surpasses anything the police state has ever shown.

The gentlemen of the Left, on the other hand, moderate their claims to the same extent as those of the Right increase theirs. In all their speeches, one can discern the broken spirit that is the result of bitter disappointment, that dejection of the ex-member of the Assembly which first let the revolution sink in the mire and afterwards, drowning in the morass of its own creation, perished with the painful cry: The people are not yet mature enough!

Even the resolute members of the Left, instead of putting themselves into direct opposition to the whole Assembly, do not abandon the hope of achieving something in the Chamber and through the Chamber, and of winning a majority for the Left. Instead of adopting an extra-parliamentary position in the parliament, the only honourable one in such a Chamber, they make one concession after another to parliamentary expediency; instead of ignoring the constitutional point of view as far as possible, they actually seek an opportunity of coquetting with it for the sake of peace.

The general debate turned on the recognition or non-recognition of the so-called Constitution. The Left, which regarded itself as the continuation of the majority of the former Agreement Assembly which had voted for refusing payment of taxes,[135] ought to have begun with the most emphatic protest against the coup d'état of December 5. But what did it do? It declared that it was prepared to accept the dissolution of the National Assembly as a fact which could no longer be altered, to give up the dispute in principle over the validity of the imposed bastard, to cover all the kicks and insults with the cloak of charity, and to pass at once to the revision!

The Right, of course, rejected this cowardly offer with the contempt it deserved and forced the Left to take up the dispute over principles.

The Left suffered the fate it deserved. Why did the gentlemen imagine that they had to achieve something where there was nothing to achieve? Why did they persuade themselves that they were destined to achieve by parliamentary means something that can only be achieved in a revolutionary way, by force of arms? But, of course, these gentlemen "*came to the top owing to parliamentary activity*", about which deputy Waldeck has so many beautiful things to say, the top where *esprit de corps* commences and revolutionary energy—*s'il y en avait*[a]—evaporates!

The first speaker of the variegated party that is called the Left was Herr *von Berg*. But one should certainly not expect to encounter again the cheerful little abbé of last year, who was able greatly to annoy the gentlemen of the Right with all kinds of piquant witticisms. Herr Berg no longer spoke as an *abbé*, but as a pastor.

He was of the opinion that it would have been desirable to draw up the draft Address in such a way that "the greatest possible majority could vote for it". The Chamber ought to have shown the country "that its representatives do not intend to sacrifice the good of the country to *mere disputes over principles*". In conclusion Herr Berg said that he missed in the draft "*the spirit of reconciliation with which we (?) are imbued*", the striving for "agreement". He prophesied that by the debate on the Address the Chamber would not "establish in the fatherland *peace and the hope of a better future*".

Indeed! Did the electors of Jülich and Düren send Herr Berg to Berlin for him to declare that the struggle for the people's right to decide its Constitution for itself is a mere "dispute over principles", to preach "reconciliation" and "agreement" in pulpit tones, and to drivel about "peace" when it is a question of *war*?

You, chaplain Berg, were elected, not because you are a preacher, but because you were a *supporter of tax refusal.* Your election did not take place in the interests of *peace*, but was from the outset a *declaration of war* against the coup d'état. You were sent to Berlin not to propose reconciliation and agreement, but to *protest*. And now, when you are a deputy, now you declare that the struggle between the sovereignty of the people and the "omnipotence of the Crown" is a mere barren dispute over principles!

Most of those who supported tax refusal were re-elected not because all their activities between May and November 1848 satisfied the electors, but because by the decision on tax refusal[b] they took up a revolutionary position, and because it could be hoped that the kicks

---

[a] If one has any.—*Ed.*

[b] See present edition, Vol. 8, p. 36.—*Ed.*

the Government had bestowed on them had opened their eyes and shown them how to behave towards the Crown and the Government in order to achieve some result. It was hoped that consequently they would all move a step to the left.

Instead of this, it has turned out that the chastisement they received in November has borne fruit; instead of moving to the left, these gentlemen have gone farther to the right. With the most well-intentioned zeal typical of the wailers,[136] they preach reconciliation and agreement. They say they want to forget and forgive the maltreatment they received, they propose peace. It serves them right that their proposals have been laughed to scorn.

The next speaker was Count *Renard*, a feudal magnate from Silesia.

Herr Renard imagines that nothing was overturned in March, but only a new factor introduced. The Crown remains the Crown, the only difference being that representation based on the *estates* (!), with the people having a *consultative* voice, is added as a "determining factor". Otherwise everything remains as it used to be. (In point of fact that is precisely what with God for King and fatherland[a] is to be imposed on us and has to be revised.) The deputy has "to represent the Constitution of the people in its entirety, that is the people *with* the sovereign, but not the people *against* the sovereign". (Why then is the sovereign still required if in any case the deputies already "represent" him?) After advancing this new theory of the state, Herr Renard also made the following statement to the Chamber: It does not exist "in order to *bargain* and *haggle* with the Crown"—i. e. to reach agreement with it—"to dispute over words or, *if you like, even about rights*"; the Government and the Chamber are by no means "advocates on behalf of two parties engaged in litigation". Anyone who regards his mandate in any other way "wages civil war in matters of theory".

Herr Renard speaks plainly enough. In the profane constitutional states, the Chamber rules through its committee, the Government, and the King's only right is that of saying yes and amen, and of giving his signature. That was also the case among us in the period of affliction, in the period of Camphausen, Hansemann and Pfuel. But in the royal Prussian constitutional monarchy by the grace of God the exact opposite holds good. The Crown rules through its Ministers, and woe to the Chambers if they venture to do anything but say yes and amen to the effusions of divine grace!

"The clearest proof," Herr Renard continued, "that there is no rift between Crown and people is afforded by the present moment, when the *German question* is

---

[a] The words are taken from Frederick William III's decree of March 17, 1813 concerning the organisation of an army reserve.— *Ed.*

being spoken of in all the provinces amid universal enthusiasm.... In many of them this enthusiasm ... is largely due to the dignity, the greatness, of our ancient royal house by divine grace, and of the *knightly* and *victorious*" (especially in Champagne, at Jena and on March 18, 1848[137]) "Hohenzollern dynasty. (Animation and cries of 'bravo'.)"

Testimony to this enthusiasm was given by the cries of "Down with the German Emperor" coming from 5,000 throats in Gürzenich[a] on March 19, the very same day when Herr Renard spoke the words quoted above. Similar testimony was the rejection in Frankfurt a few days later of the King of Prussia as hereditary emperor, and the miserable majority in Frankfurt of four whole votes in favour of a hereditary emperor in general.[138]

No, finally exclaimed Renard, who incidentally is not at all a fox[b]:

"No one should or will succeed by corrosive poison in killing the *new life* in the wound that strives to be healed, or in converting the split that has possibly arisen" (so it is there after all!) "into an unbridgeable gulf!"

Most worthy Renard! May the evil-minded never succeed "by corrosive poison in killing the new life in the wound" which last spring was inflicted on your purse crammed with feudal privileges, a wound which now thanks to the return of divine grace "strives to be healed", or in "converting into an unbridgeable gulf the split that has possibly arisen" between your income and expenditure!

Herr Jacoby came to the rostrum. He too, although he spoke more resolutely than Berg and was clearer and more precise in his arguments, could not refrain from practising diplomacy. The recognition of the Constitution in the Address was *inappropriate*, because it ought not to occur *incidentally*, and it was untimely, because the Constitution had not yet been revised, definitely sanctioned and given allegiance to by oath. As if the recognition of such a Constitution could ever be appropriate and timely!

Herr Jacoby, too, "had no wish to renew the old dispute" about the dispersion of the Agreement Assembly; the question whether it was an act of salvation or the aim and goal of a diplomatic scheme he would "leave to impartial history". "Impartial history" will record that the people who spoke so loudly when they had a majority, now, when they are in a minority, behave with the humility of schoolboys who have been punished.

"As far as recognition of the Constitution by the people is concerned, I have to reply that our Assembly is the sole legitimate and the sole authorised organ for such recognition."

---

[a] See this volume, pp. 490-91.— *Ed.*

[b] A pun on Renard—the name of the speaker and the French word for fox.— *Ed.*

No, Herr Jacoby, your Assembly is nothing of the sort. Your Assembly is nothing but the organ of the electoral delegates selected by means of the grand criterion of "independence" [139] on the basis of the imposed so-called electoral law, it is an organ which in the main owes its existence to government intrigues. Your Assembly may recognise the Constitution, but that is merely a recognition of the imposed Constitution by the imposed Constitution itself. The people will show little concern about that and "impartial history" will quite soon have to register that this so-called Constitution, despite recognition of it—if that were ever to take place—was trampled underfoot in the course of the European revolution and disappeared no one knows how.

Herr Jacoby probably knows that as well as we do; the Right in the Chamber knows that he knows it; so why all this nonsense about a legal basis, especially when one wants to leave dubious the legal basis of the dispersed Assembly!

Herr *Scherer,* a barrister and deputy from Düsseldorf-Elberfeld, was greatly shocked by d'Ester's draft Address. He considered that the deputation which presented such an Address to the King must "entail an armed uprising". People whose actions entail armed uprising, Herr Scherer, speak to kings in quite a different way!

This draft "casts a flaming torch in the country," but Herr Scherer believes that "it will not cause a conflagration, but only *harm its bearers*"!

It is impossible to speak more clearly. Herr Scherer gives the Left the well-meant advice to withdraw the draft, otherwise they will be apprehended one fine day in spite of the article guaranteeing immunity.[140] Very philanthropic of you, Herr Scherer!

Next Herr *Waldeck* rose to speak. He proved to be unchanged: on the Left, but not farther to the left than is expedient if one wants to be regarded as *possible.* Herr Waldeck began by expressing his annoyance that the Right always wanted to make him responsible for the unfortunate dispute over the November coup d'état. Herr Waldeck and "his party" had "clearly stated that in their opinion this dispute over principles ought not to have arisen at all". In his opinion, "the Assembly is unanimous" (that is bad enough!) "about what it ought to do with the Constitution"—namely, to revise it. Herr Waldeck then once more explained why the dispute over principles was superfluous, and again appealed to the better feelings of the Right:

"Cannot you for the time being *very well leave* this question *open?*... You will lose nothing as far as your views are concerned, *but do spare the views of others!*"

A worthy speech of one of the dispersed "representatives of the people" to the same majority that rubs its hands in glee when it thinks of the successful dispersal of the National Assembly.

"But do spare the views of others!" The great man begs for *mercy*.

When, however, the work on the Constitution has been completed, then the Minister of the future "hopes" that

"this Assembly, *owing to its parliamentary activity, will really have reached the high level* essential for *fully recognising* the *consequences* of such a declaration" (on the validity of the Constitution)!

Indeed! Do not our new-baked knights of the rostrum, who have hardly seven months of parliamentary activity behind them, already behave as precociously wisely as if they had sat for fifty years on the benches of St. Stephen's Chapel [141] and had been members of all the Paris Chambers from the "introuvable" of 1815 to the "introuvable" of February 24!

But this is true. In their short career our knights of the rostrum have become imbued with as much parliamentary self-satisfaction, and have become as divested of all revolutionary energy — *si jamais il y en avait*[a] — as if they had grown grey in the grandiloquent proceedings of parliament.

After Herr Waldeck came a speech from His one-time Excellency, the formerly omnipotent Herr von *Bodelschwingh*.

Just like Herr Manteuffel, so too his previous chief has become a constitutionalist "by order of His Majesty". It is quite amusing to hear the last Prime Minister of the absolutist regime defend constitutional monarchy.

Prior to February, Herr Bodelschwingh used to be ranked as the best orator of the Government of the time. In the United Diet,[142] he still proved himself the most skilful. But when one reads his present speech, one is alarmed for the sake of the man himself by the silliness and insipidity of this strange disquisition. Herr Bodelschwingh has become a constitutionalist by order; apart from this word, however, he has remained exactly as before, we do not know whether by order or not. He excused himself by saying that he had lived "in rustic seclusion"; but it could really be thought that he has let himself be *buried* for a whole year.

He acknowledges that by the extremely innocent draft Address of the Left he

"had been enlightened about their views in a manner and to an extent of which he *had not even an inkling* before his appearance in the Chamber".

---

[a] If they ever had any.— *Ed.*

*Quel bonhomme!*[a] When Herr Bodelschwingh still ruled over Prussia his numerous spies must have kept him remarkably badly informed for our money if he can now believe that since then such views have suddenly appeared out of nowhere!

The Left had stated that it was here not on the basis of the Charter imposed under martial law, but on the basis of universal suffrage. What did Herr Bodelschwingh reply?

"If our seats are the outcome of universal suffrage, then there is no need for all the formalities" (of the election test). "*We need only appear in the market place and say: Elect me!* I do not know how many particles of universal suffrage you regard as requisite in order to lay claim to entry in this Chamber. Take as many as you like, in this way it would be easy to obtain sufficient votes; by the acknowledgement of this right the Chamber would soon be so filled that we could no longer remain here; for my part at least I would renounce my seat, and the sooner the better."

If a Westphalian peasant, or if Herr von Bodelschwingh at the time when he was still a Minister, had uttered this profound wisdom about universal suffrage, we would not have been surprised. The interesting feature of the above-quoted passage is·that it proves that one could be a Prussian Prime Minister and in control of the whole carefully scrutinised bureaucracy without "having even an inkling" of the most immediate questions of European interest. But after universal suffrage has been in operation *twice* in France, after what the *Left* calls universal suffrage has been in operation twice in Prussia, and has even thrust a seat in the Chamber upon Herr Bodelschwingh himself—after this to be able to indulge in such fabulous fantasies about universal suffrage, one must have been an antediluvian Prussian Minister! However, we must not forget that Herr Bodelschwingh was buried and has only been resurrected in order to enter the Chamber "by order of His Majesty"!

Herr Bodelschwingh said further:

"Even if we are not at all of the opinion that this Constitution will become valid only through its revision, nevertheless we are completely **confident** that the Crown will not refuse its sanction ... to the *wishes* (!) ... of the Chambers ... being *conscious* that we do not need to quarrel and find fault with the Government as if we faced an enemy, but being convinced instead that we confront a Crown which like ourselves *is only concerned for the good of the fatherland* ... in good and bad days alike we must be firmly united with our sovereigns ... the foundation for piety, respect for the law, public spirit, etc."

Herr Bodelschwingh imagined he was still speaking in the United Diet. His *basis* now as previously is that of *confidence*. But the man is quite right! What the Left has called universal suffrage has, by means

---

[a] What a simpleton!—*Ed.*

of provisions about independence, indirect elections and Manteuffel's manoeuvres, brought into existence a Chamber which has no need to be ashamed of being addressed as "Exalted United Diet".

After an unimportant speech by deputy Schulze-Delitzsch, there came to the rostrum His one-time Excellency, Herr Count Arnim. Unlike Herr Bodelschwingh, he has *not* been asleep during the past year. He knows what he wants.

It is clear, he said, why we want to recognise the Constitution immediately and in its entirety.

> "For is it so certain *that the business of revising the Constitution will lead to a result?* How is this to be achieved? What fundamental law will then be valid? Precisely, therefore, because in this situation an agreement between the three powers on the points to be revised is doubtful, precisely *for that reason* we are concerned that even in *this case the people should have a Constitution.*"

Is that clear enough? That is already the second delicate hint in this one sitting.

Then deputy d'Ester opposed the Commission's draft. His speech was by far the best coming from the Left in this general debate. The audacity and vigour with which the deputy from Mayen attacked the gentlemen of the Right made a pleasant impression in the midst of this dismal and tedious debate. But d'Ester, too, could not speak without diplomatic concessions and parliamentary contortions. He said, for example, that he fully agreed that the revolution must be ended. While this statement of the deputy might, perhaps, be excused as due to parliamentary considerations, the member of the democratic Central Committee [143] ought never to express himself in this way, and the man who immediately afterwards began a debate with Vincke on the respective "degree of culture" ought not to incur even the suspicion of being capable of such twaddle. Moreover, in any case no one believed him.

Finally, deputy *Riedel* sounded a note of triumph because "*the Crown has reassumed its right to legislate*". An ironic cry of "bravo" made him aware that he had been telling tales out of school. He took fright and added: "Provisionally, of course!"

A third delicate hint for the deputies!

The Chamber proceeded to the special debate. We shall save it for tomorrow.

Written by Engels on March 25, 1849        Printed according to the newspaper

First published in the *Neue Rheinische*        Published in English for the first
*Zeitung* No. 259, March 30, 1849        time

# FROM THE THEATRE OF WAR.—
## THE CONFUSED SITUATION IN SERBIA

Today we must begin our reports from Hungary with news of a victory which, if it were true, would spread the greatest joy among the German democrats.

We have received the following from Breslau:

"*Breslau*, March 23. Just now, news has arrived from Ratibor that *Dembiński* **has taken Pest by storm**. *Görgey*, who had already occupied the heights of Raab with his army, is marching as a vanguard on Vienna, which Dembiński intends to occupy soon.

"In Bohemia, the outbreak of a terrible revolution is expected at any moment, which will in the main spread among the oppressed rural population and lead to a veritable civil war. The national hatred between Germans and Czechs has almost completely disappeared; the old Czech deputies Palacky and company have been booed, while the German Left and its Bohemian President Borrosch have received one ovation after another. Moreover, *a state of siege has already been proclaimed in Prague*."

We have received the same news by way of the democratic correspondence in Berlin. According to it, a deputy has received the following communication:

"*Ratibor*, March 23. Just after winning a major battle, and following a number of previous important victories Dembiński **has taken Pest by storm**. *Görgey*, who had previously occupied the heights of *Raab* with his army corps—to cut off the line of retreat of the Austrian army, in case it escaped—is marching on *Vienna* as the vanguard of the Hungarian advance. In that city *Dembiński* will probably disturb the Easter ceremony of washing the feet,[144] and take upon Austria the revenge it so richly deserves.

"*Prague* is in a state of siege, with the indispensable 26 guns trained on the city. It is true that a revolution has not broken out there but is expected, and it is to be hoped that in this way it will be provoked. And if that occurs, if Bohemia rises against the Cabinet—post-horses will become expensive in Olmütz."

This news was communicated to Minister *Manteuffel* who, quite alarmed, replied that the Ministry had not yet received any dispatches about it.

Unfortunately, though, this news is obviously false in the version here available and at the very least premature. The positions of the armies ascertained according to the latest reports do not admit the possibility that the Hungarians have captured Pest by now.

Our news from Pest goes up to the 18th. The most recent Vienna papers, which could have extended it to the 19th, have not yet come to hand. The *Breslauer Zeitung* has a Hungarian report of the 18th, which does indeed mention a Magyar victory over Jellachich at Izsak and Alpar. These two places lie to the right and left of the highway which leads from Pest to Szegedin via Kecskemét, about the level of Felegyhaza, where, as we know, Jellachich is supposed to have been defeated once before; though whether this is the same battle or a new action, it is not possible to judge. In any case, as the Magyar report says, the news of this Hungarian victory has been reflected on the Pest money market in a *rise* of 20 per cent in the Hungarian banknotes. Dispersed corps, as well as large numbers of wounded are also said to have arrived in Pest. Incidentally, the same report adds afterwards that the events of the Magyar war do not seem to have been confirmed to the extent the money market assumed. As regards monetary affairs in Pest the Magyar report writes:

"There is no stock exchange in Pest, and current monetary transactions which have become considerable only since the ban on Hungarian banknotes, were temporarily conducted in a coffee-house. But yesterday the local military authorities had one of the main dealers arrested, and by this *argumentum ad hominem* brought about a partial stoppage of the exchange of banknotes. Despite this, Hungarian banknotes maintained yesterday's level, though many dealers view the above-mentioned arrest as foreshadowing the complete invalidation of Hungarian banknotes even for private dealings.

"The contribution which Pest was not scheduled to pay till May must now by order of His Highness Prince Windischgrätz be paid within 24 hours. The imperial salt office now sells only for hard coin."

In addition, the report talks of an alliance between the Magyars and the Turks, in consequence of which the Magyar operations would be directed not against Pest but towards the Banat and the Turkish borders. But this item sounds rather fantastic.—Palóczy, who retired because of old age, is reported to have been replaced by Paul Almasy as President of the Hungarian National Assembly in Debreczin.

According to other, Austrian, reports Jellachich is said rather to have gained a victory over the Magyars at Szegedin (or Felegyhaza).

The action in question is obviously the one already mentioned above. But so long as the Austrian Bulletins do not break their obstinate silence about the operations on the Theiss, and so long as their reports of any victories are not confirmed by other, unbiased news, so long we shall believe the Magyar report that Jellachich has suffered a welcome defeat at Felegyhaza.

What confirms us in this belief is the following item from the *Lithographierte Correspondenz* published in Vienna *under martial-law supervision:*

"The news from Hungary is as yet still far from satisfactory: **it is known that considerable mishaps have occurred there**, and that even officers of the highest rank have been called to account. Among them even Count Wrbna is mentioned."

Today there is no word from the Banat. Not a word of Jablonowsky, Götz, and the rest of the missing corps of the Austrian army.

On the other hand, from Transylvania we hear today nothing but *compliments for Bem.* Thus the *Deutsche Allgemeine Zeitung* writes:

"The reports from the camp agree, however, that Bem has proved his ability once more in the latest encounter at Mediasch, for he took up such advantageous positions that during the entire engagement he may be said to have manoeuvred rather than fought."[a]

And even the *Siebenbürger Bote*, whose war reports, as we well know, express the official view, says:

"*Whoever has not seen for himself the impressive bearing of Bem, his tenacity on the field of battle, can have no true conception of this general's ability.* While his position seems to be shrouded in a veil, he leaves the ground he occupies only with sudden brisk movements, and if his troops were as reliable as his skill in offering battle from such well-chosen positions—which, as it were, always strikingly display the closest correlation—we would have to fight engagements that are not only interesting but brilliant. Bem fought with his 5,000-6,000 strong force from 9 in the morning till 6 in the afternoon, from three positions, with a tenacity which shows what he can do not only now but in future as well."[b]

The Imperial Government has realised, incidentally, that the Serbs are not to be trifled with. The *Napredak* (Forward) of Karlowitz writes on March 13 that, late at night on the 8th, a letter from Minister Stadion arrived in Becskerek for the Patriarch,[c] in which the Ministry confirms the provisional Serb provincial government and at the same time expresses the wish that the Serb newspapers should

---

[a] "Hermannstadt, 9. März", *Deutsche Allgemeine Zeitung* No. 84 (supplement), March 25, 1849.— *Ed.*

[b] "Mediasch, 7. März", *Der Siebenbürger Bote* No. 30, March 9, 1849.— *Ed.*

[c] Rajachich.— *Ed.*

say what kind of government the people would want to be installed in the "Voivodina". Moreover, Minister Stadion demands two representatives from the Voivodina; accordingly, Paskowich, Zivanovich and Šuplikac have also been sent off to Vienna, in addition to Bogdanović. The commission in Becskerek has already begun negotiations about the setting up of the Serb Diet. The majority of the deputies favours an early calling of a National Assembly, at which the voivode should also be elected.

Several of the Uhlans who recently dispersed the district council in Hatzfeld went on to Kécsa and seized the arms of the Serbs. Then they rode to Serb Crnja intending to dissolve the district court there, but the Serbs declared they would not obey the military command and would defend their rights to the last drop of blood. Had the Uhlans permitted themselves the slightest transgression, blood would have flowed. In Kómlos and Masdorf, too, the Uhlans wanted to dissolve the councils, but the Romanians and Germans there immediately denounced that intention, so that it came to the knowledge of the Patriarch. In this way Rukavina wanted to dissolve the district courts and national offices in the whole area. It was fortunate that he did not go further; had the Uhlans continued to molest the Serbian villages, not one of them would have kept his head on his shoulders. When the Patriarch was informed of the seizure of the arms, he flew into a rage. Now we hear that Rukavina has yielded and the Uhlans (Schwarzenberg) have been put under the command of Todorovich.

Whether this is the end of the Serbian disorders remains to be seen. In any case, Windischgrätz and Jellachich have been compromised and disowned by the Government, an outcome which we find especially pleasing in the case of the fanatic Jellachich.

Written by Engels about March 26, 1849     Printed according to the newspaper

First published in the *Neue Rheinische*    Published in English for the first
*Zeitung* No. 256, March 27, 1849    time

# THE WAR IN ITALY AND HUNGARY

*Cologne*, March 27. The war in Italy has begun.[145] By this war the Habsburg monarchy has assumed a burden beneath which it will probably succumb.

As long as Hungary was not in a state of open war against the monarchy as a whole, but was only in a fluctuating state of war against the Southern Slavs, it was no great feat for Austria to get the better of the Italians, who were only half revolutionised, and were split up and crippled by the triple treachery of the sovereigns. Nevertheless, what an effort it involved! Before Radetzky could win his victories at the Mincio,[146] the Pope[a] and the Grand Duke of Tuscany[b] had first to withdraw their troops—directly or indirectly—from the Venetian region, Charles Albert and his partly incompetent, partly venal generals had first actually to betray the Italian cause and above all at times the Magyars and at times the Southern Slavs had to be induced by a policy of duplicity and seeming concessions to send their troops to take up positions in Italy. It is known that only the mass transfer of the South-Slav border regiments to Italy rendered the disorganised Austrian army capable of fighting again.

Furthermore, as long as the armistice with Piedmont continued, as long as Austria had merely to maintain its army in Italy in its former strength without having to increase it excessively, Austria could throw the main body of its 600,000 soldiers against Hungary, it could push back the Magyars from one position to another and, by means of the daily arriving reinforcements, could in the end even succeed

---

[a] Pius IX.— *Ed.*
[b] Leopold II.— *Ed.*

in crushing Hungary's armed power. In the long run, Kossuth, like Napoleon, would have had to suffer defeat owing to the superiority of force.

But the war in Italy considerably changes the situation. From the moment when the termination of the armistice became certain, Austria had to double the number of its troops sent to Italy, it had to divide its newly enrolled recruits between Windischgrätz and Radetzky. Thus it is to be expected that neither of them gets enough.

Whereas for the Magyars and Italians, therefore, it is only a question of gaining time—time for the purchase and manufacture of arms, time for training the *Landsturm* and national guards to be soldiers fit for service in the field, time for revolutionising the country—Austria, compared with its opponents, becomes weaker every day.

While the war itself draws Rome, Tuscany and even Piedmont ever more deeply into the revolution compelling them day by day to display greater revolutionary energy, and while they can wait for the rapidly approaching crisis in France, meanwhile in Austria the third disorganising element, the *Slav opposition* is daily gaining ground and improving its organisation. The imposed Constitution[147] which, in gratitude for the Slavs having saved Austria, is throwing them back to their condition before the March events, the many insults suffered by the Slavs through bureaucratic and military excesses—these are facts that have occurred and cannot be altered in any way.

It is understandable that in these circumstances the *Kölnische Zeitung* is in the greatest possible hurry to make the imperial forces finish off the unpleasant war with Hungary. Accordingly, it announced yesterday that they crossed the Theiss in three columns[a]— a report made all the more credible by not being confirmed up to now by any communiqué. Other sources, however, report that, on the contrary, the Magyar army is advancing on Pest by forced marches and evidently intends to raise the siege of Komorn. In spite of being heavily bombarded, Komorn is holding out courageously. During the bombardment the defenders of Komorn did not fire a shot, but when the Austrians tried to take it by storm they were thrown back with heavy losses by a deadly hail of grape-shot. It is said that the Duke of Coburg's regiment of Polish Uhlans went over to the side of the Magyars at the moment when Dembiński, calmly waiting for the attack, ordered the tune of "Poland is not yet lost"[b] to be played.

---

[a] Cf. report in the section "Ungarn" in the *Kölnische Zeitung* No. 73, March 27, 1849.— *Ed.*

[b] From the Polish national anthem.— *Ed.*

This is all the news we can give today about the Hungarian theatre of war. The post from Vienna of March 23 has failed to arrive.

Let us now turn to the Italian theatre of war. Here the Piedmontese army is drawn up in a long arc along the Ticino and the Po. Its front line stretches from Arona via Novara, Vigevano, Voghera to Castel San Giovanni facing Piacenza. Its reserves are situated a few miles farther back, on the rivers Sesia and Bormida at Vercelli, Trino and Alessandria. On the extreme right wing at Sarzana on the Tuscany-Modena frontier a separate corps under the command of La Marmora is stationed, ready to attack Parma and Modena through the Lunigiani passes, to link up on the left with the right wing of the main army, and on the right with the Tuscan and Roman armies, to cross the Po and the Adige if circumstances permit and conduct operations in the Venetian region.

On the opposite side, on the left bank of the Ticino and Po, stands Radetzky. It is known that his army is divided into two corps, of which one has occupied Lombardy and the other the Venetian region. While no news at all about troop dispositions has come from the Venetian region, we hear on all sides that in Lombardy Radetzky is concentrating his whole army on the Ticino. He has withdrawn all his troops from Parma, and in Modena he has left only a few hundred men in the fortress. Varese, Como, Val d'Intelvi and Valtellina have been entirely denuded of troops, even the frontier customs guards have disappeared.

The entire fighting force at Radetzky's disposal, 50,000 strong, occupies positions from Magenta to Pavia along the Ticino and from Pavia to Piacenza along the Po.

Radetzky himself is said to have had the foolhardy plan of immediately crossing the Ticino with this army and, protected by the inevitable confusion of the Italians, of marching directly on Turin. People still remember from last year that Radetzky more than once entertained similar Napoleonic desires[148] and how he fared then. This time, however, the entire War Council opposed him, and it was decided to retreat, without any decisive battle, towards the Adda, Oglio, and, if needs be, even the Chiese, in order to obtain there reinforcements from the Venetian region and Illyria.

It will depend on the manoeuvres of the Piedmontese and the eagerness for war of the Lombards whether this retreat will take place without losses and whether the Austrians will succeed in holding up the Piedmontese for long. For the southern slopes of the Alps, namely the Como, Brienz and Bergamo Alps, Veltlin (Valtellina) and the Brescia region, now already for the most part abandoned by the Austrians, are highly suitable for national partisan warfare. The Austrians concentrated in the plain have to leave the mountains free. Here by a swift advance with light troops on the Austrian right wing, the Piedmontese can quickly organise guerilla detachments, which will threaten the flank and, in the event of the defeat of a single corps, also the retreat of the imperial troops, cut off their supplies and extend the insurrection as far as the Tritentine Alps. Garibaldi would be in his element here. But presumably he has not the least intention of once more entering the service of the traitor Charles Albert.[149]

The Tuscan-Roman army, supported by La Marmora, will have to occupy the line of the Po from Piacenza to Ferrara, cross the Po as quickly as possible, and after that the Adige, cut off Radetzky from the Austro-Venetian corps and operate on his left flank, or in his rear. However, this army is unlikely to arrive sufficiently quickly to have any influence on the first military operations.

But more decisive than all this is the attitude of the Piedmontese. Their army is good and bellicose; but if it is betrayed again as it was last year it is bound to be beaten. The Lombards are demanding weapons in order to fight against their oppressors; but if again, as last year, a vacillating bourgeois Government paralyses a mass uprising, Radetzky can once again enter Milan.

There is only one means to counter the treachery and cowardice of the Government: revolution. And perhaps it is precisely a new breach of his word by Charles Albert, and a new act of perfidy by the Lombard nobility and bourgeoisie, that are required for the Italian revolution to be carried through and, simultaneously with it, the Italian war for independence. But then woe to the traitors!

Written by Engels on March 27, 1849

First published in the *Neue Rheinische Zeitung* No. 257, March 28, 1849

Printed according to the newspaper

Published in English for the first time

# FROM THE THEATRE OF WAR

In spite of all the reinforcements asked for, in spite of all their numerical superiority, fortune refuses to favour the imperial forces. The *Ost-Deutsche Post*, in a report (?) from Pest dated March 20, spins the following yarn:

"Baron Hammerstein *is said to* have already crossed the Theiss and advanced to Nyiregyhaza, eight hours from Debreczin. Advancing from the other side, Puchner *must* already be near Grosswardein, and at this moment the *rumour is spreading* that Szegedin has surrendered without striking a blow."[a]

"Is said to"—"must"—"the rumour is spreading"—such is the reliable news from the theatre of war which the *Ost-Deutsche Post* publishes, and which the reliable, "critically sifting", experienced *Kölnische Zeitung* communicated to its readers in its second edition this morning without further comment.

In addition the *Ost-Deutsche Post* and following it the *Kölnische Zeitung* report:

"According to *fairly reliable* reports, the Serbs at Szegedin have received orders to join the imperial army stationed on the Theiss. The Ban[b] then took over general command of these two united corps and *set out* on the march to Debreczin with them."[c] (!!!)

This supposed report from Pest is simply the usual Viennese martial-law gossip, in which there is not a word of truth. The *Kölnische Zeitung* should know that; firstly, there was no official Bulletin, which would have been issued if there had been any successes however small; and secondly, it could have read, copied in

---

[a] "Pesth, 20. März", *Ost-Deutsche Post* No. 54, March 23, 1849.— *Ed.*
[b] Jellachich.— *Ed.*
[c] "Pesth, 20. März", *Kölnische-Zeitung* No. 74 (second edition), March 28, 1849.— *Ed.*

the *Deutsche Allgemeine Zeitung* and in the original in the *Constitutionelles Blatt aus Böhmen, a genuine report* from Pest of the 20th, in which there is *no mention* of the "reliable news" printed in the *Ost-Deutsche Post.* And the worthy Cologne paper still dares to accuse the *Breslauer Zeitung,* which does not claim to have a critical approach, of lacking a critical approach as far as reports from Hungary are concerned!

Actually, the *Constitutionelles Blatt aus Böhmen* reports quite the opposite from Pest on the 20th[a]:

> "The fall of Szegedin has *not been confirmed*; on the contrary, the imperial forces are said to have relinquished *Kecskemét* owing to *strategic considerations.* The enemy appears to have concentrated all his forces at Szegedin, and to regard it as the key to the current Austrian plan of operation. Yesterday reinforcements went also from our side to the battlefield by rail."

That is all that this report, which was actually written in Pest, says about the theatre of war.

True enough, Baron Hammerstein has moved from Galicia down the Hernad to Tokaj with reinforcements—ten battalions, it is said. But he would never have got across the Theiss there without a hard-fought and victorious action—and would not the imperial authorities have trumpeted abroad so important a victory in a Bulletin? From Tokaj to Nyiregyhaza is a good four miles,[b] i. e. in this marshy region and in this rainy season, fully two to three days' march for a regular army. And Hammerstein is supposed to have got through to Nyiregyhaza without the official report of his successful crossing of the Theiss some days previously having reached Vienna!

If Hammerstein had even got as far as Tokaj we would have received Bulletin after Bulletin full of triumphant chants. We would know where Götz is stationed and where Jablonowsky, Csorich and Schlick are stationed. We know nothing whatsoever of all this. Since February 26, the date of the ambiguous battle at Kapolna, *that is for almost four weeks,* there has been *no official mention* of the Theiss; and the unofficial reports we receive contradict each other daily.

Hence the first of the three columns at whose head the *Kölnische Zeitung* crossed the Theiss existed only in the imagination.

The second would have to be that of Schlick. But Schlick was still in Szegléd on the 17th or 18th, as the *Constitutionelles Blatt aus Böhmen* has also reported. At Szolnok, the nearest crossing-point, there could be no question of crossing the Theiss. Here even the wits of the noble

---

[a] This and the following quotation are taken from the report "Pest, 20. März" in the *Constitutionelles Blatt aus Böhmen* No. 71, March 24, 1849; they are reprinted in the *Deutsche Allgemeine Zeitung* No. 86, March 27, 1849.— *Ed.*

[b] See footnote on p. 20.— *Ed.*

Ban and robber chief Jellachich were baffled, and any attempt to cross there was given up. If however he had crossed the Theiss at Tisza-Füred, the only crossing-point in the vicinity, he would first have had to march there, to concentrate his forces there and to wage a battle. All this would have had to have happened in the short period from the 18th to the 20th, and that is impossible for obvious chronological reasons. Schlick's presence in Szegléd, far from proving that a hurried crossing of the Theiss was to take place, on the contrary, in conjunction with other reports, leads to the conclusion that Schlick was purely on a visit of inspection at Szegléd, where the right wing of his army must establish contact with the extreme left wing of Jellachich's corps.

The third column would naturally have been that of Jellachich. But according to the only news reaching us directly from Pest, it has been withdrawn "for strategic reasons" (as the imperial authorities say every time they are defeated) even beyond Kecskemét. But Kecskemét lies 12 miles from Szegedin, the only possible crossing-point of the Theiss there, and the notorious hinge of Jellachich's operations. Of what use is it to us now if the Serbs have "received orders" to "effect a junction" with him, when he is 14 miles away from them? And what is the meaning of the ridiculous remark that, as a result of this simple *plan* of joining up with the Serbs, the Ban "is marching directly on Debreczin", which is 25 miles from Szegedin, the as yet unconquered Szegedin!

Moreover, the *Ost-Deutsche Post* writes in a further flight of the imagination, Puchner *must* by now be already near Grosswardein. Indeed, if the wishes of the imperial side had anything to do with it, he would have been there long ago. But all we know so far is that, while the 30,000 Russians now stationed in Transylvania are keeping a tight rein on the Szeklers,[150] he is operating not in the direction of Grosswardein but in the opposite direction, towards Schässburg and Maros-Vásárhely.

By the way, the difficulties involved in driving the Hungarians from their strong positions behind the Theiss and capturing Debreczin, especially now that the *rainy season* is near, are indicated in the following excerpt from the *Constitutionelles Blatt aus Böhmen*:

"It would certainly be better for the military operations on the clayey roads and fields on the Theiss and on this side of it, if the *usual rainy season* were to arrive a few weeks late. During this season, *Debreczin becomes temporarily an island*, to which even in peace-time one can *make one's way only with great difficulty*. This will show you the obstacles of terrain with which our brave troops have to contend even before they reach the seat of rebellion. Moreover, on the way to Debreczin there are pusztas[151] so wide that one must ride for *almost a whole day* to reach the *only well* which supplies water for the horses. And on these plains the Austrian cavalry must contend with an enemy who is at home there and whose small, tireless horses may be called the camel of the puszta."

Hence, first the swamps of the Theiss and Körös, which form a natural trench round the heath of Debreczin, and then the Sahara of Debreczin itself, where the Austrian cuirassiers and Uhlans are supposed to fight the same battle with the Hungarian light hussars that the clumsy French cavalry had to fight against the Arab horsemen in the first years of the Algerian war.[152]

We have learnt from the Banat that a new complication has been added to the old ones in Serbia. The Romanians have been incited against the Serbs—though whether for or against the imperial authorities we do not know. Imperial intrigue is probably at the bottom of it.

The Temesvar fortress is being heavily armed—not against the Magyars, but against—the Serbs. Obviously ill-feeling among the Serbs must be growing.

As regards the capture of Peterwardein, "hoped for" repeatedly for some time, this is again dissolving in mist. The *Constitutionelles Blatt aus Böhmen* writes:

"*From the Drava*, March 18. The Vienna papers reported some time ago that imperial troops had succeeded in storming the fortress of Peterwardein. But Peterwardein cannot be stormed unless one is prepared to see 20,000 or 30,000 men slaughtered in the assault. Anyone who is a soldier and is familiar with the fortress will agree. If the fortress does not surrender hunger is the only thing that can conquer it. Unfortunately, our hopes of its speedy surrender, initially raised by bearers of the flag of truce, are growing dimmer and dimmer, and the officers who have just escaped from the fortress do not hold out an encouraging prospect, for particularly the common soldiers and the Honveds are behaving in a terroristic fashion."[a]

A new revolt is "to be hoped for" in the rear of the imperial forces. The regiment of dragoons that was occupying the Bakony Forest has been called to Pest and has arrived there. The Honved guerillas, who are roaming about in large numbers in the Bakony Forest, will immediately organise a fresh uprising and establish contact with the insurgents of the comitat of Tolna.

Written by Engels about March 28, 1849

First published in the supplement to the *Neue Rheinische Zeitung* No. 258, March 29, 1849

Printed according to the newspaper

Published in English for the first time

[a] "Von der Drave, 18. März", *Constitutionelles Blatt aus Böhmen* No. 71, March 24, 1849.— *Ed.*

# FROM THE THEATRE OF WAR[153]

[ITALY]

The military operations are beginning to appear in clearer outline. While the Piedmontese have crossed the Ticino at Buffalora, Radetzky has crossed it at Pavia and is stationed between the Ticino and the Po on Piedmontese territory.

Whether this attack is merely a diversion, or whether Radetzky actually intends to advance on Turin, is not yet clear. The latter is possible if the report sent from Turin on the 21st to the *Journal des Débats* is accurate[a]: that as a result of the addition of the Parma and Modena garrisons his army has increased to 60,000-70,000 men with 120 guns and that so far the Piedmontese have only 55,000 to 65,000 men with 100 to 110 guns to oppose to Radetzky. But these assertions are absolutely false, at least as concerns the Piedmontese army. Furthermore, La Marmora's corps, which has advanced to Parma, will force Radetzky to make further detachments.

In short Radetzky stands on Piedmontese territory. This is due to the negligence or treachery of the notorious Ramorino, who had already played an ambiguous role in Poland in 1831 and in the Savoy campaign in 1834.[154] He is to be thanked for the fact that the Austrians succeeded in pushing their way along the Po between his division and that of Durando. Ramorino was immediately removed from command and called to account for his action.

Chrzanowski is making the following dispositions of his forces in response to Radetzky's manoeuvre: Durando from Stradella, Fanti, who has replaced Ramorino, and one of the divisions moving out from the headquarters at Vigevano towards the Po will make a

---

[a] This refers to a report published in the *Journal des Débats* on March 26, 1849.— *Ed.*

frontal attack on the Austrians, while the division commanded by the Duke of Genoa, a force of 20,000, which has crossed the Ticino at Buffalora, is marching on the Lombardic bank of the river to Pavia, to cut off the Austrians' retreat.

If Radetzky has insufficient forces to resist the Piedmontese, it may well happen that the old fox will fall into a trap and be encircled and destroyed. But in any case, by his advance he has provoked a decisive battle, the outcome of which we should learn today, or, at the latest, tomorrow.

The rest of Chrzanowski's plan of operations is quite in accord with that which we indicated yesterday[a] as the more probable plan. While La Marmora is stirring up the inhabitants of the Dukedoms[b] to rebel and advancing on the extreme left wing of the Piedmontese to the Po, or across it, Favorola's division has advanced via Varese into the Lombard mountains. A Lombard revolutionary committee is accompanying him. The insurrection is spreading at a rapid pace. On the 20th, the insurgents of the Piedmontese border made contact with those from Veltlin and the Upper Comasca in Como. As soon as the Austrians left a locality, the insurrection was organised. All of them are marching upon Milan; individual Austrian detachments are said already to have been attacked and destroyed by the insurgents. On the 21st, a general insurrection was to break out throughout Lombardy. According to the *Patrie* the uprising has already broken out in Milan, but the *Patrie* lies notoriously. In any case, preparations have been made in Milan which testify to the Austrian commandant's fears of the insurrection and of reinforcements from the countryside.

Perhaps the Swiss papers will also bring important news at noon today, and, if so, we will communicate it to our readers under "Latest News".

Written by Engels on March 28, 1849

First published in the supplement to the *Neue Rheinische Zeitung* No. 258, March 29, 1849

Printed according to the newspaper

Published in English for the first time

---

[a] See this volume, pp. 150-51.— *Ed.*
[b] Parma and Modena.— *Ed.*

# FROM THE THEATRE OF WAR

The *Kölnische Zeitung* will surely have to retreat across the Theiss again with its "three columns"[a]; the campaign is taking an increasingly unhappy turn for the imperial forces.

But let us leave the *Kölnische Zeitung* to its justified sorrow, and instead turn immediately to *Transylvania*.

**Hermannstadt has been taken by Bem.** There is no doubt: the newspaper of the Vienna Stock Exchange barons, the martial-law *Lloyd*, publishes the news[b] from two separate sources. If it were not true, its publication would under martial law result in the editors being sentenced to several months "trench-digging in light chains".

Bem has calmly allowed the worthy Puchner, whom the equally worthy *Ost-Deutsche Post* had yesterday already advancing into the vicinity of Grosswardein,[c] to march against the Szeklers in the Carpathian Mountains, confronting Puchner with only about half his corps to support the Szekler *Landsturm*. Bem himself, as the *Lloyd* reports, marched quickly on Hermannstadt with 12,000 men, attacked the Russians and drove them out. The *Lloyd* asserts that only 3,000 Russians were there, but that is hardly likely, for more than double that number were there; unless the remainder marched with Puchner against the Szeklers, which is indeed possible.

In Hermannstadt, Bem's troops are said to have wrought "great havoc", which would be no more than just retribution for the barbarities of the imperial forces and the calling-in of the Russians. After a few hours Bem left the city again; naturally, after he had

---

[a] See this volume, pp. 149 and 153-54.— *Ed.*

[b] "Wien, 24. März", *Der Lloyd* No. 144 (morning edition), March 25, 1849.— *Ed.*

[c] See this volume, pp. 152 and 154.— *Ed.*

severely chastised the Saxon philistines,[155] his business there was finished.

The strategic aim of the campaign is obviously to isolate Puchner once again, and to drive away the imperial forces marching up along the Maros from the Banat. We shall soon hear how the tireless Pole has sported with them, perhaps how he has pursued them deep into the Banat and there attracted reinforcements himself.

While Puchner with the imperial and Russian forces is fighting the Szekler guerillas deep in the mountains, Malkowsky and the chivalrous hero Urban, the "Jellachich of the Bukovina", have been completely driven out of Transylvania on the northern side. According to the last Bulletin, Urban was still occupying Bistritz; from there he has been beaten back to Watra Dorna, and from Watra Dorna deep into the Bukovina. The headquarters of Malkowsky, the Supreme Commander, has already been shifted back again to Ober Wikow, fully 20 miles from Bistritz, and only 8 miles from Czernowitz on the Russian border. Thus reports the Austrian correspondent. In Czernowitz itself, he goes on, the greatest anxiety rules; the precautionary measures taken by the imperial authorities, abatis, the occupation of the passes, the call-up of the *Landsturm* etc. show that the danger is near. But the Hungarians will take care to penetrate into the Bukovina no further than is necessary to secure the border. They know too well that the Russians are only waiting for the signal to invade. In Novoseliza, right on the border between the Bukovina and Russia, there are 10,000 Russian troops, and the whole frontier with Moldavia is swarming with Russians.

The most important aspect of the matter is simply this:

(1) Bem can operate independently down the Maros with part of his troops, while the rest of his corps, along with the Szeklers, suffices to keep Puchner and the Russians busy;

(2) In the north, where previously Bem himself had to drive out the imperial forces every time, the insurrection has spread to such an extent that it can cope with Malkowsky and Urban even without Bem;

(3) Bem therefore not merely operates in distinguished fashion as a military leader, but at the same time he has also organised the Transylvanian insurrection and made it more formidable than ever;

(4) The Romanians, the majority of the Transylvanian population, who initially behaved with such fanaticism against the Magyars and Szeklers, either have lost all spirit for further fighting because of the successes of the latter, or must even have joined them, impelled by their hatred of the Russian invasion. Without this, Bem's latest successes would have been quite impossible.

At last we have some news about the position of the imperial forces on the *Theiss.* The *Lloyd* reports from Pest on the 20th that *Götz* is in Tokaj, *Jablonowsky* in Miskolcz, *Schlick* in Erlau, and *Jellachich* in Szegléd.[a]

This means that in this sector the imperial forces are in precisely the same positions on *March* 20 as they were on *January* 20. Compare Army Bulletin No. 19 and our comments on it in No. 214 of the *Neue Rheinische Zeitung.*[b]

Hence, for two months the imperial forces have been roaming around in the area between the Danube, the Carpathians and the Theiss, with varying fortunes. When the Theiss was frozen, they were stationed in front of it and tried to advance across the ice; the Magyars drove them back with casualties. Then it was said that the drifting ice prevented them from getting across. It did not prevent the Magyars from following the imperial troops to the right bank. After this, Görgey came, drove Schlick back to the main army, joined with Dembiński, and the two advanced to within a few miles of Pest. That was four weeks ago. They retreated again, the imperial troops followed them, and since the glorious "victory" of Kapolna they have not advanced a step further; Schlick's headquarters, Erlau, *is on the battlefield of Kapolna,* so to speak.

Whether Götz is actually in Tokaj or only in its vicinity remains an open question. The positive information we have today from this region comes from the martial-law *Lithographierte Correspondenz* of the 24th from Vienna and is this: General *Hammerstein,* whose move from Galicia into Hungary with 10 battalions was so definitely reported by the Vienna newspapers and correspondents from Pest, *has still not pressed forward towards Hungary at all!!*

Schlick and Jablonowsky are harmless in their present positions for the time being. The former is said to have already started to move; but what use is that in view of "the slushy weather that has set in" and the imminent season of spring rains which we mentioned this morning?[c]

And to crown all the Ban, the chivalrous, invincible Ban Jellachich! He marched towards Szegedin, he occupied Kecskemét, and set up his headquarters in Felegyhaza, four miles further on; he was said to have so routed the Magyars at Szegedin that the city surrendered; the procession of the inhabitants to the Ban, with maidens clad in white, garlands, flags, music and all the trappings, was already

---

[a] "Pesth, 20. März", *Der Lloyd* No. 140 (morning edition), March 23, 1849.— *Ed.*
[b] See present edition, Vol. 8, pp. 300-03.— *Ed.*
[c] See this volume, pp. 154-55.— *Ed.*

described, and, lo and behold, the South-Slav Don Quixote is suddenly back at the point whence he had set out, on the selfsame spot where he rejoined his troops after they were defeated at Szolnok—at Szegléd in the Pest comitat!

Moreover, the Olmütz Government appears to be fed up with Windischgrätz's incompetent conduct of the war. It is reported that *Windischgrätz will be dismissed*, and that Master of Ordnance *d'Aspre* will take over from him as commander of the army of the Theiss. Certainly, d'Aspre burnt and plundered enough in Italy last year to appear a capable general to a Schwarzenberg-Stadion Government.

Incidentally, the 50,000 men which Windischgrätz requested as reinforcements to enable him to cope with the Magyars, are supposed to be actually supplied. As the Augsburg *Allgemeine Zeitung* reports from Vienna,[a] 50,000 men from Vienna, Moravia, Bohemia and Galicia, are said to be marching to the theatre of war, 10,000 of which alone are to reinforce the army besieging Komorn. In addition, six batteries of heavy artillery are said to have been dispatched there from Olmütz a few days ago. Whence all these troops are supposed to be coming the Gods alone may know. It would be very surprising indeed if the Government were able to draw another 50,000 men from the German and Slav provinces, infuriated by the imposition of the Constitution, in addition to the troops (about 350,000 men) already fighting in Hungary and Italy.

On the 24th, the rumour circulated on the Vienna Stock Exchange that *Komorn had capitulated* after three days' heavy bombardment. If this were the case, we would first have learnt of it through official reports, as we did of the "victory" of Kapolna, and not through Stock Exchange puffs.

The only information we have from the *Banat* comes from statements in the Vienna and Olmütz papers that Baja on the Danube was occupied on the 18th by 4,000 Magyars. Baja is located in the comitat of Bacska, hence in the part of the Voivodina claimed as Serbian, and at the same level as Theresiopel (Subotica), about eight miles away. The garrison crossed over the Danube, i. e. into the insurgent comitat of Tolna; it is attempting to move towards the forces of Colonel Horváth, which are approaching by steamship and tug and are to clear the Danube of guerillas. But probably, nothing more will even be heard of it, as the insurgents are likely to have cut it to pieces already long ago.

One hears from the Slovakian mountains that *Perczel* is now at the head of the guerillas organised there, who have already been

---

[a] "Wien, 21. März", Augsburg *Allgemeine Zeitung* No. 84, March 25, 1849.—*Ed.*

7*

mentioned several times. A correspondent writes to the *Schlesische Zeitung* from Vienna on the 22nd that Perczel was recently in Tyrnau, five miles from Pressburg and eleven from Vienna, and was threatening the former town. He has however returned from there to Neutra and is now moving towards the Moravian border to threaten Olmütz. Everywhere he incites the Slovaks to rebellion, and arms and organises guerilla forces. He has laid under contribution all the villages and localities which have provided recruits for the royal imperial army; he is having hanged all those clergymen who previously were in agreement with Hurban.

It is evident that the so-called Slovak deputation which, with Hurban at its head, was recently in Olmütz,[156] is by no means representative of the Slovaks, and that these on the contrary prefer to side with the Magyars. Soon Perczel is likely to concentrate here the same formidable force with which Görgey conducted his brilliant campaigns.

To sum up: the imperial forces are suffering defeats everywhere, and what they need to crush the Magyar revolution is nothing more than—50,000-60,000 *Russians!*

But, in addition to the Slav movement and the Italian war, there is something else which may give a different turn to the whole Hungarian revolutionary war and change it into a European conflict, i.e. the Turkish affair. Turkey is Europe's most sensitive spot: movements in Turkey immediately bring England and France into collision with Russia. And it seems that at all events Turkey wants to move against Russian encroachments upon the Romanian provinces, and Russian intrigues in the Slav Danube provinces. A correspondent writes from Czernowitz (Bukovina) on March 16:

"Letters from Jassy bring us the news that the Turks have marched into *Galatz* as well as *Wallachia* in significant strength, 100,000 men, it is said, *to protest arms in hand against the Russian occupation of the Danube principalities.*"

And the Austrian correspondent adds from *Zara* in Dalmatia on March 13 that considerable military preparations have been going on for a fortnight in the neighbouring town of Mostar, and all men of the region capable of bearing arms have been called to the colours. In April, all men from 16 to 40 years of age are to be called up and only one man is to be left behind with each family for its support. In Zara one does not know what to make of it.[a]

If it is confirmed that the Porte wishes seriously to oppose Russia—and the French papers too have been reporting this for

---

[a] "Zara, 13. März", *Constitutionelles Blatt aus Böhmen* No. 70, March 23, 1849.— *Ed.*

some time—a new and scarcely avoidable impulse will be given to a European war. And this war will be upon us before we realise it and bear the European revolution in its train.

*Postscript.* At Hochwiesen (two miles from Schemnitz) a guerilla force which advanced from Komorn under the leadership of Ernst Simonyi has been driven back, the *Wiener Zeitung* reports.[a] This and a few fires is all that this official paper has today about Hungary!

A correspondent writes from Pest that the general offensive was to have begun on the 20th. Heavy artillery has gone to support Schlick. Theresiopel has not yet been taken, despite the reinforcement of Todorovich there by 5,000 Serbian volunteers. On the other hand, the Honveds are said to have been driven out of Baja again.

Written by Engels about March 29, 1849

First published in the *Neue Rheinische Zeitung* No. 259, March 30, 1849

Printed according to the newspaper

Published in English for the first time

---

[a] "Pesth", *Wiener Zeitung* No. 71, March 24, 1849.—*Ed.*

# FROM THE THEATRE OF WAR

## [ITALY]

As we were able to inform most of our readers yesterday,[a] two engagements have taken place simultaneously, at Vigevano and Mortara, in one of which the Austrians gained advantages, in the other the victory went to the Piedmontese.

Today we have more definite news. We shall relate it in chronological order.

Ramorino's treachery is, according to a report of the *Constitutionnel*, beyond doubt. His orders were to prevent the Austrians from crossing the Ticino with the Lombard division from Vigevano. He sent a battalion of riflemen which occupied the crossing. An Austrian regiment made its appearance on the morning of the 20th and was held back for five hours, from 5 a.m. to 10 a.m. In the meantime, instead of the regiment, an entire imperial brigade arrived at the Ticino. The Lombard battalion commander, Manara, astonished still to be left without any aid, retreated to Vigevano, the division's headquarters. Vigevano was deserted by Ramorino's troops. The Lombards retreated still further and eventually met a Piedmontese corps, which they were able to join. During this time, Ramorino had led his division off on marches which flagrantly contradicted the orders he had received. He was, however, arrested on the same day and, let us hope, will be shot.

As a result of Ramorino's treachery, the Austrians succeeded in concentrating the main body of their forces in the Lomellina, between the Po and the Ticino, thus driving a wedge into the Piedmontese army. Durando and the entire corps stationed south of the Po are cut off from the main army.

On the 21st, Radetzky with two columns marched north towards Vigevano and Mortara, on the road leading to Vercelli. At Vigevano,

---

[a] See this volume, pp. 156-57.— *Ed.*

one of the columns was halted by Piedmontese troops. For four hours they fought against numerically superior imperial forces at Sforzesca and Gambolo, without retreating. At last, the Savona brigade arrived at about four o'clock and *drove back the Austrians with casualties.* 1,500 prisoners are said to have fallen into the hands of the Piedmontese.

Immediately afterwards, at 6 o'clock, Mortara was attacked by the imperial forces; after defending themselves bravely, the Piedmontese eventually withdrew from this position under the protection of the reserve division.

This division continued the battle into the night, and only then did Mortara fall into the hands of the enemy.

So much is certain. But from here on the reports are contradictory. According to one, the Duke of Savoy had resumed the offensive on the 22nd, and put two Hungarian regiments to flight; according to another, Radetzky is advancing along the Vercelli road.

In Paris, a telegraphic dispatch said to have been received on the 26th puts Radetzky only four miles from Turin. Even the *Journal des Débats*, which is favourably disposed towards the Austrians, has to admit that this report is unfounded and could not possibly have been received in Paris on the 26th.[a] It even makes the effort to prove this by comparing the dates and distances involved.

It further admits that Radetzky has got himself into a position in which one defeat will finish him off.

"If the Piedmontese army has time to concentrate in Radetzky's rear, it will be able to put him into a most difficult position."

But this is precisely what the *Journal des Débats* doubts. Firstly, it says, the Piedmontese army has been drawn up along far too long a line, taking up positions from Novara to Castel San Giovanni, and even having other detached corps at Arona and Sarzana, or now at Parma; and secondly, it must be assumed that Radetzky, when he decided to cross the Ticino, had with him the whole of his available forces, 70,000 men with 120 cannon.

*Firstly,* the Piedmontese army has, indeed, been deployed since the 21st in such a way that the corps which directly confronts Radetzky is certainly too weak *by itself* to withstand him. That is the result of Ramorino's treachery. But this is not the issue. The Duke of Genoa is operating on the right flank of the Austrians, the Piedmontese reserves are stationed on their left flank at Casale and Alessandria, and Durando is in their rear at Stradella. Radetzky is literally encircled, and his retreat in case of a defeat is as good as cut off. It is

---

[a] "Paris, 26 mars", *Journal des Débats*, March 27, 1849.—*Ed.*

a curious assumption that these distinct Piedmontese corps would not operate together (and the Duke of Genoa and the reserve corps of the main army are close enough to do so). By his treachery, Ramorino was able to put the Piedmontese at a momentary disadvantage, but he could not thereby *decide* the outcome of the campaign.

*Secondly,* the Austrian army between the Ticino and the Po is by no means 70,000 strong. The *Journal des Débats* really argues too naively when it asserts: because Radetzky had an alleged 70,000 men under his command between the Adda and the Ticino, he must have led the same number across the Ticino. Clearly, he must have left behind a considerable number on the Lombardic bank of the Po and in Pavia, as well as on the Lambro and the Adda, to cover his base of operations. According to a report in the *Basler Zeitung* (which enthusiastically supports the imperial cause), the Austrians had 8,000 men at Gallarate, 20,000 at Magenta, 25,000 at Pavia and 25,000 at Piacenza. Only the first three corps, together 50,000-53,000 men, could be taken across the Ticino in case of extreme necessity; the corps at Piacenza barely sufficed to cover the Po from Piacenza to Pavia.

Even without the outermost formations dispatched to Como via Arona and to Parma via Sarzana, the Piedmontese army will therefore probably completely suffice to hold out against Radetzky.

Moreover, that Radetzky has left Lombardy largely stripped of troops is clear even from the hasty transfer of the troops from the Venice area, from Verona to Lombardy, from Padua to Verona. In the Tirol a corps of 7,000 riflemen is said to have been mobilised. Venice will thus be fairly denuded of troops, and the encirclement from the landward side will surely soon cease of its own accord.[157]

In Paris, the rumour was circulating on the 27th that the Duke of Genoa had defeated the Austrians. 12,000 Austrians, encircled by three Piedmontese divisions, were said to have laid down their arms. We regard this rumour as scarcely more trustworthy than that spread on the 26th about the defeat of the Piedmontese.

A letter from *Parma* says that 7,000 *Tuscans* and 8,000 *Romans* have joined La Marmora.

The Roman general Zambeccari has routed an Austrian corps on the Modena-Bologna border.

Written by Engels on March 29, 1849

First published in the supplement to the *Neue Rheinische Zeitung* No. 259, March 30, 1849

Printed according to the newspaper

Published in English for the first time

# [LATEST NEWS FROM HUNGARY]

**Hungary**. A correspondent writes to the Augsburg *Allgemeine Zeitung* on March 21 from Pest:

"It appears certain that *Kaschau and a few other districts in northern Hungary have been re-occupied by the Hungarians*. At least, yesterday's post bound for Kaschau did not get as far as *Gyöngyös*, and has returned here."[a]

Gyöngyös is in the rear of Schlick's position at Erlau, and about eleven miles from Pest.

| | |
|---|---|
| Written by Engels on March 30, 1849 | Printed according to the newspaper |
| First published in the supplement to the *Neue Rheinische Zeitung* No. 259, March 30, 1849 | Published in English for the first time |

---

[a] "Pesth, 21. März", Augsburg *Allgemeine Zeitung* No. 85, March 26, 1849.— *Ed.*

# FROM THE THEATRE OF WAR.—
# MORE RUSSIAN TROOPS

Following Bem's victories, another **20,000 Russians** *have marched into Transylvania.*

The most recent news from Transylvania brings confirmation of the Magyars' victory. In Hermannstadt, Bem had the building of the General Command and the dwelling of the Saxon Count battered down; after this, he attacked and dispersed the national guards with grape-shot, and then gave the town over to plunder for a couple of hours. He then withdrew from the town and went on to Schässburg, where he wrought even worse havoc. Kaschau has again been occupied by a Magyar raiding party, and in Schemnitz, too, Honveds [158] have once again turned up.

Written by Engels on March 30, 1849

First published in the *Neue Rheinische Zeitung* No. 260, March 31, 1849

Printed according to the newspaper

Published in English for the first time

# THE DEFEAT OF THE PIEDMONTESE

[*Neue Rheinische Zeitung* No. 260, March 31, 1849]

*Cologne,* March 30. Ramorino's treachery has borne fruit. The Piedmontese army has been *totally defeated* at Novara and driven back to Borgomanero at the foot of the Alps.[159] The Austrians have occupied Novara, Vercelli and Trino, and the road to Turin lies open to them.

So far any more detailed information is lacking. But this much is certain: without Ramorino, who allowed the Austrians to drive a wedge between the different Piedmontese divisions and isolate some of them, the Austrian victory would have been impossible.

Nor can there be any doubt that Charles Albert also was guilty of treachery. But whether he committed it merely through the medium of Ramorino or in some other way as well, we shall only learn later on.

Ramorino is the adventurer who after a more than doubtful career during the Polish war of 1830-31 disappeared during the Savoy campaign of 1834[160] with the entire cash resources for the war on the same day that matters took a serious turn, and who later, in London, for £1,200 drew up for the ex-Duke of Brunswick a plan for the conquest of Germany.

The mere fact that such an adventurer could even be given a post proves that Charles Albert, who is more afraid of the republicans of Genoa and Turin than of the Austrians, was from the outset contemplating treachery.

That, after this defeat, a revolution and proclamation of a republic in Turin is expected arises from the fact that the attempt is being made to prevent it by the abdication of Charles Albert in favour of his eldest son.[a]

---

[a] Victor Emmanuel II.— *Ed.*

The defeat of the Piedmontese is more important than all the German imperial tricks taken together. It is the defeat of the whole Italian revolution. After the defeat of Piedmont comes the turn of Rome and Florence.[161]

But unless all the signs are deceptive, precisely this defeat of the Italian revolution will be the signal for the outbreak of the European revolution. The French people sees that to the same extent that it becomes more and more enslaved by its own counter-revolution inside the country, the armed counter-revolution abroad approaches closer and closer to its frontiers. The counterpart of the June victory and Cavaignac's dictatorship in Paris was Radetzky's victorious march to the Mincio, the counterpart to the presidency of Bonaparte, Barrot and the law on association[162] is the victory at Novara and the Austrians' march to the Alps. Paris is ripe for a new revolution. Savoy, which for a year has been preparing its secession from Piedmont and union with France, and which did not want to participate in the war, Savoy will want to throw itself into the arms of France; Barrot and Bonaparte will have to reject it. Genoa, and perhaps Turin, if there is still time for it, will proclaim a republic and call on France for help; and Odilon Barrot will solemnly reply to them that he will be able to protect the integrity of Sardinia's territory.

But if the Ministry does not wish to know it, the people of Paris knows very well that France must not tolerate the Austrians in Turin and Genoa. And the people of Paris will not tolerate them there. It will reply to the Italians by a victorious uprising and the French army, the only army in Europe that has not been in the open battlefield since February 24,[a] will join it.

The French army is burning with impatience to cross the Alps and measure its strength against the Austrians. It is not accustomed to opposing a revolution which promises it new renown and new laurels, and which comes forward with the banner of war against coalition. The French army is not "My glorious army".[163]

The defeat of the Italians is bitter. No people, apart from the Poles, has been so shamefully oppressed by the superior power of its neighbours, no people has so often and so courageously tried to throw off the yoke oppressing it. And each time this unfortunate people has had to submit again to its oppressors; the result of all the efforts, of all the struggle, has been nothing but fresh defeats! But if the present defeat has as its consequence a revolution in Paris and

---

[a] On February 24, 1848 the French monarchy was overthrown.— *Ed.*

leads to the outbreak of a European war, the foretokens of which are everywhere evident; if this defeat gives the impetus for a new movement throughout the Continent—a movement which this time will have a different character from that of last year—then even the Italians will have cause for congratulating themselves on it.

[*Neue Rheinische Zeitung* No. 261 (second edition), April 1, 1849]

*Cologne*, April 1. According to the latest reports from Italy, the defeat of the Piedmontese at Novara is by no means so decisive as was reported in the telegraphic dispatch sent to Paris.

The Piedmontese have suffered defeat; they are cut off from Turin and thrown back to the mountains. That is all.

If Piedmont were a republic, if the Turin Government were revolutionary and if it had the courage to resort to revolutionary measures—nothing would be lost. But Italian independence is being lost not because of the invincibility of Austrian arms, but because of the cowardice of Piedmont royalty.

To what do the Austrians owe their victory? To the fact that owing to Ramorino's treachery, two divisions of the Piedmontese army were cut off from the remaining three, and these three isolated divisions were beaten owing to the numerical superiority of the Austrians. These three divisions have now been pressed back to the foot of the Pennine Alps.

From the outset it was an enormous mistake of the Piedmontese that they opposed to the Austrians merely a regular army, that they wanted to wage an ordinary, bourgeois, genteel war against them. A nation that wants to conquer its independence cannot restrict itself to the *ordinary* methods of warfare. Mass uprising, revolutionary war, guerilla detachments everywhere—that is the only means by which a small nation can overcome a large one, by which a less strong army can be put in a position to resist a stronger and better organised one.

The Spaniards proved it in 1807-12,[164] the Hungarians are proving it now as well.

Chrzanowski was defeated at Novara and cut off from Turin; Radetzky stood 9 miles from Turin. In a *monarchy* such as Piedmont, even in a constitutional one, the outcome of the campaign was thereby decided; Radetzky was petitioned for peace. But in a republic the defeat would have been *by no means decisive*. If it were not for the inevitable cowardice of the monarchy, which never has the courage to resort to extreme revolutionary means—if this cowardice had not held it back from this course—Chrzanowski's defeat could have become fortunate for Italy.

Had Piedmont been a republic that did not have to pay any regard to monarchical traditions, there would have been a way open to it to end the campaign quite differently.

Chrzanowski was driven back to Biella and Borgomanero. There, where the Swiss Alps prevent any further retreat, and where the two or three narrow river valleys make any dispersal of the army practically impossible, it was easy to concentrate the army and by a bold advance nullify Radetzky's victory.

If the leaders of the Piedmontese army had any revolutionary courage, if they knew that in Turin there was a revolutionary government ready to take the most extreme measures, their course of action would have been very simple.

After the battle at Novara there were 30,000-40,000 Piedmontese troops at Lago Maggiore. This corps could be mobilised in two days and could be thrown into Lombardy, where there are less than 12,000 Austrian troops. This corps could occupy Milan, Brescia and Cremona, organise a general uprising, smash one by one the Austrian corps advancing singly from the Venetian region, and so completely destroy Radetzky's whole basis of operations.

Instead of marching on Turin, Radetzky would have had immediately to turn round and go back to Lombardy, pursued by the levy en masse of the Piedmontese, who of course would have had to support the uprising in Lombardy.

Such a *really* national war, like that which the Lombards waged in March 1848, and by which they drove Radetzky beyond the Oglio and the Mincio—such a war would have drawn the whole of Italy into the struggle and a quite different spirit would have permeated the Romans and Tuscans.

While Radetzky still stood between the Po and the Ticino, pondering whether he should advance or retreat, the Piedmontese and Lombards could have marched right up to Venice, relieve the siege there, draw in La Marmora and the Roman troops, harrass and weaken the Austrian Field Marshal by countless guerilla groups, split up his forces and finally defeat him. Lombardy was only waiting for the Piedmontese to arrive; it rose up even before their arrival. Only the Austrian fortresses held the Lombardy towns in check. Ten thousand Piedmontese were already in Lombardy; if another 20,000-30,000 had marched in, Radetzky's retreat would have been impossible.

But a mass uprising and a general insurrection of the people are means which royalty is terrified of using. These are means to which only a republic resorts—1793 is proof of that. These are means, the application of which presupposes *revolutionary terror*, and where has there been a monarch who could resolve to use that?

What ruined the Italians, therefore, was not the defeat at Novara and Vigevano; it was the cowardice and moderation that monarchy forces on them. The lost battle at Novara resulted merely in a *strategic* disadvantage; the Italians were cut off from Turin, whereas the way to it lay open to the Austrians. This disadvantage would have been entirely without significance if the lost battle had been followed by a *real revolutionary war*, if the remainder of the Italian army had forthwith proclaimed itself the nucleus of a national mass uprising, if the conventional strategic war of *armies* had been turned into a *people's* war, like that waged by the French in 1793.

But, of course, a monarchy will never consent to a revolutionary war, a mass uprising and terror. It would make peace with its bitterest enemy of equal rank rather than ally itself with the people.

Whether or not Charles Albert is a traitor—Charles Albert's *crown*, the *monarchy* alone, would have sufficed to ruin Italy.

But Charles Albert is a traitor. All the French newspapers carry news about the great European counter-revolutionary plot of all the great powers, about the plan of campaign of the counter-revolution for the final suppression of all the European peoples. Russia and England, Prussia and Austria, France and Sardinia, have signed this new Holy Alliance.[165]

Charles Albert received orders to start a war against Austria, to let himself be defeated, thereby giving the Austrians an opportunity to restore "peace" in Piedmont, Florence and Rome, and to arrange for martial-law constitutions to be imposed everywhere. In return for this, Charles Albert was to receive Parma and Piacenza and the Russians were to pacify Hungary; France was to become an empire, and thus peace was established in Europe. That, according to the French newspapers, is the great plan of the counter-revolution, and this plan explains Ramorino's treachery and the defeat of the Italians.

But the monarchy, as a result of Radetzky's victory, has suffered a fresh blow. The battle at Novara and the paralysis of the Piedmontese which followed it prove that in extreme cases, when a people needs to exert all its strength in order to save itself, nothing hinders it so much as the monarchy. If Italy is not to perish because of the monarchy, then above all the monarchy in Italy must perish.

[*Neue Rheinische Zeitung* No. 263, April 4, 1849]

Now at last the events of the Piedmontese campaign right up to the victory of the Austrians at Novara lie before us frankly and clearly revealed.

While Radetzky deliberately caused the false rumour to be spread that he would keep on the defensive and retreat towards the Adda, he secretly concentrated all his troops around Sant Angelo and Pavia. Owing to the treachery of the pro-Austrian reactionary party in Turin, Radetzky was *fully* informed of all Chrzanowski's plans and arrangements and of the entire position of his army. On the other hand, he succeeded in completely deceiving the Piedmontese as to his own plans. This was why the Piedmontese army was drawn up on both sides of the Po, the sole calculation being to advance simultaneously from all sides in a concentric movement against Milan and Lodi.

Nevertheless, if strong resistance had been offered by the Piedmontese army in the centre, it would have been impossible to envisage the swift success that Radetzky has now achieved. If Ramorino's corps at Pavia had barred his way, there would still have been time enough to contest Radetzky's passage across the Ticino until reinforcements had been brought up. In the meanwhile the divisions on the right bank of the Po and at Arona could also have arrived; the Piedmontese army drawn up parallel to the Ticino would have covered Turin and been more than sufficient to put Radetzky's army to flight. One had, of course, to rely on Ramorino doing his duty.

But he did not do it. He allowed Radetzky to cross the Ticino, and this meant that there was a break-through in the centre of the Piedmontese army and the divisions on the other side of the Po were isolated. Thereby, in fact, the outcome of the campaign was already decided.

Radetzky then put his entire force of 60,000-70,000 men with 120 guns between the Ticino and the Agogna and took the five Piedmontese divisions along the Ticino in the flank. Thanks to his enormously superior force, he repelled the four nearest divisions at Mortara, Garlasco and Vigevano on the 21st, captured Mortara thereby compelling the Piedmontese to withdraw to Novara, and threatened the only road to Turin still open to them—that from Novara via Vercelli and Chivasso.

This road, however, was already lost for the Piedmontese. In order to concentrate their troops and, in particular, to be able to bring up Solaroli's division stationed on the extreme left flank round Arona, they had to make Novara the nodal point of their operations, whereas otherwise they could have taken up a new position behind the Sesia.

Being therefore already as good as cut off from Turin, nothing was left to the Piedmontese but either to accept battle at Novara or to go into Lombardy, organise a people's war and to leave Turin to its fate, the reserves and the national guard. In that case, Radetzky would have taken good care not to advance farther.

But this presupposes that in Piedmont itself preparations were made for a *mass uprising* and precisely this was not the case. The bourgeois national guard was armed; but the mass of the people were unarmed, however loudly they demanded the arms stocked in the arsenals.

The monarchy did not dare to appeal to this irresistible force that had saved France in 1793.

The Piedmontese had, therefore, to accept battle at Novara, however unfavourable their position and however great the enemy's superiority of force.

40,000 Piedmontese (ten brigades) with relatively weak artillery confronted the entire Austrian army numbering at least 60,000 men with 120 guns.

The Piedmontese army was drawn up under the walls of Novara on both sides of the Mortara road.

The left flank, two brigades commanded by Durando, had the support of a fairly strong position, La Bicocca.

The centre, three brigades commanded by Bès, backed on a farmstead, La Cittadella.

The right flank, two brigades commanded by Perrone, backed on the Cortenuova plateau (the Vercelli road).

There were two reserve corps, one consisting of two brigades under the Duke of Genoa stationed on the left flank, the second consisting of a brigade and the guards under the Duke of Savoy, the present King, stationed on the right flank.

The disposition of the Austrians, judging from their communiqué, is less clear.

The second Austrian corps under d'Aspre was the first to attack the left flank of the Piedmontese, while behind it the third corps under Appel, as well as the reserves and the fourth corps, were deployed. The Austrians were completely successful in establishing their line of battle and simultaneously delivering a concentric attack on all points of the Piedmontese battle formation with such a superiority of force that the Piedmontese were crushed by it.

The key to the Piedmontese position was the Bicocca. If the Austrians had captured it, the Piedmontese centre and left flank would have been trapped between the (unfortified) town and the canal, and they could have been either scattered or forced to lay down their arms.

Hence the main attack was directed against the Piedmontese left flank, the chief support of which was the Bicocca. Here the battle raged with great violence, but for a long time without result.

A very lively attack was launched also against the centre. La Cittadella was lost several times but several times it was retaken by Bès.

When the Austrians saw that they were encountering too strong a resistance here, they again turned their main strength against the Piedmontese left flank. The two Piedmontese divisions were thrown back to the Bicocca and finally the Bicocca itself was captured by storm. The Duke of Savoy with his reserves hurled himself on the Austrians, but it was of no avail. The superiority of the imperial forces was too great; the position was lost, and that decided the battle. The only retreat left to the Piedmontese was towards the Alps, to Biella and Borgomanero.

And this battle, prepared for by treachery and won by superior force, the *Kölnische Zeitung*, which has so long been hankering for an Austrian victory, calls:

"a battle which in the history of war will *shine for all time* (!), since the victory won in it by old Radetzky is the result of *such skilful combined* movements and *such truly magnificent bravery* that *nothing like it has occurred since the days of Napoleon, the great demon of battles* (!!!)."[a]

Radetzky or, rather, Hess, his chief of the general staff, carried out his plot with Ramorino quite well, we admit. It is also true that since Grouchy's treachery at Waterloo,[166] certainly no such magnificent villainy has occurred as that of Ramorino's. Radetzky, however, is not in the same class as Napoleon, the "demon of battles" (!), but in that of *Wellington*; the victories of both of them always cost more *ready money* than bravery and skill.

We shall not discuss at all the rest of the lies which the *Kölnische Zeitung* spread yesterday evening, i.e. that the democratic deputies have fled from Turin, and that the Lombards "behaved like a cowardly rabble" etc. They have already been refuted by the latest

---

[a] Published in the section "Italien" in the *Kölnische Zeitung* No. 79, April 3, 1849.— *Ed.*

events. These lies prove nothing but the joy of the *Kölnische Zeitung* that great Austria has crushed—and that by means of treachery—little Piedmont.

Written by Engels between March 30
and April 3, 1849

Printed according to the newspaper

First published in the *Neue Rheinische
Zeitung* No. 260, No. 261 (second edition),
No. 263, March 31, April 1 and 4, 1849

Published in English for the first
time

# [FROM THE THEATRE OF WAR]

Recent news from the theatre of war is entirely lacking. Only individual details about events of which we already know are at hand. In the following we give the most important of these:

Lieutenant-Field Marshal *Schulzig* has been recalled because of his incompetent conduct of operations in Hungary, and transferred to the post of Commandant in Styria. The first of the much vaunted royal imperial Austrian generals of whom an example is made. More are in prospect.

Jellachich is said to be in Felegyhaza and his outposts four hours from Szegedin, which is said to be encircled and cut off from supplies from the Banat. A glance at any large-scale map giving the location of the swamps around Szegedin shows that this report is an empty boast.

About 2,500 Hungarian insurgents sought to effect an entry into Galicia in the district of Stryj, but were repulsed with casualties.

It is learnt that *as a rule the cadres of the Hungarian army reserve battalions consist of Polish veterans.*

The most recent order of Field Marshal Windischgrätz that no one *can be forced* to accept Hungarian banknotes (!!)[a] has had no effect at all in Pest.

In another issue of the *Lithographierte Correspondenz* from Vienna we read:

"The Hungarians are continually advancing on Pest and will make every effort to relieve Arad, Komorn and Peterwardein, efforts that may be successful, since the Hungarian army is daily growing larger and more enthusiastic, while the imperial

---

[a] This order, of March 21, 1849, was published in the *Wiener Zeitung* No. 74 (evening supplement), March 27, 1849.— *Ed.*

troops are reduced in numbers and disheartened as well by strenuous marches, bad provisioning and continuous skirmishes. Most recently a very violent engagement took place at Török Szent Miklos, in which both parties suffered heavy losses, the Hungarians however were left in possession of the battlefield. At Szegedin, a heavy encounter between the Hungarian army of the South under Vetter and Damjanich and the Serbian army corps is expected any day now. The Serbs have actually gone back to Serbia,[a] lock, stock and barrel, and the unit numbering about 8,000 men will be greatly missed by the imperial generals. Peterwardein is still occupied by Hungarian troops and, as I learnt yesterday, the force there has resolved, after throwing into the casemates all suspect officers, to blow up the ancient rocks of Peterwardein rather than surrender. Hence the navigation on the Danube may well have been opened from Karlowitz, but not further upstream; for any boat that ventured near Peterwardein, which completely commands the whole Danube, would be sent to the bottom of the river. Komorn has been bombarded since March 17 without any success; large siege artillery is being sent by steamship down to Komorn every day. Bem has taken Hermannstadt and driven out the 3,000 Russians and 2,000 Austrians who were garrisoned there."

On Bem's capture of Hermannstadt, a Vienna correspondent of the *Börsen-Halle* writes:

"A look at the map shows the daring with which the insurgent leader has effected this coup, for, as the reports say, he made a 26 hours' forced march with 12,000 men from Vásárhely and attacked Hermannstadt before daybreak, surprised and disarmed the Russian garrison there which in part was still in barracks, and is said to have captured several guns. It is also reported that several Russians have been hanged. The Russian protection, which was promised with the arrival of the Russian relief-force, has consequently been of very little help to the unfortunate inhabitants of Hermannstadt."

A correspondent, who is an enthusiast of the royal imperial cause, has written as follows to the *Breslauer Zeitung* from the Hungarian border:

"The rumour of Prince Windischgrätz's resignation is daily growing stronger. For Windischgrätz is said to be not only disgruntled by the unsatisfactory progress of the war, which he attributes to the oft requested but never granted reinforcements to his troops, but to be particularly offended by the tutelage the Ministry has recently found it expedient to impose upon him in respect of the civil administration of the country. The affair of the banknotes caused the first rift in the *entente cordiale*[b] between Windischgrätz and the Ministry, and the dispatch of Baron Kübek to Ofen to superintend the Hungarian finances was not designed to restore the shattered harmony either. It is asserted that Baron Welden in Vienna, recently promoted to the rank of Master of Ordnance, is destined to replace the austere Marshal in Hungary. Welden's post as Governor of the capital city of the Empire will be taken by Master of Ordnance Count Nugent, since the notorious incidents in Friuli in spring last year[167] have made it impossible for this general to remain in the field.—An air of mystery continues to hang over the terrible fate of *Maklar*. After the battle of Kapolna, this beautiful market town was badly damaged; hence Prince Windischgrätz caused compensation of 1,000 florins to be granted to it. Later it was said to have been razed

---

[a] The reference is to the troops sent by the principality of Serbia to the Hungarian front.— *Ed.*

[b] Friendly understanding.— *Ed.*

to the ground because of the alleged hold-up there of five royal imperial ammunition waggons. This report, however, is denied in Hungarian newspapers appearing in Pest under the eye of the Field Marshal, although the facts concerning the destruction of Maklar appear to have been incontrovertibly established."

The same correspondent sends the following details about Komorn, from which it follows that the capture of the fortress is out of the question. An "assault" on a fortress, particularly one as impregnable as Komorn, an assault to be made before the walls are breached, would be sheer madness. Nevertheless, the correspondent predicts the assault. One sees how the Austrian officers take the journalists in with the craziest nonsense.

In addition, we learn that the so-called Palatine line, which is supposed to have been taken long ago by the imperial forces, is still in Hungarian hands, and that only now the direct-fire batteries[168] have been brought into action against it. Hence there is still no question of the capture of this outwork.

The correspondent writes:

"The Komorn fortress has been shelled assiduously since the 20th of this month, but so far with little success. Two thousand shells are intended to be fired into the area of the fortress. Should the garrison still not surrender, a general assault will be ventured, which the royal imperial troops are impatiently awaiting, since their bivouac is not very inviting in 12 degrees of frost and, moreover, the townships in the whole of the surrounding area are so impoverished and plundered of everything that their inhabitants come into the Austrian camp to beg and gladly pay 30 Kr. for a loaf of army bread merely to be able to still their hunger. The batteries set up on the Sandberg alongside the Danube are intended to clear the island and dismantle the enemy guns of the outer works of the Palatine line; another battery is shelling the road running from the bridgehead through Neu-Szöny; long-distance mortars and rocket batteries commanded by First Lieutenant Jäger, well-known from Italy, complete the list. The garrison is courageously defying death, for the fortress commandant Mek, a young man who has risen in nine months from an artillery sergeant[169] to the rank of the Colonel, sees the scaffold in front of him and will sell his life dearly.

"In Debreczin the insurgent officers lead an extremely gay life, for money is available there in abundance; a glass of punch costs 1 florin C. M., and quite ordinary cylinder clocks which cost 35 florins in Germany, fetch 200 florins there. Gold and silver are also disappearing from circulation in the seat of the Hungarian junta; payments are now made solely in banknotes, not as though the Hungarian Government were short of talers and ducats, not at all; but solely because it is keeping hard cash under lock and key, both to increase Austria's embarrassments and to preserve hard coin ready for all eventualities. As everybody knows, the cunning of the agitator Kossuth has succeeded in getting his emissaries to spread the myth that the National Bank in Vienna is no longer solvent and has suspended payments. *Even in Pest the manoeuvre succeeded* and Prince Windischgrätz is *not a little angered* by this successful ruse of the enemy."

Written by Engels about March 31, 1849

First published in the *Neue Rheinische Zeitung* No. 261, April 1, 1849

Printed according to the newspaper

Published in English for the first time

# [FROM THE THEATRE OF WAR]

*Der Lloyd* reports—and it is well known that *Der Lloyd* is an honourable man—*that the Magyars under Görgey have moved across the Theiss and are at Neograd.*[a] Neograd is *seven miles*[b] *to the north of Pest* and about 20 miles this side of the Theiss. Görgey has also occupied Kaschau and Gyöngyös, that is why the mail dispatched to Kaschau was returned to Pest even before it had reached Gyöngyös. The aim of this campaign is to relieve Komorn.

The Austrian papers had triumphantly proclaimed that Dembiński had relinquished his command because of disagreements with Görgey. Now the matter is being resolved. After some dissension between the generals, Kossuth succeeded in reconciling them. They have come to the following arrangement—Görgey retains the supreme command of all insurgent armies, while Dembiński becomes chief of the Hungarian general quartermaster staff, and the campaign *must* be conducted in strict accordance with the plans of operation laid down by him. Vetter, the former Austrian Staff Officer and currently General of the malcontents, assumes supreme command over Dembiński's corps; a Frenchman named Duchatel is in command of the forces at Arad.

Some time ago *Schlick* was in real danger of being taken prisoner; he was attacked by several Hungarian hussars and only the arrival of a Croat detachment saved him.

The *Constitutionelles Blatt aus Böhmen* relates the following information on the Hungarian war, which shows the enormous

---

[a] Engels, probably, refers to the article "Pesth, 24. März" in *Der Lloyd* No. 147 (evening edition), March 27, 1849.—*Ed.*

[b] See footnote on p. 20.—*Ed.*

heroism with which the Magyars are fighting. The Magyar army is not a regular, organised, well-trained army. It has not even enough rifles to arm the newly arriving recruits of the *Landsturm*. Hence, behind each Magyar front line stands a crowd of unarmed and untrained men, who are only waiting to take up *the muskets of those who have fallen* and to fill the gaps torn in the Magyar ranks by the Austrian guns. And it is these improvised soldiers who hold at bay the royal imperial army and its Russian allies.

The well-known story of the recognition of Francis Joseph as King of Hungary by the Debreczin National Assembly has been put into circulation again by the martial-law *Figyelmezö* (Observer) in Pest. Only this time the actual recognition is said to have been given on the basis of the Pragmatic Sanction, and on condition that the Hungarian Constitution be recognised. It is also said that Kossuth along with 15 others voted against it.[170]

About Transylvania, the *Constitutionelles Blatt aus Böhmen* has received a report from Czernowitz (Bukovina), according to which the *whole of Transylvania except Kronstadt was in the hands of the Magyars*, and Bem was about to enter this town as well. It is "believed" that Malkowsky will advance towards Transylvania after he has only just been driven out! 30,000 Russians are expected to move in immediately.[a]

Moreover, that Hungary *can only be subjugated by the Russians* is as good as *admitted* by the Austrian Ministers. We shall have to wait and see whether they will have the courage to let the Russians come.

The situation in the Banat looks bad. We quote the following report on the battle of Szolnok, sent from Kecskemét on March 15, from a Slav paper, the *Morawské Nowiny* (Moravian Newspaper):

"At 8 in the morning on March 5 a great battle was fought at Szolnok. Two battalions of infantry, half a cavalry regiment and three artillery batteries were on our side; but the mass of the enemy troops was enormous. As soon as we confronted them on the battlefield, they assaulted us with guns as well as with their entire infantry. When we realised that it was no longer possible to withstand them, we retreated. Then the enemy began to assail us forcefully from two sides, until we were wedged in between the narrow banks of the rivers Zagyva and Theiss which merge at Szolnok. Now things really began to happen; the hussars rushed upon us and cut into us so terribly that many of our men jumped into the water and were drowned. When we realised the great danger, we put up resistance and fired on the enemy. Luckily, our aim was good, and the hussars literally rained down from their horses and were compelled to retreat. Fortunately we succeeded in fighting our way out of this confined area on the banks of the rivers, where we were as good as captured already. It was terrible to see soldiers and horses drowning, and our men and the Magyars

---

[a] "Cernowic, am 21. März", *Constitutionelles Blatt aus Böhmen* No. 74, March 28, 1849.— *Ed.*

lying in pools of blood. Among our men, barely 34 of a company of 380 were left after this battle, and, although greatly weakened, we are nevertheless advancing. At Szolnok we threw away our knapsacks and reached Kecskemét (by way of Körös), where we are now expecting the enemy at any hour, since Kossuth is only three hours away from us." [a]

*Der Lloyd* carries the following report about the fighting at Theresiopel:

"*Semlin*, March 19. After their capture of Zombor, intoxicated with victory, the Serbs under the command of Dragich and Stein and the Serb auxiliary corps under the leadership of Milija Stanojevich set off towards Maria-Theresiopel via Bajmok and Pacs. But the Serbs from the Serb principality, who together with the Austrian Serbs were just about to storm Theresiopel, suddenly received orders to return to their homeland, orders which they obeyed without question. When the Magyars heard of the recall of the Serbs, they sallied out of Theresiopel, which had not yet been cut off from Szegedin whence they obtained substantial reinforcements, and fell on the small Serb force left with the encouraging battle-cry: 'Forward, have no fear, the Turkish Raizen [171] are no longer here!' The battle lasted fully three hours. Our forces had two guns of their own, an eighteen-pounder from Knićanin and a Racksa twelve-pounder, and held on bravely. The enemy simulated a retreat. Deceived by this into abandoning their advantageous positions, the Serbs impetuously pursued the enemy, who turned round unexpectedly, defeated the Serbs and put them to flight, capturing the guns mentioned above. In this battle the Chaikists [172] suffered the heaviest losses, 200 of them ending their lives on the battlefield." [b]

Incidentally, the spirit that reigns among the Serbs is shown by the following proclamation issued by Lieutenant-Field Marshal Rukavina in Temesvar:

"For some time now, among the population of this area opinions have emerged and remarks are being made openly in nearly all inns and coffee-houses, which show an ill will that can no longer be tolerated. Accordingly, the honourable mayoralty should with all the severity at its command, as the civil police authority, initiate in this respect a supervision which will give full attention to the inns and coffee-houses and will not tolerate in such places anything directed against the person of the Monarch, the Government, or existing conditions in general, and will eradicate any provocations by word or deed; it should make all innkeepers and coffee-house owners responsible for immediately reporting to the local commander and to the civil authorities concerned everyone who allows himself anything of that kind so that such persons can be arrested in good time. Anyone who neglects to make such a report will be punished for the first offence with arrest and a fine of 100 florins C.M., for the second offence with more rigorous detention and a fine of 200 fl., and for any repetition of the offence with trial by martial law and the closing down of his business. Similarly, all citizens who, having knowledge of such traitorous incitements, omit to report them and this comes afterwards to the knowledge of the local authorities, will become subject to martial law. Hereafter, not only will the honourable mayoralty itself take the

---

[a] "Kecskemet, 15. März (M. N.)", *Constitutionelles Blatt aus Böhmen* No. 74, March 28, 1849.— *Ed.*

[b] "Semlin, 19. März", *Der Lloyd* No. 143 (evening edition), March 24, 1849.— *Ed.*

necessary measures within the fortress, but will also fully inform the lower courts of the contents of this decree and call for its strict application."[a]

Moreover, the *Südslavische Zeitung* has a report on the disagreements between Patriarch Rajachich and Lieutenant-Field Marshal Rukavina:

"*Becskerek*, March 13. The Serb Central Committee [173] and the Constitutional Committee yesterday sent a deputation to the Patriarch with the request that he convene a National Assembly as soon as possible. The Patriarch replied that he could not immediately comply with this request, as many areas in the Banat are still under Rukavina's authority, in particular the comitat of Krasso and the Wallacho-Illyrian regiment. In private conversation the Patriarch expressed the opinion that the National Assembly will probably be convened after Easter.—In some districts petitions to the Patriarch for the early convening of a National Assembly are being signed."[b]

Written by Engels on April 1, 1849

First published in the *Neue Rheinische Zeitung* No. 261 (second edition), April 1, 1849

Printed according to the newspaper

Published in English for the first time

---

[a] "Temešvar, 17. März", *Constitutionelles Blatt aus Böhmen* No. 73, March 27, 1849.— *Ed.*

[b] "Bečkerek, 13. März (Südsl. Ztg.)", *Constitutionelles Blatt aus Böhmen* No. 74, March 28, 1849.— *Ed.*

# FROM THE THEATRE OF WAR

The latest news completely confirms our report printed yesterday[a] that the Magyars have advanced to the vicinity of Neograd. In the Miskolcz area, Görgey has broken through the dispositions of the imperial army and thereby—according to the *Lithographierte Correspondenz* from Vienna based on a message from Pest dated the 26th—forced Lieutenant-Field Marshal Ramberg to *withdraw as far as Waitzen* on the Danube, 20-25 miles beyond Miskolcz.

This report at last tells us something of Götz's and Jablonowsky's corps, which have been missing for so long, for it is precisely these two brigades which are commanded by Ramberg. They have thus moved to the Theiss by way of Kaschau, and here they have been driven back over the Hernad by the Magyars. While in Vienna the story has been put about that they were in Tokaj they have had to withdraw to Miskolcz—four miles further to the west, to avoid losing contact with the main army. And here all at once they are thrown back to 20-25 miles from Miskolcz thanks to a new, bold march by Görgey. Instead of advancing along the Theiss, the only alternative open to them is to try to obstruct the Magyars in their march on Komorn at the bend of the Danube where it leaves its easterly course to turn south.

A peculiar fate of all imperial units marching towards the Theiss from the High Carpathians is to be thrown out of their predetermined line of operations and back on to the main army operating from Pest. Schlick was the first to march down the Hernad to Tokaj. He had scarcely arrived when he was expelled by Görgey, who in the course of his brilliant retreat or rather triumphal march through Upper Hungary managed to get into Schlick's rear. Lieutenant-Field

---

[a] See this volume, p. 181.—*Ed.*

Marshal Schlick had no alternative but to withdraw down the Theiss, unite with Windischgrätz and abandon eastern Upper Hungary to the Magyars. Ramberg thereupon descended the Hernad, and we have seen that he shared the same fate.

The great strategic advantage which the Magyars have thus gained is the liberation of by far the greatest part of Upper Hungary as far as the mountain towns and the Jablunka, the extension of their right wing to the Carpathians, the connection established with the volunteer corps in North-Eastern Slovakia and the opening of a road for the relief of Komorn. Even if they could not achieve all this without simultaneously bringing about a greater concentration of the imperial army, it is hardly a disadvantage for them in a country like Hungary where, owing to the terrain both in the mountains and on the plain, much more depends upon strategic combinations and success in guerilla warfare than upon large-scale battles. Precisely the deployment of the imperial army into a long battle-line outflanking the Magyars is the danger here, and precisely this deployment of the imperial troops is always disrupted; indeed, the position at present is that the Magyars are threatening to outflank the imperial troops.

Here, nothing can help the imperial forces once and for all, except reinforcements from Galicia strong enough to hold the Upper Theiss. And these can only be provided by the *Russians*, either by occupying Galicia and thus giving the royal imperial forces there a free hand, or by participating themselves in the march into Hungary. We recall that Hammerstein was supposed to have marched over the Carpathians with 12,000 Austrians and advanced to the Upper Theiss,[a] and that this rumour proved to be false. Now it is being repeated, and indeed in an improved version.

The *Russians themselves* are supposed to be on their way to Hungary. The *Österreichischer Correspondent* writes from Pest:

"A traveller who arrived here by train assured us that he had learned from a reliable source *that the Russians had entered Galicia and intended to march immediately from there into Hungary.*"

This may help—nothing else will so easily. Whether these rumours are true or not, in any case they demonstrate the great significance the imperial generals attribute to the possession of Upper Hungary.

In the course of this new expedition of Görgey's the estates of several Hungarian magnates, among others the Pallavicini estates and those of Count Szirmay, have been utterly devastated. These

---

[a] See this volume, pp. 152-53.— *Ed.*

gentlemen had betrayed their countrymen and intended to organise volunteer corps against the Magyars.

*60,000 Russian* troops are said to have marched into Transylvania.

On the 25th, there were reports in Pest that the *fortress of Arad* had been *stormed* and *captured* by the Magyars under the Frenchman Duchatel. 3,000 Magyars are said to have been killed.

Moreover, a number of martial-law inspired rumours are circulating in Vienna and Pest. Bem is said to be dead, Dembiński to have lost his right arm etc.

The following additional report is taken from the *Constitutionelles Blatt aus Böhmen*, which once again only reached us this morning:

> In Pest on the 25th, there was not the slightest news either of Schlick or of Jellachich. They were presumed to be remaining inactive and awaiting reinforcements. "Moreover, the current state of the weather is too unfavourable to permit a campaign to be undertaken through the sea of mud of the Hungarian pusztas. The day before yesterday it snowed incessantly, while today and yesterday, a fine rain drizzled from the skies with great persistence. Already yesterday the post was delayed by ten hours."[a]

On the other hand the regular navigation between Pest and Esseg on the Danube is said to have been re-opened—it remains to be seen for how long. In any case, Jellachich's march on Kecskemét has resulted in cutting off the Tolna comitat insurgents from the main force of the Magyars and apparently frustrating the movement the Magyars certainly intended to make from Szegedin towards the Danube. This movement was designed to achieve the same outflanking on the right wing of the imperial forces as the one Görgey has as good as executed on the left.

Komorn is still being unsuccessfully bombarded. A battle was fought in the fortress itself; the party inclined to surrender was defeated, and the revolutionary Magyars have now introduced a reign of terror, shooting every traitor. The Austrian siege troops have to endure the greatest hardship, snow and rain. On March 24 the snow lay 4 feet deep.

The Augsburg *Allgemeine Zeitung* has published an article, "Three Months of the Hungarian War",[b] containing admissions all the more important given the dyed-in-the-wool black-and-yellow[c] views of the author. We shall return to it.

Written by Engels on April 2, 1849

First published in the *Neue Rheinische Zeitung* No. 262, April 3, 1849

Printed according to the newspaper

Published in English for the first time

---

[a] "Pest, 25. März", *Constitutionelles Blatt aus Böhmen* No. 75, March 29, 1849.— *Ed.*

[b] Augsburg *Allgemeine Zeitung* No. 88 (supplement), March 29, 1849.— *Ed.*

[c] The Austrian imperial colours.— *Ed.*

# FROM THE THEATRE OF WAR

Today the news that the Hungarians have advanced by way of Gyöngyös into the area of Waitzen, 5 hours from Pest, is reaching us from all directions. Now nobody dares doubt it any more; the *Kölnische Zeitung,* the Augsburg *Allgemeine Zeitung,* the *Constitutionelles Blatt aus Böhmen,*[a] all agree on this. The Austrians have had to retreat in all haste to Waitzen from Hatvan and Gödöllö on the worst country roads. Their flank is threatened by the Hungarians, who are simultaneously beginning to present a danger to the siege area around Komorn.

As a result of these successes on the part of the Hungarians the spirits of the inhabitants of Pest have risen again. Proclamations by Madarász, the Debreczin Minister of Police, in which the inhabitants of the two capitals[174] are urged to hold out in view of their impending liberation, have been distributed in great numbers in Pest.

Görgey has the supreme command of the advancing Magyar corps. The rumour about Dembiński's resignation on the grounds of his disagreements with Görgey is being repeated. *Vetter,* who together with Bem drafted the original plans of campaign, is said to have assumed command in his place.

Another piece of news which is similarly beyond doubt now is that of the entry of *30,000 new Russian auxiliaries into Transylvania.* The

---

[a] Engels refers to the following reports: "Pesth, 24. März", *Kölnische Zeitung* No. 78 (second edition), April 1, 1849; "Pesth, 27. März", Augsburg *Allgemeine Zeitung* No. 92, April 2, 1849; "Pest, 27. März", *Constitutionelles Blatt aus Böhmen* No. 78, April 1, 1849.— *Ed.*

*Lloyd*[a] and several issues of the *Lithographierte Correspondenz* from Vienna announced this unanimously and simultaneously, and also the news that the *Bukovina too has been occupied by the Russians.*

Incidentally, the *Lloyd* reports in addition that Bem has been *utterly defeated* by the Russians and *compelled to retreat into Wallachia.*[b] We are unable to judge whether the first part of this report is true or not, but it can scarcely be doubted that the second part is completely false. Bem had pursued the Russians as far as the Roterturm Pass, but had been unable to force this pass. If he was defeated, then it was only because of the newly arrived Russians, and these, needed precisely at Hermannstadt, had no means of access other than the Roterturm Pass. Thus Bem could not possibly have been expelled to Wallachian territory through this pass. To the right of the Roterturm Pass lie three other passes leading to Wallachia; but to reach these Bem would first have had to take Kronstadt, which was occupied by imperial troops and Russians and in addition covered by Puchner who had taken up positions on the Küküllo (Kokel). Here too, therefore, it would have been impossible for Bem to get across. Finally, the fifth of the Transylvanian-Wallachian passes, the Sill Pass, lies to the left of Hermannstadt. If he had used this pass then he would have been acting like a lunatic. If he was defeated at Hermannstadt the following courses were open to him: 1) the road along the Maros into Hungary, 2) the road to Klausenburg, and 3) the road to Maros-Vásárhely. In all three cases he would be able to remain at the place of battle and fall back upon Magyar corps to reinforce his troops. Crossing the Sill Pass on the other hand would have meant trampling on the most elementary rules of strategy, cutting himself off voluntarily from the Maros, his basis of operations, and crossing the frontier in a fit of dejection as it were. Thus, until we hear that hitherto unknown and unprecedented imperial advances have cut him off from an otherwise secure retreat we can at most believe in his defeat through Russian superiority, but not in his crossing into Wallachian territory.

No news has been received about the capture of the *Arad citadel* by the Magyars. On the other hand even the most black-and-yellow[c] newspapers admit that a considerable Hungarian army is concentrating in and around Alt-Arad, this "Magyar Saragossa",[175] and that evidently important battles are in preparation there.

Incidentally, Bem has exercised the same salutary terrorism against the Russians in Transylvania as against the Saxons and the

---

[a] "Wien, 29. März", *Der Lloyd* No. 152 (morning edition), March 30, 1849.— *Ed.*

[b] "Neuestes", *Der Lloyd* No. 151 (evening edition), March 29, 1849.— *Ed.*

[c] The Austrian imperial colours.— *Ed.*

Romanians. Thus among other things he is said to have ordered the hanging of 300 Cossacks captured by his troops in the attacks on Hermannstadt, and to have said of the deed that it had been one of the most satisfying of his life.

As a punishment for this and other atrocities, the *Lloyd* reports, the Russians ordered the hanging of six captured staff officers of Bem's after the battle they are alleged to have won.[a]

Komorn and Peterwardein will soon surrender, hopes the royal imperial press. One knows by now how often and how long these facts, so desirable to the imperial side, have been "hoped for". The rain has not let up, the roads are turning more and more into quagmires, the post arrives later every day, and military operations must also be restricted for the present.

In brief, the state of the royal imperial cause in Hungary is such that the Olmütz Government is seriously considering negotiations. It is said that a peace congress is to be held in Miskolcz. Of this the *Ost-Deutsche Post* writes:

"The Government appears to have made new decisions concerning Hungary. One of these is said to be the repeated demand for a surrender, in conjunction with the promise of full immunity (amnesty) for all those troops and officers who return to subordination."[b]

The Serbs are growing more and more serious. The following dispatch in the *Lloyd* shows that they are demanding more than a merely rhetorical independence:

"*Semlin*, March 21. Besides the deputies sent to Vienna by the Serbian National Congress upon the demand of the Government, about whom I informed you in my dispatch the day before yesterday, a further two elected deputies, Alexander Kostich and Georg Stojakovich, have departed for Ofen to bring back from the Governor's palace all the documents concerning the Serbian nation as well as the Serbian National Funds and other institutions."[c]

In short, if it were not for the Russians we should be shouting "*Finis Austriae!*" much sooner than "*Finis Hungariae!*" Now even the neighbouring journalist[d] realises this at last.

Written by Engels on April 3, 1849          Printed according to the newspaper

First published in the *Neue Rheinische*          Published in English for the first
*Zeitung* No. 263, April 4, 1849          time

---

[a] "Neuestes", *Der Lloyd* No. 151 (evening edition), March 29, 1849. The newspaper mentioned that five officers were to be hanged.— *Ed.*

[b] "Wien, 28. März", *Ost-Deutsche Post* No. 59, March 29, 1849.— *Ed.*

[c] "Semlin, 21. März", *Der Lloyd* No. 147 (evening edition), March 27, 1849.— *Ed.*

[d] An allusion to the journalist Schwanbeck reporting the Hungarian war for the *Kölnische Zeitung.— Ed.*

# FRENCH FOREIGN POLICY

*Cologne,* April 3. The sitting of the French National Assembly on March 31 was marked by the speech of the "versatile little man", Monsieur *Thiers,* who with cynical frankness and unambiguous clarity defended the Vienna Treaties of 1815 [176] and upheld them as the basis of the present political situation of Europe. Was the little man not perfectly justified in ridiculing the contradiction of allowing these treaties to exist in fact while disavowing them in legal phraseology? And that was the cautious course of action of the Provisional Government [177] as it was that of Cavaignac. Barrot's foreign policy was the necessary consequence of Cavaignac's policy, just as Cavaignac's foreign policy was the necessary consequence of Lamartine's policy. Lamartine, like the Provisional Government as a whole, of whose foreign policy he was the agent, betrayed Italy and Poland on the pretext of not hindering the internal development of the French Republic. The clang of arms would have sounded a dissonant note in Lamartine's oratorical propaganda. Just as the Provisional Government pretended that it could abolish the contradiction between the bourgeois class and the working class with a phrase about "fraternisation" and spirit away the class struggle, so it did also with regard to the contradiction between nations and foreign war. Under the aegis of the Provisional Government the oppressors of the Poles, Italians and Hungarians reconstituted themselves simultaneously with the French bourgeoisie, which at the end of June put into effect Lamartine's policy of fraternisation. Cavaignac maintained peace with foreign countries in order calmly to wage civil war within France and not endanger the destruction of the defeated red republic, the workers' republic, by the respectable moderate republic, by the bourgeois republic. Under Cavaignac the old Holy Alliance was re-established in Europe, as in France was the new Holy Alliance of the legitimists, Philippists, Bonapartists and "respectable" republicans. The Government of this duplicate Holy Alliance is that of Odilon Barrot.[178] His foreign policy is the policy of this Holy Alliance. He needs the victory of the counter-revolution abroad, in order to complete the counter-revolution in France itself.

At the sitting of the National Assembly on March 31 the Provisional Government repudiated Cavaignac. Cavaignac rightly maintains that he is the legitimate offspring of the Provisional Government and, for his part, repudiated Odilon Barrot, who imperturbably takes delight in believing that the meaning of the February revolution lies in the Vienna Treaties of 1815. Flocon states—without being disavowed by Odilon Barrot—that two days ago the Government formally imposed an interdict on Italy, and all Frenchmen, Poles and Italians who want to go there *are being refused passports.* Does not Barrot deserve to become the Prime Minister of Henry V?

Incidentally, in his rejoinder to Thiers, Ledru-Rollin admitted:

"Yes, I must confess that I acted wrongly; the Provisional Government ought to have sent its soldiers to the frontiers, not in order to conquer, but to defend our oppressed brothers, and from that moment there would have been no more despots in Europe. But if we hesitated at that time to begin a war, the blame lay on the monarchy, which had exhausted our finances and emptied our arsenals." [a]

Written on April 3, 1849

First published in the *Neue Rheinische Zeitung* No. 263, April 4, 1849

Printed according to the newspaper

Published in English for the first time

---

[a] See *Le Moniteur universel* No. 91, April 1, 1849.—*Ed.*

# [THE COMEDY WITH THE IMPERIAL CROWN]

*Cologne,* April 3. Herr Brandenburg yesterday told the Second Chamber what the King[a] will do about the "German question". The temptation was too great: "the loyal Eckarts" of the *Neue Preussische Zeitung* with all their warnings have been ignored. The *King of Prussia* **will accept** *the proffered crown,* and in the near future therefore we may be able to look forward to solemn entry of His Christian-Germanic royal imperial Majesty into the residence of the "Imperial Government".

But, while accepting the imperial crown from the hands of the plebeian Frankfurt parliament, Frederick William at the same time gives a gentle kick to this parliament and the illusion of its sovereignty.

The Prime Minister

"recognises that the decision of the Frankfurt Assembly is a *big step forward* towards the realisation of German unity. But he has to take into account also the rights of the governments. He considers that *the decision will take effect only with the voluntary consent of the sovereigns and that it will be binding only for those German states the sovereigns of which have given this voluntary consent.* The Prussian Government for its part will make every effort to bring about this voluntary unification".[b]

Very cunning! The imperial crown is always acceptable, particularly when it is an aim in life that has been desired in vain for a long time—compare von Radowitz's well-known pamphlet: How Frederick William IV did *not* become German Emperor.[c] But to the

---

[a] Frederick William IV.— *Ed.*

[b] From the statement made by Brandenburg, the Prime Minister, at the sitting of the Second Chamber on April 2, 1848.— *Ed.*

[c] [Radowitz, J. M.,] *Deutschland und Friedrich-Wilhelm IV,* Hamburg, 1848.— *Ed.*

crown proffered by the Frankfurt parliament there adheres too much plebeian dirt, too much unpleasant memory of the unhappy days of the rule of the sovereign people, for a king by the grace of God and, moreover, one who has been rehabilitated, to be able to place it on his head without more ado.

Only when the other sovereigns, also crowned by the grace of God, have given their consent to it, only then will the new crown be cleansed by the grace of God from all sinful stains caused by the March events and consecrated; only then will he who has been chosen by 290 professors and Höfräte take it into his hands and say, as he did earlier in Berlin: "By the grace of God do I have this crown, and woe to him who encroaches on it!" [179]

What new stage in the German imperial chaos will result from the imperial comedy, and especially from recognition or non-recognition on the part of the individual governments, is a matter which we leave to the wisdom of the *Kölnische Zeitung* to determine.

Written by Engels on April 3, 1849          Printed according to the newspaper

First published in the special supplement          Published in English for the first
to the *Neue Rheinische Zeitung* No. 263,          time
April 4, 1849

# [THE CALL-UP OF THE ARMY RESERVE IN PRUSSIA] [180]

*Cologne*, April 3. In Posen the whole army reserve of the Grand Duchy has been called up and has already been marched off to Schleswig-Holstein.[181]

In the area of Cleves the army reserve has similarly been called up and sent to Schleswig-Holstein.

And now—we hear—the whole *Eighth* (Rhenish) *Army Corps is to be mobilised* and **all army reserves in the Rhine Province are to be called up.** It is reported that the Eighth Army Corps is to move to the French border. It is quite impossible to understand what purpose it will serve there.

However, the reason for the army reserve on the Rhine being called up at all can most certainly be understood. In all those provinces whose loyalty to the House of Hohenzollern and to the Royal Prussian Monarchy by God's Grace is suspect they intend to *render harmless all young men capable of bearing arms* by placing them in rank and file under the command of Prussian officers and throwing them amongst troops of the line in an army corps. They then intend to send these suspect army reserves, which are thus being kept in check by martial law and other royal Prussian measures, together with other more reliable troops into foreign provinces in order to use them as need arises for suppressing the spirit of recalcitrance, which has recently been gaining ground.

By law the army reserve is only to be used against *external enemies.* To make this very law provide the excuse for the Government to trample it into the dirt, the Danish war has been expressly invented. Once the army reserve has been transported to Schleswig-Holstein, then the means will very soon be found to transport it even further, to East Prussia or to Silesia. Our Rhenish young men are to perform the same honourable services there for which the Silesian army reserves were used in Posen last April and May.[182]

The same ethnic baiting, which the royal imperial Austrian Government is pursuing on a grand scale by....

Written by Engels on April 3, 1849

First published (in Russian) in the journal *Voprosy istorii KPSS* No. 12, 1970

Printed according to the manuscript

Published in English for the first time

# WAGE LABOUR AND CAPITAL[183]

[I]

[*Neue Rheinische Zeitung* No. 264, April 5, 1849]

*Cologne*, April 4.[a] From various quarters we have been reproached with not having presented the *economic relations* which constitute the material foundation of the present class struggles and national struggles. We have designedly touched upon these relations only where they directly forced themselves to the front in political conflicts.

The point was, above all, to trace the class struggle in current history, and to prove empirically by means of the historical material already at hand and which is being newly created daily, that, with the subjugation of the working class, the class which had made February and March, its opponents were simultaneously defeated—the bourgeois republicans in France and the bourgeois and peasant classes which were fighting feudal absolutism throughout the continent of Europe; that the victory of the "respectable republic" in France was at the same time the downfall of the nations that had responded to the February revolution by heroic wars of independence; finally, that Europe, with the defeat of the revolutionary workers, had relapsed into its old double slavery, the *Anglo-Russian* slavery. The June struggle in Paris, the fall of Vienna, the tragicomedy of Berlin's November,[b] the desperate exertions of Poland, Italy and Hungary, the starving of Ireland into submission[184]— these were the concentrated expressions of the European class struggle between bourgeoisie and working class, by means of which we proved that every revolutionary upheaval, however remote from the class struggle its goal may appear to be, must fail

---

[a] In separate editions of *Wage Labour and Capital*, including that of 1891, the dates printed at the beginning of each article are omitted.— *Ed.*

[b] In the 1891 edition "1848" is added here.— *Ed.*

until the revolutionary working class is victorious, that every social reform remains a utopia until the proletarian revolution and the feudalistic counter-revolution measure swords in a *world war*. In our presentation, as in reality, *Belgium* and *Switzerland* were tragicomic genre-pictures akin to caricature in the great historical tableau, the one being the model state of the bourgeois monarchy, the other the model state of the bourgeois republic, both of them states which imagine themselves to be as independent of the class struggle as of the European revolution.

Now, after our readers have seen the class struggle develop in colossal political forms in 1848, the time has come to deal more closely with the economic relations themselves on which the existence of the bourgeoisie and its class rule, as well as the slavery of the workers, are founded.

We shall present in three large sections: 1) the relation of *wage labour to capital,* the slavery of the worker, the domination of the capitalist; 2) *the inevitable destruction of the middle bourgeois classes and of the peasant estate[a] under the present system*; 3) *the commercial subjugation and exploitation of the bourgeois classes of the various European nations* by the despot of the world market— *England.*

We shall try to make our presentation as simple and popular as possible and shall not presuppose even the most elementary notions of political economy. We wish to be understood by the workers. Moreover, the most remarkable ignorance and confusion of ideas prevails in Germany in regard to the simplest economic relations, from the accredited defenders of the existing state of things down to the **socialist miracle workers** and the **unrecognised political geniuses** in which fragmented Germany is even richer than in sovereign princes.

Now, therefore, for the first question: **What are wages? How are they determined?**

If workers were asked: "How much are your wages?" one would reply: "I get a franc[b] a day from my bourgeois"; another, "I get two francs", and so on. According to the different trades to which they belong, they would mention different sums of money which they receive from their respective bourgeois for a particular labour time or[c] for the performance of a particular piece of work, for example,

---

[a] The 1891 edition has "*the so-called burgher estate*" instead of "*the peasant estate*".— *Ed.*

[b] 1 franc equals 8 Prussian silver groschen. (In the 1891 edition the word "mark" is used everywhere instead of "franc".)—*Ed.*

[c] The words "for a particular labour time or" are omitted in the 1891 edition.— *Ed.*

# Neue
# Rheinische Zeitung
## Organ der Demokratie.

№ 264.  Köln, Donnerstag, den 5. April  1849.

Heute Morgen wurde ein Extra-Blatt zu Nro. 263 ausgegeben.

**Uebersicht.**

**Deutschland.** Köln. (Lohnarbeit und Kapital. — Zur schlesischen Milliarde. [Die "Reptilie".] — Mobilisirung des 8. Armeekorps). Barmen. (Die Frage der Fabrikarbeiter). Berlin. (Geschäftsübersetzung in der Reichskammer.) ...

**Deutschland.**

*Köln, 4. April.* ...

*Köln, 4. April.* Napoleon bearbeitete 1806 — 1807 das übermächtige Preußen ...

---

The *Neue Rheinische Zeitung* No. 264, April 5, 1849 with the beginning of Marx's *Wage Labour and Capital*

weaving a yard of linen or type-setting a printed sheet. In spite of the variety of their statements, they would all agree on one point: wages are the sum of money paid by the bourgeois[a] for a particular labour time or for a particular output of labour.

The bourgeois,[b] therefore, *buys* their labour with money. They *sell* him their labour for money.[c] For the same sum with which the bourgeois has bought their labour,[d] for example, two francs, he could have bought two pounds of sugar or a definite amount of any other commodity. The two francs, with which he bought two pounds of sugar, are the *price* of the two pounds of sugar. The two francs, with which he bought twelve hours' labour,[e] are the price of twelve hours' labour. Labour,[f] therefore, is a commodity, neither more nor less than sugar. The former is measured by the clock, the latter by the scales.

The workers exchange their commodity, labour,[f] for the commodity of the capitalist, for money, and this exchange takes place in a definite ratio. So much money for so much labour.[g] For twelve hours' weaving, two francs. And do not the two francs represent all the other commodities which I can buy for two francs? In fact, therefore, the worker has exchanged his commodity, labour,[f] for other commodities of all kinds and that in a definite ratio. By giving him two francs, the capitalist has given him so much meat, so much clothing, so much fuel, light, etc., in exchange for his day's labour. Accordingly, the two francs express the ratio in which labour[f] is exchanged for other commodities, the *exchange value* of his labour.[f] The exchange value of a commodity, reckoned in *money* is what is called its *price. Wages* are only a special name for the *price of labour*,[h] for the price of this peculiar commodity which has no other repository than human flesh and blood.

---

[a] The 1891 edition has "capitalist" here instead of "bourgeois".— *Ed.*

[b] The 1891 edition has "capitalist" here and the words "it seems" are added.— *Ed.*

[c] In the 1891 edition here follows the passage: "But this is merely the appearance. In reality what they sell to the capitalist for money is their labour *power*. The capitalist buys this labour power for a day, a week, a month, etc. And after he has bought it, he uses it by having the workers work for the stipulated time".— *Ed.*

[d] The 1891 edition has "the capitalist has bought their labour power" instead of "the bourgeois has bought their labour".— *Ed.*

[e] The 1891 edition has "use of labour power" instead of "labour".— *Ed.*

[f] The 1891 edition has "labour power" instead of "labour".— *Ed.*

[g] The 1891 edition has "so long a use of labour power" instead of "so much labour".— *Ed.*

[h] The 1891 edition has "the price of labour power, commonly called the *price of labour*" instead of "the *price of labour*".— *Ed.*

Let us take any worker, say, a weaver. The bourgeois[a] supplies him with the loom and yarn. The weaver sets to work and the yarn is converted into linen. The bourgeois takes possession of the linen and sells it, say, for twenty francs. Now are the wages of the weaver a *share* in the linen, in the twenty francs, in the product of his labour? By no means. Long before the linen is sold, perhaps long before its weaving is finished, the weaver has received his wages. The capitalist, therefore, does not pay these wages with the money which he will obtain from the linen, but with money already in reserve. Just as the loom and the yarn are not the product of the weaver to whom they are supplied by his bourgeois, so likewise with the commodities which the weaver receives in exchange for his commodity, labour.[b] It was possible that the bourgeois found no purchaser at all for his linen. It was possible that he did not get even the amount of the wages by its sale. It is possible that he sells it very profitably in comparison with the weaver's wages. All that has nothing to do with the weaver. The capitalist buys the labour[b] of the weaver with a part of his available wealth, of his capital, just as he has bought the raw material—the yarn—and the instrument of labour—the loom—with another part of his wealth. After he has made these purchases, and these purchases include the labour[b] necessary for the production of linen, he produces only with the *raw materials and instruments of labour belonging to him.* For the latter include now, true enough, our good weaver as well, who has as little share in the product or the price of the product as the loom has.

*Wages are, therefore, not the worker's share in the commodity produced by him. Wages are the part of already existing commodities with which the capitalist buys for himself a definite amount of productive labour.*[b]

Labour[b] is, therefore, a commodity which its possessor, the wage-worker, sells to capital. Why does he sell it? In order to live.

But[c] labour is the worker's own life-activity, the manifestation of his own life. And this *life-activity* he sells to another person in order to secure the necessary *means of subsistence.* Thus his life-activity is for him only a *means* to enable him to exist. He works in order to live. He does not even reckon labour as part of his life, it is rather a sacrifice of his life. It is a commodity which he has made over to another. Hence, also, the product of his activity is not the object of his activity. What he produces for himself is not the silk that he weaves, not the gold that he draws from the mine, not the palace that he builds.

---

[a] The 1891 edition has here and below "capitalist" instead of "bourgeois".— *Ed.*

[b] The 1891 edition has "labour power" instead of "labour".— *Ed.*

[c] The 1891 edition has after this: "the exercise of labour power".— *Ed.*

What he produces for himself is *wages*, and silk, gold, palace resolve themselves for him into a definite quantity of the means of subsistence, perhaps into a cotton jacket, some copper coins and a lodging in a cellar. And the worker, who for twelve hours weaves, spins, drills, turns, builds, shovels, breaks stones, carries loads, etc.—does he consider this twelve hours' weaving, spinning, drilling, turning, building, shovelling, stone-breaking as a manifestation of his life, as life? On the contrary, life begins for him where this activity ceases, at table, in the public house, in bed. The twelve hours' labour, on the other hand, has no meaning for him as weaving, spinning, drilling, etc., but as *earnings*, which bring him to the table, to the public house, into bed. If the silkworm were to spin in order to continue its existence as a caterpillar, it would be a complete wage-worker.

Labour[a] was not always a *commodity*. Labour was not always wage labour, that is, *free* labour. The *slave* did not sell his labour[a] to the slave owner, any more than the ox sells its services to the peasant. The slave, together with his labour,[a] is sold once and for all to his owner. He is a commodity which can pass from the hand of one owner to that of another. *He is himself* a commodity, but the labour[a] is not *his* commodity. The *serf* sells only a part of his labour.[a] He does not receive a wage from the owner of the land; rather the owner of the land receives a tribute from him. The serf belongs to the land and turns over to the owner of the land the fruits thereof. The *free labourer*, on the other hand, sells himself and, indeed, sells himself piecemeal. He sells at auction eight, ten, twelve, fifteen hours of his life, day after day, to the highest bidder, to the owner of the raw materials, instruments of labour and means of subsistence, that is, to the capitalist. The worker belongs neither to an owner nor to the land, but eight, ten, twelve, fifteen hours of his daily life belong to him who buys them. The worker leaves the capitalist to whom he hires himself whenever he likes, and the capitalist discharges him whenever he thinks fit, as soon as he no longer gets any profit out of him, or not the anticipated profit. But the worker, whose sole source of livelihood is the sale of his labour,[a] cannot leave the *whole class of purchasers, that is, the capitalist class*, without renouncing his existence. *He belongs not to this or that bourgeois, but to the bourgeoisie, the bourgeois class*,[b] and it is his business to dispose of himself, that is to find a purchaser within this bourgeois class.[c]

---

[a] The 1891 edition has "labour power" instead of "labour".— *Ed.*

[b] The 1891 edition has "*not to this or that capitalist, but to the capitalist class*" instead of "*not to this or that bourgeois, but to the bourgeoisie, the bourgeois class*".— *Ed.*

[c] The 1891 edition has "capitalist class" instead of "bourgeois class".— *Ed.*

Now, before going more closely into the relation between capital and wage labour, we shall present briefly the most general relations which come into consideration in the determination of wages.

*Wages,* as we have seen, are the *price* of a definite commodity, of labour.[a] Wages are, therefore, determined by the same laws that determine the price of every other commodity.

The question, therefore, is, *how is the price of a commodity determined?*

---

[a] The 1891 edition has "labour power" instead of "labour".— *Ed.*

[II]

[*Neue Rheinische Zeitung* No. 265, April 6, 1849]

*Cologne,* April 5. By what is the *price* of a commodity determined? By competition between buyers and sellers, by the relation of inquiry to delivery, of demand to supply. Competition, by which the price of a commodity is determined, is *three-sided.*

The same commodity is offered by various sellers. With goods of the same quality, the one who sells most cheaply is certain of driving the others out of the field and securing the greatest sale for himself. Thus, the sellers mutually contend among themselves for sales, for the market. Each of them desires to sell, to sell as much as possible and, if possible, to sell alone, to the exclusion of the other sellers. Hence, one sells cheaper than another. Consequently, *competition* takes place *among the sellers,* which *depresses* the price of the commodities offered by them.

But *competition* also takes place *among the buyers,* which in its turn *causes* the commodities offered to *rise* in price.

Finally, *competition* occurs *between buyers and sellers;* the former desire to buy as cheaply as possible, the latter to sell as dearly as possible. The result of this competition between buyers and sellers will depend upon how the two above-mentioned sides of the competition are related, that is, whether the competition is stronger in the army of buyers or in the army of sellers. Industry leads two armies into the field against each other, each of which again carries on a battle within its own ranks, among its own troops. The army whose troops beat each other up the least gains the victory over the opposing host.

Let us suppose there are 100 bales of cotton on the market and at the same time buyers for 1,000 bales of cotton. In this case, therefore, the demand is ten times as great as the supply.

Competition will be very strong among the buyers, each of whom desires to get one, and if possible all, of the hundred bales for himself. This example is no arbitrary assumption. We have experienced periods of cotton crop failure in the history of the trade, when a few capitalists in alliance have tried to buy, not one hundred bales, but all the cotton stocks of the world. Hence, in the example mentioned, one buyer will seek to drive the other from the field by offering a relatively higher price per bale of cotton. The cotton sellers, who see that the troops of the enemy army are engaged in the most violent struggle among themselves and that the sale of all their hundred bales is absolutely certain, will take good care not to fall out among themselves and depress the price of cotton at the moment when their adversaries are competing with one another to force it up. Thus, peace suddenly descends on the army of the sellers. They stand facing the buyers as *one* man, fold their arms philosophically, and there would be no bounds to their demands were it not that the offers of even the most persistent and eager buyers have very definite limits.

If, therefore, the supply of a commodity is lower than the demand for it, then only slight competition, or none at all, takes place among the sellers. In the same proportion as this competition decreases, competition increases among the buyers. The result is a more or less considerable rise in commodity prices.

It is well known that the reverse case with a reverse result occurs more frequently. Considerable surplus of supply over demand; desperate competition among the sellers; lack of buyers; disposal of goods at ridiculously low prices.

But what is the meaning of a rise, a fall in prices; what is the meaning of high price, low price? A grain of sand is high when examined through a microscope, and a tower is low when compared with a mountain. And if price is determined by the relation between demand and supply, what determines the relation between demand and supply?

Let us turn to the first bourgeois we meet. He will not reflect for an instant but, like another Alexander the Great, will cut this metaphysical knot with the multiplication table. If the production of the goods which I sell has cost me 100 francs, he will tell us, and if I get 110 francs from the sale of these goods, within the year of course—then that is sound, honest, legitimate profit. But if I get in exchange 120 or 130 francs, that is a high profit; and if I get as much as 200 francs, that would be an extraordinary, an enormous profit. What, therefore, serves the bourgeois as his measure of profit? The *cost of production* of his commodity. If he receives in exchange for this commodity an amount of other commodities which it has cost less to produce, he has lost. If he receives in exchange for his commodity an amount of other commodities the production of which has cost more, he has gained. And he calculates the fall or rise of the profit according to the degree in which the exchange value of his commodity stands below or above zero—the *cost of production.*

We have thus seen how the changing relation of demand and supply causes now a rise and now a fall of prices, now high, now low prices.

If the price of a commodity rises considerably because of inadequate supply or disproportionate increase of the demand, the price of some other commodity must necessarily have fallen proportionately, for the price of a commodity only expresses in money the ratio in which other commodities are given in exchange for it. If, for example, the price of a yard of silk material rises from five francs to six francs, the price of silver in relation to silk material has fallen and likewise the prices of all other commodities that have remained at their old prices have fallen in relation to the silk. One has to give a larger amount of them in exchange to get the same amount of silks.

What will be the consequence of the rising price of a commodity? A mass of capital will be thrown into that flourishing branch of industry and this influx of capital into the domain of the favoured industry will continue until it yields the ordinary profits or, rather, until the price of its products, through over-production, sinks below the cost of production.

Conversely, if the price of a commodity falls below its cost of production, capital will be withdrawn from the production of this commodity. Except in the case of a branch of industry which has become obsolete and must, therefore, perish, the production of such a commodity, that is, its supply, will go on decreasing owing to this flight of capital until it corresponds to the demand, and consequently its price is again on a level with its cost of production or, rather, until the supply has sunk below the demand, that is, until its price rises again above its cost of production, for the *current price of a commodity is always either above or below its cost of production.*

We see how capital continually migrates in and out, out of the domain of one industry into that of another. High prices bring too great an immigration and low prices too great an emigration.

We could show from another point of view how not only supply but also demand is determined by the cost of production. But this would take us too far away from our subject.

We have just seen how the fluctuations of supply and demand continually bring the price of a commodity back to the cost of production. *The real price of a commodity, it is true, is always above or below its cost of production; but rise and fall reciprocally balance each other,* so that within a certain period of time, taking the ebb and flow of the industry together, commodities are exchanged for one another in accordance with their cost of production, their price, therefore, being determined by their cost of production.

This determination of price by cost of production is not to be understood in the sense of the economists. The economists say that the *average price* of commodities is equal to the cost of production; that this is a *law.* The anarchical movement, in which rise is compensated by fall and fall by rise, is regarded by them as chance. With just as much right one could regard the fluctuations as the law and the determination by the cost of production as chance, as has actually been done by other economists. But it is solely these fluctuations, which, looked at more closely, bring with them the most fearful devastations and, like earthquakes, cause bourgeois society to tremble to its foundations—it is solely in the course of these fluctuations that prices are determined by the cost of production. The total movement of this disorder is its order. In the course of this industrial anarchy, in this movement in a circle, competition compensates, so to speak, for one excess by means of another.

We see, therefore, that the price of a commodity is determined by its cost of production in such manner that the periods in which the price of this commodity rises above its cost of production are compensated by the periods in which it sinks below the cost of production, and vice versa. This does not hold good, of course, for separate, particular industrial products but only for the whole branch of industry. Consequently, it also does not hold good for the individual industrialist but only for the whole class of industrialists.

The determination of price by the cost of production is equivalent to the determination of price by the labour time necessary for the manufacture of a commodity, for the cost of production consists of 1) raw materials and instruments of labour,[a] that is, of industrial products the production of which has cost a certain amount of labour days and which, therefore, represent a certain amount of labour time, and 2) of direct labour, the measure of which is, precisely, time.

---

[a] The 1891 edition has "depreciation of instruments" instead of "instruments of labour".— *Ed.*

Now, the same general laws that regulate the price of commodities in general of course also regulate *wages*, the *price of labour*.

Wages will rise and fall according to the relation of demand and supply, according to the turn taken by the competition between the buyers of labour, the capitalists, and the sellers of labour,[a] the workers. The fluctuations in wages correspond in general to the fluctuations in prices of commodities. *Within these fluctuations, however, the price of labour will be determined by the cost of production, by the labour time necessary to produce this commodity—labour.*[b]

*What, then, is the cost of production of labour*[c]*?*

*It is the cost required for maintaining the worker as a worker and for developing him into a worker.*

The less the period of training, therefore, that any work requires the smaller is the cost of production of the worker and the lower is the price of his labour, his wages. In those branches of industry in which hardly any period of apprenticeship is required and where the mere bodily existence of the worker suffices, the cost necessary for his production is almost confined to the commodities necessary for keeping him alive.[c] The *price of his labour* will, therefore, be determined by the *price of the necessary means of subsistence*.

Another consideration, however, also comes in.

The manufacturer in calculating his cost of production and, accordingly, the price of the products takes into account the wear and tear of the instruments of labour. If, for example, a machine costs him 1,000 francs and wears out in ten years, he adds 100 francs annually to the price of the commodities so as to be able to replace the worn-out machine by a new one at the end of ten years. In the same way, in calculating the cost of production of simple labour,[d] there must be included the cost of reproduction, whereby the race of workers is enabled to multiply and to replace worn-out workers by new ones. Thus the depreciation of the worker is taken into account in the same way as the depreciation of the machine.

The cost of production of simple labour, therefore, amounts to the *cost of existence and reproduction of the worker*. The price of this cost of existence and reproduction constitutes wages. Wages so determined are called the *wage minimum*. This wage minimum, like the determination of the price of commodities by the cost of production

---

[a] The 1891 edition has "the buyers of labour power" and "the sellers of labour power" instead of "the buyers of labour" and "the sellers of labour".— *Ed.*

[b] The 1891 edition has "*labour power*" instead of "*labour*".— *Ed.*

[c] In the 1891 edition the words "and capable of working" are added here.— *Ed.*

[d] The 1891 edition has here and in the next paragraph "simple labour power" instead of "simple labour".— *Ed.*

in general, does not hold good for the *single individual* but for the *species*. Individual workers, millions of workers, do not get enough to be able to exist and reproduce themselves; but the *wages of the whole working class* level down, within their fluctuations, to this minimum.

Now that we have arrived at an understanding of the most general laws which regulate wages like the price of any other commodity, we can go into our subject more specifically.

[III]

[*Neue Rheinische Zeitung* No. 266, April 7, 1849]

*Cologne*, April 6. Capital consists of raw materials, instruments of labour and means of subsistence of all kinds, which are utilised in order to produce new raw materials, new instruments of labour and new means of subsistence. All these component parts of capital are creations of labour, products of labour, *accumulated labour*. Accumulated labour which serves as a means of new production is capital.

So say the economists.

What is a Negro slave? A man of the black race. The one explanation is as good as the other.

A Negro is a Negro. He only becomes a *slave* in certain relations. A cotton-spinning jenny is a machine for spinning cotton. It becomes *capital* only in certain relations. Torn from these relationships it is no more capital than *gold* in itself is *money* or sugar the *price* of sugar.

In production, men enter into relation not only with nature.[a] They produce only by co-operating in a certain way and mutually exchanging their activities. In order to produce, they enter into definite connections and relations with one another and only within these social connections and relations does their relation with nature,[b] does production, take place.

These social relations into which the producers enter with one another, the conditions under which they exchange their activities and participate in the whole act of production, will naturally vary according to the character of the means of production. With the invention of a new instrument of warfare, firearms, the whole

---

[a] The 1891 edition has "not only act on nature but also on one another" instead of "enter into relation not only with nature".— *Ed.*

[b] The 1891 edition has "action on nature" instead of "relation with nature".— *Ed.*

internal organisation of the army necessarily changed; the relationships within which individuals can constitute an army and act as an army were transformed and the relations of different armies to one another also changed.

*Thus* the social relations within which individuals produce, *the social relations of production, change, are transformed, with the change and development of the material means of production, the productive forces. The relations of production in their totality constitute what* are called *the social relations, society,* and, specifically, a society at *a definite stage of historical development,* a society with a peculiar, distinctive character. Ancient society, feudal society, bourgeois society are such totalities of production relations, each of which at the same time denotes a special stage of development in the history of mankind.

*Capital,* also, is a social relation of production. It is a *bourgeois production relation,* a production relation of bourgeois society. Are not the means of subsistence, the instruments of labour, the raw materials of which capital consists, produced and accumulated under given social conditions, in definite social relations? Are they not utilised for new production under given social conditions, in definite social relations? And is it not just this definite social character which turns the products serving for new production into *capital?*

Capital consists not only of means of subsistence, instruments of labour and raw materials, not only of material products; it consists just as much of *exchange values.* All the products of which it consists are *commodities.* Capital is, therefore, not only a sum of material products; it is a sum of commodities, of exchange values, of *social magnitudes.*

Capital remains the same, whether we put cotton in place of wool, rice in place of wheat or steamships in place of railways, provided only that the cotton, the rice, the steamships—the body of capital—have the same exchange value, the same price as the wool, the wheat, the railways in which it was previously incorporated. The body of capital can change continually without the capital suffering the slightest alteration.

But while all capital is a sum of commodities, that is, of exchange values, not every sum of commodities, of exchange values, is capital.

Every sum of exchange values is an exchange value. Every separate exchange value is a sum of exchange values. For instance, a house that is worth 1,000 francs is an exchange value of 1,000 francs. A piece of paper worth a centime[a] is a sum of exchange values of

---

[a] In the 1891 edition the word "pfennig" is used here and below instead of "centime".— *Ed.*

one-hundred hundredths of a centime. Products which are exchangeable for others are *commodities*. The particular ratio in which they are exchangeable constitutes their *exchange value* or, expressed in money, their *price*. The quantity of these products can change nothing in their quality of being *commodities* or representing an *exchange value* or having a definite *price*. Whether a tree is large or small it is a tree. Whether we exchange iron for other products in ounces or in hundredweights, does this make any difference in its character as commodity, as exchange value? It is a commodity of greater or lesser value, of higher or lower price, depending upon the quantity.

How, then, does any amount of commodities, of exchange values, become capital?

By maintaining and multiplying itself as an independent social power, that is, as the power *of a portion of society*, by means of its *exchange for direct, living labour*.[a] The existence of a class which possesses nothing but its capacity to labour is a necessary prerequisite of capital.

It is only the domination of accumulated, past, materialised labour over direct, living labour that turns accumulated labour into capital.

Capital does not consist in accumulated labour serving living labour as a means for new production. It consists in living labour serving accumulated labour as a means for maintaining and multiplying the exchange value of the latter.

What takes place in the exchange between capital and wage labour[b]?

The worker receives means of subsistence in exchange for his labour,[c] but the capitalist receives in exchange for his means of subsistence labour, the productive activity of the worker, the creative power whereby the worker not only replaces what he consumes but gives to the accumulated labour a greater value than it previously possessed. The worker receives a part of the available means of subsistence from the capitalist. For what purpose do these means of subsistence serve him? For immediate consumption. As soon, however, as I consume the means of subsistence, they are irretrievably lost to me unless I use the time during which I am kept alive by them in order to produce new means of subsistence, in order during consumption to create by my labour new values in place of

---

[a] The 1891 edition has "*labour power*" instead of "*labour*".— Ed.
[b] The 1891 edition has "between capitalist and wage-worker" instead of "between capital and wage labour".— Ed.
[c] The 1891 edition has "labour power" instead of "labour".— Ed.

the values which perish in being consumed. But it is just this noble reproductive power that the worker surrenders to capital in exchange for means of subsistence received. He has, therefore, lost it for himself.

Let us take an example: a tenant farmer gives his day labourer five silver groschen a day. For these five silver groschen the labourer works all day on the farmer's field and thus secures him a return of ten silver groschen. The farmer not only gets the value replaced that he has to give the day labourer; he doubles it. He has therefore employed, consumed, the five silver groschen that he gave to the labourer in a fruitful, productive manner. He has bought with the five silver groschen just that labour and power of the labourer which produces agricultural products of double value and makes ten silver groschen out of five. The day labourer, on the other hand, receives in place of his productive power, the effect of which he has bargained away to the farmer, five silver groschen, which he exchanges for means of subsistence, and these he consumes with greater or less rapidity. The five silver groschen have, therefore, been consumed in a double way, *reproductively* for capital, for they have been exchanged for labour power which produced ten silver groschen, *unproductively* for the worker, for they have been exchanged for means of subsistence which have disappeared forever and the value of which he can only recover by repeating the same exchange with the farmer. *Thus capital presupposes wage labour; wage labour presupposes capital. They reciprocally condition the existence of each other; they reciprocally bring forth each other.*

Does a worker in a cotton factory produce merely cotton textiles? No, he produces capital. He produces values which serve afresh to command his labour and by means of it to create new values.

Capital can only increase by exchanging itself for labour,[a] by calling wage labour to life. The wage labour[b] can only be exchanged for capital by increasing capital, by strengthening the power whose slave it is. *Hence, increase of capital is increase of the proletariat, that is, of the working class.*

The interests of the capitalist and those of the worker are, therefore, *one and the same*, assert the bourgeois and their economists. Indeed! The worker perishes if capital does not employ him. Capital perishes if it does not exploit labour,[a] and in order to exploit it, it must buy it. The faster capital intended for production, productive

---

[a] The 1891 edition has "labour power" instead of "labour".—*Ed.*

[b] The 1891 edition has "The labour power of the wage-worker" instead of "The wage labour".—*Ed.*

capital, increases, the more, therefore, industry prospers, the more the bourgeoisie enriches itself and the better business is, the more workers does the capitalist need, the more dearly does the worker sell himself.

The indispensable condition for a tolerable situation of the worker is, therefore, the *fastest possible growth of productive capital*.

But what is the growth of productive capital? Growth of the power of accumulated labour over living labour. Growth of the domination of the bourgeoisie over the working class. If wage labour produces the wealth of others that rules over it, the power that is hostile to it, capital, then the means of employment [*Beschäftigungsmittel*], that is, the means of subsistence, flow back to it from this hostile power, on condition that it makes itself afresh into a part of capital, into the lever which hurls capital anew into an accelerated movement of growth.

*To say that the interests of capital and those of labour*[a] *are one and the same is only to say that capital and wage labour are two sides of one and the same relation. The one conditions the other, just as usurer and squanderer condition each other.*

As long as the wage-worker is a wage-worker his lot depends upon capital. That is the much-vaunted community of interests between worker and capitalist.

---

[a] The 1891 edition has "*workers*" instead of "*labour*".— *Ed.*

[IV]

[*Neue Rheinische Zeitung* No. 267, April 8, 1849]

*Cologne*, April 7. If capital grows, the mass of wage labour grows, the number of wage-workers grows; in a word, the domination of capital extends over a greater number of individuals. Let us assume the most favourable case: when productive capital grows, the demand for labour grows; consequently, the price of labour, wages, goes up.

A house may be large or small; as long as the surrounding houses are equally small it satisfies all social demands for a dwelling. But let a palace arise beside the little house, and it shrinks from a little house to a hut. The little house shows now that its owner has only very slight or no demands to make; and however high it may shoot up in the course of civilisation, if the neighbouring palace grows to an equal or even greater extent, the occupant of the relatively small house will feel more and more uncomfortable, dissatisfied and cramped within its four walls.

A noticeable increase in wages presupposes a rapid growth of productive capital. The rapid growth of productive capital brings about an equally rapid growth of wealth, luxury, social wants, social enjoyments. Thus, although the enjoyments of the worker have risen, the social satisfaction that they give has fallen in comparison with the increased enjoyments of the capitalist, which are inaccessible to the worker, in comparison with the state of development of society in general. Our desires and pleasures spring from society; we measure them, therefore, by society and not by the objects which serve for their satisfaction. Because they are of a social nature, they are of a relative nature.

In general, wages are determined not only by the amount of commodities for which I can exchange them. They embody various relations.

What the workers receive for their labour[a] is, in the first place, a definite sum of money. Are wages determined only by this money price?

In the sixteenth century, the gold and silver circulating in Europe increased as a result of the discovery of America.[b] Hence, the value of gold and silver fell in relation to other commodities. The workers received the same amount of coined silver for their labour as before. The money price of their labour remained the same, and yet their wages had fallen, for in exchange for the same quantity of silver they received a smaller amount of other commodities. This was one of the circumstances which furthered the growth of capital and the rise of the bourgeoisie in the sixteenth century.

Let us take another case. In the winter of 1847, as a result of a crop failure, the most indispensable means of subsistence, cereals, meat, butter, cheese, etc., rose considerably in price. Assume that the workers received the same sum of money for their labour as before. Had not their wages fallen? Of course. For the same money they received less bread, meat, etc., in exchange. Their wages had fallen, not because the value of silver had diminished, but because the value of the means of subsistence had increased.

Assume, finally, that the money price of labour remains the same while all agricultural and manufactured goods have fallen in price owing to the employment of new machinery, a favourable season, etc. For the same money the workers can now buy more commodities of all kinds. Their wages, therefore, have risen, just because the money value of their wages has not changed.

Thus, the money price of labour, nominal wages, do not coincide with real wages, that is, with the sum of commodities which is actually given in exchange for the wages. If, therefore, we speak of a rise or fall of wages, we must keep in mind not only the money price of labour, the nominal wages.

But neither nominal wages, that is, the sum of money for which the worker sells himself to the capitalist, nor real wages, that is, the sum of commodities which he can buy for this money, exhaust the relations contained in wages.

---

[a] The 1891 edition has here and in the two paragraphs below "labour power" instead of "labour".— Ed.

[b] The 1891 edition has "the discovery of richer and more easily worked mines in America" instead of "the discovery of America".— Ed.

Wages are, above all, also determined by their relation to the gain, to the profit of the capitalist—comparative, relative wages.

Real wages express the price of labour in relation to the price of other commodities; relative wages, on the other hand, express the price of direct labour in relation to the price of accumulated labour, the relative value of wage labour and capital, the reciprocal value of the capitalist and worker.[a]

Real wages may remain the same, they may even rise, and yet relative wages may fall. Let us suppose, for example, that all means of subsistence have gone down in price by two-thirds while wages per day have only fallen by one-third, that is to say, for example, from three francs to two francs. Although the worker can command a greater amount of commodities with these two francs than he previously could with three francs, yet his wages have gone down in relation to the profit of the capitalist. The profit of the capitalist (for example, the manufacturer) has increased by one franc; that is, for a smaller sum of exchange values which he pays to the worker, the latter must produce a greater amount of exchange values than before. The value of capital relative to the value of labour has risen.[b] The division of social wealth between capital and labour has become still more unequal. With the same capital, the capitalist commands a greater quantity of labour. The power of the capitalist class over the working class has grown, the social position of the worker has

---

[a] In the 1891 edition Engels changed the part of the paragraph beginning with the words "relative wages" in the following way: "relative wages, on the other hand, express the share of direct labour in the new value it has created in relation to the share which falls to accumulated labour, to capital.

"We said above, page 14 [see this volume, p. 202]: 'Wages are not the worker's share in the commodity produced by him. Wages are the part of already existing commodities with which the capitalist buys for himself a definite amount of productive labour power.' But the capitalist must replace these wages out of the price at which he sells the product produced by the worker; he must replace it in such a way that there remains to him, as a rule, a surplus over the cost of production expended by him, a profit. For the capitalist, the selling price of the commodity produced by the worker is divided into three parts: *first*, replacement of the price of the raw materials advanced by him together with replacement of the depreciation of the tools, machinery and other means of labour also advanced by him; *secondly*, the replacement of the wages advanced by him, and *thirdly*, the surplus left over, the capitalist's profit. While the first part only replaces *previously existing values*, it is clear that both the replacement of the wages and also the surplus profit of the capitalist are, on the whole, taken from the *new value created by the worker's labour* and added to the raw materials. And *in this sense*, in order to compare them with one another, we can regard both wages and profit as shares in the product of the worker."—*Ed.*

[b] In the 1891 edition this sentence reads: "The share of capital relative to the share of labour has risen."—*Ed.*

deteriorated, has been depressed one step further below that of the capitalist.

What, then, is *the general law which determines the fall and rise of wages and profit in their reciprocal relation?*

*They stand in inverse ratio to each other. The exchange value of capital,*[a] *profit, rises in the same proportion as the exchange value of labour,*[b] *wages, falls, and vice versa. Profit rises to the extent that wages fall; it falls to the extent that wages rise.*

The objection will, perhaps, be made that the capitalist can profit by a favourable exchange of his products with other capitalists, by increase of the demand for his commodity, whether as a result of the opening of new markets, or as a result of a momentarily increased demand in the old markets, etc.; that the capitalist's profit can, therefore, increase by overreaching other capitalists, independently of the rise and fall of wages, of the exchange value of labour[c]; or that the capitalist's profit may also rise owing to the improvement of the instruments of labour, a new application of natural forces, etc.

First of all, it will have to be admitted that the result remains the same, although it is brought about in reverse fashion. True, the profit has not risen because wages have fallen, but wages have fallen because the profit has risen. With the same amount of labour,[d] the capitalist has acquired a greater amount of exchange values, without having paid more for the labour on that account; that is, therefore, labour is paid less in proportion to the net profit which it yields the capitalist.

In addition, we recall that, in spite of the fluctuations in prices of commodities, the average price of every commodity, the ratio in which it is exchanged for other commodities, is determined by its *cost of production.* Hence the overreachings within the capitalist class necessarily balance one another. The improvement of machinery, new application of natural forces in the service of production, enable a larger amount of products to be created in a given period of time with the same amount of labour and capital, but not by any means a larger amount of exchange values. If, by the use of the spinning jenny, I can turn out twice as much yarn in an hour as before its

---

[a] The 1891 edition has "*Capital's share*" instead of "*The exchange value of capital*".— *Ed.*

[b] The 1891 edition has "*labour's share*" instead of "*the exchange value of labour*".— *Ed.*

[c] The 1891 edition has "labour power" instead of "labour".— *Ed.*

[d] The 1891 edition has "other people's labour" instead of "labour".— *Ed.*

invention, say, one hundred pounds instead of fifty, then[a] I will receive for these hundred pounds no more commodities in exchange than formerly for the fifty pounds, because the cost of production has fallen by one-half, or because I can deliver double the product at the same cost.

Finally, in whatever proportion the capitalist class, the bourgeoisie, whether of one country or of the whole world market, shares the net profit of production within itself, the total amount of this net profit always consists only of the amount by which, on the whole, accumulated labour has been increased by living labour.[b] This total amount grows, therefore, in the proportion in which labour augments capital, that is, in the proportion in which profit rises in comparison with wages.

We see, therefore, that even if we remain *within the relation of capital and wage labour, the interests of capital and the interests of wage labour are diametrically opposed.*

A rapid increase of capital is equivalent to a rapid increase of profit. Profit can only increase rapidly if the exchange value[c] of labour, if relative wages, decrease just as rapidly. Relative wages can fall although real wages rise simultaneously with nominal wages, with the money value of labour, if they do not rise, however, in the same proportion as profit. If, for instance, in times when business is good, wages rise by five per cent, profit on the other hand by thirty per cent, then the comparative, the relative wages, have *not increased* but *decreased.*

Thus if the income of the worker increases with the rapid growth of capital, the social gulf that separates the worker from the capitalist increases at the same time, and the power of capital over labour, the dependence of labour on capital, likewise increases at the same time.

To say that the worker has an interest in the rapid growth of capital is only to say that the more rapidly the worker increases the wealth of others, the richer will be the crumbs that fall to him, the greater is the number of workers that can be employed and called into existence, the more can the mass of slaves dependent on capital be increased.

We have thus seen that:

Even the *most favourable situation* for the working class, the *most rapid possible growth of capital,* however much it may improve the material existence of the worker, does not remove the antagonism

---

[a] In the 1891 edition the words "in the long run" are added here.— *Ed.*

[b] The 1891 edition has "direct labour" instead of "living labour".— *Ed.*

[c] The 1891 edition has "price" instead of "exchange value".— *Ed.*

between his interests and the interests of the bourgeoisie, the interests of the capitalist. *Profit and wages* remain as before in *inverse proportion.*

If capital is growing rapidly, wages may rise; the profit of capital rises incomparably more rapidly. The material position of the worker has improved, but at the cost of his social position. The social gulf that divides him from the capitalist has widened.

Finally:

To say that the most favourable condition for wage labour is the most rapid possible growth of productive capital is only to say that the more rapidly the working class increases and enlarges the power that is hostile to it, the wealth that does not belong to it and that rules over it, the more favourable will be the conditions under which it is allowed to labour anew at increasing bourgeois wealth, at enlarging the power of capital, content with forging for itself the golden chains by which the bourgeoisie drags it in its train.

[V]

[*Neue Rheinische Zeitung* No. 269, April 11, 1849]

*Cologne,* April 10. Are *growth of productive capital and rise of wages* really so inseparably connected as the bourgeois economists maintain? We must not take their word for it. We must not even believe them when they say that the fatter capital is, the better will its slave be fed. The bourgeoisie is too enlightened, it calculates too well, to share the prejudices of the feudal lord who makes a display by the brilliance of his retinue. The conditions of existence of the bourgeoisie compel it to calculate.

We must, therefore, examine more closely:

*How does the growth of productive capital affect wages?*

If, on the whole, the productive capital of bourgeois society grows, a *more manifold* accumulation of labour takes place. The capitals increase in number and extent. The *numerical increase* of the capitals increases the *competition between the capitalists.* The *increasing extent* of the capitals provides the means for *bringing more powerful labour armies with more gigantic instruments of war into the industrial battlefield.*

One capitalist can drive another from the field and capture his capital only by selling more cheaply. In order to be able to sell more cheaply without ruining himself, he must produce more cheaply, that is, raise the productive power of labour as much as possible. But the productive power of labour is raised, above all, by *a greater division of labour,* by a universal introduction and continual improvement of *machinery.* The greater the labour army among whom labour is divided, the more gigantic the scale on which machinery is introduced, the more does the cost of production proportionately decrease, the more fruitful is labour. Hence, a general rivalry arises among the capitalists to increase the division of labour and machinery and to exploit them on the greatest possible scale.

If, now, by a greater division of labour, by the utilisation of new machines and their improvement, by more profitable and extensive exploitation of natural forces, one capitalist has found the means of producing with the same amount of labour or of accumulated labour a greater amount of products, of commodities, than his competitors, if he can, for example, produce a whole yard of linen in the same labour time in which his competitors weave half a yard, how will this capitalist operate?

He could continue to sell half a yard of linen at the old market price; this would, however, be no means of driving his opponents from the field and of enlarging his own sales. But in the same measure in which his production has expanded, his need to sell has also increased. The more powerful and costly means of production that he has called into life *enable* him, indeed, to sell his commodities more cheaply, they *compel* him, however, at the same time to sell more commodities, to conquer a much *larger* market for his commodities; consequently, our capitalist will sell his half yard of linen more cheaply than his competitors.

The capitalist will not, however, sell a whole yard as cheaply as his competitors sell half a yard, although the production of the whole yard does not cost him more than the half yard costs the others. Otherwise he would not gain anything extra but only get back the cost of production by the exchange. His possibly greater income would be derived from the fact of having set a larger capital into motion, but not from having made more of his capital than the others. Moreover, he attains the object he wishes to attain, if he puts the price of his goods only a small percentage lower than that of his competitors. He drives them from the field, he wrests from them at least a part of their sales, by *underselling them.* And, finally, it will be remembered that the current price always stands *above* or *below the cost of production,* according to whether the sale of the commodity occurs in a favourable or unfavourable industrial season. The percentage at which the capitalist who has employed new and more fruitful means of production sells above his real cost of production will vary, depending upon whether the market price of a yard of linen stands below or above its hitherto customary cost of production.

However, the *privileged position* of our capitalist is not of long duration; other competing capitalists introduce the same machines, the same division of labour, introduce them on the same or on a larger scale, and this introduction will become so general that the price of linen is reduced not only *below its old,* but *below its new cost of production.*

The capitalists find themselves, therefore, in the same position relative to one another as *before* the introduction of the new means of production, and if they are able to supply by these means double the product at the same price, they are *now* forced to supply the double product *below* the old price. On the basis of this new cost of production, the same game begins again. More division of labour, more machinery, enlarged scale of exploitation of division of labour and machinery. And again competition brings the same counteraction against this result.

We see how in this way the mode of production and the means of production are continually transformed, revolutionised, how *the division of labour is necessarily followed by greater division of labour, the application of machinery by still greater application of machinery, work on a large scale by work on a still larger scale.*

That is the law which again and again throws bourgeois production out of its old course and which compels capital to intensify the productive forces of labour, *because* it has intensified them — the law which gives capital no rest and continually whispers in its ear: "Go on! Go on!"

This law is none other than that which, within the fluctuations of trade periods, necessarily levels out the price of a commodity to its *cost of production.*

However powerful the means of production which a capitalist brings into the field, competition will make these means of production universal and from the moment when it has made them universal, the only result of the greater fruitfulness of his capital is that he must now supply *for the same price* ten, twenty, a hundred times as much as before. But, as he must sell perhaps a thousand times as much as before in order to outweigh the lower selling price by the greater amount of the product sold, because a more extensive sale is now necessary, not only in order to make profit[a] but in order to replace the cost of production — the instrument of production itself, as we have seen, becomes more and more expensive — and because this mass sale becomes a question of life and death not only for him but also for his rivals, the old struggle begins again *all the more violently the more fruitful the already discovered means of production are. The division of labour and the application of machinery, therefore, will go on anew on an incomparably greater scale.*

---

[a] The 1891 edition has "more profit" instead of "profit".— *Ed.*

Whatever the power of the means of production employed may be, competition seeks to rob capital of the golden fruits of this power by bringing the price of the commodities back to the cost of production, by thus making cheaper production—the supply of ever greater amounts of products for the same total price—an imperative law to the same extent as production can be cheapened, that is, as more can be produced with the same amount of labour. Thus the capitalist would have won nothing by his own exertions but the obligation to supply more in the same labour time, in a word, *more difficult conditions for the augmentation of the value of his capital.* While, therefore, competition continually pursues him with its law of the cost of production and every weapon that he forges against his rivals recoils against himself, the capitalist continually tries to get the better of competition by incessantly introducing new machines, more expensive, it is true, but producing more cheaply, and new division of labour in place of the old, and by not waiting until competition has rendered the new ones obsolete.

If now we picture to ourselves this feverish *simultaneous* agitation on the *whole world market,* it will be comprehensible how the growth, accumulation and concentration of capital results in an uninterrupted division of labour, and in the application of new and the perfecting of old machinery precipitately and on an ever more gigantic scale.

*But how do these circumstances, which are inseparable from the growth of productive capital, affect the determination of wages?*

The greater *division of labour* enables *one* worker to do the work of five, ten or twenty; it therefore multiplies competition among the workers fivefold, tenfold and twentyfold. The workers do not only compete by one selling himself cheaper than another; they compete by *one* doing the work of five, ten, twenty; and the *division of labour,* introduced by capital and continually increased, compels the workers to compete among themselves in this way.

Further, as the *division of labour* increases, labour *is simplified.* The *special skill* of the worker becomes worthless. He becomes transformed into a simple, monotonous productive force that does not have to use intense bodily or intellectual faculties. His labour becomes a labour that anyone can perform. Hence, competitors crowd upon him on all sides, and besides we remind the reader that the more simple and easily learned the labour is, the lower the cost of production needed to master it, the lower do wages sink, for, like the price of every other commodity, they are determined by the cost of production.

*Therefore, as labour becomes more unsatisfying, more repulsive, competition increases and wages decrease.* The worker tries to keep up the amount of his wages by working more, whether by working longer hours or by producing more in one hour. Driven by want, therefore, he still further increases the evil effects of the division of labour. The result is that *the more he works the less wages he receives,* and for the simple reason that he competes to that extent with his fellow workers, hence makes them into so many competitors who offer themselves on just the same bad terms as he does himself, and that, therefore, in the last resort he *competes with himself, with himself as a member of the working class.*

*Machinery* brings about the same results on a much greater scale, by replacing skilled workers by unskilled, men by women, adults by children. It brings about the same results, where it is newly introduced, by throwing the hand workers onto the streets in masses, and, where it is developed, improved and replaced by more productive machinery, by discharging workers in smaller batches. We have portrayed above, in a hasty sketch, the industrial war of the capitalists among themselves; *this war has the peculiarity that its battles are won less by recruiting than by discharging the army of labour. The generals, the capitalists, compete with one another as to who can discharge most soldiers of industry.*

The economists tell us, it is true, that the workers rendered superfluous by machinery find *new* branches of employment.

They dare not assert directly that the same workers who are discharged find places in the new branches of labour. The facts cry out too loudly against this lie. They really only assert that new means of employment will open up for *other component sections of the working class,* for instance, for the portion of the young generation of workers that was ready to enter the branch of industry which has gone under. That is, of course, a great consolation for the disinherited workers. The capitalist gentlemen will never want for fresh exploitable flesh and blood, and will let the dead bury their dead. This is a consolation which the bourgeois give themselves rather than one which they give the workers. If the whole class of wage-workers were to be abolished owing to machinery, how dreadful that would be for capital which, without wage labour, ceases to be capital!

Let us suppose, however, that those directly driven out of their jobs by machinery, and the entire section of the new generation that was already on the watch for this employment, *find a new occupation.* Does any one imagine that it will be as highly paid as that which has been lost? *That would contradict all the laws of economics.* We have seen how modern industry always brings with it the substitution of a more simple, subordinate occupation for the more complex and higher one.

How, then, could a mass of workers who have been thrown out of one branch of industry owing to machinery find refuge in another, unless the latter *is lower, worse paid?*

The workers who work in the manufacture of machinery itself have been cited as an exception. As soon as more machinery is demanded and used in industry, it is said, there must necessarily be an increase of machines, consequently of the manufacture of machines, and consequently of the employment of workers in the manufacture of machines; and the workers engaged in this branch of industry are claimed to be skilled, even educated workers.

Since the year 1840 this assertion, which even before was only half true, has lost all semblance of truth because ever more versatile machines have been employed in the manufacture of machinery, no more and no less than in the manufacture of cotton yarn, and the workers employed in the machine factories, confronted by highly elaborate machines, can only play the part of highly unelaborate machines.

But in place of the man who has been discharged owing to the machine, the factory employs maybe *three* children and *one* woman! And did not the man's wages have to suffice for the three children and a woman? Did not the minimum of wages have to suffice to maintain and to propagate the race? What, then, does this favourite bourgeois phrase prove? Nothing more than that now *four times* as many workers' lives are used up in order to gain a livelihood for *one* worker's family.

Let us sum up: *The more productive capital grows, the more the division of labour and the application of machinery expands. The more the division of labour and the application of machinery expands, the more competition among the workers expands and the more their wages contract.*

In addition, the working class gains recruits from the *higher strata of society* also; a mass of small industrialists and small rentiers are hurled down into its ranks and have nothing better to do than urgently stretch out their arms alongside those of the workers. Thus the forest of uplifted arms demanding work becomes ever thicker, while the arms themselves become ever thinner.

That the small industrialist cannot survive in a war,[a] one of the first conditions of which is to produce on an ever greater scale, that is, precisely to be a large and not a small industrialist, is self-evident.

---

[a] The 1891 edition has "contest" instead of "war".— *Ed.*

That the interest on capital decreases in the same measure as the mass and number of capitals increase, as capital grows; that, therefore, the small rentier can no longer live on his interest but must throw himself into industry, and consequently, help to swell the ranks of the small industrialists and thereby of candidates for the proletariat—all this surely requires no further explanation.

Finally, as the capitalists are compelled, by the movement described above, to exploit the already existing gigantic means of production on a larger scale and to set in motion all the mainsprings of credit to this end, there is a corresponding increase in earthquakes,[a] in which the trading world can only maintain itself by sacrificing a part of wealth, of products and even of productive forces to the gods of the nether world—in a word, *crises* increase. They become more frequent and more violent, if only because, as the mass of production, and consequently the need for extended markets, grows, the world market becomes more and more contracted, fewer and fewer markets[b] remain available for exploitation, since every preceding crisis has subjected to world trade a market hitherto unconquered or only superficially exploited. But capital does not *live* only on labour. A lord, at once aristocratic and barbarous, it drags with it into the grave the corpses of its slaves, whole hecatombs of workers who perish in the crises. Thus we see: *if capital grows rapidly, competition among the workers grows incomparably more rapidly, that is, the means of employment, the means of subsistence, of the working class decrease proportionately so much the more, and, nevertheless, the rapid growth of capital is the most favourable condition for wage labour.*

(To be continued) [185]

Written by Marx on the basis of lectures delivered by him in the second half of December 1847

First published in the *Neue Rheinische Zeitung* Nos. 264-267 and 269, April 5-8 and 11, 1849

Printed according to the newspaper

---

[a] The 1891 edition has "industrial earthquakes" instead of "earthquakes".— *Ed.*
[b] The 1891 edition has "new markets" instead of "markets".— *Ed.*

# THE SOUTHERN SLAVS
# AND THE AUSTRIAN MONARCHY

Not a word from the theatre of war. Not a syllable confirming the fabulous report of Bem's crossing into Wallachia, which may now be regarded as pure martial-law rumour, since after the arrival of the alleged courier no Bulletin has appeared.

There is, on the other hand, interesting news of the Austrian Slavs. Among the *Czech* townspeople and peasants, says the Augsburg *Allgemeine Zeitung*,[a] *Kossuth*'s name is regarded with the same respect and wonder as Napoleon's, and people were arrested in Prague for raising a cheer for Kossuth. The *Südslavische Zeitung* writes from *Vinkovci*, March 24:

"Travellers today brought us the news that extraordinary excitement reigns in *Semlin*. Street processions in Hungarian costume, Hungarian freedom songs, *Eljens* and *Zivios*[b] for Kossuth resounding through the town."

Todorovich has withdrawn from Kanizsa to Kikinda (between the Theiss and the Maros), and has thus by no means united with Jellachich. The blockade of Szegedin and Theresiopel has therefore been *completely raised*. This retreat obviously took place as a result of the discontent among the Serbs.

The cause of this dampening down of the Serbian lust for plunder is Austria's vacillating policy, making promises to the Serbs today, to the Magyars tomorrow, and regarding the rich Hungarian aristocracy (which can easily be restored to power and influence again after an Austrian victory) as a better ally in the long run than the chaos of classes, interests and conditions of the South-Slav and especially the Serbian provinces.

---

[a] "Prag, 25. März," Augsburg *Allgemeine Zeitung* No. 91, April 1, 1849.— *Ed.*

[b] "Long live!" in Hungarian and Serbo-Croatian.— *Ed.*

For the amusement of our readers we print the latest martial-law rumour:

Kossuth is said to be involved in negotiations with the Government and to be making the following condition for Hungary's complete and immediate submission: the acceptance of the Constitution drafted by the Imperial Diet [186] for the whole monarchy and his appointment as the Governor of Hungary!!!

Baja has *not* yet been retaken, Nugent bombarded it in vain.

Bem has imposed a contribution of 100,000 florins on Hermannstadt. The Romanians are quite discouraged; a *Landsturm* can no longer be raised.

Written by Engels on April 4, 1849

First published in the supplement
to the *Neue Rheinische Zeitung* No. 264,
April 5, 1849

Printed according to the newspaper

Published in English for the first
time

# THE WAR IN HUNGARY

*Cologne*, April 5. It is a fact that the Austrians, when they win battles in Hungary, only do so because of the longer and more regular arms drill of their soldiers; they win them not *because* of their commanders but *in spite of their commanders*. The thoroughly exercised military drill and the coherent *compact mass* resulting from this is their only strength. This compact military mass has been employed by the generals from the inception of the war until now with a mediocrity, with a lack of talent which is quite unparalleled. There is no grand design, no daring, no dexterity in manoeuvres, no trace of a worked out plan, no attempt to surprise the enemy or to impress him. With a triviality of calculation which does not go beyond the four fundamentals of strategy (*s'il y en a*[a]), the Austrian armies keep marching directly toward the point to be conquered sticking as punctiliously as possible to a straight line, unconcerned about what is happening to the right or to the left of them, and if an unexpected manoeuvre by the Magyars throws them out of this line then they are at a loss and good for nothing until they have once again found some other straight line leading to their appointed goal. Nothing creates a more dreadful impression than to see that even the most unexpected and brilliant manoeuvres of the Hungarian generals are incapable of imparting even the slightest animating thought to the unwieldy body of the Austrian army and of inducing it to produce an adroit idea, however slight. It is nothing but the simple and honest old strategy of the Coburgs, Clerfayts, Wurmsers

---

[a] If such there be.— *Ed.*

& Co., of yore, which has, thank God, for about a hundred years been harping on the axiom that a straight line is the shortest distance between two points.

Thus while the Austrians slowly but by no means surely plod forward and demonstrate an unparalleled poverty of strategic thought, we find an astounding wealth of strategic genius at the head of the Magyar army. The whole campaign is conducted according to a plan whose mastery becomes daily more evident; and between the individual elements of this great plan a series of episodes occur each of which is more brilliantly contrived and more surprisingly and dextrously executed than the last. The Magyars, though inadequately drilled and armed, oppose everywhere the most subtle calculation, the most masterly use of the terrain, the clearest overall view of the situation and the most daring and swift execution to the indolent and mindless but well-drilled mass of the Austrian armies. Superiority in genius is here doing battle with superiority in numbers, weapons and arms drill. Observing the bold, rapid marches of the Magyar corps, it is hardly possible to grasp how an almost completely untrained, poorly armed and ill-equipped army can undertake such movements and carry them through to completion. We need only recall Görgey's brilliant march from Pest through the Slovakian mountain towns, along the Carpathians, through the Zips to the Theiss and from there back to within six miles[a] of Pest again, and Bem's repeated lightning triumphal expeditions through Transylvania.

Today's reports from the Theiss, admittedly unofficial but nevertheless coming unanimously from the most various sources and therefore less subject to doubt than all the martial-law bulletins, at last permit us to pass sound judgment on the latest movements between the Theiss and the Danube.

Once again these movements form one of the most brilliant and inspired manoeuvres perhaps ever to figure in the history of war. By means of manoeuvres whose design was as bold and superior as their execution was lightning fast, the Magyar commanders Görgey and Dembiński (and this manoeuvre is the best proof that he still holds his command) have completely disconcerted an army which would certainly have proved superior to them in regular, open pitched battle, they have driven it back a whole 20 miles, frustrated all its plans and even threatened its line of retreat.

The most recent dispositions of the two armies are known:

---

[a] See footnote on p. 20.— *Ed.*

The Magyars on and behind the Theiss: Görgey at Tokaj, Dembiński at Polgar and Tisza-Füred, Vetter at Szolnok, Damjanich at Szegedin.

The imperial forces on the opposite bank: Ramberg along the Hernad up to Miskolcz, Schlick from Miskolcz to Szegléd, Jellachich from Szegléd to Kecskemét and Felegyhaza.

Suddenly Görgey broke away from the Theiss, marched by way of a detour (evidently through the Zemplen comitat) north towards Kaschau and threw Ramberg's division (the Götz and Jablonowsky brigades) out of the Sáros and the Abauj comitat. Götz and Jablonowsky—at least so the Augsburg *Allgemeine Zeitung* would have it[a]—held Eperies and Kaschau, but on the other hand the open country was everywhere swept clean of imperial troops. Only stopping briefly Görgey now proceeded along the Hernad once more towards the south, driving the remnants of Ramberg's troops constantly before him, took Miskolcz and then headed west; by way of Rimaszombat he went to Losoncz, and took up a position on the Ipoly (Eipel) between Losoncz and Balassa-Gyarmat. His vanguard is said to have pushed forward as far as Nograd.

The heroic Ramberg beat a hasty retreat by way of Hatvan on the very worst roads to *Waitzen* on the Danube, *four miles above Pest.* There he immediately built a pontoon bridge to withdraw his corps to the right bank of the Danube and thus put the river between Görgey and himself.

While Görgey was advancing by way of Miskolcz, Dembiński crossed the Theiss at Czibakháza and with 30,000 men broke through Schlick's disposition at its weakest point between Jasz-Berény and the battlefield of Kapolna, marched through the middle of the country occupied by the enemy and linked up with Görgey on the other side of the Mátra mountains.

To cover Pest Schlick left part of his forces behind at Hatvan (the same place the Magyars had visited in February). With the other part he "pursued", as they say, Dembiński's army. What is meant by this "pursuit" is absolutely incomprehensible unless he is anxious to be cut off and thrown back against the Hernad into a purely Hungarian area.

At the same time Jellachich's army was being pushed back by Damjanich from Szegedin and Vetter from Szolnok. As is well known, Jellachich had occupied Kecskemét and advanced his headquarters another four miles to Felegyhaza. Damjanich expelled

---

[a] Engels refers to the article "Pesth, 27. März" in the Augsburg *Allgemeine Zeitung* No. 92, April 2, 1849.—*Ed.*

him from there, forced him to leave Kecskemét, defeated him at Nagy-Körös and drove him back to Szegléd. According to the latest reports Jellachich is said to have abandoned this place as well and withdrawn his headquarters to Pilis, *four miles from Pest.*

*Thus the Austrians are being driven back at all points,* and the theatre of war is again situated but a few miles from Pest.

But this time the Magyars are operating with completely different forces, and have taken up a disposition quite different from that of six weeks ago when they stood at Hatvan.

Then they were drawn up in a line from the Mátra mountains on the right to the Theiss on the left. To begin with they only had the aim of threatening Pest.

This time things are different. The main thing now is to relieve Komorn and support the insurrection on the right bank of the Danube in the rear of the imperial forces. Hence the much greater degree of daring and the much greater ingenuity in the co-ordination of the movements.

The Magyars are positioned in two long curved lines, the one drawn up to the north-east of Pest and the other to the south-east of it. The first extends from Erlau and Gyöngyös, occupied by Dembiński, to Balassa-Gyarmat and Neograd, where Görgey is. While Dembiński holds Schlick in check and threatens Pest, Görgey has driven Ramberg over the Danube and presents such a serious threat to the besieged area of Komorn, hardly two days' march distant, that troops from there have already been sent against him and the encirclement of the fortress is at present very slack. At the same time he is in a position to cause the adjoining Magyar comitats on the Danube, particularly Gran, to rise again in revolt, to interrupt river communications between Pest and the besieging army and, in the rear of the Austrians, to call into being an enemy who at the least will force them to weaken their main army. In the event of a defeat he once again has the possibility of a retreat into the Slovakian mountains.

The second Magyar army is positioned to the south-east of Pest, one flank on the Danube, the other on the Theiss, its centre in Kecskemét, Nagy-Körös, or perhaps by now already in Szegléd. This corps threatens Pest from the other side, and is equally capable of throwing auxiliary troops across the Danube into Stuhlweissenburg and the Tolna comitat to support the insurrection here too. Only some thousand Honveds[187] with light artillery and a few hussars would be needed to rouse the whole of the Bakony Forest from the Danube to the Raab into full rebellion in the rear of the main Austrian army, to isolate the besieging troops at Komorn and to necessitate the detachment of whole army corps against the rebels. Thus weakened, the imperial army would be unable to put up much resistance against the united Hungarian armies.

And the Hungarians undertake these rapid and daring marches at a time when, thanks to the bad weather and the muddy roads, the Austrian army cannot take a single step forward, but only steps backwards!

Incidentally, one can see from the whole design that something more serious is intended this time than last. Previously single corps, but now it is the whole main army of the Austrians that has been pressed back under the walls of Pest. Pest itself is obviously the goal. This is recognised very clearly in the town itself. The Hungarian banknotes[188] have *risen again*. The reserve has been returned to Pest from Gödöllő (three miles away) and its baggage carried over the Danube to Ofen. The garrison of Pest and Ofen was confined all day long to its barracks and to the citadel.

In short, the Austrians have been forced back towards Pest on all sides, the Magyar army is more concentrated than ever, Szegedin has been liberated, the link-up between Jellachich and the Serbs has been foiled, the siege area of Komorn has been breached, the mountain towns threatened, the guerillas in Slovakia and on the right bank of the Danube supported and Pest more seriously threatened than ever—these are the immediate results of this concentric movement of the four Magyar Theiss corps, its conception was as bold and skilful as its execution has been precise and rapid.

In *Transylvania* Bem's situation is also beginning to clarify. First of all Bem defeated Puchner and drove him to Hermannstadt. On March 10 he sent a representative under a flag of truce and demanded surrender. Instead of an answer the Russian general ordered the representative to be whipped with the knout. Thereupon Bem attacked and took the town on March 11. No quarter was given to the Russians, a revolutionary committee was set up and many Cossacks hanged. Puchner escaped to Wallachia, the Russian general is said to have remained. On March 14 Bem marched against Kronstadt. In the meantime 40,000-50,000 Russians marched in by way of the Roterturm and the Törzburg passes (near Kronstadt), attacked Bem and defeated him thanks to their double superiority in numbers. Bem withdrew into Szeklerland.[189] The story of the five hanged Polish officers has been confirmed; their names were Bilski, Prince Woroniecki, Dumanski, Podalecki and Wronski.[a] Moreover,

---

[a] "Wien, 31. März", Augsburg *Allgemeine Zeitung* No. 93, April 3, 1849. See also this volume, p. 190.— *Ed.*

another 70 or so officers and NCOs are said to have been hanged by the Russians. The rumour about Bem having been forced to enter Wallachia is scarcely mentioned any more; a second rumour sounds almost as wild, claiming that he has fled to the Magyar Theiss army. The terror inspired in the imperial forces by the name Bem is so great that they are already claiming that it was he who planned and commanded the daring move across the Theiss.

Nothing new from the Banat, except that Rukavina has *conceded* the Patriarch[a] *all his demands concerning Serbian nationhood.*

Komorn and Peterwardein are holding out. Welden himself has left for the former. *Nous verrons!*[b]

Written by Engels on April 5, 1849          Printed according to the newspaper

First published in the *Neue Rheinische*          Published in English for the first
*Zeitung* No. 265, April 6, 1849          time

---

[a] Rajachich.— *Ed.*
[b] We shall see!— *Ed.*

# FROM THE THEATRE OF WAR

No fresh news at all has arrived from the theatre of war. Only from Transylvania do we have two *Magyar* bulletins today, signed by Bem himself, brought by the Debreczin official *Közlöny*.[a]

"1. Hermannstadt Headquarters, March 15. In my dispatch of March 13 I had the fortune to declare that I had sent a corps to the Roterturm Pass (Vöröstorony) in order to sever as far as possible communications with Wallachia. This army corps was unable to advance very far, however, since the whole Austrian army was positioned in Frek, and thus only separated from the defile by a mountain ridge, and so the flank of my advancing troops was threatened. By way of a detour I gained control of this defile, however, and I shall not only hold it, but at the same time press the enemy towards Kronstadt, from where he would only be able to cross the Carpathians with great difficulty, if, that is, he should wish to escape into Wallachia. I shall commence these operations of war this very day.

"Yesterday our troops once again captured a staff officer, Colonel Kopet. The names of the two staff officers previously captured are Baron Berger (Lieutenant-Colonel) and Teichbert (Major).

"The capture of Hermannstadt was of inestimable value to us, a great number of weapons have fallen to us from all sides, while the vital artery of the enemy has been severed."

"2. Roterturm (Vöröstorony) Headquarters, March 16. My operations yesterday designed to dislodge the Russians from the Roterturm Pass were crowned by such good fortune that we had ejected the Russians from this strong position by 11 o'clock the same night. The 'March 15', the anniversary of the Liberty of Nations, could not have been celebrated in more worthy fashion.[190] Today at 5 o'clock in the afternoon the Russians have taken to the wildest headlong flight. Four Austrian generals: Puchner, Pfersmann, Gräser and Jovich have fled to Wallachia with approximately 3 companies. I myself have inspected the Roterturm Pass most carefully, and have made such arrangements that the Russians will find it hard to penetrate here again with hostile intent. I have dispatched another part of my army in pursuit of the Austrians, who according to the statements of prisoners of war are demoralised and making for Kronstadt in disorder. Their main force is at Fogaras, the rearguard, however, has

---

[a] The following passage is from *Közlöny* No. 59, March 22, 1849.— *Ed.*

just left Frek. The enemy had demolished the bridge over the Olt behind him, which hindered the energetic pursuit of him for a time. Now that the bridge has been rebuilt I shall continue the pursuit with the utmost vigour. I hope to take Kronstadt within 3 or 4 days, thereby the imperial Austrian army will be partly destroyed, and partly dispersed, and in any case rendered harmless as far as the internal tranquillity of this country is concerned. And then the return to obedience of those Wallachian bands which still operate in isolation will be so much the easier.

"*Post scriptum.* After taking Kronstadt I shall immediately leave for Hungary with an army corps."

(As our readers already know, General Bem did not succeed in taking Kronstadt.)[a]

The extent to which the Pest revolutionaries have been encouraged by the recent gains of the Magyar army may be inferred from the following report in the *Deutsche Allgemeine Zeitung.*

"*Pest,* March 30. A *secret committee* appears to exist here which *is in contact with the Debreczin revolutionary government.* For a large number of printed posters in the Hungarian language are daily found in every street, containing partly war bulletins from the Debreczin Government, and partly its orders and decrees. By means of such posters Bem's capture of Hermannstadt was already known here on March 22. The police *have not yet succeeded* in tracking down these secret information centres. If one is to believe such a poster, countless copies of which were distributed yesterday, *then the Hungarian Lieutenant-Colonel Gaal stormed and captured the fortress of Arad on March 23.* But the imperial officer commanding the fortress, Lieutenant-Field Marshal Baron Berger, is said to have made good his escape.—The Ban, Master of Ordnance Baron *Jellachich,* is[b] ... here. The plan of advancing on *Szegedin has been abandoned.* The theatre of war has *shifted back about 40 miles nearer the Austrian border,* and thanks to this an area of about 300 square miles has been abandoned to the Magyars. The imperial army is now altogether *restricted to the defensive.* Among the officers the conviction is also generally expressed that *without substantial reinforcements a decisive victory is scarcely conceivable.*—Yesterday the Jewish community here had to pay a fine of 40,000 guldens because two local Jews were sentenced for deliveries made to Debreczin.—Colonel Horváth is advancing on Baja, which the insurgents have occupied with 4,000 men. His task is to clear the Danube line and to destroy the insurgents' ships."

According to this, Jellachich, after three or four attempts on the Theiss, has returned to Pest for the fifth time; and just as he previously discovered that the Theiss cannot be crossed at Szolnok and marched towards Szegedin, he has now discovered that Szegedin cannot be taken. These repeated retreats are the "laurels" of the "chivalrous Ban Jellachich"! "Poor Jellachich! Poor *Kölnische Zeitung*"!

Herr Welden has issued a bloodcurdling proclamation to the garrison at Komorn, which has the following positive content after many inflated words:

"Wherefore I grant a further grace of 12 hours so that every man may return to the royal imperial flag. Upon the expiry of this grace, however, I shall continue with the

---

[a] See this volume, p. 235.—*Ed.*

[b] There is a blank in the newspaper due to bad printing.—*Ed.*

destruction of Komorn so long as I have one trusty soldier and my cannon the wherewithal to shoot. God will assist us! Outside Komorn, March 26, 1849."[a]

The rumour that the Russians have entered Galicia is emphatically contradicted.

Martial-law reports announce: "We still lack *consoling* (!!!) news from Hungary."

Letters from Jassy announce that in Moldavia great preparations for some war or other are being made, especially as Russian troops in great numbers are arriving from all directions and General Paskevich is expected any day now.

The *Neue Oder-Zeitung* today prints a document of the erstwhile Palatine of Hungary, Archduke *Stephan*,[191] from which it becomes clear that the betrayal of Hungary which is now practically complete was contemplated and projected as early as March last year. The document reads as follows:

"*Your Majesty*, the condition of Hungary is so critical at the moment that the most violent eruption can be expected any day. Anarchy reigns in Pest. The authorities have been ousted from their spheres of action by committees of public safety, and—while the Governor's Council at least maintains the outward form of its authority under the powerful leadership of Count Zichy—the Exchequer has been reduced to practically nothing. The nobility" (it appears to be implied from the context later on that the rural population is meant, since the nobility has already enjoyed rights) "has rebelled in several places in order to win real rights for itself.

"In this anomalous and dangerous situation every man expects his salvation from the impending formation of a responsible government.[192]

"Even if we regard this plan as a calamity, the question now at issue, however, is which is the least calamity?

"I shall now attempt briefly to adduce the three means by which *alone* I can still hope to achieve anything in Hungary. The first means would be to remove the whole of the armed forces from the country and abandon it to total devastation; passively to observe the destruction and arson, and passively to watch the bitter struggles between the nobility and the peasants.

"The second would be to negotiate with Count Batthyány (who is now the people's only hero;—if we hesitate for long his star too is likely to fade—) concerning the proposed legislation, in order to save as much as can still be saved. One must know in advance, however, what is to be done if in the event of his dissatisfaction he should perhaps resign.

"Finally, the third means would be to furlough the Palatine immediately and to send to Pressburg a Royal Commissioner invested with extraordinary powers and accompanied by a considerable military force, who after dissolving the Diet there would leave for Pest and there continue to run the government with a strong hand as long as conditions demand it.

"I frankly confess that I myself recoil in horror from the first alternative. It is immoral, and it is perhaps also not proper for a government to forsake its subjects completely, some of whom at least are well disposed, and to abandon them as victims

---

[a] The proclamation is given in the report "Pressburg, 31. März", *Der Lloyd* No. 157 (evening edition), April 2, 1849, and is dated March 30, 1849.— *Ed.*

to all the cruelties of a rebellion (!). Moreover, the example this would set to the undisciplined rude masses would produce the most damaging effect in the other provinces.

"The second alternative on the other hand is a good one, and although at first glance it has the semblance of separation, yet for the present it is the only means of retaining this province, provided that the gentlemen to be newly appointed are capable of exercising complete influence over internal developments—which can admittedly no longer be claimed with complete certainty in advance. With the coming of more propitious times much may be organised differently which might cause a separation at present. I am not certain that one might not achieve something by way of proper negotiations through Batthyány and Deák—but solely through them—for if they deliberate in Pressburg [193] everything is to be feared. At this juncture, however, I must, as a faithful servant of the state, make so free as to draw Your Majesty's attention to a circumstance of the greatest significance: what will happen if in the event of unsuccessful negotiations Batthyány should hazard everything and be ready to resign?

"Here I consider it my duty not to exaggerate but to observe in accordance with the truth that one must be prepared for this eventuality in order to be able to meet with armed force the demonstrations along the Danube and on the road from Pressburg to Vienna which will certainly be instigated by the youth of Pressburg and a section of the nobility. In this case the third alternative would remain, provided that neither the will nor the possibility of its employment were lacking. This third means would have to be used with great dispatch. Four questions arise in this connection, however:

"a) is there sufficient money available? That is, is it not impossible to send a fairly large military force, by which I understand at least 40,000 to 50,000 men, to Hungary? Or

"b) is this force available and able to be concentrated quickly? Is, further,

"c) a Royal Commissioner available who is both willing and fitted to take over this task? Finally, however,

"d) is there also no doubt that this means is sufficient for achieving the end desired? And whether later in the winter an accommodation will not be brought about, and whether the other hereditary provinces will remain tranquil upon perceiving this? Will one not need a substantial military force in Galicia and in Italy?

"If to all these questions, which I am unable to judge from my own position, a favourable answer can be given according to which the execution of the plan is possible without illusions and without, for instance, calculations which perhaps later prove to be incorrect, then I have no further comment to add against its being carried out, provided that the settlement with Count Batthyány is attempted, and in addition that the dignitaries of the country, who have to be summoned in any case, are asked.

"I frankly confess that in the present state of affairs I must pronounce myself to be for the second alternative, and I do not doubt that the dignitaries of the country—although I have not yet spoken with them—are of the same opinion. I have definite knowledge only of the opinion of Supreme Judge of the country Mailáth.

"If, however, Your Majesty in Your wisdom should consider the first or the third means to be more to the purpose, then Your Supreme Highness will without doubt command me in accordance with the prevailing laws and customary practice as to whether for the time being I shall remain in Vienna in this event or whether I ought to travel elsewhere.

Your Majesty's most faithfully obedient subject,<br>
*Stephan* m. p.[a]

Vienna, March 24, 1848."

---

[a] Manu propria—with one's own hand.— *Ed.*

We refrain from all further discussion of this document, which is self-revealing indeed. In the margin of the original document there are comments by Archduke Stephan in his own hand and a dispatch note: "Stephanus 23 March 1848" and "Kiads Marcz 24èn 1848" (i.e. dispatched on March 24, 1848).

We have found the following additional information in the papers which have arrived this morning:

The village of Aszod, four miles from Pest on the road to Hatvan, was captured by the Magyars. They had already left it again the following day, however, in order to advance further in the direction of Neograd and the Waag. The Slovakian guerillas have once again been so encouraged by Görgey's sudden appearance on the Eipel that they are ranging as far as the Moravian border.

Götz and Jablonowsky are in Waitzen. The report that they had held Eperies and Kaschau against Görgey was therefore *untrue*. The whole of the Zips, and indeed *the whole* of *Upper Hungary,* are thus once more in the hands of the Magyars, and the imperial forces now occupy only the western and southern borders, also the land between the Danube and the Drava and the immediate environs of Pest.

"Ban Jellachich," states the Pest Observer (*Figyelmező*), "is not only a hero, but also an *astute diplomatist.* He caused a sensation in Kecskemét. He summoned the Gipsy bands of Körös and Kecskemét, marched through the town to the accompaniment of the most genuine Hungarian melodies, and has so enthused the whole population with his Magyar conduct that they declared: 'Even if he were to land us in the middle of the Theiss, we should follow him!!'"[a]

Ban Jellachich is daily revealing himself as more of a buffoon and a Don Quixote.

The Augsburg *Allgemeine Zeitung* reports the following fact, which may once again serve as proof of the genuinely revolutionary character of the Hungarian war:

"While the young Count Esterházy holds a command in the fortress of Komorn and will probably be executed for high treason should this be taken, the old Count Esterházy, the young Count's father, has just presented 160 casks of wine to the siege troops as encouragement for them to storm the fortress!"[b]

Written by Engels about April 6, 1849

First published in the *Neue Rheinische Zeitung* No. 266, April 7, 1849

Printed according to the newspaper

Published in English for the first time

---

[a] A similar account is also published in "Wien, 31. März", *Der Lloyd* No. 155 (evening edition), March 31, 1849.— *Ed.*

[b] "Pesth, 29. März", Augsburg *Allgemeine Zeitung* No. 93, April 3, 1849.— *Ed.*

# FROM THE THEATRE OF WAR

Today we have gladdening news. *Bem's bulletins,* which we printed yesterday,[a] are *confirmed to the very last letter.*

**Bem has driven the Russian garrison of Hermannstadt right out of Transylvania, has destroyed the Austrian army and is advancing on Kronstadt. Puchner and his generals have fled to Wallachia.**

Bem had captured Hermannstadt on March 11 and beaten the Russians so soundly that only 2,000 of them found their way over the Roterturm Pass into Wallachia. The remainder, between 2,000 and 6,000 men (the reports are contradictory) were partly cut down, partly taken prisoner. On March 12 and 13 Bem pursued them to the defile.

In the meantime unlucky old Puchner had set out from Mediasch to pursue Bem. He arrived before Hermannstadt exactly fifteen hours too late and stationed his troops at Frek on the Aluta, to one side of Hermannstadt and the Roterturm. Now, on March 15, Bem drove the Russians right out of the defile and on March 16 he destroyed the Austrian army. The childish old Puchner and his generals Pfersmann, Gedeon and Schurter likewise escaped into Wallachia together with three companies. Command of the defeated corps was assumed by Major-General Kalliani; he fled with his men in great disorder to Fogaras on the Aluta, eight to ten miles from Hermannstadt.

Bem fortified the Roterturm Pass in such a way that, as he affirms, the Russians will no longer get through. Then he immediately headed for Kronstadt, hoping to take it in 3-4 days. The Russians, who immediately sent considerable forces to Transylvania (20,000

---

[a] See this volume, pp. 237-38.— *Ed.*

men with 50 cannon are mentioned), will probably arrive too late as they are taking a circuitous route through Wallachia, and perhaps Bem will still succeed in occupying and fortifying the Törzburg, Tömös and Boha passes (two to three miles from Kronstadt) before the Russians get there. That the latter are counting on considerable resistance and only very uncertain success is evident from the fact that they are sending a second corps of occupation into Transylvania by way of the Bukovina.

The capture of Hermannstadt was of incalculable significance for Bem. All the depots of arms, munitions and provisions of Puchner's army were here. All these supplies have fallen into his hands and such a skilled and active insurrectionary general as Bem, who can obtain soldiers with ease, will be able to make excellent use of precisely these weapons.

The capture of Kronstadt completes Bem's conquest of Transylvania. He promises, as soon as he succeeds in this enterprise, to head for Hungary with an army. Even if the Russians, who are exerting themselves to the utmost to revenge the humiliating reverse they have suffered, do not permit him to reach the Theiss, it will nevertheless be possible for the fast-moving Bem to create a diversion by marching into the Banat, and just there his presence may prove decisive.[194]

To avoid the suspicion that these facts, which incidentally *reach us from all sides simultaneously,* are fabricated, we print the few melancholy lines in which the *official Wiener Zeitung* itself announces them:

"According to reports from Bucharest Master of Ordnance Puchner was in Rimnik (Wallachia) on March 19. Bem had occupied the Roterturm and the Russians the quarantine.[a] A courier from Kronstadt brought the news to Czernowitz on March 26 that the royal imperial Transylvanian corps, after arriving too late for the relief of Hermannstadt, had retired to Kronstadt in order to cover the town. On account of illness Master of Ordnance Puchner has handed over the command of this corps to Major-General Kalliani, and he himself has withdrawn to Rimnik with the General Command."

The martial-law reports of the arrival of two Russian columns by way of the Roterturm and the Törzburg passes[b] were thus *totally untrue.* Unfortunately for the *Kölnische Zeitung* they were not published by Magyar but by genuine imperial journals. On the contrary, this time the "Magyar boasting" has been corroborated word for word.

---

[a] See this volume, p. 279.— *Ed.*

[b] Ibid., p. 235.— *Ed.*

Let us turn from Transylvania to the *Banat*. Here on March 16 and 18 the Szegedin and Theresiopel Magyars inflicted serious defeats on the Serbs at Kanizsa on the Theiss. After this they are said to have advanced into the Banat as far as Zenta and to have caused great devastation. As a result of these defeats the Patriarch[a] ordered the *Landsturm* to be recalled in the whole of the Voivodina. However, the latest news from this area (Semlin, March 28) mentions a new victory of the Serbs over the Hungarians by which the former are said to have regained their previous advantageous position.[b]

Baja on the Lower Danube is still occupied by a band of insurgents. Colonel Horváth received the order to expel them, to clear the Danube line completely and to this end to destroy the insurgents' ships. These pirate barges appear to be the principal reason for refusing the request of the steamship transport company agency here to be allowed to sail the stretch of the Danube to Esseg.

Horváth, however, returned with his mission unaccomplished. He does not appear to have got further than Kis-Körös (eight to ten miles from Baja).

There is very little to be heard from the *Theiss* today. An Austrian column which had dared advance as far as Losoncz was suddenly attacked by the Honveds and completely wiped out. In an imperial bread store at Gödöllö (three miles from Pest) considerable supplies have been spoilt by the rain. The state of things here may be judged from the following dirge from a Vienna correspondent of the *Constitutionelles Blatt aus Böhmen*:

"I am very much afraid of this Hungarian business, and were I a Minister I should be unable to sleep in peace because of it. Would you find it incredible if I were to report that *Windischgrätz will actually be relieved of his command*? Things have gone so far that *the plans of the battle at Kapolna have been sent* to the Emperor *at Olmütz to demonstrate the Marshal's incompetence.* The officers before Komorn have held their own council of war, and it took Welden's energy and the proven confidence of the troops in him to settle a great many differences. Welden is expected to return tonight and thus we shall already be able to read a report on the operations at Komorn tomorrow evening; my wish is that it may be favourable, but I dare not hope so."[c]

An issue of the *Lithographierte Correspondenz* from Vienna states that Dembiński *has crossed the Danube* below Pest with an army corps and *is threatening Stuhlweissenburg.* This remains to be proved. Several days ago we were already saying that Magyar corps would cross the

---

[a] Rajachich.— *Ed.*

[b] "Semlin, 28. März", *Constitutionelles Blatt aus Böhmen* No. 81, April 5, 1849.— *Ed.*

[c] "LC Wien, 3. April", *Constitutionelles Blatt aus Böhmen* No. 81, April 5, 1849.— *Ed.*

Danube in this area[a]; it is quite possible that they are threatening Weissenburg; but whether merely guerillas are involved or considerable army corps cannot yet be ascertained. In any case it may be assumed that Dembiński is not commanding them; according to the latest reports he and his troops have taken up positions significantly further northwards, on the Zagyva and the Mátra mountains.

From the camp at Komorn Herr Welden has brought back a long account of the operations against the fortress, which in spite of all its rhetoric and deliberate vagueness does not give the least consolation to the imperial side. Not the faintest prospect of capture. It merely contains a dry enumeration of events to date. The following is an extract from it:

"In the summer of 1848 Komorn was re-equipped, provided with nearly 300 cannon and victuals for at least a year; in the month of September the Magyars raised the red-green-and-white flag[b] there and handed over the general command to Baron Jessenak. The garrison of the fortress still comprises the following military units: 6 companies of the Alexander regiment,[195] 2 companies of Prussian infantry, 8 Honved battalions, 700 Honved artillery troops and two squadrons of Austrian hussars who changed sides. All attempts at attacking the fortress with the enormous masses of troops under Windischgrätz came to nothing; the encirclement commenced in January with the advance on Leopoldstadt was abandoned as futile, and only towards March 10 did the Austrians make an attack in earnest. Siege equipment, cannon and technical detachments were sent down from Vienna; in vain, however, for the bad weather conditions and the bottomless roads hindered both the transport and the mounting of the cannon. On March 24, 42 twelve- and 18-pound cannon, mortars and howitzers opened a murderous fire on the fortress from the Sandberg. The besieged troops replied likewise with heavy fire and on March 31 in particular tried to hinder the erection of the batteries; on this day the siege troops threw a bridge across the Danube at Nemes-Oers. On the day mentioned the Austrian Lieutenant-Field Marshal Simunich began the closer encirclement of Komorn; he ordered the troops to march in part along the Waag and after they had taken up their positions pickets of the besieged caused considerable damage with intensive small arms fire, to Sossay's brigade in particular.— The damage inflicted on the enemy section which crossed the Danube by the Hungarians with the fire they maintained from 10 o'clock in the morning to 4 o'clock in the afternoon is naturally given out as very slight by the official press. At the same time Veigl's brigade too advanced on the Waag bridgehead in three sections, while the raiding party under Cremeville formed the reserve. The first section moved on Batföldre which the Hungarians had set fire to, the second against the fortified brick wall, and the third moved by way of Lisza on the left bank of the Danube against the powder tower where the fire was liveliest. The Austrian side suffered very considerable losses during this operation.— Thus the western, northern and eastern sides of Komorn were surrounded by a line of fire; finally, 42 pieces of artillery were bombarding the fortress and the Danube bridgehead from the Sandberg. During the night four 24-pounders forced the bridgehead and bombarded

---

[a] See this volume, pp. 234-35.— Ed.

[b] The national colours of Hungary.— Ed.

the fort with red-hot cannon-balls. In the course of April 1 another 12 heavy cannon and two 60-pound mortars arrived and were disembarked opposite Nemes-Oers."[a]

The only positive thing to emerge from this account is that the *Palatine redoubts* so often alleged to have been conquered by the imperial forces are *still in the hands of the Hungarians*, as is also the *Danube bridgehead*, and that there can be no talk yet of direct-fire batteries, let alone breach batteries.[196]

In *Debreczin* spirits are high and the mood is very cheerful. Bem has sent seven captured Russian cannon there, which have been decked with garlands and put on public display. It is said that the Debreczin National Assembly *has been convoked for April 15 in Pest*.[197]

A report has arrived from Croatia which indicates a curiously sudden indulgence of the imperial Government towards the Slavs. As is known the Southern Slavs had protested against the continuation of the military dictatorship in the Military Border area.[198] The imposed Constitution declared that in the border area everything must remain as of old. Hence particularly the discontent of the Croats and the Serbs, who saw their country split by this into two halves set against each other. Now, when the Slavs are needed more than ever, the following poster was suddenly put up on March 30 in Agram:

"We learn from a reliable source that *all the decisions of our world-historic Diet*[199] of the year 1848 and in particular *Article 26* concerning the future state of the *Military Border area* have been *ratified* by His Majesty our youthful Emperor and King Francis Joseph. The man to whom, besides the grace of the Emperor, our thanks are most due for this favourable turn of events, will be divined in the heart of every true patriot. Southern Slavs! Dear brothers! Do not despair! We shall thus have a fatherland and consequently love Austria again; then shall the gaping wounds of our people, inflicted on so many battlefields in the struggle for the power and the glory of Austria, be healed. Then, brothers, will it be our glory so courageously to have contributed to reconstruction in the South of Europe in which we shall take our allotted place as members in the free dwelling house of so many nations, and forgetting the pain and tribulation of the past, we shall be able to exclaim: Long live the constitutional King and Emperor Francis Joseph! Long live the darling of the nation, the brave Ban Jellachich!"[b]

There was no signature at all on this poster, but it was considered to have originated with Minister Kulmer and to be semi-official. The decisions of 1848 referred to demanded: subordination of the civil

---

[a] "Bericht über die Verhältnisse vor Comorn", *Wiener Zeitung* No. 79, April 3, 1849; *Die Presse* No. 80, April 4, 1849.— *Ed.*

[b] "Freudige Nachricht", *Agramer Zeitung*, March 31, 1849. Printed also in *Der Lloyd* No. 157 (evening edition), April 2, 1849 and in *Österreichischer Correspondent* No. 77, April 4, 1849.— *Ed.*

administration of the Military Border area to the ministries concerned, so that only the military organisation should remain with the Ministry of War, and the restriction of the borderers' obligation to service abroad by fixing a definite contingent in proportion to the rest of the monarchy. For hitherto the civil administration in the border area has also been made over to the military authorities, and all borderers between 16 and 60 years of age could be enlisted for active service abroad. It was precisely the borderers thus conscripted whose massive presence decided the war in Austria's favour in Italy in August and in Hungary on the Drava and in the Banat in October last year. If the poster in Agram is not merely a royal imperial Austrian puff, then the trick of being able to stamp soldiers out of the earth has come to an end with it.

Written by Engels about April 7, 1849

First published in the *Neue Rheinische Zeitung* No. 267, April 8, 1849

Printed according to the newspaper

Published in English for the first time

# [FROM THE THEATRE OF WAR]

The Hungarian correspondent of the *Breslauer Zeitung* reports today that on March 20 Bem captured *Kronstadt* and moreover without striking a blow. The remainder of the Austrians and Russians are said to have withdrawn to Wallachia. Hermannstadt and Kronstadt had each to pay 1,000 florins in cash per day to the Russians and in addition they were subjected to the most shameless requisitioning and thieving. Bem has proclaimed a general amnesty in these two towns. The Saxons are said to have at once publicly declared that the Austrians had *compelled* them to call in the Russians (this is certainly not true).

On March 29 the imperial forces under Welden are said to have attempted (?) to take Komorn by storm and to have suffered so great a defeat that they have abandoned the siege of Komorn; only an observation corps[200] still remains at Gönyö. Wimpffen's Italian battalion is said to have gone over to the Hungarians. We print these news items with the greatest reservation, although recently the essential facts in the reports of the Hungarian correspondent have as a rule proved correct.

Banknotes continue to be printed by the Hungarians in *Debreczin*, for a considerable amount of currency paper has been smuggled in.

"On March 15, the anniversary of the Hungarian insurrection,[201] a great public celebration was held near Debreczin and a large number of people assembled there. Two whole oxen and many pigs and lambs were roasted, there was plenty of wine and Gipsies played Hungarian airs and marches. A number of speeches were made and toasts proposed with the indispensable *Eljen.*[a] There are no troops stationed in Debreczin and the national guards are on duty. They wear bright red ribbons on their shakos and hats. Incidentally, half the companies of every battalion in the

---

[a] Long live (in Hungarian).— *Ed.*

country must always be in the field to face the enemy, and after three months they are relieved by the other three companies that stayed at home. This explains the strength of the military forces of the insurgents and also why their battalions are unable to withstand any bayonet charge by the imperial troops" (*Constitutionelles Blatt aus Böhmen*).

Schlick and Jellachich are again (for the tenth time) holding a council of war in Pest. According to Austrian reports, General Jablonowsky has advanced towards Losoncz.

"Business letters sent from Lemberg on the 31st of this month have caused a new wave of anxiety. The leading business houses report from there that the entire garrison of Lemberg is expected to leave for Hungary and it is feared that after its departure a revolutionary move or diversion in favour of the Hungarians will take place" (*Lithographierte Correspondenz*).

It seems that the Agram poster announcing the concessions [a] is all humbug. Up to now no one has come forward to defend it, and it is generally believed to be an imposture.

Written by Engels on April 8, 1849

First published in the *Neue Rheinische Zeitung* No. 267 (second edition), April 8, 1849

Printed according to the newspaper

Published in English for the first time

---

[a] See this volume, p. 246.— *Ed.*

# AUSTRIAN LAMENTATIONS

Not the smallest news item from anywhere, especially since the Breslau newspapers, generally the best informed, did not arrive today because of the recent holiday.

From Komorn the *Wiener Zeitung* officially reports the following unenlightening fact:

"In connection with the operations and events at Komorn announced on April 3, we learn from the latest reports:

"Closer encirclement began on April 2; the remaining heavy guns were brought into No. 8 battery during the night of April 1, and at daybreak the 24-pounders of this very aptly sited battery began firing hot shots against the old fortress. The enemy returned the fire only moderately from the Palatine line, the old fortress, and the bridgehead." [a]

Now even the *Constitutionelles Blatt aus Böhmen* has to admit that the army on the Theiss has been substantially decimated by fever:

"The incidence of sickness in the flooded areas on the Theiss is said to be enormous."

The same paper reports "From the Drava, March 30" that in the Banat things are also beginning to take a disagreeable turn for Austria. Listen to the lamentations of the royal imperial martial-law correspondent on this most unwelcome "concurrence" of circumstances:

"The terrain of operations has special difficulties; moreover, among the border troops the army has also less experienced ranks and has been weakened by garrisoning. The size of the area of Hungary and Transylvania should likewise be considered and taken into account. The rebels, on the other hand, are more concentrated and are pushing towards the Banat. Hence, the imperial Serbian corps

---

[a] *Wiener Zeitung* No. 81, April 5, 1849.— *Ed.*

of Major-General Todorovich, which, as I reported last time, had marched from the area of Theresiopel towards Kikinda, is in *serious trouble*, or even—if the news about Karlowitz is not misleading—dispersed.

"The siege corps at Peterwardein has received 3 battalions as reinforcements, and is working hard on the entrenchments. When (!) Komorn is taken (!) a considerable number of troops will no doubt be moved to this point, for *next to Transylvania no area needs reinforcements more urgently than this one*, not only because of the fortress but because of the probability of enemy pressure. The mood in the Voivodina is very black, not among the lower orders, but in the middle and upper strata of society. The extent to which this makes itself felt in the Mitrowic Odbor[202] and the atmosphere there may be judged by the fact that Lieutenant-Colonel Puffer, who when a captain distinguished himself by his resolution during the well-known outrage in Reichenberg, does not think it advisable for him *as a German* to take up the regimental command of the Peterwardein regiment, although a section of the regiment has petitioned for his appointment as colonel."[a]

In conclusion, here is the deeply affecting distress call of a Vienna correspondent of the same paper who has at last seen a glimmer of light and already has an inkling of what is going on:

"Now blows are coming thick and fast from Hungary! What used to be whispered here in the night can now be read in plain words in the evening edition of the *Wiener Zeitung*: the valiant Puchner has been pushed into Wallachia—he does not even appear to have kept his entire corps together, otherwise he would surely have been able to hold his ground at the Roterturm Pass. *Where are our friends, the Russians?* And why do our troops not push into Transylvania from Hungary? The areas on the Theiss are said to be completely impassable, *but how is it that the Magyars find a way through the areas on the Theiss and across it?* In Szegedin bread is very dear and in Komorn it is said to be very bad—such is the pass we have come to—*but Honveds are still to be had cheaply, in masses, and, it appears, of tolerable quality.* 'Oh, Lord in Heaven, behold!' If this goes on, then—ah well, *we must not prophesy!*"

This is "the Austria of old,
For feats and victories oft extolled!"[b]

Written by Engels about April 9, 1849

First published in the *Neue Rheinische Zeitung* No. 268, April 9, 1849

Printed according to the newspaper

Published in English for the first time

---

[a] "Von der Drave, 30. März", *Constitutionelles Blatt aus Böhmen* No. 81, April 5, 1849.— *Ed.*

[b] From Ernst Moritz Arndt's poem "Des Teutschen Vaterland" (music by Gustav Reichardt).— *Ed.*

# FROM THE THEATRE OF WAR

That Bem is master of all Transylvania is no longer open to doubt. The Austrians who have hurriedly withdrawn from Hermannstadt to Kronstadt and the Russian garrison there, offered no resistance. Allegedly "for lack of ammunition" they also left Kronstadt without striking a blow, and withdrew to Wallachian territory. Some 22,000 men, 3,000 horses and 50 guns are supposed to be there, besides 8,000 Russians, and on the Bessarabian-Moldavian border another corps of 15,000 men which has already received orders to cross the Pruth. Thus reports the *Wiener Zeitung*.[a]

Whether the information in the *Wiener Zeitung* is correct remains to be seen. This much is, however, certain: *if* it is correct, Bem's forces must have swollen enormously to be able to drive out 25,000 Austrians with 50 guns and 6,000 to 10,000 Russians from an area so rich in advantageous positions as the environs of Kronstadt. In spite of the Russians we can therefore be easy about the fate of Transylvania. For nobody will be taken in by the fib that the imperial troops had to flee "for lack of ammunition" when Kronstadt is their second main depot after Hermannstadt.

All the reports received so far show that the *Wiener Zeitung* has given only a fifth of the real number of *Russian* soldiers in Wallachia.

Quoting an eye witness, a Saxon from Hermannstadt, the Magyar correspondent of the *Neue Oder-Zeitung* confirms a report carried earlier by the *Breslauer Zeitung* about the capture of Hermannstadt. Bem is said to have restrained his troops from any excesses and to have promised a general amnesty except for those who called in the Russians. But these are said to have already fled.

---

[a] *Wiener Zeitung* No. 82 (evening supplement), April 5, 1849.—*Ed.*

According to a Cracow report in the same paper the "depressing news" which the Royal Imperial Consul in Belgrade, Herr Mayerhofer, is taking to Vienna is said to convey that the Turkish Government has protested against the Russian intervention in Transylvania which is being conducted from Turkish territory, asserting its exclusive right to intervene from its own territory.

Incidentally, even the royal imperial martial-law reports admit that Bem, far from being threatened in his position, is rather himself *threatening Wallachia and Bucharest.* Should circumstances indicate an incursion there as appropriate, he will appeal to the suppressed Wallachian revolution[203] and to the ambition of the Turks which has been offended by the Russian invasion. The Russian appetite for the Danube provinces and the alliance of the Austrians and Russians have moreover roused much sympathy for the Magyar cause among the Turks.

No changes have occurred in the positions of the two armies on the *Theiss* since yesterday's news. Yet the lamentations of the Austrians are becoming more frequent, and their situation apparently more depressing every day. Some 13,000 soldiers are said to be lying wounded and sick in Pest, and the active army on the Theiss to have dwindled to 45,000 men. Windischgrätz is reported to have handed over the command to Jellachich (?). The courage and power of the Magyars, on the other hand, are growing day by day. They are drawn up in a great semi-circle round Pest from Waitzen to Szegléd; their mobile units patrol as far as Komorn and the Moravian border. Kossuth has had banknotes issued for another 15 million guldens, and thereby covered the costs of his army for a further six months.

The Imperial Command is making every effort to improve the situation of the army on the Theiss. A corps has withdrawn from the close encirclement of Komorn (where 5,000 Austrians are said to have already died of sickness or in battle) and has marched towards Pest; three battalions have marched from Vienna, and two squadrons of cuirassiers and one regiment and one battalion of infantry from Olmütz. In addition considerable preparations are being made in Moravia and Galicia. Ten thousand Russians are to be called to Lemberg, so that Hammerstein can at last move off to Hungary with the entire Austrian garrison (see under "Poland"[a]). The best officers of Radetzky's army, Lieutenant-Field Marshal Baron Hess, generals Benedek and Mayerhofer have been called to Hungary, and in spite of all this the Austrians' hope of success is so

---

[a] The reference is to a report from Lemberg (Lvov) which was published in the section "Poland" in the same issue of the *Neue Rheinische Zeitung.—Ed.*

slight that they do not intend to "begin operations in Hungary in earnest before May".

In the *south*, things are equally disagreeable for the imperial forces. True enough, there is again talk of the victory of the Serbs at Zenta and of the inevitable cruelties which they afterwards committed. On the other hand, the bonds between Serbs and Austrians are now so far dissolved that the latter have to fear the worst.

"Recently, Lieutenant-Field Marshal Rukavina has declared categorically that the three Banat border regiments, and—as regards the internal administration—also the three comitats, Temes, Krasso and Torontal, must obey his orders unconditionally, failing which he would be forced to take the most serious measures against all offenders. This declaration and the half-hearted action of the General Staff excited the greatest hostility among the people, and after fruitless endeavours to win Rukavina back to the national cause, the Patriarch[a] yesterday felt obliged to dispatch the courier Jovan Nedeljkovich to His Highness Prince zu Windischgrätz with the request for 20,000 rifles to arm those Serbs who are fit to bear arms, and to instruct generals Rukavina and Todorovich to work more sincerely in the Serbian national cause, *failing which he would find himself in the most disagreeable position of having to treat with the Magyars.* People are looking anxiously into the future."

This is how they write to the Austrian papers from Semlin.

Moreover, the Magyars have made another incursion into *Galicia.* The *Wiener Zeitung* writes:

"A band of 800 Hungarian insurgents attacked the village of Brzywka in Sambor district, situated hard on the Hungarian border, drove away all the cattle and then withdrew. The verger, who wanted to raise the alarm by ringing the church bell, was shot by the insurgents."[b]

Written by Engels on April 9-10, 1849

First published in the *Neue Rheinische Zeitung* No. 269, April 11, 1849

Printed according to the newspaper

Published in English for the first time

---

[a] Rajachich.— *Ed.*

[b] *Wiener Zeitung* No. 82 (evening supplement), April 5, 1849.— *Ed.*

# FROM THE THEATRE OF WAR

Nothing has happened in the theatre of war. The imperial forces have held a big council of war in Pest and have decided to confine themselves to the defensive for the next four weeks and in the meantime round up reinforcements (50,000 men are mentioned!). The Magyars, however, are acting so challengingly that Windischgrätz could not help showing his teeth—loose already—once more, despite this decision. On April 4 he advanced to Gödöllö three miles[a] from Pest, and made his headquarters there. The *Ost-Deutsche Post* concludes from this that a battle is near. At Hatvan and also at Szegléd people say they have heard gun-fire, but what happened there is as yet quite unknown.[204]

Because of an announcement recently disseminated by the insurgents that Kossuth's paper money[205] is to be regarded as legal tender and must be accepted on pain of martial-law treatment, the Government again insists that these money tokens are invalid and worthless and gives particular warning against accepting the ten-florin notes recently issued by Kossuth, since they will not only be subject to confiscation, but anyone on whom they are found is liable to penalties.

Baja, which had briefly fallen into the hands of the imperial forces, has been regained by the Magyars, who in general seem to be making considerable progress in the Banat. The Austrians can spread as many martial-law rumours as they like, such as that Szegedin has been conquered and is in flames; their own papers are forced to contradict them and to admit that the Magyars are making

---

[a] See footnote on p. 20.— *Ed.*

considerable progress in the Bacska (between the Danube and Theiss).

Komorn is being heavily bombarded, but what good is that with a fortress in which *every building is bomb-proof.* To show their contempt for the imperial cannon, the garrison the other day made a man in dressing-gown and white nightcap walk about on the wall and dust it very carefully with a white handkerchief. The imperial cannon-balls whistled by on all sides, but the genial Hungarian did not allow himself to be at all disturbed in his absorbing occupation.

There is nothing new from Transylvania. A martial-law report asserts that the Russians have invaded in superior strength and retaken the position recently conquered by the Magyars. Such brazen lies have rarely been told. Another report claims that, on the contrary, Bem has already arrived at the Theiss and declared that Transylvania was secure and that he had left 20,000 men there to garrison the country and the passes. The one assertion is as false as the other. Bem holds the whole of Transylvania and is still there, and in a few days he will perhaps hold all the country to the Danube and the Pruth.

Written by Engels about April 11, 1849

First published in the *Neue Rheinische Zeitung* No. 270, April 12, 1849

Printed according to the newspaper

Published in English for the first time

# [THE EXTRADITION OF POLITICAL REFUGEES]

*Cologne*, April 12. By the issue of warrants for the arrest of Austrian, German and non-German so-called political criminals, especially Kossuth, Bem, Perczel and other Hungarian heroes, the Prussian Government has already proved the close connection between Prussian constitutional freedom and blood-stained royal imperial martial law. That an *entente cordiale* between Potsdam and Olmütz [206] existed, despite the question of the imperial crown, the German question, the Schleswig-Holstein and other questions, was a fact which could be overlooked only by the diplomatising literary moles from the *Kölnische Zeitung* and other shrewd journals. But that this *entente cordiale* was to sink to the lowest depths of vileness, to the infamy of the *extradition of political refugees* to the Austrians—that is what our glorious Government still had in store for us.

*If Robert Blum had escaped from Vienna into Prussia, the Prussian Government would have handed him over to his executioners.*[207]

*On April 4 of this year* the Prussian Government *handed over* the Viennese cadet *Höcke*, a comrade-in-arms of Robert Blum's, *to the bloodhounds of Austrian martial law.* The *Oberschlesische Lokomotive* published the following report from *Ratibor* dated April 4:

"Yesterday at midday the Viennese cadet *Höcke* was brought here in a special conveyance under police guard from Breslau, to which town he had fled not long ago, being charged with high treason for his part in the October revolution in Vienna. In a letter to his family in Vienna, Höcke had given his Breslau address. This letter must have shared the fate of many others, i.e. it was opened at some Austrian post station, for soon afterwards the police authorities in Breslau received the order to arrest the aforesaid Höcke at the place where he lived, and to hand him over to the Austrians.

"Accordingly, the prisoner arrived here at noon yesterday under escort, where a very serious illness, from which he has suffered for a long time, delayed the continuation of his journey to judgment by court martial. He was put in the town gaol under a strong military guard, but already at 5 a.m. today he was taken across the frontier under the escort of two men of the town guard and a policeman. The much-vaunted Prussian human feeling did not allow him on this last journey of two-and-a-half hours to leave the vehicle even once, although it was a necessity in view of his illness. Nor was he allowed any kind of refreshment, for the purchase of which no money was available although, according to the prisoner's statement, 80 talers were taken from him when arrested in Breslau, and the cost of transport, as we know for certain, amounted to only (!) 30 talers.

"It is the most urgent duty of German newspapers forcefully to draw the attention of the Austrian fugitives to the danger to which they are exposed by staying on Prussian, and especially Silesian, soil. The old extradition treaty continues to operate in all its old glory.[208] The great German fundamental law, called martial law, is recognised in Prussia just as it is in Austria, and it is being put into effect with relish."

Such an example from the heroes of martial law in the various countries where a state of siege has been proclaimed should not be given us in vain. Just as they assist one another now, so the democrats of all nations, too, will assist one another when the day of reckoning comes.

The royal and ministerial scum of half Europe found a safe refuge in England last spring.[209]

We assure Herr Manteuffel, Herr Brandenburg and Co. that in the next revolution which they themselves are so busily expediting, no obstacle will be put in the way of England handing *them* over to the victorious German people thirsting for revenge. Arrangements for that have already been made.

Written by Engels on April 12, 1849        Printed according to the newspaper

First published in the *Neue Rheinische*        Published in English for the first
*Zeitung* No. 271 (second edition),        time
April 13, 1849

# FROM THE THEATRE OF WAR.—
## THE GERMAN NAVY

*Schleswig-Holstein.* The Danes have left Hadersleben and the town has been re-occupied by the imperial army.[210] A few particulars have come in on the fighting in the Sundewitt area, according to which losses on both sides were fairly high. The imperial army has taken a number of prisoners.

North-German papers are still largely occupied with that remarkable stroke of luck in the port of Eckernförde.[211] This unique and quite unexpected event will probably figure as the greatest imperial military feat until the next German revolution. It has become clear that the Danes had definite orders to carry out the crazy attempt on Eckernförde. Obviously, in the prevailing circumstances they were bound to suffer such a defeat. Moreover, this whole affair shows what a droll institution the German Navy is. For the German Navy, which still exists only on paper, in spite of all the money, earrings, bracelets and false jewels sent to Frankfurt, is now at last to become a reality. It is to be built from—the wreckage of the Danish battleship *Christian den ottende* which was blown to smithereens! We are not joking. All Eckernförde, along with the victorious imperial troops stationed there, is busy fishing for splinters, gun-carriages, water kegs, yards, etc. as these are driven ashore, and storing them for the building of the German Navy. The Hamburg *Börsen-Halle* reports all this with appropriate seriousness. For our part, we predict that the gloriously captured *Gefion* will be brilliantly recaptured by the Danes as soon as she shows herself on the high sea.

Four Danish blockade ships, three frigates and a corvette, are already again lying off the Elbe. The frigate *Havfruen* is lying off the Oder. This is a good opportunity for the German Navy to show itself, but it will fight shy of that. The whole German Navy served no other purpose except for too much boasting and excellent profits for the Hamburg, American and English shipping companies which palmed off their discarded ships on the Frankfurt imperial powerlessness for vast sums of money. The whole flotilla, which is lying in the Elbe and can already be seen in lithographs in all the picture shops, is unseaworthy; still less can the lightly-built ex-merchantmen and ex-steamboats from the Weser, promoted to warships, carry the weight of the guns or withstand the recoil of firing them. Not to mention the elegantly equipped erstwhile transatlantic steamships which the other day brilliantly ran aground and are lying in the Weser.

The whole story of the German Navy is sheer plagiarism, it has all *happened before*. Many years ago the Belgian model state (on the water Germany's model state as well) bought from a Liverpool shipping company the steamship *The British Queen* for 1,200,000 francs in order to open up a steamship line between Antwerp and New York. On the masts of this ship was hoisted the black-red-and-gold flag which the German fatherland also has in common with the Belgian model state.[212] But what happened? On the very first voyage it became clear that *The British Queen* was not seaworthy, and this cast-off Liverpool ship was lying in the Antwerp dock ever since until at last, some little time ago, it was resold for 130,000 francs under the description "old wood".

That is the German Navy! When the Danes next take a German ship, they will auction it also in Copenhagen for "old wood".

That the Germans will never become a naval power is the fault of their geographical position. But they could have a navy which would at least protect their coasts and rule in the Baltic, in spite of Danes and Russians. But even that they will never get so long as the black-red-and-gold and black-and-white [213] imperial trash prevails. A German Navy will only be possible when the red flag is hoisted on its masts.

Written by Engels about April 12, 1849        Printed according to the newspaper

First published in the *Neue Rheinische*        Published in English for the first
*Zeitung* No. 271, April 13, 1849        time

# FROM THE THEATRE OF WAR.—
# WINDISCHGRÄTZ'S COMMENTS
# ON THE IMPOSED CONSTITUTION

As the Breslau and Vienna letters and journals did not arrive tonight, little material is available today on the events of the Hungarian war. The imperial side once again speaks of victories which it claims to have won over the Hungarians. Jellachich is said to have captured 17 guns from the Magyars at Szegléd, Jablonowsky is again said to have advanced to Losoncz, Schlick to have thrown back the Magyars all along the line at Hatvan etc. This was reported to the Augsburg *Allgemeine Zeitung* from Pest on April 4.[a] Other reports of the same date say nothing of this and assert that the Austrian army is still in full retreat and that the Magyars of Pest have never been more cheerful than they are at present. Certainly, the Magyars' resolute advance has remarkably thwarted Windischgrätz's well-intentioned plan to impose a four weeks' truce on the Hungarians until he had received reinforcements of 50,000 men. Windischgrätz realises that he cannot avoid a decisive battle now, decisive for the imperial side if he is beaten, but not at all decisive if the Magyars are beaten. The Hungarians can always retreat into the impassable swamps and the pusztas[214] on the Theiss, behind which they are entrenched as in the most formidable fortress; the imperial troops, who have no basis of operations, having behind them 60 miles of hostile country, must retreat in a rout towards Vienna in case of defeat, just as Napoleon had to retreat towards the Rhine after the battle of Leipzig.[215] Few will escape, and those who do will no longer form an army.

---

[a] The news items mentioned by Engels can be found in the Augsburg *Allgemeine Zeitung* Nos. 99 to 101, April 9 to 11, 1849 under the datelines "Pesth, 4. April", "Pesth, 5. April" and "Pesth, 6. April".— *Ed.*

Moreover, the sole definite advantage which the imperial troops have gained by their concentration at Pest appears to be that Görgey, since he has been joined by Klapka and his corps, which had been roving in Slovakia till then, has given up his plan to advance to Komorn by the side of the mountains. He has marched a little further south, so as to meet Schlick's corps head-on, jointly with the main Magyar force which is at Hatvan and Gyöngyös. The victory of the Magyars in this area is of course much more important than a passing raid, even a highly successful one, against the Komorn siege force.

In the *south*, the Magyars have gained decisive advantages at the points where fighting is still in progress, namely in the Bacska. The alleged victory of the Serbs at Zenta has vanished into—the martial-law—thin air. Moreover, we learn now that the Magyars have moved from Theresiopel and Szegedin to the south with irresistible force, driving the Serbs before them; that they have occupied Zombor and Verbasz, conquered the entire Bacska etc. and are threatening the siege area of Peterwardein. Verbasz lies, in fact, only a few miles from Peterwardein, and we shall receive important news from this area shortly. It was Vetter-Damjanich's corps which carried out this surprisingly rapid march, having left behind an observation brigade against Jellachich, who was retreating to the north. This march is of the greatest importance, not only for the relief of Peterwardein, but particularly because of the Serbs. It is known that they are already on very strained terms with the imperial side and have threatened several times to negotiate with the Magyars. And nothing would be more likely to bring these negotiations to a rapid conclusion than just such a sudden and surprising display of strength by the Magyars in the Voivodina.

In the *north*, General Hammerstein, who is in command in Lemberg, is said to have started for Hungary with 15 battalions. We recall that news of his departure was carried once before in all the papers; he was reported to have crossed the Theiss and to have advanced to Nyiregyhaza, 8 miles from Debreczin, and there was not a word of truth in it. We refer the reader, by the way, to our report from Lemberg [a] of the day before yesterday, which indicated no such rapid departure.

According to the *Lloyd* of April 7,[b] 20,000 Russians have already started for **Transylvania** and General Muraviev is approaching in haste from Bessarabia with a corps of 20,000 men. The Turks too

---

[a] Published in the *Neue Rheinische Zeitung* No. 269, April 11, 1849.—*Ed.*

[b] "Wien, 6. April", *Der Lloyd* No. 166 (morning edition), April 7, 1849.—*Ed.*

have marched to the border to guard Wallachia. The Turkish troops, about 6,000 men who hitherto were garrisoning Galatz and Ibrail, made for Bucharest on March 21 and in a few days a new Turkish garrison is expected in Galatz.

Needless to say, these reports are again purely martial-law rumours.

From the Bukovina we learn that Malkowsky, whom various martial-law papers had already drawn up between Bistritz and Maros-Vásárhely, is not on Transylvanian soil at all. So far from advancing, he has, on the contrary, had to send a considerable part of his troops from the Bukovina to Galicia. These are now at Delatyn, about 15 miles from the border of the Bukovina, where a Magyar invasion is feared.

We conclude with a document which the Pest *Figyelmező*[a] quotes with the following introductory remark:

"The following explanation of the Austrian Constitutional Charter[216] with reference to Hungarian conditions has been issued. Although it has not reached us officially, it has however been communicated to the Royal Commissioners for distribution in the country, therefore we shall not delay its publication."

### The document itself reads:

"By order of His Majesty Our Emperor and King Francis Joseph I, I, as Plenipotentiary of His Majesty, make hereby known the following declarations and explanations relating to the constitutional Charter in force throughout the Empire from March 4, as far as the Charter concerns Hungarian conditions. His Majesty Our Most Gracious Emperor and King has deigned to issue and to publish a constitutional Charter for the one and indivisible monarchy which intimately links the whole realm in a mutual connection, bestows unity upon the whole while maintaining the independence and capacity for development of the individual parts and at the same time guarantees equal rights to every nation. His Majesty wishes this Charter, accompanied by the Manifesto to His peoples issued by His Majesty, to be made known without delay also to the inhabitants of the Kingdom of Hungary in their language. His Majesty is fully confident in the belief that the peoples of Hungary will recognise the enlargement and guarantee of their political rights, vouched for by this constitutional Charter under which they are authorised to take their constitutional share in the common affairs of the realm, which in future will embrace with the bond of common rights the peoples united under a single ruler by the Pragmatic Sanction.[217] His Majesty expects that His peoples will see in this Charter a strong guarantee of their permanence, of their well-being and of a constitutional future, and will know how to appreciate those beneficial fruits which are bound to result from the welding together of material interests and the community of truly liberal political institutions. In carrying out this great work, which has become the task of His life, it has been the endeavour of the Emperor duly to consider Hungarian conditions; it is His supreme desire that this great work of unification, which commends itself to all the peoples for their own good, should come into force with just consideration of the existing conditions and careful thought for those institutions which time and

---

[a] Reprinted in the article "Pesth, 4. April," *Die Presse* No. 83, April 7, 1849.— *Ed.*

experience have proved to be beneficial to the community and vitally necessary; that accordingly the legally guaranteed freedom of religious belief be maintained, while the free sphere of action for Hungarian national law should remain untouched and limited only by the power necessary to maintain the unity of the realm and its strong government, and handled in the constitutional spirit; a sphere of action which makes necessary the passing of an internal national reform taking cognisance of the concessions which Our illustrious predecessor[a] in government made to the agricultural class in the spring of 1848. No sooner will peace and order be restored and the armed uprising, which unfortunately is still in existence in part of the realm, put down, than His Majesty will assign to Hungarian national law its legal sphere of action. It is for the joint co-operation of His order- and peace-loving peoples with His Majesty and His troops to restore the desired state of affairs with all speed. Until then, His Majesty will regard it as His duty and His right to employ every means with the help of which order, peace and a settled internal administration can be achieved, the numerous wounds inflicted on the unfortunate country can be healed, and a renewal of revolutionary ventures can be made impossible. His Majesty will know how to live with their rights and how to respond to their profession, and He confidently expects that all men of goodwill will endeavour to support Him in this, so that they and their compatriots may participate in the benefits which they must extend to everyone by helping in the rebirth of a great realm and the unification of all forces towards a great aim.

Given at my headquarters in Ofen, March 20, 1849.

Prince *Windisch-Grätz,* Field Marshal."

Written by Engels about April 12, 1849

First published in the *Neue Rheinische Zeitung* No. 271, April 13, 1849

Printed according to the newspaper

Published in English for the first time

---

[a] Ferdinand I.— *Ed.*

# [RUMOURS OF THE EXTERMINATION
OF THE REBELS]

At last we perceive again an official royal imperial sign of life in the Vienna papers which came this morning. The following poster was displayed in Pest and Ofen:

"A brigade of the corps of His Excellency the Ban[a] yesterday encountered an enemy detachment on the way from Jasz-Bereny. Although the enemy was numerically superior to our troops, he was at once attacked, dispersed and deprived of 17 guns. This is the *beginning of operations* which will end with the extermination of the rebels (!!).

Ofen, April 5, 1849

Count Lad. Wrbna,
Lieutenant-Field Marshal and Commander
of the 2nd Army Corps"

A commentary on this bulletin is provided by the *Ost-Deutsche Post* in a report from Pest, also dated April 5, where we read:

"Yesterday an encounter took place. The air was pregnant with rumours. Commotion grew when about 7 p. m. the pontoons were brought back, followed by ammunition carts, empty gun-carriages and individual small detachments of soldiers. At the same time an order went out to the inhabitants of the houses on the fortified bank of the Danube next to the suspension bridge to keep themselves in readiness for the evacuation of their quarters. Today waggons full of wounded came in and the rumour spread that the Ban had suffered a reverse and the insurgents were closing in on the city from Szegléd. The soldiers coming in were from his corps."[b]

This looks more like a defeat than a victory, and it is well known that the *Ost-Deutsche Post* is by no means on the side of the Magyars.

This then is, in Herr Wrbna's words, "the beginning of operations which will end with the extermination of the rebels". We therefore

---

[a] Jellachich.— *Ed.*

[b] "Pest, 5. April," *Ost-Deutsche Post* No. 68, April 8, 1849.— *Ed.*

have every prospect to learn of more serious fighting shortly. By the way, even the *Kölnische Zeitung* no longer believes Herr Wrbna's tale of the "extermination of the rebels".

It appears that the gentlemen of the Pest War Council are offended that their incompetence is to be alleviated by bringing in allegedly more capable officers from Italy. *À tout prix* they want to "exterminate the rebels" before the victors of Novara arrive.[218] *Nous verrons.*

Written by Engels about April 12, 1849

First published in the *Neue Rheinische Zeitung* No. 271, April 13, 1849

Printed according to the newspaper

Published in English for the first time

# [A MAGYAR VICTORY]

*Cologne*, April 12. We are publishing a second edition today, not to inform our readers of yesterday's basically quite unimportant debates at Frankfurt but to report something much more important, namely that the *Magyars have gained a significant victory over the imperial army, and that the imperial army, beaten all along the line, has withdrawn to below the walls of Pest.* (See "Hungary".[a])[219]

Written by Engels on April 12, 1849

First published in the *Neue Rheinische Zeitung* No. 271 (second edition), April 13, 1849

Printed according to the newspaper

Published in English for the first time

---

[a] See this volume, pp. 268-70.— *Ed.*

# [A MAGYAR VICTORY]

After a prolonged period of depression the *Kölnische Zeitung* suddenly raises its shrewd head and speaks:

"After a long interval the Austrians have recommenced operations and the blow now about to fall *will, in all probability, be decisive.*"[a]

Thus the *Kölnische Zeitung* gratefully refers to the 40,000 Russians and 50,000 Austrians who were recently marshalled against Hungary and who were especially provided in order to extricate the *Kölnische Zeitung* from the complicated situation in which it had landed itself as a result of its bellicose military operations in Hungary.

The *Kölnische Zeitung* proposes but Dembiński disposes.

A few hours after our worthy paper has ascribed such "decisive", miraculous powers to the Austrian attack, in strange disregard of the failure of its threefold victorious march to Debreczin, the report has been received in Cologne that

**"Dembiński has beaten the Austrians all along the line and driven them back to the walls of Pest".**

"Truly, that's how it is. It really is so. I have had it in writing." Windischgrätz himself does not deny it. Bulletin No. 34 has arrived.[b] In it Windischgrätz whines about the superiority of the enemy, especially in light cavalry, which is decisive on the Hungarian plains, and also about the "numerous cannon" at the disposal of the

---

[a] This and the following quotation are taken from a report published in the section "Ungarn" in the *Kölnische Zeitung* No. 88, April 13, 1849.— *Ed.*

[b] "34. Armee-Bulletin. Vom 9. April 1849."— *Ed.*

Magyars and declares that *he wants to wait for reinforcements from Pest.*
The Bulletin reads:

"*Vienna,* April 9. Communications from His Highness Field Marshal Prince
Windischgrätz, from Pest on the evening of the 7th, give the outcome of the
reconnaissance-in-force—mentioned previously—undertaken against enemy troops
on the 4th and 5th of this month and led by the Field Marshal in person. For these
enemy troops commanded by Görgey and Klapka, allegedly 50,000 men with a
considerable number of cannon and *extremely strong in cavalry,* had advanced from
Miskolcz to Mezö-Kövesd towards Gyöngyös, while their advance guard under
Dembiński moved forward almost to Hatvan.

"It was this which was attacked on the 2nd of this month by Lieutenant-Field
Marshal Count Schlick and driven back to Hort with considerable losses in cannon and
in prisoners. Another body of insurgents on the right bank of the River Theiss
between Szolnok and Jasz Apáti was advancing towards Baron Jellachich, the Master
of Ordnance.

"The 3rd corps under Lieutenant-Field Marshal Count Schlick was drawn up
behind the Zagyva while the first corps was deployed near Tapio-Bicske. This being
the situation, the Field Marshal wanted to estimate the disposition and strength of the
enemy for himself and therefore came to Gödöllö on the 4th, where a part of the 2nd
Army Corps had likewise been sent, leaving its left wing in position in Balassa-
Gyarmat and Vadkert.

"The reconnaissance undertaken revealed the whole strength of the enemy who,
anticipating an attack, directed his main forces first against the third and then against
the first army corps.

"There must have been approximately *four enemy corps* which had now joined
forces near Gyöngyös and Szolnok and attempted to attack our centre around
Tot-Almas.

"An advance by the third corps, in the enemy's right flank, a splendid encounter
near Tapio-Bicske which, as already stated, was fought by Master of Ordnance Baron
Jellachich, *brought home* to the Field Marshal the *superiority of the enemy, especially in light
cavalry,* in a quite open terrain. In order to make contact with his reserves which were
coming up from all sides, he issued orders to the first and third corps as well as to the
second corps, hitherto held in reserve between Waitzen and Pest, to join forces thus
establishing a long concentrated position in front of Pest so that the city would remain
encircled by a great arc extending from Palotta and Keresztúr to Soroksar.

"In the course of this manoeuvre which *the enemy followed with great speed* and
launched his attack especially against the first army corps drawn up near Isaczeg while
supposing that he was engaging the third army corps deployed near Gödöllö,[a]—battle
was joined about midday on the 6th during which the Fiedler Brigade, reinforced by a
detachment from the Lobkowitz division, forced the enemy to retreat, which he
afterwards sought to cover by a large-scale attack by 12 squadrons of cavalry. But this
was thwarted by a flank attack made by two squadrons of Kress' light cavalry and one
squadron of Max Auersperg's cuirassiers, as a result six more cannon were captured
from the enemy who left many dead on the battlefield, for the well-directed fire of our
guns wreaked havoc in his ranks. Master of Ordnance Baron Jellachich, too, made a
spirited attack on the enemy and then took up the positions assigned to him.

"His Highness the Field Marshal is *determined* there *to await reinforcements* which at
this moment are advancing against Hungary from all sides and since his army is
completely concentrated this enables him to operate in all directions with such forces
as circumstances may require."

---

[a] See this volume, p. 274.— *Ed.*

We must, alas, reserve our comments on this edifying and, as we hope, final Bulletin of the imperial army until tomorrow owing to lack of space.

We can merely add today that according to reports in the *Breslauer Zeitung*, the Magyar army commanded by *Dembiński has* partly *cut off* the corps commanded by Jellachich from the main army and that the same is said to have happened to a part of the corps commanded by Schlick. We shall know by tomorrow night to what extent these reports are correct. But this much is certain: since the beginning of the campaign the imperial forces have not suffered two such reverses as those inflicted by Bem in Transylvania and Dembiński near Gödöllö. May it do them good!

Written by Engels on April 13, 1849

First published in the *Neue Rheinische Zeitung* No. 271 (second edition), April 13, 1849

Printed according to the newspaper

Published in English for the first time

# AN AUSTRIAN DEFEAT

We are returning to the two Army Bulletins issued by Windischgrätz.

The 33rd Bulletin[a] begins:

"His Highness, Field Marshal Prince zu Windischgrätz *had learned* that important rebel forces are concentrating between Gyöngyös and Hatvan and has therefore ordered Lieutenant-Field Marshal Count Schlick to undertake a reconnaissance in that area."

"Had learned"! Windischgrätz undoubtedly "learned" this in a most poignant fashion in the battles which forced his troops to retreat from Kaschau to Waitzen and from Felegyhaza to Pilis, a distance of from 20 to 30 miles, in face of the victorious Magyars.

But to come to the point.

This "reconnaissance" by Schlick on April 2 initiated a series of engagements which lasted for five days and ended on the 6th with the general retreat of the imperial forces to the walls of Pest. Let us try to describe the course of these engagements on the basis of the totally inadequate information available and especially on the basis of the imperial Bulletins themselves in order not to ascribe too great an advantage to the Hungarians.

According to Bulletin No. 34[b] the position of the imperial forces was as follows:

The Austrian army was extended in a long line from Balassa-Gyarmat via Waitzen and Aszod to Szegléd. The second army corps commanded by Ramberg constituted the left wing, and its most

---

[a] Dated April 7, 1849, published in the *Wiener Zeitung* No. 84, April 9, 1849 and in *Der Lloyd* No. 169 (evening edition), April 9, 1849.— *Ed.*
[b] See this volume, pp. 268-70.— *Ed.*

advanced brigades (Götz and Jablonowsky) occupied positions not at Losoncz, as was previously boasted, but six miles further back near Balassa-Gyarmat, Vadkert and Waitzen. Schlick with the third corps were in the centre and had taken up positions in the vicinity of Hatvan and Aszod behind the Zagyva. Jellachich with the first corps made up the right wing which was extended from Szegléd to the vicinity of Jasz-Bereny and was likewise behind the Zagyva, but a little further back.

This was the position of the imperial forces according to the Bulletins.

Confronting them were two of the main bodies of Magyars. The northern corps under Dembiński, Görgey and Klapka advanced on Schlick from the direction of Gyöngyös. A second corps, whose commanders are not named, confronted Jellachich and was a few miles from his main forces, from Jasz Apáti to Szolnok. The River Zagyva separated the hostile forces along the whole line.

Schlick moved out of his position on April 2 and crossed the Zagyva near Hatvan. But, as was stated in Bulletin No. 33,

"*the strength of the enemy forces was so much superior to his own* that he found it preferable to establish himself in a strong position near Gödöllö until the arrival of more reinforcements. In the course of this withdrawal Capt. von Kalchberg of the Prohaska Infantry was ordered to destroy the bridge behind Hatvan.

"Captain Kalchberg and his very brave company carried out this order with most exemplary endurance under very fierce cannon and small-arms fire, thus delaying the enemy to such an extent that he was hardly able to molest the retreating corps."

So—a lost engagement for the Austrians and a retreat halfway back to Pest. All they could achieve was reduced to the fact that "the retreating corps *could hardly be molested*".

The Zagyva near Hatvan is only a small, narrow stream, hardly seven miles from its source. The demolition of the bridge could, at best, only delay pursuit by artillery, perhaps also by the infantry, but certainly not by hussars. And it is precisely pursuit by light cavalry which is most unpleasant for a retreating army in this undulating terrain merging into plains.

In Bulletin No. 34 this first Austrian reverse is already transformed into a victory.

"It was this" (the Magyar advance guard commanded by Dembiński) "which was attacked on the 2nd of this month by Lieutenant-Field Marshal Schlick and driven back to Hort with considerable losses (!) in cannon and in prisoners (!!)."

Windischgrätz credits his readers with such short memories that he believes they will already have forgotten by the 9th of April what he had printed on the 7th.

If this passage means anything at all, it is that "considerable losses in cannon and in prisoners" applies not to the Magyars but to the *imperial forces.*

As a result of this reverse, Windischgrätz was compelled to concentrate his forces further. The Csorich division from the left wing (2nd corps) was hurriedly sent for and moved from Waitzen to Gödöllö. Jellachich was ordered to move up and maintain contact with Schlick. Windischgrätz himself went to Gödöllö on the 3rd and to Aszod on the 4th. (This was stated in Bulletin No. 33. According to Bulletin No. 34 Windischgrätz came to Gödöllö only on the 4th. This is how these Bulletins agree!)

Jellachich moved his corps in a north-westerly direction from Szegléd closer to Gödöllö. It was attacked during the course of this operation near Tapio-Bicske, on the 4th. The Bulletin now declares:

"Major-General Rastic quickly went over to the offensive, attacked the superior advancing enemy forces with the bayonet and threw them back, on this occasion 12 cannon were seized, four of which were harnessed and immediately taken to safety, while the remaining 8 were spiked. We took many more prisoners but we also deplore the loss of brave Major Baron Riedesel and Cavalry Captain Gyurkovics of the Banderial hussars.[220]"

At first, it was 17 cannon that had been captured; then it was 14, finally it was 12, but these were harnessed and taken to safety. Now, at last, it is admitted that although 12 cannon *were* captured, eight of them had, unfortunately, to be left behind. They were, however, spiked, so it is said. Not much value can be attached to this either. But it is precisely the fact that eight captured cannon had to be left behind, which shows how victorious the action near Tapio-Bicske was. If one is victorious one remains master of the battlefield, and if one is master of the battlefield one is also master of unharnessed cannon on it.

The "glorious action" near Tapio-Bicske is thus at bottom, once again, a reverse, the second suffered by the imperial forces during their "reconnaissance-in-force".

Now however Windischgrätz himself took charge of the army and achieved the following gains:

"On the 5th of this month the Field Marshal launched an attack on the enemy forces stationed near Hatvan in the course of which a division[221] of Civalart's Uhlans and three squadrons of Kress' light cavalry attacked four divisions of enemy hussars with remarkable bravery and gained a brilliant success with the small loss of two dead and ten wounded.

"Sixty dead hussars, including two officers, were left on the battlefield. In addition the insurgents suffered forty wounded and thirty-two taken prisoner, including one officer."

Windischgrätz relates some incidental deeds of heroism performed by a few squadrons of the imperial cavalry on this occasion; but what we are not told is what was the outcome of the *whole* "attack". Obviously in this case too an isolated, momentarily favourable episode is singled out from an engagement that was, on the whole, unsuccessful, in order to cover up the adverse results of the whole action.

The result of this engagement was—the retreat of the imperial forces to the walls of Pest. These engagements, Windischgrätz tells us, brought home to him "the superiority of the enemy, especially in light cavalry, in the quite open terrain" and he was therefore compelled to concentrate, as quickly as possible, all three army corps in the immediate vicinity of Pest.

Incidentally, this movement of his troops was the result far less of strategical calculations than of dire necessity. Windischgrätz admits that the enemy

"*followed* him *with great speed* and launched his attack especially against the first army corps drawn up near Isaczeg while supposing that he was engaging the 3rd army corps deployed near Gödöllö."

Thus during a hard pressed retreat the only satisfaction Windischgrätz had was that the Magyars routed a different corps from the one they intended.

In the course of this retreat battle was again joined on the 6th

"during which the Fiedler Brigade, reinforced by a detachment from the Lobkowitz division, forced the enemy to retreat, which he afterwards sought to cover by a large-scale attack by 12 squadrons of cavalry. But this was thwarted by a flank attack made by two squadrons of Kress' light cavalry and one squadron of Max Auersperg's cuirassiers, as a result six more cannon were captured from the enemy who left many dead on the battlefield, for the well-directed fire of our guns wreaked havoc in his ranks".

Even the *Kölnische Zeitung* has not written a more colossal piece of nonsense about strategic matters. A brigade, reinforced by a divisional detachment, compels the victorious and overwhelmingly superior Magyars to retreat! In order to cover this retreat the Magyars launch a large-scale attack with *twelve* squadrons of hussars—against such a small force of infantry! But even better: these *twelve* Magyar squadrons are put to flight by *three* squadrons of the imperial cavalry, and, finally, six cannon are captured!! One can see that Windischgrätz, accustomed to victory, was forced once again to single out a few favourable incidents from an engagement which, taken as a whole, ended most unfavourably and so to provide an historical fable much more fantastic than all the Münchausen stories in the world put together.

Things went no better with the brave Ban Jellachich.

"He, too, made a spirited attack on the enemy and then took up the positions assigned to him."

These few words provide sufficient proof that Jellachich had to face an arduous engagement and to fight his way through in order to be able to withdraw to Pest. What the losses were we shall soon know.

Windischgrätz, in this position in front of Pest, is now

"determined to await those reinforcements which at this moment are advancing against the Hungarians from all sides and since his army is fully concentrated, this enables him to operate in all directions with such forces as circumstances may require".

Görgey and Dembiński may already have foiled the noble Field Marshal's well-intentioned plan as also his final ludicrous boasting.

If the two Bulletins are taken together, it emerges that the imperial forces have been driven back all along the line and are confining themselves to the defence of Pest. No doubt we shall soon be hearing about Dembiński's assault of Pest or the measures he is taking in the rear of the imperial forces.

All non-official dispatches report that the defeats suffered by the imperial forces are far more significant than the Bulletins admit. The sound of uninterrupted gun-fire all along the line has been heard in Pest since the 2nd. The withdrawal in the streets of Pest began from the 3rd and 4th onwards. Munition and pack-waggons, reserve gun-carriages, waggons carrying wounded, individual un-armed men who were not wounded, alternated. Defence measures were taken in the whole town, at various points houses were requisitioned for the military; personnel are held ready to destroy the pontoon bridges at a moment's notice.

In Pest, Hungarian banknotes rose in value, in Breslau Austrian securities fell, following private letters from Pressburg which spoke of a *decisive victory by the Magyars near Gödöllö*. We will disregard for the time being the report in the *Breslauer Zeitung* that Jellachich had been cut off and that Schlick was threatened with the same fate, since the gains made by the Hungarians, already *admitted* by the imperial forces, are quite sufficient.

The *Kölnische Zeitung* threatens that within twelve days 30,000 Italian troops will be arriving in Hungary. We shall examine this tomorrow. In addition, it talks menacingly about the advance of 40,000 Russians on Transylvania and finally about 18 battalions commanded by Hammerstein which are to force their way across the

Zips.[a] The Russians are not yet there and Hammerstein has so far only given the *order* for the mustering of an army corps near Dukla on the Galician-Hungarian frontier. By the time he has finished doing this the Magyars may be far off.

Written by Engels on April 13, 1849

First published in the *Neue Rheinische Zeitung* No. 272, April 14, 1849

Printed according to the newspaper

Published in English for the first time

---

[a] The reference is to the item "Wien, 8. April" and a report published in the section "Ungarn" in the *Kölnische Zeitung* No. 88, April 13, 1849.— *Ed.*

# FROM THE THEATRE OF WAR

No further definite news has arrived from Pest today. The Vienna *Lithographierte Correspondenz* reports though that the Austrian army has evacuated Pest completely, has withdrawn to the right bank of the Danube and that the Hungarian generals entered Pest on the evening of the 7th, greeted by a torchlight procession and general jubilation. This report, however, is certainly premature. The battle around Pest which began on the 2nd and which raged right under the walls of Pest on the 5th and 6th, continued on the 7th and, if we may believe one isolated report, still continued on the 8th. It is not hard to grasp that the victory at Pest is not such an unimportant matter as many would like to believe. The imperial forces have two advantages, firstly, their rear is covered by the Danube, the Ofen fortress and by the town itself whose fortified approaches would suffice to hold up the enemy in the event of a retreat while the defeated imperial forces crossed the river. Secondly, their positions are more concentrated than those of the Magyars. They form a semi-circle around Pest and the Magyars, in their turn, form a larger semi-circle around the imperial forces. Added to which is the fact that the clumsy, slow but stubborn and obedient character of the Austrian army makes it pre-eminently suited to a defensive position. It is therefore probable that the imperial forces have continued to fight around Pest for two more days.[222] But that in the end they were cut to pieces and driven across the Danube cannot be doubted in view of the reports coming in from all sides about the unexpected strength and incredible bravery of the Magyar army. The retreat of the imperial baggage trains through Pest and across the Danube was going on continuously for 48 hours. The thunder of gun-fire resounded about the gates of the city.

At any rate these reports seem to indicate that the Magyars do not want to compel the imperial forces to abandon their position around

Pest by means of strategic manoeuvres but are waging the decisive battle under the walls of Pest itself. In our opinion, and according to reports so far received, success cannot be in doubt.

It was reported in Vienna that *Kossuth* is with the Magyar army, that Klapka has been badly wounded; according to other reports he was taken prisoner near Jasz-Bereny etc. If this last report were true we would already have read it in the Bulletins.

We shall take this opportunity to give some information about Klapka. He is not a Pole as has been asserted here and there, but a Hungarian, a Magyar Slav from Temesvar where his father as mayor was head of the municipal council for many years. While he was still a youth his lust for adventure drew him to military life. He distinguished himself greatly in mathematics and military science in the School of the Bombardier Corps in Vienna and in 1841 was posted to the Hungarian Guard of Nobles. The morale and spirit of this corps were not such as to make a peacetime garrison post on the frontiers of the monarchy—to which he was transferred after six years—seem attractive and he resigned his commission as a first lieutenant. Later we find him in Bucharest offering his services to the *Hospodar*[a] as an organiser of artillery. Even the idea of a journey to India seemed to attract him. But then came March 1848 and by April he was already in Pest, in the closest contact with the Radical Party. He now rose, for he was a most ardent Magyar and after Görgey was the most outstanding talent in the National Army of Insurrection.

Incidentally, the Magyars seem to have spread out suddenly from all sides. The masses of reserve troops between the Theiss and Maros, which Kossuth trained to become efficient soldiers, have suddenly appeared on the battlefield. The *Hungarians are victorious* not only in Transylvania, not only around Pest, but also in the *Banat and are surging forward with incredible speed.* As we wrote yesterday, the Banat as well as the whole of Bacska have been occupied by them. We did not want to report that a Magyar corps under Perczel had fought its way through the besieging Austrians to Peterwardein, because it seemed to us to be too incredible to be true. And yet it seems to be beyond doubt, for the *Agramer Zeitung*, the organ of the Croat Government, itself prints it. Perczel and Batthyány (ex-commandant of Peterwardein) have broken through the blockading cordon and entered the fortress with fresh troops. The siege appears to have been completely abandoned. Nugent has again turned westwards towards Zombor where the Magyars have occupied the town and its

---

[a] George Bibesco.— *Ed.*

environs. Everything imperial has withdrawn from Peterwardein and its environs to Syrmien and Slavonia.

As a result of these recent advances by the Magyars, the *Serbs in the Banat are completely isolated* just as Puchner had been previously isolated in Transylvania. It is clear that this isolation can only have a favourable influence on the negotiations which still continue between the Serbs and the Magyars.

In *Transylvania,* finally, Bem's conquests seem to be completely secured. The Austrian soldiers who fled into Wallachia and whose numbers have only now been officially made known, are *abandoning any attempt to return to Transylvania.* By way of Wallachia they will go to the Banat. Happy journey!

The following is the official report about this printed in the *Wiener Zeitung* itself:

"Latest reports from Transylvania say that the royal imperial troops arrived in the vicinity of Hermannstadt on March 13, and were drawn up near Geroldsau in order to link up with the Russians holding the Falmatsch position. On the 15th the royal imperial troops marched towards Kronstadt and the Russians in accordance with the royal imperial quarantine regulations entrenched themselves in the most extreme border area. The Transylvanian headquarters, Lieutenant-Field Marshal von Puchner and several royal imperial generals as well as 1,200 men of the royal imperial infantry who had also withdrawn into Wallachia had set off for Rimnik. The Transylvanian royal imperial army corps arrived in Kronstadt on the 18th with the aim of holding this town which was occupied by the Russians under the command of General Engelhardt. The rebels, under the command of Bem, arrived likewise in the vicinity of Kronstadt. Meanwhile, however, General Lüders had given orders to evacuate Kronstadt. This, together with the fact that the royal imperial troops had no munitions, were short of many other necessities and were exhausted, determined the officer commanding these troops, General von Kalliani, to evacuate Kronstadt and on March 20 to move on to Wallachia together with the Russians. The army corps consisted of 8,140 men of the infantry and artillery, 900 cavalrymen and 42 cannon. Major Baron Hayde, who was in command of 1,200 infantrymen and 240 cavalrymen, hurried towards Törzburg and was expected in Campulung, in Wallachian territory, on March 21. Thus there were now 12,000 men of the royal imperial forces in Wallachia. The main force under General Kalliani is stationed in Campina, Ploeşti and Konkurrenz and is to rest for 10 or 12 days. The Government of the country has helped as much as possible with regard to supplies. The former Hungarian Minister of War[a] is said to be now in command in Hermannstadt and Bem—to lead the rebels in Kronstadt, from whence it is believed he will seek to march to Bukovina. The number of refugees who have left Transylvania to seek protection in Wallachia is very large. The royal imperial Major von Reichetzer, the Adjutant of the General Command, arrived in Bucharest from Craiova on March 27, in order to organise the march of the royal imperial troops from Campina to the Banat by way of Craiova and Orsova."[b]

[a] Lázár Mészáros.— *Ed.*

[b] "Siebenbürgen, 9. Apr.", *Wiener Zeitung* No. 86 (evening edition), April 10, 1849.— *Ed.*

From this it follows: (1) that Bem must have a very considerable army if he was able to defeat over 12,000 Austrians and 10,000-15,000 Russians; (2) that the Russians, too, are at present not keen on returning to the Transylvanian area and thus Transylvania is at last *secured* and with Transylvania the rear of the Hungarian revolutionary army.

The 40,000 Russians thus do not seem to be willing to come to the aid of the *Kölnische Zeitung*.[a] But it still has Hammerstein's 15 battalions and Haynau's 30,000 men.

*Eh bien!* According to the most recent and direct reports Schlick was still in Lemberg trying to induce its citizens to send him a petition inviting the Russians to come in. At the same time he gave orders for an army corps to be *assembled* near Dukla, 25 miles  from Lemberg. Three or four weeks at least must elapse before this corps can be concentrated there and equipped with munitions, provisions, transport etc. and who knows where the Magyars will be by then.

As far as Haynau's famous 30,000 men are concerned, who are supposed to arrive on Hungarian soil within 12 days (!), these are even more harmless. Haynau had to abandon the blockade of Venice and advance into Lombardy. We know how the Brescians kept him occupied on March 31 and April 1.[223] We know that he cannot leave his position until he is relieved by Radetzky—and Radetzky is still not able to do this. And when he is finally relieved, he has still to cover between 150 and 170 German miles[b] before arriving at Pest. True, part of the journey can be covered by rail, but when it is a matter of transporting 30,000 men along with their artillery, cavalry, baggage train etc., railways do not speed things up very much. The "twelve days" can therefore easily become six weeks and meanwhile the Magyars will have time enough to teach Windischgrätz's army some very serious lessons. Who knows—perhaps the Magyars will meet Herr Haynau halfway!

Written by Engels on April 14, 1849

First published in the *Neue Rheinische Zeitung* No. 273, April 15, 1849

Printed according to the newspaper

Published in English for the first time

---

[a] See this volume, p. 275.— *Ed.*
[b] See footnote on p. 20.— *Ed.*

# [PARLIAMENTARY DECISIONS ARE DISREGARDED.— MANTEUFFEL'S SPIES]

*Berlin*, April 13. Of course no notice at all is being taken of the motion passed by the Second Chamber that goods up to 5 lbs. should be post-free. The decision has been taken and although it is the custom in constitutional states for the House to decide matters of this kind independently, Herr von der Heydt has different ideas about these things. To date he has not even thought it worth the trouble to express his opinion on the matter in question.

As is well known, Herr *von Meusebach* is the most indispensable of all government counsellors. Nobody understands how to make the best and most valuable use of his eyes and ears, as he does, and always to provide his friend Manteuffel with the best and up-to-the minute reports about the frame of mind and intentions etc. of the Berliners. It is quite natural that the author of the "Revelations" should have great skill in matters which in ordinary language are called spying! He makes use of various literary rogues for these noble aims. His most intimate friends and most skilful tools are *Gödsche*, the well-known columnist of the *Kreuz-Zeitung*, and *Röhrdanz*, the writer.*

A note has also arrived from Mecklenburg which expresses opposition to the definite acceptance of the imperial crown by the King of Prussia.[224]

Written by Marx on April 13, 1849

First published in the *Neue Rheinische Zeitung* No. 273 (second edition), April 15, 1849

Printed according to the newspaper

Published in English for the first time

---

* Herr Röhrdanz was suspected of similar activities in Paris as early as 1844 and is hereby challenged to answer these accusations. *The Editors of the "Neue Rheinische Zeitung".*

# STATEMENT

*Cologne,* April 14. Citizens *K. Marx, K. Schapper, Fr. Anneke, H. Becker* and *W. Wolff* (as deputy) met today as the District Committee of Rhenish Democratic Associations.

Citizens Marx, Schapper, Anneke and Wolff issued the following joint statement.

"We consider that the present organisation of the Democratic Associations includes too many heterogeneous elements for any possibility of successful activity in furtherance of the cause.

"We are of the opinion, on the other hand, that a closer union of the Workers' Associations is to be preferred since they consist of homogeneous elements, and therefore we hereby from today withdraw from the Rhenish District Committee of Democratic Associations.[225]

*"Fr. Anneke, K. Schapper, K. Marx, H. Becker, W. Wolff* (deputy)"

Written on April 14, 1849

First published in the *Neue Rheinische Zeitung* No. 273 (second edition), April 15, 1849

Printed according to the newspaper

Published in English for the first time

## [FROM THE THEATRE OF WAR]

*The imperial troops have been driven further and further back; the Magyars have reached the Rakos plain,[226] the field where the Hungarian kings used to be elected, half an hour from Pest, and are offering battle.*

This is the latest news from Pest, of the 8th. The other information received is less certain. For instance, somebody has written to the *Breslauer Zeitung* that Windischgrätz would not accept battle and had already retreated to Pest with his troops. Those with pro-imperial views believe that the Magyars would not dare attack Pest, on the one hand because of the strong entrenchments thrown up there, on the other so as not to expose their capital to destruction. In the meantime things look grim in Pest. Windischgrätz returned first to Pest, then to Ofen, but without giving any indication of how the battle is going. Of course, this has deeply hurt the "loyal subjects" and greatly cheered the Magyars.

At the same time Herr Wrbna has had the following proclamation posted up on the 7th of this month:

"The cities of Ofen and Pest are in a state of siege, hence all meetings in squares and streets are prohibited; but as this order has not been observed for some days, I feel compelled to remind the inhabitants herewith that they must stay at home and also avoid unnecessary travel; patrols are authorised *to intervene in any gathering with full use of arms. A further consequence of any kind of riotous movement would be the immediate bombardment of the city,* for which everything is in readiness."

Many loyal subjects of His Apostolic Majesty, who no longer feel safe in Pest, have already moved across to Ofen, into the fortress; refugees from Pest have already arrived even in Vienna. The Pest Magyars are jubilant; the Austrians, on the other hand, are threatening. Two loaded twelve-pounders from the Ofen side of the pontoon bridge, and many heavy guns from the Ofen citadel, are aimed at Pest, to give emphasis to Welden's threat.

The intensity of the Magyar attack is said to exceed all expectations of the Austrians. In particular the countless Magyar hussars have been giving no rest by day or by night to the imperial troops for five days, and the audacity of these hussars is beyond all Austrian calculation.

The imperial troops, by the way, have mustered everything so as to stand their ground. The garrisons of Waitzen and Vesprim have gone to Pest; reinforcements are approaching by forced marches from Komorn, Vienna etc., but will in any case be too late for the decisive battle.

On April 11 the news spread at the Vienna Stock Exchange that the Hungarians had been beaten off at Pest. We regard this rumour as a mere speculators' bluff. Not much more trustworthy is another rumour according to which Görgey is said to have relieved Komorn with one Magyar corps, and to have compelled the siege army to march against him and so relinquish the fortress. Nothing is more probable than that Hungarian or Slovak volunteers in the comitats of Neutra, Gran and Nograd are raiding and harassing the Komorn siege corps; but that the main Magyar army should send off Görgey with an important corps while it is waging a decisive battle at Pest, is not credible.

The matter of Jellachich's victory, announced in the 33rd Bulletin (he thereupon "took up the positions assigned to him", as the comical placard-maker Welden expressed it in the 34th Bulletin), is also given away by the *Lloyd,* reporting from Pest that the people there had to believe that the Ban was a prisoner, and were much surprised to get further news from him.[a]

Further details are available about the Magyar army. Klapka is *not* a prisoner, as some papers have maintained, but is in charge of a detachment in the Magyar centre. The left wing of the Hungarian army is led by Damjanich, a Banat Serb, who earlier led an army corps against Nugent and Dahlen in the Baranya comitat and then in the Bacska and at Szegedin. If some martial-law papers say that he has *now* sold (!) himself to the Magyars, this is a lie as silly as it is contemptible. The earlier Austrian Bulletins are there to prove the contrary.

The decisive battle was to be fought on the 8th. We know that it was fought, and fought very violently; but as regards the outcome we only have the rumours quoted above.

---

[a] "Pest, 8. April", *Der Lloyd* No. 171 (evening edition), April 10, 1849.— *Ed.*

If Windischgrätz is driven to the right bank of the Danube, he can immediately withdraw his troops beyond the Raab and relinquish Komorn. He has not a single line of defence as far as the Leitha,and whether he can hold even that will depend entirely on the morale of his beaten army. In any event, with Windischgrätz's defeat Hungary will for the time being be cleared of imperial troops, while a rebuff of the Magyar attack would not take the Austrians further than the Theiss. On the Theiss the old game of trick-track would in the meantime begin again, until royal imperial reinforcements of 50,000-60,000 men arrive.

It is confirmed in the Banat that the Magyars have conquered the whole of the *Bacska* and have relieved Peterwardein. The Nugents, *père et fils,* have once again made fools of themselves.

In conclusion we give the following details from a Vienna *Lithographierte Correspondenz* concerning certain Hungarian generals and the Hungarian army:

Among the Hungarian generals *Görgey* deserves special mention. He is still very young, but most talented and extremely active, untiring and personally courageous; it is perhaps not saying too much to describe him as the soul of all the military operations, since, as everyone knows, Kossuth, in his career as a lawyer, had little opportunity to distinguish himself in the military sciences. Among the foreigners the Englishman *Guyon* is outstanding. His daring knows no limit. For instance, recently he stormed a mountain (which can only be reached by a road with seven bends and which was held by an adequate garrison of Austrian troops and guns) at the head of his column, with a loss of 400 men, although it would have been possible to bypass it, but with considerable loss of time.

The courageous Guyon shrinks from no obstacle and is as cool-headed as he is fearless, one of the most daring partisans of this in its way unique campaign. The *Honveds,* who initially were poorly clad and fed, are now in much better shape. In the winter it was not uncommon to find some ill-clad Honveds frozen to death by the road. They have learned to bear the hardships of the campaign and fight with the courage of disciplined troops. The lull Windischgrätz granted the Hungarians at the beginning they used in the best possible way, and in particular they proceeded with the training of the Honveds by employing them in small raids so as to accustom them gradually to warfare.

In the meantime their military training was completed as far as possible. At present the Honveds are significantly advanced in their development and have already distinguished themselves in individual engagements. The main strength of the Hungarian army, of course, is its excellent cavalry which daily arouses more respect in the Austrian cavalry; even the Wallmoden cuirassiers, known for their courage, have often had opportunity to get to know the might of the Hungarian hussars and have succumbed to their impetuous attacks more that once.

Written by Engels about April 15, 1849          Printed according to the newspaper

First published in the *Neue Rheinische*          Published in English for the first
*Zeitung* No. 273 (second edition), April 15.          time
1849

# FROM THE THEATRE OF WAR

Still no decisive news from the Rakos plain. On the 8th there appears to have been little fighting; the main battle was expected on the 9th. The most contradictory rumours have been circulating in Vienna. According to one the Hungarians have marched victoriously into Pest; according to another they were beaten and Schlick had encircled 5,000 Honveds[227] and taken them prisoner. What is certain is that neither a Bulletin nor a telegraphic dispatch, nor any other official report has arrived, and that, for the time being, is sufficient proof that as far as the imperial side is concerned matters are not going very well. Moreover, Windischgrätz is said to have sent his son with his *resignation* to Olmütz. The Supreme Command in Hungary has been offered to both Hess and Welden; both have so far rejected the offer as they have not been given a completely free hand.

The black-and-yellow[a] side in Pest relies on the Hungarians not wishing to subject their own capital to bombardment and flames. Dembiński, moreover, is said to have declared against it, saying that Poland had been vanquished in 1831[228] only because much too great strategic importance had been ascribed there to Warsaw, the capital.

In the Bacska the Magyars are pressing irresistibly forward. It is confirmed that Perczel and Batthyány have marched into Neusatz. Neusatz lies directly opposite Peterwardein on the other (left) bank of the Danube, and like Peterwardein itself is occupied by the Magyars. The fortifications of Sz. Thomas, so stubbornly defended by the Serbs last year, have been stormed by the Magyars; Zombor and Becse (Base) are also in their hands. They are threatening the left bank of the Theiss; Patriarch Rajachich has had to leave

---

[a] The Austrian imperial colours.— *Ed.*

Becskerek and is going via Pancsova to Semlin. Kničanin has suddenly reappeared on the battlefield to help the Austrians in their predicament.

Transylvania is safe. The *Constitutionelles Blatt aus Böhmen* reports the following from Czernowitz:

"*Czernowitz*, April 5. It has been settled, 60,000 Russians are to occupy Galicia and remain there as a garrison. Lieutenant-Field Marshal Baron von Hammerstein is going to Hungary with 25 battalions and a proportionate number of cannon. Today Lieutenant-Field Marshal von Malkowsky is departing to relieve Lieutenant-Field Marshal Puchner who is ill. All Transylvania is barricaded, Bem is commanding an army of 100,000 men, including 10,000 men of the Polish Legion, a legion of Vienna academics[229] and proletarians. The Bukovina is again afraid of an incursion of Hungarians who, according to recent travellers, have a particular sympathy for the Bukovina. Moreover, the departure of the 4th battalion of Baron Sivkovich's regiment has indeed been stopped for the time being, because there appears, after all, to be some inclination to resistance."[a]

For Bem is recruiting very actively among the Transylvanian Wallachians and Saxons. Anyone able to carry arms is put into the Honveds, trained and used against the Austrians. Clearly, Bem is taking heavy vengeance for the Austrian recruiting system which forced Viennese prisoners to fight against Magyars, and Hungarian prisoners to fight against Italians. In Hermannstadt a great banquet was held to celebrate the fraternisation of Wallachians and Magyars.

As a result of the news from Hungary all the Ministers have been summoned to Olmütz by telegraph.

Yesterday's *Abend-Lloyd*[b] reports as authentic that Lieutenant-Field Marshal Wohlgemuth has taken over the command of the army corps which is concentrated at Komorn.

Written by Engels about April 16, 1849

First published in the *Neue Rheinische Zeitung* No. 274, April 17, 1849

Printed according to the newspaper

Published in English for the first time

---

a "Černowic, 5. April", *Constitutionelles Blatt aus Böhmen* No. 87, April 12, 1849.— *Ed.*

b A reference to the item "Neustes" published in *Der Lloyd* No. 173 (evening edition), April 11, 1849.— *Ed.*

# FROM THE THEATRE OF WAR.—
## PEASANT WAR IN THE BUKOVINA

The Magyars have suddenly broken off the fighting at Pest and marched off to Waitzen, leaving their outposts behind. Waitzen is situated north of Pest on the Danube just at the corner where it leaves the eastern direction and turns south. *Waitzen, the key to the road to Komorn, has been taken by the Hungarians.* Jellachich is on the *right bank of the Danube* at Szent Endré!

This news was known in Vienna on the 13th at midday and had a "very depressing effect". As early as the 14th Welden was supposed to go to the army fighting in Hungary.

Further details on this new turn in the fighting and this strategically most important success of the Hungarians are still lacking. Hence we cannot know whether the Hungarian army is really marching to Komorn to relieve it or whether it simply wants to entice the imperial troops from their fortified positions at Pest and engage them in battle in the open field without exposing Pest to the danger of bombardment.

The rest of the news is contradictory to the highest degree. Nothing at all is known either about the position of the Magyar army in the recent battles at Pest, or about the details of the battle itself. Windischgrätz is not allowing anybody to leave the Pest lines. We know only that nothing happened on the 8th (Easter Sunday) except some outpost skirmishes. Nor were any guns fired on the 9th. This was the day when the Magyar main force appears to have started for Waitzen. Two Austrian brigades marched off in the same direction.

South of Pest, at Raczkeve, the Magyars under Vetter are said to have attempted to throw a bridge over the Danube, but to have been prevented from doing so.

Otherwise the most fantastic and contradictory rumours are circulating. The fear of the Black-and-Yellows makes Bem arrive from Transylvania with 20,000 men and operate against Kalocsa on the Danube (on the border of the Bacska), so as to go from there to the right bank and to advance in the rear of the Austrians. In this area, by the way, Perczel is taking one important position after another from the Serbs. Peterwardein, recently besieged, is now the main support point of his operations.

Another rumour born of the Austrians' fear makes Görgey stand already at Bruck on the Leitha, a few hours' march from Vienna!

Incidentally, the Serb Voivodina has at last been promised by the Government that it shall join the ranks of the independent crown lands. It may be doubted whether this will tend to make the mood of the Serbs—now moving daily further towards unity with the Magyars—more favourable towards the Government. The Serbs no longer trust a Government which has so often tried to trick them. The correspondent of the *Constitutionelles Blatt aus Böhmen* writes from the Drava:

"Perhaps I shall soon write to you *while in flight!*"[a]

From Transylvania not a word. Just as little news from Galicia concerning the alleged entry of the Russians. On the other hand the long lost nation of the Huzuls[230] has reappeared in the Bukovina, with its peasant king, Kobylica, at its head. Here, in this most remote corner of the united monarchy, the struggle is developing between peasants and nobility which the implementation of the imposed redemption laws[231] is bound to produce everywhere in Austria. Kobylica *is directly allied with the Magyars.* Just listen to the *Bucovina* (which appears in Czernowitz) of April 4 on this subject[b]:

"The notorious *Kobylica* with his dangerous agent Birla Mironiuk has reappeared in the mountains among the (Ruthenian[232]) Huzuls and is deluding the villages with dangerous misrepresentations; he is egging them on to trespass on the baronial woods and pastures and maintain a rebellious attitude: he would soon come *with a Hungarian army* to help them. The excitement this has induced has taken on a dubious character particularly in the neighbourhood of Berhometh, hence the District Office has seen fit to dispatch a complete company to this area and to take other energetic measures. In accordance with the instructions of the local District Office the company has been stationed in and around Berhometh. District Commissioner Wex is in charge of the official action which is to comprise, first, prevention of trespass and damage to baronial woods and fenced pastures in the area, questioning and punishing the guilty

---

[a] "Von der Drave, 7. April", *Constitutionelles Blatt aus Böhmen* No. 88, April 13, 1849.— *Ed.*

[b] The following report under the date-line "Bukowina. Czernowitz, 4. April" was also published in the *Ost-Deutsche Post* No. 72, April 13, 1849.— *Ed.*

severely, the instruction and surveillance of the villages, the harshest and most relentless treatment of all disturbers of the peace and agitators, keeping an eye and a tight rein on rural people and capturing Kobylica and his agent Birla Mironiuk.—These strong measures should at last bring about the definitive pacification of the Ruthenian mountain villages."

## Good luck to the Austrian peasant war!

Written by Engels about April 17, 1849

Printed according to the newspaper

First published in the *Neue Rheinische Zeitung* No. 275, April 18, 1849

Published in English for the first time

# ELKEMANN

*Cologne*, April 18. Yesterday in Berlin the Second Chamber voted on the question whether the entire Bill to suppress the right of association, brought in by Herr Manteuffel, should be rejected lock, stock and barrel or not. Rejection of the Bill failed by 137 votes to 141. Thus the Left was in a minority of only four votes. Among these four votes, all of which were of the Left Centre, was Pastor *Elkemann* from *Worringen,* deputy of the *rural constituency of Cologne and Mülheim.* One may ask his intermediate and primary electors whether the Pastor, who acted the extreme liberal at the time, was elected by them to help get rid of the few still remaining civil liberties?

Written by Engels on April 18, 1849

First published in the *Neue Rheinische Zeitung* No. 276, April 19, 1849

Printed according to the newspaper

Published in English for the first time

# FROM THE THEATRE OF WAR

The Hungarians' plan of operations after Windischgrätz was pushed back by them to the Danube is now fairly clear. While Dembiński kept the Austrian centre under Schlick "fully occupied" (Augsburg *Allgemeine Zeitung*[a]), Görgey with greatly increased strength turned on the imperial army's left wing at Waitzen, commanded by Windischgrätz himself, beat him back and took Waitzen. Almost every report maintains complete silence about what has become of Jellachich and the Austrian right wing. As we wrote already yesterday, one report makes him stationed at Szent Endré, between Ofen and Waitzen on the right bank of the Danube.[b] This is today confirmed directly from Pest. He can only have marched there to cover the threatened left wing by abandoning his earlier position on the right wing. Besides the great strength of the Hungarians at Waitzen, the fact that the Croats can no longer be brought into the firing line by the "chivalrous" Ban and show a daily growing respect for the Hungarian hussars, may perhaps explain this otherwise quite inexplicable movement. At the same time, they have been plundering and raping in Pest and its neighbourhood with such gusto that the Croat Don Quixote felt compelled to have a number of those keenest on plundering shot summarily. Also we are still hearing of desertions among the Croats. Evidently, this most charming of all the corps gathered at Pest can therefore only be used as a reserve. This is also confirmed in a Vienna report of the *Deutsche Allgemeine Zeitung*, according to which 5,000 to 6,000 Croats are said to have been sent to Pest to serve as a reserve.

---

[a] "Wien, 12. April", Augsburg *Allgemeine Zeitung* No. 105, April 15, 1849.— *Ed.*
[b] See this volume, p. 288.— *Ed.*

On the other hand, the Magyars have by no means kept their left wing, facing the Austrian right wing, inactive. It is beyond doubt that they have already crossed the Danube at least at one point below Pest, and that without meeting with any significant resistance, since all the imperial troops of this area have marched to Pest. Vetter, who is here in command (he was previously a major in the 37th imperial infantry regiment), is operating against Pentele and Földvar, and is according to consistent rumours already on the march to Stuhlweissenburg. In the Bacska Batthyány's and Perczel's main force seems also to be pressing ahead against the Danube and Drava, so as to cut off Nugent and the Serbs from direct contact with the Austrian main army, or to force Nugent to make a hurried retreat to Esseg or Agram.

Thus, Windischgrätz is threatened on all sides and outflanked both on the left and the right. Tonight we may receive definite information that Görgey is at Gran and Vetter at Stuhlweissenburg. God knows what will become of the imperial troops when both their lines of retreat are thus cut off.

Now that the Magyars have had time to train, the imperial side speaks with one voice of how they fight. The *Ost-Deutsche Post* says:

"The fanaticism of our opponents and the money which is apparently at their disposal, attract to them masses where we only have ranks. Like an impetuous mountain torrent they break through the strong wall facing them."[a]

And the Augsburg *Allgemeine Zeitung*:

"The hussars fight with a bravery which makes any advance of the imperial army impossible without considerable reinforcements. These Magyars are no Piedmontese (!), even Radetzky's entire army would find it hard going here."[b]

The Black-and-Yellows in Pest, on the other hand, are completely demoralised. They flee from Pest in droves, some to Ofen, others in the direction of Gran or even so far as Raab.

Benedek has arrived in Vienna. He is to command the advance guard of Hammerstein's corps which, according to the Austrian martial-law boasts, is already in Kaschau! Haynau's corps will *not* go to Hungary. We said at once that it could not be spared in Italy.[c]

Herr Welden, remembered for his incendiarism, the man who wanted to take Komorn by storm like an Italian village, is now to help the imperial troops in their predicament. He has departed for the theatre of war.

---

[a] "Pest, 11. April", *Ost-Deutsche Post* No. 73, April 14, 1849.— *Ed.*
[b] "Wien, 12. April", Augsburg *Allgemeine Zeitung* No. 105, April 15, 1849.— *Ed.*
[c] See this volume, p. 280.— *Ed.*

In the Banat and in the Bacska things are likewise daily getting worse for the imperial side. The *Südslavische Zeitung* bewails the fall of Szent Thomas, christened Srbobran (Serb Bulwark)[a] by the Serbs as the scene of their heroic deeds of last year. The Bacska has been abandoned altogether by the imperial troops; Nugent is on the defensive beyond the Danube and will be glad if he can keep Syrmien. The mood of the Serbs is becoming more and more "sinister"; if they formerly hated the Magyars, now this has given place to *hatred of the Germans.* The bad turn the war has taken is directly ascribed to a deliberate, planned abandonment of the Serbs by the Austrian officers. Kničanin is again expected with Serb auxiliaries; according to others the well-known Vučič is to command them. Moreover, the Austrian Government has at last recalled Rukavina and pensioned him off, and thus initiated a series of concessions to the Serbs.

Not a word from Transylvania. Yesterday the *Kölnische Zeitung* had the Russians and Puchner march in again. The news came from the *Bukurester Zeitung,* it passed from there into the *Wiener Zeitung* and finally into the *Kölnische.* But it merely gave the positions which Puchner and the Russians occupied after the capture of Hermannstadt by Bem, before they fled through the Roterturm Pass. The *Kölnische Zeitung* could have known that as well as we; but in its pleasure at seeing the imperial troops at last advance again at any point, it fell into the trap and promptly reprinted this ancient news, *deliberately* put into the *Wiener Zeitung* to confuse the reader. That is how history is made.

Written by Engels on April 18, 1849

First published in the *Neue Rheinische Zeitung* No. 276, April 19, 1849

Printed according to the newspaper

Published in English for the first time

---

[a] This report of the *Südslavische Zeitung* was reprinted in the article "Mitrović, 5. April" in the *Ost-Deutsche Post* No. 74, April 15, 1849.— *Ed.*

95

# SITTING OF THE SECOND CHAMBER IN BERLIN. APRIL 13

*Cologne,* April 19. For a change, let us return once more to our dear Second Chamber in Berlin. It has checked the elections, issued Addresses, produced standing orders, and with quite exceptional interest it has discussed a question which, as is well known, belongs to the feature section of the *Neue Rheinische Zeitung,* i.e. the question of the German Emperor.[233] All this passed quite unnoticed in view of the cannonades at Novara and Pest, and even the "naval battle" at Eckernförde and the storming of the Düppel fortifications[234] made a greater impression than all the speeches from the Right and the Left in the Prussian people's representative body.

Now, however, when the honourable Chamber is busy with the three gagging laws[235]—the law on posters, the law on associations and the law on the press—when it has already finished dealing with one of them, the law on posters, now the matter more closely concerns us, now it will be more interesting to see how our deputies do their utmost to make up deficiencies in the imposed Constitution.

Let us look at the verbatim report of the 26th sitting on April 13.[a]

First of all Deputy Lisiecki put a question to the Ministry about the use of the Polish army reserve in the war against Denmark.

According to § 61 of the law on the army reserve, [236] it can only be mobilised in the event of unexpected hostile attacks on the country. Its entire organisation is so constituted that in general it is only to be employed when the standing army and reserves are insufficient. But now the army reserve is being mobilised in the war against little

---

[a] *Stenographische Berichte über die Verhandlungen der durch das Allerhöchste Patent vom 5. Dezember 1848 einberufenen Kammern. Zweite Kammer.* Bd. 2, S. 462-65.— *Ed.*

Denmark, which can be dealt with by the troops of the line of a single army corps!

That is not all. Although the allegedly German part of Posen could be tricked into joining the German Confederation only through breach of faith and brutal violence, although, according to all the treaties, the part of Posen lying on the other side of the famous demarcation line has nothing to do with the German Confederation,[237] part of the army reserve sent to Schleswig from Posen has been taken from both sides of the demarcation line.

These army reserve men of purely Polish nationality, half of whom do not even belong to the German Confederation, are being sent to Schleswig to let themselves be killed there for the greater glory of *Germany* as *German* imperial troops with the *German* black-red-and-gold[a] imperial cockade on their helmets!

The Croats decided the outcome of the "*German* war" in Lombardy; the Czechs, Ruthenians[238] and, again, the Croats decided the outcome of the "German" struggle against Vienna; the *Poles* will decide the outcome of the "German" war in Schleswig. It is with such soldiers that nowadays the "victories of German arms" are being won!

And that is how the King keeps the promise he gave the Poles on April 11 through his plenipotentiary commissioner[b]:

"Accordingly, no recruits born in the Grand Duchy of Posen are to be incorporated in a Silesian or other German regiment and, conversely, no German recruits are to be incorporated in a Polish regiment. The training and commanding of troops are to be in their own language ... all arms of the Polish military service are likewise to form a *completely independent entity*" etc.

Lisiecki enumerated these various points in a calm, but resolute, tone. In conclusion he drew attention to the special malice shown by recruiting three battalions of the army reserve precisely in the one province which last year had suffered heavily from the civil war imposed on it by Prussia.

Herr Strotha, Minister of War, rose to speak.

The Minister delivered a lecture to the Assembly at some length to the effect that

"the entire Prussian army organisation is based on a combination of troops of the line and the army reserve, and in war this combination in the composition of corps and divisions reaches as far as the composition of brigades", that the dispatch of "mere troops of the line without the army reserve to a distant theatre of war essentially hinders the organic formation of several troop units and gives rise to many kinds of serious drawbacks when mobilising the remaining units" etc.

---

[a] The colours of the movement for the unification of Germany.— *Ed.*

[b] Wilhelm Willisen.— *Ed.*

All this was very suitable for opening the eyes of the philistines and civil officials in the Chamber to the organisation of "My glorious army".[239]

It may be so. It is possible that "the troops of the line of My glorious army" cannot manage without "the army reserve of My glorious army". It may be that the dangerous potato war[240] with Denmark compels the Government to set in motion all the chicanery of the glorious Prussian military organisation. But why is it that precisely the *Poles* have been made the victims of this fate, which derives from the glorious Prussian military organisation?

Because—well, "because *it is justified by the immediate circumstances!*"

That is all we are told. That is how a Prussian Minister of War answers questions.

There still remains the reply to the legal question: should not German troops be used in German imperial wars? On this Herr Strotha stated:

1) "The Grand Duchy of Posen, with the exception of a small part ... belongs to Germany."

That is the Prussian translation of last year's phrases to the effect that Posen should become Polish, "with the exception of a small part" of the frontier, which must become German. Things have now gone far enough for the phrases to be dispensed with and the perpetrated swindles to be admitted in blunt words.

2) "The delimitation of military areas in the entire Grand Duchy of Posen has so far undergone no change. Accordingly (!), therefore (!), the three mobilised battalions consist to the extent of about half of inhabitants from one side of the demarcation line and one half of inhabitants from the other side of the demarcation line."

In plain language that means: the whole farce with the demarcation line merely served to incorporate two-thirds of Posen into Germany directly, and the remaining one-third indirectly. And in order that the Poles finally abandon the illusion that this demarcation line has any practical meaning, we have at this very time recruited our imperial troops from those districts through which the demarcation line passes.

3) "In utilising troops of the line drawn from the Grand Duchy of Posen, no other consideration has ever been taken into account than that demanded by *state reasons.*"

And if the solemn pledges of March and April 1848 in regard to the troops of the line have been trampled under foot, then why should not the same happen in regard to the army reserve? Cannot a

Polish army reserve man become as good a "soldier of the imperial troops" as a Polish regular soldier?

We have taken into consideration only "state reasons"!

And what are these "state reasons"?

They are quite obvious. Men capable of bearing arms and trained in the use of arms who live in areas not yet sufficiently merged in the "Prussian fatherland" are to be removed from their homeland. Objectionable primary electors who voted in an un-Prussian way are to be punished. The authorities wish to inculcate in these primary electors a better notion of the duties of a citizen by making them undergo a supplementary course of instruction in the school of "My glorious army". By this Prussian treatment many a hated elector will be provoked to insubordination and then, with the greatest nonchalance, he can under martial law be awarded 15 years' confinement in irons and perhaps even gunpowder and lead.

It is for this that the army reserve has been mobilised in Posen and also in part of the Rhine Province and Westphalia. Herr Strotha does not mention the Rhine Province, nevertheless the Clever battalion has already been sent to Schleswig. Or does Herr Strotha want to introduce a demarcation line in the Rhine Province as well and declare: The Rhine Province, "with the exception of a small part", belongs to Westphalia?

But what has not yet happened can happen. Although up to now the greater part of the Rhine Province has been spared from mobilisation, we are nevertheless aware that, in spite of all official denials, *there exists a firm intention* to mobilise also the army reserve of the *Eighth* Corps, i.e. of the Rhine Province. Preparations for this have already been made, and the order will not be long in coming.

Of course, this also is dictated by "state reasons" and is justified by the "immediate circumstances".

And if the Rhenish deputies put down a parliamentary question, Herr Strotha will reply to them just as he now replies to Herr Lisiecki: the matter "is in fact already settled" since "the Rhenish division is already concentrated at Flensburg"!

After Herr Strotha had concluded his speech, Herr Lisiecki wanted to make a factual correction. But the standing orders forbid factual corrections to replies by Ministers. And the standing orders are quite right. What un-Prussian insolence to imagine that a ministerial reply could be capable of undergoing factual correction!

Written by Engels on April 19, 1849

First published in the *Neue Rheinische Zeitung* No. 277, April 20, 1849

Printed according to the newspaper

Published in English for the first time

# THE SLOVAKS.—
## THE SO-CALLED DEMBIŃSKI BULLETIN

Owing to the non-arrival of the Berlin train we are without any recent news from the theatre of war. The Augsburg *Allgemeine Zeitung*, which now carries all the news from Vienna and Hungary one day late, has nothing new either, of course. The report of its "reliable" Vienna correspondent on the latest military events contains nothing but nonsense and most glaringly contradicts geography. For example, he says that the insurgents want to erect a bridge "at Szent Endré",[a] though two arms of the Danube and an island four miles[b] long and a half mile wide lie between Szent Endré and the Magyars etc.

The *Constitutionelles Blatt aus Böhmen* yesterday carried a long article "from Slovakia",[c] which in the last analysis amounts to a doleful lamentation about the Austrian Government doing nothing to foster pan-Slavist separatist aspirations against Hungary among the Slovaks. Every line indicates how much they deplore that it is quite impossible to arouse pan-Slavist Magyar hatred in the Slovaks, that the Slovak peasants give their allegiance above all to the party which definitely assures them of liberation from their feudal burdens, that the Magyar nobility is naturally pro-Magyar and the German middle class of the towns is also favourably inclined towards the Magyars. The notorious boasting at the Olmütz Court about the "Slovak trusted representatives"[241] is disowned even here:

"The common people naturally know little or nothing of the election of 'Slovak trusted representatives'; educated Slovaks shrug their shoulders at a blunder that

---

[a] "Wien, 13. April", Augsburg *Allgemeine Zeitung* No. 106, April 16, 1849.— *Ed.*
[b] See footnote on p. 20.— *Ed.*
[c] "Aus der Slovakei", *Constitutionelles Blatt aus Böhmen* No. 89, April 14, 1849.— *Ed.*

could hardly have been worse. Kollár, the only poet among them, is a name everywhere popular and respected; the rest are lawyers whom not a soul knows in Slovakia, who have never wielded a pen in favour of the Slovaks, never taken a step, never spoken a word which could have given them a claim to the honourable title of 'trusted representatives' of a nation, even if in other respects their honourable private character is in no way disputed. In Slovakia they are, Kollár excepted, 'mistrusted representatives'. To put a Hungarian lawyer in charge of Slovak affairs is an unfortunate idea. Perhaps this was why the *Slovenski pozornik* (Slovak Observer), mentioning the trusted representatives in its first issue, did not even bother to give their names, Kollár again excepted, to whom due respect is paid."

Since last night, an alleged "27th Battle Report of General Dembiński to Kossuth", dated Gödöllö, April 7,[a] is being circulated here in Cologne. This report is printed in Frankfurt, whence false news on Austria has already come more than once. But even if it is not genuine, it is a good imitation made from the available material. Dates and military positions are everywhere sufficiently in accord with those of the Austrian Bulletins; the Bulletin only contains something new on the fighting which took place before April 2. The main content is as follows:

Dembiński, acting here as commander of the centre and General-in-Chief (Vetter has the right wing, Görgey the left), has first totally defeated an enemy corps at Erlau and then beaten the rearguard again at Gyöngyös. In this second battle the Hungarians are said to have captured 16 cannon and made 1,200 prisoners, which, however, is somewhat exaggerated.

On the 5th the Austrians were driven from Hatvan to Gödöllö, where a major battle took place on the 6th. Here the Hungarians were completely victorious, took 26 cannon, 7 flags, 38 ammunition carts and 3,200 prisoners, and drove the Austrians back to the walls of Pest. The imperial troops are said to have lost 6,000 dead and wounded, the Hungarians 2,000.

As can be seen, the Bulletin contains nothing new except that it gives figures; these, even if it were genuine, are probably not too correct. In the first flush of victory enemy losses always tend to be exaggerated.

So it is really immaterial whether the Bulletin is genuine or simply a fake, since it only gives known *results*.

What makes its authenticity very suspect, however, is the date. A Bulletin from Gödöllö dated the 7th could not have been received again on the 10th printed in Debreczin. Had it been printed by the army and distributed in Pest or Ofen, we would have heard the news

---

[a] This report was published in the *Kölnische Zeitung* No. 95, April 21, 1849.— *Ed.*

already in other ways. Moreover, the leaflet gives its source only in the words "translated from the Hungarian". It neither says where the original was printed nor whence it comes. Even if the content can be accepted as authentic, its form is certainly very suspect. But, as we have said, it is immaterial whether this leaflet is authentic or fabricated, since it reports nothing new at all.

Written by Engels about April 19, 1849

First published in the *Neue Rheinische Zeitung* No. 277, April 20, 1849

Printed according to the newspaper

Published in English for the first time

# [FROM THE THEATRE OF WAR]

According to the letters and papers which have arrived from Eastern Germany only this evening (Thursday), the Hungarians are masters of the left bank of the Danube to the point at which the Gran flows into it from the north, five miles below Komorn. On the 12th Pest was still besieged by a Hungarian corps which could be observed quite clearly from the roofs with the naked eye, and which is supposed to have occupied the Pest railway station. To avoid exposing it to bombardment, and because from here it would be impossible to effect a crossing of the Danube under the guns of Ofen, this corps has not attacked the city itself.

The most contradictory rumours are current about the battle at Waitzen, but they all agree that the left wing of the Austrians has suffered a complete defeat there. One report asserts that Götz is not dead but severely wounded and in the hands of the Hungarians. After their defeat, part of the Austrian corps which linked up at Waitzen retreated across the Danube, while another part, two brigades strong, drew back behind the Gran. Here, five brigades of reinforcements, which have arrived from Austria etc., are said to have been stationed for a considerable time (!), the force is estimated at 25,000 men (!!) by the *Wanderer*. These five brigades are probably not more than a few regiments who marched away from the former siege corps of Komorn, for had five brigades been stationed on the Gran, four miles from Waitzen, they would hardly have remained there while the Hungarian guns thundered at Waitzen!

The *Wanderer* is nothing but a martial-law paper printing reassuring news. It had to report that Waitzen had been captured by the Magyars without a battle, and that only one volunteer corps was stationed there, whereas all the other papers speak of a violent battle and it is certain that Götz, Jablonowsky and Csorich were there, not counting the troops which Windischgrätz took with him when he personally went there. The *Wanderer* further believes that there is no threat at all to Pest (!!), otherwise the imperial forces would surely have removed their wounded and constructed a second pontoon bridge. But the imperial generals have never shown much concern for their wounded, and all they do care for, the baggage, munitions and above all the money, has long been dispatched to Ofen. They have even **stolen** *the gold and silver reserve of the Hungarian National Bank*, 1,700,000 guldens C.M.,[242] which were kept as backing for the Hungarian 1- and 2-florin notes, and incorporated them in the state treasury in Ofen. As concerns the second bridge, the Austrians obviously have much greater need of their pontoon trains on the long battle-front from Pest to Waitzen and Gran than in Pest, which no longer forms their centre but their left flank.

This *Wanderer* has now also suddenly to estimate the imperial army at 100,000, namely 50,000 men at Pest, plus the above non-existent 25,000 at Gran, plus the 10,000 reinforcements from Galicia under Vogl, plus Nugent's force, a total of 100,000 men; that is supposed to be reassuring. We are quite willing to believe that Windischgrätz had 50,000 men before the recent battles, and now still has 40,000. But the 25,000 men at Gran amount to 10,000 at most, scattered along both sides of the Danube from Raab and Gran to Neuhäusel, the remainder of the siege corps at Komorn, reinforced by newly arrived troops. Vogl is still in Galicia, and Nugent is hard-pressed in Syrmien. The imperial forces were indeed over 200,000 strong at the beginning of the war, but the Hungarians have made a clean sweep and scattered the imperial troops to all points of the compass. Puchner is in Wallachia, Knićanin back in Serbia, the Banat volunteers have gone home, large numbers of Croats have been disbanded, and of the whole army at most 120,000 effective troops are scattered over the wide Hungarian territory; of these, perhaps 50,000-55,000 face the main Magyar army.

The rumour persists that a Magyar corps has crossed the Danube south of Pest in the Bacska area and is marching on Stuhlweissenburg, but there is as yet no positive information on this corps' position.

Komorn is already virtually relieved. The siege area has been considerably reduced by the advance of the Magyars. As a substantial part of Windischgrätz's troops had earlier been moved to Pest, the remainder obviously had to march to Gran, to face the Magyars approaching from that direction. Even prior to this, the garrison is said to have made a sortie against the weak besieging troops, scattered them and captured all the siege artillery. Now a report in the *Ost-Deutsche Post* says, moreover, that Komorn has sufficient provisions *for two years*, and that its garrison is united and resolved to defend it to the utmost.

In the small area of Upper Hungary still occupied by the imperial forces, the end of their rule is now approaching. According to the *Österreichischer Correspondent*, a Magyar column reputed to be composed of 800 infantrymen, 200 cavalrymen and five guns, under the command of a Polish officer, Bernicki, marched into Leutschau on April 4, into Neudorf on the 5th, and into Rosenau on the 6th. One of Welden's battalions garrisoning the neighbouring area was called to Eperies, which was threatened by this movement. Nevertheless, the Magyar corps captured Eperies and drove the royal imperial troops, together with the notorious Slovak *Landsturm*, into the Carpathians, to the Galician border.

The name of *Bem*, who at one time was said to be at Debreczin and at another time already at Kalocsa on the Danube, currently looms like a spectre over the *Banat.* It is also reported from Alt-Orsova, on the 2nd of the month, that Bem is preparing an expedition of 10,000 against the Banat. Rukavina is, incidentally, not pensioned off there but merely relieved of the civil administration, which has been transferred to the Patriarch.[a] Rukavina retains command of the Banat Military Border area,[243] and Major-General Mayerhofer, serving under him, will be in command on the Syrmien border.

By the way, the Magyars have not rested content with the seizure of the Bacska. They have crossed the Theiss and occupied the districts of Kikinda and Neu-Becse.

In their hour of greatest need the imperial authorities have no other cure but to take radical measures. The official report of Windischgrätz's dismissal and Welden's appointment to supreme command in Hungary has at last arrived. At the same time, Wohlgemuth has set off with Welden (whom *Böhm* replaces in Vienna) for Hungary, where he is to command a corps of six brigades. Benedek has gone to Galicia to be given a command in Vogl's corps of 10 battalions; the corps is said to be marching via Eperies. Wrbna is to be retired.

But not even that is the end of this revolution in the army.

They have realised that *without the Russians they cannot cope with the Magyars. Russian assistance has* therefore *been directly asked for.* **30,000 Russians are expected to arrive in Hungary via Cracow.**

---

[a] Rajachich.— *Ed.*

In the Banat also the endangered slogan: *svoboda a slavjanstvo* (freedom and Slavdom) will be kept up with *Russian assistance*. Already there is talk of the approach of Russian troops and, to hasten matters, delegates were sent to Duhamel in Bucharest from an assembly held in Semlin on the 5th.

We may hope that the arrival of the Russians will everywhere be too late, and that they will find that the war has already taken so decisive a turn that the most they will be able to do is to look on while the brave Magyars and the Viennese, who may also soon reappear on the field of battle, prepare an ignominious end for

"the Austria of old,
For feats and victories oft extolled".[a]

Today again the latest Vienna and Breslau papers have not arrived.

Written by Engels on April 19, 1849

First published in the *Neue Rheinische Zeitung* No. 277 (second edition), April 20, 1849

Printed according to the newspaper

Published in English for the first time

---

[a] From Ernst Moritz Arndt's poem "Des Teutschen Vaterland" (music by Gustav Reichardt).— *Ed.*

# ["MAGYAR RODOMONTADE"
## OF THE *KÖLNISCHE ZEITUNG*]

We have been informed that none of the current issues of the Vienna and Breslau newspapers arrived yesterday evening with the last train from Berlin. Hence the assertion of the *Kölnische Zeitung* that it has nevertheless received these Vienna newspapers is simply "Magyar rodomontade".

Written by Engels on April 20, 1849

First published in the *Neue Rheinische Zeitung* No. 278, April 21, 1849

Printed according to the newspaper

Published in English for the first time

# THE NEW CROATIAN-SLAVONIAN-DALMATIAN
## ROBBER STATE

*Agram.* While in Hungary proper the royal imperial united monarchy is being shaken in its very foundations by the victorious Magyar armies, the national separatist movement in the South-Slav countries is continually creating new difficulties for the Austrian Government. The Croats have now conceived the idea of a Croatian-Slavonian-Dalmatian triune kingdom, to serve as the focal point for pan-Slav aspirations in the south. This trinity of Pandours, Serezhans and Haiduks, this kingdom of red-coats, was at once "taken in hand", to use the Austrian Croat-German phraseology, by the Croatian-Slavonian Committee of the Diet, and the appropriate Bill produced by the Committee is available in print.[244] The document is remarkable.[a] There is not a trace in it of hatred for the Magyars or of any precautions against *Magyar* transgressions. But it plainly bears the marks of *hatred for the Germans,* of safeguards against *German* transgressions and of the pan-Slav alliance *against the Germans.* That is what our constitutional-patriotic wailers of the Holy Roman Empire have got for their enthusiasm for the Croats.[245] We have already earlier informed our readers that the same hatred and the same mistrust of the Germans is prevalent in the Serbian Voivodina.[b]

The trinity of red-coated cut-throats begins its existence at once with conquests. Apart from the fact that it tears from Hungary the whole of Croatia and Slavonia, it demands the Mur Island, i.e. the

---

corner of the comitat of Zala lying between the Drava and the Mur, and the Quarnero islands of the district of Istria and Trieste, i.e. a small fragment of *Germany* as well as one of Hungary.

In addition it demands the following rights: (1) the internal relations of Croatia-Slavonia with Dalmatia are to be decided by their respective Diets; (2) their relations with the Serbian Voivodina are to be decided by mutual agreement; (3) also,

"*closer political union* is to be established with the remaining neighbouring *Slav* provinces of the Austrian Empire on the basis of mutual agreement",

i.e. a *pan-Slav separatist union*[246] to be formed *against the Germans and the Magyars* within the royal imperial united monarchy. And this right of separatism is, according to the Pandour-Serezhan way of thinking, the first right of man:

"This *natural* (!) right of union cannot *under any pretext* be either denied or hindered in either the triune kingdom or in the Austro-Slav areas which wish to unite with the kingdom by reason of" (Croat German!) "the same or related nationality."

That is, our first, "natural" right of man is the revival of the Prague Slav Congress[247] as the *legislative authority*. How naive a demand to put to a Schwarzenberg-Stadion Government!

These conquests and pan-Slav alliances are followed by a solemn declaration:

"The triune kingdom has never been a *German* country" (*Dieu merci!*), "nor does it wish to become such or even a part or *member of the German Empire*, and consequently the triune kingdom cannot in future be drawn, without its express consent, into *any kind of union* with *Germany* which Austria may enter into either now or in the future."

Such solemn declarations vis-à-vis the *Germans* are considered to be urgently necessary, although to our knowledge no one has ever regarded Croatia and other areas inhabited by cut-throats as a "German country", and although Germany at the moment has not the slightest wish to incorporate the Otočac[248] and Serezhan gentlemen into the German Empire.

There is not a single mention of the *Magyars* in the whole document, not a single paragraph designed to safeguard the desired triune robber state against the much-lamented Magyar oppression!

But the object of the whole thing is quite clear: the united, centralised Austria for which the Government is striving and in which the Germans as the most civilised nation will in the long run certainly be morally dominant, frightens the pan-Slav trinity a thousand times more than the Magyars, whom they consider to be defeated. Moreover, it is clear that among these petty robber nations hatred of the Germans far exceeds their hatred of the Magyars. And yet these petty robber nations are the allies of the *Kölnische Zeitung*, that German patriot!

These general principles are then followed by a long series of stipulations with which the South-Slav robber states seek to safeguard themselves against Austrian centralisation, i.e. against German oppression.

Thus the document proposes that all functions which this law does not expressly assign to the central government shall remain the prerogative of the provincial government. The authority of the central government, however, is only recognised in the following fields: (1) foreign affairs, with the exception of the above proviso regarding relations with Germany, changes in which require a two-thirds majority in the Diet; (2) financial administration, insofar as this is absolutely necessary; (3) military affairs, but only insofar as they concern the standing army; (4) commercial affairs; (5) roads and waterways.

Furthermore, in addition to representation in the Imperial Diet, the trinity of robber states demands

"consideration for the sons of the triune kingdom in appointments to relevant central government posts on the basis of the population proportions and the necessary qualifications"

(elegant Croat German again!), dealings with the central government to be conducted in the official language, a separate robber-state Minister in the central government, and a separate administrative section for the robber states in every relevant ministry.

Apart from that, the robber states will be governed by a "State Council of the Triune Kingdom", and the armed forces, the army as well as the Banderial units,[249] the levy in mass and the National Guard will be under the command of the Ban. But the Ban may command only the army according to the orders of the Central Authority; for his command of the remaining sections of the armed forces he is responsible to "the nation".

In internal affairs, the following changes are demanded: (1) the triune robber state shall provide contingents of troops no larger than any other Austrian province in relation to the size of its population; and (2) in civil matters the Military Border is to be subject to the ordinary civil administration and jurisdiction; the military administration and military jurisdiction operate only for those borderers who are actually under arms. But with that the whole of the royal imperial Military Border will automatically cease to be. We shall return to this.

This is the draft plan for the new triune Otočac-Pandour-Croat robber state which they want to set up on the south-eastern borders of Germany if the revolution and the Magyars permit it.

Written by Engels about April 20, 1849

First published in the *Neue Rheinische Zeitung* No. 278, April 21, 1849

Printed according to the newspaper

Published in English for the first time

# THE RUSSIANS

*Cologne,* April 21. When the *Neue Rheinische Zeitung* began to be published almost eleven months ago, it was the first newspaper to point out the concentration of Russian armies on our Eastern frontier.[a] At that time many virtuous citizens spoke of exaggeration, of unnecessary cries of alarm etc.

It has become clear whether we were exaggerating or not. The Russians, who at first were merely protecting their frontiers, passed more and more to the offensive as the counter-revolution achieved successes. The June victory in Paris brought them to Jassy and Bucharest; the fall of Vienna and Pest brought them to Hermann-stadt and Kronstadt.

A year ago Russia was not prepared for war; at that time, in the first panic terror at the omnipotence of the sudden revolution, it was easy to drive the 30,000-40,000 Russians out of Poland and establish a free Poland. That was what was called for, but the desire for it was lacking. The Russians were given time to arm, and now a Russian army of 500,000-600,000 men surrounds us from the Niemen to the Danube and Aluta. Along the Prussian frontier alone, according to the *Ostsee-Zeitung,* some 150,000 men are stationed; the remainder are in the interior, on the Galician frontier, in Moldavia, Wallachia, Lithuania, Podolia and Volhynia, and in the fortresses of Novo-Georgievsk (Modlin), Brest-Litovsk, Demblin and Zamosye, which according to the *Ostsee-Zeitung* have depots with arms and reserves for 250,000 men.

The same newspaper writes:

---

[a] See the article "The Russian Note" (present edition, Vol. 7, pp. 307-13).— *Ed.*

"Food depots are set up with the aid of requisitioning notes, which oblige every landowner to deliver a certain quantity of produce that is to be used as provisions for the army. Next year these notes will be accepted in payment of taxes. This, therefore, is the source of the recently spread rumour that the Russian Government in Poland has ordered taxes to be collected one year in advance."

What the state of affairs is as regards the acceptance of these notes we learn from another quarter.

At the end of last year and the beginning of this year, Polish landlords had to make enormous deliveries, but these were taken into account in the payment of taxes. It was believed that thereby everything was settled, but it turns out now that the taxes until the end of this year have to be paid in advance.

Even from this compulsory method of ensuring supplies for the army it is evident what enormous masses of Russian troops must be concentrated in Poland.

Another newspaper, the Posen *Zeitung des Osten*, reports from Posen on April 13:

"The number of Russian troops in the West is as follows: Within the Polish Kingdom is the Rüdiger Corps—half of the Fourth Rüdiger Corps together with reserves, altogether approximately 120,000 men. In Lithuania is the so-called Grenadier Corps (formerly the Shakhovskoy Corps), and part of the First Corps. The Guards are expected to arrive later—there has been talk of their arrival for several months already. In Volhynia, where the staff headquarters is in Dubno, is the remaining part of the Fourth Chegodayev Regiment. In Kiev there is a Second Auxiliary Corps, in Krzemieniec a mobile corps (Pavlov's) of about 6,000-8,000 men. Finally in Moldavia and Wallachia is the Lüders Corps with about 65,000 men."

As to why these troops are there, they themselves very naively make the following admission:

"Rank-and-file Russians, as well as the officers, are less reserved in their conversation. It is noteworthy that to the question why they are stationed on the frontier they all give the same reply, viz: Our Emperor[a] is the brother-in-law of the King of Prussia.[b] After the French were defeated by the Russians in the great war, all the land right up to Paris belonged to the Emperor; he entrusted the administration to various small German *knyazes*[c] (princes), and appointed his brother-in-law, the Prussian *knyaz*, as supreme military governor. Now the French and Germans have risen in revolt, and so the German *knyazes* as well as the supreme governor have asked for help from the Emperor, and that is why we are stationed here on the frontier. If calm is not soon established, we shall cross the frontier and restore order."

But that is not all. Emperor Nicholas has ordered another call-up of recruits of eight men per thousand to be carried out in the western part of his Empire. The order lists 21 provinces where recruits are to be called up.

---

[a] Nicholas I.— *Ed.*
[b] Frederick William IV.— *Ed.*
[c] Here and later on Engels uses the Russian word *knyaz*.— *Ed.*

That is how things look on the other side of the frontier. Half a million armed and organised barbarians are only waiting for an opportunity to fall on Germany and turn us into feudal serfs of the orthodox Tsar.

Just as Transylvania was once before occupied by the Russians, just as at the present time the incursion of 30,000 Russians into that same region is being demanded, and another 30,000 to be sent across Galicia, just as the Banat Serbs are also imploring the orthodox Tsar for help, so it will be with us. We shall yet reach the point when the Government and the bourgeoisie *invite the Russians into our country*, as happened recently in Transylvania. And things are bound to go that way. The victory of counter-revolution in Vienna and in Berlin has not sufficed for us. But when Germany has once felt the Russian knout, it will behave somewhat differently.

The Russians are the true liberators of Germany, we said in June last year.[a] We repeat this also today, but today we are no longer the only ones to say it!

Written by Engels on April 21, 1849

First published in the *Neue Rheinische Zeitung* No. 279, April 22, 1849

Printed according to the newspaper

Published in English for the first time

---

[a] See "The Agreement Assembly of June 15" (present edition, Vol. 7, p. 90).— *Ed.*

# FROM THE THEATRE OF WAR

The *Wiener Zeitung* which failed to arrive the evening before yesterday, and following it, all the Vienna evening papers report:

"The Hungarian insurgents' plan to relieve Komorn has been completely thwarted. The advantage they gained by their temporary occupation of Waitzen has also been wrested from them, for Lieutenant-Field Marshal Csorich's division has driven them out of this position again. With the imposing reinforcements proceeding to the royal imperial army from all directions, a most successful resumption of the offensive by the royal imperial troops already in the very near future can be predicted."[a]

This royal imperial martial-law report, however, can already now almost certainly be affirmed to be a *pure lie.* If there were anything in it, a Bulletin would have been issued within the next 24 hours at the latest, and that has not happened. Moreover, all the other reports contradict this assertion, made without either a date or any detail.

We have no wish to repeat the many rumours circulating in Vienna and Breslau, to the effect that Komorn has been relieved, Görgey is marching on Vienna, Dembiński and Vetter have outflanked the imperial army and cut off its retreat to Vienna, that the *Landsturm* has been raised in all comitats on both sides of the Danube etc. So long as the postal connection between Pest and Vienna is not cut, little credence can be given to these rumours.

Up to the 18th, there was no mention of the post from Pest having failed to arrive in Vienna. The latest news from there was dated the afternoon of the 14th. This contains not a word about the recapture of Waitzen.

---

[a] *Wiener Zeitung* No. 91 (evening supplement), April 16, 1849.— *Ed.*

It will be remembered that some days ago the *Ost-Deutsche Post* already reported that Waitzen had been recaptured. It is quite possible that Waitzen had to be taken twice, and that the imperial forces re-occupied it temporarily before finally being driven out. The fact that at a moment of great peril the official paper designed to dispense reassuring news writes with jesuitical reservations about this temporary re-occupation, is quite consistent with the previous practice of the Bulletins.

On the 14th nothing at all was known in Pest of the alleged capture of Waitzen. On the contrary, the *Lloyd* in a report of this date wrote:

> "For the present, the Hungarians are behaving pretty arrogantly in Waitzen. They send off letters and parcels which pass through and arrive here safely, except that they are first opened and searched and officially sealed by the Hungarian Defence Council.[250] Under such a cover a dispatch arrived here yesterday containing the news that Major-General Götz was buried in the Hungarian camp with full military honours. Twelve battalions are said to have been paraded for the solemn occasion."[a]

All the other Pest news of the same date simply provides further evidence of the fear of the Austrians there. The *Spiegel* has this report:

> "I am writing to you when I am just on the point of bringing my family to safety. Last night it was rumoured that all Germans were to be murdered (!). This and similar rumours are following each other at a frantic pace; the fanaticism of the Magyars threatens to erupt at any moment."

Visits to the camp are prohibited, the bell-towers are occupied; the Magyars in Pest are said to have intended to ring the alarm at the first attack from outside. Outside Pest itself, little has happened since the 11th. At noon on the 14th a few skirmishes took place when the Hungarian outposts showed themselves in the vicinity. It is also claimed that the thunder of guns has been heard.

The royal imperial finances appear to be in a bad way too. Windischgrätz announced on the 10th that the *imperial authorities* are now issuing *Hungarian paper money*, drafts on the Hungarian revenues, *at a fixed rate of exchange*, in denominations of 5, 10, 100 and 1,000 florins. With these scraps of paper the royal imperial army will pay for the provisions supplied to them, and so, just before quitting, they will steal a few millions from Hungary. Such a dirty system of robbery as carried on by the honourable friends of the *Kölnische Zeitung*, a system composed of elements from all levels of civilisation, from the plundering by Croat-Tartar nomads down to the most modern paper-money swindling and fraudulent bill-jobbing, is wholly unprecedented.

---

[a] "Pest, 14. April", *Der Lloyd* No. 181 (evening edition), April 16, 1849.— *Ed.*

And while even the Austrian banknotes are subject to exchange fluctuation, these notes must be accepted at their full face value in private dealing!

All these items of news confirm the expectation of an imminent Austrian retreat from Pest rather than the claim that Waitzen has been taken.

An occupation of Waitzen is moreover almost impossible on strategic grounds. By all reports, the imperial forces have been everywhere thrown back over the Danube and the Gran, Pest being the sole point they hold on the left bank. Pest could not be left without cover; hence the attack could only take place from the right bank, the imperial armies would have had to cross the Danube under fire of the superior Hungarian artillery and then to drive a superior army out of Waitzen. To do all this would be quite impossible; and even if it were possible, it could not be done without a great battle. But no one, not even the *Wiener Zeitung*, knows anything about such a battle. All this is supposed to have been done by Csorich's division. *One* division!

Windischgrätz is happily in Olmütz. Welden is not yet with the army, but he has sent out in advance pompous proclamation to his soldiers, these "heroes (!) on whom the gaze of half the world (!) is fixed", a proclamation which could have been written by the *Kölnische Zeitung* in those glorious days of its Theiss manoeuvres. He describes his opponents as "infamous villains", who have made Hungary into a "tool of venal Poles", threatens them with destruction, and then adds: "But once more we offer our hand in reconciliation to our brother who has been led astray!"[a] Herr Welden *therefore wants to negotiate*. The Magyars will be much obliged.

Little is heard of the reinforcements which the Austrians are supposed to have already received. Eight battalions (?) are said to be stationed at Neuhäusel on the Waag; that is how much the five brigades on the Gran[b] must have shrunk already.

Six battalions are reported to be on the march from Vienna and the Fleischhackerstrasse is said to be choked with the waggons on which the reinforcements are arriving.

A reserve camp of 25,000 men is *supposed* to be formed on the Marchfeld near Vienna, another at Pettau (Styria) of 15,000 men, and a third of 20,000 to 30,000 men at Tábor and Budweis in Bohemia—everything to be quite ready by the 10th of May! Where

---

[a] "An die K. K. Armee in Ungarn." Proklamation von F. Welden. Vom 17. April 1849.— *Ed.*

[b] See this volume, p. 302.— *Ed.*

are these troops to come from!! Haynau's corps is *not* coming, Radetzky cannot spare it. Instead he has sent all his light cavalry. Finally, Vogl is said to be expected in Eperies.

We defer the news from the Banat and Transylvania until the second edition, since it contains nothing of urgency.

Written by Engels about April 21, 1849

Printed according to the newspaper

First published in the supplement to the *Neue Rheinische Zeitung* No. 279, April 22, 1849

Published in English for the first time

# [FROM THE THEATRE OF WAR]

The post from Vienna has failed to arrive; we are therefore able to learn details from the field of battle on the Upper Danube only indirectly, in snatches. △, the "best-informed" Vienna correspondent of the Augsburg *Allgemeine Zeitung,* also asserts that Waitzen has been re-occupied by the imperial forces, and that only one Magyar battalion was encountered there, because—the bulk under Görgey *had already marched off to Komorn!* In this way the thing can indeed be explained, and such an occupation of Waitzen is not only possible but even a mistake of the Austrians, who are now threatened in their rear. Welden has not gone to Pest either but to Neuhäusel on the Waag, where indeed some Austro-Moravian rearguard appears to be stationed. He is marching from there against the Magyars who strongly attacked the retreating imperial forces at *Gran.* The outcome of this engagement is not yet known.[a]

The following report in the *Constitutionelles Blatt aus Böhmen* shows what a lion's den this Hungary is, where the footsteps of many warriors go in but few come out.

"If this thing drags out to the summer, Kossuth's supporters will gain an ally in the fever, which may well be very much more dangerous to the Austrian troops, unaccustomed to the climate, than the Russians, whose entry is expected in the enemy's rear, will be to their opponents. All the proved bravery of our troops is useless against the fever, and it is precisely to the regions where the fever rages most fiercely that the war will shift as soon as the insurgents are forced back from Pest to the east."

Very great alarm reigns in the *Banat.* While from Peterwardein Perczel strikes terror into the countryside and already threatens Slavonia, while the Danube navigation from Pest to Mohacs continues to be disrupted, Bem is recently reported to be advancing

---

[a] "Wien, 15. April", Augsburg *Allgemeine Zeitung* No. 109, April 19, 1849.— *Ed.*

on Temesvar with a strong force. He is said to have called upon Temesvar and Arad to surrender to him within a week. The Serbian Voivodina is in its death throes; Kničanin intends to return there with 8,000-10,000 men, but only after Todorovich, Albert Nugent, Bosnich etc. have been retired. Nugent senior[a] has already been dismissed; Castiglioni, the bombardier of Cracow,[251] has been appointed as his successor, and one deputation after another is going to Bucharest to seek Russian assistance. Puchner too is on the march to the Banat.

*Transylvania* is still wholly in Bem's hands. The Russians have been expelled entirely from their last position at the Roterturm Pass. The Magyar party among the Transylvanian Romanians is conducting a strong agitation in favour of Bem and supports his recruiting drive in the country. The organisation of the army is proceeding at a marvellous pace. Moreover, Bem has captured 21 guns with 6,000 shells and 5,000 rifles with one million rounds of ammunition in Hermannstadt. He has persuaded most of the Transylvanian refugees in Bucharest to return, by declaring a general amnesty and simultaneously threatening to confiscate the property of all who stay behind.

We learn from *Galicia* (April 12) that the Hungarians are advancing nearer and nearer to the Carpathians, while nothing is heard of Vogl's alleged advance into Hungary. Almost the entire Cracow garrison has marched off to Hungary. It is expected to be *replaced by Russians.*

An indication that the imperial forces no longer feel secure in Slovakia is given by the transfer of their treasury from Schemnitz to Troppau.

Finally, we give a (Magyar) report from the *Neue Oder-Zeitung* on the strength of the Magyar army:

The Hungarian army is daily increasing in numbers, daily becoming better organised and more disciplined. According to authentic reports, when the Banat and Transylvanian armies are included as well as the Peterwardein and Komorn garrisons, the army now has 32 regular battalions of infantry and Szeklers,[252] 23 regiments of cavalry (hussars, Uhlans, cuirassiers), 105 Honved battalions, 15,000 national cavalry, hence a total of 197,000 infantry and 30,000 regular cavalry, excluding national cavalry, national guards and *Landsturm.*

Written by Engels about April 21, 1849

First published in the *Neue Rheinische Zeitung* No. 279 (second edition), April 22, 1849

Printed according to the newspaper

Published in English for the first time

---

[a] Laval Nugent.— *Ed.*

# THE DEBATE ON THE LAW ON POSTERS

[*Neue Rheinische Zeitung* No. 279 (second edition), April 22, 1849]

*Cologne*, April 21. (The debate in the Chamber.) We return to the sitting of April 13.[a] After the reply[b] to Deputy Lisiecki's question, the next item on the agenda was the debate on the *law on posters*.[253]

After Herr Rohrscheidt had read the report of the Central Commission, Herr Wesendonck moved an amendment for the rejection of the government Bill *en bloc*.

Herr Arnim (Count) rose to speak. He said that the amendment was impermissible, being tantamount to a motion to proceed to the Order of the Day. But government Bills cannot be passed over in this way. That is established by the standing orders.[c]

Now at last the gentlemen of the Left realise what the Right intended by para. 53 of the standing orders. In relation to government Bills the Chamber cannot resolve to proceed to the Order of the Day. This seemingly innocent provision, however, meant neither more nor less than the following: you are not entitled to reject any government motion *en bloc*, but must debate every one of its paragraphs, even if there were a thousand of them.

But that was too much even for the Centre deputies. After a rather lengthy debate during which each of the sides displayed the greatest possible acumen in exegesis, the Chairman finally proceeded with the discussion by declaring Wesendonck's amendment permissible.

The floor was taken by Herr Rupp, the great Rupp, who was suspended from his post, persecuted, at one time hounded by all the

---

[a] See this volume, pp. 295-98.— *Ed.*
[b] Given by the Minister of War K. A. Strotha.— *Ed.*
[c] "Geschäfts-Ordnung für die Zweite Kammer."— *Ed.*

newspapers, and expelled from the Gustavus-Adolphus Union[254] of blessed memory. Herr Rupp delivered a speech after which, in the opinion of the Berlin *National-Zeitung*, which is no less great and no less enlightened than Herr Rupp, there remained little more for the Left to say, not only in the general debate but also in the special debate. Let us take a look at this exhaustive speech of pure reason delivered by Rupp, the Friend of Light.

This exhaustive speech is, indeed, a true product of the *enlightened* spirit, of the spirit of the "free communities",[255] i.e. it exhausts nothing but the platitudes which can be uttered on the subject of posters.

Herr Rupp began his speech by pointing out the difference between the arguments in support of the law on posters put forward by the Government and the Central Commission. Whereas the Government presented the law as a mere police measure in the interests of road traffic and aesthetics, the Central Commission, which eliminated this clumsy Prussian trick, put the political motives in the foreground. This afforded wide scope for declamations by the enlightened preacher.

"Thus this Bill is indisputably one of the most important subjects for discussion by the present Assembly. Now we shall not want to say" (we shall not want to say!) "that it is so much (!) a matter of indifference to us whether there are a few more or a few less posters in the world, since (!) the *lofty* character of right and freedom consists precisely in the fact that even what seems to be most insignificant, when linked with it, immediately itself acquires a *higher significance*"!![a]

Having established the "lofty character" and "higher significance" of posters by this pastoral introduction, and having put his audience in a pious frame of mind, Herr Rupp could calmly give free rein to "the eternally clear, pure and smooth" stream of his pure reason.

First of all, Herr Rupp made the exceedingly shrewd remark "that very often measures have been taken against imaginary dangers, with the result that real dangers are created".

This platitude evoked delight and cries of "bravo" from the Left.

After this, Herr Rupp with equal profundity of thought pointed out that the Bill contradicts ... the imposed Constitution,[256] which Herr Rupp does not recognise at all!

It is a strange policy of the Left—to appeal to the imposed Constitution and to cite the kicks received in November as arguments against further kicks!

---

[a] See *Stenographische Berichte über die Verhandlungen der durch das Allerhöchste Patent vom 5. Dezember 1848 einberufenen Kammern. Zweite Kammer.* Bd. 2, Berlin, 1849, S. 467.— Ed.

If the Government considers—Herr Rupp continued—that this Bill does not infringe freedom of the press, but only concerns the use of the streets and squares for the distribution of printed matter, then one could equally well say that freedom of the press prevailed also under the censorship, since it was not the use of the press but only the distribution of its products that was put under control.

One must have lived in Berlin under the censorship to appreciate the whole novelty of this proposition, which already years ago used to be current among all the pettifogging liberals, and which nevertheless was once more greeted by the Left with hilarity and cries of "bravo".

Herr Rupp then quoted the article on freedom of the press in the imposed Constitution and proved in detail that Manteuffel's Bill was in crying contradiction to the Manteuffel Constitution.

But, my dear Herr Rupp, *tout bonhomme que vous êtes,*[a] have you not yet realised that Manteuffel imposed the Constitution only in order subsequently to annul the few liberal phrases contained in it either by retaining the old gagging laws[257] or introducing new ones.

Indeed, Herr Rupp even went so far as to explain to the Right with some thoroughness that although later on, during the revision of the Constitution, they could include the law on posters in this Constitution, but at present they must reject it, otherwise they would be anticipating the revision of the Constitution!

As though the gentlemen of the Right were concerned with consistency, and not with putting the speediest end to the bad press, associations, agitation, commercial distrust, and other more or less revolutionary achievements!

To these weighty arguments, Herr Rupp then added the following banalities:

1) Posters are condemned because they spread *agitation*. But the prevention of agitation is not a matter for the state in which the rule of law prevails but for a police state.

2) I want a strong government. But a government that cannot tolerate agitation and posters is not a strong government.

3) Germans like to follow a leader.

4) The absence of posters did not prevent March 18 ("Neither horse, nor rider"[b]—etc.).

---

[a] However credulous you are.— *Ed.*

[b] From the Prussian anthem *Heil Dir im Siegerkranz* written by B. G. Schumacher on the basis of the poem "Lied für den dänischen Unterthan" by H. Harries, a Schleswig pastor.— *Ed.*

5) Revolutions are the result of despotism.

From this Herr Rupp drew the conclusion that the law on posters must be rejected in the interests of Manteuffel.

"Gentlemen," he exclaimed imploringly, "protect the Government from the self-deception to which this law, like every law of a police state, exposes it!"

According to Herr Rupp, the rejection of Manteuffel's Bill would not be a vote of *no* confidence in Manteuffel, but, on the contrary, a *vote of confidence* in him. Herr Rupp wants Manteuffel to become the desired "strong government", and for that reason he does not want to weaken Manteuffel by adopting the law on posters. You think Herr Rupp is joking? He has no such intention. Herr Rupp is a Friend of Light, and a Friend of Light never jokes. Friends of Light cannot tolerate laughter any more than their worthy cousin, Atta Troll.

But the last trump card Herr Rupp played set the crown on his whole speech.

"The rejection of this law will contribute not a little to *calm* that section of the population which cannot agree to recognise the Constitution *prior* to its revision."

Herr Rupp's concern is "to *calm* that section of the population" which has not yet reached the level of Manteuffel!

That, however, is the nature of the gentlemen of the Left! They are tired of turbulent movement and since they are now deputies and realise that they can do nothing against the sabre dictatorship, all they want is that the unpleasant questions of principle should at last be settled, the Constitution revised *pro forma* with a view to declaring it valid, and an oath of allegiance sworn to it, and "the revolution brought to an end". Then a comfortable life will begin for them, a life of constitutional routine, declamation based on nothing, dealing with nothing, leading to nothing, intriguing, patronage, ministerial reshuffling etc.; that Olympian life of idleness and luxury which the Frenchmen of the type of Odilon,[a] Thiers and Molé enjoyed for 18 years in Paris, and which Guizot liked to call the "*play* of constitutional institutions". If only the unpleasant revolutionary movement were to recede somewhat, a Waldeck Ministry would indeed no longer be an impossibility! And after all the people are not yet mature enough for a republic!

After Herr Rupp's speech precisely *everything* still remains to be said. It was a question in the first place not of restriction of the freedom of the press *in general*, but above all of restriction of the

---

[a] Barrot.— *Ed.*

freedom of the press in regard to *posters*. What had to be done was to examine the effect of posters, to defend "street literature", and most particularly to champion the right of the *workers* to the *literature provided free of charge* in the form of posters. It was not a matter of glossing over the right of agitation by means of posters, but *frankly to champion* that right. But Herr Rupp said not a word about this. The old phrases about freedom of the press which we had sufficient opportunity of examining in all its aspects during 33 years of censorship—these old phrases were once more trotted out by Herr Rupp at length in a solemn tone, and because he said everything that the gentlemen from the *National-Zeitung* know about the subject, that newspaper considers he has exhausted the subject.

After the "enlightened" Rupp, the "obscurantist" Riedel was given the floor. But Herr Riedel's speech is too good to write about it in haste. *A demain donc, citoyen Riedel!*[a]

[*Neue Rheinische Zeitung* No. 283, April 27, 1849]

*Cologne*, April 23. Deputy *Riedel* certainly delivered the most classic speech of the whole debate. Whereas some restraint was still being shown by the ministerial bench, whereas even Manteuffel still employed certain pseudo-constitutional phrases, and only the clumsy parvenu, von der Heydt, at times forgot his constitutional role, Herr Riedel from Barnim-Angermünde was not in the least embarrassed to speak as a dyed-in-the-wool representative of Uckermark.[258] Never before has an electoral constituency been so worthily represented as that of Herr Riedel.

Herr Riedel began by asking: what are posters? And he gave the answer:

"Posters in the proper meaning of the word are public statements intended to have a *reassuring* effect on people's minds."

That, according to Herr Riedel's etymology, is the "definition" of posters.

For the time being we do not want to dispute with Herr Riedel about the derivation of the word "poster" [*Plakat*]. We only draw his attention to the fact that if he had read the Bill attentively, he could have saved himself all his etymological exertions. This Bill is concerned not only with "posters" but also with "*pasted notices*",

---

[a] Till tomorrow, therefore, Citizen Riedel.— *Ed.*

which "in the proper meaning of the word" are simply intended to be pasted up.

Instead of this, Herr Riedel expressed his righteous indignation at the most scandalous misuse of the word "poster".

"As a rule, posters serve merely to inflame *passions*, to kindle an *impure fire of hatred* or *revenge* particularly against the authorities.... As a rule, therefore, posters are precisely the opposite of what their name implies. Hence their use is usually a misuse" (i.e. a misuse of their *name*) "and therefore the question arises: Ought the local police authorities to help promote this mischief of posters?" (i.e. this misuse of the name "poster"). "Ought the police to make themselves in some measure the accomplices in the mischief caused by the misuse" (of the name) "of posters" (for notices which are in no way posters, i.e. reassuring notices)?

In short, ought posters in future to be employed "in accordance with their definition" (i. e. in accordance with the definition of the word "poster") or not?

What a great mistake Manteuffel committed in ascribing the law on posters to motives concerned with police duties and beautifying the streets! What a mistake it was for the Central Commission to advocate the law for political reasons! The law is necessary—for etymological reasons and should really be entitled: a law to return the use of the word "poster" to the "proper meaning of the word".

In this connection, however, the thorough Herr Riedel has committed a thorough blunder. If we, at the risk of boring our readers to death, were to enter into a discussion with Herr Riedel on etymology, we would, with Diez's grammar in hand, prove to him that the derivation of the [German] word *Plakat* [poster] is not at all from the Latin *placare*,[a] but is only a distortion of the French *placard*, which is connected with the French word *plaque*, which itself is of German origin. Hence Herr Riedel's whole reassurance theory falls to the ground.

That, of course, is a matter of indifference to Herr Riedel, and rightly so. For this whole reassurance theory is merely a schoolmaster's *captatio benevolentiae*[b] behind which is an outright appeal to the fears of the propertied classes.

Posters "inflame passions", they "kindle an impure fire of hatred or revenge particularly against the authorities", they

"serve as a call to the *unreasoning mass* to demonstrations which menacingly (!) violate order and go beyond the limits of legitimate freedom".

And therefore posters must be prohibited.

---

[a] To placate, pacify, soothe.— *Ed.*

[b] Attempt to gain favour.— *Ed.*

In other words: the united feudal lords, bureaucrats and bourgeois successfully accomplished their coup d'état last autumn by force of arms, and now, with the help of the Chambers, want to impose on us the supplementary laws that are still required in order that these gentlemen can enjoy their victory in peace. They are heartily sick of "passions", they will use every means to extinguish "the impure fire of hatred and revenge against the authorities", who for them after all are the most desirable authorities in the world, to establish "order" and to restore "legitimate freedom" to the level that suits them. And what sort of level that is can be judged from the fact that Herr Riedel calls the great majority of the people an "*unreasoning mass*".

Herr Riedel cannot find words bad enough to describe this "unreasoning mass". He continues:

"These communications" (by means of posters) "are mostly read by just that class of people who are least of all accustomed to written communications, who are not able to test and judge the credibility of written communications with the caution and distrust that is of course displayed by the public accustomed to reading and acquainted with the deceptions of the press...."

Who then form this unreasoning mass, this class least of all accustomed to written communications? Is it the peasants of Uckermark? By no means: since, firstly, they are the "backbone of the nation", secondly, they do not read posters, and, thirdly, they elected Herr Riedel. Herr Riedel has in mind none but the *urban workers*, the proletariat. Posters are a chief means of influencing the proletariat. By its very position the proletariat is revolutionary; being the class which is as much oppressed under a constitutional regime as under absolutism, the proletariat is quite prepared to take up arms again; it is precisely from the proletariat that the chief danger threatens, and therefore away with everything that could keep alive the revolutionary fervour in the proletariat!

And what is more conducive to keeping alive revolutionary fervour among the workers than posters, which convert every street corner into a huge newspaper in which workers who pass by find the events of the day noted and commented on, the various views described and discussed, and where at the same time they meet people of all classes and opinions with whom they can discuss the contents of the posters; in short, where they have simultaneously a newspaper and a club, and all that without costing them a penny!

It is just this, however, that the gentlemen of the Right do not want. And they judge correctly. For it is from the side of the proletariat that the greatest, indeed the sole danger threatens them; why should they, who hold the reins of power, not strive by every means to remove this danger?

No one could raise any objection to this. With God's help we have been living for about six months under a sabre dictatorship. We do not harbour the slightest illusion about the fact of being in a state of open war against our enemies, or about the means by which alone our party can come to power. We shall not be so ridiculous as to make moral reproaches against the present ruling triple alliance of junkers, bureaucrats and bourgeois because they strive in every way to enslave us. If the highly moral preacher's tone and bombastic moral indignation of the wailers[259] were not in any case obnoxious to us, we would beware of such an empty phrase-mongering polemic if only because we still intend to take revenge on our enemies.

But what we find peculiar is that the gentlemen who are now in power, and who have an official majority, do not speak as frankly as we do. Herr Riedel, for example, is as genuine an Uckermark man as anyone could wish for and yet he could not refrain from asserting at the end of his speech:

"It has certainly never been my intention to put any kind of barrier in the way of *free expression of opinion.* I regard the spiritual struggle ... for the truth as a sacred right of free peoples, which no one may call in question."

And in another passage Herr Riedel speaks of his wish

"to allow the distribution of posters on the same basis as that on which literary works in general can be distributed".

What, after all the preceding explanations, are these phrases intended to mean? The existing government and the constitutional monarchy in general cannot nowadays remain in power in civilised countries, if the press is free. Freedom of the press, free competition between opinions means giving freedom to the class struggle in the sphere of the press. And the kind of order that they ardently desire is precisely the stifling of the class struggle, the gagging of the oppressed classes. Hence the party of law and order has to abolish free competition between opinions in the press; by means of press laws, bans etc., it must as far as possible ensure its monopoly of the market; it must, in particular, wherever possible directly suppress the literature provided free of charge in the form of posters and leaflets. The gentlemen are well aware of all this; why do they not say as much frankly?

In fact, Herr Riedel, why do you not propose immediate restoration of the censorship? There is no better means for repressing "passions", extinguishing "the impure fire of hatred and revenge against the authorities", and safeguarding "the limits of legitimate freedom"! *Voyons, citoyen Riedel, soyons francs!* [a] After all, it will come to that in the end!

Herr Riedel resumed his seat. The floor was given to *Simons,* the Minister of Justice, barrister from Elberfeld, the offspring of a Wuppertal bourgeois family of an equal rank to that of von der Heydt.

Herr Simons set about his task with tremendous thoroughness. It is noticeable that he is still new to the Ministry of Justice.

Posters are pasted up in public streets and squares, said the Minister of Justice. Consequently

"one must look for the *definition of public streets and squares*"!!

True, Herr Riedel had established the "definition" and "proper meaning of the word" poster in a way deserving our thanks. But that is not the point at all. On the contrary, it is a question of the "definition of streets and squares". And here the Minister of Justice wins immortal laurels.

Can one imagine a finer school for teaching the ABC than this Chamber where people argue seriously about the definition of streets and squares, about schoolboyish points of grammar, and so forth?

What then is the "definition of streets and public squares"?

It is as follows: streets etc.

*cannot* "be made available for any random and public use", *because* "such a definition of streets etc. *cannot be proved*"!

Hence the reason why we have a so-called Minister of Justice is precisely to give us such profound explanations. In fact, one understands now why Herr Simons found it embarrassing to be presented to the Chamber.

Of course, after such a brilliant performance, the remainder of the Minister's speech is not worth mentioning. Under the cloak of remarkable erudition in French jurisprudence, Herr Simons brought out some forgotten recollections from his former practice as a Public Prosecutor. Then come statements like the following:

"This question of need must *certainly* (!) be given an affirmative answer, that *at least* (!!) is *my* opinion (!!!), *bearing in mind the doubts* (!!!!) that have been raised (!!!!!)."

Finally, Herr Simons wanted

"to sanction the legal foundation for restricting posters".

---

[a] Well, Citizen Riedel, let us be frank.— *Ed.*

*To sanction a foundation!* Where did you learn such language, Herr Simons?

After such oratorical feats as those of Herr Riedel and Herr Simons, we cannot, of course, dwell on Herr Berends' speech which followed them. Herr Berends correctly felt by instinct that the ban on posters was aimed directly against the proletariat, but his development of the theme was rather feeble.

The general debate came to an end. For rejecting the Bill *en bloc* there were 152 votes, and against it 152 votes. Among others of the Left who were absent *without special permission* was Herr *Kyll* from Cologne. If Herr Kyll had been present the Bill on posters would have been rejected out of hand. Hence we owe it to Herr *Kyll* that the Bill was adopted in part.

We shall not dwell on the special debate. Its result is well known: the itinerant traders in books have been placed under police surveillance.

For this they can thank Herr Kyll!

Written by Engels on April 21 and 23, 1849

First published in the *Neue Rheinische Zeitung* No. 279 (second edition) and No. 283, April 22 and 27, 1849

Printed according to the newspaper

Published in English for the first time

# FROM THE THEATRE OF WAR

In the welter of contradictory rumours, some of which are evidently invented by the imperial side, we can be certain of only two facts: firstly, the Magyars have crossed the Gran, and on the left bank of the Danube at Parkány, opposite Gran, have defeated the corps assembled there under Simunich; secondly, they have disappeared from Pest for the second time, and nobody can say where they have gone.

Hence, little can be said about their present position or intentions. It is most likely that they will station themselves along the left bank of the Danube from Waitzen to Komorn, so as, after successfully relieving Komorn, to cross the Danube under the protection of this fortress's guns and to cut off the retreat of the main imperial army.

The corps defeated at Parkány was made up of the remnants of the Götz brigade, the Simunich division and troops drawn from the corps besieging Komorn that could be spared there.

According to remarks made by Austrian officers in Pest, it is more doubtful than ever that Waitzen has been re-occupied by the imperial forces.

The imperial side is spreading the rumour that Jellachich has defeated the Magyars at Pest and forced them to retreat to Gödöllö. But this rumour is deprived of all significance by the simultaneous and much better established news that the Magyars left Pest during the night, while the peasants in the area kept their watch-fires burning till daybreak to deceive the Austrians.

One part of the Magyar army is said to have moved to the north from Parkány via Ipolyság, so as to be able together with the volunteer forces raised all over Upper Hungary to prevent the entry of Vogl's corps. According to reports received via Pest and

Pressburg, Vogl is at Zboró (six miles[a] from Eperies); direct reports via Cracow and those in the Bohemian and Moravian papers which are best informed on these areas know nothing of this so far. Vogl's entry has moreover been reported so often that by now no one believes in it any longer. In Pest and Ofen, and also among the troops, the rumour is being disseminated by the imperial side that Kossuth has resigned his post as President of the Hungarian Defence Council and taken to flight so as not to stand in the way of the negotiations which are now said to be about to begin (Welden's proclamation may be remembered[b]).

Two days ago it was reported that an imperial sharpshooter on patrol had shot Kossuth in the Hungarian camp. This report appears to have found no credence, hence this new invention.

The Magyars will take care not to waste precious time on negotiations so that the defeated and weakened Austrians can gather their reinforcements at their leisure and then, supported by 50,000-60,000 Russians, throw their adversaries back across the Theiss again!

Böhm in Vienna has published the report that Komorn continues to be encircled, and that even the bridge from the citadel to the bridgehead on the right bank of the Danube has been destroyed by the royal imperial artillery. What truth there is in that remains to be seen.

Transylvania is still in the hands of the Magyars. Under Bem's direction, it has been converted into a gigantic fortress, unassailable from the Moldavian-Wallachian-Bukovina border. The Magyars make sorties from there into the Bukovina. Thus, on April 9, six companies of Szeklers with two guns advanced as far as Pojana-Stampi, beat the Austrians and retreated across the border with 14 oxen and some horses as booty. Clearly, these raids keep the movement among the peasants in the area very much alive. Kobylica has promised to bring in a Hungarian army on the 12th and to make the peasants masters of all the land.

Perczel still continues to advance in the Bacska. He has invaded the territory of the Chaikist battalion,[260] occupied Gospodincze, and is now in Tschurug on the Theiss, the largest base of the battalion. The Chaikist territory occupies the extreme angle between the Danube and the Theiss, east of Peterwardein.

Both Puchner and the Russians are said to have arrived at Orsova on the borders of the Banat; 10,000 Russians are expected there. In

---

[a] See footnote on p. 20.— Ed.
[b] See this volume, p. 316.— Ed.

addition, Stratimirovich has emerged again and is rallying volunteer forces against the Hungarians in the Chaikist battalion.

On the other hand, a report from Semlin, dated April 13, says:

"The arrival of the steamboat passengers yesterday presented a sorry sight. The entire personnel of the general command of Transylvania, among them General Pfersmann and General Appel, disembarked. Their shabby garments and their pale countenances betrayed their misfortunes. After an hour's rest, they continued their journey to Vienna by way of Agram. They carried with them the substantial war-chest and the archives."[a]

In the Voivodina, Rajachich is to assume the civil and Mayerhofer the military administration. The Serbs intend to hold a grand National Assembly on May 20 and to elect a new voivode. Knićanin has the best chances. We have the draft Constitution of the Voivodina before us; long faces will be pulled over it at Olmütz. We shall return to it.

We have just received a letter from Lemberg dated April 16; it says nothing at all of Vogl's entry into Upper Hungary.

Written by Engels about April 23, 1849

First published in the *Neue Rheinische Zeitung* No. 280, April 24, 1849

Printed according to the newspaper

Published in English for the first time

---

[a] "Semlin, 13. April", *Der Lloyd* No. 183 (evening edition), April 17, 1849.— *Ed.*

# FROM THE THEATRE OF WAR

On the 16th, the Hungarians undertook a reconnaissance along the whole line of the imperial army stationed at Pest. The attack did not begin until four in the afternoon; the bombardment lasted until nearly six. No exchange of infantry fire developed; the losses on both sides were small. The attack began with the Hungarian hussars surprising the imperial forces while cooking, causing great confusion; and when the Austrians had won enough time to bring their artillery into operation against them, the Hungarians disappeared equally suddenly. What purpose the Hungarians sought to achieve by this attack is not yet clear. It is supposed that the battle outside Pest was merely a cover for the Hungarians to cross the Danube, and the Magyar correspondent of the *Breslauer Zeitung* actually claims to know that the attempt was successful. However, perhaps by their sudden reappearance before Pest, the Hungarians merely wished to prevent the imperial forces from drawing off larger sections of troops to Gran and the Komorn road. Nevertheless, Welden, who journeyed on from Pressburg on the 17th, is reported to have ordered 10,000 men from Ofen to Gran on the 18th.

The fortification of Ofen with woolsacks is still going on.

We have no further definite news from the theatre of war at Waitzen and Gran. It is still uncertain who is in possession of Waitzen, but probably it is still occupied by the Hungarians.

Concerning the action at Gran, martial-law reports are again circulating the rumour that the Magyars were defeated there and 2,000 were taken prisoner. Of course, there is not a tittle of truth in this. At most, the imperial forces may have succeeded in holding their ground on the Gran.

Naturally, the story of Kossuth's alleged flight[a] has dissolved again into pure fable. While the Austrian officers talk of negotiations the Magyars attack, and Kossuth has announced that he intends to recruit another 50,000 men (the Magyar correspondent even mentions a figure of 200,000). Everywhere the *Landsturm* is being called up, and many thousands of them armed with pitchforks and scythes are reported to be marching behind the regular army. The latter is said already to number 35 hussar regiments.

News comes from the Banat that on the 13th Perczel in the area of the Chaikist battalion was driven back at Titel and Wilowa by Stratimirovich; Todorovich, too, is reported to have sent two battalions there.

The journal *Bucovina* paints a heart-rending picture of conditions in that province. Destitution and misery are so intense in the Bukovina that in certain localities there are people who for some weeks past have been living on minced straw or crushed acorns mixed with maize meal.

Written by Engels about April 24, 1849

First published in the *Neue Rheinische Zeitung* No. 281, April 25, 1849

Printed according to the newspaper

Published in English for the first time

---

[a] See this volume, p. 331.— *Ed.*

# THE HUNGARIAN WAR

*Cologne*, April 25. Today we have no new information from the theatre of war. That which we already published yesterday about the *departure* of a corps of substantial size *from Pest to Gran*,[a] has been fully corroborated, and this is a most important fact. It obviously constitutes *the first step towards the abandonment of Pest.*

We do not know the strength of the departed corps, nor how many men still remain in Pest. Some papers report that 10,000 men marched away; if this is so, 5,000-7,000 men at most can have remained in Pest. The *Wanderer*, a martial-law sheet *pur sang*,[b] which has connections with the military camp, speaks of a "departure of the *whole camp*" to Gran having occurred during the night, after Welden had been in Pest for some hours and then returned to Gran. The *Wanderer* relates:

"The march towards Waitzen and the neighbouring area began at 4 a.m. The whole army stationed on the Ofen bank of the Danube as far as Komorn is crossing the river and today will take the offensive against the insurgents at all points, while Schlick and the Ban,[c] operating beyond Waitzen, are attacking them in the rear and on the flanks. Already yesterday it was said at headquarters that decisive results were expected within three days."

The strategic reason which the *Wanderer* gives for the Austrian withdrawal is more than ludicrous. According to it the plan is for the main imperial army to cross the Danube between Komorn (this is how far the retreat has already gone!) and Gran and attack the

---

[a] See this volume, p. 333.— *Ed.*
[b] Thoroughbred.— *Ed.*
[c] Jellachich.— *Ed.*

Magyars in the front,while Jellachich *and* Schlick (! *i.e.*two out of the three army corps!) will cross over to Waitzen and cut off their retreat.

But if the imperial forces have made such progress that they can already think of such decisive manoeuvres, why do they not remain at Pest, where they are in complete command of the Danube crossing, on the left bank of the river, and march up along that bank towards Waitzen and Balassa-Gyarmat? In this way, with "Schlick and Jellachich's" assistance, they could completely cut off the Hungarians from their base of operations, and totally destroy them after winning one battle, while in case of a defeat their own retreat to Pest could not be cut off?

However, the *Wanderer's* glosses are the more certainly pure phrases as the small number of reinforcements arrived in the last few days do not allow the imperial side to think even remotely of resuming the offensive.

It is as clear as daylight: what is happening is that *the imperial forces are retreating from Pest* and taking up new positions in the area from Komorn to Gran and Szent Endré along the right bank of the Danube and the Gran so as to oppose the Magyar pressure on Komorn. Incidentally, this very "*speedily*" performed withdrawal is the best commentary on the supposed imperial victory at Parkány on the Gran.

What these manoeuvres seem to suggest is that Welden, in the crude fashion in which he conducts warfare, intends to provoke a decisive battle at all costs and as speedily as possible. His rashness will probably end badly for him.

△, the "best-informed" Vienna correspondent of the Augsburg *Allgemeine Zeitung,* a black-and-yellow[a] bureaucrat and an authority for the *Kölnische Zeitung,* but otherwise an impudent braggart and extremely ignorant of geography, is again lying with remarkable impertinence when he speaks of *two* Magyar corps marching with all haste towards Kaschau to meet Lieutenant-Field Marshal Vogl's forces. One of these corps is said to be 30,000 strong, the other to be commanded by Görgey (!)—but Lieutenant-Field Marshal Wohlgemuth is alleged to be following hard on their heels and if he could get to Miskolcz before them (the Austrians are now on the march to Miskolcz!!!), the Magyars would have to retreat over the Theiss!![b] A brilliant strategist, this "best-informed" correspondent of the best-informed Augsburg *Allgemeine Zeitung.*

---

[a] The Austrian imperial colours.— *Ed.*

[b] "Wien, 19. April", Augsburg *Allgemeine Zeitung* No. 112, April 22, 1849.— *Ed.*

These lies show the lengths to which those on the imperial side have to go to sustain the spirit of their troops even to some extent.

In a similar way, they also sought to capture Komorn, the fortress they could not capture by force of arms. They sent spies to spread among the garrison the rumour that Debreczin had long ago been taken by the imperial forces; that Mack was already inclined to capitulate, but Esterházy was not. Fortunately, a Magyar spy got through to Komorn and brought the news of the latest Magyar victories.

In the Banat, the Magyars are already beginning the encirclement of Temesvar.

From Galicia, there is still no news at all of Vogl's alleged entry into Hungary with his fictitious twelve battalions, reports of which were so grandly trumpeted abroad. It appears that the plans for the disposition of the troops concerned have been changed so frequently, because Galicia cannot be trusted to keep calm, that they have not yet even been assembled on the border.

There is nothing new from Transylvania. We shall print only an excerpt from a report about Bem, sent to the Augsburg *Allgemeine Zeitung* from the Wallachian border. These admissions from the Augsburg *Allgemeine Zeitung* are the most striking confirmation of what we have so often said about Bem:

"At this moment, *the whole of Transylvania* is obedient to the irresistible authority of Bem, a leader who is as *bold* as he is fortunate, whose *genius* and *exceptional energy have decimated the best troops of two emperors*[a] *and driven them from the country*. With relatively few and for the most part inexperienced forces, this extraordinary man has been able to set at nought the immense sacrifices demanded by this unprecedentedly bitter struggle, and to frustrate the brilliant feats of arms of the Austrian troops, nay, even the universally feared Russian intervention. Bem's successes are all *the more amazing* as he has succeeded in conquering a country in which the majority of the inhabitants, and especially the Saxons and Romanians, without exception, remained loyal to their Emperor and readily made every sacrifice, however hard. In face of so sad an outcome of this war, as protracted as it is destructive, all previous sacrifices, indeed even the summoning of foreign assistance, appear as sheer waste, while the reconquest of the country demands new sacrifices which are the heavier as the tireless Bem *has increased his power tenfold* by promptly levying soldiers and contributions. The inhabitants of Hermannstadt alone are reported to have been afflicted with a levy of four million florins C. M., payable within three days. What is equally distressing is the fact that this so lamentable misfortune, which could have been averted by prudence and strong measures, has led to an extraordinary cooling off in the sympathies which the populations thus afflicted previously gave so cordially to the Government, while their spirits have been crushed and their energy crippled by the imposed Constitution. All this is very natural, considering the enormous distance between the rights demanded in the well-known petitions of the Romanians and Saxons and those granted in the Constitution of March 4, and the obstinacy with which the Vienna Government

---

[a] Francis Joseph I and Nicholas I.— *Ed.*

withholds the concessions promised in Olmütz to the Romanian deputation.[261] The common sense of the people sees that fundamentally it is all the same whether its rights are neglected or curtailed by the arrogance of the Hungarians or by an all-powerful Government."[a]

| | |
|---|---|
| Written by Engels on April 25, 1849 | Printed according to the newspaper |
| First published in the *Neue Rheinische Zeitung* No. 282, April 26, 1849 | Published in English for the first time |

---

[a] "Von der walachischen Gränze, 8. April", Augsburg *Allgemeine Zeitung* No. 110, April 20, 1849.— Ed.

# LASSALLE[262]

*Cologne,* April 26. We have to report a fact which testifies that *en fait de justice*[a] there is no longer anything impossible. Herr Nicolovius, Public Prosecutor General, clearly intends to surpass even the laurels which Herr Hecker in his time won for himself.

From our previous reports[b] it will be recalled that during the criminal court trial against Lassalle, von Ammon I, deputy Chief Public Prosecutor in Düsseldorf, for three weeks concealed in his office desk and withheld from the examining magistrate a letter of Lassalle's in which the latter requested a farmer[c] from Schönstein to arrange for a reinforcement of some 100 men to march to Düsseldorf in the event of a struggle and that von Ammon only handed the letter to the examining magistrate when the latter informed him that the investigation had been concluded. It will be recalled that because of this letter—which, incidentally, was so far from containing a direct call for an uprising that neither the Court nor the indictment board included it among the grounds for prosecution—the investigation had to be begun afresh, and this was the reason why Lassalle's trial was not already concluded in the previous session of the Assize Court.

Lassalle protested at the time to the Public Prosecutor General against this deliberate dragging out of the case by Herr von Ammon I.

The Public Prosecutor General, instead of making any reply to Lassalle, sent the latter's complaint to the Public Prosecutor's office

---

[a] As regards jurisdiction.— *Ed.*
[b] See present edition, Vol. 8, pp. 344-46, 463-65 and 474-76.— *Ed.*
[c] Stangier.— *Ed.*

in Düsseldorf with instructions to instigate proceedings against Lassalle for this complaint on the basis of Article 222 because in it Herr von Ammon *had been insulted!*

*Pends-toi, Figaro, tu n'aurais pas inventé cela!*[a]

Thus, a letter to Herr Nicolovius is alleged to constitute an insult to Herr von Ammon within the meaning of Article 222! Already once before, on the occasion of the trial of the press, which we had the pleasure of conducting against Herr Zweiffel and Herr Hecker, we explained that Article 222 does not even apply to public insults by the press but only to insults levelled at officials when they are actually present.[b]

But even if Article 222 were also applicable to insults through *printed* matter, it would still certainly not occur to anyone to maintain that a letter to a third person could be an insult to an official. According to the practice adopted hitherto in the police courts, it was always requisite that the material containing the insult should be addressed to the insulted person himself or that it should be publicly disseminated. Herr Nicolovius now discovers that if one writes in insulting terms to *a third person* about an official, that is an insult to the official! It seems, therefore, that one must beware of speaking about officials in a disrespectful tone in one's private correspondence!

The fact that Lassalle's letter was addressed to the *official authority superior* to Herr von Ammon and was therefore a *complaint,* a *protest,* makes the matter still more impossible.

For the law even makes it obligatory for complaints against wrongful actions of officials to be addressed to the superior authority. If, therefore, the substance of the complaint was true, it was perfectly in order; if it was false then the Public Prosecutor General should have instituted legal proceedings on the basis of Article 373—because of a *calumniatory complaint.* But in that case it would be the easiest thing in the world for Lassalle on the basis of the documents to prove the truth of his complaint, whereas this proof is of no avail to him when brought before a police court on a charge of insulting an official.

The case came before the Court in Düsseldorf. But this Court, too, found that an insult has to be made either publicly, or in the presence of the insulted person, and dismissed the case. The Public

---

[a] Hang yourself, Figaro, you would not have thought of that! (Beaumarchais, *La folle journée, ou le mariage de Figaro,* Act V, Scene 8.)—*Ed.*

[b] See "The First Trial of the *Neue Rheinische Zeitung*" (present edition, Vol. 8, pp. 304-12).—*Ed.*

Prosecutor's office opposed this, and our local Cologne indictment board, which has often been tested and has always proved reliable, actually decided to institute legal proceedings based on Article 222 against Lassalle, who is now happily burdened with a police court case.

What else will be achieved with the help of Article 222, if things continue in this way?

Incidentally the Lassalle case will come before the Assize Court on May 3.

Written by Engels on April 26, 1849

First published in the *Neue Rheinische Zeitung* No. 283, April 27, 1849

Printed according to the newspaper

Published in English for the first time

342

# FROM THE THEATRE OF WAR

We begin our news today with the following report from the *Neue Oder-Zeitung*:

"From private sources we have received the important news that a big battle was fought between Gran and Komorn on the 20th and 21st. Welden led a reserve corps and held the heights near Gran. A large part of the royal imperial forces, including the Jablonowsky and Simunich brigades, was spread out on the plain between Gran and Komorn. The Magyars attacked all the positions of the imperial forces with such fierceness that the latter were thrown into confusion right from the outset. Despite the most courageous defence of the soldiers, Welden had to retreat. *In addition to the great loss in dead and wounded suffered by the royal imperial army, 20 guns and 2,000 prisoners fell into the hands of the insurgents.*

"According to another report, which generally confirms the news of the Hungarian victory mentioned above, **the immediate consequence of this victory has been the relief of Komorn.**"

Evidently, this Job's news is already known in higher circles, for Government Counsellor von Festenburg, who accompanied Master of Ordnance Welden to Hungary, arrived in Vienna as a courier on the night of the 21st, and between then and the departure of the mail on the evening of the 22nd, not a word transpired either on the reason for his arrival or on the content of the dispatches he brought.

We have to await confirmation of this report, however probable it may seem. The letters from Breslau take us up to the evening of the 23rd; news of the Magyar victory at Komorn on the 21st could hardly have reached Breslau by then. But a letter from another Breslau source also reports that news *of the capture of Gran by the Magyars* came with the train which arrived there on the morning of the 23rd.

We were quite correct in our estimate of the butcher Welden. He was eager to mark his arrival in the field at once by a great battle and to spread his fame far and wide. According to all the reports from Vienna, this battle actually took place on the 20th and 21st.

All the newspapers now unanimously recognise that the departure of the main imperial forces from Pest was *actually the beginning of their retreat* from the city. It even appears that they have become convinced of the impossibility to hold Ofen, and that they intend to give this up as well. All the woolsacks requisitioned for the ramparts have been returned to their owners and the sand-bagging of the ramparts has also ceased. According to the Magyar correspondent of the *Breslauer Zeitung*, the Magyars are said to have already occupied Neu-Pest (the first suburb). There are, by the way, not many of them left; their main corps, as we know, departed long ago, the unmounted *Landsturm* has for the most part been disbanded, and only the mounted *Landsturm,* armed with the *fokos* (a strong staff with a small brass axe at one end) are still at Pest, along with some Honveds and a few guns.

According to △ , the "best-informed" correspondent of the Augsburg *Allgemeine Zeitung,*[a] who, incidentally, cannot spell any Magyar or Serb name correctly, the Magyars are no longer stationed along the Danube but along the Gran, from the Leva down to the confluence of the Gran and the Danube. Their main force is said to be located in Ipolyság (a few miles[b] to the rear). Wohlgemuth, who has 5,000 men, is said to be facing their right flank.

More recent reports state that this right flank has wheeled round, crossed the Gran and advanced towards Neutra, driving Wohlgemuth back to the town. Even the *Lloyd* admits this.[c] There is no definite news of the positions of the imperial forces. Vienna newspapers and *Lithographierte Correspondenz* still have "Schlick and Jellachich operating beyond Waitzen in the rear of the insurgents", as if it were possible to get "beyond" Waitzen without first getting "*into*" it! And Waitzen is and will remain in the hands of the Magyars, despite all the martial-law lies of the black-and-yellow press.

The butcher Welden is ruining himself by his brutal impatience to attack. If he stayed on the defensive, covered by the Danube and the Gran, and if his main force were united with the corps besieging Komorn, he might succeed in holding his ground until the arrival of reinforcements. But he wants to get all the credit for putting down the Magyar revolution, with the result that by now he together with his entire army may have perished.

---

[a] "Wien, 20. April", Augsburg *Allgemeine Zeitung* No. 113, April 23, 1849.— *Ed.*
[b] See footnote on p. 20.— *Ed.*
[c] "Neuestes", *Der Lloyd* No. 191 (evening edition), April 21, 1849; No. 194 (morning edition), April 24, 1849.— *Ed.*

For at last we have more definite news about the Galician reinforcements. Some of them are concentrated on the Jablunka Pass. These are said to be under Benedek's command and to be rapidly advancing on the mountain towns. The others—eight battalions, 1,200 cavalry and 15 guns—are reported to have marched from Lemberg on or about the 16th and a reserve force of six battalions, 800 cavalry and nine guns was supposed to be following. These troops, whose numbers are obviously much exaggerated, were supposed to be marching over the Carpathians in three columns, and to be operating directly against the main Hungarian army and not in the direction of the Theiss. But remarkable obscurity still persists as to when they will arrive.

Hence a report from Breslau that Vogl has been surrounded in the mountains at Munkács and his entire corps destroyed, is false. Munkács lies far to the east of Vogl's line of operations. It is, however, possible that an Austrian column invaded there from Galicia and was beaten.

Concerning Komorn, the imperial forces also had very philanthropic intentions: The brigadier commanding the corps of sappers and engineers, Major-General von Zitta, who himself had built the Komorn fortress, is said to be leading the last attempt to force the capitulation of the fortress which, according to his own declaration, cannot be taken by assault. It is reported that he is attempting to flood the casemates in order to drive out the garrison from this bomb-proof refuge and confront it with the alternative of either surrendering Komorn or seeking shelter from the devastating rain of fire in the ruins of the town.

But this kind intention will surely have been frustrated by recent events.

It is now officially reported that Nugent in the south has very politely but firmly been recalled. His son, who abandoned Zombor to the Magyar *Landsturm* without a fight, is said to be court-martialled. What a farce! Stratimirovich's victory does not prevent the Magyars from keeping the Bacska occupied; the flight of the Serbs across the Danube and the Theiss is continuing. Mayerhofer is now in command in Nugent's place but is now almost without troops, as they have nearly all been sent to Ofen.

It is confirmed that Bem is in the Banat. He has equipped the Szekler *Landsturm* well with arms from the Hermannstadt and Kronstadt arsenals and, leaving to it the guarding of the country, is advancing with 30,000-40,000 of his best troops reinforced with Wallachian and Saxon recruits. He is reported to have already taken Temesvar.

The new Hungarian banknotes devised by Windischgrätz have now been issued, but no one will accept them. All exchanges and shops are closed. The Magyar report writes about this:

"Despite the martial-law threat, all the banking-houses and merchants have refused to accept the notes. With the Hungarian army in the vicinity, the imperial military authorities have not deemed it advisable to employ force, and further issue of the banknotes has been deferred until better times. But there is already circulating here a decree of the Hungarian Government, branding these banknotes as 'maliciously manufactured, forged bills' and warning everybody against accepting them. Another of Kossuth's proclamations outlaws those commissars installed by Windischgrätz who have dared partially to reintroduce the compulsory labour abolished by the Diet of 1848.[263] The peasants of Duna Vecse, Germans, have already taken advantage of the proclamation and killed one of these commissars."

Fresh support for the Magyars, which just now, on the eve of their probable victory, is of the greatest significance, is *the Polish peasant rising* which is about to break out in Galicia. About this movement, which the Cracow martial-law sheet *Czas* (The Times) seeks as far as possible to conceal, the Vienna *Lithographierte Correspondenz* writes:

"Forced recruiting has caused a serious situation in the vicinity of *Cracow*. **Three thousand peasants have moved to the large forest near Chrzanov and are camping there.** Attempts to persuade them amicably to come out have merely elicited the response: 'We would rather die here than in Hungary; what have the Hungarians done to us?' Many of the young people, who do not wish to serve against the Hungarians either, have fled from Cracow to the forest, and there are fears that this example will prove contagious and that a *general rising* might develop. It is well known that Cracow is almost totally denuded of troops."

At this moment talk of Russian assistance is more widespread than ever. The rumours are self-contradictory. But it is a fact that between Kalisch and Bucharest 200,000 Russians are already drawn up and ready to invade Galicia and Hungary so soon as the orthodox Tsar gives the order. 40,000 are stationed at Cracow, 50,000 at Brody (Radziwilow), and the remainder partly further to the rear, partly further to the south in Podolia, Bessarabia and the Danube principalities.

We had almost forgotten to inform our readers that *the first defeat of the Austrians on the Gran has been confirmed.* It was Wohlgemuth who was there in command and did not take 2,000 Hungarian prisoners but rather suffered these losses himself. This accounts for his otherwise inexplicable positions at Leva and later at Neutra.

Written by Engels about April 26, 1849          Printed according to the newspaper

First published in the *Neue Rheinische*          Published in English for the first
*Zeitung* No. 283, April 27, 1849                 time

# [HUNGARIAN VICTORIES]²⁶⁴

*Cologne,* April 26. In the confused news reaching us today from the Hungarian theatre of war via Vienna and Breslau, three clear, definite and undeniable facts stand out:

(1) *The imperial forces have evacuated Pest and Ofen;*

(2) *The Hungarians have won a victory between the Gran and the Waag;*

(3) *Komorn has been relieved.*

The battle itself took place between Leva and Neutra, and it was Wohlgemuth who suffered a complete defeat. He was forced to retreat five miles. Görgey thereupon marched on Komorn with his entire force and, according to the latest news, reached Neuhäusel and Sz. Peter on the Waag, an hour from Komorn.

No credence can be given to a martial-law report that the encirclement area of Komorn has been re-established.

The outposts of the Magyar vanguard are reported to be already at *Tyrnau, five miles from Pressburg.* According to other reports they are *two miles* from Pressburg, and people claim to have seen them even on the March a few hours from Vienna!

Ofen and Pest were completely evacuated on the 21st and 22nd. The imperial headquarters was last located in *Gran,* from there it has probably been transferred to Raab.

In the south, the Magyars are overrunning wider and wider areas. They are even *threatening Semlin* on the Turkish frontier, as the *Wiener Zeitung* admits.

The Hungarians are reported to have invaded Wallachia from Transylvania and defeated the Russians.

In short, the Magyar revolutionary army is advancing victoriously on all fronts. The entire might of all the 36 million Austrians has

# Außerordentliche
# Beilage zu Nr. 283 der N. Rh. Ztg.

Freitag, 27. April 1849.

———— ❦ ————

**\* Köln,** 26. April. Aus den verworrenen Nachrichten, die uns heute über Wien und Breslau vom ungarischen Kriegsschauplatz zukommen, treten drei Thatsachen klar, bestimmt und unleugbar hervor:

    **1) Die Kaiserlichen haben Pesth und Ofen geräumt.**

    **2) Die Ungarn haben zwischen der Gran und der Waag einen Sieg erfochten.**

    **3) Komorn ist entsetzt.**

Die Schlacht selbst hat zwischen Lewa und Neitra stattgefunden, und zwar war es Wohlgemuth, der hier eine vollständige Niederlage erlitt. Er mußte sich fünf Meilen weit zurückziehen. Görgei rückte hierauf mit seiner ganzen Heeresmacht gegen Komorn und stand nach den letzten Nachrichten bei Neuhäusel und St. Peter an der Waag, eine Stunde von Komorn.

Ein Standrechtsbericht, der die Wiederherstellung des Komorner Cernirungsrayons meldet, verdient keinen Glauben.

Die Vorposten der magyarischen Avantgarde sollen schon bei Tyrnau, fünf Meilen von Preßburg stehn. Nach andern Berichten stehn sie zwei Meilen vor Preßburg, ja selbst an der March, wenige Stunden von Wien, will man sie gesehen haben!

Die vollständige Räumung von Ofen und Pesth fand am 21. und 22. statt. Das kaiserliche Hauptquartier befand sich zuletzt in Gran. Von dort wird es wohl nach Raab verlegt sein.

Im Süden dehnen sich die Magyaren immer weiter aus. Selbst Semlin, an der türkischen Gränze, ist bedroht, — die Wiener-Zeitung gibt es zu.

Von Siebenbürgen aus sollen die Ungarn nach der Walachei eingefallen sein und die Russen geschlagen haben.

Kurz, die magyarische Revolutionsarmee dringt auf allen Punkten siegreich vor. An der Kühnheit und dem Enthusiasmus eines kleinen Volks von kaum fünf Millionen scheitert die ganze Macht der 36 östreichischen Gesammtmillionen, scheitert die siegreiche Armee, vor der „halb Europa anstaunt", wie Welden sagt. Dieselben Erfahrungen wie die Kaiserlichen vor 50 Jahren bei Jemmappes und Fleurus machten, machen sie jetzt wieder in Ungarn: mit der Revolution ist nicht gut Krieg führen!

**\* Berlin,** 25. April. In der zweiten Kammer wurde über den Berliner Belagerungszustand debattirt. Manteuffel erklärte, er werde ihn nicht aufheben. Die Debatte wurde vertagt.

**Dresden,** 25. April. Seit heute Morgen ist allgemein das Gerücht verbreitet, daß das Ministerium seine Entlassung gegeben habe.

                                            (D. A. Z.)

**\* Paris,** 25. April. Der Bericht über die Ausgaben der provisorischen Regierung ist vertheilt. Lamartine und Marrast werden wegen persönlicher Schwindeleien kompromittirt, dagegen wird man Ledru Rollin wegen Ausgaben angreifen, die er im Interesse der Revolution gemacht hat.

                                 Redakteur en chef **Karl Marx.**

———— ❦ ————

Druck von J. W. Dietz, unter Hutmacher Nr. 17.

Engels' article "Hungarian Victories" published in the *Neue Rheinische Zeitung* No. 283 (special supplement), April 27, 1849

been frustrated and the victorious army which in Welden's words "amazed half Europe" has been balked by the daring and enthusiasm of a small nation of barely five million people. The imperial forces are learning once again in Hungary the lesson they were taught at Jemappes and Fleurus 50 years ago[265]: it is unwise to make war on revolution!

Written by Engels on April 26, 1849

First published in the special supplement to the Neue Rheinische Zeitung No. 283, April 27, 1849

Printed according to the newspaper

Published in English for the first time

# FROM THE THEATRE OF WAR

We shall briefly supplement the news we published this morning in a special edition.

When Welden arrived in Gran, where he set up his headquarters, he made, according to the *Wiener Zeitung*,[a] the following dispositions: Wohlgemuth with his alleged "five brigades"—in reality only 16,000 men—in the Neutra area was to prevent the Magyars who were advancing via Leva from reaching Komorn. Further south, between the Danube and the Gran, the Veigl brigade was to protect the Komorn siege corps. The bulk of the imperial forces, concentrated at Gran and Szent Endré, was to attempt to take Waitzen and thereby to reach the Magyars' rear. The official paper admits the superior strength of the Hungarians, especially in light cavalry and artillery.

At the same time it is admitted that 2,000 Hungarians have crossed the Danube at Duna Földvar and are raising the local area in revolt. Between Földvar and the eastern corner of the Plattensee there are about ten miles of mostly swampy country; if the Magyars have occupied this easily defensible region, they are covered on their right flank by the whole length of the Plattensee (10-12 miles long) and can organise the insurrection quite unhindered behind this natural moat. Burits' imperial brigade, and Horváth's mobile column which has been sent towards Stuhlweissenburg against them, will be unable to do much harm.

After Wohlgemuth's defeat on the Gran (in which Welden with the bulk of the imperial forces appears to have remained quite calmly at Gran as a "reserve"), and after the relief of Komorn, which now offers the Hungarians an invaluable point of support, Welden must

---

[a] *Wiener Zeitung* No. 97 (evening supplement), April 23, 1849.— *Ed.*

give up his position at Gran and will perhaps have to fight a bloody battle to effect his retreat to Raab, which leads past the guns of the Komorn bridgehead. Raab, the junction of the two roads to Pest, and the line of the River Raab are the only positions south of the Danube which are perhaps still possible for the imperial forces. But here too the closeness of Komorn and the difficult terrain, broken up into a mass of islands by innumerable branches of the Danube, will prevent regular contact between the bulk and Wohlgemuth's corps. There is not a single defensible position other than the line of the March and Leitha, *which means retreating to Austrian territory.*

During the departure from Pest and Ofen the greatest confusion prevailed. The "loyal ones" are wailing; the *moral impression* created by the occupation of the *two cities* by the revolutionary troops is *immense.*

Everywhere the peasants and Jews have been driven into the arms of the Magyars by the Windischgrätz-Stadion tyranny. The Slovak peasants, who are indebted to Kossuth for freeing them from feudal burdens, and upon whom Windischgrätz wanted to reimpose the former compulsory labour, are enthusiastic supporters of the Magyars, and are aiding them everywhere with reports, fire-signals etc.

The Serb National Committee in Semlin has applied for protection to *the consuls of the three great powers* in Belgrade. The English Consul has declined, since the Committee is allegedly not a regular legal authority. Mayerhofer is hurrying to Belgrade. To what depths has "venerable" Austria descended!

Written by Engels on April 27, 1849

First published in the *Neue Rheinische Zeitung* No. 284, April 28, 1849

Printed according to the newspaper

Published in English for the first time

# [HUNGARIAN ADVANCES.—EXCITEMENT IN VIENNA]

*Cologne,* April 27. Today is *Kossuth's birthday;* the leader of the Hungarian revolution is 43 years old today.[266]

Today an *official* royal imperial *Bulletin* (No. 35) already *confirms* the reports of Hungarian advances which we published this morning: that Wohlgemuth has been defeated, Pest and Ofen are taken, and Komorn is relieved.[a] It is now established that the Hungarians have already passed not only the Gran and the Neutra but even the *Waag,* and that Wohlgemuth has been *driven back to Tyrnau,* five miles from Pressburg. Altogether *only four comitats* in Hungary are *still* in imperial hands, and on all sides it is conceded that *on Hungarian soil not a single defensible position is left to the imperial forces.*

*Great excitement* prevails in **Vienna.** The people throng the streets as in the revolutionary days of last year. The military, usually so impudent, have again become remarkably restrained. Vienna is waiting for the Hungarians to cross the Leitha to effect its **fifth revolution,**[267] a revolution which will not be simply an Austrian, but simultaneously a European one.

*Eljen Kossuth! Eljenek a Magyarak!*[b]

Written by Engels on April 27, 1849

First published in the special supplement to the *Neue Rheinische Zeitung* No. 284, April 28, 1849

Printed according to the newspaper

Published in English for the first time

---

[a] See this volume, pp. 350-51.— *Ed.*
[b] Long live Kossuth! Long live the Magyars!— *Ed.*

# MAGYAR ADVANCES

*Cologne,* April 28. No commentary is necessary on the royal imperial Army Bulletin No. 35,[a] the main points of which we have already this morning communicated to our readers.[b] It reads as follows:

"Concerning events in the army in Hungary. After the movement back towards Pest made by the Austrian army early this month, in order to concentrate in positions protecting the two cities, the enemy almost daily attempted attacks on the same which, though they were without results, nevertheless gave him proof that our main strength was gathered at Pest and Ofen. Soon afterwards he attacked Waitzen, where two brigades were stationed commanded by General Götz—in the fighting the latter died the death of a hero—and advanced up the Danube via Leléd and Kemend. Believing that we were kept sufficiently busy at Pest, the enemy then marched in two strong columns, one on the left bank of the Gran and the other via Ipolyság, towards Leva. Here he assembled about 30,000 of his best troops on the 18th and crossed the Gran in three columns at Kalna, Bars and Sz. Benedek.

"Lieutenant-Field Marshal von Wohlgemuth—in command of five brigades totalling about 15,000 men from Moravia and Austria, which as a reserve were drawn up behind the Gran—made aware of this movement, left Kemend on the night of the 18th to march toward the enemy between Malas and Bese.

"Meanwhile the enemy drew up his entire force—outnumbering ours by two to one—in battle order between Verebely and Nagy Sallo. An attack launched on Nagy Sallo by Prince Jablonowsky's brigade was indeed completely successful, one column already having reached the town, when entry had to be given up because the town was ablaze. The enemy took advantage of this to outflank us on our right between the Gran and Nagy Sallo, at the same time attempting a similar manoeuvre against our left flank from Verebely. A most stubborn battle had already raged from early morning till afternoon; with his proven composure, Lieutenant-Field Marshal von Wohlgemuth made a fighting retreat, leading his very tired troops from one position to

---

[a] "35. Armee-Bulletin. Vom 24, April."—*Ed.*
[b] In the special supplement to the *Neue Rheinische Zeitung* dated April 28 but issued in the morning of April 29, 1849 (see this volume, p. 352).—*Ed.*

another; the enemy, on the other hand, extended his outflanking manoeuvre even towards Neutra.

"Lieutenant-Field Marshal Wohlgemuth had already previously been given orders to continue his retreat behind the Neutra and even back across the Waag, if things took an unfavourable turn, so as to cover both the valley of the Waag and Pressburg, and beyond the Waag to effect a junction, by way of Schütt Island, with the corps besieging Komorn, where in the meantime the bombardment was continued in the most lively manner.

"The commanding general, Master of Ordnance Baron Welden, who had arrived in Gran on the 17th, convinced that the main force of the enemy could have made the outflanking movement through the mountains to relieve Komorn, immediately ordered the Ban[a] to sally forth from Pest with his entire force and to attack the enemy, but not to follow up advantages too quickly. On the 19th, the Ban advanced *in all directions* (!!!!), but the enemy gave way before him so rapidly that he was not even within reach of our artillery (!).

"On the 20th, another enemy column, which up to then had been held in reserve at Paszto on the River Ipoly, moved down the right bank of the Gran with the left wing of the enemy towards Kemend and Gran, and immediately attacked the Csorich division, stationed there as a reserve, which, since on that day Lieutenant-Field Marshal Wohlgemuth had already passed Neuhäusel, retreated fighting towards Gran and dismantled the pontoon bridge there so as to defend this point as strongly as possible. The commanding general arrived at Ofen on the 20th.

"Given this military situation, it appeared to the commanding general that to continue to hold Pest and Ofen would have great disadvantages for further military operations, especially since the Danube from Komorn to Waitzen had been taken by the enemy, and neither city offered a useful pivot for the operations. The Master of Ordnance therefore set about concentrating his troops in a secure position, and is convinced that, with the reinforcements placed at his disposal which are marching to his aid, he will soon be in a position to renew the offensive successfully.

"Messages from Pest of the 21st of this month report that the enemy made an attack at Czinkota on that day, but after not very stubborn fighting he was forced back everywhere by our troops which were advancing towards him.

"According to news of the 17th of this month, just arrived from Semlin from the Master of Ordnance Count Nugent, the state of things on the Lower Danube is taking an increasingly favourable turn: the Chaikist area[268] has again been cleared of the enemy; the position at Peterwardein has been much strengthened by the well-placed entrenchments constructed under the energetic direction of Colonel Mamula, and through the troop reinforcements moving on Peterwardein from all directions the corps being formed there will soon be in a favourable position to resume the offensive and advance on Szegedin."

This Bulletin confirms everything that we have already reported from the theatre of war. Moreover, it is written more clearly than the previous imperial hushing-up proclamations.

At Komorn, to which fresh troops and fresh cattle for slaughter have been brought by the Hungarians, many guns were left behind by the imperial forces, which, though in part spiked, fell into the hands of the Hungarians. Now, 24 hours after we pointed it out in

---

[a] Jellachich.— *Ed.*

our newspaper, all the papers bewail the fact that the imperial troops no longer have a single defensible position in Hungary, and will have to withdraw beyond the Leitha and March.

The imperial authorities have glaringly failed in their attempt to issue the new Hungarian banknotes, *alias* "forged bills". The *Ost-Deutsche Post* relates the following story:

"A high-ranking staff officer went into the vault of a money-changer the other day, demanding that he change 2,000 florins of the new paper money into Austrian banknotes, and even offered them at a premium. The money-changer declined to do so, under the pretext that he had only a few Austrian notes. However, he was willing to change a few 100 florins, though without any premium. The officer replied: you are a money-changer, you *must* have notes, and if you do not change them I will have your vault locked up. After some argument between them the notes were exchanged. On the following day, the money-changer's wife received from that same staff officer a little packet of 5-florin notes in new Hungarian bills. She said that she could not change them. Shortly afterwards, the officer himself appeared, accompanied by an adjutant. In the meantime, the money-changer also arrived and declared that he was certainly willing to change silver money and ducats, but not the banknotes, for, he reasoned, not without logic, *if the bills were valid, the General had no need to change them* and could use them as well as the money-changer; *if they were no good, he did not want to change them,* for he could not use them. He had payments to make in Vienna, and he was so far not aware that the new bills would be accepted in payment there. If he were to change them for the General hundreds of people would immediately turn up with similar requests which he would be unable to satisfy. The General replied that it was beneath his dignity (!!!) to answer him, and ordered the mayor to be fetched, instead of whom a town councillor appeared and locked up the vault on the General's order." [a]

## The news from Hungary has had a tremendous effect in Vienna:

"*As in the days of the barricades last year,* crowds were moving up and down the streets. A stranger might suppose that the masses of people swarming hither and thither like ants were there in response to the warm spring weather, but to anyone even moderately familiar with the physiognomy of the capital, it was clear that mighty levers of curiosity, hope and feverish tension must have agitated the Viennese, encouraging them despite the ubiquitous glint of bayonets, despite the vigilance of the police, to a form of passive resistance expressed in crowds gathering at street corners, loud and fearless political beer-hall talk, and a thousand other variations. *Former legionnaires*[269] in ranks four and five deep marched past the guards as though on parade, with bold provocative glances; former *national guards* shook hands with one another as though asking 'Well, will it start soon?' while those in favour of 'calm at any price' despondently and fearfully crept along keeping close to the houses as though Kossuth were at the gates of Vienna.

"That the 'loyal ones' have a guilty conscience was clearly and strikingly shown yesterday. In inns and coffee-houses, cries of *Eljen*[b] were raised to Kossuth. 'I am biding my time, and it will come,' says Perceval to the Queen. Today the tumult seems

---

[a] "Pesth, 21. April", *Ost-Deutsche Post* No. 81, April 24, 1849.— *Ed.*
[b] Long live!— *Ed.*

to have died down somewhat, at least the sound of tramping and the buzzing of voices are not as audible today as yesterday."

Another letter from *Vienna* reports:

"The turn in the Hungarian events has produced a simply indescribable despondency among the majority of the city's inhabitants" (i.e. the bourgeoisie). "The numerous refugees arriving here hourly from Pest increase the anxieties, and only now vent is given to the universal execration of Windischgrätz (!). Already loud shouts of 'treason' can be heard (!!). However, the city is quiet. Both yesterday and today, troop reinforcements have gone from here to the battlefield. On the other hand, the arrival of fresh troops is again expected here; two battalions have already arrived since yesterday.

"The courier coach with the mail from Pest has already failed to turn up today, and we must be prepared for that city being cut off once again by Kossuth."

A third correspondent, who already sees half a step further, makes the following observation:

"A ministerial crisis is inevitable, Schwarzenberg will have to follow Windischgrätz, public opinion must have its victims, otherwise — I doubt if I need say more."

It is obvious that it will now be a matter of crises quite different from ministerial crises!

Important news has come in from the south:

*Vetter* has advanced towards Stuhlweissenburg and the Plattensee with a Magyar column.

Further to the south, *Perczel* too has crossed the Danube and *recaptured Vukovar*, on the road to Fünfkirchen.

*Karlowitz* in Syrmien has been attacked and *bombarded* by the Magyars.

We hear from several quarters that *Bem* has invaded Wallachia and driven the Russians back to Rimnik Vatitza, three and a half miles from the border.

In short: the Magyars are advancing victoriously at all points, and the Austrian "united monarchy", the centre of European counter-revolution, will be destroyed within a fortnight, unless a miracle happens.

But it is on the ruins of the "united monarchy" that the European revolution will arise anew.

Written by Engels on April 28, 1849

First published in the *Neue Rheinische Zeitung* No. 285, April 29, 1849

Printed according to the newspaper

Published in English for the first time

# [DISSOLUTION OF THE SECOND CHAMBER]

*Cologne*, April 28. The rumour already current in the town at midday today was confirmed this evening: the King and his martial-law Government **have dissolved the Second Chamber**.[270]

The details can be found below, *de dato* Berlin.[a]

By this act the King and his martial-law Ministers have once again *broken their word*. According to the imposed martial-law Charter of December 5,[271] the Chambers were expressly convened "to revise the Constitution". Only after the *first* Parliament convened under this Constitution had revised this botchwork was the latter to be regarded as complete and definitively valid. This is how it was imposed in December of last year.

Hence the Chambers had at least a *partially constitutional mandate*. So long as they had not carried out this mandate, so long as they together with the Crown had not revised the Constitution, *they could not be dissolved*, any more than the Assembly of blessed memory convened to agree upon the Prussian Constitution.[272]

Nevertheless it has been dispersed—this miserable Second Chamber, summoned under the sabre dictatorship and the menace of the bayonet, by means of bribery, intimidation and deception!

This is what is called "Prussian honour", "Prussian loyalty"!

If the Ministers had waited a few more weeks, perhaps the Austro-Hungarian revolution would have spared them the trouble and dispersed both Chambers.

As for the significance of this new coup d'état, it is quite obvious. We are going to be made to experience the **rule of the sabre raised**

---

[a] The reference is to the report published under the date-line "Berlin, 28. April" in the same issue of the *Neue Rheinische Zeitung.*—*Ed.*

**to the second power**. We shall have most graciously foisted on us laws on the press, on associations, on civil disturbances, on posters etc., to such an extent that the German philistine's eyes will fill with tears. There will be persecution, disciplinary punishment, arrests; the state of siege will be made universal and, to cap it all, finally a new Constitution will be introduced, and an electoral law with property qualifications as well as a House of Lords, a Constitution in which the present first Chamber will figure as the *second.*

In short, things will be pushed as far as Prussian pluck will permit.

We, for our part, wish only that Herr Manteuffel will once more convene the United Diet [273] of blessed memory.

Written by Engels on April 28, 1849

First published in the *Neue Rheinische Zeitung* No. 285 (second edition), April 29, 1849

Printed according to the newspaper

Published in English for the first time

# [POSEN]

*Cologne*, April 28. Our readers will be thankful to us if from time to time we examine the "splendour and might" of our Hohenzollern royal family and the simultaneous wonderful prosperity of the chief supports of its noble throne, the bug-ridden knights of Brandenburg who have been transplanted into every province.

In this instructive investigation we deal today with the Polish part[a] of our fatherland in the narrower sense. Already last summer, on the occasion of the glorious pacification and reorganisation of Poland carried out by shrapnel and caustic,[274] we tested the German-Jewish lies about the "predominantly German population" in the towns, "the large German landed estates" in the countryside, and the royal-Prussian merit for the growth of general well-being. Readers of the *Neue Rheinische Zeitung* will recall that we learned from official figures and reports of the Archbishop of Gnesen and Posen[b] to the bourgeois transitional Minister Camphausen[c] that in the parts of the territory included within the Prussian demarcation lines, not about one half, but hardly one-sixth, of the population is Germans,[d] whereas the lying statistics of the Prussian Government step by step increased the alleged German population the more the progress of the counter-revolution seemed to make possible a new division and a new diminution of the Polish part of Posen. We discovered that in

---

[a] i.e. Grand Duchy of Posen under Prussian rule.— *Ed.*

[b] Przyluski.— *Ed.*

[c] "Korrespondenz des Erzbischofs von Posen Przyluski mit dem Berliner Kabinet." *Neue Rheinische Zeitung* Nos. 5, 7, 10, 14, 38, 39 of June 5, 7, 10, 14, and July 8 and 9, 1848.— *Ed.*

[d] "The Frankfurt Assembly Debates the Polish Question" (present edition, Vol. 7, pp. 337-81).— *Ed.*

connection with these figures the German national simpletons and money-grubbers of the Frankfurt parliamentary swamp always counted as Germans the Polish Jews as well, although this meanest of all races, neither by its jargon nor by its descent, but at most only through its lust for profit, could have any relation of kinship with Frankfurt. We discovered that in fact relatively very few of small German landowners were ensconced in individual districts of Posen, and then only as a result of treacherous Prussian speculation on Polish poverty, since, by the Cabinet Order of 1833, all *auctioned* estates could be sold exclusively to Prussian junkers from the backwoods, to whom the Government advanced money for that purpose. Finally, we discovered that the benefits and services rendered by the Hohenzollern paternalism consisted in the fact that after the March revolution, out of cowardice, the finest promises were given of a "national reorganisation", and then, with the growth of the counter-revolution, by means of a five times repeated and ever greater partition, the noose was fastened more tightly round the neck of the country, whereupon "reorganisation" was made dependent on "pacification" i.e. the surrender of weapons. Finally, when this condition was fulfilled, "My glorious army"[275] was let loose on the unarmed, trustful country in order in alliance with the Jews to plunder the churches, set fire to the villages, beat the Poles to death in public places with ramrods or brand them with caustic and, after having taken revenge for their belief in the "March promises", pay honour to God and his Christian-Germanic Majesty on this field of corpses.

Such was the charitable work of Prussian "reorganisation" in Posen. Let us now deal also with the origin of large-scale Prussian landownership, the domains and estates. Their history is no less instructive as regards the "splendour and might" of the Hohenzollern family and the value of its beloved rogue knights.

In 1793 the three crowned thieves divided the Polish booty among themselves according to the same right by which three highwaymen divide among themselves the purse of a defenceless traveller.[276] Posen and South Prussia on that occasion received the Hohenzollerns as *hereditary* rulers in exactly the same way as the Rhine Province in 1815 received them as *hereditary* rulers,—in accordance with the right of trafficking in people and of kidnapping. As soon as this right of trafficking in people and of kidnapping is abolished, the Poles, like the Rhinelanders, will cancel with a *red* stroke the title-deed of their *hereditary* Hohenzollern Grand Duke.

The first thing by which in plundered Poland the Hohenzollern Father of the country manifested his Prussian benevolence was the confiscation of the lands formerly belonging to the Polish Crown and Church. In general we have not the slightest objection to such confiscation; on the contrary, we hope it will soon be the turn of *other* crown lands. We ask however for what purpose were these confiscated estates used? In the interest of "the general well-being" of the country, for which the Brandenburg paternal regime was so benevolently concerned during the work of pacification and reorganisation in 1848? In the interests of the people whose sweat and blood created those estates? We shall see.

At that time Minister Hoym, who for twenty years had administered the province of Silesia quite free from any supervision and used that power for the most junker-like swindling and extortions, was entrusted with the administration of South Prussia as well, in reward for his services to God, King and country. In the interests of the "splendour and might" of the dynasty and in order to create a splendid and mighty class of devoted junkers from the backwoods, Hoym proposed to his lord and master[a] that he should bestow as many as possible of the confiscated Church and Crown lands to so-called "*deserving persons*". And that was done. A host of rascally knights, favourites of royal mistresses, creatures of the Ministers, accomplices whom one wanted to silence, were presented with the largest and richest estates of the plundered country and thereby "German interests" and "predominantly German landownership" were implanted among the Poles.

In order not to arouse royal cupidity, Hoym had as a precaution assessed these estates for the King at a quarter or sixth part of their value, and sometimes even less; he was afraid, and probably not without reason, that if the King were to learn the true value of these estates, he would think of his own "paternal" pocket before anything else. During Hoym's four years of administration after the "pacification",[277] from 1794 to 1798, there were in this manner given away: in the Posen administrative region 22, in the Kalisch, formerly Petrikau, region 19, in the Warsaw region 11, altogether 52 larger and smaller groups of estates, which in total contained not less than *two hundred and forty-one* separate estates. The King was told that the value of these estates was $3\,^1/_2$ million talers, but their true value exceeded **twenty million talers.**

*The Poles will know from whom during the coming revolution they will have to extract these 20 million talers, that Polish milliard, stolen from them by the right of traffic in people.*

---

[a] Frederick William II.— *Ed.*

In the Kalisch region alone the area of the estates given away amounted to *more than a third of all the Crown and Church lands*, and the income from these estates, even according to the miserable estimates of the value of the grants in 1799 alone, was 247,000 talers annually.

In the Posen administrative region the Owinsk estate with its extensive forests was presented to Tresckow, a haberdasher. At the same time the adjacent Crown estate of Szrin, which had not a single tree, was declared a state domain and had to buy its timber at government expense from Tresckow's forests.

Finally, in other regions, the deeds of gift expressly freed the estates from ordinary taxes, and moreover freed them "*in perpetuity*", so that no Prussian King should ever have the right to impose new taxes on them.

We shall now see in what manner the stolen estates were given away and to which "*deserving persons*". The extent of the services of these junkers from the backwoods, however, compels us for the sake of coherent exposition to deal with this subject in a special article.[278]

Written by Engels on April 28, 1849

First published in the *Neue Rheinische Zeitung* No. 285 (second edition), April 29, 1849

Printed according to the newspaper

Published in English for the first time

# [FROM THE THEATRE OF WAR]

The imperial army is *disintegrating*. The Croats have openly rebelled and forced their Ban, Jellachich, to go with them from Pest down the Danube by steamship to the south, probably so that they may protect their homeland. Jellachich had to give way, and hence the whole of the First Army Corps is on the march southwards.

Welden has indeed withdrawn his headquarters to Raab. Though he insists that Ofen is still garrisoned (by 6,000 men commanded by Schlick, they say), this however is very doubtful.

Another rumour, though immediately disavowed by other sources, has it that Wohlgemuth, who has just been defeated, has now defeated Görgey!!!

The Pest mail of the 22nd arrived in Vienna 24 hours late.

A letter from Pressburg to Breslau of April 24 says

"that the Komorn siege artillery, sailing up the Danube, has just arrived and that the Austrian troops are withdrawing to Pressburg".

Finally the correspondent expresses the fear that all correspondence will probably be interrupted quite soon. The last mail was also missing in Pressburg.

Welden's proclamation, mentioned previously, runs thus:

"To reassure the public we herewith announce that according to news just received from the headquarters of Lieutenant-Field Marshal Baron Welden, Ofen continues to be occupied by an adequate force, and the main army, continuously following the enemy's movements on the right bank of the Danube, is in process of being concentrated. At the same time we announce that Komorn is still under continuous bombardment and is being kept under observation by our troops. In addition, Csorich's division continues to occupy Gran and covers the Danube crossing.

"The Commanding General and Deputy Governor,
Baron von Böhm, Lieutenant-Field Marshal." [a]

The Austrian retreat towards Vienna is now called "concentration".

The martial-law paper *Die Presse* reports the following on the latest operations:

"The Hungarians were above all concerned to get possession of the left bank of the Danube above Waitzen by a rapid movement under cover of the mountains. Thus they achieved a double purpose: the insurrection gained scope and strength, and they could hope in this way to relieve Komorn, the key to the Danube. The execution of this plan was concealed from the Austrian general by sham attacks on our troops by a few brigades, and since he allowed himself to be deceived it was in the main successful. The insurgents crossed the Eipel and Gran and were thus able to bypass General Wohlgemuth, stationed at Kemend with 15,000 men. This bypassing was executed with far superior numbers of insurgents and could not have been prevented even by Wohlgemuth's most energetic and devoted resistance. The Magyars extended the line of their bypassing to Neutra, and, while their right wing reached the flank of the royal imperial troops between Sallo and the river Gran, their left wing threatened the rear. It seems therefore to have become impossible for General Wohlgemuth to carry out his intention of retreating across the Waag, thus covering Pressburg and occupying the Schütt Island in conjunction with the corps besieging Komorn, for he withdrew to Neuhäusel." [b]

The (Italian) Mazzuchelli regiment is reported to have gone over to the Hungarians.

In Pest, a proclamation [c] issued by Havas, the royal commissioner, warns the inhabitants against attempts on the departing royal imperial troops, as the destruction of the city would ensue; Havas exhorts them not to place any obstacles in the way of the withdrawal of the troops.—The military hospitals have been placed under the protection of the municipality. The guns have disappeared from Ofen's ramparts. The imperial side must be in a bad way if it has to resort to such proclamations.

*The Hungarian banknotes are—al pari*[d]; the Austrian notes have dropped considerably.

The *Pester Zeitung* has engaged a Magyar editor; the *Figyelmező* has ceased to appear.

The retreat from Pest is said to be the result of a 48-hour cease-fire granted by the Magyar forces outside Pest to the imperial forces.

---

[a] "Kundmachung, von Böhm. Wien, 24. April 1849."—*Ed.*

[b] "Wien, 24. April", *Die Presse* No. 98, April 25, 1849.—*Ed.*

[c] Of April 22, 1849, *Der Lloyd* No. 197 (evening edition), April 25, 1849.—*Ed.*

[d] At par.—*Ed.*

The *Neue Oder-Zeitung* writes:

"The Magyar army is reported to amount to 200,000 men, including the *Landsturm*. In newly occupied areas, Kossuth likewise calls up the *Landsturm*, so that his combat forces will soon amount to 300,000 men, etc. etc. The fact is that since March 4 the energy of the Croat troops has declined, and Jellachich is having to employ all his prestige to restrain them."

General of the Cavalry Hammerstein has not left Lemberg to this day, and the First Deutschmeister battalion[279] marched off to Stryj only on the 14th of this month, to replace a battalion stationed there and destined for Hungary. The report that Lieutenant-Field Marshal Vogl is with the corps which consists of 20,000 men and is already on Hungarian soil has thus proved incorrect. The entire force now on the way to Hungary probably consists of 53 companies of infantry, six squadrons of cavalry and four artillery batteries, formed up in three columns. The first is commanded by Major-General Barco, the second by Major-General Benedek, and the third by Colonel Ludwig. Lieutenant-Field Marshal Vogl is in charge of the operations.

As a precautionary measure, Lieutenant-Field Marshal Simunich has sent guns to Vienna; but already yesterday they were sent back to Hungary by steamship.

Since the 25th, more fresh troops have arrived in Vienna and others have marched off. Commercial and banking circles have recovered a little from their fears. In the suburbs, especially Josefstadt and Wieden, considerable excitement prevails, and last night, particularly in the former, people drank immoderately in most inns; nay, Hungarian tunes were demanded and chanted.

Two days previously, in the Josefstadt transport depot, a detachment of the Hungarian Alexander infantry regiment,[280] which is in process of reorganisation, was worked on by emissaries. But the battalion was quickly sent away, and some of the "agitators"[281] were arrested. Today was the first day of recruiting by the drawing of lots and up to now it has passed off quietly, although in the suburbs those liable to conscription had been greatly incited. The Government has taken stringent police measures to check the throng of "agitators" and to remove strangers. Kossuth's proclamations to the sister nation in Vienna, in which it is called upon to aid in the restoration to the throne of the legitimate Emperor Ferdinand, have been read here. In addition, the rumour was circulating that a cabinet council decided yesterday to reject Russian intervention in the Austro-Hungarian question.

Although somewhat belatedly, we are reprinting a letter from Pressburg which appeared in the *Constitutionelles Blatt aus Böhmen*, because it contains much that is interesting.

"The stage-coaches to the Upper Comitats were discontinued already last week; soon afterwards, mail also was dispatched only to Neutra, and—yesterday morning it was already reported that the Hungarians had entered Neuhäusel (three to four hours from Komorn). During the day, a traveller arriving here from Tyrnau showed me a proclamation issued by the military commandant there, which refuted the rumour that the Hungarians had entered Neutra as well, but in such a way that from the few lines one might easily infer the opposite. Yesterday afternoon, this doubt was strengthened by the dispatch by train to Tyrnau of a detachment from the garrison here, provided with guns. Late in the evening, I was told by an acquaintance who had arrived the same day from Neuhäusel that this town was already occupied by an insurgent force of nearly 40,000-45,000 men together with a considerable number of guns, and the royal imperial troops, about 12,000-15,000 men, had withdrawn to Sellye (two hours up-river towards Pressburg), because of the great superiority of the enemy. I was still quite unwilling to believe this strange news, when I heard an imperial army sergeant confirm this sad fact. Both agreed that the troops had run out of ammunition and for that reason alone had to retreat. An observation that unfortunately one has had to hear more than once since the beginning of the unhappy civil war in Hungary.

"Our trades people here were however greatly surprised when this morning they wanted to travel by train to the market in Tyrnau, and found that railway journey there had been suspended. In answer to their enquiries they were told that last night almost the whole of our garrison, together with artillery, had been hurriedly sent off to Tyrnau, for which purpose all the carriages had been requisitioned.—It has become known that a fairly heavy encounter between our troops and the enemy army has taken place at Neuhäusel, on which occasion the Nassau infantry regiment is said to have suffered heavily. It is also said that the Tyrnau railway carriages which left last night will bring back here a large number of royal imperial troops today.

"A camp of about 18-20 battalions is soon to be formed outside one of the city lines. It is certain that already last week, the innkeeper in the Schlossberg fort which is now fairly heavily fortified, was given definite instruction by the military commandant here to lay in all necessary provisions for at least three to four weeks, and the garrison here is expecting at any moment the order to move into that fort with bag and baggage.—The announced issue of the new compulsory notes naturally did not produce a good mood. The standing questions regarding these notes are: (1) To what amount are they to be issued? (2) Will the Bohemian, Silesian and Austrian industrialists accept them at their full value?

"*Postscript.* Just now we hear that the Hungarian advance guard is already at Szered."[a]

The same newspaper carries a report from Vienna about Transylvanian affairs:

"A considerable number of refugees from Transylvania arrived here recently. Some of them, who came directly from Hermannstadt—directly now means through Wallachia and via Esseg—relate the events there in almost identical terms. The

---

[a] "Pressburg, 22. April", *Constitutionelles Blatt aus Böhmen* No. 98, April 25, 1849.—*Ed.*

murder stories are in large part invented; looters were shot, and the strictest discipline was soon established. Bem put up to public auction all the belongings of the officers which they left behind, with the exception of General Puchner's belongings and correspondence: these he forwarded to him by some Honveds, together with a polite letter. They were, however, intercepted by the Russians, and none of the refugees was able to say anything about what had happened to either the Honveds or the documents. Incidentally, they depict the condition of the country as deplorable, and the conduct of the Russians towards the refugees as really shocking, but all agree that they were moved by the kindness and considerateness of the Turks."

Written by Engels about April 28, 1849

First published in the *Neue Rheinische Zeitung* No. 285 (second edition), April 29, 1849

Printed according to the newspaper

Published in English for the first time

# FROM THE THEATRE OF WAR

No reports of further victories. On the contrary, we hear now that the Austrians are retreating in the greatest confusion on all fronts.

The brutal butcher Welden has landed himself in a fine mess. He is as good as cut off from Vienna, and the only line of retreat still open to him is that to Styria via Vesprim, along the Plattensee and through the pathless mountains.

Wohlgemuth, completely cut off from the main body of the army, is in a totally indefensible position between Sellye on the Waag and Bös on the Danube, on the Schütt Island. The path to Pressburg is open to Klapka's right wing, which faces Wohlgemuth there.

Pest is now actually occupied by the Hungarians (on the evening of the 23rd). The imperial forces were given sufficient time for their retreat, since on that condition they promised not to bombard Pest. The pretence of the imperial forces to wish to defend Ofen is without significance, for Ofen could have been held only by threatening to bombard Pest.

Welden has again been in Ofen. He obviously does not know where to turn.

Jellachich's Croats have had to turn back; the Danube below Pest was occupied by the Hungarians with artillery. But they will nevertheless attempt to break through to Croatia.

Jablonowsky has already passed through *Raab* with his brigade, which is going to Oedenburg.

There is great excitement in Vienna. The workers are rejoicing. The mail to Hungary has not been dispatched from there for the past three days.

Fifty thousand Russians are said to have received orders to march into Transylvania from the north and south.

The Olmütz Ministry has now *certainly requested Russian intervention in Hungary as well.*

The Berlin *National-Zeitung* quotes the following alleged conditions under which the Hungarians would be willing to conclude peace:

(1) Recognition of the Kingdom of Hungary in its old boundaries, hence including Croatia, Slavonia and the Military Border.[282]

(2) Union with Transylvania as resolved and determined last year by the Transylvanian and Hungarian Assemblies.[283]

(3) A general amnesty throughout Austria; the immediate release of all the October prisoners [a] and compensation for the families of those murdered.

(4) Demobilisation to Hungary of the Hungarian regiments still serving in Italy and the other parts of the Empire.

(5) Recognition of the Hungarian Constitution of 1848.[284]

(6) Hungary to remain under the government of a provisional executive power originating from the Assembly, until the succession to the throne is established by law, and the King, who is to be elected, has been crowned in Buda-Pest and has sworn loyalty to the Constitution.

(7) Galicia to enter into the same relationship to the Austrian union of states in which Hungary stands now and will stand in future, and be called the Polish Kingdom of Galicia; hence Galicia will be linked with Austria in a personal union and will have its own army and its own finances.

(8) The share of Hungary in the Austrian National Debt to be determined by the Hungarian Assembly by a simple majority.

Written by Engels on April 30, 1849

First published in the *Neue Rheinische Zeitung* No. 286, May 1, 1849

Printed according to the newspaper

Published in English for the first time

---

[a] Those arrested when the October 1848 uprising in Vienna was crushed.— *Ed.*

# THE COUNTER-REVOLUTIONARY PLANS
# IN BERLIN

*Cologne,* April 30. The plans of our counter-revolutionary Government are gradually being revealed.

It was intended that a new stage of the Prussian counter-revolution should date from April 27. It was desired to provoke the Berlin people into street fighting, perhaps to allow the insurrection *à la* Cavaignac to achieve "considerable magnitude", then to crush it by Cavaignac's means and with superior force such as Cavaignac possessed, to proclaim martial law, to favour a few deputies and a good number of agitators [285] with powder and shot, and finally, by new dictated measures to get rid of the troublesome fetters which even the martial-law Charter of December 5 still imposed on our counter-revolution.

The provoked uprising would have provided a sufficient excuse for asserting that the people "were not yet mature enough" for the freedom most graciously bestowed on them, and that it was impossible to govern under such an electoral law and such a Constitution.[286] "To avoid bloodshed", and therefore in the interests of the people, the last remnants of freedom had to be destroyed. "To avoid bloodshed", a state of siege had to be proclaimed throughout the country with the exception of Further Pomerania! All that could be asserted only after a decent-sized revolt in Berlin, with the requisite disturbances in Breslau, Magdeburg, Cologne etc., had taken place and had been successfully suppressed with the aid of grape-shot.

Hence the brutal behaviour of the constables against the Left assembled in the Konversationshalle,[287] and the cordon of troops encircling Dönhoff Square; hence the rapid fire on an unarmed peaceful crowd, which *could not* disperse because all the streets were barred to it.

The calm behaviour of the people despite all provocation upset the calculations of the counter-revolutionaries. They have no pretext for issuing dictates, but dictate they *must*. Perhaps this evening already we shall learn what new turn these gentlemen have decided on.

What extensive plans were envisaged is evident from all the circumstances. Firstly, from the simultaneous dissolution of the Chamber in Hanover, secondly and in particular, from Herr Radowitz's journey to Berlin.

Herr Radowitz is the heart and soul of the Prussian counter-revolution. He drafted the plan for the counter-revolution of November last, but he himself still remained behind the scenes and intrigued in Frankfurt on behalf of the Prussian hereditary imperial crown. *This time* Radowitz himself went to Berlin in order, it is said, to come out in the open at last and to become *Prime Minister*. A **Radowitz Government** — that is the heart of the matter! [a]

Furthermore, we definitely know the following facts:

1) In the course of *last week all Chefpräsidenten* received from their *Oberpräsidenten* a document informing them of the *forthcoming dissolution of the Chamber* and directing them to take all necessary precautionary measures.

2) A ministerial rescript was sent to all government authorities stating:

1. That *all burgomasters* are obliged to report *daily* to the appropriate government authorities about the impression produced by the dissolution of the Chamber. The government authorities, for their part, must present *collective reports* on this subject to the Ministry.

2. *For the present new elections would* **not** *be held*; on the other hand, *measures will be taken* against *many members of the "so-called" Left.*

3. *All precautionary measures* should be taken to suppress any attempt at revolt.

The rescript is signed: *Manteuffel.*

Herr Manteuffel, or rather Herr Radowitz, his superior, could not have rendered a better service to the developing *Hungarian-Polish-German* revolution than precisely at the present time to come forward openly with his plans for the restoration of the absolutist regime.

Written by Engels on April 30, 1849

First published in the *Neue Rheinische Zeitung* No. 286, May 1, 1849

Printed according to the newspaper

Published in English for the first time

---

[a] Goethe, *Faust*, 1. Teil, 1. "Studierzimmerszene".— *Ed.*

# LASSALLE

*Cologne*, May 1. The day after tomorrow the indictment against *Lassalle* on the charge of direct incitement to take up arms against the royal power will come before the Assizes in Düsseldorf.

It will be recalled that Lassalle, Cantador (head of the Düsseldorf civic militia) and the street-vendor Weyers were arrested last November when the state of siege was proclaimed in Düsseldorf, and an investigation was begun against them on account of the above-mentioned "crime under Articles 87 and 102 of the *Code pénal*".[288]

The investigation proceeded as slowly as possible. Whereas the simultaneously instituted tax-refusal trial of the Rhenish District Committee of Democrats took place already on February 8 in Cologne,[289] one assize period after another elapsed in Düsseldorf before the Cologne indictment board had even referred the case to the Assizes. But Marx, Schneider and Schapper were at liberty, whereas Lassalle was kept in the Düsseldorf remand prison; yet the *Code d'instruction criminelle*[290] lays down that the case of an arrested person should have *priority* in being dealt with!

In prison Lassalle was given a quite special kind of preference. The *Neue Rheinische Zeitung* has often enough had occasion to report examples of the tenderness with which he was treated by the myrmidons of the royal-Prussian judiciary.[a] Whereas all sorts of favours were conferred on Cantador—for, despite his political activity, Cantador had a great many friends among the Düsseldorf bourgeoisie—Lassalle had once again[291] to experience the arbitrary

---

[a] See present edition, Vol. 8, pp. 344-46, 463-65, 474-76 and this volume, pp. 339-41.— *Ed.*

tyranny to which a royal-Prussian prisoner under examination is subjected. Without speaking of the pettier annoyances, we shall merely recall the brutal way in which Herr Morret, the prison governor, treated Lassalle in the presence of the examining magistrate, Herr Ebermeyer (whom we now have the pleasure of having here, in Cologne). Lassalle sent a complaint to the Public Prosecutor's office. The Public Prosecutor General, Herr Nicolovius, decided: the action in question is *neither a crime nor an offence* and therefore cannot be the subject of legal proceedings!

We recall further that the physician considered that outdoor walks were absolutely necessary for Lassalle's health, to which the Public Prosecutor's office gave its consent, *whereas the government authority prohibited them*, although according to the law a prisoner undergoing examination does not come under the jurisdiction of the government authority but solely under that of the Public Prosecutor.

The difficulties involved in gaining access to Lassalle in the prison, the excuses, evasions etc. are familiar to everyone who has ever tried to penetrate into the interior of the Düsseldorf "institution".

The investigation was at last concluded and the case should have gone to the Court. There was then still enough time to bring the case for trial at the last Assizes, which were held in February and March. But they wanted to prevent this at all costs. When the dossiers were submitted to the deputy Chief Public Prosecutor, the "gracious" Herr von Ammon I, for his final conclusion, Herr Ammon suddenly produced a letter from Lassalle to a certain Stangier, a farmer in the Altenkirchen district, in order to base a fresh charge on it. But this letter had for several weeks already lain quietly in the office desk of Herr Ammon, without the idea occurring to him of adding it to the dossiers as a new point in the indictment. Now, when everything was ready and the time for the Assizes was at hand, now Herr Ammon came forward with the letter. Then, of course, new interrogations of witnesses had to take place and the case was delayed for several weeks. And this period was just sufficient to *make it impossible* for Lassalle's case to be dealt with at the *Assizes then about to be held.*

The letter, which Herr Ammon, *as he himself admitted*, had kept for a fairly long time in his office desk, was moreover so unimportant that neither the Court nor the indictment board paid any attention to it or listed it as an additional reason for indictment!

In short, the Assizes were successfully avoided, and the next session began only in May. One deputation after another went to the Public Prosecutor General Herr Nicolovius, and asked for the case to be expedited or for an extraordinary session of the Assizes to be called. Herr Nicolovius promised to do all he could and stated that in no case would Lassalle be imprisoned for as much as six months. And now! It is hardly two weeks short of six months.

The Court at last decided: all three accused were referred to the indictment board. But here a difficulty arose: people were quite convinced that in the whole Düsseldorf Circuit no jury could be found that would convict Herr Cantador. Hence in order to free Cantador, Lassalle also would have to be acquitted, even by people who would otherwise have convicted him. And it was precisely the conviction of Lassalle that was desired by the authorities in Düsseldorf, the Government, and even the very high and supreme camarilla. The hostility to Lassalle "does not even stop short of the throne".

This is what has happened:

"The indictment board drops the case against Cantador and sets him free, whereas Lassalle and Weyers remain in prison and have to come before the Assizes."

Yet the charge against Cantador was exactly the same as against Lassalle, except for a single speech which Lassalle made in Neuss.[292]

And it is precisely this speech in Neuss that is seized on and for which Lassalle is committed to the Assizes.

Let us briefly recall the whole course of events.

At a time when at any day an open struggle could break out between the now defunct National Assembly and the Crown, Düsseldorf was, as is well known, one of the greatest centres of agitation of all the towns in the Rhine Province. The civic militia here was completely on the side of the National Assembly and, moreover, was led by a democrat. It was ready to turn passive resistance into active resistance as soon as Berlin gave the signal for it. Arms and munitions were available. Lassalle and Cantador stood at the head of the whole movement. They not merely called on the citizens to arm themselves against the Manteuffel Government, they actually provided them with arms. *Here, in Düsseldorf*, was the centre of their activity. *It was here, therefore*, if any crime had actually been committed, that *this crime must have taken place.* But where is it supposed to have taken place? Not in Düsseldorf, but—in Neuss!!

Lassalle was at a meeting in Neuss and called for armed reinforcements to be sent to Düsseldorf. This call did not even have any result, because matters never reached the point of fighting. And yet Lassalle's crime is supposed to consist in this!

Consequently, Lassalle has not been committed for trial at the Assizes on account of his main activity, on account of the *actual* arming, or the *actual* uprising, that was on the point of breaking out in Düsseldorf. There was no "crime" in that. Even the indictment board, decrepit though it is, had to admit that. The alleged crime consisted in a quite *fortuitous, incidental* action which was *totally dependent* on the main action in Düsseldorf and *absolutely meaningless* apart from it;—it consisted not in the *organisation* of armed force against the government authorities in Düsseldorf, but in a call to the inhabitants of Neuss to support that organisation!

*But, of course, Cantador was not in Neuss* when Lassalle made this terrible speech; Cantador did not *call on* the inhabitants of Neuss for armed resistance, Cantador merely—*organised* the inhabitants of Düsseldorf for armed resistance and called on the Düsseldorf *civic militia, which is itself part of the Government's armed force,* to resist the Government. That is the difference, and that is why Cantador was set free, and Lassalle kept in prison up to the present session of the Assizes.

But that is not all. Lassalle also directly appealed to the farmer Stangier for armed reinforcements to be sent to Düsseldorf. This letter is in the dossiers and is cited word for word in the indictment (see *Neue Rheinische Zeitung* No. 277, second edition). Did the indictment regard *this letter* as a reason for committing Lassalle to the Assizes? By no means. Even the Court, which had put forward *nine* counts against Lassalle, eight of which were dropped by the indictment board, never thought of including this letter among them. But this letter contains *exactly the same* alleged "crime" as that committed by Lassalle in Neuss.

Rarely has anything more inconsistent, more contradictory and more incomprehensible been fabricated than this decision of the indictment board to send the case for trial.

But what is certainly commendable is the following: even according to the decision of the Cologne indictment board, in all the agitation that was carried out in Düsseldorf last November, in the direct call for resistance to the Government, in the arming, in the procurement of ammunition, in the direct and open opposition of the civic militia to the Government, in the oath sworn by the civic militia that they would fight, arms in hand, against the Government and in support of the National Assembly—*in all this there was no crime.* The Cologne indictment board has said so.

And it is true that on this point it agrees with the Cologne Court, and indeed with the Cologne Public Prosecutor's office. During the investigation of the case against the Rhenish District Committee, they both calmly ignored the call to arm against the "enemy", took no notice of the criminal case involved, and confined themselves merely to the fact of a call to revolt punishable by a police court, and it came before the Assizes only because it was issued through the press.

Lassalle was dealt with much more cunningly. First of all criminal proceedings were instituted, and the police court kept in reserve. For in case he were to be acquitted in connection with the speech made in Neuss, he was committed for trial to the police court on account of his call for resistance to officials (revolt) supposed to be contained in two Düsseldorf speeches.

We need merely to recall here the course of the trial of the Rhenish District Committee. The case is completely analagous. At that trial it was argued that the matter under consideration was either a *crime* (the same as that of which Lassalle is accused) or nothing at all, and that it was not possible to call for armed resistance to the Government without at the same time calling for resistance to all the individual officials who constitute the Government. The jury's verdict was an acquittal.

Lassalle will be in the same position when, after his indubitable acquittal by the jury, he comes before the police court. But meanwhile they have a pretext to apply for the prolongation of the arrest, and in addition it is easier to manipulate the police court than the jurymen!

Tomorrow we shall deal with the indictment itself, and from it, too, prove the absurdity of this whole trial.

Written by Engels on May 1, 1849

First published in the *Neue Rheinische Zeitung* No. 287, May 2, 1849

Printed according to the newspaper

Published in English for the first time

# A PRUSSIAN KICK FOR THE FRANKFURT ASSEMBLY

*Cologne*, May 1. Another new item in the history of the Prussian counter-revolution. The King gives the Frankfurt Assembly a determined kick and contemptuously casts in its face the proffered gold-tinsel crown of an imaginary empire.[293]

If at the right time the Frankfurt Assembly had acted with energy, it could now order *the arrest* of this Hohenzollern, who is filled with insolence, and commit him to the Assize Court for "insult to the National Assembly" (Law of September 1848, published also in Prussia[294]). As yet there exists no "imperial" law that declares the individual sovereigns exempt also from responsibility in regard to the "empire"; and the imperial irresponsibility has been rejected by the Hohenzollern.

The new Prussian "imperial" Note of April 28 softens the "imperial" kick by a few kind observations about the so-called German imperial Constitution. This innocent botchwork is depicted in the Note as a supreme example of all that is bad and as an extreme product of revolution and secret republicanism "exceeding all bounds".

St. Paul's Church as a robbers' cave of carbonari![295] Welcker and Gagern as secret republicans, "Möros with a dagger under his cloak"[a]! Bassermann, the man who sees spectres, himself turned into one of the "Bassermannic characters"[296]! That, of course, is flattering for the worthy Frankfurt deputies after all the scorn with which they have been treated by the people, after all the curses

---

[a] Schiller, "Die Bürgschaft".— *Ed.*

heaped on them by the defeated barricade fighters of Frankfurt and Vienna, and there are people of all shades of opinion, right down to Herr Vogt, who are capable of really believing such nonsense.

The Prussian Note is the last threat to the Frankfurt Assembly even before it is actually dispersed. Once more the stubborn Hohenzollern proffers his hand for a "reconciliation". And, in point of fact, after the Assembly has gone *so far* it could truly make one little step further and become *completely* a tool of Prussia.

Meanwhile, however, a section of the people, and especially the peasantry and the lower middle class of the small south German states, cling to the Assembly and to the so-called imperial Constitution. The army is favourably disposed towards the imperial Constitution. The people regard every step, however small, towards the unification of Germany as a step towards abolition of the petty sovereigns and liberation from the oppressive burden of taxation. The hatred of Prussia, too, plays a part here. The Swabians even made a revolution in support of the so-called imperial Constitution[297]; it was, of course, a storm in a teacup, but all the same it was something.

Hence, if the worthy Frankfurt deputies possessed the slightest degree of courage, it would not be possible to disperse the Frankfurt Assembly without the use of force. They now have a last opportunity of atoning at least for a small part of the grievous sins they have committed. If simultaneously with the victories of the Hungarians, the break-up of Austria, and the fury of the people in Prussia at the Hohenzollern-Radowitz-Manteuffel betrayals, Frankfurt and South Germany were to rise up openly in defence of the imperial Constitution, they could form a temporary centre for a new revolutionary uprising based on Hungary.

But then the worthy deputies would not have to shrink from *proclaiming civil war* either and, in the extreme case, if it comes to making a decision, they would have *to prefer a united and indivisible German republic to a restoration of the German Federal Diet.*[298]

But anyone who supposes the Frankfurters capable of *that* is greatly mistaken. These gentlemen will make a little noise, offer a little resistance, enough to satisfy at least to some extent the requirements of decency, and then they will agree to everything that the stubborn Hohenzollern dictates to them. Here and there, perhaps, the people will erect barricades and—will be betrayed as on September 18.[299]

That would be the end of the famous imperial bombastic dramatical performance, if it depended on the *Frankfurt gentlemen.*

But perhaps the Hungarian hussars, the Polish Uhlans, and the Viennese proletarians will have a word to say, and then matters can nevertheless take a different turn.

Written by Engels on May 1, 1849

First published in the *Neue Rheinische Zeitung* No. 287, May 2, 1849

Printed according to the newspaper

Published in English for the first time

# [THE DISSOLUTION]

*Cologne*, May 1. Deputies who arrived here yesterday from Berlin report that *the Chambers have been dissolved in Dresden* as well.[300]

Hanover, Berlin, Dresden—in Munich there has so far only been an adjournment—do you, honest German citizen, now realise what tune is to be played?

Last year, when the Frankfurt Assembly was convened, Prussia ordered all the small states to *convene* their Chambers. Now, exactly one year later, Prussia orders them to *dissolve* all the Chambers. Then it was Camphausen, now it is Manteuffel. On each occasion there was the same aim, the same intention. Despite all the phrases, Camphausen and Manteuffel go arm in arm.

And there are still people in Germany who defend the sovereigns!

Written by Engels on May 1, 1849

First published in the *Neue Rheinische Zeitung* No. 287, May 2, 1849

Printed according to the newspaper

Published in English for the first time

# [FROM THE THEATRE OF WAR]

*Cologne*, evening of May 1. Reports just received from Berlin and Vienna confirm the continued withdrawal of the imperial troops. In Pressburg, where on the 27th nothing was known about attacks by the Hungarians, there are continuous commotion, confusion and retreat.

An encounter took place near Komorn. A force consisting of two divisions of imperial troops under Schlick drove the Hungarians from the Sandberg near Acs and this is now presented as a victory. But, on looking at the map and discovering that Acs is situated on the *right* bank of the Danube, *a mile*[a] *from Komorn*, the fact emerges that, even according to this official account, **the Hungarians have crossed the Danube near Komorn and are in command of the road from Gran to Pressburg.** And Schlick still talks about the royal imperial troops surrounding (!) Komorn!!

Welden's headquarters, transferred from Pest to Kapolna, from Kapolna to Raab, is now moving even further back, to **Oedenburg**, hard by the Styrian border and to the south of Vienna.

Jellachich has actually received orders to cut his way through to Croatia and to drum up as many men to escort him as possible.

North of the Danube, Wohlgemuth has temporarily disappeared from the scene. He was driven off Schütt (the big island in the Danube); and the Csikos (mounted *Landsturm*) patrolled with impunity from Komorn to Szerdahely, halfway to Pressburg. Wohlgemuth must have withdrawn towards Pressburg and the March.

---

[a] See footnote on p. 20.— *Ed.*

From Pressburg and Vienna swarms of black-and-yellow [a] supporters are already in flight, some up the Danube, some to Prague.

It is reported that intervention by the Russians is imminent. One paper even maintains they have taken up positions near Lundenburg, on the border between Austria, Moravia and Hungary, but this is obviously a complete fabrication. It is expected that, as in Transylvania, they will be used as reserve and garrison troops in the towns, thus leaving all the Austrian troops free to concentrate on the Hungarians. *It is said that 15,000 Russians are to come to Vienna as a garrison.*

A *Prussian staff officer* has also arrived in Olmütz "for the purpose of reaching an understanding with the Austrian Government". When "My glorious army" [301] marches in, the Bohemians will soon discover the meaning of this "understanding"!

Tomorrow evening we shall probably have news of further decisive Magyar successes.

Written by Engels on May 1, 1849

First published in the special supplement to the *Neue Rheinische Zeitung* No. 287, May 2, 1849

Printed according to the newspaper

Published in English for the first time

---

[a] The Austrian imperial colours.— *Ed.*

# LASSALLE

*Cologne,* May 2. Yesterday we promised to return to the indictment against Lassalle.[a]

Lassalle is charged with a "crime under Articles 87 and 102 of the Criminal Code".[b]

Article 87 is directed against an "attempt or a plot the aim of which is to incite (*exciter*) the citizens or inhabitants to take up arms against the imperial power".

Article 102 imposes the punishments (mainly the death penalty) laid down in the preceding Articles of the section (which includes Article 87) on all those who by speeches in public places or at public meetings, or by the display of posters, incite (*excitent*) the citizens to commit these crimes. Only in the event of the incitement being unsuccessful is the penalty mitigated to exile.

Of what is Lassalle being accused?

Since under a single charge he is alleged to have sinned against Article 87 and *simultaneously* against Article 102, he can only be accused:

of having called for the commission of crimes listed in Article 87 in the manner of Article 102, i.e.

of having incited the citizens to prepare an attempt or a plot the aim of which is an incitement to take up arms against the royal power, i.e.

of having *incited* the citizens to *incitement* to take up arms!

---

[a] See this volume, p. 376.— *Ed.*

[b] i.e. Napoleon's *Code pénal* which was in force in the Rhine Province of Prussia.— *Ed.*

To the ordinary human mind, that is fairly obvious nonsense. But that is how the Public Prosecutor's office and the indictment board wanted it!

The point is that Article 102, which makes incitement to commit the crimes envisaged in Articles 86-101 equivalent to the commission of the crime itself, is, if the incitement is successful, quite properly applicable to all of these Articles. It applies even to the remaining items of this same Article 87. For all these Articles are directed against *definite actions*, to the commission of which instigation *is possible*. Article 87, for example, which is directed against commission of an attempt or a plot, speaks also about an attempt or plot against the life and person of the Emperor, and about an attempt or plot aimed at altering or destroying the form of government or the order of succession to the throne. All these are things to which one can "incite" people. Incitement to regicide, or to a revolution, is a possible fact; incitement to a plot the aim of which is regicide or a revolution can also occur. But "*incitement* to prepare an attempt or plot for the purpose of *inciting* people to take up arms against the royal power", in short, *incitement to incitement*, is a crime as impossible and as absurd as "an *attempt* at a remote *attempt* at high treason", which in the good old times of Prussian Law [302] cost many an unfortunate member of a students' association ten years imprisonment in a fortress, or as the notorious *suspect de suspicion d'incivisme* (suspected of suspicion of lack of civic sense), which people wearing legitimist spectacles claim to have found in the prison lists of the time of the Terror in 1793.

Alternatively, if the "incitement to incitement to take up arms" is really a crime that is logically and juridically possible, then for Lassalle to come simultaneously under the passage in question of Article 87 and under Article 102, he should have been indicted not for the speech in Neuss, but for the address to the National Assembly, which states: "We beseech the National Assembly: Issue a call to arms!" [303]

Here is the "incitement to incitement to take up arms". But it has not even occurred to this *ne plus ultra* of an indictment to see a crime in these words.

How did it happen that, out of the long series of Articles in the section in question, the Public Prosecutor's office selected and combined with Article 102 precisely the passage to which Article 102 *does not apply at all?*

Quite simply. The crime envisaged by Article 87 involves the *death penalty. But in the whole of the Rhine Province no jury could be found* that would assist in condemning Lassalle to death. The prosecution therefore preferred to include Article 102 as well, which prescribes mitigation of the punishment to *exile* in cases where the incitement to "crime" is unsuccessful. It was thought that a jury prepared to do this could be found.

Hence, in order to get rid of Lassalle, the prosecution invented an *impossible crime* and combined two passages of the law which in combination are *sheer nonsense.*

Therefore, either Lassalle is *guilty* of having violated Article 87, and then one should have the courage to condemn him *to death* outright, or he is not guilty of having violated Article 87, and then he has not violated Article 102 either, and must certainly be *acquitted.* But to violate Article 87 in the passage quoted *and* Article 102 at the same time is an impossibility.

Note the craftiness of the prosecution. The charge against Lassalle really comes under Article 87 (death penalty). But they do not dare to bring that charge against him; so he is charged under Article 87 in combination with Article 102 (*exile*). And if that does not succeed, if the jury acquits him, he will be brought before the police court and charged under Articles 209 and 217 (*six days' to one year's imprisonment*). And all this for one and the same fact, for his activity as an agitator during the movement to refuse payment of taxes!

Let us now look at the actual *corpus delicti*—the speech in Neuss on November 21.

Lassalle is charged with having directly incited the people to take up arms against the royal power.

According to the statements of the three witnesses referred to in the indictment, Lassalle did directly incite the inhabitants of Neuss *to arm* themselves, to procure ammunition, to safeguard by force of arms the liberties they had won, to support the National Assembly by effective action etc. However *incitement to take up arms in general* is by no means an offence, and still less a crime, most certainly not since the revolution and the law of April 6, 1848[304] which guarantees to every Prussian the right to bear arms. According to the *Code pénal,* incitement to take up arms is punishable only if the arming is directed against individual officials (revolt) or against the royal power, or against another section of the citizens (riot). The present case relates especially to incitement, and indeed to *direct* incitement to take up arms against the royal power.

In all three statements of the witnesses, however, there is *not a single word* about taking up arms against the royal power, they mention only taking up arms *to protect the National Assembly.* But the National Assembly was a legally constituted, legally existing body, an essential part of the legislative authority, and here indeed an essential part even of the *constituent* authority. Just as the constituent authority stands high above the executive authority, so the National Assembly stood above the "royal Government". To call for the universal arming of the people for the protection of this body, which alongside the King is the supreme legislative authority in the country, is regarded by our Public Prosecutors as a serious crime!

The only passage in which the sensitive nose of a Public Prosecutor could discover a remote reference to the "royal Government" was that concerning the gun-batteries in Neuss. But did Lassalle incite the people of Neuss to arm themselves in order to seize the batteries on the left bank of the Rhine, and in particular did he do so "directly", as is asserted in the résumé of the indictment and as is required for a conviction?

On the contrary! Neither "directly" nor indirectly did he incite them to do so. He merely said that the people of Düsseldorf were *expecting* that the people of Neuss would seize these batteries. And this mere expression of an "expectation" is, in the opinion of the worthy Public Prosecutors, an *excitation directe*, a *direct incitement* to take up arms against the royal power!

Thus, in the quite *real* arming of *Düsseldorf*, openly organised for the protection of the National Assembly and clearly directed against none other than the Prussian troops, i.e. against the royal Government (*le gouvernement de l'empereur*), there is no crime at all, there is merely the offence of resistance to individual officials; but in that mere statement, in those few words, there is a serious crime!

For what Lassalle *did*, they do not dare to accuse him; but what he *said* is supposed to be a serious crime. And what did he say? That it was expected that the people of Neuss would seize the batteries. And who did he say was expecting it? Was it perhaps Lassalle himself? On the contrary, it was the people of Düsseldorf!

Lassalle said that third persons expect you to do such and such, and according to the logic of the public prosecution that is a "direct appeal" to you actually to do what is expected.

In Berlin, the Ministers have now dissolved the Chamber and are preparing for further dictatorial measures. Let us suppose that today universal suffrage were to be arbitrarily abolished, the right of association suppressed, freedom of the press destroyed. If we say: We expect that the people will reply to this disgraceful perfidy by erecting barricades—then, according to the Public Prosecutors, we have "directly incited" the citizens of Berlin to arm themselves against the royal power. And if things turn out as the Public Prosecutors desire, we would be sentenced either to death or exile, depending on the circumstances!

The secret of the whole court action against Lassalle consists in its being an arbitrary trial of a troublesome agitator. In a concealed form it is a trial on a charge of "stirring up discontent"[305] such as prior to the March days we, too, had the pleasure of enjoying here on the Rhine. In the same way, the trial instituted against Weyers is in a concealed form a trial on a charge of lèse-majesté. Weyers said: "death to the King" and "the King ought not to be allowed to have the crown a quarter of an hour longer". And these few words, quite innocent from the point of view of the Code pénal, are similarly alleged to contain a "direct·incitement to take up arms"!

And even if Lassalle had actually called for arming against the royal power, what would this mean? Let us adopt the constitutional standpoint and speak in accordance with constitutional ideas. At that time, in November, was it not the duty of every citizen not only to "call for arming", but to take up arms himself in defence of the constitutional representatives of the people against a perfidious "royal Government" which, with the aid of soldiers, drove the Assembly of people's representatives from one building to another, dispersed their sittings, allowed soldiers to use their official documents as spills and for lighting stoves, and finally sent the representatives packing? According to the decisions of the United Diet, and according to Herr Camphausen's famous "legal basis", not to mention the achievements of March 19,[a] was not the Assembly an "entity on a footing of equality" with the Crown? And should one not be allowed to defend such an Assembly against encroachments by the so-called "royal Government"?

Moreover, we have seen that it has become second nature for the "royal Government" to bestow kicks on the people's representatives. Hardly two months after the convocation of the imposed Chambers this same "royal Government" disperses them at the first objectionable decision—disperses the very Chambers which were supposed to revise the Constitution! The Chambers have now recognised the validity of the imposed Constitution, and now we know still less whether we have a Constitution or not. Who knows what will be imposed on us tomorrow?

And the people who foresaw all that and acted accordingly, who strove energetically to oppose these violent activities of an arrogant camarilla, and who, according to the views of all constitutional

---

[a] i.e. achievements of the March revolution of 1848 in Prussia.— Ed.

*countries* and especially *England,* kept *completely to a legal basis,* these people are arrested on orders from Manteuffel, Simons and Co., held for six months in prison and are finally brought before the Assize Court charged with *incitement to riot!*

Written by Engels on May 2, 1849

First published in the *Neue Rheinische Zeitung* No. 288, May 3, 1849

Printed according to the newspaper

Published in English for the first time

# PROHIBITION OF THE MEETING
# OF THE RHENISH MUNICIPAL COUNCILS

*Cologne,* May 2. It is with especial satisfaction that we inform our readers that the meeting of the representatives of municipal councils of the Rhine Province convened by the praiseworthy Cologne municipal council has been **prohibited** by a simple government order.[306] The "good citizens", who felt so "comfortable" when meetings of democrats were prohibited in September,[307] can now offer thanks to their lords and masters. In September 1848 the democrats' right of assembly was destroyed at least by the respectable violence of the state of siege; the Cologne municipal council's right of assembly, on the other hand, has met its end *by a kick* at a time when the legal basis is in finest flower.

Written by Engels on May 2, 1849

First published in the *Neue Rheinische Zeitung* No. 288, May 3, 1849

Printed according to the newspaper

Published in English for the first time

# [FROM THE THEATRE OF WAR]

*Cologne*, evening of May 2. The Hungarians are taking advantage of the Austrians' hasty retreat and confusion to make a rapid advance on Vienna, on the one hand, and, on the other, to occupy the whole of Upper Hungary up to the Jablunka Pass and the Moravian border. The *Slovakian mountain towns* are in their hands, and from there they have advanced to the Jablunka Pass. The Pass itself seems to have been taken by them already, for the thunder of artillery has been heard in Neutitschein (near Teschen), indicating that fighting has already occurred on *this side* of the Carpathians.

As a result of this swift operation Slovakia has been entirely cleared of imperial troops, the Hungarians thereby gaining an area of 300-350 square miles, with more than 2 million inhabitants providing a source of fresh recruits. The Slovaks, who were formerly in part indifferent, in part even anti-Magyar, are now definitely on the side of the Magyars, since the latter have abolished the feudal burdens of the Slovak peasants and made a number of concessions with regard to language and nationality.

It is expected that the Magyars will cross the Little Carpathians (border range between Moravia and Hungary) and direct the spearhead of their attack against *Olmütz.* By dispatching a corps over the Jablunka they could also destroy the railway line to Vienna, thus considerably delaying the Russians' march on that city. Almost all regular troops have been withdrawn from the whole of Moravia; the national guard has replaced them everywhere.

On the other flank, the Magyars are advancing directly on Vienna and have, according to our Breslau correspondent, already **occupied Raab**. The Austrian headquarters has been transferred to *Oedenburg,* and the commissariat from Pressburg to *Hainburg* (6 miles from

Vienna). Here the Austrians are expected to make another stand. Indeed, this position, between the Danube and Neusiedler Lake and behind the Leitha, is the only possible one remaining before Vienna.

The line along which the Austrians are attempting to rally their forces for a fresh battle is as follows: the right wing is concentrated around Oedenburg, from the southern tip of Neusiedler Lake nearly up to Güns and the Styrian mountains which it touches on the right; the centre stretches from the northern tip of Neusiedler Lake up to the Danube near Hainburg, blocking the road to Vienna; the left wing, Wohlgemuth's corps, on the other side of the Danube near Pressburg, is in a position it cannot possibly hold and from which it will certainly have to withdraw across the River March. As a result the war will be carried into the territory of Austria itself, and Kossuth will continue to wage it there as well. **Kossuth has declared his intention of forestalling the Russians and being in Vienna on May 10.** And Kossuth has shown that he knows how to keep his word. He wanted to be in Pest on April 24 and he entered it on that very day.

There is complete obscurity about what has happened to Jellachich. Some sources state that he is already near Mohacs, not far from the Slavonian border (an impossibility since the distance from Pest to Mohacs is much too great). According to other rumours, from black-and-yellow[a] sources, he has again taken up his position on the Rakos plain[308] near Pest. The latter is, of course, even less true than the former.

From the south no direct confirmation has as yet been received of the capture of Semlin by the Magyars. The rest of the news from this area is contradictory; so is that about the arrival of the Russians. All that is certain is that the Russian troops encamped on the Cracow border have been concentrated and are on the point of marching into Austria.

Written by Engels on May 2, 1849

First published in the special supplement to the *Neue Rheinische Zeitung* No. 288, March 3, 1849

Printed according to the newspaper

Published in English for the first time

---

[a] The Austrian imperial colours.— *Ed.*

# THE CONGRESS OF RHENISH TOWNS

*Cologne*, May 3. The congress of Rhenish municipal councils will take place after all, although in a less official form, and not until next *Tuesday*.[309]

It goes without saying that we are expecting *nothing at all* from this assembly composed of bourgeois elected on the basis of three classes according to the property qualification with the mass of the people debarred from voting. A deputation is to be sent to Berlin, which *will not even be allowed into the presence* of Herr von Hohenzollern.

But it may be that the congress will not take place at all. On Sunday various party congresses will be held here in Cologne.[310] The Government is trying *at all costs* to provoke a conflict between the people and the army, in order to be able to muzzle us Rhinelanders, just as the Berliners have been muzzled.

It depends on the *workers of Cologne* whether this subtle Prussian plan will be frustrated. By their calm behaviour, by unshakeable equanimity in the face of the provocations of the soldiers, the Cologne workers can deprive the Government of any excuse for acts of violence.

Decisive events are at hand. Vienna, Bohemia, South Germany, Berlin, are in a ferment and await the right moment. Cologne can play its part, it can play a very powerful part, but it cannot *begin* any decisive action.

Let the workers of Cologne bear in mind, especially next Sunday, that all the provocations of the Government aim only at causing an outburst of *such* a kind as will occur *at a moment unfavourable for us but favourable for the Government.*

Only by great events can revolutions be carried through but if one accepts the challenges of the Government, the most that can result is a revolt.

*Workers of Cologne, remember the 25th of September!*[311]

Written by Engels on May 3, 1849

First published in the *Neue Rheinische Zeitung* No. 289, May 4, 1849

Printed according to the newspaper

Published in English for the first time

# [THE THIRD PARTY IN THE ALLIANCE]

*Cologne*, May 3. We have pointed out a hundred times that in the coalition of Russia and Austria Herr von Hohenzollern and his Ministry are the "third party in the alliance".[a] A hundred times the honest German citizen has indignantly rejected such an assertion.

Very well then: it is now firmly established that one of the secret reasons for the dissolution of the Chambers was that, by a secret agreement with the Olmütz *knyaz*[b] and the orthodox supreme Tsar in St. Petersburg,[c] the Russians' subordinate *knyaz*[d] in Sans-Souci[312] **has pledged his word to put 40,000 Prussians into Bohemia** to keep the people there in subjection and as reserves against the Hungarians. This was spoken of openly even in the St. Paul's Church.[e] It was impossible to persuade even the deputies of the Centre and part of those of the Right in Berlin to keep silent about it. They were therefore dispersed.

But that is not all: the Berlin *National-Zeitung* reported from Berlin on May 1:

We have just learned from a very reliable source: **"Yesterday morning the Management Board of the Upper Silesian Railway received a telegram from the Minister of the Interior that 30,000 Russian soldiers would be transferred from Cracow by means of the Upper Silesian Railway (consequently, from Cracow via Mislowitz, Kosel, Ratibor, Oderberg) to Austria.** The Board of the Upper Silesian

---

[a] Schiller, "Die Bürgschaft".— *Ed.*

[b] Francis Joseph I.—The Russian word "knyaz" means "Prince".— *Ed.*

[c] Nicholas I.— *Ed.*

[d] Frederick William IV.— *Ed.*

[e] The German National Assembly met in the St. Paul's Church at Frankfurt.— *Ed.*

Railway is informed **that the royal Prussian Government has no objection to this** and it trusts that the Railway Board will not hinder this transport in any way."

The telegram was signed: **von Manteuffel.**[a]

That then is what we have come to: The Government of the imperial Russian subordinate *knyaz* in Potsdam not only issues *warrants for the arrest* of Kossuth, Bem and Görgey,[b] it even allows 30,000 Russian police agents to be sent by rail *through Prussian territory* to Hungary—and what is more, it sends 40,000 Prussian soldiers to Bohemia in order to hold down a people which has been contemptuously trampled under foot and which is thirsting for revenge!

Hear that, Rhinelanders! It is for this, therefore, that we are being subjected to the *Russo-Prussian rule of violence,* so that our sons and brothers, Rhinelanders like ourselves, shall be sent to Bohemia and perhaps to Hungary, in order that **in the service of the Russian Tsar** they will help to suppress the last people that is defending the revolution of 1848 arms in hand!

It is for this we were betrayed to Prussia in 1815, so that the disgrace would fall on us, too, for having allowed the Russians, with bands playing and banners flying, to be marched against the Magyar revolutionary army through *our* territory, through a country joined *with us* into a single state.

It was only by *force* that we became Prussian *subjects* and have remained Prussian *subjects. We were never Prussians.* But now, when we are being led against Hungary, when Russian robber bands are setting foot on Prussian territory, now we feel that we are Prussians, indeed **we feel what a disgrace it is to bear the name of Prussian!**

Written by Engels on May 3, 1849

First published in the supplement to the *Neue Rheinische Zeitung* No. 289, May 4, 1849

Printed according to the newspaper

Published in English for the first time

---

[a] *National-Zeitung* No. 116 (supplement), May 2, 1849.— *Ed.*

[b] See present edition, Vol. 8, pp. 269-70 and this volume, pp. 257-58.— *Ed.*

# [FROM THE THEATRE OF WAR]

*Cologne,* evening of May 3. As the flight of the imperial troops from Hungary becomes ever wilder, and the pursuit by the Magyars more inexorable, so much the more confused and contradictory become the reports on events in the theatre of war. They agree only in one respect: that the imperial troops are daily suffering fresh defeats.

The following facts, however, emerge as pretty well certain:

*Firstly:* The battle at *Acs,* which the imperial forces depicted as a victory, was a *defeat.* This follows from the fact that Schlick, who claims to have won a victory here, immediately afterwards retreated to Raab. The *Lithographierte Correspondenz,* too, states that the outcome of the encounter at Acs proved to be disadvantageous for the imperial troops, and that the Zanini regiment, apart from a few officers, went over to the Hungarians.

*Secondly:* On April 28, in the region of Hungarian Altenburg (halfway between Raab and Pressburg), *the Austrians were defeated again.* Various reports concur in stating this. Many wounded were brought across the Leitha and the whole surrounding area is crowded with them. On the 29th and 30th, some 2,000 are said to have been brought to Vienna itself. Some say that Welden's headquarters is in Pressburg, others that it is in Bruck on the Leitha (on Austrian soil). At Raab, too, where Schlick is supposed to have been on the 27th, the pursuing Hungarians are said to have engaged him in a murderous battle.

From this news it would appear that the bulk of the Austrian army has already been driven out of Hungary. And it is beyond doubt that it is for the most part already on Austrian soil, and in Hungary it merely occupies Pressburg and Oedenburg. In addition, what we predicted is now confirmed, namely that the Hungarians have crossed the Danube at Komorn and are advancing on both sides of this river in a concentric movement against Vienna. The clearance of Slovakia by the Hungarians is now confirmed by the *Wiener Zeitung* as well.

*Thirdly*: It is practically certain that Jellachich, too, has been *completely defeated*. He himself, as the *Wiener Zeitung* reports, has already arrived in Esseg, which means that, since he only left Pest on the 23rd or 24th, and was already in Esseg on the 26th, he has made a much quicker journey than his corps. It is said that this corps has been *completely destroyed* and that the greater part of the survivors have gone over to the Magyars. According to one report, the battle took place at Kis-Bér, but this is impossible since this place, situated a few miles south of Komorn, is quite outside Jellachich's route. Apart from that this report contains also various other impossibilities. The news of Jellachich's defeat, however, appears in all newspapers and correspondents' reports.

***A manifesto issued by Kossuth proclaims the independence of Hungary and its neighbouring territories from Austria and declares the separation of these territories from the Habsburg-Lorraine dynasty because the latter unleashed such a calamitous war against Hungary.***[313]

From the *south*, no news has come of further advances of the Magyars. Perczel is said to have moved with his main army towards Pest. Rukavina has asked for help from the Serbs in order to fortify Temesvar, but the Serbs have refused it. On the contrary, they are demanding the immediate convocation of the Serbian National Assembly for election of the voivode and constitutional establishment of the Voivodina.

The Hungarians are said to have obtained 80,000 rifles from England via Turkey. The Grosswardein factory supplies them with 300 daily.

Meanwhile, in Vienna joy and excitement prevail among the people, and consternation in the Government. On April 30, *indescribable despondency* was evident on the *Stock Exchange*. Petty traders came from the suburbs and gave accounts of *mounting unrest*. In the afternoon, well-known barricade personalities were noticed in the streets.

The Government is in the throes of complete break-up. Not only has Stadion resigned, but it is already the turn of *Schwarzenberg*, who is to be replaced by Colloredo-Waldsee.

The Russians are coming. The Russian General von Berg has already travelled via Cracow to Vienna. 12,000-15,000 Russians of all branches of the service,including four squadrons of cavalry and two artillery batteries, were *expected in Cracow* on May 1 and 2. It is said that the orthodox Tsar[a] *himself will come to the neighbourhood* to supervise the operations.

*The Russians have already marched into the Bukovina,* according to a note from Czernowitz of April 28.

(The Viennese and Prague newspapers have not reached us this evening.)

Written by Engels on May 3, 1849

First published in the supplement to the *Neue Rheinische Zeitung* No. 289, May 4, 1849

Printed according to the newspaper

Published in English for the first time

---

[a] Nicholas I.— *Ed.*

# [NEWS FROM SOUTHERN GERMANY]

*Cologne,* May 3. We have today received several letters from various parts of Southern Germany; they are all unanimous in conveying the heartening news that everywhere the people are impatiently awaiting the moment when they can at last confront the barefaced counter-revolution of the rulers "by the grace of God" and their worthy accomplices with a genuine revolution—not like that of March—and avenge the acts of violence and infamy that, day after day, for so long have been perpetrated against the people's rights. Everywhere the people are organising themselves into companies, electing leaders, providing themselves with arms and ammunition etc. It is particularly encouraging, however, to learn that the spirit prevailing amongst the majority of the military there precludes the possibility of once again setting the soldiers like murderous dogs and wild beasts upon their brothers and making them run amuck against their own flesh and blood.

The justified anger of the people has reached a level that makes an imminent outbreak appear inevitable. It is to be hoped that this time the storm will rage so mightily through all Germany that at last the whole pack of divinely appointed martial-law addicts, robber knights and traitors to the people will be uprooted utterly and finally from German soil.

Written by Engels on May 3, 1849

First published in the supplement to the *Neue Rheinische Zeitung* No. 289, May 4, 1849

Printed according to the newspaper

Published in English for the first time

# NEWS FROM HUNGARY

*Cologne*, May 4. We have received the following reports from Vienna dated May 1:

In the concluding days of last month, and especially yesterday, April 30, an unusual amount of activity could be observed in the streets of the capital. There was general excitement as the news spread about the withdrawals of troops from the Hungarian border. Evidence of the heavy losses and defeats sustained by the Austrian side is provided by the continuous transports of maimed and wounded, who for the past two days have been coming, brought in hundreds of carts, to the military hospitals in Vienna. The latter are already so full that all the corridors and the spaces between the beds are being used to accommodate patients. The men brought back under these conditions are in a wretched state, which cannot but remind one of Napoleon's retreat from Russia—pale, emaciated, tattered apparitions, their wounds are covered with makeshift bandages of rags, they lie on the bare planks of the carts. One cannot look upon this picture of suffering without shedding tears of pity. The majority of the wounded received incurable fatal injuries—many losing their noses and chins—in the course of the Hungarian cavalry attacks. In short, it is impossible to describe how badly these poor devils have been mauled. In addition, ten carts laden with caps of all branches of the service, together with cavalry harness, arrived here yesterday, followed by about 500 unmounted horses which had lost their riders in the battle.

Altogether, things look very bad for the Austrian cause in Hungary; a week ago the royal imperial troops were still in Pest, and now their headquarters has been in Oedenburg for several days already; the Austrian army is no longer withdrawing but is in full flight; the Oedenburg supply column has just arrived with soldiers of all branches of the service and military baggage. I met a sergeant-major I know who belongs to an Upper-Austrian regiment formerly stationed in Vienna. According to his account there can be no doubt about the Hungarians' victory, since the latter are taking advantage of the Austrian troops' utter confusion, allowing them no time to rally, but continually attacking with fresh energy and forcing them to fall back. The Hungarian army is far superior to them and is fanatically devoted to its cause, whereas the Austrians, as a result of fatiguing and pointless marches, discouraging losses and setbacks, and as a result of bad leadership having been left in the lurch at decisive moments by their officers, are naturally not defending the cause of the dynasty with the necessary determination. The ignorance displayed by the royal imperial generals and officers, on whose training during the pre-March period such a vast amount was spent, is said to be unparalleled; they lead the troops straight to the slaughter-house. Inquiries are already being held on five generals. The *Hrabowski Regiment* (Upper Austrians), which only recently returned from Italy, *has changed sides almost to a man*, and so has the Lower-Austrian *Hess Regiment*; in general it is considered that the *German troops are not such reliable tools for the designs of the dynasty as the Slav troops are.* Altogether *five regiments* have changed sides, apart from the countless number of Croats. *A quite unprecedented and incredible demoralisation has set in in the army.* The war in Hungary is being carried on under the command of the Polish General Dembiński. The Polish contingent consists of ten legions, with a total strength of 36,000 men and about 25 generals; they are said to perform unparalleled feats and the royal imperial troops fear them most of all.

On Sunday, April 29, there was a big battle near Wieselburg, with the Austrian losses amounting to 6,000 dead and wounded — so that there are grounds for believing that a sensational defeat has been suffered, and that this accounts for the transports of the wounded.

The army corps commanded by the Ban[a] is thought to have been completely routed.

The Hungarian insurgents have advanced with a force numbering 15,000 men and 30 pieces of ordnance north-westward into the Turocz comitat and at present hold the county town, St. Martin, as well as Mossocz. It is said they intend to cross the Waag, to occupy the Kisuca valley and block the roads from Silesia and Galicia.

In St. Martin, from which town the Slovakian *Landsturm* received many volunteers, there is said to be great fear that vengeance will be meted out by the insurgents. Slovakia, too, seems to be falling very much under Magyar influence.

In Pressburg on the 29th the post from Pest failed to arrive for the fourth day in succession. In the heath on the outskirts of the town earthwork and redoubts are being built.

Written by Engels on May 4, 1849

First published in the *Neue Rheinische Zeitung* No. 291, May 6, 1849

Printed according to the newspaper

Published in English for the first time

---

[a] Jellachich.— *Ed.*

# LONGING FOR A STATE OF SIEGE

*Cologne*, May 5. It is still being rumoured that on Sunday, on the occasion of the district congresses of the various parties,[314] a *state of siege* will once again be imposed on the good city of Cologne.

From all kinds of small preparations by the military authorities, it is clear that at any rate they are preparing themselves for all eventualities. That is not all. Measures are being taken which definitely indicate a desire to provoke disturbances.

Why otherwise has "My glorious army"[315] been suddenly permitted, to the great astonishment of the soldiers themselves, to remain out of barracks until *10 p.m.* instead of 9 p.m.?

There is likewise again talk of *arrests.* We are quite ready to believe in it. The desire for such action has been in existence for a long time. Moreover, it is known that already on one occasion by means of such arrests the plan of provoking disorders proved completely successful.

We repeat, it is of the utmost importance that the democrats, and especially the *workers*, of Cologne do everything possible so that tomorrow the powers that are eager for a state of siege will *not* be given *even the slightest excuse* that will serve them as a cover for their acts of violence.

It is primarily the *bourgeoisie* that is endangered by the latest counter-revolutionary actions. The bourgeoisie has convened the congress of the towns. Let the *bourgeoisie have the honour of saying the first word.* Let us wait to see what these gentlemen will decide on Tuesday. We are convinced that many a worthy democrat will be greatly disappointed by the results of this pompous "congress of the towns".[a]

---

[a] See this volume, p. 392.— *Ed.*

One thing is certain: if the state of siege is proclaimed before Tuesday then the congress of the towns will not take place and no one will be more pleased at this than precisely the gentlemen *who convened it.*

If tomorrow the workers allow themselves to be provoked into disorders they will only be pulling the *chestnuts out of the fire for the bourgeoisie,* and at the same time for the *Government.* The question is whether they wish to be used for this purpose at a time when all Germany is on the threshold of *civil war,* and when perhaps they will soon have the opportunity to *come forward with their own demands.*

Written by Engels on May 5, 1849

First published in the *Neue Rheinische Zeitung* No. 291, May 6, 1849

Printed according to the newspaper

Published in English for the first time

# [THE SITUATION IN HUNGARY]

Apart from the news received from our Vienna correspondent (see under Cologne[a]) there is a complete lack of definite information about the events in the theatre of war. We are therefore restricting ourselves today to a few items of news from the Hungarian-Moravian border that clearly bear the imprint of fear of the Magyars.

The *Constitutionelles Blatt aus Böhmen* writes:

"From the Galician-Silesian border, April 28. The outcome of the clash near Neutra is that the Magyars have penetrated into the Zips as well as into the north-western foot-hills of the Carpathians. Neumarkt, Budatin and Sillein are in their hands. For some days they have been threatening the passes near Csacze and Jablunka, whither the imperial observation corps has been withdrawn. To avert a Magyar invasion of Silesia, an infantry division has been sent to Csacze, the infantry division stationed at Bielitz since last January has been moved to Jablunka, and, finally, a battalion has been withdrawn from Troppau and stationed in the neighbourhood of Friedek.—Since the day before yesterday fleeing Slovaks have been passing through Saybusch and Andrichau; the Imperial Commissioner from Sillein has been in Teschen for the last four or five days.

"The day before yesterday (the 26th) brisk artillery fire coming from the direction of Sillein or Teplitz could be heard in Saybusch until 6 o'clock in the evening.—However, only those who regard the recent occurrences in Cracow[316] and Görgey's simultaneous advance as parts of a co-ordinated plan think it likely that the Magyars will pay a visit to Galicia."[b]

In another report from Silesia published by the same paper it is stated:

"From Karwin, a small Prussian town, about two hours' journey from Troppau, reports have been received that from the castletower many beacons could be observed

---

[a] See this volume, pp. 400-01.— *Ed.*

[b] This and the following quotations are taken from the *Constitutionelles Blatt aus Böhmen* No. 103, May 1, 1849.— *Ed.*

in the Carpathians on the 24th, and it is believed that they were signals to mobilise the *Landsturm* in Galicia.

"A host of insurgents, about 15,000 in number, most of them horse-, cattle- and swine-herdsmen, conscripted from their pusztas[317] for the war, and accompanied by several cannon, are said to have advanced up to St. Martin and, on the evening of the same day, even as far as Sillein (about $2^1/_2$ post stages from Jablunka). Counts Pongrácz and Révay, the royal commissioners, fled to avoid death at the hands of the Magyars; Major Wenk crossed to this side of the Waag and called on all the imperial garrisons stationed in Slovakia to concentrate at certain frontier points so as to maintain communications with Moravia and Silesia.

"The borders are manned and all men in the towns and villages capable of bearing arms have been mustered for the *Landsturm* that is to go into action under the command of Archducal Justiciary Peter in the event of an invasion by the Magyars.—Kossuth's supporters are doing all they can to make the Slovaks waver. Thus, a song is going the rounds in which every Slovak loyal to the King, a 'German alien', is called a traitor to his country; some people are unfortunately led astray by this and have been ensnared. These are the bitter fruits of a mistaken policy pursued by a military leader[a] who let himself be lulled to sleep by the perfidious *Magyar nobility,* and whose anti-national measures repressed a people prepared to sacrifice everything in order to humble the Magyars (!?!)."

From Ofen we learn that the garrison left behind by the imperial troops is thought to consist of four infantry battalions, two to three cavalry squadrons and 83 well-manned pieces of ordnance. The fortress has provisions for six weeks.

Written by Engels about May 5, 1849

First published in the supplement
to the *Neue Rheinische Zeitung* No. 291,
May 6, 1849

Printed according to the newspaper

Published in English for the first
time

---

[a] Windischgrätz.— *Ed.*

# [FROM THE THEATRE OF WAR]

The Hungarians continue to advance. They are said to have already made incursions into Styria (near Fürstenfeld on the Raab), into Moravia (near Friedland on the Jablunka) and Galicia (near Raycza on the Moravian border). On the 29th Raab was still in the hands of the imperial troops; since then it is thought to have been abandoned. Pressburg was fortified by the imperial troops; according to some reports it has already been evacuated.

In the south, the imperial troops must be in a bad way. They are said to be *evacuating Fünfkirchen*, between the Danube and the Drava. Jellachich's corps, it now appears, was completely scattered, and *two regiments of Croats were taken prisoner* and put into the ranks of the Honveds. A report also mentions the encirclement and capture of Simunich.

Bem's troops are really in the Banat, near Lugos and Karánsebes and are threatening the fortresses of Arad and Temesvar.

The rumours about the expansion of the Magyar army are beginning to assume fantastic proportions. They say that 250,000 Magyars are under arms. While Görgey was fighting Wohlgemuth with a force of 45,000, 18 battalions attacked Jellachich, and in addition to this, Dembiński's corps, the strongest of all, has not been in action since the battle of Kapolna. Guyon and Klapka are now in command at Raab. The Hungarian Assembly *has been convoked* for May 10 *in Pest*. The Russians, 8,000 strong, are said to have entered Cracow.

Written by Engels about May 5, 1849

First published in the *Neue Rheinische Zeitung* No. 291 (second edition), May 6, 1849

Printed according to the newspaper

Published in English for the first time

# [KOSSUTH'S PROCLAMATION]

We are publishing the following passages from a proclamation by Kossuth, dated Gödöllö, April 7, and taken from the *Neue Oder-Zeitung*:

"The nation's valiant army has driven out that enemy whose traitorous commissioners in Nograd and Somogy had once more started *to subject the people to the yoke of labour services which had been abolished by law and which we shall never permit to be inflicted on you again*. It has driven out the enemy who in the past month issued an imperial decree that where the terrier has been abolished, *the tenant has to pay half the value of the abolished labour services and tithes out of his own pocket, although the Hungarian law exempted you from this payment*. It is our firmest resolve to uphold this law in defence of your freedom.

"Our valiant army is driving from your borders the enemy whose Emperor[a] dared to state: 'Hungary does not exist and will never again exist', and who dared to partition us from our brothers in Transylvania, to tear Croatia from Hungary, to cut up our own fatherland and to turn our most fertile regions into a special Rascian Kingdom,[318] for the benefit of those Rascian robbers with whom he did not scruple to ally himself for the purpose of exterminating the Hungarian nation.

"Our valiant army is driving from your borders the enemy who, wherever he went in his flight, robbed like a common highwayman, who, not content with stealing as much as he could eat and drink, destroyed and laid waste what he was unable to consume, in order to leave famine in his wake; what is more, with inhuman ferocity and out of sheer predatory, malignant instincts he snatched the pillows from under the heads of your children, scattering the feathers to the winds. He did not even spare your churches; he tore the marble slabs from the altars, gutted the roofs of the chapels, while some of the *officers stole the silver spoons* from those who gave them food: thus behaves the enemy that the Austrian Emperor sent to our country, to destroy it, to exterminate our nation, and to make our people slaves and beggars!

"I prophesied to you months ago that Hungary's freedom, autonomy and independence would blossom out of the tyranny of the Austrian Emperor.

"And, thank God, it is so. Praised be the holy name of the Lord for this, and the nation's blessing and eternal thanks also to the valiant Hungarian army, to those who

---

[a] Francis Joseph I.— *Ed.*

gladly sacrificed their lives and blood for the fatherland, who with unshaken courage defeated the united force of the enemy and who with their continuing victories are hastening towards the glorious goal, making you, O Hungarian people, by the sacrifice of their heroic blood free and happy! The enemy boasted of fictitious victories in order to deceive the Hungarian people and to plunge them into desperation.

"That is a characteristic piece of cowardice, for only a coward is capable of lying. The enemy deceived you with lying reports that he had driven our troops out of Transylvania, that Jellachich had taken Szegedin by storm, although he never came anywhere near it.

"Yes, and what is more—now that the enemy has been defeated four times within five days, and forced out of his strongest position, Windischgrätz, Schlick and Jellachich with their whole army in flight from Poroszlo, Pest and Waitzen—now, while I am writing this in Gödöllö, in the very same room where 24 hours ago Windischgrätz dared to dream of Hungary's subjugation—now, whilst his whole defeated army is on the run and we have snatched the whole of Transylvania, two-thirds of Hungary, from the tyrant's clutches—even now he is still not ashamed of spreading the lies in the venal Pest journals that he won a victory near Jasz-Bereny. To remove any doubt in the matter, I give you—my brothers, my friends!—the comforting assurance that I and the splendid leaders of our heroes are in Gödöllö with our army, whither our intrepid Honveds fought their way at bayonet's point. We are in Gödöllö from whose outskirts our artillerymen went into action, shelling the arrogant enemy out of his positions; in Gödöllö from whose outskirts our hussars pursued the fleeing enemy up to the Danube at Pest.—And over there in Transylvania the imperial enemy no longer exists. This Emperor sent the wild Muscovites against us, but Bem and our Hungarian army in Transylvania expelled the enemy and his Muscovite protectors, down to the last man, from the sacred soil of Transylvania.

"And down in the Bacska, Perczel took St. Tamas whose capture cost so much blood on other occasions. And he liberated Peterwardein, which was enmeshed by Austrian treachery, and freed the prosperous Alföld from the Rascian robbers. But up here, where the enemy's main force planned to subjugate Hungary, Commander-in-Chief Görgey with his generals Damjanich, Aulich, Klapka and Gaspar defeated Schlick near Hatvan, Jellachich near Tapio-Bicske, Windischgrätz and Schlick rejoined by Jellachich near Isaczeg; and now that they and our victorious troops have taken Gödöllö, they are already standing on the Rakos plain. A few more days, and Hungary will be free and no wicked enemy will violate the soil of our fatherland.

"This is the joyful news I give you, my brothers! Long live the free Hungarian fatherland!"

Written by Engels about May 7, 1849

First published in the *Neue Rheinische Zeitung* No. 292, May 8, 1849

Printed according to the newspaper

Published in English for the first time

# FROM THE THEATRE OF WAR

The Austrian army continues to retreat. On April 28 Raab was evacuated; on the 29th, the Hungarian outposts had reached Hochstrasse, two miles[a] from Wieselburg. On the other side of the Danube, the Austrian corps stationed near Dioszeg has also withdrawn to Lanschütz (4 hours from Pressburg). Even on the 30th one could not travel from Pressburg further than Karlsburg (one and a half miles from Pressburg, on the southern bank).

The Austrian High Command is in Laxenburg, $1^1/_2$ hours from Vienna.

Slovakia is now completely in the hands of the Hungarians who were welcomed with open arms by the inhabitants. The Hungarians have found a mass of weapons there since Windischgrätz had disarmed the rural population and the confiscated rifles were collected and piled up in the county towns. There is no sign of the Slovak *Landsturm;* Bloudek has disappeared, the guerilla commander Janiczek has gone over to the Magyars. From Slovakia the Hungarians threaten Moravia, Austrian Silesia and Galicia. There is talk of an invasion corps numbering 40,000-60,000 men to transfer the theatre of war to Russian and Prussian Poland. A surprise attack on Prerau, the junction of the Polish-Silesian-Austrian railway lines, must certainly be expected.

In connection with the sudden stoppage in the advance of the Russians, we refer to our report from Breslau.[b] It is true that there is still talk about a large Russian corps advancing on Transylvania; for the present, however, all these reports are unreliable.

---

[a] See footnote on p. 20.— *Ed.*

[b] "Breslau, 4. Mai", *Neue Rheinische Zeitung* No. 292, May 8, 1849.— *Ed.*

It is now confirmed that in the south Bem has invaded the Banat with a considerable force, occupied the mountain passes between the Maros and the Danube, has taken Lugos and is even supposed to have captured *Temesvar*. As a result of this and the advance of parts of Perczel's corps over the Theiss towards Kikinda District, the Serbian Voivodina has dissolved into thin air.

Jellachich, whose defeat has been repeatedly confirmed, has been appointed commander with full authority over the Southern Army (Croatian-Slavonian-Banat) that is being formed.

This "Southern Army" consists on paper of 30,000 men; in actual fact it numbers at the most 8,000 plus a few thousand men from Serbian robber bands.

Written by Engels about May 7, 1849

First published in the *Neue Rheinische Zeitung* No. 292, May 8, 1849

Printed according to the newspaper

Published in English for the first time

# [THE PRUSSIAN ARMY
# AND THE REVOLUTIONARY UPRISING
# OF THE PEOPLE]

*Cologne*, May 7. The elements now in ferment in Germany are daily becoming more distinct; the situation is becoming more firmly defined.

While one of the centres of the German counter-revolution, Austria, has its hands more than full in dealing with Hungary, the other centre, Prussia, is sending its armed hordes in all directions against the revolutionary uprising of the people.

In *Dresden,* that patient town of art and luxury, the people are taking up arms and replying with barricades and musket-fire to the traitorous proclamations of the royal Government.[319] The greater part of the troops are coming over to the side of the people; the struggle is as good as decided; but suddenly *Prussian battalions* appear and side with the royal traitor[a] against the people.

In the Palatinate, too, the people are taking up arms against the daily more insolent Bavarian counter-revolution; here, too, *Prussian battalions* stand ready in order to invade at a suitable moment and put an end both to the Frankfurt Assembly and to the uprising in the Palatinate.

In whatever direction one looks in North and South-West Germany, everywhere there are *Prussian battalions* ready to carry through the counter-revolution by force of arms.

And so that there should be no lack of Prussian battalions, whether in our country or in neighbouring states, *recruiting into the army reserve* is taking place everywhere[b] in accordance with our glorious military organisation.

---

[a] Frederick Augustus II.— *Ed.*
[b] See this volume, pp. 195-96.— *Ed.*

Thus the centres of the counter-revolution are in one place the Austrian army, in another the Prussian army. Day by day the new revolution opposes an increasingly vigorous and universal resistance to the counter-revolution.

The Dresden Provisional Government is still in existence and rallies the forces of the people in the whole country.

The Palatinate Defence Council[320] is still in existence and every day more and more people of the Palatinate gather around the banner of the revolution.

Finally, in Rhenish Prussia, the army reserve is *refusing to march.* Even in Elberfeld, in black-and-white[a] Wuppertal, the army reserve is refusing to move beyond its place of assembly.

And lastly, in Austria the most important occurrence is the *Hungarian revolution which is irresistibly advancing.* The post from Vienna has not arrived—perhaps because the Magyars have torn up the Moravian railway line. That they have *broken into Moravia* is definitely established. Reports in writing from Ratibor inform us that already eight days ago bombardments from whole batteries were heard in Golkowitz on the Austrian frontier, and on May 3 in Loslau, and likewise in Prussian Upper Silesia. At all events, the battles must have taken place on this side of the Jablunka.

Incidentally, the *victory of the Hungarians is more certain than ever before.* It is quite definite that *the Russians will not come.* A few more days, therefore, and the Hungarians will be in Vienna, the Hungarian revolution will have been accomplished and the second German revolution will be ushered in in the most magnificent way.

Written by Engels on May 7, 1849

First published in the special supplement to the *Neue Rheinische Zeitung* No. 292. May 8, 1849

Printed according to the newspaper

Published in English for the first time

---

[a] The colours of the Prussian monarchy.— *Ed.*

# [A QUESTION TO THE WORKERS]

*Cologne,* May 7. The Prussian gentlemen seem to be making every effort to provoke a riot.

The day before yesterday the artillerymen (concerning whom, incidentally, the Government is labouring under a great illusion) were paid 15 silver groschen per man as a "supplement" for the previous month. True, the infantry also received this supplement.

The officers of one regiment stationed here have *directly called on* their soldiers to start a riot tomorrow.

This evening a scuffle between soldiers and civilians has already taken place on Neumarkt Square.

Once more we ask the workers *whether they want to let the Prussian gentlemen dictate the moment for the uprising?*

Written by Engels on May 7, 1849

First published in the special supplement to the *Neue Rheinische Zeitung* No. 292, May 8, 1849

Printed according to the newspaper

Published in English for the first time

# THE TSAR AND HIS SUBORDINATE KNYAZES[a]

*Cologne*, May 8. It is said that the French ambassador[b] in Berlin has *protested against the entry of the Prussians into Saxony.*

At last, therefore, the French Government has noticed that the East-European counter-revolution menaces it as well, and that the new Holy Alliance [321] has as its ultimate, supreme aim nothing other than the conquest, and this time, perhaps, the *partition of France.*

We know positively that in the treaty which has been concluded between the orthodox Tsar and his two subordinate *knyazes* from Olmütz and Potsdam[c] the ultimate aim of the alliance is declared to be the conquest of France, the abolition of the Republic and the elevation of the "legitimate King", the "son of holy Louis", the idiot *Henry of Bordeaux to the throne of France and Navarre.*

That Odilon Barrot is involved in this plot is hardly doubtful.

This is what they expect you to do, Prussian soldiers of the army reserve! You are being called away from your hearths and homes, from your wives and children, in order first of all to fight against your brothers in Germany and Prussia, to help in suppressing the small remnant of the freedom which you won last year—and then to fight against the Hungarians who are coming to the aid of your threatened freedom—and when you have completed this work to the satisfaction of your *knyazes* and your supreme lord and master, Tsar Nicholas, then you will be led across the Rhine against the nation whose heroic uprisings in 1789-94, 1830, and 1848 procured you all the freedoms you enjoy.

---

[a] "Knyaz" is the Russian word for "prince".— *Ed.*

[b] F. V. E. Arago.— *Ed.*

[c] The Austrian Emperor Francis Joseph and the Prussian King Frederick William IV.— *Ed.*

It is for this that last year as fighters at the barricades, and as the awe-inspiring mass of the people, you won a few liberties for yourselves, so that now, as soldiers of the army reserve, you yourselves will help to suppress these liberties once more and finally, in the service of your supreme master, the Russian Tsar, destroy also the two bulwarks of liberty—Hungary and France!

Written by Engels on May 8, 1849

First published in the *Neue Rheinische Zeitung* No. 293, May 9, 1849

Printed according to the newspaper

Published in English for the first time

# [THE APPROACHING REVOLUTION]

*Cologne*, evening of May 8. The revolution is drawing nearer and nearer. While in Dresden the people are displaying the utmost courage in their struggle against the Saxon and Prussian mercenaries,[322] and armed reinforcements are pouring in from all quarters to repulse the Prussian invasion; while in the Palatinate the people are rallying round the Defence Council,[323] the people's militia is mobilising and arming itself, the military are siding with it and the government officials are acquiescing, the whole of Germany is seething with unrest. Franconia is only waiting for the moment when it, too, can break away from Bavaria; the people there are in a state of great unrest, and the peasantry especially wait with impatience the outbreak of the struggle. We shall be in a position to supply details about this tomorrow. In Baden and Württemberg even the military have declared themselves in favour of the imperial Constitution. Similar reports have been received from Thuringia, Hesse-Cassel and Darmstadt.

Finally in Prussia the movement is gaining momentum with every day that passes and becoming more revolutionary. Breslau is in a state of profound unrest; the minor riots, the mustering of troops, the patrols, the groups of people gathering in the streets, are all harbingers of graver events. The whole of Silesia is in a similar state of tension in anticipation of the news from Hungary and Vienna. Berlin is quiet, held down by the rule of the sabre. On the Rhine and in Westphalia the plans of Hohenzollern despotism are miscarrying because of the resistance of the army reserve which refuses to allow itself to be used as a tool for new coups d'état. The whole of the Berg Country, the District of Hagen, Mülheim an der Ruhr, Krefeld—in short, precisely the regions with the largest number of black-and-white supporters have suddenly gone over to *open insurrection*.

The Brandenburg-Manteuffel clique is in the meantime doing its best to provoke the people into revolution. The *Staats-Anzeiger*[a] which arrived today contains a circular addressed to all heads of provincial administrations, calling on them to take energetic measures against all "revolutionary" activities in support of the imperial Constitution, and also correspondence between Imperial Commissioner Bassermann and Herr Brandenburg in which the latter states: 1) Prussia refuses once and for all to recognise the imperial Constitution, and 2) the Central Authority[324] is to abstain from interference in Prussia's internal affairs, such as dissolution of the Chamber, proclamation of a state of siege etc., once and for all.

We commend these last samples of Hohenzollern arrogance to the people of the Rhine. It seems that through its contemptuous dismissal of even the most trivial concessions the dynasty intends to drive the people into revolution.

If it comes to another revolution, Herr von Hohenzollern, *who knows whether the people will leave it at "Hats off!" this time!*[325]

Written by Engels on May 8, 1849

First published in the special supplement to the *Neue Rheinische Zeitung* No. 293, May 9, 1849

Printed according to the newspaper

Published in English for the first time

---

[a] *Preussischer Staats-Anzeiger* No. 125, May 8, 1849.— *Ed.*

15*

## THE DEEDS OF THE HOHENZOLLERN DYNASTY [326]

*Cologne,* May 9. It seems that in the last days of its existence and of the existence of the Prussian state, the Government of Herr von Hohenzollern wants once again to justify to the full the ancient reputation of the Prussian and Hohenzollern name.

Who does not know the description in Heine's poem:

> A child with a head as large as a pumpkin,
> With the drooping moustache of a grey-haired bumpkin,
> With spider-like arms, lengthy but strong,
> With the paunch of a giant but guts not so long,
> A changeling....[a]

Who does not know the treacheries, the perfidies, the legacy-hunting, by means of which that family of corporals which bears the name of Hohenzollern rose to greatness?

It is well known that the so-called "Great Elector"[b] (as though any "Elector" could ever be "great"!) perpetrated the first betrayal of Poland when he, Poland's ally against Sweden, suddenly went over to the side of the Swedes in order to be able to plunder Poland more thoroughly by the Peace of Oliva.[327]

People are well acquainted with the absurd figure of Frederick I and the brutal coarseness of Frederick William II.

It is well known that Frederick II, inventor of patriarchal despotism, the friend of Enlightenment with the help of flogging, sold his country by auction to the highest bidders among French entrepreneurs; it is well known that he allied himself with Russia and

---

[a] Heinrich Heine, "Der Wechselbalg" in *Zeitgedicht.—Ed.*
[b] Frederick William.— *Ed.*

Austria in order to carry out the rape of Poland,[328] an act which still today, after the revolution of 1848, remains a permanent blot on German history.

It is well known that Frederick William II helped to accomplish the rape of Poland and that he gave away the stolen Polish national and church estates to his courtiers.

It is well known that in 1792 he entered into a coalition with Austria and England to suppress the glorious French Revolution and invaded France; it is likewise well known that his "glorious army" was most ignominiously driven out of France.

It is well known that he then left his allies in the lurch and hastened to conclude a peace with the French Republic.[329]

It is well known that, while pretending to be enthusiastically in favour of the legitimate King of France and Navarre,[a] he bought the crown jewels of this same king for a song from the French Republic and thus profited from the misfortune of his "dear brother".

It is well known that he, whose whole life was a typical Hohenzollern mixture of opulence and mysticism, senile lasciviousness and infantile superstition, trampled on the free expression of opinions by means of the Bischoffswerder edicts.[330]

It is well known that his successor, *Frederick William III*, the "Just", betrayed his old allies to Napoleon in exchange for Hanover, thrown to him as a bait.

It is well known that immediately after this he betrayed Napoleon to these same former allies, when being in the pay of England and Russia he attacked the French Revolution embodied in the person of Napoleon.

It is well known what the result of this attack was: the unprecedented defeat of the "glorious army" at Jena,[331] the sudden outbreak of a moral sickness of the whole Prussian body politic, a series of acts of treachery, baseness and sycophancy on the part of Prussian officials from which Napoleon and his generals turned away in disgust.

It is well known that in 1813 Frederick William III, by fine words and magnificent promises, actually induced the Prussian people to believe that they were fighting a "war of liberation" against the French, although it was solely a matter of suppressing the French Revolution and restoring the old rule by the grace of God.[332]

It is well known that the fine promises were forgotten as soon as the Holy Alliance made its triumphant entry into Paris on March 30, 1814.

---

[a] Louis XVI.— *Ed.*

It is well known that at the time of Napoleon's return from Elba, the enthusiasm of the German people had already cooled down again to such an extent that the Hohenzollern had to try to revive their flagging zeal by the promise of a Constitution (the Edict of May 22, 1815—four weeks before the battle of Waterloo).[333]

People recall the promises contained in the Act of Federation and the Vienna concluding document: freedom of the press, a Constitution etc.[334]

It is well known how the "just" Hohenzollern kept his word. The Holy Alliance and congresses for the suppression of nations, Carlsbad decisions, censorship, police despotism, rule of the nobility, arbitrary bureaucratic rule, high-handed administration of justice by ministerial orders, persecution of demagogues, mass sentences, squandering of financial resources, and—no Constitution at all.[335]

It is well known that in 1820 the people were given a guarantee that taxes and state debts would not be increased, and how the Hohenzollern kept his word: by transforming the Overseas Trading Company into a secret loan bank for the state.[336]

It is well known how the Hohenzollern responded to the appeal of the French people during the July revolution: by massing troops on the frontier, by suppressing his own people, by crushing the movement in the smaller German states, and by the final enslavement of these states under the knout of the Holy Alliance.

It is well known that this same Hohenzollern violated neutrality during the Russo-Polish war[337] by allowing the Russians to pass through his territory and thus to attack the Poles from the rear, by putting the Prussian arsenals and depots at the disposal of the Russians, and by affording every defeated Russian corps a safe refuge in Prussia.

It is well known that all the efforts of the Hohenzollern subordinate *knyaz*, in unison with the aims of the Holy Alliance, were directed towards strengthening the rule of the nobility, the bureaucracy and the army, and crushing by brute force all freedom of speech, all influence on the Government exerted by the "limited understanding of the subject"[338] and moreover not only in Prussia but in the rest of Germany as well.

It is well known that there seldom has been a reign in which such praiseworthy intentions were implemented by more brutal and violent means than that of Frederick William III, particularly in 1815-40. Never and nowhere have there been so many arrests and sentences, never were the fortresses so filled with political prisoners, as under this "just" ruler. Moreover, it should be borne in mind what innocent simpletons these demagogues were.

Ought we to speak also of the Hohenzollern[a] who, according to the monk of Lehnin, "will be the last of his tribe"?[339] Ought we to speak about the rebirth of Christian-Germanic grandeur, about the emergence of ghastly financial distress, about the Order of the Swan, and about the supreme court for censorship, about the United Diet and the General Synod, about the "scrap of paper",[340] about the vain attempts to borrow money, and all the other achievements of the glorious epoch of 1840-48? Ought we to prove, by referring to Hegel, why precisely it will have to be a comedian who closes the series of Hohenzollerns?[341]

It will not be necessary. The data given suffice for a full characterisation of the Hohenzollern Prussian name. True, there was a moment when the splendour of this name was dimmed, but since the pleiad of Manteuffel and Co.[b] surrounds the crown, the old grandeur has been revived. Once again, as formerly, Prussia is a vice-regal province under Russian supremacy; once again the Hohenzollern is a subordinate *knyaz* of the autocrat of all the Russias, and superior *knyaz* over all the little boyars of Saxony, Bavaria, Hessen-Homburg, Waldeck etc., once again the limited understanding of the subject is reinstated in its old right, that of obeying orders. "My glorious army", as long as the orthodox Tsar[c] himself is not making use of it, is allowed to establish in Saxony, Baden, Hessen, and the Palatinate the order which has prevailed for eighteen years in Warsaw, and in its own country and in Austria it is permitted to glue together the pieces of the shattered crowns with the blood of the subjects. We care as little about the word given earlier in a moment of fear and distress as did our deceased forefathers, and as soon as we have set our house in order we shall march with bands playing and banners flying against France and we shall conquer the land where the vines of Champagne grow, and we shall destroy the great Babylon, the mother of all sin!

Such are the plans of our august rulers; such is the safe harbour towards which our noble Hohenzollern is steering. Hence the ever more frequent dictates and coups d'état; hence the repeated kicks for the cowardly Frankfurt Assembly; hence the states of siege, arrests and persecutions; hence the intervention of the Prussian soldiery in Dresden and South Germany.

But there exists another power, to which, it is true, the gentlemen from Sans-Souci pay little heed, but which will nevertheless interpose

---

[a] Frederick William IV.— *Ed.*
[b] i.e. the members of the Brandenburg-Manteuffel Government.— *Ed.*
[c] Nicholas I.— *Ed.*

its word like a clap of thunder. That power is the **people,** the people who, in Paris and on the Rhine, in Silesia and in Austria, in furious anger await the moment for the uprising, and who—who knows how soon—will give their due deserts to all the Hohenzollerns, and all the superior and inferior *knyazes.*

Written by Marx on May 9, 1849

First published in the *Neue Rheinische
Zeitung* No. 294, May 10, 1849

Printed according to the newspaper

# [THE SITUATION IN ELBERFELD]³⁴²

"*Elberfeld*, May 8. After several posters appealing to the people to support the army reserve in their refusal of military duty, as well as a proclamation by the army reserve against the King[a] and Government, had been torn down by the police, the latter were attacked and *forced to fasten the posters to the offices and doors* while the people watched them. Towards the evening, as the crowds grew larger and larger, the rumour spread that troops were on their way. And so the *army reserve took up arms* and forced the burgomaster to accompany them to the railway station to try and persuade the regular troops to turn back. However, when they were passing the officers' mess von Carnap took refuge in it and the people then demolished the building. Whilst the army reserve marched to the station to prevent the troops from entering the town, the armed forces appeared on the scene, causing confusion among the crowd and lashing out at them to such an extent that a number of casualties had to be carried away.

"But the crowd gathered again and went to the town hall where the civic militia had in the meantime been mounted to defend the building. It contains a great deal of ammunition, and the demand was raised that this should be handed over. After this demand had been refused, an attempt was made to force an entry, but this was unsuccessful. A hail of stones had in the meantime smashed several window-panes. At 8 o'clock this morning, the army reserve, *fully armed*, have taken up positions near Böttcher on Engelnberg *where they await the arrival of the military.*

"*Many proletarians armed with weapons have joined them, as well as army reserve units from other parts. The civic militia* are equally active, but will *not attack the army reserve* and only control the crowd. If the military arrive and attack the army reserve, then alas! They will have to come in large numbers if they are to achieve anything." *D. Z.*[b]

(This morning artillery left Cologne at an early hour bound for Elberfeld, in order to riddle with grape-shot the honest workers of the Berg Country who are not willing to be used unlawfully as tools by a traitorous camarilla. We trust that the artillery will *do its duty.*)

Written by Engels on May 9, 1849

First published in the *Neue Rheinische Zeitung* No. 294, May 10, 1849

Printed according to the newspaper

Published in English for the first time

---

[a] Frederick William IV.— *Ed.*
[b] *Düsseldorfer Zeitung.— Ed.*

# [FROM THE THEATRE OF WAR]

New victories are reported from the Hungarian border! The news about the **defeat of the Austrians** near *Hochstrasse* that we published a few days ago[a] has been fully confirmed. The island of Schütt is almost completely in the hands of the Magyars.

A **second defeat** has been sustained by the imperial troops near *Szered* on the Waag, about five miles[b] from Pressburg. Here Görgey fought his way across the Waag, driving the imperial troops nearly back to Pressburg.

In both these battles the Austrian cavalry in particular suffered heavy losses. Galician and German cavalrymen arrived in Vienna in carts and on foot, without their horses and sabres, often shouldering their saddles, their ragged, mud-stained and dejected appearance causing dismay amongst the black-and-yellow[c] supporters. The routed and ragged remnants of the Hurban corps also passed through Pressburg.

In this town general confusion prevailed among the imperial forces; they expected that a decisive battle would take place here on the 4th or 5th of May, and had given up hope of holding the town. Many black-and-yellow supporters fled from it.— Tyrnau, to the north-west of Szered, was also evacuated by the imperial troops and the railway line connecting it with Pressburg was torn up.

It is certain that the Magyars intend to make *Moravia and Lower Austria* the theatre of war, i.e. *to take Vienna*. Even the Vienna

---

[a] See this volume, p. 409.— *Ed.*

[b] See footnote on p. 20.— *Ed.*

[c] The Austrian imperial colours.— *Ed.*

*Lithographierte Correspondenz* admits that the whole of Lower Austria is ardently awaiting the arrival of the Magyars.

In the *Bukovina*, the peasant agitator Kobylica is causing the Government increasing anxiety.

In the *Bacska*, Perczel is exacting heavy war-contributions from the Serbs who also have to raise recruits. But at the same time he has guaranteed their language and nationality and abolished the Military Border.[343]

The Austrian reports now maintain that the alleged deposing of the Habsburg dynasty was a bluff originating from the Austrian Government with the aim of inciting the other provinces against the Magyars. According to other sources the National Assembly revoked its decisions because of their adverse effect on the people. *Se non è vero è ben trovato.*[a]

In the south, according to the *Vjestnik* [Вѣстникъ] and the *Serbske Novine* [Србске Новине], Perczel has crossed the Theiss, captured Kikinda District, forced the Serbs to retreat everywhere and now threatens Werschetz. Everyone there has fled to Pancsova. A corps is supposed to have advanced to the outskirts of Temesvar (whose capture by Bem is thus not confirmed). Bem is reported to have taken up his position near Orsova, ready to receive the Austrians and Russians advancing from Wallachia. The Serbs have completely lost their confidence in General Todorovich's conduct of the war. The South-Slav papers are unanimous in admitting that the Banat cannot be held and it will be completely reconquered by the Magyars in a few weeks' time.

Written by Engels on May 9, 1849

First published in the special supplement to the *Neue Rheinische Zeitung* No. 294, May 10, 1849

Printed according to the newspaper

Published in English for the first time

---

[a] Even if it's not true it's well invented.— *Ed.*

# [COUNTER-REVOLUTIONARY OFFENSIVE AND VICTORY OF THE REVOLUTION][344]

*Cologne,* May 9. The counter-revolution is advancing swiftly, but the revolution advances still faster.

While the counter-revolution has gained advantages in *Dresden,* which make its victory probable, and has managed to introduce a *state of siege, censorship* and *martial law* by successfully provoking a revolt in *Breslau,*[345] the revolution can point to quite different victories.

We do not speak of the rapidly growing *open rebellion of the army reserve* in Rhenish Prussia, involving the most black-and-white[a] districts, nor of the South-German movement, which is being betrayed everywhere by the governments, the bourgeoisie and the Frankfurt National Assembly[346]; we speak only of those great events which, coming from outside, can give strong support and unity to the small, isolated and deceived German movements — we speak of the Magyar and the French revolutions.

While the *Magyar revolution* is gaining one victory after another, and after the next decisive battle (which must have taken place on May 5 or 6 at Pressburg) will march directly on Vienna and liberate the city, *France* suddenly enters a stage when the movement is developing again openly and in broad daylight. The underground development of the past months comes to a close; the defeat of the French army at Rome[347] has exposed and discredited the entire Government. The people reappears upon the scene — the people, the ultimate, supreme judge. Whether it happens at the elections or in the course of an open revolution, the French people will shortly

---

[a] The colours of the Prussian monarchy.— *Ed.*

give an impetus to the movement, an impetus which all Europe will feel.

The European dynasties will soon see that the chosen people of the revolution has not changed; the French revolution of 1849 will speak to them, not in Lamartinian phrases, but in the language of guns.

Written by Engels on May 9, 1849   Printed according to the newspaper

First published in the special supplement
to the *Neue Rheinische Zeitung* No. 294,
May 10, 1849

# [THE UPRISING IN ELBERFELD
# AND DÜSSELDORF][348]

*Cologne,* May 11. From Elberfeld we learn that after twice attacking the people, the soldiery drawn up on the market square were repulsed with several dead and wounded. The colonel of the 16th regiment had his horse shot from under him; he himself was severely wounded. Captain Uttenhoven is reported to have fallen, riddled with bullets in front and—behind (!); it is said that his own men fired at him. The soldiers' attack aroused the most tremendous fury. The majority of the civic militia fought on the side of the people.

The dissolved town council is said to have been replaced by a committee of public safety, and four members of the former council have joined it. The house of the chief burgomaster, von Carnap, was totally demolished; the mahogany furniture from the Hotel von der Heydt was used to build one of the most valuable barricades. A total of about 40 barricades is supposed to be in the town.

At the time of dispatch of this news which, however, cannot be vouched for in every point, the town had been evacuated by the troops, and large reinforcements from the surrounding districts were advancing to support the people of Elberfeld.

When the news that fighting had begun in Elberfeld reached Düsseldorf on the evening of the 9th, a truly heroic struggle was waged at Düsseldorf railway station against the troops who were being sent from Cologne to Elberfeld as reinforcements[a]; and there was soon fierce barricade fighting in all streets. The alarm tocsins were rung the whole night through, and the grape-shot fired by the military was answered by the bullets of the people. Towards morning, the soldiery gained the upper hand, however, and it is

---

[a] See this volume, p. 423.— *Ed.*

reported that during the day posters were put up on the street corners proclaiming a state of siege and martial law.

There are thought to be about 20 dead among the casualties suffered by the people; they include the well-known forwarding agent Hartmann and a Polish painter who, after springing in front of the advancing soldiers and urging them not to fire on their brothers, was cut down by their bullets and fell dead to the ground.

The military are said to have later shot down defenceless men, women and children, thus marking their victory by even more bloodshed.

Written by Engels about May 10, 1849

First published in the special supplement to the *Neue Rheinische Zeitung* No. 295, May 11, 1849

Printed according to the newspaper

Published in English for the first time

# THE NEW PRUSSIAN CONSTITUTION

*Cologne*, May 12. In November of last year, after the dispersal of the people's representatives, the Potsdam member of the Trinity,[349] blessed by divine grace and the state of siege,[a] imposed a Constitution which was to be revised by the Chambers soon to be convened. As we know, the new representatives of the people suffered a fate similar to that of the old ones; the latter were dispersed by Wrangel's bayonets, the former received from Manteuffel a simple little notice of dissolution,[350] ordering them to go home. That put an end, too, to the revision of the Constitution.

Thus the Christian-Germanic sovereign and his accomplices, the whole host of lay-abouts, parasites and vampires sucking the blood of the people, whether of high-born lineage or without ancestry, whether decorated with orders or undecorated, have acquired free scope for planting whatever kind of fruit they like.

In November of last year, the royalty, bureaucracy and junkers were still compelled to use various hypocritical statements and to accept articles of the Constitution which seemed very liberal. The November Constitution had to be framed in a way that would make it possible to ensnare the numerically large, *stupid* part of the so-called "Prussian people".

*Now* all such subtle diplomatic considerations have become superfluous. Is not brother-in-law Nicholas already on German soil with 20,000 men? Has not Dresden been demolished by artillery shelling? Does there not exist the closest alliance of Prussia with the cowardly fugitive in Königstein, with imperial Max in Munich,[351]

---

[a] Frederick William IV.— *Ed.*

with the bulldog Ernest Augustus of Hanover, with the whole counter-revolutionary gang inside and outside Germany?

Certainly, this moment has been used by the Hohenzollern to the best advantage. He had a new Constitution drawn up for his "beloved" subjects, and he sanctioned and imposed it in Charlottenburg on May 10.

The latest royal-Prussian Constitution, *the only one sincerely intended*, which also has the advantage over the November Constitution of consisting of only seventeen paragraphs, reads as follows:....[a]

Written by Marx on May 12, 1849

First published in the *Neue Rheinische Zeitung* No. 297, May 13, 1849

Printed according to the newspaper

Published in English for the first time

---

[a] There followed the "Verordnung über den Belagerungszustand" ("Decree on the State of Siege") of May 10, 1849, which the *Neue Rheinische Zeitung* published under the heading "The Latest Prussian Constitution".— *Ed.*

# THE SANGUINARY LAW IN DÜSSELDORF

*Cologne*, May 12. The "new Constitution", the abolition of ordinary laws and law-courts, together with the announcement of murderous privileges conferred by the sovereign[a] on "My glorious army", already came into force in *Düsseldorf* yesterday.

After the defeat and massacre of the people, the commander immediately asked Berlin for instructions. From Herr von Hohenzollern's accomplices, Brandenburg-Manteuffel, an order was received by telegraph to proclaim the **sanguinary law** and to set up murderous military courts.

By Articles 1 and 6 of the army orders the right of association is abolished, and Articles 5, 6, 7, 24, 25, 26, 27, and 28, of the imposed "Schnaps" Charter[352] are made invalid.

Last year, under the rule of "citizen and communist" Drigalski,[353] when a state of siege was proclaimed the Düsseldorf press was put under *censorship*, a measure which gave rise to loud protests and great indignation even among the majority of the feeble Agreers' company. Today, after the new Hohenzollern achievements, when at the side of the subordinate *knyaz* in Potsdam there are no Chambers, but instead snub-nosed Cossack kinsmen, today the powers that be are not content with *censorship*, but proceed simply to *suppression* of the press.

According to Article 7, Düsseldorf newspapers, and the *Neue Rheinische Zeitung* as well, are *prohibited* in the Düsseldorf area. According to Article 8, nothing but official "information" may be published.

---

[a] Frederick William IV.—*Ed.*

Under "citizen and communist" Drigalski's rule by the sabre, the victims of arbitrary arrests were at least not removed from the jurisdiction of the ordinary law and its regular judges. Today the law and the courts have been suspended and murderous special military courts have been set up.

Article 9. Anyone who by word of mouth, in writing, in the press, or in representational form, incites resistance to the legal (!) orders of the authorities will come before a court martial.

Article 10. Anyone who is caught in open or armed resistance to the *measures* of the legal authorities, or who by traitorous action exposes the troops to danger or harm, *will be summarily shot in accordance with martial law.*

**The laurels of the murderer Windischgrätz allow no rest to the reinvigorated Hohenzollern!**

Written by Marx on May 12, 1849

First published in the *Neue Rheinische Zeitung* No. 297, May 13, 1849

Printed according to the newspaper

Published in English for the first time

# THE UPRISING IN THE BERG COUNTRY

*Cologne*, May 12. At the present time the attention of the entire Rhine Province is concentrated on Elberfeld, a place which is now raising the "banner of revolt" higher than any other Rhenish town.[a] The dissolution of the Chamber[354] was the signal for the movement in the otherwise so peaceful Wuppertal. The most addle-pated "wailers"[355] and the most miserable "hypocrites" had to admit that the guilt of the reaction exceeded all bounds, and carried away by the enthusiasm of those courageous workers whose energy we have never doubted, they have taken up arms and joined the ranks of those heroes on the barricades who are resolved to wage a struggle to the death against the monarchy.

In view of the confused reports which reach us from the battle arena itself, it is impossible to separate the truth from the lies. This much at least seems certain: that the whole population has taken up arms, that streets and houses are barricaded, that from neighbouring places—Solingen, Remscheid, Gräfrath, from localities of the Ennepe highway, in short, from the entire Berg Country—armed reinforcements are hurriedly arriving. It seems certain, too, that the insurgents are already not restricting themselves to the occupation of Elberfeld and Barmen but are extending their measures of defence to the most important points of the environs.

It is confidently asserted that the insurgents also plan to hasten to the aid of Düsseldorf in order to clear that city of Prussian troops. The army reserve, which now for the first time has definitely sided with the people, is playing the main role in these operations. The fighters do not lack munitions and money since several of the richest

---

[a] See this volume, pp. 423 and 428-29.— *Ed.*

merchants have readily opened their coffers. Thus, it is said that one trading house alone has given the Elberfeld Committee of Public Safety 500 friedrichsdors.

Under these circumstances, of course, it is not surprising that the royal mercenaries are getting ready to attack in order wherever possible to crush the people in the Berg Country as well and perpetrate the same atrocities as in Breslau, Dresden, Erfurt etc. It is to be hoped that this time things will turn out differently.

The artillery parked at Wesel will move from there to Elberfeld. It is said that the attack has been fixed for next Monday.

We cannot vouch for these reports. But whatever the plans of the counter-revolution may be, Elberfeld will have to face a struggle in which it can truly perform a great service to our country.

Written by Marx on May 12, 1849

First published in the *Neue Rheinische Zeitung* No. 297, May 13, 1849

Printed according to the newspaper

Published in English for the first time

# [THE VENAL BASENESS
# OF THE *KÖLNISCHE ZEITUNG*]

*Cologne*, May 13. We draw our readers' attention to the recent issues of the *Kölnische Zeitung*, in particular to today's issue, that of Sunday, May 13.

Probably never before has the "*most vulgar artlessness*" gone so closely hand in hand with *venal baseness* as in the latest leading articles and reports of our admirable contemporary.

Only a few days ago, at the congress of the Rhenish municipal councils,[356] we saw the *owner* of the *Kölnische Zeitung, Herr Joseph Dumont,* hastily rising to support the decisions adopted there. Today we see the same man, through his henchman Brüggemann, expressing in every line the most brutal pleasure at the failure of the revolts which were precisely the consequence of those decisions of the Rhenish municipal councils.

In return, however, the *Kölnische Zeitung* has also the good fortune to be *imposed* on the Rhenish towns, together with the state of siege, as their sole newspaper.

Truly, what is being simultaneously imposed on these towns is *blood and*—**dirt!**

Written by Marx on May 13, 1849

First published in the *Neue Rheinische Zeitung* No. 297 (second edition), May 13, 1849

Printed according to the newspaper

Published in English for the first time

# THE *KREUZ-ZEITUNG*

*Cologne*, May 15. The rascally Prussian newspaper does us the special favour of compiling an anthology of unpatriotic expressions published in the *Neue Rheinische Zeitung* about the "imperial-Russian subordinate *knyaz* in Olmütz" and the "Prussian bug-ridden knights".[a] The selection is limited to the dispatches from Breslau and is accompanied at the end by the following outburst of indignation of the covertly frivolous "crusader":

"Compared to this *Chimborazo insolence*, how flat is the announcement of the wedding of the Prussian King published in the French *Moniteur* in 1793: '*Le jeune tyran de Prusse vient d'épouser une demoiselle de Mecklenbourg*'!"[b]

In order to complete as fully as possible the account of the "Chimborazo insolence" of the *Neue Rheinische Zeitung*, we ask the rascally newspaper to be so good as to reprint the Premier-Cologne from No. 294 of our newspaper "The Deeds of the Hohenzollern Dynasty".[c] We hear that Frau von Hohenzollern[d] is a zealous reader of the rascally sheet and we do not adopt so "exclusive" an attitude that we begrudge the respectable lady some historical studies on the family of her spouse for her amusement.

Written by Marx on May 15, 1849

First published in the *Neue Rheinische Zeitung* No. 299, May 16, 1849

Printed according to the newspaper

Published in English for the first time

---

[a] See this volume, pp. 359 and 414.— *Ed.*

[b] "The young tyrant of Prussia recently married a young lady of Mecklenburg." (From a report in the section "Berliner Zuschauer" published in the *Neue Preussische Zeitung* [*Kreuz-Zeitung*] No. 107, May 10, 1849.) A reference to Luise von Mecklenburg-Strelitz.— *Ed.*

[c] See this volume, pp. 418-22. The Premier-Cologne—leading article datelined *Cologne.— Ed.*

[d] Queen Elizabeth, the wife of Frederick William IV.— *Ed.*

# [A NEW PRUSSIAN KICK
## FOR THE FRANKFURT ASSEMBLY]

*Cologne*, May 15. No sooner had the Holy Alliance of the knout imposed a brand-new state-of-siege Constitution on Prussia[a] than it favoured us today with a second document of no less interest. Those nationally-assembled milksops of Frankfurt, who by their radical philistinism, cowardice and doltishness so faithfully assisted the paid traitors of the German people for a whole year in working for the counter-revolution, are now reaping what they sowed.[357] If it were possible for some glimmer of light to occur in the minds of our National Assembly deputies, and for their breasts to be filled not merely with indignation inspired by March beer, but at least with a small degree of *revolutionary indignation and energy*, then that ought to be effected by the following "royal order" of the subordinate *knyaz* in Charlottenburg[358]:

*"Royal Order*

"We, Frederick William, by the grace of God King of Prussia etc. etc., hereby, on the proposal of our Ministry, order the following:

§1

"**The mandate of the deputies elected in the Prussian state to the German National Assembly on the basis of the Decrees of the German Confederation of March 30 and April 7, 1848, and of Our Order of April 11, 1848, has ceased to be valid.**

§2

"**This Our present Order is to be put before the deputies by Our Plenipotentiary in Frankfurt am Main for their guidance and with the**

---

[a] See this volume, pp. 430-31.— *Ed.*

**directive to refrain from any participation in the further proceedings of the Assembly.**

"Given in Charlottenburg, May 14, 1849

*Frederick William*
Count von Brandenburg, von Ladenberg, von Manteuffel,
von Strotha, von der Heydt, von Rabe, Simons"

Written by Marx on May 15, 1849

First published in the special supplement
to the *Neue Rheinische Zeitung* No. 299,
May 16, 1849

Printed according to the newspaper

Published in English for the first
time

# THE NEW MARTIAL-LAW CHARTER

[*Neue Rheinische Zeitung* No. 299, May 16, 1849]

*Cologne*, May 15. We still have to report on the latest paternal intentions of the subordinate *knyaz* in Potsdam[a] towards his "hereditary" subjects, acquired by plunder and traffic in people. We are referring to the newly *imposed martial-law Charter*,[b] this sole true promise of all the Hohenzollern promises, in which Prussian glory is at last revealed even to the most stupid and credulous simpletons in its fullest natural nakedness, divested of the last traces of its hypocritical comedian's tinsel.

The dispersal of the inoffensive Berlin Chambers, which were supposed to "*revise*" the imposed Constitution of December 5, was only, as is well known, the necessary preparation for the Russians' entry into German territory. But the agreement arrived at between the Potsdam Bashkirs and the kindred dog-nosed Cossacks of the orthodox Tsar had another purpose besides that of the notorious Trinity's campaign against Hungary,[359] in which Prussia, true to its cowardly, perfidious nature, stood at the gates like a police agent with orders for arrests, while the Austrian and Russian executioners were intended to institute the murder hunt within the country. The true aim of this Hohenzollern alliance was through the entry of the Russians to inspire the Potsdam hero with the necessary *courage to take revenge* on the revolution for the *confession of* **cowardice** *wrung from him in March of last year*.

We have no need to make excursions into history in order to prove the innate and natural *cowardice* of the Hohenzollerns at all times, nor perhaps do we even need to go back to the ancestors of this noble

---

[a] Frederick William IV.— *Ed.*
[b] See this volume, pp. 430-31.— *Ed.*

clan who ambushed unarmed travellers from behind bushes and hedges, and thus as highwaymen laid the foundations for the "splendour of the dynasty". Nor do we need to recall the boastful campaign of Frederick William II against the French Republic, in which the great Hohenzollern was the first to turn tail thus betraying the German "imperial troops" in order together with Russia to set about a new rape of Poland [360]; still less is it necessary for us to mention the pitiful role his successor, Frederick William III, played in the imperial wars before driving "His people" into battle with the aid of lying promises.[a] The history of the "March achievements" was only a continuation of the old "hereditary" cowardice and perfidy. The Agreement Assembly was the first concession made by this *cowardice* to the revolution, a concession which superseded the famous boasting about a "scrap of parchment" [361]; the Assembly was dispersed when the fall of Vienna gave the reinvigorated Hohenzollern the necessary courage for that action. The imposed Constitution with the Chambers that were "to revise" the Constitution was the second act of cowardly hypocrisy, since the "unweakened Crown" [362] at that time still considered a few liberal concessions to be necessary. The [Second] Chamber was dismissed when the conspiracy with the Russian Tsar and master[b] had reached the desired conclusion. But only the *actual* entry of Russians into German territory, only the *reliable* proximity of the protecting Cossacks, gave the Hohenzollern the courage to come out with the latest plan: abolition of the last hypocritical "constitutional guarantees" by the introduction of the most unrestricted, most arbitrary sabre dictatorship, by the suspension of the old, even the pre-March, laws and law-courts, by revenge with "gunpowder and lead" on the revolution for the cowardice of the Hohenzollerns proclaimed in the March concessions.

That is the historical origin of the recently imposed martial-law Constitution. Let us now look at its content.

Under Articles 1 and 2, "for the event of a disturbance" not only every commandant of a fortress can declare his fortress to be in a state of siege, but every "commanding general" can declare *the whole area occupied by the army corps* to be in a state of siege.

"For the event of a disturbance", *c'est-à-dire*, if the commandant or general sees fit to foresee the "event of a disturbance". Or is it possible that the Hohenzollern Ministers, in whose stylistic exercises the most remarkably abundant lack of grammatical knowledge usually predominates, intended to say: "in the event of a distur-

---

[a] See this volume, p. 419.— *Ed.*
[b] Nicholas. I.— *Ed.*

bance"? The interpretation will be left to the well-tested understanding of the generals and commandants.

"For the event of a disturbance", therefore, a commandant can declare his fortress, and a commanding general a whole province, to be in a state of siege. The limits of this "event" are not defined. Whether the "event of a disturbance" must show itself within the fortress or province or needs only threaten the fortress or province from a greater or lesser distance—that, too, will have to be decided only by the "tact" of the general or the commandant, and "tact", according to the weighty word of Lieutenant-General Tietzen, is the first requirement of a Prussian officer.

But the power of the general "for the event of a disturbance" has, on the other hand, been most remarkably restricted in the interests of all enthusiasts for the legal basis. Only "for the event of a war" are generals and commandants *on their own initiative* able to declare provinces and fortresses in a state of siege. "For the event of a disturbance", however, according to Article 2 of the new Charter, the proclamation of a state of siege emanates from the Ministry; "for this event" the commandant has the right to declare his fortress, and the general his province, in a state of siege only *provisionally,* subject to being confirmed or (!) rescinded by the Ministry. A pleasant safeguard for subjects threatened by a disturbance! Do we not have "responsible" Ministers? Is not the "legal basis" saved by the merely "provisional power" of the commandant's or general's dictatorship, by the existence of a final instance in the person of the "responsible" Minister? True, under Articles 7 and 13 the "provisional power" of the commandant or general gives them the right *provisionally* to suspend the ordinary law-courts, *provisionally* to set up courts martial, which then, likewise *provisionally,* pass *death sentences* (Article 8) and *provisionally* carry out the death sentences within 24 hours (Article 13, § 7). But the "legal basis" is always saved by the final confirmation of the "responsible" Minister—long live the legal basis! Our sole secret wish in this context is that the advocates of the legal basis should be the first to experience *provisional* execution in the name of God and His Majesty the Christian-Germanic subordinate *knyaz.*

[*Neue Rheinische Zeitung* No. 300, May 17, 1849]

*Cologne,* May 16. Cervantes somewhere talks about a worthy *alguacil*[a] and his clerk, who for the protection of public morality kept

---

[a] A Spanish police agent.— *Ed.*

two women of no ambiguous reputation.[a] These obliging nymphs appeared at big fairs or other festive occasions in such attire that already from far off the bird could be recognised by its plumage. If they managed to entrap some new arrival they immediately contrived to inform their lovers of the hotel to which they had gone. The *alguacil* and his clerk then broke into the room to the immense fright of the women, created a jealous scene and allowed the stranger to escape only after long pleading and payment of a suitable monetary compensation. In this way they combined advantage for themselves with the interests of public morality, for the victim took care for some time not to give way to his improper inclinations.

Like these guardians of morality, the Prussian heroes of order have a simplified procedure for ensuring normal tranquillity under martial law. The provocative dispatch of some pillars of legality reeking of liquor, a few provocative sabre blows among the people, and the rebellious desires thereby aroused in some remote town or village provide an opportunity for proclaiming a state of siege and thus safeguarding the *whole province* against further improper disturbances and cheating it of its last remnant of constitutional rights.

Under Article 5 of the new martial-law Charter, on the proclamation of a state of siege the "military commander" can *district by district* invalidate Articles 5-7 and 24-28 of the latest "acquisitions" imposed in December.

Let us see what still remains when we subtract from the March promises the Articles abolished by the imposition of the new martial-law Charter. "For the event of a disturbance" by the arbitrary decision of a "military commander" there cease to exist:

Article 5 of the December Constitution: "*Freedom of the person* is guaranteed."
Article 6: "The home is *inviolable.*"
Article 7: "No one may be deprived of his *legally appointed* judge."
Article 24: "Every Prussian has the right etc. freely to express his *thoughts.*"
Article 25: "Offences committed by word of mouth, writing etc. are punishable in accordance with the *general* penal laws."
Article 26: "If the author of a written work is known and within reach of the power of the court, the printer, publisher and distributor are *not liable to punishment.*"
Article 27: "All Prussians have the right to assemble peacefully and without weapons in *closed premises.*"
Article 28: "All Prussians have the right to unite in *societies* for purposes which do not contravene the penal laws."

As soon as a military commander proclaims a state of siege, "for the event of a disturbance", "freedom of the person" is *no longer*

---

[a] M. Cervantes, "Coloquio de los perros" in *Novelas ejemplares.—Ed.*

guaranteed, homes are *no longer* declared inviolable, the "*legal*" courts, freedom of the press, protection of printers, and the right of association, cease, and even the "*societies*" of the philistines—casinos and balls—whose "purposes do not contravene the penal laws", can only exist *par grâce de M. le commandant,* but not at all by "right".

At the same time Article 4 of the new martial-law Charter lays down that

> "with the proclamation of the state of siege" (*pur et simple*) "the executive power is transferred to the *military* commander, and the civil-administrative and municipal authorities must *carry out* the orders and *commissions* of the military commander".

By this paragraph all the usual forms of municipal and administrative government are safely abolished and the oxen of the snub-nosed, arrogant bureaucracy harnessed under the yoke of the sovereign military dictatorship as "lackeys for executing *commissions*".

Articles 8 and 9 contain the punishments by which the energetic Hohenzollern intends to defend his safety and order even when he is protected by bayonets and guns. This new penal law has at any rate the advantage of brevity over all the tediously agreed theories of law.

> Article 8: "Anyone who in a place or region declared to be in a state of siege is guilty of deliberate arson, of deliberately causing an *inundation*" (what prudence!), "or who uses open violence and dangerous weapons to attack or *resist the military forces or representatives of the civil and military authorities,* **will be punished by death.**"

"Resistance to the military forces or representatives of the authorities"! The deeds of "My glorious army" are well known; it is known also that the worthy Pomeranians, Prussians and Upper Silesian Poles, who in the interest of unity are being so zealously grafted into the Western provinces, following the example of His Majesty, derive their courage only from the circumstances and after having disarmed the citizens, as in Düsseldorf, Breslau, Posen, Berlin, and Dresden, they crown the state of siege by the murder of unarmed men, women and children.[a] Hence the "hereditary" subjects of the Potsdam Bashkir *knyaz* are given the highly commendable freedom, after a state of siege has been proclaimed, either to allow themselves to be "lawfully" murdered by the courageous executors of the benevolence of the sovereign, or by offering "resistance" to allow themselves to be shot in accordance with martial law.

---

[a] See this volume, pp. 429 and 435.— *Ed.*

Ought we also to discuss the provisions of Article 9, by which the dissemination of reports which "mislead" the authorities and the *violation* of any "*prohibition* issued in the interests of public security" etc. are punishable by up to one year's imprisonment, and even the most ordinary police and gendarme functions are henceforth made more perfect in accordance with martial law?

Ought we to deal with the cowardly perfidy with which the Hohenzollern sovereign, and his accomplices Simons-von der Heydt-Manteuffel decree the formation of courts martial consisting of *three* "senior officers" and two civil judges *appointed* by the military commander, in order to preserve the semblance of "legal" procedure in the eyes of the stupid bourgeois and yet at the same time to be sure of a conviction owing to the preponderance in the number of military executioners?

Ought we to take note of the various provisions of Article 13 on "procedure at courts martial", in which there is nowhere any mention of the testimony of witnesses, but under which judgment can obviously be pronounced in the spirit of the murderer Windischgrätz "in accordance with the *coincidence* of circumstances"?

Ought we to take note of the provisions that there is no appeal against sentences of courts martial, that death sentences are merely confirmed by the "military commander" and are carried out within twenty-four hours, and lastly that *even after the lifting of the state of siege*, in cases where sentences of courts martial have not yet been carried out, the "ordinary courts" can only convert the court-martial punishment into a legally imposed punishment, but must "*accept* the fact *as proven*" and cannot decide on the correctness or incorrectness of the charge?

Ought we, finally, to examine the last and best Article of this new Constitution which has been strengthened by the Cossacks, according to which "*even apart from the state of siege*", consequently "**not** for the event of a disturbance", Articles 5, 6, 24-28 of the December acquisition, "personal freedom", "inviolability of the home", "freedom of the press" and the "right of association" can be *abolished district by district?*

After all these splendid things there is no need for us to express our heartfelt good wishes to all well-intentioned Prussians on the new, *solely true* promises, on the finally true outburst of paternal benevolence resulting from the proximity of the Cossacks. We sincerely rejoice at this bloody castigation of the bourgeois who are so frantic for order, and of the miserable dolts who yearn for a basis of legality.

But the people will soon feel that this new "acquisition" has filled
its cup to overflowing, it will wreak vengeance on this lying cowardly
race that plagues the land, and the Rhine Province above all will not
let slip the long-desired hour when we shall cry out: *Ça ira!*[363]

> The pitiful ranks of knights
> Will soon be riding off.
> **They shall be offered a stirrup-cup**
> **From bottles of iron to quaff!**[a]

| | |
|---|---|
| Written by Marx on May 15 and 16, 1849 | Printed according to the newspaper |
| First published in the *Neue Rheinische Zeitung* Nos. 299 and 300, May 16 and 17, 1849 | Published in English for the first time |

---

[a] Heinrich Heine, *Deutschland. Ein Wintermärchen*, Caput VIII.— *Ed.*

# [ELBERFELD]

*Cologne*, May 16. The *Neue Rheinische Zeitung*, too, was represented at the Elberfeld barricades.[364]

In order to refute various false rumours, we owe it to our readers to give them a brief report on this matter.

On May 10, *Friedrich Engels*, editor of the *Neue Rheinische Zeitung*, went from Cologne to Elberfeld and took with him from Solingen two cases of cartridges which had been captured by the Solingen workers at the storming of the arsenal of Gräfrath. On arriving in Elberfeld, Engels made a report to the Committee of Public Safety on the situation in Cologne, and put himself at the disposal of the Committee. The military commission at once entrusted him with the management of fortification works by issuing the following authorisation:

"The military commission of the Committee of Public Safety hereby empowers Herr Friedrich Engels to inspect all the barricades in the town and to complete the fortifications. All posts at the barricades are hereby requested to assist him wherever necessary.

"Elberfeld, May 11, 1849

(signed) *Hühnerbein, Troost*"

On the following day the artillery too was put at his disposal.

"Citizen F. Engels is hereby empowered to instal artillery at his discretion, and also to requisition the artisans necessary for this purpose, the costs involved being borne by the Committee of Public Safety.

"Elberfeld, May 12, 1849

Committee of Public Safety
On behalf of which
(signed) *Pothmann, Hühnerbein, Troost*"

On his very first day in Elberfeld, Engels organised a company of sappers and completed the building of barricades at several exits from the town. He attended all the meetings of the military commission and proposed that it appoint Herr *Mirbach* as Chief Commandant, which was unanimously agreed to. In the following days Engels continued his activity, he made changes to a number of barricades, decided on the positions for new ones, and strengthened the sapper companies. From the moment of Mirbach's arrival, Engels put himself at his disposal and took part also in the war councils held by the Chief Commandant.

During his whole stay in Elberfeld, Engels enjoyed the absolute confidence of the armed workers of the Berg Country and the Mark, as also of the volunteer corps.

On his very first day in Elberfeld, Engels was asked by Herr Riotte, a member of the Committee of Public Safety, about his intentions. Engels stated that he had come, firstly, because he had been sent there from Cologne; secondly, because he believed that he could perhaps be usefully employed in a military respect; and, thirdly, because, having been born in the Berg Country, he considered it a matter of honour to be there when the first armed uprising of the people of the Berg Country took place. He said that he desired to concern himself exclusively with military matters and to have nothing to do with the political character of the movement, since it was obvious that up to now only a movement under the black-red-and-gold flag[a] was possible here, and therefore any action against the imperial Constitution had to be avoided.

Herr Riotte was in full agreement with this statement.

On the morning of the 14th, while Engels was accompanying Chief Commandant Mirbach to a general muster on the Engelnberg, Herr Höchster, also a member of the Committee of Public Safety, approached him and stated that although there was absolutely nothing to be said against his behaviour, nevertheless his presence evoked the utmost alarm of the Elberfeld bourgeoisie; they were afraid that at any moment he would proclaim a red republic and that by and large they wished him to leave.

Engels said that he wanted neither to impose his services, nor cravenly to desert his post, and he requested, without otherwise undertaking any kind of obligation, that the above-mentioned request should be presented to him in black and white, over the signatures of all members of the Committee of Public Safety.

---

[a] The colours symbolise Germany's unity, and in this case they denote the unification of the country in accordance with the imperial Constitution.— *Ed.*

Herr Höchster put the matter before the Committee of Public Safety and on the same day the following decision was adopted:

"*While fully appreciating* the activity hitherto shown in this town by Citizen Friedrich Engels of Barmen, recently resident in Cologne, it is requested that he should from today leave the precincts of the local municipality *since his presence could give rise to misunderstandings as to the character of the movement.*"

Already before the decision was adopted Engels stated that he would comply with the request of the Committee of Public Safety only if Mirbach ordered him to do so. Mirbach had arrived in Elberfeld at his suggestion, and therefore he could not leave before Mirbach had released him.

On the morning of the 15th, after considerable pressure from the Committee of Public Safety, Mirbach finally signed the requisite order, which was later also made public in the form of a poster.

The armed workers and volunteer corps were highly indignant at the decision of the Committee of Public Safety. They demanded that Engels should remain and said they would "protect him with their lives". Engels himself went to them and calmed them down, referring them to Mirbach and stating that he did not intend to be the first to refuse obedience to the Commandant who had been invited at his suggestion and in whom, moreover, he had absolute confidence.

Engels then took part in one more reconnaissance of the environs and, after handing over his post to his adjutant, departed from Elberfeld.

Let the workers of the Berg Country and the Mark, who have shown such astonishing affection for and devotion to a member of our editorial board, bear in mind that the present movement is only the prologue to another movement a thousand times more serious, in which the issue will concern their own, the workers', most vital interests. This new revolutionary movement will be the result of the present movement and as soon as it occurs Engels—on this the workers can confidently rely—like all the other editors of the *Neue Rheinische Zeitung*, will be at his post, and no power on earth will induce him to forsake it.

Written by Engels on May 16, 1849

First published in the *Neue Rheinische Zeitung* No. 300 (second edition), May 17, 1849

Printed according to the newspaper

Published in English for the first time

# [THE WORTHY SCHWANBECK]

One of the editors of the *Kölnische Zeitung*, worthy Schwanbeck, has issued a statement[a] about his misfortunes in Elberfeld, in which he also alleges that an "editor of the *Neue Rheinische Zeitung*"[b] acted as an informer against him. All that the editor of the *Neue Rheinische Zeitung* referred to knows about the affair is as follows. Whilst holding an official appointment in Elberfeld,[c] he was asked by a member of the Committee of Public Safety to identify two gentlemen who claimed to have come from Cologne and who were being detained in the cells at the town hall; one of these gentlemen was none other than worthy Schwanbeck. He declared in the presence of the latter that he would make it his business to see that that gentleman was to be expelled from the town the next morning, which was indeed done. He also recounted to his friend, the member of the Committee of Public Safety, an episode concerning Herr Schwanbeck's connection with Police Inspector Brendamour, which had already been made public by Herr C. Cramer in the *Wächter am Rhein*.[d] That was the extent of the "informing".

Incidentally whether, as worthy Schwanbeck maintains, "there is nothing to spy on in Elberfeld", no one is in a better position to say than the Prussian officer who is still detained as a spy in Elberfeld and who was promptly arrested whilst roaming around there under a false name.

<table>
<tr><td>Written by Engels on May 16, 1849</td><td>Printed according to the newspaper</td></tr>
<tr><td>First published in the *Neue Rheinische Zeitung* No. 300 (second edition), May 17, 1849</td><td>Published in English for the first time</td></tr>
</table>

---

[a] *Kölnische Zeitung* No. 117, March 17, 1849.— *Ed.*
[b] Frederick Engels.— *Ed.*
[c] See this volume, pp. 447-49.— *Ed.*
[d] Cramer, C., "Polizeispione", *Der Wächter am Rhein* No. 51, May 6, 1849.— *Ed.*

# [THE SUMMARY SUPPRESSION OF THE *NEUE RHEINISCHE ZEITUNG*][365]

*Cologne*, May 18. Some time ago Berlin demanded that the local authorities re-introduce a state of siege in Cologne. It was intended to use martial law to suppress the *Neue Rheinische Zeitung*, but this met with unexpected resistance. The municipal authorities of Cologne then turned to the Public Prosecutor's office here in order to achieve the same purpose by arbitrary arrests. But this failed on account of the legal scruples of the judiciary, just as it had failed twice before on account of the common sense of the Rhenish juries.[366] There was nothing for it but to resort to a *police ruse*, and this, for the time being, has achieved its purpose. *The "Neue Rheinische Zeitung" ceases publication for the present.* On May 16, its editor-in-chief *Karl Marx* received the following government note:

"The tendency of the *Neue Rheinische Zeitung* to provoke in its readers contempt for the present government, and incite them to violent revolutions and the setting up of a social republic has become stronger in its latest pieces" (!). "The right of hospitality" (!) "which he so disgracefully abused is therefore to be withdrawn from its editor-in-chief, Dr. *Karl Marx*, and since he has not obtained permission to prolong his stay in these states, he is ordered to leave them within 24 hours. If he should not comply voluntarily with this demand, he is to be forcibly conveyed across the frontier.

"*Cologne*, May 11, 1849

Royal Government
*Moeller*

To Herr *Geiger*, Royal Police Superintendent, here."

Why these absurd phrases, these official lies?

The trend and tone of the latest pieces of the *Neue Rheinische Zeitung* do not differ a whit from its first "sample piece". In that "first piece" we wrote among other things:

"The project of Herr Hüser" (in Mainz) "is only part of the grand plan of the Berlin reactionaries who seek to ... deliver us defenceless into the hands of the army."[a]

*Eh bien, Messieurs, qu'en dites-vous maintenant?*[b]

As to our tendency, did not the Government know it? Have we not declared before the jury that it was now "*the duty of the press to undermine the whole basis of the existing order*"[c]? Regarding the Hohenzollern subordinate *knyaz* one can read the following in the issue of October 19, 1848:

"The King is consistent. He would always have been consistent had it not been for the unfortunate fact that the March days interposed that fateful scrap of paper between His Majesty and the people. At this moment His Majesty, just as he did before the March days, seems again to believe in Slavdom's '*legs of iron*'; and perhaps the people in Vienna will turn out to be the magician who will transform the iron into clay."[d]

*Est-ce clair, Messieurs?*[e]

And the "*social republic*"? Have we proclaimed it only in the "latest pieces" of the *Neue Rheinische Zeitung*?

Did we not speak plainly and clearly enough for those dullards who failed to see the "*red*" thread running through all our comments and reports on the European movement?

The November 7 issue of the *Neue Rheinische Zeitung* says, "Assuming that *arms* will enable the counter-revolution to establish itself in the whole of Europe, *money* would then kill it in the whole of Europe. European *bankruptcy*, *national bankruptcy* would be the fate nullifying the victory. Bayonets crumble like tinder when they come into contact with the salient 'economic' facts. But developments will not wait for the expiry of the bills of exchange drawn by the European states on the new European society.

"The crushing counter-blow of the June revolution will be struck in *Paris*. With the victory of the '*red*' republic in Paris, *armies* will be rushed from the *interior* of their countries to the frontiers and across them, and the *real strength* of the fighting parties will become evident. We shall then remember this June and this October and we too shall exclaim:

---

[a] See the article "Hüser" (present edition, Vol. 7, p. 20).— *Ed.*

[b] Well, gentlemen, what do you say now?— *Ed.*

[c] "The First Trial of the *Neue Rheinische Zeitung*"; Speech by Karl Marx (present edition, Vol. 8, p. 317).— *Ed.*

[d] Marx, "Reply of the King of Prussia to the Delegation of the National Assembly" (present edition, Vol. 7, pp. 474-75).— *Ed.*

[e] Is that clear, gentlemen?— *Ed.*

"**Vae victis!**[a]

"The purposeless massacres perpetrated since the June and October events, the tedious offering of sacrifices since February and March, the very cannibalism of the counter-revolution will convince the nations that there is only one means by which the murderous death agonies of the old society and the bloody birth throes of the new society can be *shortened,* simplified and concentrated, and *that* is by *revolutionary terror.*"[b]

*Est-ce clair, Messieurs?*

From the very beginning we did not consider it necessary to conceal our views. During a polemic with the judiciary here, we told you:

"*The actual opposition of the 'Neue Rheinische Zeitung' only begins with the tricolour republic.*"[c]

And at that time we were speaking with the prosecution. We summed up the old year, 1848, in the following words (cf. the issue of December 31, 1848):

"The history of the Prussian bourgeoisie, like that of the German bourgeoisie in general between March and December, shows that a purely *bourgeois revolution* and the establishment of *bourgeois rule* in the form of a *constitutional monarchy* is impossible in Germany, and that only a feudal absolutist counter-revolution or a *social republican revolution* is possible."[d]

Did we therefore have to advance our social republican tendency only in the "last pieces" of the *Neue Rheinische Zeitung*? Did you not read our articles about the *June revolution,*[e] and *was not the essence of the June revolution the essence of our paper?*

Why then your hypocritical phrases, your attempt to find an impossible pretext?

*We have no compassion and we ask no compassion from you. When our turn comes, we shall not make excuses for the terror.* But the *royal terrorists,* the terrorists by the grace of God and the law, are in practice brutal, disdainful and mean, in theory cowardly, secretive and deceitful, and in both respects *disreputable.*

---

[a] Woe to the conquered!— *Ed.*

[b] Marx, "The Victory of the Counter-Revolution in Vienna" (present edition, Vol. 7, pp. 505-06).— *Ed.*

[c] Marx, "Public Prosecutor 'Hecker' and the *Neue Rheinische Zeitung*" (present edition, Vol. 7, p. 488).— *Ed.*

[d] Marx, "The Bourgeoisie and the Counter-Revolution" (present edition, Vol. 8, p. 178).— *Ed.*

[e] See present edition, Vol. 7, pp. 124-27, 130-49.— *Ed.*

The Prussian Government's piece of paper goes even to the absurd length of speaking about the "*right of hospitality which was disgracefully abused*" by *Karl Marx,* the editor-in-chief of the *Neue Rheinische Zeitung.*

The right of hospitality which the insolent intruders, the anterior Russians (Borussians), forced upon *us, inhabitants of the Rhineland,* on our own land—this hospitality was indeed "disgracefully" abused by the *Neue Rheinische Zeitung.* We believe that we have thereby rendered a service to the Rhine Province. We have saved the revolutionary honour of our country. From now on the *Neue Preussische Zeitung* alone will enjoy the full right of citizenship in the Rhine Province.

In parting we should like to remind our readers of the words printed in the first issue we published in January:

"The table of contents for 1849 reads: **Revolutionary rising of the French working class, world war.**"[a]

And in the East, a revolutionary army made up of fighters of all nationalities already confronts the alliance of the old Europe represented by the Russian army, while from Paris comes the threat of a "red republic".

Written by Marx on May 18, 1849          Printed according to the newspaper

First published in the *Neue Rheinische Zeitung* No. 301, May 19, 1849

---

[a] Marx, "The Revolutionary Movement" (present edition, Vol. 8, p. 215).—*Ed.*

# [HUNGARY]<sup>367</sup>

*Cologne,* May 18. At a moment when the actual entry of Russian troops turns the Magyar war into a *European* war, we are compelled to discontinue our reports on its further course. The only thing we can still do is once more to provide a brief survey of the development of this grand East-European revolutionary war for our readers.

It will be remembered that in the autumn of 1847, even before the February revolution, the Diet at Pressburg,<sup>368</sup> under the leadership of *Kossuth,* adopted a number of revolutionary decisions, such as those providing for the right to sell landed property, the peasant's right to live where he likes, the commutation of feudal obligations, the emancipation of the Jews and equal taxation of all classes. On the very day the February revolution began in Paris (February 22) the Diet permitted Croats and Slavonians when dealing with their internal affairs to use their own language for official purposes and finally, by demanding a separate responsible ministry for Hungary, it made the first step towards a *separate Hungary.*

The February revolution broke out, and with it came the collapse of the resistance of the Viennese Government to the demands of the Hungarians. On March 16, the day after the Viennese revolution, consent was given for the formation of an independent Hungarian Government thereby reducing the association between Hungary and Austria to a mere personal union.

The now independent Magyar revolution made rapid progress. It abolished all political privileges, introduced universal suffrage, did away with all feudal obligations, labour services and tithes without payment—compensations being payable by the state—brought about the union with Transylvania and compelled the appointment of Kossuth as Minister of Finance and the dismissal of the rebellious Ban Jellachich.

Meanwhile the Austrian Government recovered from the blow. While the supposedly responsible ministry at Vienna remained powerless, the camarilla at the Innsbruck Court grew steadily more powerful. It relied on the imperial army in Italy, on the national desires of the Czechs, Croats and Serbs and on the stubborn narrow-mindedness of the Ruthenian [369] peasants.

The Serbian insurrection, instigated with the help of money and emissaries from the Court, broke out in the Banat and Bacska on June 17. On the 20th Jellachich had an audience with the Emperor at Innsbruck and was reappointed Ban. Jellachich returned to Croatia, renounced allegiance to the Hungarian Government and on August 25 declared war against it.

The treachery of the Habsburg camarilla was plainly evident. The Hungarians tried once more to persuade the Emperor to return to constitutional methods. They sent a deputation of 200 members of the Diet to Vienna; the Emperor replied evasively. Feeling ran high. The people demanded guarantees and forced a change in the Government. Traitors, who sat in the Pest Government too, were removed, and on September 20 Kossuth was appointed Prime Minister.[370] But only four days later the Palatine Archduke Stephan, the representative of the Emperor, escaped to Vienna and on the 26th the Emperor issued the well-known manifesto to the Hungarians[371] in which he declared that the Government was rebellious and dismissed it, appointing the Magyarophobe Jellachich governor of Hungary and encroaching on the most important revolutionary gains of Hungary.

The manifesto, not having been countersigned by an Hungarian Minister, was declared null and void by Kossuth.

Meanwhile Jellachich, taking advantage of the disorganisation and treachery prevailing among the nominally Hungarian, but in reality old imperial, officers and general staff, advanced as far as Stuhlweissenburg. There he was defeated by the Hungarian army, despite its treacherous leaders, and driven back into Austrian territory to the very walls of Vienna. The Emperor and the old traitor Latour then decided to send reinforcements to Jellachich and to reconquer Hungary with the aid of German and Slav troops. But the revolution broke out in Vienna on October 6, and for the time being put an end to the royal imperial schemes.

Kossuth immediately marched with a Magyar corps to the assistance of the Viennese people. At the Leitha he was prevented

from moving immediately on Vienna by the indecision of the
Vienna Imperial Diet, the treachery of his own officers and the bad
organisation of his army, which consisted for the most part of the
*Landsturm.* He was finally obliged to arrest more than a hundred
officers, send them to Pest and have some of them shot. Only after
this did he dare to attack. But it was too late—Vienna had already
fallen, and his undisciplined *Landsturm* men were thrown back at
Schwechat by the regular Austrian troops.[372]

The truce between the imperial troops and the Magyars lasted six
weeks. While both armies did their utmost to strengthen their forces,
the Olmütz camarilla carried out a coup which it had been preparing
for a long time. It forced the idiot Ferdinand—who had compromised himself by concessions to the revolution and was now
useless—to abdicate and placed on the throne Sophia's son, the boy
Francis Joseph, whom it intended to use as its tool. On the basis of
the Hungarian Constitution the Pest Diet rejected this change of
sovereigns.

Finally in the middle of December the war started. Hungary by
then was practically surrounded by the imperial army. The offensive
was launched from all sides.

From Austria three army corps, no less than 90,000 strong, under
the supreme command of Field Marshal Windischgrätz, advanced
southward from the Danube. Nugent with about 20,000 men
marched from Styria along the left bank of the Drava. Dahlen with
10,000 men marched from Croatia along the right bank of the Drava
to the Banat. Several border regiments, the garrison of Temesvar,
the Serbian *Landsturm* and the Serbian auxiliary corps of Kničanin,
totalling 30,000 to 40,000 men commanded by Todorovich and
Rukavina, fought in the Banat itself. Puchner with 20,000-25,000
men was in Transylvania as was also Malkowsky with 10,000-15,000
men, who had invaded it from the Bukovina. Finally Schlick with a
corps of 20,000-25,000 men moved from Galicia towards the Upper
Theiss.

The imperial army thus numbered at least 200,000 regular, mostly
battle-hardened troops, not counting the Slav, Romance and Saxon
*Landsturm* men and national guards who took part in the fighting in
the south and in Transylvania.

Against this colossal fighting force Hungary could pit an army of
perhaps 80,000-90,000 trained soldiers, including 24,000 men who
had formerly served in the imperial army, and in addition 50,000 to
60,000 poorly organised Honveds[373] and *Landsturm* men. This army
was commanded for the most part by traitors similar to the officers
whom Kossuth had had arrested at the Leitha.

But whereas Austria, a country kept down by force, financially ruined and almost moneyless, could not yield another recruit for the time being, the Magyars still had great resources at their disposal. The Magyars' enthusiasm for liberty, reinforced by their national pride, waxed stronger every day, providing Kossuth with eager fighters in numbers unheard-of for such a small nation of 5 million. The Hungarian printing-press placed inexhaustible financial resources in the form of banknotes at Kossuth's disposal and every Magyar accepted these national assignats as if they were hard silver coin. Rifle and gun production was in full swing. All the army lacked was weapons, experience and good leaders, and all this could be procured in a few months. It was therefore only necessary to gain time, to entice the imperial troops into the heart of the country where they would be worn down by unceasing guerilla warfare and weakened by having to leave behind strong garrisons and other detachments.

Hence the plan of the Hungarians to withdraw slowly into the interior, to train the recruits in continuous skirmishes and as a last resort to place between themselves and their enemies the Theiss line with its impassable swamps, which form a natural moat around the heart of the Magyar lands.

According to all calculations, the Hungarians should have been able to hold the area between Pressburg and Pest for two to three months even against the superior strength of the Austrians. But severe frosts suddenly set in, and for several months all rivers and swamps were covered with a thick layer of ice capable of bearing the weight even of heavy guns. This deprived the terrain of all features favouring defence, and made all fortifications built by the Magyars useless and liable to be outflanked. And so it happened that before twenty days had passed the Hungarian army was thrown back from Oedenburg and Pressburg to Raab, from Raab to Mor, from Mor to Pest, and even had to leave Pest and withdraw beyond the Theiss at the very beginning of the campaign.

The other corps fared no better than the main army. In the south Nugent and Dahlen continued their advance towards Esseg, which was occupied by the Magyars, and the Serbs gradually approached the Maros line; in Transylvania Puchner joined Malkowsky at Maros-Vásárhely; in the north Schlick descended from the Carpathians to the Theiss and made junction with Windischgrätz at Miskolcz.

The Austrians seemed to have practically put an end to the Magyar revolution. They had two-thirds of Hungary and three-fourths of Transylvania in their rear, the Hungarians were attacked in front, on both flanks and in the rear. A further advance of a few miles[a] would have enabled all the corps of the Emperor to make junction and draw the ring tighter until Hungary was crushed in it as in the coils of a boa constrictor.

It was essential now—while on the front the Theiss still formed an insuperable barrier to the enemy—to gain some breathing space on one flank or another.

This was done at two points: in Transylvania by Bem, and in Slovakia by Görgey. Both carried out operations which show that they are the most gifted commanders of our time.

On December 29, Bem arrived at Klausenburg, the only town in Transylvania still held by the Magyars. Here he quickly concentrated the reinforcements he had brought and the remnants of the defeated Magyar and Szekler[374] troops, and marched to Maros-Vásárhely, defeated the Austrians and drove Malkowsky first across the Carpathians into the Bukovina and from there into Galicia, where he pushed on towards Stanislav. Then, swiftly turning back into Transylvania he pursued Puchner to within a few miles of Hermannstadt. After several skirmishes and a few swift drives in various directions, the whole of Transylvania was in his hands apart from two towns, Hermannstadt and Kronstadt, and these too would have been taken if the Russians had not been called in. The 10,000-strong Russian auxiliary troops tipped the scales and forced Bem to fall back on Szeklerland. There he organised an uprising of the Szeklers, and having succeeded in this, he had the Szekler *Landsturm* engage Puchner, who had reached Schässburg, while he bypassed Puchner's positions, moved straight on Hermannstadt and drove the Russians out, then defeated Puchner who had followed him, marched on Kronstadt and entered it without firing a shot.

Transylvania was thus won and the rear of the Magyar army cleared. The natural defence line formed by the Theiss now found its continuation and complement in the Carpathian mountain range and the Transylvanian Alps, from the Zips down to the borders of the Banat.

Görgey at the same time made a similar triumphal march in North-Western Hungary. He set out with a corps from Pest to Slovakia, for two months kept in check the corps of generals Götz, Csorich and Simunich operating against him from three directions, and finally, when his position became untenable against their superior forces, fought his way through the Carpathians to Eperies and Kaschau. There he appeared in the rear of Schlick and forced

---

[a] See footnote on p. 20.— *Ed.*

him hurriedly to abandon his position and his whole operational base and retreat to Windischgrätz's main army, while he himself was already marching down the Hernad to the Theiss to join the main body of the Magyar army.

This main army, which was now commanded by Dembiński, had likewise crossed the Theiss and had repulsed the enemy all along the line. It had reached Hatvan, six miles from Pest, when a stronger concentration of enemy forces compelled it to retreat again. After offering vigorous resistance at Kapolna, Maklar and Poroszlo it recrossed the Theiss just at the moment when Görgey reached the Theiss at Tokaj. The union of the two corps was the signal for a new magnificent advance of the Hungarians. Newly trained recruits arriving from the interior strengthened the Hungarian army in the field. Polish and German legions were formed, capable leaders had been trained or enlisted, and in place of the leaderless, unorganised mass of December, the imperial troops were suddenly faced by a concentrated, brave, and numerous army which was well organised and excellently led.

The Magyars crossed the Theiss in three columns. The right wing (Görgey) moved northwards, outflanked the Ramberg division, which had been following it, at Eperies and quickly drove this division back through Rimaszombat towards the main imperial army. The latter was defeated by Dembiński at Erlau, Gyöngyös, Gödöllö and Hatvan, and hastily retreated to Pest. Finally the left wing (Vetter) dislodged Jellachich from Kecskemét, Szolnok and Szegléd, defeated him at Jász-Berény and compelled him, too, to retreat to the walls of Pest. There the imperial forces stood along the Danube from Pest to Waitzen, surrounded in a wide semi-circle by the Magyars.

To avoid exposing Pest to bombardment from Ofen, the Hungarians had recourse to their well-tried tactics of dislodging the Austrians from their positions by manoeuvres rather than by open frontal attacks. Görgey captured Waitzen and forced the Austrians to fall back beyond the Gran and Danube; he defeated Wohlgemuth between the Gran and Neutra, thereby relieving Komorn, which was besieged by imperial troops. Since its line of retreat was threatened, the imperial army had to decide on a hurried withdrawal. Welden, the new Commander-in-Chief, retreated in the direction of Raab and Pressburg, and Jellachich was obliged, in order to pacify his extremely refractory Croats, to hastily retreat with them down the Danube into Slavonia.

During their retreat, which rather resembled a stampede, Welden (and especially his rearguard commanded by Schlick) and Jellachich suffered further considerable reverses. While the latter's hard-pressed corps was slowly fighting its way through the Tolna and Baranya comitats, Welden was able at Pressburg to concentrate the remnants of his army which were by no means capable of offering any serious resistance.

Simultaneously with these astonishing victories of the Magyars over the main Austrian army, Moritz Perczel pressed forward from Szegedin and Tolna towards Peterwardein, relieved it, occupied Bacska and moved into the Banat, in order to link up there with Bem who was advancing from Transylvania. Bem had already taken Arad and besieged Temesvar; Perczel stood at Werschetz close to the Turkish frontier; the Banat was thus conquered in a few days. The fortified Transylvanian mountain passes were at the same time held by the Szeklers, the passes in Upper Hungary by the *Landsturm*, and Görgey with a considerable army stood at the Jablunka Pass on the Moravian-Galician frontier.

In short, in a few more days the victorious Magyar army, driving the remnants of the mighty Austrian legions before it, would have entered Vienna in triumph and put an end to the Austrian monarchy for all time.

Hungary's separation from Austria had been decided in Debreczin on April 14[375]; the alliance with Poland, openly proclaimed since the middle of January, was turned into reality by the 20,000-30,000 Poles who joined the Hungarian army. The alliance with the German Austrians, which had existed since the Viennese revolution of October 6 and the battle at Schwechat, was similarly preserved and sustained by the German legions within the Hungarian army, as well as by the fact that the Magyars were faced with the strategic and political necessity of occupying Vienna and revolutionising Austria so as to secure recognition of their declaration of independence.

Thus, the Magyar war very soon lost the national character it had had in the beginning, and assumed a clearly European character, precisely as a result of what would seem to be a purely national act, as a result of the declaration of independence. Only when Hungary proclaimed her separation from Austria, and thereby the dissolution of the Austrian monarchy, did the alliance with the Poles for the liberation of both countries, and the alliance with the Germans for the revolutionisation of Eastern Germany acquire a definite character and a solid basis. If Hungary were independent, Poland restored, German Austria turned into the revolutionary focus of Germany, with Lombardy and Italy winning independence—these plans, if carried out, would destroy the entire East-European system of states: Austria would disappear, Prussia would disintegrate and Russia would be forced back to the borders of Asia.

The Holy Alliance,[376] therefore, had to make every effort to stem the impending revolution in Eastern Europe—the Russian armies rolled towards the Transylvanian and Galician frontiers; Prussia occupied the Bohemian-Silesian frontier and allowed the Russians to pass through her territory towards Prerau, and within a few days the first Russian army corps stood on Moravian soil.

The Magyars, who clearly understood that in a few weeks they would have to deal with numerous fresh troops, did not advance on Vienna as quickly as was expected at the beginning. They could not take Vienna, just as they could not take Pest, by a frontal attack without shelling the city, and this they were not prepared to do. Again, as at Pest, they were compelled to resort to outflanking manoeuvres, and this required time and the assurance that their own flanks and rear were secure. But it was here that the Russians menaced their rear, while if Vienna were in direct danger strong detachments of Radetzky's army could be immediately expected from the other direction.

The Hungarians therefore acted very wisely when, instead of advancing swiftly on Vienna, they confined themselves to steadily forcing the imperial armies out of Hungary, enveloping them in a wide arc from the Little Carpathians to the foot-hills of the Styrian Alps, dispatching a strong corps towards the Jablunka, fortifying and covering the Galician mountain passes, attacking Ofen and rapidly proceeding with the recruitment of 250,000 men, especially from the reconquered western comitats. In this way they secured their flanks and rear and assembled an army which had no more need to fear the Russian contingents than the once colossal imperial army. 200,000 soldiers of this redoubtable black-and-yellow[a] army had invaded Hungary and barely 50,000 of them had returned; the rest were either killed, wounded, sick, taken prisoner or had changed sides.

True, the Russians threaten to send even more gigantic armies. Some speak of 120,000 soldiers, others of 170,000. According to the *Triester Freihafen,* the mobile army in the field is expected considerably to surpass 500,000 men. But Russian exaggerations are well known: of the figures they give only half are on the nominal rolls, and of the numbers on the nominal roll again less than half are really there. If, after deducting the number of troops required for the occupation of Poland, the effective Russian aid amounts to from

---

[a] The Austrian imperial colours.— *Ed.*

60,000 to 70,000 men, the Austrians can be glad. And the Magyars will be able to deal with that number.

The Magyar war of 1849 has strong points of resemblance with the Polish war of 1830-31.[377] But the great difference is that the factors which were against the Poles at that time now act in favour of the Magyars. Lelewel, as we know, unsuccessfully urged, first, that the mass of the population be bound to the revolution by emancipating the peasants and the Jews, and secondly, that all three partitioning powers be involved in the war and this war turned into a *European* war, by raising an insurrection throughout the old Polish territories. *The Magyars started at the point* which the Poles only achieved when it was *too late.* The Hungarians' first measure was to carry out a social revolution in their country, to abolish feudalism; their second measure was to involve Poland and Germany in the war, thus turning it into a European war. It started with the entry of the first *Russian* corps into German territory, and will take a decisive turn when the first *French* battalion enters German territory.

By becoming a European war, the Hungarian war is brought into reciprocal interaction with all other factors of the European movement. Its course affects not only Germany, but also France and England. The English bourgeoisie cannot be expected to let Austria become a Russian province and it is certain that the French people will not calmly look on while the counter-revolution comes closer and closer to attacking them. Whatever the outcome of the French elections,[378] the army at any rate has declared for the revolution. And the army today is the decisive force. If the army wants war—and it does want it—then war it will be.

War will come. Paris is on the threshold of revolution, whether as a result of the elections or of the army's fraternisation with the revolutionary party at the ballot-box. While in Southern Germany the core of a German revolutionary army is being formed, which prevents Prussia from taking an active part in the Hungarian campaign, France is on the point of playing an active role in the struggle. A few weeks, perhaps even a few days, will decide everything, and soon the French, the Magyar-Polish, and the German revolutionary armies will celebrate their fraternisation on the battlefield before the walls of Berlin.[379]

Written by Engels on May 18, 1849        Printed according to the newspaper

First published in the *Neue Rheinische Zeitung* No. 301, May 19, 1849

# ["TO MY PEOPLE"]

*Cologne,* May 18. "To my people!"[a] Not—"To my glorious army!"[380] Have the Russians perhaps been defeated? Has the wind shifted and once again, as in March of last year, knocked the military cap from the head of the "unweakened" servant of Russia? Are the "loyal subjects", living under a state of siege, once more in full rebellion?

When in 1813 the old "monarch of blessed memory"[b] likewise derived from the *advance of the Cossacks* the necessary courage to shake off his abject cowardly role and the bloody punishments of the revolutionary empire, then—in spite of the Cossacks, Bashkirs and the "glorious army" made famous by battles at Jena and Magdeburg and by the surrender of Küstrin to 150 Frenchmen—it was only the lying promises of an "*Appeal to My People*"[381] which made possible the crusade of the Holy Alliance against the successors to the French revolution. And now! Has not the reinvigorated Hohenzollern, as a result of the incursion of the Cossacks into German territory, obtained sufficient courage to renounce his cowardly role of the post-March period and to cancel the "scrap of paper interposed between him and his people" owing to the revolution?[382] Has not "My glorious army" in Dresden, Breslau, Posen, Berlin, and on the Rhine, worthily wreaked vengeance on the revolution by the valiant slaughter of unarmed men, women and children with shrapnel and caustic?[383]

Have not the last cowardly concessions made in March—abolition of censorship, freedom of association, arming of the people—once

---

[a] Appeal issued by Frederick William IV on May 15, 1849.— *Ed.*
[b] Frederick William III.— *Ed.*

more been abolished by the recently imposed martial-law Constitution,[a] "*even apart from the state of siege*"?

No, the son of the hero of Jena and Magdeburg still does not feel safe enough in spite of the alliance with the Cossacks, in spite of the privileges in regard to murder and courts martial afforded to the uncurbed "glorious" military horde. *The unweakened Crown is afraid, it appeals "To my people", it "feels compelled" to address an appeal for help and support against "internal and external enemies" to the downtrodden besieged "people"* which has been battered by grapeshot.

"In these difficult times, Prussia is called upon to protect Germany against internal and external enemies. Therefore, I call My people to arms already now. It is a matter of establishing law and order in our state and in the other German states where our help is required; it is a matter of creating Germany's unity, of protecting her freedom from the rule of terror of a party that is ready to sacrifice morality, honour and loyalty to its passions, a party which has succeeded in casting a net of delusion and folly over a section of the people."

"That is the gist of the royal address," exclaims the filthy police agent Dumont,[b] and the venal police *claqueurs* of Dumont have indeed discovered the "gist".

"External enemies"! By that is meant the "party of terror", the party which terrifies the valiant Hohenzollern, the party which demands our interference in the "*other* **German** *states*". The people of the Rhine Province, Silesia and Saxony are called upon "in the name of German *unity*" to put an end to the revolutionary movements in the foreign *German* states of Baden, Bavaria, and Saxony! And to this end the bait with which the Hohenzollern gladdened the hearts of the people in 1813 is repeated, the well-tried "royal word" is pledged once again, promising the "people" a castrated recognition of the Frankfurt Constitution, promising them the "protection of law and liberty" against "godlessness". "I and My house wish to serve the lord." [384] Is the well-tried pledge of a "Hohenzollern's royal word" not worth a crusade against the "party which terrifies the Crown that promises so much"?

The powerful subordinate *knyaz* of imperial Russia recalled the Prussian deputies from Frankfurt only in order now, in accordance with his March promises, to put himself "at the head of Germany". The Agreement Assembly and the imposed Chamber were dismissed, the "scrap of paper" was replaced by a martial-law Constitution and murderous military courts solely in order to guarantee the people the "protection of law and liberty!"

---

[a] See this volume, pp. 440-46.— *Ed.*

[b] "Die Ansprache des Königs", *Kölnische Zeitung* No. 118, May 18, 1849.— *Ed.*

And freedom of the press has been suppressed, *censorship* has been imposed on the press in Erfurt, newspapers are directly banned throughout Posen, in Breslau, in the Silesian provincial towns, and even the *National-Zeitung* in Berlin. In Düsseldorf censorship has been re-introduced *de jure*, but the press has been totally abolished *de facto* (the Düsseldorf newspapers, the *Neue Rheinische Zeitung* etc.), and finally only the police cesspool of the *Kölnische Zeitung* and the rascally newspaper in Berlin[a] were imposed on the "free" subjects. All this has been done so that there should not be the slightest doubt about the value of the "royal word".

And the word of the Hohenzollern does indeed merit that the people don military uniforms to strengthen the royal courage so as to procure—under the army reserve law—a royal bounty of one taler monthly for the wives they leave behind as a "safeguard against begging".

Written on May 18, 1849

First published in the *Neue Rheinische Zeitung* No. 301, May 19, 1849

Printed according to the newspaper

Published in English for the first time

---

[a] *Neue Preussische Zeitung (Kreuz-Zeitung).— Ed.*

# TO THE WORKERS OF COLOGNE[385]

Finally we warn you against any revolt in Cologne. In the military situation obtaining in Cologne you would be irretrievably lost. You have seen in Elberfeld that the bourgeoisie sends the workers into the fire and betrays them afterwards in the most infamous way. A state of siege in Cologne would demoralise the entire Rhine Province, and a state of siege would be the inevitable consequence of any rising on your part at this moment. The Prussians will be frustrated by your calmness.

In bidding you farewell the editors of the *Neue Rheinische Zeitung* thank you for the sympathy you have shown them. Their last word everywhere and always will be: **emancipation of the working class!**

**The Editorial Board of the *Neue Rheinische Zeitung***

Written on May 18, 1849

First published in the *Neue Rheinische Zeitung* No. 301, May 19, 1849

Printed according to the newspaper

# Neue
# Rheinische Zeitung
## Organ der Demokratie.

№ 301.     Köln, Samstag, den 19. Mai.     1849.

## Abschiedswort der Neuen Rheinischen Zeitung.

Kein offner Hieb in offner Schlacht —
Es fällen die Rücken und Tücken
Es fällt mich die schleichende Niedertracht
Der schmutzigen West-Kalmücken!
Aus dem Dunkel flog der tödtend Schaft,
Aus dem Hinterhalt fielen die Stiche —
Und so lieg' ich nun da in meiner 'raft,
Eine stolze Rebellenleiche!

Auf der Lippe den Trotz und den zuckenden Hohn,
In der Hand den blitzenden Degen,
Noch im Sterben rufend: „Die Rebellion!"
So bin ich mit Ehren erlegen.
O gern wohl besträuten mein Grab mit Salz,
Der Preuße zusammt dem Czare —
Doch es schicken die Ungarn, es schickt die Pfalz
Drei Salven mir über die Bahre!

Und der arme Mann im zerriß'nen Gewand,
Er wirft auf mein Haupt die Schollen!
Er wirft sie hinab mit der fleißigen Hand,
Mit der harten, der schwielenvollen.
Einen Kranz auch bringt er aus Blumen und Mai'n,

Zu rub'n auf meinen Wunden;
Den haben sein Weib und sein Töchterlein
Nach der Arbeit für mich gewunden.

Nun Ade, nun Ade, du kämpfende Welt,
Nun Ade, ihr ringenden Heere!
Nun Ade, u pulvergeschwärztes Feld,
Nun Ade, or Schwerter und Speere!
Nun Ade - doch nicht für immer Ade!
Denn sie tödten den Geist nicht, ihr Brüder!
Bald richt' b mich rasselnd in die Höh',
Bald kehr' b reißiger wieder!

Wenn die letzte Krone wie Glas zerbricht,
In des Kampfes Wettern und Flammen.
Wenn das Volk sein letztes „Schuldig!" spricht,
Dann stehn wir wieder zusammen!
Mit dem Wort, mit dem Schwert, an der Donau, am Rhein, —
Eine allzeit treue Gesellin
Wird dem Throne zerschmetternden Volke sein
Die Geächtete, die Rebellin!

**F. FREILIGRATH.**

## An die Arbeiter Kölns.

Wir warnen Euch schließlich vor jem Putsch in Köln. Nach der militärischen Lage Kölns wäret ihr rettungslos verloren. Ihr habt in Elberfeld gesehen, wie die Bourgeoisie Arbeiter ins Feuer schickt und sie hinterher aufs Niederträchtigste verrath. Der Belagerungszustand in Köln würde die ganze Rheinprova demoralisiren und der Belagerungszustand wäre die nothwendige Folge jeder Erhebung von Eurer Seite in diesem Augenblicke. Die Preußenhorden an Eurer Ruhe verzweifeln.

Die Redakteure der Neuen Rheinien Zeitung danken Euch beim Abschiede für die ihnen bewiesene Theilnahme. Ihr letztes Wort wird überall und immer sein: Emanzipation der arbeitenden Klasse!     **Die Redaktion der Neuen Rhein. Zeitung.**

## Deutschland.

※ Köln, 18. Mai. Vor einiger Zeit wurde vollends auf agrarie dürftige Behörde die Forderung gestellt, amtlich den Belagerungszustand über Köln zu verhängen, die „Neue Rheinische Zeitung" [...]

## Proklamation an die Frauen.

Seit dem 1. Juni 1848, wo die „Neue Rhein. Zeitung" wie ein fremmer Wundervstern drohend und prächtig in Ländern und Herren herausstieg und wo das Frauleein wie humoristischer Kommenistand einherzrin flackerte, daß dieser Feuergeweih so unwiderstehlg [...]

Eine Polizeithate seine Zuflucht zu nehmen und man hat für den Augenblick seinen Zweck erreicht. Die Neue Rheinische Zeitung dört erscheinen [...]

„In ihrem neuesten Stücken (3) tritt die N. Rh. 3. mit der Aufreizung zur Verachtung der bestehenden Regierung, zum gewaltsamen Umsturz und zur Einführung der socialen Republik offenbar hervor. Es ist daher ihrem Redacteur en chef, dem Dr. Karl Marx, das Gastrecht (!), welches er so [...]

Köln, den 11. Mai 1849.

König. Regierung.
Weiler

An den König. Polizeidirektor Herrn Geiger hier.

**Georg Weerth.**

The last issue of the *Neue Rheinische Zeitung* (No. 301, May 19, 1849) which was printed in red ink

# KARL MARX
and
# FREDERICK ENGELS

## ARTICLES AND STATEMENTS

May-July 1849

Neue

Deutsche Zeitung.

Organ der Demokratie.

№ 129.  Frankfurt. Samstag, 2 Juni  1849.

## Karl Marx

### LETTER
### TO THE *FRANKFURTER JOURNAL*

The esteemed Editorial Board of the *Frankfurter Journal* is requested to print the following statement in its newspaper in large type and in a prominent position, and if this is only possible on payment for its insertion, please obtain the amount from Herr J. Weydemeyer, editor of the *Neue Deutsche Zeitung*.

Bingen, May 31

**Dr. Karl Marx**

### STATEMENT[386]

The *Editorial Board of the "Neue Rheinische Zeitung"* owes its correspondents and the public the statement that it has nothing in common with the news-sheet published in *Cologne* under the title *Westdeutsche Zeitung*. The undersigned editorial board reserves to itself the right to communicate further when and where the *Neue Rheinische Zeitung* will again make its appearance.

**The Editorial Board of the *Neue Rheinische Zeitung***
***Karl Marx, Ernst Dronke, Friedrich Engels,***
***F. Freiligrath, Georg Weerth, F. Wolff, W. Wolff***

The Statement was published in the *Neue Deutsche Zeitung* Nos. 129 and 133, June 2 and 7, 1849; and in the *Neue Kölnische Zeitung* No. 126 (second edition), June 3, 1849

Printed according to the newspaper text checked against the manuscript; the covering letter is printed according to the manuscript

Published in English for the first time

12ter Jahrgang.
Der Bote erscheint täglich, und zwar das Hauptblatt
viermal, das Plauderstübchen dreimal.

Der

Erste Hälfte.
Halbjähriger Abonnementpreis 3 fl. 20 fr. im
ganzen Königreiche Bayern.

# Bote für Stadt und Land.

## Pfälzisches Volksblatt.

**Nr. 110.**     Kaiserslautern, Sonntag 3. Juni     **1849.**

## Frederick Engels

### [THE REVOLUTIONARY UPRISING
### IN THE PALATINATE AND BADEN][387]

*Kaiserslautern,* June 2. The counter-revolutionary German newspapers try in every way to cast suspicion on the revolution in the Palatinate and Baden. They are not ashamed to assert that the trend of the entire uprising is tantamount "to betraying" the Palatinate, Baden and, indirectly, the whole of Germany "to the French". They thereby seek to conjure up afresh the counter-revolutionary hatred of the French stemming from the so-called good old times, believing that in this way they will be able to deprive us of the sympathy of our brothers in North and East Germany. The filthy, lying newspapers which accuse the Palatinate and Baden of having sold themselves to France happen, however, to be precisely those which are in favour of the *Russian invasion* of Hungary, the Russians' march through Prussia, and even the new Holy Alliance[388] between Russia, Austria and Prussia. As proof of this, we name only one of these newspapers: the *Kölnische Zeitung.*

Thus, the fact that the Russians march into German, into Prussian, territory in order to suppress Hungarian freedom is no betrayal of the country! If the King of Prussia[a] concludes an alliance with the Croats and the Russians in order that the last remnants of German freedom shall be trampled under the hooves of Cossack horses, that is no betrayal of the country! If all of us, if the whole of Germany from the Niemen to the Alps is sold by cowardly despots to the Russian Emperor,[b] that is no betrayal of the country! But if the Palatinate enjoys the sympathy of the French and especially of the

---

[a] Frederick William IV.— *Ed.*
[b] Nicholas I.— *Ed.*

Alsatian people, if it does not out of foolish self-conceit reject the expression of this sympathy, if it sends persons to Paris to obtain information about the state of feeling in France and about the new turn which will take place in the policy of the French Republic,[389]—that is indeed betrayal of the country, that is high treason, and means selling Germany to France, to the "hereditary enemy", to the "enemy of the Empire". That is how the counter-revolutionary newspapers argue.

It is true, gentlemen "by the grace of God", that the Palatinate and Baden did do all this and neither of them will be ashamed of its actions. Of course, if that is betrayal of the country, then the entire people of the Palatinate and Baden consists of two-and-a-half million traitors to their country. The people of the Palatinate and Baden did certainly not make a revolution in order to support the despots in the imminent great struggle between the free West and the despotic East. The people of the Palatinate, and those of Baden, made their revolution because they do not want to share the guilt of the despicable acts in the destruction of freedom by which Austria, Prussia and Bavaria have so shamefully distinguished themselves in recent months, and because they have not allowed themselves to be misused for the enslavement of their brothers. The army of the Palatinate and Baden joined the movement without reservations; it disclaimed loyalty to the perfidious sovereigns and has to a man sided with the people. Neither the citizens nor the soldiers want to fight in the ranks of the Croats and Cossacks against freedom. If the despots of Olmütz, Berlin and Munich still find soldiers who have sunk so deep as to put themselves on a level with Bashkirs, Pandours,[390] Croats and similar predatory rabble, and to fight under the same flag as such hordes of barbarians, so much the worse. It may occasion us sorrow, but we shall never treat such mercenaries as German brothers; we shall treat them as Cossacks and Bashkirs, and it will not worry us if a treacherous imperial ex-Minister of War stands at their head.[391]

But at the present time when we are on the threshold of a European war, a *people's war,* it is altogether ludicrous to speak of "betrayal of the country" and similar accusations smacking of demagogue[392] hunting. In a few weeks, perhaps even in a few days, the huge armies of the republican West and the enslaved East will advance against each other to fight out a great struggle on German soil. Germany—to such lengths has she been brought by her sovereigns and the bourgeois—Germany will not be asked at all for her permission. Germany does not want the war, the war will be brought into this country without its consent and it will be unable to prevent it. Such is the glorious position of Germany in relation to the imminent European war, thanks to the March rulers, the March Chambers, and not least to the March National Assembly. There can be no talk of *German* interests, of *German* freedom, of *German* unity, of *German* welfare, when it is a question of the freedom or enslavement, of the weal or woe, of the whole of *Europe.* Here all questions of nationality cease, here there is only one question! Do you want to be *free,* or do you want to be *Russian?* And in this situation the counter-revolutionary newspapers still talk of "betrayal of the country", as if *there was still anything that could be betrayed* in relation to the Germany that will soon enough be abandoned to the two contending armies as an inert arena! It is true that last year things were different. Last year the Germans could have undertaken the struggle against Russian oppression, could have liberated the Poles and so waged the war on *Russian* territory and at *Russia's* expense. Now, on the contrary, thanks to our sovereigns, the war will be waged on *our* soil, and at *our* expense; as matters stand now, the European war of liberation is for Germany at the same time a civil war in which Germans fight against Germans.

We owe that to the treachery of our sovereigns and the supineness of our people's representatives, and if anything is betrayal of the country, it is that! In short, in the great struggle for freedom which is spreading through the whole of Europe, the Palatinate and Baden will stand on the side of freedom against slavery, of revolution against counter-revolution, of the people against the sovereigns, of revolutionary France, Hungary and Germany against absolutist Russia, Austria, Prussia and Bavaria; and if the wailers[393] call that betrayal of the country, in the whole of the Palatinate and the whole of Baden nobody cares two hoots about it.

Written on June 2, 1849

First published in *Der Bote für Stadt und Land* No. 110, June 3, 1849

Printed according to the newspaper

Published in English for the first time

Freiheit, Wohlstand, Bildung für Alle.

# Der Volksfreund.

## Eine Wochenschrift für Westfalen.

Redacteur: G. A. Wolff in Lemga.

№ 26.     Lemgo, den 29. Juni.     **1849.**

Der »Volksfreund« erscheint jeden Freitag und kostet in der Expedition (F. L. Wagener) vierteljährlich 6 Sgr. — Alle Postämter
und Buchhandlungen des In- und Auslandes nehmen Bestellungen auf das Blatt an. — Insertionen (Anzeigen) werden zu 8 P.
die gespaltene Zeile oder deren Raum aufgenommen.

## Karl Marx

## THE 13th OF JUNE [394]

*Paris*, June 21

You are sufficiently acquainted with the Paris population to realise *a priori* the absurdity of the accusation of cowardice. Nevertheless, I can understand that in Germany especially the day of June 13 remains completely enigmatic and is bound to give rise to all kinds of malicious misinterpretations.

The chief actor in the drama of June 13 was not the *people*, but the "Mountain". Behind the "Mountain", it is true, there was in turn a secret committee,[395] which pushed matters forward and more or less compelled Ledru-Rollin to play that particular role.

The chief error of the "Mountain" was its *certainty of being victorious*. It was so sure of this that it believed everything could be achieved by a peaceful demonstration. Thus it afforded the Government the opportunity of defeating it without having to strike a blow against it. The procession which made its way from Château d'eau through the boulevards was entirely unarmed. The Government, for its part, being fully informed on all details by its spies, had quietly and unnoticed arranged for all important points to be occupied by the National Guard, sharpshooters from Vincennes and other troops. The procession was completely encircled and even if it had been armed could not have offered any resistance. How much less could it do so, being unarmed! *Changarnier*, who had taken all necessary measures, was clever enough not to allow the alarm to be sounded. As if by magic, it was suddenly seen that all decisive points were occupied by troops. You can therefore understand that the unarmed masses quickly dispersed in order to get weapons, but even the arms depots which had been prepared in advance for the eventuality of an uprising were found to have been seized by the Government and put under military guard. The uprising was thus outwitted.

That is the whole secret of this unprecedented day in the history of the French revolution. You may perhaps have read in the German newspapers of *barricades* which were said to have been easily captured. These barricades consisted of nothing but a few chairs which were thrown on to the street in order to halt for a moment the cavalry which were attacking unarmed people with their sabres.

In addition, there were some other circumstances which made the shameful outcome of June 13 inevitable.

At the very moment when Ledru-Rollin and his colleagues in the Conservatoire des Arts[396] were occupied with constituting themselves as the Provisional Government, the secret socialist committee was engaged on the same task. It wanted to constitute itself as the Commune. Hence, even before the existing power was overthrown, the uprising had already split into two camps, and the important thing is that the *People's Party* was not the party of the "*Mountain*". This fact alone explains a great deal. The secret committee had wanted to start the outbreak already some days previously and by night. In that way the Government would have been taken by surprise. But the "*Mountain*" and the "Friends of the Constitution" (the party of the *National*)[397] allied with it were opposed to this. They wanted to have the initiative in their hands. Ledru-Rollin's speech in the Chamber[398] was to be the pledge that the "Mountain" had decided on serious action. Thus on the one hand, those advocating immediate vigorous action were frustrated and preparations were made for a peaceful demonstration. On the other hand, the people who saw that Ledru-Rollin had so strikingly committed himself in the National Assembly, believed he possessed immense connections within the army and a profoundly conceived and far-reaching plan etc. How surprised, therefore, they must have been when it became obvious that Ledru-Rollin's power was a mere illusion and that precautionary measures and preparations for an attack had been taken only by the Government. Thus you see how the two revolutionary parties paralysed and deluded each other. The people's recollections of the more than ambiguous behaviour of the "Mountain" and of Ledru-Rollin in particular during May and June,[399] and finally the cholera, which raged especially in the working-class districts, did the rest. Taken as a whole, June 13, 1849 is only the retaliation for June 1848. On that occasion the proletariat was deserted by the "Mountain", this time the "Mountain" was deserted by the proletariat.

However grievous June 13 is bound to be for our party throughout Europe, the good thing about that day is that, with the exception of Lyons,[400] the counter-revolutionary party in the National Assembly arrived at *sole power* without much bloodshed. That party will not only disintegrate, its extreme faction will soon reach a point when it will seek to discard even the irksome semblance of the Republic, and then you will see *how it will be blown away with a single breath and there will be a repetition of the February, but on a higher level.*

*K. M.x.*

Written on June 21, 1849

First published in the newspaper *Der Volksfreund* No. 26, June 29, 1849.

Printed according to the newspaper

Published in English for the first time

# Karl Marx

## TO THE EDITOR OF THE NEWSPAPER
### *LA PRESSE*[a]

Your item published in *La Presse* of July 26 concerning my stay in Paris, which has been reprinted word for word by other newspapers, contains such erroneous assertions that I am compelled to write a few lines in reply.

In the first place, the *Neue Rheinische Zeitung*, of which I was the owner[401] and editor-in-chief, was never banned. Its publication was suspended only for five days because of the state of siege. When the state of siege was lifted, the newspaper reappeared, and continued to appear during the following seven months. Since the Prussian Government could not see any possibility of legally prohibiting the newspaper it had recourse to a strange measure: It got rid of the owner, that is to say, it forbade me to reside in Prussia.[b] As regards the legality of this measure, this will be decided by the Prussian Chamber of Deputies which is shortly to meet.

After being forbidden to stay in Prussia, I went first of all to the Grand Duchy of Hesse, in which—as in other parts of Germany—I was not forbidden to reside. I did not go to Paris as a refugee, as your newspaper asserts, but of my own accord with a regular passport and with the sole aim of collecting additional material for my work on the history of political economy, which I had begun already five years earlier.[402]

---

[a] Émile de Girardin.— *Ed.*
[b] See this volume, p. 451.— *Ed.*

Neither was I ordered to leave Paris *immediately;* on the contrary, I was given time to address a complaint to the Minister of the Interior.[a] This complaint has been handed in and I now await the result.[403]

Kindly accept etc.,
**Dr. K. Marx**

Written about July 27, 1849

First published in the newspaper *La Presse*, July 30, 1849

Printed according to the newspaper

Translated from the French

Published in English for the first time

---

[a] J. A. S. Dufaure.— *Ed.*

17°

# Frederick Engels

## REPUDIATION [404]

It has come to the ears of the undersigned, who served in Willich's volunteer corps during the campaign in the Palatinate and Baden, that the following accusations are being made against that corps:

1) Willich's corps is said to have deserted Becker's in the Black Forest [405];

2) it is said not to have acknowledged Becker as commander-in-chief;

3) it is said to have crossed into Switzerland whilst Becker's corps was still eight German miles[a] behind.

As regards the first accusation, let the following facts speak for themselves: Willich was positioned in Furtwangen with orders to hold the Simonswalder Thal and the defiles leading to the Höllenthal. He advanced the larger part of his troops over the mountains towards Simonswald and St. Märgen. Becker was positioned in Triberg and St. Georgen, on Willich's right. To our great astonishment Becker suddenly appeared in Furtwangen with his whole corps. He explained this strange manoeuvre to Willich by saying that the troops stationed in Triberg had left their posts in defiance of their officers and he himself had gone after them, from St. Georgen, to persuade them to re-occupy Triberg. And in fact Becker and his corps did march off again towards evening. Meanwhile Willich went to headquarters in Donaueschingen to see how matters stood. The enemy, who had broken through to Villingen by crossing Württemberg, had already reconnoitred the territory up the road. In Donaueschingen it was first of all intended to take up a position near Hüfingen, an hour's march further back;

---

[a] In the manuscript the word "German" is written in pencil. For the "German mile" see footnote on p. 20.— Ed.

later, however, it was decided to retreat to the Swiss frontier and defend the Wutachthal. As soon as this decision was taken, Willich sent two dispatches to Furtwangen. From there the information was passed *first* to Becker and only then to Willich's companies, which were in advanced positions, although along the difficult mountain tracks it would take longer to reach the latter. By the time Willich's corps had assembled in Furtwangen, Becker could therefore also have arrived there. Willich himself went as far as Neustadt to meet his corps, and there he delayed departure until the arrival of two companies from Becker's corps. From Bondorf he sent another dispatch to Becker notifying him that the enemy was already advancing well towards Lenzkirch and that the route through Bondorf[a] was therefore to be preferred. And Becker did in fact take this route and reached Tiengen with his whole corps without being attacked, whilst Willich with one company and four cannon faced the enemy first forming the rearguard based on Stühlingen and later the right flank at Ofteringen and Wutöschingen. It is clear that there can be no question of any "desertion" here.

The second accusation refers to the fact that the captain of one of Willich's companies stationed in Furtwangen refused to leave the post where Willich had stationed him and to march with Becker. He acted rightly. Willich's corps had formed voluntarily and had put itself voluntarily under Willich's command. It consisted exclusively of men who knew what they were fighting for. It is self-evident that such a corps ceases to exist if it is broken up and dispersed. Furthermore, Willich had been specifically ordered to hold this position with his corps, and the withdrawal of the company in question would have thwarted all his arrangements.

The third accusation has even less foundation. It is public knowledge that at the last council of war held in Jestetten[406] Becker advocated crossing on to Swiss soil, whereas Willich was for continuing the struggle. It is public knowledge that from Tiengen Becker marched with the main part of the army to Baltersweil while Willich covered his retreat with 350 men and four cannon near Erzingen, and from Baltersweil to Jestetten whilst Willich occupied the position the army had vacated at Baltersweil. It is public knowledge that Willich remained for a further 24 hours with his corps in this position—the artillery had already left him—whilst Siegel crossed into Switzerland at Rafz and Becker a few hours later at Rheinau; that we only left the position after facing the enemy outposts for several hours without being attacked; that we spent that

---

[a] In the manuscript: "Lenzkirch"—evidently a slip of the pen.— *Ed.*

night still bivouacking on German soil and only entered Swiss territory the following morning[a]—the last to do so.

It is by no means our purpose to become involved in the unedifying disputes which have broken out between the various leaders of the Baden army. We merely ask that false reports should not be circulated about our corps and our leaders.

Canton Vaud, July 26, 1849

*Koehler*, Captain[b]

Written by Engels on July 26, 1849

First published in the *Beiträge zur Geschichte der deutschen Arbeiterbewegung* No. 2, 1967

Printed according to the manuscript

Published in English for the first time

---

[a] July 12, 1849.— *Ed.*

[b] The words "*Koehler*, Captain" are written in pencil and not in the same handwriting as the manuscript as a whole.— *Ed.*

# APPENDICES

# REPORT ON MARX'S EXPULSION
# SENT BY THE COLOGNE GOVERNMENT AUTHORITIES
# TO THE MINISTER OF THE INTERIOR
# VON MANTEUFFEL

Meanwhile Marx is still staying here, although furnished with neither residence permit nor card, and the newspaper of which he is editor continues with its destructive tendencies, deriding and ridiculing all that men normally respect and hold sacred, and urging the overthrow of the existing constitution and the establishment of a social republic, and its effects are all the more damaging since its impertinence and humour constantly attract new readers.

The earlier investigation into his affairs resulted in his acquittal, as did the one subsequently opened against him for direct incitement to rebellion.[407]

The commandant of the local fortress has now called on the police authorities to expel Marx from here as a dangerous person. We enclose the application in question, along with the report of the Police Superintendent,[a] and we can only concur with the latter's view that his expulsion from this town without his simultaneous removal from the Prussian state would achieve nothing; nor do we see any objection to proceeding forthwith with Marx's expulsion if he gives any specific cause. Whether on the other hand it would be expedient to expel him at the present moment merely on the grounds of the dangerous tendencies of the newspaper which he has been editing in like manner for some considerable period, appears to be more doubtful. It is possible that taking such a step might provoke a demonstration by the democratic party in sympathy with Marx. For this reason and because the Royal Ministry of the Interior had

---

[a] Geiger. See also this volume, pp. 496-97.— *Ed.*

previously seen fit in its directive of August 12[a] last to take note of the measures we have taken regarding Marx,[408] we consider it necessary to assure ourselves of Your Excellency's agreement as to the expulsion of Marx from the state before proceeding.

Written on March 10, 1849

First published in the *Frankfurter Zeitung und Handelsblatt* No. 176, June 27, 1913

Printed according to the manuscript

Published in English for the first time

---

[a] Presumably a slip of the pen; it should read September 12.— *Ed.*

# INVITATION
## OF THE DEMOCRATIC ASSOCIATION IN SOLINGEN TO MARX, FREILIGRATH, ENGELS, SCHAPPER AND WOLFF[409]

Solingen, March 11, 1849

To Herr Karl Marx, Editor-in-Chief
of the *Neue Rheinische Zeitung,*
Cologne

Dear Citizen,

In accordance with the decision of a general meeting of the Democratic Association here, a grand democratic banquet will be held here on the 18th inst. to celebrate the anniversary of the March revolution of last year.

Because of your devotion to this cause, we take the liberty of inviting you to participate in this festival, together with citizens Freiligrath, Engels, Schapper and Wolff, and ask you to be so good as to inform them, in the hope that you will respond to our invitation.

With our democratic fraternal greetings,

On behalf of the Festival Committee,
*H. Schaeffer*

P. S. In addition, we ask you to publish the accompanying announcement in the Wednesday issue of the *Neue Rheinische Zeitung* and to collect the payment for the insertion through the post-office from the undersigned.

On behalf of the above-named Committee,
*H. Schaeffer*

First published in *Der Bund der Kommunisten,* Bd. I, Berlin, 1970, S. 919

Printed according to the manuscript

Published in English for the first time

# BANQUET IN GÜRZENICH

*Cologne,* March 20. Yesterday evening a banquet was held in Gürzenich to mark the anniversary of last year's barricade battles in Berlin. Whereas even at the bourgeois concert of March 18 "to celebrate the promise" of a Constitution etc. etc., the biggest hall of our city was fairly well filled, yesterday there was not room enough to hold half the public streaming towards it. While 5,000-6,000 persons stood crowded in the hall side by side, several thousand more tried in vain to get in. The hall had filled so rapidly that even a number of speakers succeeded only after 9 o'clock in forcing their way through.

*Karl Schapper* was in the chair and opened the meeting with a toast to the sovereign people, the sole source of all legal power. Further toasts were drunk as follows: *H. Becker:* to the memory of those who died on March 18 and 19; Citizen *Wachter:* to the improvement of the German Michel; Citizen *Weyll:* to the *complete* revolution, not an incomplete one; Citizen *Rittinghausen:* to the downfall of the German Emperor; *C. Cramer:* to the democratic women present at our banquet; *W. Wolff,* editor of the *Neue Rheinische Zeitung:* to the Italian republics; *E. Dronke,* editor of the *Neue Rheinische Zeitung:* to the proletarian revolution; *P. Nothjung:* to the victory of the Magyars and Kossuth; *H. Bürgers,* editor of the *Neue Rheinische Zeitung:* to the overthrow of Austria; *F. Wolff,* editor of the *Neue Rheinische Zeitung:* to the accused on trial in Bourges[410]; *F. Engels,* editor of the *Neue Rheinische Zeitung:* to the June insurgents in Paris; *K. Schapper:* to the English Chartists and their revolutionary leaders, Ernest Jones and G. J. Harney; *Carl Cramer:* to the Poles; *Chr. Esser,* editor of the *Arbeiter-Zeitung*[a]: to the Red Republic.

---

[a] i.e. the newspaper *Freiheit, Brüderlichkeit, Arbeit.—Ed.*

The banquet, which went off entirely peacefully and orderly, concluded at about 11 p.m. with unanimous cheers for the Red Republic. In contrast to the concert held by the wailers,[411] in Gürzenich on March 18, we are glad to note that never before has there been a festival in Cologne which has brought together such a numerous and at the same time so judicious a public as that at the banquet held yesterday evening under the auspices of the red flag.

First published in the *Neue Rheinische Zeitung* No. 251, March 21, 1849

Printed according to the newspaper

Published in English for the first time

# LETTER
## FROM THE MINISTER OF THE INTERIOR VON MANTEUFFEL TO THE OBERPRÄSIDENT OF THE RHINE PROVINCE, HERR EICHMANN, TOGETHER WITH A COPY OF THE INSTRUCTIONS REGARDING THE EXPULSION OF MARX SENT TO THE ROYAL GOVERNMENT AUTHORITIES IN COLOGNE

To the Royal Oberpräsident,
His Honour Herr *Eichmann,*
at *Coblenz*

In response to the courteous communication of 29th ult. from Your Honour regarding the expulsion of *Dr. Carl Marx,* I have today dispatched the instructions to the Royal Government Authorities in Cologne, a copy of which I enclosed herewith for your information.

At the same time I grant Your Honour full discretion to issue the appropriate instructions to the said Government Authorities concerning those points which you most particularly wish to see observed in case of the expulsion of the aforesaid *Marx.*

Berlin, April 7, 1849

The Minister of the Interior

*v. Manteuffel*

*Copy*

To the Royal Government Authorities at Cologne

Consequent upon the report of 10th ult.,[a] for which the supporting documents are returned enclosed, I would reply to the Royal Government Authorities that I for my part see no objection to the proposed expulsion of *Dr. Carl Marx,* who is no longer a subject of this polity. The Royal Government Authorities however need no

---

[a] See this volume, pp. 487-88.— *Ed.*

special authorisation to this end; indeed it must be left to the latter to judge whether there is sufficient cause for such a step. It would seem desirable, it is true, to proceed with the expulsion of the aforesaid *Marx* on the direct occasion of a specific, unequivocal offence on his part; however, such an occasion is unlikely to be wanting, since, as I am informed, he has very recently once again evoked grave suspicion of treasonable activities endangering the state.[412]

Accordingly I simply leave the decision as to further action to the discretion of the Royal Government Authorities, and look forward to receiving a fuller account of the issue of the affair in due course.

Berlin, April 7, 1849

The Minister of the Interior
signed *v. Manteuffel*

First published in the *Zeitschrift für Geschichtswissenschaft*, Berlin, 1969, No. 5

Printed according to the manuscript

Published in English for the first time

# DECISIONS OF THE GENERAL MEETING
# OF THE COLOGNE WORKERS' ASSOCIATION
# HELD ON APRIL 16, 1849[413]

The meeting unanimously resolves:

1. To withdraw from the Union of Democratic Associations of Germany and to join instead the Union of German Workers' Associations, the Central Committee of which is in Leipzig.[414]

2. With the aim of a closer union of the purely social party, to authorise the Committee of the Workers' Association to convene in Cologne a provincial congress of all Workers' Associations of the Rhineland and Westphalia, prior to the holding of the general Workers' Congress in Leipzig.[a]

3. To send delegates to the Congress of Workers' Associations of Germany which will take place shortly in Leipzig.

First published in the newspaper *Freiheit, Brüderlichkeit, Arbeit* No. 22, April 22, 1849

Printed according to the newspaper

Published in English for the first time

---

[a] See this volume, p. 495.— *Ed.*

# FROM THE MINUTES OF THE COMMITTEE MEETING OF THE COLOGNE WORKERS' ASSOCIATION HELD ON APRIL 17, 1849

...5. In accordance with the decision of yesterday's general meeting: To convene here on the first Sunday in May a congress of representatives of all the Workers' Associations of the Rhineland and Westphalia.

For the implementation of this decision, the Committee appoints a provisional provincial committee of six members, consisting of citizens K. Marx, W. Wolff, K. Schapper, Anneke, Esser and Otto, and calls upon it to send invitations, with a statement of reasons, to the Associations concerned....

First published in the newspaper *Freiheit, Brüderlichkeit, Arbeit* No. 22, April 22, 1849

Printed according to the newspaper

Published in English for the first time

# LETTER
## FROM THE ROYAL GOVERNMENT AUTHORITIES IN COLOGNE TO THE OBERPRÄSIDENT OF THE RHINE PROVINCE, HERR EICHMANN, REGARDING THE EXPULSION OF MARX

*Cologne, April 19, 1849*
re. No. 2474

To the Royal Oberpräsident of the Rhine Province
His Honour Herr *Eichmann,*
at *Coblenz*

We have the honour to communicate to Your Honour a copy, enclosed, of the order issued to the local Police Superintendent relating to the expulsion of the writer *Carl Marx*, in execution of the directive of 13th inst.

Royal Government
Department of the Interior
*Birck   Wenzel*

To the Royal Police Superintendent
Herr *Geiger*, in *Cologne*

*Copy*

Following your report of 1st ult., for which the supporting documents are returned enclosed, we decided to ask the Minister of the Interior concerning the expulsion of *Dr. C. Marx*, informing him at the same time that although we were in no doubt that his expulsion from the state should be carried out forthwith if he gives any specific cause, but that on the other hand it was more doubtful whether his expulsion should take place merely on the grounds of the dangerous tendencies of the newspaper which he has been editing in like manner for some considerable period.[a] We hereby send you for your information a copy of the Minister's instructions of 7th inst.,[b] as communicated to us, and instruct you to arrange and carry out the expulsion of the aforesaid *Marx* from the state when direct cause is next given for such action by an unequivocal offence on the part of the aforesaid *Marx*. We would furthermore observe that we have no knowledge of the allegations which, as we are informed by the Minister, have quite recently brought upon the aforesaid *Marx* the grave suspicion of treasonable activities endangering the state,[415] and request you to apprise us forthwith of whatever knowledge you may have of them, so that we may determine whether to proceed with the expulsion on those grounds.

Cologne, April 19, 1849

Royal Government
Department of the Interior
(signed) *Birck*
Copy signed *Perker*

First published in the *Zeitschrift für Geschichtswissenschaft*, Berlin, 1969, No. 5

Printed according to the manuscript

Published in English for the first time

---

[a] See this volume, p. 451.— *Ed.*
[b] See this volume, pp. 492-93.— *Ed.*

# RESOLUTION OF BRANCH No. 1
## OF THE COLOGNE WORKERS' ASSOCIATION[416]

1. Considering that in the newspaper *Freiheit, Arbeit* Dr. Gottschalk describes Citizen Karl Marx as a friend and co-thinker of Franz Raveaux, deputy of the Assembly in Frankfurt, whereas Citizen Marx stated at the committee meeting of February 8 that, although at present he supported the candidature of Raveaux and Schneider II, he was a long way from agreeing with these persons in principle; that, on the contrary, the first named precisely during the period when he was most prominent was mercilessly attacked in the *Neue Rheinische Zeitung;* but that at the present moment there could be no question of red democrats and colourless democrats, since for the time being the main thing was to oppose the absolute monarchy, and to achieve this aim both red and colourless democrats would have to unite against the wailers;

2. furthermore, that Dr. Gottschalk took the opportunity of the Democratic Congress in Frankfurt[417] to state that he was able to utilise the Cologne workers just as much for a red monarchy as for a red republic, thus alleging that the workers themselves were merely a machine blindly obedient to him;

3. that the attacks against Raveaux in the above-mentioned newspaper are of a very base, malicious nature because they make his bodily infirmity a subject of reproach and call it a sham;

4. that the other attacks in the newspaper are for the most part wholly without foundation, and owing to their silliness are not even worth refuting, but nevertheless betray petty hatred and spite and the base, malicious character of their author;

5. that Dr. Gottschalk after his acquittal had a plan, about which he spoke to a number of members of the Workers' Association, to re-organise the Workers' Association and for this purpose to place

himself (as president), together with five others chosen by him as committee members, at the head of the Association, this betrays a despotic frame of mind and conflicts with the most elementary democratic principles;

6. that in attempting to set up such a new organisation he has deserted the party of the real proletarians, and has thrown himself into the arms of the petty bourgeois by desiring to raise the monthly subscriptions of members to five silver groschen;

7. that Dr. Gottschalk made changes in the newspaper of the Association, as a result of which its publication was interrupted for fourteen days,[418] without having been authorised to do so by the Association, in fact without even giving any direct notice of this to the Association or its Executive Committee; this is a violation of the rights of the Association that is totally unjustifiable and because of Dr. Gottschalk's departure shortly afterwards, it even cannot be defended on the grounds of necessity or urgent reasons;

8. that Dr. Gottschalk, after his acquittal, instead of fulfilling the expectations of the Cologne workers and resuming his previous progressive activity among them, to the astonishment of all went away without saying a single word of farewell to them or thanking them for their loyal support;

9. that Dr. Gottschalk, owing to excessive sensitivity, went into exile of his own accord, and from Brussels he issued a declaration which certainly could not serve in the least to explain or justify his behaviour, since in it he, a republican, speaks of his being called back either by "*the hitherto supreme arbiter in the country*" or by "*the voice of the people*",[419] therefore considering the supreme arbiter to be something other than the voice of the people as a whole; that by the supreme arbiter in this passage he could only have meant the King,[a] thereby putting himself directly on the side of the legitimists and monarchists; that, on the other hand, in this declaration he once again mocks the people by expecting that it would call back someone who acknowledges and appeals to a supreme arbiter other than the voice of the people itself; that he plays the part here of the most ignoble type of time-server, seeking to keep a path open for himself to both the King and the people;

10. that Dr. Gottschalk has not deigned to give any reply to the request of the Workers' Association that he should explain his so-called declaration, a declaration which is incomprehensible, and especially that he should state what he understands by "the hitherto supreme arbiter";

---

[a] Frederick William IV.— *Ed.*

11. that Dr. Gottschalk, without being called back by anyone, nevertheless returned to Germany, whereby the whole story of his voluntary banishment is dissipated into thin air and is bound to seem a badly calculated electoral manoeuvre, bearing in mind that in the meantime his brothers and friends have been working very actively for his election to the Berlin Assembly;

Considering all this, branch No. 1 of the Cologne Workers' Association declares:

that it in no way approves of Dr. Gottschalk's behaviour after his acquittal by the jury at the trial here, and that it emphatically and indignantly repudiates the imputation that the Workers' Association would allow itself to be misused in the interests of a red monarchy or misled by spiteful personal attacks on individuals, or permit a president with a subservient committee to be foisted on it, or call back a voluntary exile who, in order to be redeemed, appeals for clemency simultaneously to the King and to the people, or in general to allow any individual whoever he may be, to treat the Workers' Association as if it consisted of stupid boys.

First published in the newspaper *Freiheit, Brüderlichkeit, Arbeit* No. 24, April 29, 1849

Printed according to the newspaper

Published in English for the first time

# DECISIONS OF THE GENERAL MEETING OF THE COLOGNE WORKERS' ASSOCIATION HELD ON APRIL 23, 1849

1. The general meeting will be held in future every Wednesday.

2. The provisional committee, consisting of Karl Marx, Karl Schapper, Wilhelm Wolff, Friedrich Anneke, Esser and Otto, elected by the Committee for the purpose of convening here in Cologne a congress of the Workers' Associations of the Rhineland and Westphalia, is confirmed.

First published in the newspaper *Freiheit, Brüderlichkeit, Arbeit* No. 24, April 29, 1849

Printed according to the newspaper

Published in English for the first time

# REPORT ON THE CONVOCATION OF THE CONGRESS OF WORKERS' ASSOCIATIONS

Recently, a number of its members has resigned from the district committee of the Democratic Associations of the Rhine Province, and simultaneously the Workers' Association here has announced its withdrawal from the Union of Rhenish Democratic Associations.[a] This step is due to the conviction that, in view of the heterogeneous elements in the Associations in question, there is little to be expected from them that would be advantageous for the interests of the working class or the great mass of the people.

The more urgent, therefore, is it firmly to unite the homogeneous elements, and to bring about vigorous cooperation of all the Workers' Associations.

As the first measure for this purpose, the Workers' Association here considers it necessary to set up a provisional committee of all the Workers' Associations of the Rhine Province and Westphalia, and it appoints the undersigned as members of this committee with the task of undertaking the necessary steps to achieve the above-mentioned aim.

The provisional committee herewith invites all Workers' Associations and all other associations which, although hitherto not bearing this name, nevertheless *resolutely support the principles of social democracy*, to send delegates to a provincial congress to be held on the first Sunday of next month (**May 6**).[b]

The subjects on the agenda will be:

1. Organisation of the Rhenish-Westphalian Workers' Associations;

---

[a] See this volume, pp. 282 and 494.— *Ed.*

[b] See this volume, p. 495.— *Ed.*

2. Election of delegates to the General Congress of All German Workers' Associations to be held in the month of June in Leipzig;
3. Discussion and formulation of the proposals to be sent with the delegates to the Congress in Leipzig.

Delegates elected to the preliminary Congress to be held here are requested to report their arrival, furnished with their mandates, not later than 10 a.m. on May 6 here at *Simon's* hotel Kranz in the Altenmarkt.

Cologne, April 24, 1849

*K. Marx* (absent), *W. Wolff, K. Schapper, F. Anneke, C. J. Esser, Otto*

N. B. It is requested that communications by letter should be addressed to *Karl Schapper*, President of the Workers' Association, Unter Hutmacher No. 17.

First published in the supplement to the *Neue Rheinische Zeitung* No. 282, April 26, 1849

Printed according to the newspaper

Published in English for the first time

# FROM THE MINUTES OF THE COMMITTEE MEETING
## OF THE COLOGNE WORKERS' ASSOCIATION
## HELD ON MAY 1, 1849

The representatives of the various branches of the Association reported on their situation and activities.

The former Democratic Association in Deutz too has joined the Workers' Association in Cologne, as branch club No. 10. At the present time it consists of 230 members. [...]

The president[a] announced the receipt of assenting communications from Bingen, Leipzig and Mannheim. The first two of these concern the separation of the Workers' (Social) Party[420] from the democrats; the last one thanks us for sending the article "Wage Labour and Capital" published in the *Neue Rheinische Zeitung* and promises that it will be discussed. [...]

First published in the newspaper *Freiheit, Brüderlichkeit, Arbeit* No. 28, May 13, 1849

Printed according to the newspaper

Published in English for the first time

---

[a] Karl Schapper.— *Ed.*

# MARX'S RECEIPT FOR A FINANCIAL CONTRIBUTION TOWARDS THE PUBLISHING EXPENSES OF THE *NEUE RHEINISCHE ZEITUNG*[421]

I acknowledge that I have received an advance of 50 talers from Herr von Frisch.

*Dr. K. Marx,*
Harburg, May 6

First published in the *Zeitschrift für Geschichtswissenschaft*, Berlin, 1974, No. 4

Printed according to the manuscript

Published in English for the first time

# CONGRESS OF THE DEMOCRATIC AND WORKERS' ASSOCIATIONS[422]

*Cologne*, May 6. The Congress of the Democratic Associations of the Rhine Province began early today under the chairmanship of Dr. *Becker*. Represented were: the Democratic Club in Aachen, the Democratic Association in Bonn, the Democratic Association in Coblenz, the Democratic-Constitutional Association in Neuwied, the Political Association in Opladen, the Democratic Association in Lamersdorf, the Democratic Association in Uckerath, the Democratic Workers' Association in Honnef, the Citizens' Association in Eupen, the Democratic Association in Plittersdorf, the Democratic Association in Lohmar, the Democratic Socialist Association in Hersel, the Democratic Readers' Association in Xanten, the Democratic Association in Kessenich, the Democratic Association in Saarburg, the Democratic Association in Burscheid, the Citizens' Association in Neuss, the Democratic Association in Siegburg, the Democratic Association in Eitorf, the Democratic Association in Winterscheidt, the Workers' Association in Lennep, the People's Association in Eschweiler, the Democratic Association in Mülheim an der Ruhr, the Democratic Association in Sieglar. (46 persons.)

The Workers' Congress, presided over by Schapper, had delegates from the Associations in Solingen, Eschweiler, Aachen (Workers' Association and Army Reserve Association), Heinsberg, Coblenz, Barmen, Ratingen, Stolberg, Eilendorf, Hamm, Münster, Kreuznach, Hersel, Honnef, Overath, Mülheim an der Ruhr, Scheiderhöhe, Königswinter, Merzenich, Bork, Wiesedorf, Bielefeld, Ems, Bonn, Cologne (Workers' Association and Cigarmakers' Association). (120 persons.)

In the afternoon the two meetings united for a joint consultation.

A number of private discussions took place with the Democratic-Constitutional Associations that were in session in Deutz. Many representatives of these Associations declared that in all probability their Associations would be wholly merged in the District Federation of Democrats.

First published in the *Düsseldorfer Zeitung*, May 8, 1849, reprinted in the journal *Beiträge zur Geschichte der deutschen Arbeiterbewegung*, Berlin, 1968, No. 2

Printed according to the newspaper

Published in English for the first time

# ENGELS' EXPULSION FROM ELBERFELD

*Elberfeld,* May 15. The state of affairs remains the same, calm and order was not disturbed yesterday; the appearance of the city was unaltered. Today a poster was pasted up at street corners announcing that the Committee of Public Safety has appointed a Herr von Mirbach as Commander-in-Chief of the armed forces*; another announcement of the Committee declares that Herr Engels, one of the editors of the *Neue Rheinische Zeitung,* has been expelled.[a] In another poster the Committee of Public Safety decrees that everywhere only the black-red-and-gold[b] flag is allowed to be flown, and it calls on towns and villages in the neighbourhood of Elberfeld for assistance. We learn from Essen that the army reserve men there who have returned from leave have gone to Wesel. The private letter which gave us this information adds that a *state of siege has been proclaimed in Essen.* According to the announcement of the colonel responsible for this action, the reason for it was that he believed he could not mobilise the army reserve in any other way.

First published in the *Neue Kölnische Zeitung* No. 113, May 17, 1849

Printed according to the newspaper

Published in English for the first time

---

* In this connection, we are in a position to report that Herr von Mirbach, for reasons which will later become evident, did not accept the position of Commander-in-Chief, and also that for the same reasons Herr Anneke left Elberfeld voluntarily and was not expelled, as has been reported. Dr. Gottschalk, who is supposed to have shared the fate of expulsion with Anneke, has not been in Elberfeld at all, but is living quite peacefully at Bad Ems. [Editorial note in the *Neue Kölnische Zeitung.*]

---

[a] See this volume, p. 449.— *Ed.*

[b] Colours symbolising Germany's unity, here symbolising adherence to the imperial Constitution worked out by the Frankfurt National Assembly.— *Ed.*

# THE DEMOCRATIC AND WORKERS' PRESS
# ON MARX'S EXPULSION AND THE SUPPRESSION
# OF THE *NEUE RHEINISCHE ZEITUNG*

*TRIER'SCHE ZEITUNG*

*Cologne*, May 18.... It is rumoured that all democrats who are not domiciled in Cologne will be deported by police action; this measure is said to be primarily aimed at the editorial personnel of the *Neue Rheinische Zeitung*. It is a fact that Karl Marx was already yesterday served with such an order. At midday yesterday, Fr. Engels left for the Rhine Palatinate.[423]

First published in the supplement to the *Trier'sche Zeitung* No. 120, May 20, 1849

Printed according to the newspaper

Published in English for the first time

*NEUE KÖLNISCHE ZEITUNG*

*Cologne*, May 19

> From out of the dark did the fatal shaft fly,
> From ambush blows fell thick and fast—
> So now in the flower of my manhood I lie,
> A proud rebel that's breathed his last!

F. Freiligrath

"Abschiedswort der *Neuen Rheinischen Zeitung*"[a]

The *Neue Rheinische Zeitung* has ceased to exist.
Our issue therefore has a black mourning border.
The most interesting news items from south and east pale against

---

[a] "Farewell Word of the *Neue Rheinische Zeitung*", first published in the *Neue Rheinische Zeitung* No. 301, May 19, 1849.— Ed.

the sudden mournful tidings that the *Neue Rheinische Zeitung* has appeared today for the last time.

And what an appearance it has!!

*Red, red, red* was ever its battle-cry, but today the whole garb is red. The red print of the newspaper has greatly surprised its readers,—the spirit which once more blazes out from these breath-taking lines of print has made us profoundly lament that the newspaper has now ceased to exist!

No other newspaper can henceforth serve us as a substitute for this loss.—We shall seek in vain in the most brilliant periodicals of all countries for articles like those of the blood-stained June of 1848, nowhere shall we find again such conclusive documentation regarding the "good financial administration of Prussia",[a] or the "Silesian milliard",[b] or "Wage Labour and Capital".[c] It must be admitted that by the glorious downfall of the *Neue Rheinische Zeitung* democracy in the Rhineland has suffered a reverse. We mourn—but Freiligrath's poetry, which has attained its everlasting pinnacle in his "farewell word" today, does not leave us without consolation:

> Farewell, brothers, but not forever farewell,
> For the spirit they never can slay!
> I'll rise up again soon with a rattling of mail,
> I'll return better armed for the fray!

First published in the *Neue Kölnische Zeitung* No. 115, May 20, 1849

Printed according to the newspaper

Published in English for the first time

### NEUE DEUTSCHE ZEITUNG

*Cologne*, May 19. The last number of the *Neue Rheinische Zeitung* printed in red ink has just been published here. At last it, too, has succumbed to the blows of divinely-graced Prussianism. Since the Government was unable to get at it by judicial proceedings, and in spite of all provocations it could not find a reason for imposing a state of siege, it finally had to have recourse to deporting its editor-in-chief,[d] and it prepared orders for the deportation or arrest

---

[a] Marx, "Prussian Financial Administration under Bodelschwingh and Co." and "Further Contribution on the Old-Prussian Financial Administration" (see present edition, Vol. 8, pp. 379-89, 418-20).— *Ed.*

[b] W. Wolff, "Die Schlesische Milliarde", *Neue Rheinische Zeitung*, March-April 1849.— *Ed.*

[c] See this volume, pp. 197-228.— *Ed.*

[d] Marx.— *Ed.*

of the other editors in case even that measure should not have the desired effect.—Day by day the German people will increasingly learn to appreciate the blessing which their representatives in Frankfurt intended to bestow on them by establishing a Prussian hereditary emperor.

First published in the *Neue Deutsche Zeitung* No. 119, May 22, 1849

Printed according to the newspaper

Published in English for the first time

## DEUTSCHE LONDONER ZEITUNG

*Cologne*, May 19. The *Neue Rheinische Zeitung* has for the time being ceased publication; its last number today is printed entirely in *red*. The following order has been issued against its editor-in-chief:

"The tendency of the *Neue Rheinische Zeitung* to provoke in its readers contempt for the present government, and incite them to violent revolutions and the setting up of a social republic has become stronger in its latest pieces. The right of hospitality which he so disgracefully abused is therefore to be withdrawn from its editor-in-chief, Dr. *Karl Marx*, and since he has not obtained permission to prolong his stay in these states, he is ordered to leave them within 24 hours. If he should not comply voluntarily with this demand, he is to be forcibly conveyed across the frontier".

"Cologne, May 11, 1849.                           Royal Government. *Moeller*

To Herr *Geiger*, Royal Police Superintendent, here." [a]

Today a poster has been pasted up in the streets of Cologne, inviting attendance at a meeting to discuss the speedy establishment of a new democratic organ.

Such, you constitutional Germans, are your new achievements!—A German, a Prussian, is expelled from Germany "because he abuses hospitality"—a newspaper is suppressed because it spoke the *truth,* because Prussia's reactionary martial-law newspapers were unable to cope with the wit and stylistic acumen of the noble-minded Marx. Yes, Herr von Hohenzollern, the truth told you by the *Neue Rheinische Zeitung* is painful, very painful—(we shall reproduce in our next issue an article from the newspaper, "The

---

[a] See this volume, pp. 496-97.— *Ed.*

Deeds of the Hohenzollern Dynasty")[a]—and when press trials, and all other acts of trickery, proved of no avail, for eight to ten times the tortures of the Prussian Inquisition came to naught in the face of the sound common sense of a Rhenish jury, recourse was had to the ultimate means—suppression of the newspaper. In vain did the bankrupt brains of Prussian reaction assail the *Neue Rheinische Zeitung,* they could not get at it by judicial measures. The martial-law newspapers of drunken Frederick William could not refute the exposition which Marx gave of the edicts of the hypocrite in Potsdam,[424]—and worst of all was the fact that the circulation of the *Neue Rheinische Zeitung* increased so quickly and was so extensive, and that the paper met with universal approval.

The Hohenzollern on his throne, surrounded by "My glorious army" and with a legion of quill-drivers at his service, trembles before a *single* democratic newspaper; he cannot sleep in peace because it tells the naked truth —so it must be suppressed.

Things have come to such a pass with the monarchy that it has to proceed to use brute force to suppress a newspaper which, by the irrefutable pungency of its truth, threatened to give the miserable, ailing existence of the monarchy a still more wretched ending!

This is the Prussian guaranteed freedom of the press. Such is the interpretation of the Prussian Constitution—of the German Imperial Constitution!

First published in the *Deutsche Londoner*          Printed according to the newspaper
*Zeitung* No. 217, May 25, 1849
                                                    Published in English for the first
                                                    time

## DEMOCRATIC REVIEW[425]

...The German kings and princes—gore-dyed with the blood of their "subjects",—are labouring hard for the establishment of the Red Republic. The thrice-perjured King of Prussia[b] is determined to earn for himself the title of "Most Infamous". On the 27th of April, the Prussian Chamber of Representatives was dissolved and the same evening, crowds having collected in the streets, the people were fired on and mercilessly butchered. From that time martial law has been the only law throughout Prussia, arrests are continually taking place, and the prisons are crowded. Early in May, insurrections broke out

---

[a] The article was reproduced in the *Deutsche Londoner Zeitung* No. 218, June 1, 1849.— *Ed.*

[b] Frederick William IV.— *Ed.*

in the Rhine provinces. In some of the insurgent towns, the patriots have been put down, in others they have been sold by the bourgeoisie, and in others they yet maintain their stand.

That admirable journal, the *New Rhenish Gazette,* has been forcibly suppressed, and its chief editor, Dr. Marx, expelled from Cologne. The last number of the *Gazette* appeared on the 19th May, printed in *red ink;* it proclaimed in every line "war to the knife" against his Prussian kingship, and all the oppressors and betrayers of the German people....

First published in the journal *Democratic Review,* Vol. 1, June 1849, p. 25

Printed according to the journal

514

# THE EDITORS OF THE *NEUE RHEINISCHE ZEITUNG*

*Cologne*, May 19. ... What has happened to the individual editors of the *Neue Rheinische Zeitung* is as follows: for his actions in Elberfeld Fr. Engels is being prosecuted like a criminal[a]; Marx, Dronke and Weerth, since they are not Prussian subjects, have to leave Prussia; F. Wolff and W. Wolff are being threatened with judicial proceedings, the former because he has not done military service, the latter because of political offences alleged to have been committed by him earlier in the old provinces. The Court has today refused to free Korff on bail.[b]

(*Düsseldorfer Zeitung*)

Reprinted in the *Deutsche Zeitung* No. 140, May 22, 1849 and the *Trier'sche Zeitung* No. 122, May 23, 1849

Printed according to the newspaper text

Published in English for the first time

---

[a] See this volume, pp. 447-49.— *Ed.*
[b] See this volume, pp. 521-22.— *Ed.*

# DEPARTURE OF EDITOR KARL MARX
## FROM COLOGNE

*Cologne.* Yesterday morning Herr Karl Marx, the former editor-in-chief of the *Neue Rheinische Zeitung,* accompanied by some of the other editors, left Cologne and went to the region of the Upper Rhine; his activity there will be as successful as it has been here.[426]

First published in the *Neue Kölnische Zeitung* No. 116, May 22, 1849

Printed according to the newspaper

Published in English for the first time

# THE SECOND TRIAL
## OF THE *NEUE RHEINISCHE ZEITUNG*

*Cologne*, May 29. Today the police court passed sentence in a case which has been pending since September of last year concerning a charge of libelling deputies of the Frankfurt National Assembly.[427] Summoned before the court were: K. Marx, E. Dronke, G. Weerth, H. Becker, H. Korff, and the printers Dietz and Bechtold. The first three did not attend. With the exception of Korff, all were acquitted. Korff (as former responsible manager of the *Neue Rheinische Zeitung*) was sentenced to one month's imprisonment and payment of one-seventh of the costs, on the charge of insulting the "comical Stedtmann". The court very incisively rejected the accusation against Weerth in regard to Schnapphahnski-Lichnowski.

First published in the *Neue Deutsche Zeitung* No. 128, June 1, 1849

Printed according to the newspaper

Published in English for the first time

# TRIAL FOR LIBELLING DEPUTIES
# OF THE GERMAN NATIONAL ASSEMBLY

Proceedings of the session of the Police Court of the Royal Provincial Court in Cologne on May 29, 1849.

The persons here listed:
*Georg Weerth,* writer,
*Dr. Carl Marx,* formerly editor of the *Neue Rheinische Zeitung,*
*Joh. Wilh. Dietz,* proprietor of a printing-press,
*Hermann Korff,* formerly responsible manager of the *Neue Rheinische Zeitung,*
*Arnold Bechtold,* foreman at the Langen printing works,
*Dr. Herm. Becker,* lawyer,
*Dr. Ernst Dronke,* writer,
were summoned as of today to answer charges of libelling deputies of the German National Assembly. Of the accused, only Dietz, Korff, Bechtold and Becker appeared; the court will therefore find against those absent *in contumaciam.*[a]

The representative of the Public Prosecutor's office, *State Public Prosecutor Bölling,* set out the substance of the indictment. *G. Weerth,* he said, is accused: of having libelled Prince *Lichnowski* in the short novel entitled *Leben und Taten des berühmten Ritters Schnapphahnski* [*Life and Deeds of the Famous Knight Schnapphahnski*], printed in the literary section of the *Neue Rheinische Zeitung* in the months of August and September last year, by imputing to him actions which, if they were true, would bring him into disrepute or render him liable for prosecution. Dr. *Carl Marx* is similarly accused of libelling Prince

---
[a] In their absence.—*Ed.*

Lichnowski. In No. 95 of the *Neue Rheinische Żeitung* of September 6, 1848, in an article dated Breslau, August 29, Prince Lichnowski was charged with having called upon the electors of his district not to elect any town-dweller as deputy, since such a man would only work for the alleviation of municipal taxes and the increase of rural taxes. The State Public Prosecutor read out some passages from this article and sought to show that it contained insults directed at Prince Lichnowski. Dr. Marx, as editor-in-chief, was necessarily liable for the content of this article, whose author he refused to name. *Korff* is accused of: 1) having libelled the German National Assembly deputy, Stedtmann, in the article dated Frankfurt, September 12 contained in No. 102, p. 4, col. 4 of the *Neue Rheinische Zeitung* of September 14, 1848, by imputing to him an action which, if it were true, would bring him into disrepute; and 2) having libelled the deputies in the German National Assembly in Frankfurt who voted approval of the armistice with Denmark,[428] by accusing them of having betrayed the nation, in the proclamation which was printed in No. 110, p. 4, col. 2 of the *Neue Rheinische Zeitung* of September 23, 1848. The two articles on which the charge is based were read out. In the first the deputy *Stedtmann* is specifically accused of incorporating false information in a report on a committee meeting, in the hope of being made a Minister. The indictment brought against Marx and Korff was also extended to include *Joh. Wilhelm Dietz* as printer of the *Neue Rheinische Zeitung*. The State Public Prosecutor attempted to derive his responsibility for the contentious article from Articles 25 and 26 of the imposed Constitution and from Article 60 of the Rhenish Penal Code. The indictment against *Becker, Bechtold* and *Dronke* similarly concerns libel of the deputies who voted for the armistice with Denmark. On September 20, 1848, here in the Eiser Hall a public meeting was held, at which the Malmö armistice was discussed. *Dronke* was a speaker at this meeting and declared that the deputies who had voted approval of that armistice had betrayed the nation. The meeting adopted this declaration and resolved to publicise it by having it printed and posted at street corners. Dr. *Becker* had passed the resolution in question to *Bechtold* for printing, and the latter had printed it.

The accused, questioned more closely by the presiding magistrate, made the following statements:

*Dietz* admitted having printed the contentious articles. He did not know who the authors were. He maintained, however, that he was not responsible for the content of those articles, since the editor and responsible manager of the newspaper were known and living in Prussia. If Dr. Marx had recently been expelled from the country, that was not his fault; the former had in any case been resident in Cologne throughout the investigation.

*Korff* conceded he was manager of the *Neue Rheinische Zeitung*. The contentious articles were accepted with his approval. His defence counsel, barrister *Rath,* sought to demonstrate that there was no libel in the articles concerned. He named their author and maintained that as a result his client was absolved of all responsibility.

Dr. *Becker* admitted having passed to Bechtold for printing the proclamation from the Eiser Hall, which had been sent to him by a messenger-boy from the *Neue Rheinische Zeitung.* The content of the proclamation in question had however been unknown to him as he had not been present at the proceedings in the Eiser Hall on September 20. As secretary of the Democratic Association[429] he was charged with attending to all material for printing, and that was why the manuscript had been sent to him. Moreover the proclamation had already been published by the *Neue Rheinische Zeitung* before he had passed the manuscript to Bechtold. The defendant declared that in certain circumstances he would be ready to assume responsibility for the contents of the proclamation. In his statement he also drew attention to the fact that the indictment had been brought at the request of the Imperial Minister of Justice. The indictment, he submitted, was not directed at specific persons but at a specific party. When he attempted to elaborate on this, the speaker was asked by the presiding magistrate, at the twice repeated instance of the State Public Prosecutor, to keep to the point at issue.

*Bechtold* admitted that he had read the manuscript received from Dr. Becker and had forwarded it for printing. His defence counsel, barrister *Pheiffer,* thereupon argued that as the author of the proclamation was known, the printer could not be punished. If the prosecution intended to adduce Article 60 of the Penal Code, it would have to demonstrate that the accused intended to libel the deputies, and the Public Prosecutor's office had not even attempted to prove this. Moreover, the proclamation did not contain a libel in the legal sense, it did not contain any specific assertion which exposed the deputies to prosecution at law, nor to hatred and contempt; it only expressed a criticism of the resolution concerning the armistice.

Hereupon the State Public Prosecutor *Bölling,* in a lengthy speech, sought to justify the indictment and to refute the arguments used by the accused in their defence. In conclusion, he asked that the accused Weerth, Marx, Dronke, and Korff should each be sentenced to a three-month term of imprisonment and to a fine of 1,000 francs, and the remaining accused to a one-month term of imprisonment, and one-seventh of the costs to be imposed on each one of them.

Hereupon the court adjourned and after deliberations lasting about two hours pronounced judgment to the effect that *Korff* was sentenced to a *one-month imprisonment* for libelling the deputy Stedtmann, the charge against *Weerth* was *dismissed* because the accusations made in it were not specified, and the remaining accused were *acquitted*.

First published in the supplement
to the *Kölnische Zeitung* No. 129,
May 31, 1849

Printed according to the newspaper

Published in English for the first
time

# TRIAL FOR INTERFERENCE IN OFFICIAL FUNCTIONS [430]

On May 30 the former responsible manager of the *Neue Rheinische Zeitung, Hermann Korff*, stood again before the police court, accused of having interfered in official functions and having committed an act encroaching on these functions. In an item in the supplement to No. 297 of the *Neue Rheinische Zeitung* of May 13 of this year, Korff had invited people to come to a meeting of the 14th Company of the civic militia and to enter their name on a list. Judicial proceedings were started against Korff for making this call, and he was arrested.

In the public trial the State Public Prosecutor, *Bölling*, sought to justify the indictment and asked for the defendant to be sentenced to a two-year term of imprisonment.

The counsel for the defence, barrister *Rath*, drew attention to the fact that for some time past similar items concerning the civic militia had been appearing in the local newspapers without there having been any prosecution hitherto. The accusation against Korff, he said, is utterly and completely unfounded. The convoking of the 14th Company in a tavern is not an official function, at most it is an attempt to form a company, that is to say, an attempt at exercising an official function. But assuming that the convocation in question were an official function in the legal sense, only two possibilities were then conceivable: 1) the civic militia is still in existence—and this I maintain is the position in principle; in that case Korff was entitled to convene it. The civic militia had merely been suspended in Cologne during the state of siege[431]; with the lifting of the state of siege, all former laws and institutions came back into force; even if not in practice, but legally the civic militia was once more in existence. Or 2) the civic militia was no longer in existence, and this is the view of the authorities and the Public Prosecutor's office; in that case there was no official function either, and in that case the accusation is complete and utter nonsense.

After the prosecution had replied briefly to the counsel for the defence, barrister *Hagen* opened his address for the defendant, seeking to demonstrate that the most that could be imputed to him was a remote intention to interfere in official functions, but not in any sense an actual act, actual interference, as is required by Art. 258 of the Penal Code. The court thereupon adjourned for about a quarter of an hour to its committee room and then *acquitted* the defendant with neither sentence nor costs.

Despite this acquittal, Korff was taken back into custody by order of the State Public Prosecutor, since he intends to appeal against the verdict of acquittal.

First published in the supplement
to the *Kölnische Zeitung* No. 129,
May 31, 1849

Printed according to the newspaper

Published in English for the first
time

# FROM THE EDITORS
## OF THE *NEUE KÖLNISCHE ZEITUNG*

On his departure from here, the editor-in-chief of the former *Neue Rheinische Zeitung*, Herr Karl Marx, has arranged that reports for the *Neue Rheinische Zeitung* which still continually arrive are to be handed over to the *Neue Kölnische Zeitung* for its use. We wish to bring this to the notice of the correspondents and we request them, in order to save time, to send their reports directly to our address.

The Editors of the *Neue Kölnische Zeitung*

First published in the *Neue Kölnische Zeitung* No. 124, June 1, 1849

Printed according to the newspaper

Published in English for the first time

# A WARRANT OF ARREST

On the basis of the order for their appearance in Court issued by the royal examining magistrate, I request the civil and military authorities concerned to look out for and, if found, to arrest and bring before me, the following persons:

1. *Friedrich Engels,* editor of the *Neue Rheinische Zeitung,* born in Barmen and last residing in Cologne ...[a] who have taken refuge in flight from the investigation instituted against them on account of crimes envisaged in Article 96 of the Penal Code, and whose description I give below.

Elberfeld, June 6, 1849
For the Chief Public Prosecutor
State Public Prosecutor *Eichhorn*

*Description:* 1. *Engels.* Age 26 to 28; height 5 feet 6 inches; hair blond; forehead smooth; eyebrows blond; eyes blue; nose and mouth well proportioned; beard reddish; chin oval; face oval; complexion healthy; figure slender. Special characteristics: speaks very rapidly and is short-sighted....[b]

First published in the *Kölnische Zeitung* No. 137, June 9, 1849

Printed according to the newspaper

Published in English for the first time

---

[a] There follow the names of two other wanted men, their occupation and last residence.— *Ed.*

[b] There follow the descriptions of the two other wanted men.— *Ed.*

# MARX'S ARRIVAL IN PARIS

*Cologne*, June 9. The editor-in-chief, Karl Marx, has arrived in Paris.[432]

First published in the *Neue Kölnische Zeitung* No. 132, June 10, 1849

Printed according to the newspaper

Published in English for the first time

# NOTIFICATION OF MARX'S EXPULSION FROM PARIS ISSUED BY THE COMMISSIONER OF POLICE[433]

City of Paris
Quartier du Faubourg
St. Germain

Year eighteen hundred and forty
nine, nineteenth of July

Office of the
Prefect of Police[a]

## NOTIFICATION TO MR. MARX TO RESIDE IN THE DEPARTMENT OF MORBIHAN

We the undersigned Commissioner of Police of the Faubourg St. Germain,—

notify Mr. *Marx* (Charles), 29 years of age,[b] born at Trèves (Prussia), writer, living at rue de Lille No. 55, of the decision of the Minister of the Interior,[c] by which he is required to go to the department of Morbihan in order to reside there, and is obliged to comply with the measure adopted in respect of him.

*Dourlens*

First published in: Marx and Engels,
*Works*, Second Russian Edition,
Vol. 43, Moscow 1976

Printed according to the manuscript

Translated from the French

Published in English for the first time

---

[a] Carlier.— *Ed.*
[b] Marx was 31 at the time.— *Ed.*
[c] Dufaure.— *Ed.*

# NOTIFICATION SENT BY THE COMMISSIONER
# OF POLICE STATING THAT MARX'S PETITION
# WAS REJECTED

Monsieur Marx, Prussian refugee, rue de Lille

Quartier du Faubourg St. Germain      Paris, August 16, 1849
Sir,

In fulfilment of the orders of the Prefect of Police[a] I have the honour to inform you that the Minister of the Interior[b] has not thought it possible to accede to the petition you have addressed to him requesting him to revoke his decision. Consequently, I require you to leave Paris *without delay* in order to proceed to the department of Morbihan, where you must reside.

I have the honour to greet you,

Commissioner of Police
of the Quartier du Faubourg
Saint-Germain
*Dourlens*

First published in: Marx and Engels, *Works*, Second Russian Edition, Vol. 43, Moscow 1976

Printed according to the manuscript

Translated from the French

Published in English for the first time

---

[a] Carlier.— *Ed.*
[b] Dufaure.— *Ed.*

Passport issued to Marx by the French police on August 24, 1849 because having been expelled from Paris he intended to go to England. It bears the stamp of Boulogne, the port from which Marx embarked for England, and the date August 26, 1849. Marx's description is given on the left-hand side of the passport.

| | | | |
|---|---|---|---|
| Age | *32 years* | Nose | *Ordinary* |
| Height | *1m. 71 cm.* | Mouth | *Medium* |
| Hair | *Black* | Beard | *Black* |
| Forehead | *Round* | Chin | *Round* |
| Eyebrows | *Brown* | Face | *Round* |
| Eyes | *Brown* | Complexion | *Ordinary* |

# NOTES
# AND
# INDEXES

# NOTES

1 In this article, the editors of the *Neue Rheinische Zeitung* raised the important question of the relation between economic development and the course of the European revolution and of the influence of the economic factor on the revolutionary process. Subsequently, Marx and Engels dealt with this problem on several occasions, particularly in the period when, in the pages of the *Neue Rheinische Zeitung. Politisch-Ökonomische Revue*—the journal that continued the traditions of the periodical they had published during the revolution—they summed up the results of the revolutionary battles that had just ended. In the autumn of 1850, they elaborated the ideas expressed in this article when they wrote the following in the "Review [ May to October 1850]": "However, this much at least is certain, that the commercial crisis contributed infinitely more to the revolutions of 1848 than the revolution to commercial crisis" (present edition, Vol. 10).

The *Neue Rheinische Zeitung* was founded by Marx as a militant periodical intended to exert an effective influence upon the masses, to educate and unite them politically and ideologically and pave the way for the creation of the mass party of the German proletariat. The newspaper provided Marx and Engels with an opportunity to guide the activities of the Communist League founded by them in 1847, which they regarded as the nucleus of the future proletarian party. However, since the League was too weak and numerically small, it could not be directly transformed into the rallying centre of the proletarian forces at the time when the 1848 revolution was at its peak. As the underground activities of the League lost all sense under the conditions of revolution, Marx and Engels instructed its members, who were scattered throughout Germany, to avail themselves of every legal opportunity to join the emerging workers' associations and democratic societies. In this context, a revolutionary proletarian newspaper became the main instrument for directing and co-ordinating the activities of the Communist League members, of mobilising the masses to resolve the tasks of the bourgeois-democratic revolution.

It was decided to publish the *Neue Rheinische Zeitung* in Cologne, the capital of the Rhine Province, which was more advanced economically and politically than the other regions of Germany (here the working class was fairly strong and the *Code Napoléon* was in operation, which provided for somewhat greater freedom of the press than did the Prussian Law). The name, *Neue Rheinische Zeitung*, was chosen in order to stress the intention to continue the revolutionary-democratic traditions of the *Rheinische Zeitung,* which was edited by Marx in 1842 and 1843. In view of the specific conditions and the absence of the mass workers' party in Germany, Marx, Engels and their followers entered the political scene as the Left, in fact the proletarian, wing of the democratic movement. This predetermined the stand adopted by the *Neue Rheinische Zeitung,* which was put out under the subtitle *Organ der Demokratie* (Organ of Democracy). Only after mid-April 1849, when the German workers' class consciousness underwent certain changes, did the newspaper's editors take steps to set up an independent mass political party of the German proletariat, organisationally separate from petty-bourgeois democracy.

The first issue came out in the evening of May 31, but was dated June 1, 1848. The editorial board consisted of Karl Marx (editor-in-chief), Heinrich Bürgers, Ernst Dronke, Georg Weerth, Wilhelm Wolff, Ferdinand Wolff and Frederick Engels. In October 1848, the poet Ferdinand Freiligrath became one of its editors. All the editors were members of the Communist League. Common views, a strict division of functions and good co-ordination were characteristic of the work of the editorial board. Besides reading and answering letters and assisting the editor-in-chief, every editor dealt with a specific range of problems. The editorial board had correspondents in various parts of Germany and abroad. It established contacts with a number of democratic periodicals in other countries.

As a rule, Marx and Engels wrote the editorials, formulating the paper's stand on the most important questions of the revolution. These articles were marked "*Köln" and "**Köln". Sometimes editorials marked with one asterisk were printed in other sections of the paper under the heading of News from Italy, France, Hungary, Switzerland and other countries. In addition to editorials, Engels wrote articles on other subjects, such as the progress of the revolutionary and liberation movement in Italy, the revolutionary war in Hungary, the political situation in Switzerland and so on. Wilhelm Wolff contributed articles on the agrarian question, on the condition of the peasants and their movement, particularly in Silesia. He was also responsible for the Current Events section. Georg Weerth wrote feuilletons, and Ernst Dronke contributed various reports (including reports from Paris). Heinrich Bürgers' contribution to the paper was limited to a single article, which was practically rewritten by Marx; he had more success speaking at various meetings as the paper's representative. Freiligrath published his revolutionary verses in the paper.

The *Neue Rheinische Zeitung* was a daily (from September 1848 it appeared every day except Monday); it aimed to give its readers prompt information on all the most significant revolutionary developments in Germany and Europe. Often a second edition was put out on the same day; supplements were printed when there was too much material to be squeezed into the four pages of the issue, while special supplements and special editions in the form of leaflets carried the latest and most important news.

The consistent revolutionary tendency of the *Neue Rheinische Zeitung,* its militant internationalism, and articles that appeared in its columns containing political accusations against the Government, aroused the displeasure of its bourgeois shareholders in the first months of the paper's existence and led to the persecution of its editors by the Government and attacks in the feudal monarchist and liberal bourgeois press. It was particularly the paper's articles in defence of the June 1848 uprising of the Paris proletariat that frightened away the shareholders.

To make Marx's stay in the Rhine Province more difficult, the Cologne authorities, on instructions from Berlin, refused to restore his Prussian citizenship (which Marx had renounced in 1845), and on several occasions instituted legal proceedings against him and other editors of the paper. On

September 26, 1848, when a state of siege was declared in Cologne, several democratic newspapers, the *Neue Rheinische Zeitung* among them, were suspended. To avoid arrest, Engels, Dronke and Ferdinand Wolff had to leave Germany for a time. Wilhelm Wolff stayed in Cologne, but for several months he lived in hiding. When the state of siege was lifted, the paper resumed publication on October 12, thanks to the great efforts of Marx who invested all his ready money in the paper. Until January 1849, the brunt of the work, including writing leading articles, fell to Marx, since Engels had to stay in France and later in Switzerland.

Persecution of the *Neue Rheinische Zeitung* editors by the judicial authorities and the police became particularly intense after the counter-revolutionary coup in Prussia in November-December 1848. On February 7, 1849, Marx, Engels and Hermann Korff, the responsible manager, had to appear before a jury in Cologne and, the next day, Marx was summoned to court as the leader of the Rhenish District Committee of Democrats, together with Schapper and the lawyer Schneider. In both cases, Marx and his associates were acquitted thanks to skilful defence.

The paper's highly unstable financial position led to Marx continually taking steps to raise the necessary funds for its publication. Towards the end of March 1849, he insisted that Korff, who had considerably entangled the paper's financial affairs, be replaced by Stephan Adolf Naut who was closely associated with the Cologne Communists. In mid-April Marx had to undertake a trip to North-West Germany and Westphalia to raise funds among Communist League members and German democrats. In his absence (he returned to Cologne about May 8), the newspaper was managed by Engels. At the time, in the context of a new rise of revolutionary developments caused by the conflict between the Frankfurt National Assembly and the German governments, the *Neue Rheinische Zeitung* intensified its campaign for the consolidation of the revolutionary forces by publishing reports on the course of the uprising in Rhenish Prussia, Saxony and South-West Germany in defence of the imperial Constitution drafted by the Assembly. The authorities used this as a fresh pretext to persecute the paper. The number of legal proceedings against its editors rose to 23. However, the authorities' failure to win previous cases induced them to resort to another means of suppressing the revolutionary periodical. In May 1849, under the conditions of the general counter-revolutionary offensive, the Prussian Government issued an order to expel Marx from Prussia on the grounds that he had not been granted Prussian citizenship. Marx's expulsion and new repressions against other editors of the *Neue Rheinische Zeitung* resulted in the paper ceasing publication. The last issue, No. 301, printed in red ink, appeared on May 19, 1849. In their farewell address "To the Workers of Cologne", the editors wrote that "their last word everywhere and always will be: ***emancipation of the working class***" (see this volume, p. 467). p. 3

2 An allusion to the Nanking Treaty concluded by Britain as a result of the 1840-42 war with China (the so-called First Opium War). It was the first of a series of unequal treaties China was forced to conclude with European powers, reducing it to the state of a semi-colony. Under this treaty, Hong Kong was placed under British rule and five Chinese sea ports, including Canton and Shanghai, were declared open sea ports for British commerce. The Treaty was signed by Sir Henry Pottinger, Commander of the British Expeditionary Corps in China. p. 3

3 The *Corn Laws*—a series of laws in England (the first dating back to the 15th century) that imposed high duties on imported corn with the aim of maintaining high prices for corn on the home market in the interests of the landowners. The

struggle between the industrial bourgeoisie and the landed aristocracy over the Corn Laws ended in the adoption of a Bill repealing them in June 1846.  p. 3

4 The struggle between Britain and the USA for the Oregon region on the Pacific coast of North America ended in 1846 with its partition between the two powers.

In 1845-49 Britain waged wars of conquest in Northern India against the State of Sikhs, which resulted in the entire Punjab being annexed by the East India Company.
p. 4

5 In 1847, along with other European countries, Italy went through an economic crisis. In an attempt to overcome it, Pope Pius IX proposed a programme of economic and political reforms including a project to set up a customs union of the Italian states.. However, the Pope's proposals and measures, supported by the liberals, failed to prevent a revolutionary upheaval in Italy. The revolution started with a popular uprising in *Palermo* on January 12, 1848 against the absolutist regime of the Neapolitan Bourbons. The movement for a Constitution and liberation from foreign rule spread all over the country. As a result of the popular uprising in *Milan* in March 1848, the Austrian troops were driven out of the capital of Lombardy which, however, was recaptured by Austrians after the defeat of the Piedmontese troops. From November 1848, the centre of the revolutionary movement shifted to Central Italy, particularly to the Papal states where developments forced Pope Pius IX to flee from Rome. The *Roman Republic* was proclaimed on February 9, 1849.
p. 7

6 The present and following articles on the course of the revolutionary war in Hungary against the Austrian monarchy are the continuation of a series of reports by Engels on the subject which he began in February 1848 (see present edition, Vol. 8). He drew his information mainly from Austrian Command communiqués, i. e. army bulletins published in the official *Wiener Zeitung* and other Austrian newspapers. At the time Hungarian sources were almost unavailable in Germany. In spite of the biased and incomplete data contained in the Austrian bulletins, Engels managed to present a fairly exact overall picture of the hostilities. Subsequently, in his work *Revolution and Counter-Revolution in Germany*, Engels pointed out that, by reporting the true development of the revolutionary war in Hungary, the *Neue Rheinische Zeitung* had contributed more than any other paper to making the Hungarians' cause popular in Germany. The paper had explained the character of the struggle between the Magyars and the Slavs and printed a series of articles on the Hungarian war which had the honour of being plagiarised in nearly every subsequent book on the subject, not excluding those by Hungarians themselves and by "eyewitnesses" (see present edition, Vol. 11).

Engels also mentions his reports about Hungary in his letters to Marx dated April 3, 1851 and July 6, 1852 and also in his letter to H. J. Lincoln, editor of the *Daily News*, dated March 30, 1854. At that time he took up a systematic study of military science and the art of war and began to collect additional material on the Hungarian campaign (*Memoirs* by the Hungarian Commander-in-Chief Görgey, biographies of Hungarian generals, periodicals put out by the Kossuth Government). He also planned to write a book on the history of the revolutionary war in Hungary and Italy—but these plans did not materialise.

Engels started his military reports at a grievous moment for revolutionary Hungary. On December 16, 1848, the Austrian imperial army, under the command of Windischgrätz, started an offensive and at the beginning of January captured Buda and Pest (two neighbouring cities at the time). The Hungarian revolutionary Government (the Defence Council) headed by Kossuth and Parliament (National Assembly) moved to Debreczin. Simultaneously, counter-revolutionary forces launched an offensive in Galicia (the corps under General Schlick), Silesia, the Banat and other districts. Right-wing circles in Austria and Germany predicted a speedy and final defeat of revolutionary Hungary. However, from the very beginning Engels pointed to her reserves for building up her defences and possibilities for securing a turn in the war. In fact the Defence Council did take a number of energetic steps to strengthen the revolutionary army. Guerilla warfare spread in the enemy's rear. Volunteer detachments arrived from Austria to defend the Hungarian revolution and units consisting of national minorities were formed for the purpose. The Hungarian army was joined by many Polish revolutionary commanders (among them Bem, Dembiński). In February 1849, the Hungarians not only succeeded in stabilising the situation in the central area of hostilities (on the Theiss) and even in forcing the enemy to retreat along some other sectors of the front, but also in starting to concentrate forces for a counter-blow that was delivered early in April 1849.          p. 9

[7] On February 26 and 27, 1849, a *battle* between the Hungarian revolutionary army and Austrian troops took place at *Kapolna* (in Central Hungary between Pest and Debreczin) which, despite the retreat of the Hungarian troops beyond the Theiss, was not a victory for either side. Having received Windischgrätz's report on the victory at Kapolna, Francis Joseph abrogated Hungary's autonomy, which had up to that point been recognised by the Austrian ruling circles, and incorporated her into "the lands of the Austrian Empire" by the Olmütz Manifesto of March 4, 1849 (Olmütz was the seat of the Austrian Court since the people's uprising in Vienna in October 1848).                                              p. 9

[8] The 1848-49 struggle between revolutionary and counter-revolutionary forces was accompanied by an exacerbation of national contradictions in Transylvania and in other districts belonging administratively to Hungary but inhabited by other nationalities. The predominant part of the motley population of the region (Romanians, Hungarians and Szeklers, who are their off-shoot, and Germans, mainly settlers from Saxony) consisted of Romanian peasants, who were exploited by Hungarian landowners and Austrian officials. Although the advanced sections of the Romanian bourgeoisie and intelligentsia welcomed the Hungarian 1848 revolution, the erroneous policy of the Hungarian Government in the national question allowed the feudal clerical circles to use social and national antagonisms and stir up Romanians to revolt against Hungary in September 1848. The Romanian legions under the command of Colonel Urban, aided by Austrian troops under Baron Puchner, fought against the Hungarians. However, the Polish emigrant Bem, who was appointed Commander of the Hungarian army in Transylvania in December 1848, succeeded in preventing Puchner from invading Hungary from Transylvania and dealt crushing blows to the counter-revolutionary forces in Transylvania proper during January-March 1849.

A small detachment of Russian troops sent to Puchner's aid by Lüders, commander of the Tsarist expeditionary corps in Wallachia, failed to stop Bem's advance and by the end of March the latter had cleared nearly all enemy troops out of Transylvania. Bem owed his success to his policy of reconciliation of national contradictions between the Hungarians and the Romanians, in spite of the resistance of Hungarian government representatives, who were spokesmen of the Hungarian nobility (later Marx and Engels stressed this in the article "Bem" written for the *New American Cyclopaedia*). Calls for joint actions of the Romanians and Hungarians against the Habsburgs were also issued by Balčescu, a Romanian democrat; Janku, the leader of the Romanian poor peasants' guerilla movement, supported this idea.

The Hungarian revolutionaries from among the bourgeoisie and nobility were, however, too late in realising the necessity of co-operation with the oppressed nationalities and this enabled the Austrian ruling circles in general to use the Romanian national movement in Transylvania, led by the clerical-aristocratic upper sections, as a tool in the struggle against revolutionary Hungary. After the defeat of the Hungarian revolution, the Austrians established a rule of brutal national oppression in Transylvania, despite their demagogic promises to the contrary.                                                                              p. 9

[9] *Szeklers* (from *szek*—settlements)—an ethnic group of Hungarians, mostly free peasants. In the 13th century their forefathers were settled by Hungarian kings in the mountain regions of Transylvania to protect the frontiers. The majority of Szeklers sided with the Hungarian revolution.                                              p. 9

[10] The reference is to the paper money issued in 1848-49 by the Hungarian revolutionary Government. The notes were first issued in May 1848. Despite the Austrian authorities' repeated ban on the "Kossuth notes", the Hungarian paper money was a serious competitor to Austrian money, not only within Hungary but also in Austria proper. The "Kossuth notes" were in circulation until almost the end of 1849.                                                                         p. 10

[11] The reference is to the *Chief Administrative Committee of the Serbian Voivodeship* or the *Chief Odbor* in Karlowitz—an executive body elected by the Assembly (*Skupština*) of representatives of the Serbian communities in the South-Slav border regions of the Austrian Empire in May 1848. The *Skupština* proclaimed the Voivodina an autonomous region within the Empire. In the autumn of 1848, a number of Serbian cities formed local *Odbors* which were patterned on the Chief Odbor and concentrated all civil and military authority in their hands.

The Chief Odbor became the scene of struggle between the liberals headed by Stratimirovich (who was elected President) and clerical and feudal group, who professed loyalty to the Habsburgs and opposed liberal reforms. At the beginning of 1849, this group led by Patriarch Rajachich took the upper hand. They directed the Serbian national movement in the Voivodina towards still closer collaboration with the Austrian counter-revolutionary Government which, having made use of the Serbs in the struggle against revolutionary Hungary, broke its promise and, in March 1849, refused to grant them autonomy.                                  p. 11

[12] This refers to the southern part of the Austrian-Turkish border (the Military Border area—see notes 22 and 68).                                                 p. 12

[13] An allusion to the new *Constitution* of the Austrian united monarchy (*Gesamtmonarchie*) introduced by Francis Joseph on *March 4, 1849*. According to the Constitution, the Emperor and his Ministers were vested with full executive authority and the bureaucratic centralisation principle was strictly implemented in the administration of the Empire. Lombardy, Venice, Hungary and Bohemia were proclaimed Austrian crown lands and the autonomous estate institutions that existed in some national regions even before the 1848 revolution were abolished. Croatia, Serbian Voivodina and Transylvania likewise did not receive autonomy, repeated promises notwithstanding; they separated from Hungary administratively and a system of administration similar to that in other crown lands was established there. The Constitution of March 4, 1849, was a step towards the restoration of absolutism (it was finally restored by the imperial patent of December 31, 1851, which repealed constitutional rule) and was unpopular even

among the Right-wing elements in the Slav national movement in Austria, who
cherished the hope that the Habsburgs would satisfy their national demands.

p. 12

[14] The reference is to the *Hungarian National Assembly* which moved to Debreczin
early in January 1849 because of the advance of the Austrian troops on Pest. Some
of the Right-wing deputies refused to leave for Debreczin and went over to the
side of Windischgrätz who captured the capital of Hungary.                    p. 14

[15] The fortified camp and fortress of Komorn in North-Western Hungary remained
in the hands of the Hungarians in the rear of the Austrian army during its
offensive in late 1848 and early 1849. Later on the fortress, which withstood
several sieges by Austrian troops, played an important role in the operations of the
Hungarian revolutionary army.                                                p. 15

[16] The reference is to the final stage in the suppression of the 1830-31 Polish
national liberation uprising by Tsarist troops supported by Prussia and Austria.
After Warsaw was outflanked from the west and on September 6 its western
suburb seized, the Tsarist command succeeded in forcing the city to capitulate on
the night of September 7, 1831. Early in October, the remnants of the Polish
insurgent army crossed the border for Prussia and Austria, where they were
interned.                                                                    p. 18

[17] By the autumn of 1848, a democratic movement had spread among the Polish
population of Galicia that aimed at preparing a national uprising and uniting with
revolutionary Hungary. However, the Polish revolutionaries failed to rally
adequate forces for an uprising.

In connection with the victories of the Hungarian troops under Bem in
Transylvania in the first months of 1849, in particular with his march on January 5
to South Bukovina, rumours spread in Galicia of an impending advance over the
Carpathians by the revolutionary Hungarian army and the Polish legion, and this
intensified the revolutionary ferment among the Poles. Many young Polish
democrats went secretly to Hungary to serve in the Polish legion.            p. 20

[18] *Petty sessions*—a court of the Justices of the Peace in England, tries minor offences
according to a simplified legal procedure.

*Quarter sessions*—a court held quarterly by Justices of the Peace.

The expressions "petty sessions" and "quarter sessions" are given in English in
the original.                                                                p. 22

[19] An allusion to the New Year's message of greetings from King Frederick William
IV "To My Army" ("An mein Heer") which he signed in Potsdam on January 1,
1849; it was published in the *Preußischer Staats-Anzeiger* on January 3, 1849. The
*Neue Rheinische Zeitung* used this to expose the counter-revolutionary actions of
the Prussian military (see Marx's article "A New Year Greeting", present edition,
Vol. 8, pp. 222-26).                                                          p. 23

[20] See Note 9.                                                                 p. 25

[21] A considerable section of the population of Transylvania (over 200,000) were
German colonists who had come from Saxony, Flanders and the Rhine lands
(known as Teutons, Flemings, Saxons, later all German colonists came to be
known as Saxons); they had been settled there by the Hungarian kings and
Austrian emperors.

The majority of the Saxons, who were well-to-do townspeople, came out against the Hungarian revolution and sided with the imperial troops in the armed struggle. p. 25

22 *Peterwardein borderers* as well as *Serezhans* and other South-Slav army formations mentioned below performed compulsory military service on the Austro-Turkish border (in the so-called Military Border area). They were named after their regimental or company districts or communities from which the soldiers came. In 1848-49 the Austrian authorities and the Right-wing bourgeois-landowning nationalist elements drew them into the war against revolutionary Hungary. p. 25

23 This refers to the Transylvanian Saxons (see Note 21). p. 26

24 The war between the Serbs and the Hungarians broke out as far back as May 1848, as a result of the conflict between the Hungarian Government and the Serbian national movement which demanded autonomy for the Voivodina. The movement was socially and politically heterogeneous. Liberal bourgeois elements (Stratimirovich and others) and Right-wing conservative landowning elements prevailed in the movement and thus allowed the Austrian ruling circles to make use of it in the struggle against the Hungarian revolution. On the other hand, the Hungarian revolutionaries, who refused to recognise the national demands of the Serbs and other Slav peoples incorporated in the Hungarian state prompted them to side with the Habsburgs. It was only on July 28, 1849, i. e. on the eve of its downfall, that revolutionary Hungary officially declared equality for all nationalities in the country. Having consolidated their domination largely with the help of the Croats, the Serbs of the Voivodina and so on, the ruling circles of the Austrian Empire went back on their promises and not only refused to grant autonomy to the Slav and other peoples of the multinational state, but abolished even the remnants of self-government in the national regions. p. 26

25 See Note 15. p. 29

26 The *Central Committee of German Democrats* (d'Ester, Reichenbach, Hexamer) was elected at the Second Democratic Congress held in Berlin from October 26 to 30, 1848.

The *Central Committee of Democrats* mentioned below was elected at the First Democratic Congress held in Frankfurt am Main from June 14 to 17, 1848. Fröbel, Rau and Kriege were elected to the first Central Committee and Bairhoffer, Schütte and Anneke were their deputies. The Committee had its headquarters in Berlin. However, despite the decision of the Frankfurt am Main Congress to unite all democratic associations and set up the Central and district committees of German Democrats, the democratic movement in Germany still lacked unity and organisation owing to the weakness and vacillation of its petty-bourgeois leaders. p. 33

27 This refers to the Prussian National Assembly convened in Berlin on May 22, 1848, to work out a Constitution and introduce a constitutional system on the basis of an "agreement with the Crown". It was dissolved on December 5 as a result of the coup d'état in Prussia. The causes behind the coup d'état were the formation of the Brandenburg-Manteuffel counter-revolutionary Government and the publication on November 9 of a decree transferring the Assembly to the provincial town of Brandenburg. Liberal and democratic (Left) deputies failed to offer any real resistance to the instigators of the coup d'état and confined themselves to

passive resistance. The introduction of a Constitution "granted" by the King was announced simultaneously with the dissolution of the Assembly.                p. 34

[28] An allusion to the *Wahl-Manifest der radicalen Reformpartei für Deutschland* (Election Manifesto of the Radical Reform Party of Germany) written by Ruge not long before the elections to the Frankfurt National Assembly. It proclaimed "editing of the rationale of events" to be the chief task of the Assembly. The Election Manifesto was published by Ruge in Leipzig in his newspaper *Die Reform* on April 16, 1848.                p. 34

[29] The *Central March Association* which had branches in different cities of Germany was set up at the end of November 1848 in Frankfurt am Main by the Left-wing deputies to the Frankfurt National Assembly. The leaders of the March associations, which derived their name from the March 1848 revolution in Germany, were petty-bourgeois democrats including Fröbel, Simon and Vogt. These confined themselves to revolutionary phrase-mongering, were both indecisive and inconsistent in the struggle against the counter-revolution and were sharply criticised by Marx and Engels on this account.                p. 36

[30] The phrase "*Imperial Assembly*" refers to the *German National Assembly* which opened on May 18, 1848 in St. Paul's Church, in the free town of Frankfurt am Main. It was convened to effect the unification of the country and to draw up its Constitution. Among the deputies elected in various German states late in April and early in May were 122 government officials, 95 judges, 81 lawyers, 103 professors, 17 manufacturers and wholesale dealers, 15 physicians and 40 landowners. The liberal deputies, who were in the majority, turned the Assembly into a mere debating club. At the decisive moments of the revolution, the liberal majority in fact condoned the counter-revolution.

When writing this and other articles on the Frankfurt National Assembly, Marx and Engels made use of the shorthand reports of its sittings which later appeared as a separate publication, *Stenographischer Bericht über die Verhandlungen der deutschen constituirenden Nationalversammlung zu Frankfurt am Main*, Frankfurt am Main, 1848-49.                p. 36

[31] An allusion to the Left wing of the Frankfurt National Assembly which consisted of two factions: the Left (Fröbel, Vogt, Venedey and others) and the extreme Left known as the Radical-Democratic Party (Ruge, Schlöffel, Zitz, Trüzschler, Simon and others). Though the *Neue Rheinische Zeitung* supported the extreme Left rather than the more moderate groups of democrats, it criticised the former for their vacillations and halfway stand on the basic problems of the German revolution—abolition of feudal survivals and unification of the country.   p. 36

[32] The *toleration tax* was levied on the Jewish population of the Kingdom of Hungary in 1749. The arrears grew from year to year, and the 1840s witnessed the intensified struggle for the abolition of this humiliating tax. In June 1846 it was repealed on condition that all the arrears, which amounted to 1,200,000 florins, were paid off during the next five years.

This measure was a certain step towards the emancipation of the country's Jews.
                                               p. 39

[33] On *September 7, 1848* the Emperor sanctioned the law drawn up by the Austrian Imperial Diet (Reichstag) repealing the personal bondage of the peasants and making labour and other services connected with land tenure subject to redemption. The redemption sum was fixed at twenty times the amount of the peasants' annual duties. Two-thirds of this was to be paid by the peasants and one-third by the state (from taxes). Despite the halfway nature of this agrarian

reform, which did not satisfy the peasants who continued to fight for the abolition of feudal obligations without redemption, it nevertheless opened the way for the development of capitalist relations in agriculture. p. 39

[34] This article is complementary to the series of articles and reports on Switzerland written by Engels during his forced stay there (because of the order for his arrest issued by the Cologne authorities) from November 1848 to January 1849. The series started with the article "The Ex-Principality" and ended with two reports on the foreign policy of the Swiss ruling circles (see present edition, Vol. 8, pp. 7-8, 251-53). Engels ceased his writings on Swiss affairs in mid-January 1849, when he returned to Germany. Later on, however, he occasionally wrote on the subject, as this article shows. It is based on data from Swiss and German papers, but the editors of the volume are not in possession of the actual material used by Engels. p. 42

[35] *Sonderbund*—a separatist union formed by the seven economically backward Catholic cantons of Switzerland in 1843 to resist progressive bourgeois reforms and defend the privileges of the church and the Jesuits. The decree of the Swiss Diet of July 1847 on the dissolution of the Sonderbund served as a pretext for the latter to start hostilities against the other cantons early in November. On November 23, 1847, the Sonderbund army was defeated by federal forces. p. 42

[36] The reference is to the Constitution of the Swiss Republic adopted on September 12, 1848. The Constitution legalised the results of the victory won by the progressive forces over the Sonderbund and turned Switzerland from a union of individual cantons into a united federative state. In place of the former Swiss Diet, the members of which functioned as representatives of cantons, an all-Swiss Federal Assembly was set up consisting of two chambers—the National Council and the Council of States. The executive power was vested in the Federal Council (the Government of Switzerland) and the chairman of the Federal Council acted as President of the Republic. The Constitution provided for the organisation of a single post and customs department, the introduction of a unified monetary system, and a system of weights and measures. At the same time, cantons retained broad autonomous rights. p. 43

[37] In the period from the fifteenth to the mid-nineteenth centuries agreements were concluded between Swiss cantons and European states for the supply of Swiss mercenaries. In many countries they were used by counter-revolutionary monarchist forces.

In this case, the reference is to the agreements concluded in 1848 by the canton of Berne and some other cantons with the counter-revolutionary Government of Ferdinand II, King of Naples. The use of Swiss troops against the revolutionary movement in Italy aroused profound indignation among the Swiss progressive public, and this eventually led to the annulment of these agreements. p. 44

[38] An allusion to the invitation to Berne extended by the Federal Council to Professor of Military Sciences Rudolf Lohbauer, formerly a radical journalist who contributed to Prussian government periodicals. See Engels' article "Herr Müller.—Radetzky's Chicanery towards Tessin.—The Federal Council—Lohbauer" (present edition, Vol. 8, pp. 239-41). p. 45

[39] The reference is to the dissolution of the Austrian Constituent Imperial Diet (*Reichstag*) by Emperor Francis Joseph on March 7, 1849. He was prompted to do this by his mother Archduchess Sophia and the Court camarilla. The Imperial Diet opened in Vienna on July 22, 1848. Prior to this, on May 15, as a result of the

mass revolutionary actions, the Government was forced to recognise the constituent rights of the Imperial Diet to be convened. The majority of its deputies, however, representing the liberal bourgeoisie and landowners (includ- ing deputies from the Slav national districts), opposed any extension of the revolution. During the Vienna popular uprising in October 1848, the Imperial Diet transferred its seat to the Moravian town of Kremsier. There, on March 4, 1849 the consultative commission it had set up completed a Draft of Fundamental Rights providing for people's sovereignty, freedom of assembly and the press, equality of estates and nationalities, while retaining the monarchy. The draft, however, was not approved because the coup d'état took place the same day and the new, anti-democratic Constitution (see Note 13) was introduced by royal decree. Three days later the Diet itself was dissolved.                p. 47

[40] The reference is to the October-November 1848 counter-revolutionary coup d'état in Prussia which resulted in the dissolution of the Prussian National Assembly and the introduction of the Constitution imposed by King Frederick William IV (see Note 27).

The *Holy Alliance*—an association of European monarchs founded on September 26, 1815, on the initiative of the Russian Tsar Alexander I and the Austrian Chancellor Metternich, to suppress revolutionary movements and preserve feudal monarchies in European countries. During the 1848-49 revolution and subsequent years, counter-revolutionary circles in Austria, Prussia and Tsarist Russia attempted to revive the Holy Alliance's activities in a modified form.                p. 47

[41] During the popular uprising in Vienna in October 1848, Welcker and Mosle, liberal deputies of the Frankfurt National Assembly (see Note 30), were sent to Vienna to negotiate with the insurgents and the Austrian Court and Government, which moved from the capital to Olmütz. Both of them acted as commissioners of the so-called Central Authority (*Zentralgewalt*) set up by the Frankfurt Assembly on June 28, 1848 and consisting of the Imperial Regent (Archduke Johann of Austria) and an Imperial Ministry. This provisional Central Authority had neither a budget nor an army of its own, possessed no real power, and was in fact an instrument of the counter-revolutionary German princes. However, Welcker and Mosle never turned up in revolutionary Vienna and confined themselves to fruitless talks with the Austrian Ministers and audiences granted by Emperor Ferdinand and Commander-in-Chief of the counter-revolutionary army Windischgrätz. The mediatory mission of the imperial commissioners was in fact a cover for the treacherous refusal by the liberal majority of the Frankfurt Assembly to support the Viennese insurgents.

Robert Blum, who represented the Left wing of the Frankfurt Assembly, sided with the insurgents and, despite his parliamentary immunity, was shot on November 9 by an Austrian firing-squad after the uprising was suppressed.

The correspondence between Welcker and Mosle and the Austrian Ministers was published in the Appendices to the Report of the Committee of the Frankfurt Assembly for investigating Austrian affairs (see *Verhandlungen der deutschen verfassunggebende Reichsversammlung zu Frankfurt am Main*, Bd. 2, Frankfurt am Main, 1849, S. 602-19).

The *Neue Rheinische Zeitung* responded to the Welcker-Mosle mission with a critical article "Report of the Frankfurt Committee on Austrian Affairs" (see present edition, Vol. 8, pp. 88-93).                p. 48

[42] At the time when the coup d'état was being hatched and implemented in Prussia, the Frankfurt National Assembly undertook to settle the conflict between the

Prussian National Assembly and the Crown. To fulfil this mission, first Bassermann (a liberal leader) and later Simson and Hergenhahn arrived in Berlin as imperial commissioners. Gagern, Chairman of the Frankfurt Assembly, also went to the capital of Prussia to render assistance. The mediation of the imperial commissioners and Gagern proved to be helpful to the counter-revolutionaries, because it diverted the democratic forces in the German state from offering real support to the Prussian National Assembly in its struggle against the Brandenburg-Manteuffel Ministry.                                                        p. 48

[43] *Serezhans*—see Note 22.

*Huzuls*—Ukrainians living in the Carpathian mountains which formed part of Austrian Hungary. In the first half of the 19th century, up to 1918, they were subjects of the Habsburg Empire.                                                        p. 48

[44] The reference is to the *Grundrechte des deutschen Volkes*, a document passed by the Frankfurt National Assembly in December 1848 in the course of drawing up an all-German imperial Constitution ("Verfassung des deutschen Reiches vom 28. März 1849"). It was regarded by the Assembly as a component part of the Constitution and was included in it as Chapter VI.                                        p. 48

[45] An allusion to the Austrian special border troops who wore red-coats and caps and were recruited mainly from among the inhabitants of the Empire's Slav provinces (Croats, Serbs of the Voivodina etc.). In 1848 and 1849, they were used by the counter-revolution against the revolutionary movement.                p. 49

[46] An allusion to Frederick William IV's statement in his speech at the opening of the United Diet on April 11, 1847, that he was "heir to the unweakened crown and must hand it over to his successors in an unweakened state" (see *Der Erste Vereinigte Landtag in Berlin 1847*, erster Teil).                                        p. 50

[47] In the first half of the 19th century the word *poster* was used to denote any appeal, announcement or notice posted in the streets for the public to see.

The *September Laws* promulgated by the French Government in September 1835 restricted the rights of jury courts and introduced severe measures against the press. They provided for increased money deposits for periodical publications and introduced imprisonment and large fines for publishing attacks on private property and the existing political system.                                        p. 50

[48] The Prussian National Assembly dissolved by King Frederick William IV on December 5, 1848 (see Note 27), was ironically referred to by Marx and Engels as the "Agreement Assembly" ("Vereinbarungsversammlung"), because it was guided by the "theory of agreement". According to this, the Assembly was to draw up a Constitution not on the basis of sovereign and constituent rights, but by "agreement with the Crown" (the principle formulated by the Camphausen-Hansemann Government and adopted by the majority of the Assembly). The Crown used this theory of agreement as a screen to cover up preparations for a counter-revolutionary coup d'état.                                                        p. 51

[49] The so-called law on *crieurs publics* (street newspaper-sellers) adopted by the Louis Philippe Government in 1834 was intended to restrict the distribution of opposition periodicals.                                                        p. 51

[50] *Code Napoléon (Code civil)*—French code of civil law promulgated in 1804. It was introduced by Napoleon in the conquered regions of West and South-West

Germany and remained in operation in the Rhine Province even after its incorporation into Prussia in 1815.

The expression *Prussian Law* refers to the *Allgemeines Landrecht für die Preussischen Staaten* approved and published in 1794. It included the criminal, state, civil, administrative and ecclesiastical law and was strongly influenced by backward feudal juridical standards. p. 52

51 After the Rhineland's union with Prussia in 1815, the Prussian Government strove to introduce Prussian Law standards into various spheres of jurisdiction, in place of the existing French civil code. This was being done through a series of laws, edicts and instructions aimed at restoring the feudal privileges of the nobility (the right of primogeniture), introduction of the Prussian penal code, marriage laws etc. These measures, which met with great opposition in the Rhineland, were repealed after the March revolution by the decree of April 15, 1848. p. 52

52 The *Constitution imposed* ("granted") by King Frederick William IV on December 5, 1848, dissolved the Prussian National Assembly and introduced a two-chamber system; the First Chamber was transformed by age and property qualifications into a privileged chamber of the nobility. According to the electoral law of December 6, 1848, the right to vote in the two-stage elections to the Second Chamber was granted only to so-called independent Prussians. The Constitution provided for the suspension, in case of war or disorder, of freedom of the individual, inviolability of the dwelling, freedom of the press, assembly, association and so forth. The royal authority was vested with very wide powers—the King was authorised to convene or dissolve the Chambers, to appoint Ministers, declare war or conclude a peace treaty. He was vested with full executive power, while he exercised legislative power together with the Chambers. Later on, anti-democratic revisions of the Constitution were repeatedly made on the initiative of Prussian ruling circles. p. 52

53 See Note 19. p. 56

54 *Raizen (Rascians, Rascier)* is the name for Serbs of the Orthodox denomination, often used to denote Serbs in general; it probably derives from the ancient town of Rassa, the centre of the Raschka district where the first Serbian tribes settled. p. 60

55 *Honved*—literally: defender of the homeland; the name given to the Hungarian revolutionary army of 1848-49, which was set up by the decision of the Hungarian revolutionary Government on May 16, 1848, to form ten battalions of Honveds. p. 60

56 See Note 9. p. 61

57 The *Slovanská Lípa*—a Czech national society founded in Prague at the end of April 1848. The society was under the leadership of moderate liberals (Šafařík, Gauč), who joined the counter-revolution after the Prague uprising was suppressed in June 1848, whereas the provincial branches were mostly led by representatives of the radical Czech bourgeoisie. p. 62

58 The reference is to the Bills on associations and assemblies, and on posters and the press prepared by the Prussian Government.
The *September Laws*—see Note 47.
The *Prussian Law*—see Note 50. p. 65

59 See Note 46. p. 65

[60] After Napoleon was proclaimed "Emperor of the French" in 1804, he assumed the title of king of the vassal Italian state formed from the Cisalpine Republic (Northern Italy), a dependency of France. After being crowned in Milan Cathedral on May 26, 1805 with the traditional iron crown of the Lombard kings who conquered Northern Italy in the sixth century, he uttered the following phrase, "God has given it to me, woe to him who will touch it" ("*Dio mi la diede, guai a chi la tocca*"). p. 66

[61] See Note 19. p. 69

[62] An allusion to Camphausen who was formerly an oil and corn dealer. p. 69

[63] In the *Neue Rheinische Zeitung* this ironical expression was used of the commander of a division billeted in Düsseldorf, the reactionary Prussian general Drigalski (see Marx's article "Drigalski—Legislator, Citizen and Communist", present edition, Vol. 8, pp. 75-80) who in November 1848 proclaimed a state of siege in the town and appealed to the citizens to be "communists in the noble sense of the word" and make donations to the poor. The appeal signed "Citizen Drigalski" was published in the *Düsseldorfer Zeitung* No. 311, November 24, 1848. p. 70

[64] The reference is to the eastern provinces of the Kingdom of Prussia (with the exception of Posen) which historically formed its basis. They were known as the old provinces as distinct from the western ("new") provinces—Rhineland and Westphalia, which were incorporated into Prussia in 1815 by decision of the Vienna Congress. p. 70

[65] See Note 55. p. 73

[66] See Note 45. p. 73

[67] The reference is to the so-called party of Magyarisers, or the Croatian-Hungarian party, formed as far back as 1841 and consisting mainly of Croatian-Slavonian nobles and big landowners. The party aimed for a complete merger of Croatia and Slavonia (which administratively formed part of the Hungarian Kingdom within the Austrian Empire) with Hungary as a means to counteract bourgeois reforms and to retain political and social privileges. Its members waged a bitter struggle against the representatives of "Illyrism", a national trend dominated mainly by liberal landowners and commercial bourgeoisie. The Illyrians aimed at uniting the South-Slav peoples and at securing broad autonomous rights for them within the framework of the Austrian Empire, on a federative basis.

During the 1848 revolution and the increasingly acute national conflict, many Magyarisers fled to Hungary. On June 5, 1848, the sittings of the *Sabor* of the Southern Slavs opened in Agram (Zagreb). Representatives of the liberal landowners and the top sections of the commercial bourgeoisie in Croatia and Slavonia who predominated at the *Sabor* (the *Sabor* was also attended by delegates from the Serbs of the Voivodina and the Czechs), professed their loyalty to the Habsburgs and restricted the national programme to the demand for autonomy for the united Slav territories within the Austrian Empire. General Jellachich, who was close to the Right-wing Illyrians, was appointed Ban of Croatia in March 1848. After a brief conflict with the Austrian Government, which led to his dismissal, he was reinstated in September 1848. Placing Croatian and Slavonian military units at the service of Austrian reaction, Jellachich took part in the counter-revolutionary campaign against Hungary and in the suppression of the popular uprising in Vienna.

The *Banal Council*—an administrative body, headed by the Ban, exercised the functions of the Government of Croatia. p. 73

68 The reference is to the inhabitants of the so-called Military Border area, i.e. the southern border region of the Austrian Empire under a military administration. The area included part of Croatia and southern Hungary. Its population was made up of Serbs and Croats who were allotted land in return for military service, the fulfilment of state obligations and payment of duties. Borderers often rose in revolt against this system of military-feudal oppression (see also notes 22 and 45).

p. 74

69 In this item, Engels apparently made use of the material published in the *Breslauer Zeitung* and reprinted in the *Kölnische Zeitung* No. 63 (second edition), March 15, 1849.

p. 76

70 The reference is to the *Defence Council* set up on September 22, 1848 under the conditions of the intervention launched against revolutionary Hungary by the army of the Croatian Ban Jellachich. The Council, headed by Kossuth, exercised control over the Count Batthyány liberal Government. After the victory over Jellachich and the resignation of the Batthyány Cabinet the Defence Council was entrusted with governmental functions on October 8. Kossuth, its chairman, was vested with full powers in accordance with war-time conditions. In January 1849, when Austrian troops seized Pest, the Defence Council and the National Assembly transferred their seat to Debreczin.

p. 77

71 The reference is to the *French Provisional Government* formed on February 24, 1848, as a result of the overthrow of the July monarchy. The posts in this Government were mainly held by moderate republicans (Lamartine, Dupont de l'Eure, Crémieux, Arago, Marie and two men from the *National*—the opposition republican party—Marrast and Garnier-Pagès). In addition, the Government included three representatives of the petty-bourgeois party of democrat-socialists who grouped round the *Réforme*—Ledru-Rollin, Flocon and Louis Blanc, and a mechanic Albert (real name Martin). The Provisional Government stayed in power till May 10, 1848 when it was superseded by the Executive Commission formed by the National (Constituent) Assembly.

p. 79

72 The reference is to the uprising of the Paris proletariat against the bourgeois regime of the Second Republic (June 23-26, 1848). It was the climax of the 1848 revolution in France and had an impact on revolutionary events in other European countries. Marx and Engels appraised the uprising and its historic significance in a series of articles published in the *Neue Rheinische Zeitung* (see present edition, Vol. 7, pp. 130-49).

p.80

73 The *additional 45-centime tax* for every franc of all direct taxes that was introduced by the French Provisional Government on March 16, 1848, became a heavy burden, above all for the peasants who made up the majority of France's population. This measure caused the peasant masses to turn away from the revolution and to vote for Louis Napoleon Bonaparte at the presidential elections on December 10, 1848.

p. 80

74 The *legitimists*—advocates of the Bourbon dynasty overthrown in 1830, who upheld the interests of the big hereditary landowners, and the claim to the throne by the grandson of King Charles X, Comte de Chambord, who took the name of Henry V.

p. 80

75 The reference is to the restoration of the Bourbon dynasty in France, first in May 1814 and later in July 1815. After the defeat of Napoleonic France in the war against the sixth coalition, Napoleon had to abdicate in April 1814 and the Bour-

bons were restored to power. Louis XVIII became King of France. In March 1815, Napoleon regained power but his rule did not last long (the Hundred Days). After his defeat at Waterloo by British and Prussian troops he again abdicated on June 22, 1815 and Louis XVIII was again restored to the throne (July 8) with the help of the foreign armies.                                                                            p. 80

76 *Orleanists*—supporters of the Orléans dynasty which held power in France during the July monarchy (1830-48). The Orleanists upheld the interests of the financial aristocracy and the big industrial bourgeoisie.                                                   p. 80

77 On May 15, 1848, there was a revolutionary uprising of Paris workers led by Blanqui, Barbès and others against the anti-labour and anti-democratic policy pursued by the Constituent Assembly which opened on May 4. The participants in the mass demonstration forced their way into the Assembly's premises, demanded the formation of a Ministry of Labour and presented a number of other demands. An attempt was made to form a revolutionary government. However, with the help of national guards from the bourgeois quarters and regular troops, the power of the Constituent Assembly was restored. The leaders of the movement were arrested and put on trial.                                                                    p. 81

78 The trial of the leaders of the Paris workers' revolutionary uprising of May 15, 1848 was held in Bourges from March 7 to April 3, 1849. They were accused of conspiring against the Government. The court sentenced Barbès and Albert to exile and Blanqui to ten-year solitary confinement. The other defendants (among them Sobrier, Raspail) were sentenced to various terms of imprisonment or exile.                                                                                                            p. 81

79 The reference is to the article "*Ein Aktenstück des Märzvereins*" published in the *Neue Rheinische Zeitung* No. 181 of December 29, 1848, which exposed the half-hearted and inconsistent policy of a number of the Frankfurt Left leaders whose actions only helped the counter-revolution. The *Neue Rheinische Zeitung* called these leaders the "Girondists of our revolution".                                       p. 84

80 This refers to the counter-revolutionary Catholic Union attached to the Frankfurt National Assembly and headed by von Radowitz, an extreme Right-wing leader.
                                                                                                               p. 84

81 "*Thinking friends of history*" is a phrase which Marx and Engels ironically used of Camphausen and other liberals, alluding to the subtitle of the then well-known book by the liberal historian Karl von Rotteck, *Allgemeine Geschichte vom Anfang der historischen Kenntniss bis auf unsere Zeiten. Für denkende Geschichtsfreunde bearb. von Karl von Rotteck*, Bd. 1-9, Freiburg im Breisgau, 1834.                            p. 85

82 The *Feuillants*—moderate liberal constitutionalists who, during the French Revolution, withdrew from the Jacobin Club on July 16, 1791, after it had adopted a petition to dethrone the King. They formed their own political club which held meetings in the premises of the monastic order of the same name which was dissolved in 1789. The Feuillants upheld the interests of the big bourgeoisie and liberal nobility and did their utmost to prevent the revolution from developing further.                                                                                                          p. 85

83 An allusion to the stand adopted by Karl Vogt and other leaders of the March Association over the future state structure of Germany. At the concluding stage of the debates in the Frankfurt National Assembly on the imperial Constitution, Vogt and other moderate democrats began to be inclined to agree with the pro-Prussian

liberals (Gagern and others) who strove to unite Germany as an empire, with Frederick William IV, King of Prussia, at the head. p. 85

84 The *Second Chamber of the Prussian Diet* (Landtag) was convened on February 26, 1849, on the basis of the Constitution "granted" by Frederick William IV on December 5, 1848. Despite the fact that elections to it were held under conditions of virtual martial law, introduced in many provinces of Prussia and under the anti-democratic electoral law of December 6, 1848, a strong opposition was formed in the Chamber. It was made up of the majority of Left-Centre and Right-Centre deputies of the dissolved National Assembly. Though the opposition speeches of the Left were rather moderate, the Second Chamber was dissolved by the Government on April 27, 1849.

The text of the draft Address, as well as the minutes of the debates in the Chamber, were published in *Stenographische Berichte über die Verhandlungen der durch das Allerhöchste Patent vom 5. Dezember 1848 einberufenen Kammern. Zweite Kammer. Beilage zum "Preußischen Staats-Anzeiger"*, Bd. 1-2, Berlin, 1849.

Marx apparently used newspaper reports. p. 86

85 See Note 52. p. 86

86 The reference is to "Verordnung über einige Grundlagen der künftigen Preußischen Verfassung" and to "Wahlgesetz für die zur Vereinbarung der Preußischen Staats-Verfassung zu berufende Versammlung", adopted by the Second United Diet (the first document on April 6, the second on April 8, 1848). The dissolution of the National Assembly by the Prussian Government on December 5, 1848, was in blatant violation of the laws passed by the United Diet. p. 86

87 *Comité du salut public* (Committee of Public Safety)—revolutionary government of France during the dictatorship of the Jacobins (1793-94). p. 87

88 The *United Diet*—an assembly of representatives from the eight Provincial Diets of Prussia and similarly based on the estate principle. The United Diet sanctioned new taxes and loans, took part in the discussion of new Bills and had the right to address petitions to the King.

The First United Diet, which opened on April 11, 1847, was dissolved in June, following its refusal to grant a new loan. The Second United Diet was convened on April 2, 1848, after the revolution of March 18-19 in Prussia. It passed a series of laws pertaining to the principles of a future Constitution and on elections to the Prussian National Assembly, and also sanctioned the loan. The United Diet session was closed on April 10, 1848. p. 87

89 An allusion to the suppression of the Polish national liberation insurrection of 1830-31 by Tsarist troops. p. 87

90 The *Danish campaign* refers to the war between Prussia and Denmark over Schleswig-Holstein which broke out in April 1848. The national liberation movement against Danish rule arose in the duchies of Schleswig and Holstein inhabited mainly by Germans under the influence of the March 1848 revolution in the German states. Fearful of a national uprising and an extension of the revolution, Prussian ruling circles strove to come to terms with the King of Denmark in the course of the war, at the expense of all-German interests, and this also affected the war manoeuvres of the Prussian army. Engels ironically compared them with the proceedings in the *Imperial Court of Law* which were marked by unprecedented red tape and confusion (the Imperial Court of Law was

the supreme judicial institution in Germany in the 15th-18th centuries). The Imperial Court of Law ceased to exist in 1806 when the so-called Holy Roman Empire of the German nation was abolished.                                    p. 88

[91] During the suppression of the national liberation uprising in Posen at the end of April and the beginning of May 1848, Prussian troops suffered a defeat at Miloslavl and shot the Polish insurgents at Wreschen (Września) (see present edition, Vol. 7, pp. 104-05).

When speaking of the "victories" of the Prussian army, Engels is ironically referring to its savage reprisals against the popular movements in Anhalt-Bernburg in March 1848, in Mainz in May 1848 and its participation in suppressing the revolt in Frankfurt am Main in September 1848.

"*My glorious army*"—see Note 19.                                           p. 88

[92] The reference is to the armistice concluded on August 26, 1848, in the Swedish town of Malmö between Denmark and Prussia for a term of seven months. The armistice actually preserved the Danish rule in the duchies of Schleswig and Holstein, provided for the replacement of provisional authorities in Schleswig by a new government (in which the puppets of the Danish monarchy prevailed), the separation of the Schleswig and Holstein troops and other terms unfavourable to the national liberation movement in the duchies. The revolutionary-democratic changes that had been introduced there came virtually to nothing.

Later on, the ruling circles of Prussia, hoping to raise the prestige of the Prussian monarchy by taking part in this popular war and to realise their aggressive plans, resumed hostilities in March 1849 which went on with changing success. However, under pressure from Denmark's allies (England and Russia), Prussia signed a peace treaty with Denmark on July 2, 1850, temporarily abandoned its claims to Schleswig and Holstein and withdrew its military support in the war waged by the duchies. The Schleswig-Holstein troops sustained a defeat and had to give up resistance. As a result, the two duchies remained within the Kingdom of Denmark.                                                        p. 88

[93] See Note 9.                                                               p. 93

[94] This apparently refers to the *Chief Odbor* (see Note 11).               p. 98

[95] See Note 54.                                                              p. 98

[96] See Note 68.                                                              p. 99

[97] The reference is to the Hungarian National Assembly (Diet) convened in Pressburg before the 1848 revolution in the Austrian Empire. The Assembly, in which the liberal nobility predominated, put forward a demand for a Constitution. After the revolutionary demonstrations in Pest on March 15, 1848, the Assembly introduced a parliamentary system. Executive power was vested in the Hungarian Government, but the two states—Hungary and Austria—continued as monarchies under one crown.

The imperial government at first had to recognise this status of Hungary, but subsequently, as a result of the deepening conflict, tried to demolish it through armed intervention. At the same time, in the Hungarian National Assembly which held its sessions in Debreczin there was the "Party of Pacification" which consisted mainly of aristocratic elements and was striving to find a compromise with the Habsburgs and to secure recognition of the new Emperor Francis Joseph as the King of Hungary. The "Party of Pacification" was opposed by the radicals headed by Kossuth who came out for more resolute action against the Austrian monarchy.

The *Pragmatic Sanction* was a royal decree having the force of fundamental law on succession to the throne. Adopted in the Austrian Empire in 1713, it established the principle of the indivisibility of the Habsburg crown lands and the possibility of distaff succession if the Emperor had no sons.                    p. 100

98 This article was written by Engels for the *Neue Rheinische Zeitung* but was not published. It is extant in the manuscript form with slight corrections and deletions in the text made by the author. The most important versions that were crossed out are given in footnotes.                                                      p. 102

99 The reference is to the suppression of the popular uprising in Vienna by the counter-revolutionary army of Windischgrätz at the end of October and the beginning of November 1848, and also to the capture of Pest on January 5, 1849 by Austrian troops under his command in an attack on revolutionary Hungary.
                                                                  p. 102

100 Apparently Engels is here referring to the Slav group in the Imperial Diet and, in general, to the representatives of the Slav peoples' national movement who were demanding the unification of the Slav lands and autonomy within the framework of the Austrian Empire. After the publication of the imposed ("granted") Constitution on March 4, 1849, which destroyed all hopes that the national demands might be satisfied, opposition sentiments grew stronger among the Slavs.
                                                                  p. 105

101 The reference is to the conflict of the Austrian Government with the Constituent Imperial Diet and to the Constitution imposed by Emperor Francis Joseph on March 4, 1849 (see Note 39).                                       p. 105

102 See Note 35.                                                   p. 105

103 The sittings of the Frankfurt National Assembly were held in *St. Paul's Church*. Austrian ruling circles were hostile to the elaboration of an all-German Constitution by the Assembly and strove to restore the old German Confederation of 1815, in which Austria played the leading role. Schwarzenberg, head of the Austrian Government, issued a Note imbued with this idea on March 9, 1849, after the dissolution of the Austrian Diet. On April 15, 1849, the Austrian Government officially rejected the imperial Constitution adopted by the Assembly as incompatible with the unity and nature of the Austrian Empire and recalled the Austrian deputies from Frankfurt.                                     p. 106

104 The revolution in Austria began with the uprising of March 13, 1848 in Vienna. It was followed by the March 18-19 revolutionary events in Berlin which started the revolution in Prussia.                                              p. 108

105 On June 25, 1849, the anniversary of the June 1848 uprising of the Paris workers was to be celebrated.                                                p. 108

106 Camphausen was one of the shareholders of the oppositional *Rheinische Zeitung* which was published in Cologne in 1842 and 1843 and edited by Marx from October 1842 to March 1843.                                        p. 108

107 The reference is to the appeal by Frederick William IV published on March 21, 1848 under the title "To My People and the German Nation" ("An mein Volk und an die deutsche Nation"). Under the impact of the revolutionary events, the King had to give a pledge to be loyal to the tricolour banner of the revolution and to contribute to the unification of Germany.                         p. 109

[108] *Friedrichshain*—a park in Berlin where those killed in the barricade fighting during the March 18, 1848 uprising were buried.                                          p. 109

[109] The reference is to the cities of Buda (Ofen) and Pest which at the time were virtually twin capital cities of Hungary. After a successful counter-attack by the Hungarian revolutionary army and the liberation of the two capital cities from the Austrian invaders on June 24, 1849 the Hungarian authorities announced the unification of Buda and Pest into one city. However, subsequent events prevented this decree from being implemented.

The official unification of Pest and Buda and the formation of a single city of Budapest took place on January 1, 1873.                                          p. 111

[110] See Note 10.                                          p. 111

[111] See Note 21.                                          p. 112

[112] Cavalry units of the Austrian army included not only squadrons but also larger tactical formations—divisions, which usually consisted of two squadrons. p. 113

[113] The reference is to the *armistice* concluded between *Austria* and the *Kingdom of Sardiniá* (*Piedmont*) on August 9, 1848 after the defeat of the Piedmontese troops at Custozza. The Kingdom of Sardinia was to withdraw its troops from Lombardy, Parma and Venice and cede them to the Austrians.

On March 20, 1849, under pressure from the masses, King Charles Albert had to declare the armistice cancelled and to resume hostilities against Austria.
                                          p. 114

[114] *C.M.* (conventional money, or 20-gulden coins) had existed in Austria since the eighteenth century and, under the respective convention, was also introduced in Bavaria. Its standard was silver (20 guldens were to contain 234 grams of silver). In the eighteenth century, paper money was issued which, from the early nineteenth century, was called "Vienna currency". Transactions were quoted in conventional monetary units.                                          p. 114

[115] See Note 39.                                          p. 115

[116] The German term used here and elsewhere is *Feldzeugmeister* which is a higher rank in the Austrian army directly subordinate to Field Marshal. In some other armies it retained its original meaning of artillery commander.                                          p. 115

[117] See Note 67.                                          p. 116

[118] See Note 54.                                          p. 121

[119] The reference is to provincial diets (*Landtags*) introduced in Prussia in 1823. They consisted of representatives of four estates (princes, nobility, representatives of towns and rural communities). Property and other electoral qualifications secured the majority in the provincial diets for the nobility. The provincial diets were convened by the King and they were competent only to deal with questions of local economy and administration. As consultative bodies they could make proposals on Bills submitted by the Government for discussion. In 1843, under the pretext of introducing unified legislation for Prussia, King Frederick William IV submitted for discussion in the Rhenish Diet a new draft of the penal code which was to replace the more liberal French *Code pénal*. The seventh Rhenish Diet (1843) rejected the Bill, stating that the existing laws fully conformed to the moral standards, traditions and legal practices of the Rhine Province.                                          p. 125

<sup>120</sup> See Note 46.

The Rhenish legislation refers to the *Code civil* (see Note 50) and *Code pénal*—the penal code adopted in France in 1810 and introduced in the conquered regions of West and South-West Germany. It remained in operation in the Rhine Province even after its incorporation into Prussia in 1815.     p. 125

<sup>121</sup> An allusion to the rescripts (patents) of Frederick William IV of February 3, 1847, on the convocation of the United Diet (on which see Note 88).     p. 125

<sup>122</sup> At the June 2, 1847 sitting of the United Diet, Thadden-Triglaff, a Right-wing deputy, stated: "My proposal reads as follows: freedom of the press—*really* public proceedings for the gentlemen of the press and along with them the *gallows!* I would ask Messrs the stenographers to underline thoroughly both the words 'really' and 'gallows'." (*Der Erste Vereinigte Landtag in Berlin 1847*, vierter Theil, S. 2241.)     p. 125

<sup>123</sup> *Uckermark*—a northern part of the Brandenburg Province (Prussia), the mainstay of the reactionary Prussian junkers.     p. 126

<sup>124</sup> *Holy Hermandad*—a league of Spanish towns set up at the end of the fifteenth century with the approbation of the King, who sought to make use of the wealthy townspeople in their fight against the feudal magnates in an attempt to establish royal absolutism. From the middle of the sixteenth century, the armed detachments of the Holy Hermandad performed police duties. Thus the police in general has often been ironically labelled the "Holy Hermandad".     p. 126

<sup>125</sup> See Note 47.     p. 127

<sup>126</sup> The reference is to the *Vienna Congress* of European monarchs and their Ministers (September 1814 to June 1815) which set up a system of all-European treaties after the wars of the European powers against Napoleonic France. The decisions of the Congress helped to restore the feudal system and a number of former dynasties in the states that had been conquered by Napoleon, sanctioned the political disunity of Germany and Italy, the incorporation of Belgium into Holland and the partition of Poland and mapped out measures to combat the revolutionary movement.     p. 127

<sup>127</sup> See Note 50.     p. 127

<sup>128</sup> The reference is to the so-called *United Commissions* of the representatives of the Provincial Diets which met on January 17, 1848 to discuss the Bill concerning penal law ("Entwurf des Strafgesetzbuchs für die preußischen Staaten..."). Convening these commissions, the Prussian Government hoped that the apparent preparations for reform would lessen the growing public unrest. The work of the commissions was interrupted by the revolutionary outbursts that swept through Germany at the beginning of March.     p. 127

<sup>129</sup> The reference is to the edict issued by the King of Prussia on March 6, 1821 under the title "Allerhöchste Kabinetsorder vom 6ten März 1821, betreffend die Strafgesetze und das Verfahren in den Rheinprovinzen bei Verbrechen und Vergehungen gegen den Staat und dessen Oberhaupt...". It introduced the Prussian penal code into the Rhine Province with respect to high treason. This was one of the first attempts made by the Prussian Government to limit the jurisdiction of the *Code pénal* operating in the Rhine Province and introduce the old-Prussian feudal-type penal code.     p. 128

<sup>130</sup> See Note 55.     p. 133

[131] The debates in the Second Chamber of the Prussian Provincial Diet (see Note 84) were published in *Stenographische Berichte über die Verhandlungen der durch das Allerhöchste Patent vom 5. Dezember 1848 einberufenen Kammern. Zweite Kammer. Beilage zum "Preußischen Staats-Anzeiger"*, Bd. 1-2, Berlin, 1849. The discussion of the draft Address in reply to the speech from the throne was held on March 13, 1849.                                                                                      p. 135

[132] The minutes of the Prussian National Assembly (ironically referred to here as the "Agreement Assembly"—see Note 48) were published in the *Stenographische Berichte über die Verhandlungen der zur Vereinbarung der preußischen Staats-Verfassung berufenen Versammlung. Beilage zum "Preußischen Staats-Anzeiger"*, Bd. 1-3, Berlin, 1848. Later they were published as a separate edition under the title *Verhandlungen der constituirenden Versammlung für Preußen. 1848*, Bd. 1-8, Berlin, 1848; Bd. 9 (Suppl.-Bd.), Leipzig, 1849.                                    p. 135

[133] The reference is to the period between the dissolution of the Prussian National Assembly (December 5, 1848) and the convocation of the Chambers of the Prussian Provincial Diet (February 26, 1849).                                    p. 135

[134] See Note 52.                                                                    p. 135

[135] During the coup d'état in Prussia, after a series of delays, the National Assembly adopted on November 15, 1848 a decision to refuse to pay taxes from November 17 onwards in protest against government policy. However, the decision taken under the pressure of the Left deputies and democratic circles was interpreted by the majority of deputies in the spirit of passive resistance, which could hardly be effective measure in the struggle against the counter-revolutionary offensive.
                                                                                      p. 136

[136] *Wailers (Heuler)*—the name the republican democrats in Germany in 1848-49 applied to the moderate constitutionalists who, in turn, called their opponents "agitators" (*Wühler*). See also Note 245).                                    p. 138

[137] In January and February 1814, during the war against Napoleonic France, the Prussian and other coalition armies suffered a number of defeats in Champagne (including the battles at Bar-Sur-Aube, Saint Dizier, and Montmirail).
     In the battle at *Jena* on October 14, 1806, the Prussian army was defeated by the French; the defeat was followed by the surrender of feudal Prussia to Napoleonic France.
     On March 18 and 19, 1848, the imperial troops had to withdraw from Berlin as a result of the victorious uprising of the masses.                              p. 139

[138] The question of electing the King of Prussia to the throne of the German Empire was discussed in the Frankfurt National Assembly on its completion of the draft for an imperial Constitution which, though it proclaimed some civil liberties and introduced all-German central institutions, nevertheless attributed to the united German state the form of a monarchy. The liberal deputies of the Assembly who held pro-Prussian views were particularly insistent on handing over the imperial crown to the Hohenzollerns. They were opposed by the democratic wing, but pro-Prussian tendencies took the upper hand as a result of a compromise between the moderate democrats and the liberals. On March 27, 1849, the imperial Constitution was passed on second reading. On March 28, the Frankfurt Assembly elected the Prussian King Frederick William IV "Emperor of the Germans". Frederick William IV, however, rejected the imperial crown. On the causes of his

refusal to accept the crown from the Frankfurt Assembly see Engels' article "The Comedy with the Imperial Crown" (this volume, pp. 193-94).                    p. 139

139 According to the electoral law of December 6, 1848 (see Note 52) only "independent Prussians" had the right to elect to the Second Chamber. This qualification in fact deprived the poor and the dispossessed sections of the population of all electoral rights.                                       p. 140

140 The imposed Constitution of December 5, 1848, contained reservations which contravened the principle of the immunity of deputies. Article 83 in particular stated that members of both Chambers "may be called to account both for their voting in the Chamber and for the statement of their views there".      p. 140

141 *St. Stephen's Chapel*—part of Westminster Palace, where the House of Commons sat since 1547.
   *Chambre introuvable*, the name given by King Louis XVIII to the Chamber of Deputies in France which in 1815-16 consisted of extreme conservatives.
   *The Chamber of February 24, 1848*—the Chamber of Deputies in France which tried in vain to restrain the growing revolution and preserve the monarchy by replacing Louis Philippe by his grandson—the Count of Paris—in whose favour Louis Philippe abdicated on February 24, 1848.                          p. 141

142 See Note 88.                                                         p. 141

143 See Note 26.                                                         p. 143

144 An allusion to the Catholic Easter rites practised at the Viennese, Munich, Madrid and other courts. On the Thursday of Passion Week a religious ceremony of the ablution of the sovereign's feet used to be held in the cathedrals before the liturgy.
                                                                         p. 144

145 On March 12, 1849, the King of Sardinia cancelled the armistice with Austria that had been concluded on August 9, 1848, and hostilities were resumed on March 20. However, the seven-month armistice had not been used by the ruling circles of Piedmont to reorganise and strengthen the army; the key posts were left in the hands of mediocre and counter-revolutionary-minded generals. Despite the national enthusiasm with which the resumption of hostilities was met in Piedmont, in Austrian-ridden Lombardy and all over Italy, the Piedmontese army was defeated by March 23. Charles Albert abdicated. Victor-Emmanuel II, the new king, concluded an armistice with the Austrians on March 26, and on August 6, 1849, a peace treaty was signed on very onerous terms for Piedmont. It sanctioned the restoration of Austrian rule in Northern Italy and the Austrian protectorate over a number of states of Central Italy (Tuscany, Parma).              p. 148

146 The reference is to the main battle during the first stage of the Austro-Italian war (which broke out on March 25, 1848, as a result of the national liberation uprising in Lombardy and Venice against Austrian rule)—the *battle at Custozza* (on the River Mincio) on July 25 and 26, 1848, in which the Austrian army under the command of Radetzky defeated the Piedmontese troops. Then, on August 6, the Austrians captured Milan and on August 9, 1848, an armistice was concluded between Austria and the Kingdom of Sardinia, under which the latter undertook to withdraw its troops from the cities and fortresses of Lombardy and Venice and

cede them to the Austrians. At the beginning, some of the states of Southern and Central Italy (including the Kingdom of Naples, Rome and Tuscany) were forced by the patriots to take part in the war against Austria, but right from the start the counter-revolutionary ruling circles of these states sabotaged the dispatch of army detachments to the front and soon managed either to recall their troops or make them surrender to the Austrians.                                                    p. 148

[147] See Note 13.                                                                  p. 149

[148] Apparently an allusion to the actions of General Bonaparte (the future Emperor Napoleon) during his Italian campaign of 1796-97. At the beginning of the war, as a result of his bold manoeuvring of large military contingents, Bonaparte succeeded in defeating first the Austrian troops and then their allies, the Piedmontese, in the area of the Gulf of Genoa and, by threatening to march against Turin, in forcing the Kingdom of Sardinia to dissociate itself from the anti-French coalition and sign an armistice on April 28 and a peace treaty with France on May 5, 1796.                                                         p. 150

[149] In the summer of 1848, during the initial period of the Austro-Italian war, Garibaldi offered help to Charles Albert who, however, rejected it. The command of the Piedmontese army and the provisional government of Lombardy controlled by Charles Albert in no way assisted the volunteer corps formed by Garibaldi, who was left to fight the Austrian troops alone. Though Garibaldi and his corps continued to offer heroic resistance to the Austrians, even after the Austrian-Piedmontese armistice was signed on August 9, 1848, they were compelled by superior enemy forces to retreat to Switzerland.                                p. 151

[150] See Note 9.                                                                   p. 154

[151] *Pusztas*—the Hungarian plains between the Danube and Theiss.              p. 154

[152] Engels refers to the liberation war of the Algerians under the command of Emir Abd-el-Kader against the French colonialists who had occupied Algeria in 1830. The war continued from 1832 to 1847 with short intervals.                        p. 155

[153] Several items written by Engels on the war in Northern Italy were published in the *Neue Rheinische Zeitung* under the title "From the Theatre of War" which headed the majority of his reports on the revolutionary war in Hungary. However, the former were printed in the section entitled "Italy" and the latter in the "Hungary" section. To distinguish the Italian items from his Hungarian reports, the former are published in this edition with the subtitle "Italy" supplied by the editors.                                                                        p. 156

[154] During the national liberation insurrection of 1830-31 in Poland, Ramorino, who had emigrated from Italy, was appointed commander of one of the insurgents' corps. After Warsaw was stormed by Tsarist troops early in September 1831, Ramorino withdrew his corps to Austria, where it was interned.

In 1833, Italian revolutionary emigrants, members of the "Young Italy" association headed by Mazzini, proposed to Ramorino that he should lead the military expedition to Savoy intended to instigate a republican uprising in Piedmont. However, Ramorino embezzled part of the money given him by Mazzini to enlist volunteers and in fact helped to frustrate the insurgents' plan. Instead of a simultaneous entry into Savoy from Switzerland and France, only one group of patriots penetrated Savoy from Grenoble in February 1834, and was dispersed by the Piedmontese carabinieri.

At the second stage of the Austro-Italian war, Ramorino commanded one of the Piedmontese divisions made up of Lombards. On March 20, 1849, he ordered his troops to retreat from the Ticino lowlands and thus enabled the Austrians not only to enter Piedmont, but even to cut off part of the army from the main forces. After the war, Ramorino was court-martialled and executed.                p. 156

[155] The reference is to the German section of the population of Transylvania (see Note 21).                                                                        p. 159

[156] On March 20, 1849, the Slovak deputation consisting mainly of Right-wing leaders of the Slovak national movement was received by Emperor Francis Joseph. The visit to Olmütz was prompted by the fact that Slovakia was still deprived of language equality and of other national rights, even after the imposed Constitution was proclaimed on March 4, 1849. The Slovak deputation again demanded the separation of Slovakia from Hungary and autonomy within the framework of the Austrian Empire. The Austrian Court deliberately adopted a delaying policy with the aim of using the Slovaks to fight the Hungarian revolution. However, all their national demands were subsequently rejected.
                                                                         p. 162

[157] Venice, where the masses had proclaimed independence and restored the "Republic of St. Mark" as early as March 1848, took an active part in the national liberation struggle against Austrian rule. The Venetians continued to offer resistance to the Austrians even after the armistice was concluded on August 9, 1848, between Austria and Piedmont, and withstood for many months a severe blockade by sea and land. After scoring a new victory over the Piedmontese army in March 1849, the Austrians reinforced their troops besieging Venice, which was finally forced to surrender. On August 22, 1849, the Republic of Venice, the last bulwark of the revolution in Italy, collapsed. p. 166

[158] See Note 55.                                                       p. 168

[159] The *battle at Novara* between Piedmontese and Austrian troops lasted the whole day of March 22 and ended at dawn on March 23, 1849, in the defeat and retreat of the Piedmontese army.                                                      p. 169

[160] On Ramorino's part in the Polish national liberation movement and the Savoy campaign of the Italian republicans in 1834, see Note 154.                  p. 169

[161] As Engels expected, the defeat at Novara and the conclusion of a new armistice between Austria and Piedmont cardinally changed the balance of forces in Italy in favour of the home and foreign counter-revolution. In Florence, the revolutionary events in January and February 1849 led to the overthrow of Grand Duke Leopold II and the proclamation of a republic in Tuscany (the official inauguration of a republic did not take place owing to sabotage by moderate liberals). On April 11, a counter-revolutionary coup d'état took place, the democratic provisional government of Guerazzi was overthrown, and the Grand Duke returned to power. He entered the city on May 25, 1849, together with Austrian troops.
The Roman Republic, proclaimed on February 9, 1849, had to wage a grim struggle against counter-revolutionary insurgents instigated by the Catholic clergy, against Neapolitan troops, Austrians and the French expeditionary corps sent to Italy on April 6, 1849 to restore the power of Pope Pius IX over Rome. On July 3, 1849 the Republic fell under the blows of the foreign interventionists.
                                                                         p. 170

[162] On January 26, 1849, Faucher, Minister of Public Works in the Government of the liberal monarchist Odilon Barrot, submitted a Bill on the right of association to the Constituent Assembly. Its first clause ran as follows: "Clubs are prohibited". The

Bill on the right of association (better known as the Bill on clubs) was adopted on March 21, 1849, by the votes of the monarchists and moderate republicans, despite opposition from Left deputies who accused the Government of a breach of the Constitution and demanded its resignation. This decision dealt a heavy blow to freedom of assembly and association, and primarily to the workers' associations.

p. 170

[163] See Note 19.

p. 170

[164] The reference is to the liberation war waged by the Spanish people against Napoleonic rule; a prominent part in this war was played by guerilla fighters.

p. 171

[165] See Note 40.

p. 173

[166] During the 1815 campaign in Belgium, Napoleon, after defeating the Prussian army under Blücher at Ligny, ordered Marshal Grouchy to pursue the routed Prussians and prevent them from joining the Anglo-Dutch troops under Wellington. Grouchy, however, could not prevent Blücher's army from appearing, on June 18, on the battlefield of Waterloo at the most crucial moment of the battle. Grouchy with his troops failed to provide support for the French Emperor in time, and this lost them the entire campaign.

p. 176

[167] The reference is to the march of the Austrian auxiliary army under General Nugent from Triest to help the troops under Field Marshal Radetzky who were in a difficult position as a result of a popular uprising in Lombardy and Venice against Austrian rule in March 1848. Nugent's army left Triest in the second half of April 1848. Moving through the Venetian region, particularly the mountainous district of Friuli, and only meeting resistance from weak volunteer detachments, it plundered everything on its way. On April 21 Nugent barbarously shelled Udine, the main city of Friuli. At the end of May his army joined Radetzky's troops in Verona.

*Master of Ordnance*—see Note 116.

p. 179

[168] *Direct-fire batteries* (*Demontir-Batterien*) were intended for demolishing gun emplacements and guns in besieged fortresses.

*Palatine line* (Palatine—Hungarian title for a representative of the Emperor)— outer earthwork north-west of the Komorn fortress, between the Waag and the Danube; its construction was started in 1809 by order of the Hungarian Palatine, Archduke Joseph, and continued up to 1848.

p. 180

[169] The German term used here is *Feuerwerker*—a rank in the artillery corresponding to that of non-commissioned officer in other arms.

p. 180

[170] On the recognition of Francis Joseph as King of Hungary on the basis of the Pragmatic Sanction, see Note 97.

On the *Debreczin National Assembly*, see Note 14.

p. 182

[171] See Note 54.

p. 183

[172] *Chaikists*—Austro-Hungarian infantrymen who served on small sailing vessels and rowing boats (chaikas) in the Military Border area. They built pontoon bridges and transported troops along the Danube, Theiss and Sava. Recruited mainly from among the Serbs, inhabiting the Chaikist Area in Slavonia, from 1764 onwards they formed a special battalion.

p. 183

[173] See Note 11.

p. 184

[174] The reference is to Pest and Buda (see Note 109).          p. 188

[175] An allusion to the important part Saragossa played in the Spanish national liberation war against Napoleon's rule, when the city was twice besieged by the French (in June-August 1808 and December 1808-February 1809) and won fame for its heroic defence.          p. 189

[176] The reference is to the decisions of the Vienna Congress of 1814-15 (see Note 126).          p. 191

[177] See Note 71.          p. 191

[178] An allusion to the predominance of monarchists in the Government of Odilon Barrot, set up after the election of Louis Bonaparte as President of the Republic on December 10, 1848. Republican officials in the state apparatus were replaced by monarchists. Monarchist factions of legitimists (supporters of the Bourbon dynasty), Orleanists (followers of Louis Philippe) and Bonapartists formed a coalition in the Constituent Assembly, launched a struggle against the moderate republicans for political influence and strove to strengthen counter-revolutionary policy. In the Legislative Assembly convoked on May 28, 1849, this joint "party of order" was in the majority.

The *Holy Alliance*—see Note 40.          p. 192

[179] An allusion to the composition of the Frankfurt National Assembly which on March 28, 1849 resolved to elect the King of Prussia, Frederick William IV, "Emperor of the Germans". The overwhelming majority of the Assembly's deputies were government and state officials, professors and lawyers (see Note 30)

At first Frederick William IV agreed to accept the imperial crown proffered by the National Assembly on the condition that the other German states agreed, but on April 25, 1849, he finally rejected the proposal of the Frankfurt National Assembly and the imperial Constitution it had drawn up.

The phrase *"By the grace of God do I have this crown"* was pronounced by Frederick William IV on October 15, 1840 when he was crowned King of Prussia.          p. 194

[180] This article written by Engels for the *Neue Rheinische Zeitung* was not published and has survived as an unfinished manuscript.

The article was occasioned by the Prussian Government's measures to call up the army reserve. Among the pretexts for this was the war with Denmark resumed in Schleswig-Holstein. The Prussian ruling circles were obviously preparing the armed suppression of the revolutionary-democratic movement in Prussia and the rest of Germany.

The *army reserve* (*Landwehr*) appeared in Prussia during the struggle against Napoleon. "Landwehr-Ordnung" defining the rules of enrolment, recruitment and service was adopted on November 21, 1815. In the 1840s, those to be enrolled in the army reserve had to be under 40 and go through three-years active service and be not less than two years in reserve. In contrast to the regular army, enlistment to the army reserve took place only in case of extreme necessity (war, or threat of war).          p. 195

[181] On the resumption of war between Prussia and Denmark over Schleswig-Holstein, after the expiry of the truce between them at the end of March 1849, see Note 92.          p. 195

[182] The reference is to the brutal suppression by Prussian soldiers of the national liberation insurrection in Posen in March-May 1848.          p. 196

[183] In the second half of December 1847, Marx delivered several lectures on political economy in the German Workers' Society in Brussels and intended to prepare them for publication. A manuscript of the pamphlet prepared at the time and entitled *Wages* has survived. It is written in Joseph Weydemeyer's hand and its text is almost identical to that published later in the *Neue Rheinische Zeitung*. A draft outline of Marx's concluding lectures, which he had no time to prepare for publication, is extant as a manuscript written in his own hand and also bearing the heading *Wages* (see present edition, Vol. 6). As regards its contents, it supplements the work *Wage Labour and Capital*. Later, in the preface to *A Contribution to the Critique of Political Economy* (1859) (see present edition, Vol. 30), Marx pointed out that he did not manage to publish the work on "Wage Labour" based on his lectures because of the February revolution of 1848 in France and his expulsion from Belgium.

This work first appeared as a series of leading articles in the *Neue Rheinische Zeitung* of April 5-8 and 11, 1849 under the title of *Wage Labour and Capital*. When undertaking this publication, Marx edited the former text once more and wrote an introduction giving the reasons why it was necessary to discuss economic problems in a newspaper, and primarily to reveal the economic relations on which bourgeois rule and the actual slavery of wage workers were founded.

By publishing this work, Marx wished to prepare the proletarian readers of the *Neue Rheinische Zeitung* for the solution of the tasks that had become urgent by that time—the creation of the mass workers' party, and also to define the social aims set by the revolutionary organ which he edited. Marx's work helped to spread the ideas of scientific communism among the advanced section of the German proletariat. On April 11, 1849 the Committee of the Cologne Workers' Association recommended that all its branches should start discussing social problems on the basis of the articles on wage labour and capital published in the newspaper, and called upon other workers' associations in Germany to discuss these articles.

The work was not published in the newspaper in full. Issue No. 269 announced that there was to be a sequel, but this never appeared because Marx had to leave Cologne for a time on financial and other business connected with the newspaper. The *Neue Rheinische Zeitung* No. 277 of April 20 carried the following note: "*Cologne*, April 19. Owing to the temporary absence of the author, the exposition of the relationship between wage labour and capital has had to be interrupted. It will, however, be resumed shortly and then continued to the end without interruption." This was never done, however, because the *Neue Rheinische Zeitung* ceased publication. Marx's subsequent intention to put out the work as a separate pamphlet did not materialise either.

The first separate edition in the language of the original appeared in Breslau in 1880 without Marx's knowledge. In 1881 the pamphlet was republished there. A Russian translation (the first translation into a foreign language) appeared in Geneva in 1883. It was made from the Breslau edition and repeatedly republished illegally.

After Marx's death, *Wage Labour and Capital* was published in 1884 in Hottingen-Zurich as a pamphlet with a short introductory note by Engels, dated June of that year. From December 1884 to February 1885, the London newspaper *Justice*, the organ of the Social-Democratic Federation, published the first English translation made by J. L. Joynes. In March 1885 it appeared as a separate pamphlet and later was repeatedly republished. J. L. Joynes' translation was used in the workers' press of the USA, in particular by the *Workmen's Advocate*, New Haven (Connecticut), in November 1886-January 1887.

In 1891 a new edition of the pamphlet appeared in Berlin: *Lohnarbeit und*

*Kapital.* Von Karl Marx, Separat-Abdruck aus der *Neuen Rheinische Zeitung* vom Jahre 1849. Berlin, Verlag der Expedition des *Vorwärts* Berliner Volksblatt, 1891. It was edited by Engels who wrote the introduction and made certain changes and amendments in order to bring the presentation and terminology into harmony with the further development of Marx's economic teaching after 1849. Engels wrote about this in his introduction:

"In the forties, Marx had not yet finished his critique of political economy. This took place only towards the end of the fifties. Consequently, his works that appeared before the first part of *A Contribution to the Critique of Political Economy* (1859) differ in some points from those written after 1859, and contain expressions and whole sentences which, from the point of view of the later works, appear unfortunate and even incorrect. Now, it is self-evident that in ordinary editions intended for the general public this earlier point of view also has its place, as a part of the intellectual development of the author, and that both author and public have an indisputable right to the unaltered reproduction of these older works. And I should not have dreamed of altering a word of them.

"It is another thing when the new edition is intended practically exclusively for propaganda among workers.

"In such a case Marx would certainly have brought the old presentation dating from 1849 into harmony with his new point of view....

"My alterations all turn on one point. According to the original, the worker sells his *labour* to the capitalist for wages; according to the present text he sells his *labour power.*"

The 1891 edition, intended by Engels for popular propaganda, was used as the basis for many publications of this work in different languages, in particular for the English translation of 1891 printed in Glasgow by the Socialist Labour Party publishers.

In this volume, the work is reproduced in a form which was in keeping with the level of Marx's economic teaching in 1849 and in accordance with the text in the *Neue Rheinische Zeitung.* At the same time, all the major amendments made by Engels in the 1891 edition are given in footnotes. The division of the work into sections follows the sequence in which it was published in separate issues of the newspaper. The sections are numbered by the editors of the present edition. The list of misprints given in the *Neue Rheinische Zeitung* No. 270, April 12, 1849, is also taken into account.                                                                    p. 197

184  The reference is to the major events of 1848 and 1849: the insurrection of the Paris proletariat on June 23-26; the suppression of the Vienna October popular revolt by Austrian soldiers and the capture of the capital on November 1 by troops under Windischgrätz; the counter-revolutionary coup in Prussia in November, which brought about the dissolution of the Prussian National Assembly on December 5; and the rise of the revolutionary national liberation movement in Poland, Italy and Hungary.

In 1845-47, Ireland experienced a terrible famine, after continual failure of the potato crop. The real reason for this social calamity was the cruel exploitation of the Irish people under English rule, reduced to destitution by the ruling classes through the enslaving lease system imposed on the Irish peasants by the landlords. About a million died of hunger, and as many were compelled to emigrate. The effects of the famine were felt to the full in subsequent years.                p. 197

185  Engels points out in the introduction to the 1891 edition that Marx failed to prepare his lectures on wage labour and capital for the press mainly because of the rapid pace of political events at the time: popular uprisings in response to the

refusal by the ruling circles of Prussia and other states to recognise the imperial Constitution (Dresden, Iserlohn, Elberfeld, the Palatinate, Baden) and a new counter-revolutionary advance which led to the suppression of the *Neue Rheinische Zeitung*.

p. 228

[186] The reference is to the draft Constitution drawn up in Kremsier by the Austrian Constituent Imperial Diet. In early March 1849 it was dissolved by the Austrian Government which countered this draft with the Constitution imposed by the Emperor (see notes 13 and 39). The Kremsier draft, though it contained some concessions to the great-power and centralising tendencies of the German aristocratic ruling circles, envisaged a certain administrative independence for a number of national regions of the Empire and introduced provincial diets as representative institutions there.

p. 230

[187] See Note 55.

p. 234

[188] See Note 10.

p. 235

[189] See Note 9.

p. 235

[190] On March 15, 1848, a popular uprising broke out in Pest. In the middle of the day, the insurgents—craftsmen, workers, students, and peasants who had come to the fair—captured the town, crossed the Danube by the bridge and broke into Buda, where they set political prisoners free. The Austrian garrison was paralysed. The insurgents elected a Committee of Public Safety which provisionally concentrated power in its own hands. A popular meeting adopted the "12 points" drawn up by the radical opposition and demanding administration by parliament and civil liberties. The events of March 15 started the revolution in Hungary against the feudal serf-owning system and for national independence.     p. 237

[191] The Austrian Archduke Stephan was appointed Palatine of Hungary in 1847. From the very first days of the Hungarian revolution he strove to restore the Habsburgs' rule, disguising his counter-revolutionary designs by concessions to the Hungarian national liberation movement, and aiming at collusion with Hungarian magnates. In September 1848, when the Ban Jellachich, inspired by Austrian court circles, entered Hungary causing a government crisis there, Stephan made an unsuccessful attempt to seize power. On the proposal of Hungarian Right-wing leaders, the National Assembly appointed him Commander-in-Chief of the Hungarian troops. However, Archduke Stephan delayed military action and tried to come to an agreement with the Croatian Ban. Shortly afterwards, feeling himself insecure, he fled from Hungary. On September 29, 1848, Hungarian revolutionary troops defeated Jallachich's army.     p. 239

[192] The reference is to the "independent and responsible government" of Hungary formed as a result of the March uprising of 1848 and headed by Count Batthyány. The Government was dominated by representatives of the landed aristocracy and nobility, who were afraid that the revolution would be carried further and strove to compromise with the Austrian ruling circles. The radicals were represented in the Government by Lajos Kossuth (Finance Minister) and Bertalan Szemere (Minister of the Interior). The Batthyány Government (its compositon was made public on March 25) held power up to October 1, 1848. Early in October, the National Assembly transferred governmental functions to the Defence Council (see Note 70) headed by Kossuth.     p. 239

[193] An allusion to the debate on a number of Bills in the National Assembly (Diet) then in session in Pressburg: on the abolition of labour services and tithe. On

March 18, 1848, the Assembly promulgated an agrarian law annulling some of the peasants' feudal services, and passed laws on representation of the people, national independence, the press etc. These Bills were proposed under the impact of the growing revolutionary movement in the country.                    p. 240

[194] The march of Bem's army to the Banat (a district in the Serbian Voivodina, then administratively included in Hungary) took place in April 1849 after his troops had routed the Austrian army and Russian auxiliary detachments and occupied almost the whole of Transylvania. In the Banat, the troops under Bem and the Hungarian General Perczel inflicted a number of defeats on the Austrians and the Serbs of the Voivodina, whom the Austrian Government and pro-Austrian circles of the Serbian nobility and clergy had involved in the war with revolutionary Hungary (see Note 24); but they were unable to achieve any decisive successes. At the end of June 1849, large army contingents from Tsarist Russia entered Transylvania to assist the Austrian counter-revolution and this again made the presence of Bem's troops necessary in the Transylvanian theatre of war. This time he was defeated by the superior Russian troops.

Later Marx and Engels drew attention to Bem's expedition in the Banat in the article "Bem" written for the *New American Cyclopaedia* in September 1857.
                                                                         p. 243

[195] Up to 1868, regiments and other independent military units in the Austrian imperial army were named after their "patrons" or chiefs (*Inhaber*). This custom dated back to the mercenary armies when commanders maintained regiments at their own expense and therefore had the right to appoint officers. Later the commanders retained the right to give their names to the regiments, but the state assumed the responsibility of maintaining them.                        p. 245

[196] The *Palatine redoubts, direct-fire batteries*—see Note 168.

*Breach batteries* were installed at the concluding stages of a siege to destroy the bastions and other fortifications of a besieged fortress.              p. 246

[197] The *Debreczin National Assembly*—see Note 14.

This session of the National Assembly was held in Debreczin because only on April 24, 1849 did the Hungarian troops liberate Pest.                    p. 246

[198] See Note 68.                                                    p. 246

[199] "*World-historic Diet*"—the reference is to the *Sabor* of the Southern Slavs in Agram (Zagreb) on June 5, 1848 (see Note 67). Though the *Sabor* came out in favour of uniting Croatia, Slavonia and Dalmatia and of certain reforms there, on the whole, it sought compromise with the Austrian monarchy and did little to modify the former military feudal order in these regions and the enslaved position of their population. Only a small group of democratic delegates connected the struggle for the national cause with the revolutionary struggle against feudal monarchist regimes.                                                  p. 246

[200] *Observation corps* were assigned to watch the enemy on the flanks of the main theatre of military operations.                                          p. 248

[201] See Note 190.                                                   p. 248

[202] The reference is evidently to the Odbor then in session in the town of Karlowitz (see Note 11).                                                      p. 251

[203] In the summer of 1848, the anti-feudal movement and the struggle for complete liberation from the Turkish Sultan's yoke gained strength in the Danube

principalities (Moldavia and Wallachia), which were formally still autonomous possessions of Turkey. The movement in Wallachia grew into a bourgeois revolution. In June 1848, a Constitution was proclaimed, a liberal Provisional Government was formed and George Bibesco, the ruler of Wallachia, abdicated and fled the country.

On June 28, 1848, a 12,000-strong Russian army corps entered Moldavia and, in July, Turkish troops also invaded the country. In September 1848 the Turkish army, supported by the Tsarist Government, occupied Wallachia and perpetrated a massacre in Bucharest. A proclamation of the Turkish government commissioner Fuad-Effendi declared the need to establish "law and order" and "eliminate all traces of the revolution". Intervention by Russia and Turkey led to the restoration of the feudal system in the Danube principalities and the defeat of the bourgeois revolution in Wallachia. The desire to completely suppress the revolutionary movement made the two governments, despite acute Russo-Turkish contradictions, conclude a convention in Balta-Liman on May 1, 1849. This cancelled the system of the election of rulers and other progressive reforms introduced in the Danube principalities in 1848, and sanctioned the occupation of their territories by Turkish and Russian troops. The military occupation of the principalities lasted until 1851.                                                                                 p. 253

204  The bombardment of Hatvan on April 2, 1849 opened a new stage in the Hungarian offensive against the Austrian troops. It was prepared for by successful movements in the centre of military operations at the Theiss, Bem's victories in Transylvania, guerilla warfare in areas occupied by the Austrians, and vigorous measures taken by the Kossuth Government (the Defence Council) to strengthen the army and mobilise all its resources for the struggle against the enemy. When Engels wrote this report he had not yet received the news of the battle at Hatvan. Meanwhile, the victory scored by the Hungarian army there and the subsequent blows inflicted by it on the Austrians at Tapio-Bicske (April 4), Isaczeg and Gödöllö (April 5-7), Waitzen (April 10), etc. brought about a radical change in the war in favour of revolutionary Hungary. On April 19, 1849 the Hungarians routed the Austrians in a decisive battle at Nagy-Sallo, advanced further, relieved Komorn on April 22, and liberated Pest on April 24. The defeated Austrian army retreated to the western border.

The Hungarian command faced the prospect of spreading the revolutionary war into Austrian and German territory. However, because of anti-revolutionary sentiments among a number of high commanders, Görgey in particular, and the fear of diplomatic complications, it was decided to cease the pursuit of the Austrians and to turn the main forces towards the fortress of Buda, which was still held by an Austrian garrison. The siege of Buda was time-consuming (it was captured only on May 21) and this gave the Austrians the respite they needed to bring up new reserves and complete their talks withTsarist Russia about help in suppressing revolutionary Hungary (the final agreement was reached at the meeting of Francis Joseph and Nicholas I in Warsaw on May 21). All this had fatal consequences for the Hungarian revolution.                                              p. 255

205  See Note 10.                                                                            p. 255

206  *Potsdam*—a town near Berlin, the residence of the Prussian kings, where military parades and reviews of the Prussian army were held.

*Olmütz* (Olomouc)—a town in Moravia, from October 7, 1848, temporary residence of the Austrian Court which fled from Vienna where the people rose in revolt; centre of counter-revolutionary forces.                                      p. 257

[207] An allusion to the shooting of Robert Blum, a German democrat and deputy to the Frankfurt National Assembly, by sentence of an Austrian court martial (see Note 41). This crudely arbitrary act on the part of the Austrian military clique was approved by reactionary circles in Prussia. p. 257

[208] The reference is to the conventions concerning extradition of criminals, deserters, vagabonds etc. concluded by Prussia with a number of German states (Austria, Bavaria, Württemberg, Saxony, Grand Duchy of Baden etc.) and also with Russia in 1816-20. In practice, these conventions applied to persons accused of political crimes in accordance with the policy of the Holy Alliance powers (see Note 40) which strove for an international union of counter-revolutionary forces in the struggle against the revolutionary movement. p. 258

[209] In the initial period of the European revolution of 1848, various reactionary sovereigns and public figures, deprived of throne and power and seeking safety from the people's wrath, found refuge in England. Among them were: ex-King of the French, Louis Philippe (February); ex-Chancellor of the Austrian Empire, Metternich; the Prince of Prussia, Wilhelm (March); and later Lola Montez, an influential favourite of Ludwig I, King of Bavaria who was compelled to abdicate, and others. p. 258

[210] The war with Denmark over the duchies of Schleswig and Holstein renewed by Prussia at the end of March 1849 (see notes 90 and 92) was waged in the name of all the states of the German Confederation. Owing to this, military and naval contingents from Schleswig-Holstein were regarded as the nucleus of an all-German imperial army and navy, their formation being stipulated by the imperial Constitution drawn up by the Frankfurt National Assembly. p. 259

[211] On April 5, 1849 a German coastal battery fired on the Danish squadron at the harbour of Eckernförde (Schleswig); two damaged Danish ships were captured. This event, which made no essential difference to the course of war with Denmark, was claimed by the official Prussian press as a major victory. p. 259

[212] Black-red-and-gold—a symbolic combination of colours signifying the unity of Germany. The Belgian state flag, introduced during the revolution of 1830-31, after the separation of Belgium from Holland, included the same colours but arranged differently (vertical black, gold and red stripes). p. 260

[213] An ironical allusion to the strivings of the liberal majority of the Frankfurt National Assembly to place the Prussian King (black-and-white—state colours of the Prussian monarchy) at the head of united Germany (black-red-and-gold — symbol of its unity) as the "Emperor of the Germans" (see Note 138). p. 260

[214] See Note 151. p. 261

[215] In the battle of Leipzig on October 16-19, 1813 troops from Russia, Prussia, Austria and Sweden won a victory over the army of Napoleon and the states dependent on him. This victory decided the outcome of the 1813 campaign in favour of the sixth anti-Napoleon coalition (England, Spain and some other states also participated in it). As a result, Napoleon's troops were driven out of Germany and military operations moved over into France. p. 261

[216] The reference is to the Constitution imposed by Francis Joseph on March 4, 1849 (see Note 13). p. 263

[217] See Note 97. p. 263

[218] On the battle at *Novara* between the Austrian and Piedmontese armies, see Note 159.                                                                                  p. 266

[219] Here and in the two reports given below, "A Magyar Victory" and "An Austrian Defeat", Engels writes about the military events in Hungary early in April: the victory won by the Hungarian troops at Hatvan on April 2 and the subsequent blows they inflicted on the Austrian army (see Note 204).                     p. 267

[220] *Banderial hussars* (from the Latin *banderium*—banner)—the name given in medieval Hungary to cavalry detachments of nobles that under their own banners formed part of the royal army or of the armies of the big feudal lords. In this instance, the reference is to the regiment of Banderial hussars formed in July 1848 in Croatia. It took part in the marches of Jellachich's army against revolutionary Hungary.                                                                       p. 273

[221] See Note 112.                                                                              p. 273

[222] The battles for Pest were fought from April 6 to 25, 1849. They also continued after the main Austrian forces, beaten by Hungarian revolutionary troops, had been compelled to retreat north-west to the borders of Austria. After Pest was liberated, the Austrian garrison still held out in the fortress of Buda which was besieged by the Hungarians from May 4 to 21, 1849.                               p. 277

[223] In March 1849, the war between Piedmont and Austria was renewed and this served as a new impetus to the national liberation movement in Lombardy, in the rear of the Austrian army. A large popular uprising against Austrian rule took place on March 20 in Brescia. The Austrian garrison was trapped in the fortress. The Austrian troops sent against Brescia consisted partly of those which had taken part in the operations against the Republic of Venice. They were under the command of General Nugent, who was later replaced by a Master of Ordnance, Haynau. The insurgent city was severely bombarded, but continued to resist even after the truce was signed between the King of Piedmont and Austria. Brescia was taken only by a fierce assault on March 31 and April 1. Haynau inflicted brutal reprisals on the insurgents.
On the *blockade of Venice*, see Note 157.                                          p. 280

[224] The reference is to the response of the ruling circles in one of the small German states, the Grand Duchy of Mecklenburg, to the proposal by the Frankfurt National Assembly that the crown of the "Emperor of the Germans" be given to the Prussian King, Frederick William IV (see Note 138).                          p. 281

[225] The *Rhenish District Committee of Democrats* was set up at the First Rhenish Congress of Democrats held in Cologne on August 13 and 14, 1848, by a decision of the First All-German Democratic Congress in Frankfurt am Main, on the basis of the Central Commission of representatives from the three democratic organisations in Cologne—the Democratic Society, the Workers' Association and the Association for Workers and Employers—formed late in June 1848. Marx, who was on the Central Commission, also became a member of the Rhenish District Committee, together with Schapper, Moll and other prominent figures of the Communist League.
The President of the Committee was a German democrat, lawyer Schneider II. When he was elected to the Second Chamber of the Prussian Provincial Diet early in 1848, Marx acted as President. Thanks to Marx and his associates, the Committee exerted a considerable influence on the popular movement in the Rhine Province. It successfully organised resistance to the growing counter-revolutionary forces and, in particular, initiated the tax-refusal campaign during

the coup d'état in Prussia (November-December 1848). It did not confine its activities to the Rhine Province, but extended them to Westphalia as well.

Marx and other members of the Communist League decided to withdraw from the Rhenish District Committee of Democrats because of the changes that had taken place in Germany and in the working-class movement there by the spring of 1849. The rising activity of workers' associations and the markedly growing class consciousness of the German proletariat provided the opportunity to create a mass proletarian party. On the other hand, the wavering position of the petty-bourgeois democrats made necessary an ideological and organisational separation from them. Under these conditions, taking the first steps to found a proletarian party, Marx and Engels proposed the task of strengthening the independence of the workers' associations, primarily the Cologne Workers' Association, of freeing them from petty-bourgeois influence, of marshalling their activities in a single direction and achieving a unified revolutionary platform. Their withdrawal from the Committee in no way meant a break with the non-proletarian democratic trends. Marx and Engels continued to call for unity of action with democrats in the struggle against counter-revolution, believing, however, that at that stage it should not be carried out within a single organisation. At the same time, Marx established closer contacts with the representatives of the workers' associations.

These tasks and the financial problems of the *Neue Rheinische Zeitung* were the main purpose of Marx's trip to North-West Germany and Westphalia in the second half of April 1849, during which he visited Bremen, Hamburg, Bielefeld, Hamm and other towns.                                                          p. 282

226  The *Rakos plain*—a district on the left bank of the Danube where, until the sixteenth century, Hungarian assemblies of estates were held and Hungarian kings crowned. It is now within the city bounds of Budapest.          p. 283

227  See Note 55.                                                             p. 286

228  See Note 16.                                                             p. 286

229  The reference is to the men of the Vienna mobile guard and the Academic Legion who survived after the capture of Vienna by counter-revolutionary troops (November 1, 1848) and, as part of Bem's army, participated in the revolutionary war in Hungary.

The *Vienna mobile guard* was formed by Bem during the October uprising in Vienna. It consisted mainly of artisans and workers and proved itself to be the most disciplined, efficient and audacious section of the insurgents' military forces.

The *Academic Legion* was a student militarised organisation set up in March 1848 in Vienna. It also included university lecturers and other intellectuals, mostly radical democrats. The Legion played a significant part in the Austrian revolutionary movement in 1848. When the October uprising in Vienna was suppressed, it was dissolved.                                               p. 287

230  See Note 43.                                                            p. 289

231  Under the impact of the March revolution of 1848, the peasants' anti-feudal struggle assumed wide proportions within the Austrian Empire and became combined with the national liberation movement in the national border regions. Disturbances among the Ukrainian peasants of the Bukovina started in the spring of 1848 and became especially intensive when, on April 17, 1848, a law was promulgated in neighbouring Galicia abolishing feudal services. This law did not apply to the Bukovina, though it was administratively part of Galicia. The

Ukrainian peasant, Huzul Lucian Kobylica, was especially prominent among the peasants' leaders. He belonged to the radical democratic wing of the Austrian Constituent Imperial Diet to which he was elected in 1848. He helped the peasants lodge their petitions and complaints and did his best to get the lands seized by the landowners returned to the peasants. For this, Kobylica was deprived of his rights as a deputy.

In the spring of 1849, the peasants' movement in the Bukovina was rekindled. Peasants' detachments were formed, landowners' estates seized and their woods felled more often. The peasant leaders, Lucian Kobylica (who may have been in direct contact with the Hungarian emissaries) and Birla Mironiuk, called upon the peasants to store up provisions and fodder for the Hungarian troops and to join them, if the latter entered the Bukovina. The peasants' disturbances in the Bukovina were suppressed by imperial forces.

The imposed *redemption law* referred to by Engels was adopted by the Austrian Imperial Diet on *September 7, 1848* (see Note 33). p. 289

[232] *Ruthenian*—the name given in nineteenth-century West-European ethnographical and historical works to the Ukrainian population of Galicia and the Bukovina, which was separated at the time from the bulk of the Ukrainian people. p. 289

[233] The *Neue Rheinische Zeitung* Nos. 265, 266, 267, 269 and 271 of April 6, 7, 8, 11 and 13, 1849, carried a series of feature articles by Georg Weerth ridiculing the servility of the liberal majority of the Frankfurt National Assembly who wished to unite Germany under the aegis of Prussia and resolved on March 28, 1849 to elect the Prussian King, Frederick William IV, "Emperor of the Germans" (see Note 138). p. 295

[234] The *battle at Novara*—see Note 159.
The *battle for Pest*—see Note 222.
The *battle at Eckernförde*—see Note 211.

On April 13, 1849, the so-called German federal troops stormed the Danish fortifications near Düppel (a village in Schleswig). p. 295

[235] *"Gagging laws"*—the name given to the six exceptional laws passed in England in 1819 after "Peterloo"—when participants in a mass meeting for electoral reforms in St. Peter's Field near Manchester were shot by police and troops; the laws limited the freedom of assembly and the press. p. 295

[236] See Note 180. p. 295

[237] After the March revolution, an insurrection of the Poles broke out in the Duchy of Posen for liberation from the Prussian yoke. Polish peasants and artisans took an active part in this, along with members of the lesser nobility. The Prussian Government was forced to promise that a reorganising committee would be set up in Posen and that the "reorganisation" would include: formation of a Polish army, appointment of Poles to administrative and other posts, recognition of Polish as an official language, etc. Similar promises were given in the convention of April 11, 1848, signed by the Posen Committee and representatives of the Prussian Government in Jaroslawiec. On April 14, 1848, however, the King of Prussia ordered that the Duchy of Posen be divided into an eastern Polish part and a western "German" part, which was not to be "reorganised" and was to remain formally part of the German Confederation. During the months following the suppression of the uprising by Prussian troops, the demarcation line was pushed further east and the promised "reorganisation" was never carried out.

The *German Confederation*—the ephemeral union of German states founded in 1815 by decision of the Vienna Congress. p. 296

[238] See Note 232.                                                    p. 296

[239] See Note 19.                                                     p. 297

[240] *Potato war*—the name given ironically to the so-called war for the Bavarian succession between Prussia and Saxony, on the one hand, and Austria, on the other, in 1778 and 1779. The military actions consisted mainly of troop movements and of soldiers' quarrels over potatoes. The war ended with the Peace of Teschen, compelling the Austrian Habsburgs to abandon their claims to Bavarian possessions.                                                 p. 297

[241] The reference is to the deputation of the Right-wing representatives of the Slovak national movement to the negotiations with Austrian ruling circles in Olmütz in March 1849 (see Note 156).                                        p. 299

[242] See Note 114.                                                   p. 303

[243] See Note 68.                                                    p. 304

[244] The foundation of a Croatian-Slavonian-Dalmatian triune kingdom was discussed in the Croatian *Sabor* (see Note 67) as early as the summer of 1848. The scheme under consideration reflected the desire of the top bourgeoisie and landowners in the South-Slav lands for autonomy within the Austrian monarchy and a moderate Constitution. The scheme was regarded as part of a broader programme for integrating all the South-Slav lands of the Austrian Empire. The centralising Constitution imposed in March 1849 dealt a heavy blow to the Right wing of the South-Slav national movement, which cherished hopes of obtaining autonomy in collaboration with the Austrian ruling circles. The latter, however, needed the Southern Slavs for the struggle against revolutionary Hungary and Italy, and therefore supported the illusion that this scheme for autonomy could be put into effect. The Croatian *Sabor,* in particular, was allowed to negotiate unity with the representatives of Dalmatia. When the uprisings in Hungary and Italy were suppressed, the Austrian authorities curbed all attempts on the part of the South-Slav adherents of autonomy to implement their plans. Engels calls the newly conceived state *Raubstaat* meaning either a robber state or a dwarfish, dependent state.

*Pandours*—irregular infantry units of the Austrian army recruited mainly in the South-Slav provinces of the Austrian Empire.

*Serezhans*—see Note 22.

*Haiduks*—South-Slav guerillas fighting against Turkish conquerors in the fifteenth to nineteenth centuries. In the Austrian Empire, this name was given to people inhabiting an autonomous district in Hungary who provided special military contingents for the army.

*Red-coats*—see Note 45.                                              p. 307

[245] An allusion to German moderate constitutionalists (contemptuously called *wailers* by democratic circles), including members of the Frankfurt parliament, advocates of uniting Germany in the form of the German Empire. Engels ironically compares the state they planned to form with the Holy Roman Empire of the German Nation (962-1806) which included, at different times, the German, Italian, Austrian, Hungarian and Bohemian lands, Switzerland and the Netherlands and which was a motley confederation of feudal kingdoms, church lands and free towns with different political structures, legal standards and customs.
                                                                      p. 307

[246] An ironical comparison with the Swiss separatist union — *Sonderbund* (see Note 35).
                                                                      p. 308

247 The reference is to the *Congress of representatives of the Slav regions* forming part of the Austrian Empire. It met in Prague on June 2, 1848. The Right, moderately liberal wing to which Palacký and Šafařik, the leaders of the Congress, belonged, tried to solve the national problem through autonomy of the Slav regions within the framework of the Habsburg monarchy. The Left, radical wing (Sabina, Frič, Libelt, Štúr and others) wanted joint action with the revolutionary and democratic movement in Germany and Hungary. The radical delegates took an active part in the popular uprising in Prague (June 12-17, 1848) against the arbitrary rule of the Austrian authorities, and were subjected to cruel reprisals. On June 16, the moderate liberal delegates declared the Congress adjourned indefinitely.

p. 308

248 *Otočac gentlemen* (Otočaner)—soldiers of the Austrian border regiment formed in 1746 and stationed in Otočac (Western Croatia). They were recruited mainly from the South-Slav subjects of the Austrian Emperor.                              p. 308

249 See Note 220.                                                                          p. 309

250 See Note 70.                                                                           p. 315

251 When the Austrians heavily bombarded Cracow during the national liberation uprising in April 1848, Castiglioni was military commandant of the Cracow fortress.                                                                              p. 319

252 See Note 9.                                                                            p. 319

253 See Note 47.                                                                           p. 320

254 The *Gustavus Adolphus Union*—a religious organisation formed in 1832 to help Protestant communities in Catholic regions of Germany; Rupp, formerly pastor in Königsberg (he was removed from his post for criticism of church dogmas), was expelled from this Union in 1846.                                      p. 321

255 *"Friends of Light"*—a religious trend which arose in 1841 and was directed against pietism; the latter, being supported by junker circles, was predominant in the official Protestant church and was outstanding for its extreme reactionary nature and hypocrisy. The "Friends of Light" movement was an expression of bourgeois discontent with the reactionary order in Germany in the 1840s; in 1846-47 it led to the formation of the so-called *free communities*, which separated from the official Protestant church.                                                                 p. 321

256 See Note 52.                                                                           p. 321

257 See Note 235.                                                                          p. 322

258 See Note 123.                                                                          p. 324

259 See Note 136.                                                                          p. 327

260 See Note 172.                                                                          p. 331

261 See notes 13 and 39.                                                                   p. 338

262 Here the *Neue Rheinische Zeitung* continues its exposure of the legal and police persecution of Ferdinand Lassalle. Lassalle was arrested in Düsseldorf on November 22, 1848 on a charge of incitement to arm against the government during the tax-refusal campaign. The proceedings against him were delayed by the legal authorities of the Rhine Province in every possible way. During the

investigation, attempts were also made to bring a case against him for insulting government officials, etc. On Lassalle's request, expressed in his letters to Marx and Engels, the *Neue Rheinische Zeitung* came out in defence of him and of other Düsseldorf democrats under persecution. The newspaper carried a number of articles exposing the abuses of power and illegal actions by the judicial and prison authorities against Lassalle (see present edition, Vol. 8, pp. 463-65, 474-76). Marx and Engels also took part in the efforts of the Cologne democratic organisations to induce the legal authorities to speed up the investigation of the case. Subsequently, the newspaper several times published material exposing this trial (see this volume, pp. 344-46, 372-76 and 383-88) which was held on May 3 and 4. The jury acquitted Lassalle.

Below, the reference is to the Articles of the *Code pénal* (see Note 120).

p. 339

263 The reference is to the resolutions on abolition of serfdom, labour services and tithes and landowners' courts by the Hungarian National Assembly on March 18, 1848 in the atmosphere of general revolutionary upsurge. The agrarian reform carried out by the Assembly (it was elected before the March revolution according to the principle of estate representation and on the whole expressed the interests of the nobility) was half-hearted, however. The peasants had to pay redemption for the abolition of certain feudal obligations, and the terms of redemption were such that whole categories of landless and land-starved peasants were virtually unable to free themselves of labour services. During the revolution, the radical wing made repeated demands for further measures in favour of the peasants, but met with resistance from the moderate elements among the nobility. Incomplete agrarian reforms were one of the inner causes of the defeat of the Hungarian revolution of 1848-49.

p. 345

264 This item, occasioned by the news reaching Cologne that the Hungarian revolutionary army had taken Pest and Buda (here as well as in other military reports, Engels uses its German name—Ofen), was printed in the special supplement to the *Neue Rheinische Zeitung* No. 283 dated April 27; however, the supplement came out on the morning of April 28, 1849, as is pointed out in Engels' next war review (see this volume, pp. 350-51).

Hungarian troops occupied the city of Buda; but its fortress still remained in the hands of the Austrian garrison and was captured only on May 21, 1849, after a prolonged siege.

p. 346

265 Mentioned here are two big battles during the war waged by revolutionary France against the first anti-French coalition of European counter-revolutionary states—Austria, Prussia, England, Russia and others.

At *Jemappes* (Belgium) on November 6, 1792 the French army defeated the Austrian troops.

At *Fleurus* (Belgium) on June 26, 1794 the French troops defeated the Austrian army under the Duke of Coburg. This victory enabled the French revolutionary army to enter and occupy Belgium.

p. 349

266 Evidently the editors of the *Neue Rheinische Zeitung* did not have Kossuth's exact biographical data at that time and so availed themselves of the current newspaper information. In fact, Kossuth was born on September 19, 1802.

p. 352

267 When Engels expressed his hope for a new revolution in Vienna if the Hungarian army moved further, and called this probable revolt the "fifth revolution", he obviously had in mind the four revolutionary events in the Austrian capital in 1848, namely: the popular uprising of March 13 that started the revolution in

Austria   armed risings of workers, artisans and students on May 15 and 26 that
compelled the Government to make new concessions to the democratic movement
(it extended the suffrage, consented to have a one-chamber Constituent Imperial
Diet, annulled orders to dissolve the Central Committee of the National Guard
and the Academic Legion, etc.); workers' disturbances on August 23 that led to the
collision between workers and bourgeois detachments of the national guards; and
the popular revolt on October 6-31, the culminating point of the revolution in
Austria and Germany.                                                        p. 352

268  See Note 172.                                                          p. 354

269  The reference is to the former soldiers of the Academic Legion (see Note 229).
                                                                           p. 355

270  On April 27, 1849 the Prussian Government dissolved the Second Chamber
because, at its sitting on April 21, it had approved the imperial Constitution drawn
up by the Frankfurt National Assembly. The Chamber took this resolution on the
initiative of the opposition deputies, in spite of the head of the Government's
statement that the King had definitely decided to reject the imperial Constitution.
                                                                           p. 357

271  See Note 52.                                                          p. 357

272  The reference is to the Prussian National Assembly dissolved by the Government
on December 5, 1848. For its principle of "agreement with the Crown", see
Note 48.                                                                    p. 357

273  See Note 88.                                                          p. 358

274  The reference is to the suppression of the national liberation uprising in the
Grand Duchy of Posen in 1848 by Prussian soldiers and to the gross violation of
the promise originally given to the insurgents by the Government, namely to
introduce national autonomy in the eastern part of the Duchy, i. e. behind the
demarcation line (see Note 237). General Pfuel, in command of the Prussian
troops in Posen, ordered that all the insurgents who had been taken prisoner be
shaved and their hands and ears branded with caustic (in German *Höllenstein*).
This was how he got his nickname *Pfuel von Höllenstein* in democratic circles.
                                                                           p. 359

275  See Note 19.                                                          p. 360

276  In 1793 the *second partition* of Poland (the first in 1772, the third in 1795) took
place. As a result, the Polish feudal state ceased to exist. The Polish lands were
incorporated into Prussia, Austria and Russia. The second partition was carried
out by the Russian Empress Catherine and the Prussian King Frederick William II. The Austrian Emperor Francis I did not participate in it directly, but his
policy facilitated the partition and thus prepared for Austria's participation in the
third partition of Poland.
    By the second partition, the Prussian kingdom obtained Torun (Thorn) and
Gdansk (Danzig) with adjoining lands, the greater part of Great Poland (provinces
of Posen, Gnesen, Kalisch, Plotsk, etc.) and other Polish territories. The annexed
part of Great Poland was turned into a new province—South Prussia (mentioned
by Engels below), to which Warsaw was joined in 1795 after the third partition.
    By the Treaty of Tilsit in 1807, however, these lands were taken from Prussia by
Napoleon who formed them into a vassal Duchy of Warsaw but, in 1815, by
decision of the Vienna Congress, part of them—the Great Duchy of Posen—was
returned to the Prussian monarchy.                                         p. 360

<sup>277</sup> The reference here is to Prussian participation in the suppression of the Polish national liberation uprising of 1794 led by Tadeusz Kosciuszko. The insurgents wanted to restore the independence of Poland, to return the lands taken from it in 1772 and 1793, and to continue the progressive reforms interrupted by the second partition. The uprising was suppressed by troops from Tsarist Russia, Prussia and Austria which, in 1795, partitioned Poland for the third time.
p. 361

<sup>278</sup> The article mentioned was not published in the next issues of the *Neue Rheinische Zeitung*; evidently, the newspaper was suppressed before Engels managed to write it.
p. 362

<sup>279</sup> The *Deutschmeister* regiment of the Austrian imperial army was formed in 1695 and originated with the military religious "Hoch und Deutschmeister" Order. The master of the Order was the regiment's chief.
p. 365

<sup>280</sup> See Note 195.
p. 365

<sup>281</sup> See Note 136.
p. 365

<sup>282</sup> See Note 68.
p. 369

<sup>283</sup> The reference is to the decisions taken by the National Assemblies (Diets) of Hungary and Transylvania after the March revolution of 1848 to establish union between the two countries and to introduce a single administrative system. In Transylvania, the decision on the union was adopted on May 30 by the Assembly in Cluj that was elected according to the principle of estate representation which secured the predominance in it of Hungarian landowners. This decision attached a one-sided character to the union, it retained the privilege of the Hungarian minority in local administration and school matters and proclaimed Hungarian as the only official language. The ideas of the Romanian and Hungarian democrats, who regarded this union as the formation of a Hungarian-Transylvanian state based on the equality of nations, were actually rejected. This fact was used by the Right wing of the Romanian national movement in Transylvania who aimed at a union with the Habsburgs and helped the latter make use of the Transylvanian Romanians in the struggle against revolutionary Hungary.
p. 369

<sup>284</sup> The *Hungarian Constitution of 1848*—a number of laws promulgated in the second half of March 1848 by the Hungarian National Assembly in the atmosphere of revolutionary upsurge (see Note 193) concerned political organisation in the country. These laws proclaimed Hungary independent of the Austrian Empire in financial and military matters; legislative power was concentrated in the elected National Assembly, and the executive body—the Cabinet Council—was proclaimed responsible to the latter. However, Hungary remained bound to the empire by the common emperor of the Habsburg dynasty and suffrage was limited by a property qualification. Though the new Constitution preserved many of the nobility's privileges, it was an important step towards a bourgeois transformation of the political order in Hungary.
p. 369

<sup>285</sup> See Note 136.
p. 370

<sup>286</sup> On the *Prussian electoral law* and the *imposed Constitution* (called above the "martial-law Charter of December 5"), see Note 52.
p. 370

<sup>287</sup> The *Konversationshalle* at Dönhoff square—a hall in Berlin where, on April 27, 1849, Left-wing deputies assembled after the dissolution of the Second Chamber of the Prussian Provincial Diet. They were turned out by soldiers and constables

and the people who gathered near the Konversationshalle came under fire from the troops.

*Constables in Berlin*—a special detachment of plain-clothes men formed in summer 1848 for use against street gatherings and popular disturbances and for spying purposes. The name was given by analogy with special constables in England, who were used to break up the Chartist demonstration on April 10, 1848.

p. 370

[288] See Note 120.

p. 372

[289] The trial of the Rhenish District Committee of Democrats (see Note 225) was held on February 8, 1849. Marx, Karl Schapper and the lawyer Schneider II were brought before the jury and accused of instigation to revolt on the basis of that committee's appeal issued on November 18, 1848 concerning the refusal to pay taxes as a measure of struggle against the counter-revolutionary coup in Prussia. The jury returned a verdict of not guilty. For Marx's speech at this trial see present edition, Vol. 8, pp. 323-39.

p. 372

[290] *Code d'instruction criminelle*—French Criminal Code which was in force in the Rhine Province of Prussia. In this particular case, reference is to Article 300.

p. 372

[291] The first time Lassalle was imprisoned from February to August 1848. Legal proceedings were instituted against him on the charge that he had instigated the theft of a box containing documents to be used in the divorce case of Countess Hatzfeld. As a lawyer, he was employed on this case from 1846 to 1854. About Lassalle's second arrest and trial see Note 262.

p. 372

[292] On November 22, 1848 Lassalle made a speech at the popular meeting in Neuss (near Düsseldorf) in which he called upon the people to give armed support when needed to the Prussian National Assembly in its conflict with the Prussian Government. On the same day he was arrested.

p. 374

[293] After the dissolution of the Second Chamber, the Prussian Government published a Note of April 28, 1849 signed by Prime Minister Brandenburg and addressed to the Frankfurt National Assembly and the German governments. The Note contained Frederick William IV's final refusal to accept the imperial crown proffered by the Assembly, motivated by the fact that the revolutionary origin and contents of the imperial Constitution made it inacceptable to the King. At the same time, the Note stressed that the Prussian King certainly did not refuse to fulfil the mission of uniting the German lands, in collaboration with other German monarchs. It was suggested that the Frankfurt Assembly should give up the imperial Constitution and promote these dynastic plans. Simultaneously with this Note, the Prussian Government stepped up military preparations in order to put down the growing popular movement in Germany for the introduction of the imperial Constitution.

p. 377

[294] In September, the Frankfurt National Assembly discussed the Law on the Protection of the Constituent Imperial Assembly and the Officials of the Central Authority ("Gesetz, betreffend den Schutz der constituirenden Nationalversammlung und der Beamten der Centralgewalt") and adopted it on October 10, 1848. Article V read: "Public insult to the Imperial Assembly, including that made outside its sittings, is to be punished by imprisonment of up to two years." This law was also published in Prussia in *Stenographischer Bericht über die Verhandlungen der deutschen constituirenden Nationalversammlung zu Frankfurt am Main*.

p. 377

<sup>295</sup> *St. Paul's Church*—see Note 30.
*Carbonari*—members of secret political societies in Italy and France in the first half of the nineteenth century. In Italy they fought for national independence, unification of the country and liberal constitutional reforms. In France their movement was primarily directed against the rule of the restored Bourbon dynasty (1815-30).                                                                    p. 377

<sup>296</sup> In connection with the coup d'état that began in Prussia in November 1848, the Frankfurt National Assembly sent a delegation to Berlin to mediate in the conflict between the Prussian Assembly and the Government (see Note 42). On his return to Frankfurt, Bassermann, a moderate liberal member of the delegation, announced to the Assembly that the Prussian Government had a good reason for taking decisive measures, because savage-looking characters were loafing about in the streets of Berlin as they usually did on the eve of anarchist demonstrations. Hence the ironical expression "Bassermannic characters".                        p. 377

<sup>297</sup> Engels had in mind revolutionary disturbances among the broad masses in the Bavarian Palatinate caused by the declaration made by the Bavarian King Maximilian II and his Cabinet on April 23, 1849. In it they rejected the imperial Constitution and proclaimed loyalty to the former particularism of small states. The movement in the Palatinate soon led to a revolutionary upheaval there, the Palatinate's separation from Bavaria and the formation of a local provisional government.                                                                         p. 378

<sup>298</sup> This refers to the central body of the German Confederation (see Note 237) which consisted of representatives from the German states. Though it had no real power, it was nevertheless a vehicle for feudal and monarchist reaction. After the March 1848 revolution in Germany, Right-wing circles tried in vain to revive the Federal Diet and use it to undermine the principle of popular sovereignty and prevent the democratic unification of Germany.                                p. 378

<sup>299</sup> On September 18, 1848 a popular uprising broke out in Frankfurt am Main against the Frankfurt National Assembly's ratification of the armistice with Denmark concluded in Malmö (see Note 92). The wavering and indecision of the Assembly's Left wing helped defeat the uprising.                               p. 378

<sup>300</sup> The dissolution of the Second Chamber in Prussia on April 27, 1849 was followed by the dissolution of the corresponding chambers in Hanover and Saxony because the ruling circles of these states refused to recognise the imperial Constitution approved by the majority of deputies. In Saxony the Provincial Diet was dissolved by order of King Frederick Augustus II as early as April 28, 1849. This act and the Government's other counter-revolutionary measures sparked off the uprising in Dresden on May 3. It started the armed struggle for the imperial Constitution in a number of regions in Germany.                                              p. 380

<sup>301</sup> See Note 19.                                                                  p. 382
<sup>302</sup> See Note 50.                                                                  p. 384

<sup>303</sup> The address quoted here was composed by Lassalle in November 1848 on behalf of the Düsseldorf civic militia and sent to the Prussian National Assembly that same evening. The address was published in the *Neue Rheinische Zeitung* No. 149, November 22, 1848. About Lassalle's speech at Neuss, see Note 292.     p. 384

<sup>304</sup> See Note 86.                                                                  p. 385

<sup>305</sup> An allusion to the paragraphs in Prussian Law concerning the prosecution and punishment of persons guilty of "stirring up discontent".                        p. 387

306 On May 1, 1849 the Cologne municipal council, which consisted mainly of liberal bourgeois representatives, addressed all other municipal councils in the Rhine Province with a proposal to convene a meeting on May 5, 1849 in connection with the new situation that had arisen in Prussia after the dissolution of the Second Chamber. The Prussian Government banned this meeting (the ban was published in the *Kölnische Zeitung* No. 104, May 2, 1849). Even so, the Cologne municipal council convoked a congress of delegates from the Rhine cities on May 8, 1849 in Cologne. The Congress came out in favour of the imperial Constitution and demanded the convocation of the dissolved Provincial Diet. It was made clear that, if the Prussian Government ignored the Congress's resolution, the question of the Rhine Province's secession from Prussia would be raised. This threat, however, was not supported by decisive action and remained merely an empty declaration, because the liberal majority of the Congress rejected the proposal to arm the people and to resist the authorities by force.                              p. 389

307 On September 26, 1848 the authorities, frightened by the upsurge of the revolutionary-democratic movement in Cologne, declared a state of siege there "to safeguard the individual and property". The military commandant's office issued an order prohibiting all associations pursuing "political and social aims", banned all meetings, disbanded and disarmed the civic militia, instituted courts martial and suspended publication of the *Neue Rheinische Zeitung* and a number of other democratic newspapers. A protest campaign compelled the Cologne military authorities to lift the state of siege on October 2. The *Neue Rheinische Zeitung* resumed publication on October 12.                              p. 389

308 See Note 226.
                                                                        p. 391
309 See Note 306.
                                                                        p. 392
310 The organisations of the Rhine Province and Westphalia held three congresses in Cologne on Sunday, May 6, 1849: the congress of workers' associations, the congress of democratic associations and the congress of constitutional-monarchist citizens' associations (in Deutz, near Cologne).                 p. 392

311 On September 25, 1848 the Cologne authorities arrested several leaders of democratic and workers' associations and provoked premature action on the part of the workers, who began to erect barricades in the city. Marx and his associates did their utmost to prevent the Cologne workers from premature and isolated actions. On the next day, a state of siege was declared in Cologne on the pretext of "safeguarding the individual and property" (see Note 307).                 p. 393

312 *Sans-Souci*—a residence of the Prussian kings in Potsdam, built at the time of Frederick II.
                                                                        p. 394
313 At the peak of the victorious offensive of the Hungarian revolutionary troops, the National Assembly at its grand meeting in Debreczin on April 14, 1849 adopted, on Kossuth's initiative, a Declaration of Hungary's Independence. The Habsburg dynasty was dethroned and Kossuth elected head of state. In fact, a republican order was established in Hungary though, for foreign policy considerations, the name "Hungarian republic" was not used in official documents.

The *Neue Rheinische Zeitung* No. 291 for May 6, 1849 published the minutes of the session of the Hungarian National Assembly on April 14, 1849 and the text of the Declaration of Independence adopted by it. It also reproduced the respective article from the *Neue Oder-Zeitung*, supplying it with the following introductory note by the editors (probably written by Engels): "*Cologne*, May 5. The *Neue Oder-Zeitung* contains minutes of the session of the Hungarian National Assembly held in Debreczin on April 14, which decreed separation from Austria and the overthrow of the Habsburg dynasty and nominated Kossuth president of the state. Despite the poor German translation, we reproduce below the whole article word for word."                                                                   p. 397

314 See Note 310.                                                       p. 402

315 See Note 19.                                                        p. 402

316 The author of the report cited by Engels is obviously referring to the revolutionary unrest among peasants and townspeople in Galicia, subordinate to Austria. It was caused by rumours spreading in the spring of 1849 about the impending intrusion from behind the Carpathians of the Hungarian army and Polish legions fighting in its ranks. In April 1849, a large group of peasant recruits escaped from Chrzanov (near Cracow) and tried to make their way to Hungary. Some were captured by the Austrian authorities; four were shot in Cracow.
                                                                       p. 404

317 See Note 151.                                                      p. 405

318 The reference is to the schemes for a Croatian-Slavonian-Dalmatian state under the auspices of the Habsburgs. These were put forward by the Right-wing leaders of the South-Slav national movement (see Note 244).
    *Rascians*—see Note 54.                                            p. 407

319 On May 3-9, 1849 an armed uprising took place in Dresden, the capital of Saxony. It broke out because the King of Saxony refused to recognise the imperial Constitution. With workers forming the most active contingent in the barricade fighting, the insurgents occupied the greater part of the city and formed the provisional government headed by a radical democrat Tzschirner. However, the moderate policy of other members of the provisional government, desertion by the bourgeois civic militia, sabotage on the part of the liberal municipal council, the treachery of the bourgeoisie in Leipzig where they suppressed the workers' solidarity movement, weakened the insurgents' resistance to counter-revolution. The uprising was put down by Saxon troops assisted by troops dispatched from Prussia. Active in the uprising were the Russian revolutionary Mikhail Bakunin, a workers' leader Stephan Born and the composer Richard Wagner.        p. 411

320 The *Palatinate Defence Council* was formed at the beginning of May at people's gatherings in Kaiserslautern. Relying on the people's support, it demanded that the Bavarian Government recognise the imperial Constitution. However, the moderate elements on the Council strove to confine the movement to legal resistance. Only the threat of intervention by Prussia made the Palatinate petty-bourgeois democrats take more resolute action. On May 17, a provisional government of the Palatinate was formed and separation from Bavaria proclaimed.                                                          p. 412

321 See Note 40.                                                       p. 414

322 On the *Dresden uprising*, see Note 319.                           p. 416

323 See Note 320.                                                      p. 416

324 At that moment Bassermann was commissioner of the provisional Central Authority in Frankfurt (see Note 41) empowered to negotiate with the Prussian ruling circles. Despite the National Assembly's decision, the Austrian Archduke

20*

Johann, head of the Central Authority, supported the activities of the Prussian
and other governments against the imperial Constitution.                    p. 417

[325] On March 19, 1848, during the revolutionary events in Berlin, the armed people
compelled King Frederick William IV to come onto the balcony of his palace and
bare his head before the insurgents who had fallen on the barricades.     p. 417

[326] This article was reprinted in the *Deutsche Londoner Zeitung* No. 218, June 1, 1849
(see this volume, pp. 511-12). Later it was published in a slightly abridged form in
the newspaper *Der Sozialdemokrat* (Zurich) No. 2, January 8, 1886 and entitled
"Aus dem Ruhmeskranz der Hohenzollern". The name of the author was
mentioned in the editorial introduction.

The article was first published in English in the book: Karl Marx. *On Revolution,*
ed. by S. K. Padover, New York, 1971 ("The Karl Marx Library" series, Vol. 1).
                                                                            p. 418

[327] During the war between Sweden and Poland (1655-60) the Great Elector of
Brandenburg, Frederick William, sided now with the one, now with the other, of
the warring states. Taking advantage of Poland's military difficulties, he broke off
relations with Sweden in 1657 on condition that the Polish King renounced his
sovereign rights to Eastern Prussia, which was joined to Brandenburg in 1628 but
was dependent on the Polish crown. The Peace of Oliva concluded on May 3, 1660
by Sweden with Poland, Austria and Brandenburg confirmed Eastern Prussia's
independence from Poland.                                                    p. 418

[328] This refers to the first partition of Poland between Prussia, Austria and Russia in
1772. It was initiated by the Prussian King Frederick II.                   p. 419

[329] Early in 1792, supported by England and Tsarist Russia, Austria and Prussia
concluded a military alliance against revolutionary France. During the war, this
first anti-French coalition was joined by the Kingdom of Sardinia (Piedmont),
England, Holland, Spain, Naples and other states. However, the defeats inflicted
by the French army on the allied troops and the growing Austro-Prussian
contradictions compelled Prussia to withdraw from the coalition in 1795 and
conclude in Basle a separate peace with the French Republic.               p. 419

[330] In 1788 royal edicts limiting the rights of the press and freedom of worship were
issued in Prussia on the initiative of Bischoffswerder, adviser to Frederick
William II.                                                                 p. 419

[331] See Note 137.                                                         p. 419

[332] The wars waged in 1813-14 and 1815 against Napoleonic France after the defeat
of Napoleon's army in Russia in 1812 were contradictory in nature. Their
character was affected by the counter-revolutionary and expansionist aims and
policy of the ruling circles in the feudal monarchical states, and this is implied in
this article. At the same time, especially in 1813, when the struggle was aimed at
liberating German territory from French occupation, it assumed the character of a
genuinely popular national liberation war against foreign oppression. Later in a
series of articles entitled "Notes on the War" (1870), Engels stressed the
progressive nature of the people's resistance to the French rule and in his work
*The Role of Force in History* (1888) he wrote: "The people's war against Napoleon
was the reaction of the national feeling of all the peoples, which Napoleon had
trampled on."                                                              p. 419

[333] On May 22, 1815, Frederick William III of Prussia who, during the war with
Napoleonic France, had to respond to the demand for a Constitution, issued a

decree promising to convoke an all-Prussia people's representative body. However, according to the law of June 5, 1823, only provincial assemblies of the estates with limited consultative functions were formed.

The *battle of Waterloo*—see Note 166.                                    p. 420

334 The reference is to the *Federative Act (Bundesakte)* which proclaimed an ephemeral German Confederation and virtually sanctioned the political dismemberment of Germany and the maintenance of the monarchist system in the German states. This Act was signed on June 8 at the Vienna Congress and confirmed on June 9 in the Vienna concluding document. It contained vague promises of constitutional reforms and freedom of the press, but these remained a dead letter.    p. 420

335 These decisions were drawn up in August 1819 on the initiative of the Austrian Chancellor Metternich at the conference in Carlsbad by delegates of the states forming the German Confederation. They envisaged the introduction of preliminary censorship in all the German states, strict surveillance over universities, prohibition of students' societies and the establishment of a committee of inquiry to suppress so-called *demagogues* (participants in the opposition movement of that time).

The congress of the *Holy Alliance* (see Note 40), which began in *Troppau* in October 1820 and ended in *Laibach* in May 1821, openly proclaimed the principle of interference in the internal affairs of other states. Accordingly, the congress in Laibach resolved to send Austrian troops to Italy, and the congress in Verona (1822) to effect French intervention in Spain, with the aim of crushing the revolutionary and national liberation movements in those countries.    p. 420

336 According to the law of January 17, 1820 on state debt, state loans could only be made with the consent of the assemblies of estates, but this law was not observed in practice.

*Seehandlung* or *Preussische Seehandlungsgesellschaft* (Prussian Overseas Trading Company)—a trade and credit society founded in 1772 which enjoyed a number of important state privileges. It granted large credits to the Government and actually played the part of its banker and broker. In 1904 it was transformed into the official Prussian State Bank.                              p. 420

337 The reference is to the suppression of the Polish national liberation insurrection of 1830-31 by the Tsarist Government.                              p. 420

338 In a letter of January 15, 1838 addressed to the citizens of Elbing who expressed their dissatisfaction with the persecution of seven opposition professors in Hanover, the Prussian Minister of the Interior, Rochow, wrote: "Loyal subjects are expected to exhibit due obedience to their king and sovereign, but their limited understanding should keep them from interfering in the affairs of heads of state."                                          p. 420

339 Here the reference is to the so-called *Lehnin Prophecy (Vaticinium Lehninense)*—a poem in Latin which is ascribed to a certain Hermann, a monk of the Lehnin monastery (near Potsdam) who lived circa 1300. It described the crimes of the Hohenzollern dynasty which ruled in Brandenburg and prophesied their ruin in the eleventh generation.                                    p. 421

340 In 1843 Frederick William IV, who wanted to revive the romantic aspect of feudalism, issued a decree on the rebirth of the *Order of the Swan,* a medieval religious order of knights (founded in 1443 and dissolved during the Reformation). The King's intention did not materialise, however.

The *United Diet*—see Note 88.

The *"scrap of paper"*—an expression taken from the royal speech of Frederick William IV at the opening of the United Diet on April 11, 1847. The King declared that he would never agree to a Constitution which he derisively called "a written piece of paper".            p. 421

341 Marx probably had in mind the idea repeatedly expressed by Hegel that, in the process of dialectical development, there is an inevitable transition from the stage of formation and efflorescence to that of disintegration and ruin. In particular, Hegel stated in *Grundlinien der Philosophie des Rechts* that the "history of a world-historic nation contains partly the development of its principle from its latent embryonic stage until it blossoms ... and the period of its decline and fall..." (Part 3, Section 3, § 347). Marx developed this idea in his *Contribution to the Critique of Hegel's Philosophy of Law. Introduction* (end of 1843-beginning of 1844): "History is thorough and goes through many phases when carrying an old form to the grave. The last phase of a world-historical form is its *comedy*" (see present edition, Vol. 3, p. 179).            p. 421

342 The report which Engels cites from the liberal *Düsseldorfer Zeitung* and supplements with a call to the Cologne troops to join the popular movement, describes the initial stage of the Elberfeld uprising.

The *Elberfeld uprising* of workers and petty bourgeois broke out on May 8, 1849 and served as a signal for armed struggle in a number of cities in the Rhine Province (Düsseldorf, Iserlohn, Solingen and others) in defence of the imperial Constitution. The immediate occasion for the uprising was the attempts by the Prussian Government to use troops to suppress the revolutionary movement on the Rhine, to destroy democratic organisations and the press, and to disarm the army reserve troops it had itself called up which disobeyed its orders and supported the demand for the imperial Constitution. Engels played an active part in the uprising, having arrived in Elberfeld on May 11 together with a workers' detachment from Solingen (later legal proceedings were instituted against him for this— see present edition, Vol. 10). Engels' efforts to secure the disbandment of the bourgeois civic militia, the imposition of a war tax on the bourgeoisie, extensive armament of the workers in order to form the core of the Rhenish revolutionary army and to unite local uprisings, met with opposition from the Committee of Public Safety which was dominated by the representatives of the local bourgeoisie. Under pressure from bourgeois circles, Engels was deported from the city on the morning of May 15. As a result of secret negotiations between a deputation from the city bourgeoisie and the Government and of the capitulatory stand taken by the Committee of Public Safety, workers' detachments including those which came to their support from other places (the Berg Country, etc.) were forced out of the city on the night of May 16 (some managed to break through to the south, to the insurgent Palatinate) and the previous order was restored in Elberfeld. The defeat of the Elberfeld uprising led to the triumph of reaction throughout Rhenish Prussia.

The *Neue Rheinische Zeitung* and *Neue Kölnische Zeitung* devoted several articles to the events in Elberfeld (see, for instance, this volume, pp. 447-49 and 508).            p. 423

343 See Note 68.            p. 425

344 In English this article was first published in the collection: Karl Marx and Frederick Engels, *Articles from the "Neue Rheinische Zeitung". 1848-49*, Progress Publishers, Moscow, 1972.            p. 426

345 The suppression of the *uprising in Dresden*—see Note 319.

In response to the dispatch of artillery to suppress the Dresden uprising, workers and democrats in Breslau erected barricades in the city on May 6 and 7, 1849. They were, however, considerably outnumbered by the counter-revolutionary troops and were defeated. Isolated attempts to start a revolt in Saxony (the Prussian province) also failed. In the eastern districts of Prussia, the authorities managed in a very short time to overwhelm the campaign in defence of the imperial Constitution.                                                          p. 426

346 Alongside the uprising in Dresden and other towns in the Rhine Province and Westphalia, the most powerful struggle for the imperial Constitution developed in the Bavarian Palatinate and Baden (South-West Germany). Despite the limited nature of this Constitution the popular masses saw it as the only revolutionary achievement still surviving. In the Palatinate and Baden, workers, urban petty bourgeoisie and peasants rose in its defence. Soon they were joined by military units, particularly the lower ranks. In the middle of May provisional governments were set up there, the Grand Duke of Baden, Leopold, fled from the country, and the separation of the Palatinate from Bavaria was proclaimed. However, the leadership of the movement fell into the hands of moderate petty-bourgeois democrats who were hesitant, refusing to proclaim a republic and carry through a radical agrarian reform in the interests of the peasants. They chose passive defensive tactics which confined the movement to local limits and prevented the uprising from spreading outside the Palatinate and Baden. Nevertheless, the combined Palatinate-Baden insurgent army, in which there were many workers' units, put up a strong resistance to the Prussian-Bavarian-Württemberg mercenary troops who greatly exceeded the insurgents in numbers and strength. Engels took part in the campaigns and battles of this army. He was aide to August Willich, commander of one of the units which covered the retreat of its last detachments to Swiss territory on July 11 and 12. The insurgents' last stronghold—Rastatt—fell on July 23.

The uprising in the Palatinate and Baden was the culmination of the German revolution of 1848-49. Its character and course were later described by Engels in the essay "The Campaign for the German Imperial Constitution" (see present edition, Vol. 10).                                                          p. 426

347 In April 1849, President Louis Napoleon and the French Government decided to send an expeditionary corps under General Udino to Italy with the aim of intervening against the Roman Republic and restoring the secular power of the Pope. On April 30, 1849 the French troops were driven from Rome. The main blow was dealt them by Garibaldi's volunteer legion. However, Udino violated the terms of the armistice signed by the French and, on June 3, started a new offensive against the Roman Republic which had just completed a military campaign in the south against Neapolitan troops and was compelled to deliver a rebuff to the Austrians in the north. On July 3, after a month of heroic defence, Rome was captured by the interventionists and the Roman Republic ceased to exist.

                                                                    p. 426

348 Engels' article on the uprising in Elberfeld and Düsseldorf (see Note 342) was obviously written not later than May 10, before he left for insurgent Elberfeld via Solingen, where an armed struggle in defence of the imperial Constitution had also begun. It is possible that Engels sent the report to Cologne from Solingen, where he formed a detachment of armed workers on May 10. The next day he and this detachment arrived in Elberfeld where he stayed till the morning of May 15. The article was published in the special supplement to the *Neue Rheinische*

*Zeitung* No. 295, May 11, and probably the editors themselves supplied it with the same date. p. 428

349 Marx has in mind the close bond between the three monarchs—the Prussian King, the Russian Tsar and the Austrian Emperor. p. 430

350 The majority of the Prussian National Assembly which continued its sittings in Berlin despite the King's order to transfer the Assembly to Brandenburg was dispersed by General Wrangel's troops on November 15, 1848.

The Second Chamber was dissolved on April 27, 1849 (about this see Note 270) on the basis of the Brandenburg-Manteuffel Government's memorandum, sanctioned by the King. p. 430

351 The Saxon King Friedrich Augustus II found refuge in the fortress of Königstein to which he fled from Dresden during the uprising in May 1849.

*Imperial Max in Munich*—King of Bavaria, Maximilian II, nominated by certain deputies of the Frankfurt National Assembly for German emperorship. p. 430

352 The reference is to the Constitution imposed by the Prussian King on December 5, 1848 (see Note 52). p. 432

353 See Note 63. p. 432

354 See Note 270. p. 434

355 See Note 136. p. 434

356 See Note 306. p. 436

357 Marx's prediction of the Frankfurt National Assembly's inglorious end, which was brought about by its own compromise with and connivance in the counter-revolution, came true. In compliance with the orders of the Austrian, Prussian and other governments which recalled their deputies from Frankfurt, the Assembly's liberal majority, scared by the uprisings in defence of the imperial Constitution and the possibility of a civil war, disavowed this Constitution—their own creation—and resigned. The moderate democrats who thus proved to be in the majority lacked the courage to join the insurgents and continued to cherish hopes of introducing a Constitution by peaceful means. Early in June 1849, when the threat of dissolution arose, the "rump" of the Assembly transferred its sittings to Stuttgart (Württemberg). The imperial regent, who took an openly counter-revolutionary stand, was replaced by a five-man imperial administration (Karl Vogt, Ludwig Simons and others) which, because of its refusal to take revolutionary measures and its wavering and equivocal policy, was a complete failure. On June 18, 1849, the "rump" was dispersed by Württemberg troops. p. 438

358 *Charlottenburg*—a royal palace in the town of the same name west of Berlin (it became a suburb in the twentieth century); built in 1695 for Sophia Charlotte, wife of the Great Elector of Brandenburg, it later became one of the residences of the Prussian kings and also a place of their burial. p. 438

359 This refers to the joint action taken against revolutionary Hungary by the three monarchs—the Austrian Emperor, the Russian Tsar and the Prussian King. This counter-revolutionary plot is also exposed in Engels' article "The Third Party in the Alliance" (see this volume, pp. 394-95). p. 440

360 In April 1795 Prussia concluded the separate Basle peace treaty with France and withdrew from the first anti-French coalition, and in October of that same year it

signed the Petersburg convention with Russia and Austria on the *third partition of Poland* (see Note 276). p. 441

[361] "*Scrap of parchment*"—paraphrased expression from the royal speech of Frederick William IV at the opening of the United Diet in 1847 (see Note 340). p. 441

[362] See Note 46. p. 441

[363] *Ça ira!*—a popular song during the French Revolution. p. 446

[364] See Note 342. p. 447

[365] On May 19, 1849 the *Neue Rheinische Zeitung* came out for the last time. The Government and the police had long awaited a suitable moment to suppress the newspaper. In April and early May 1849, the Minister of the Interior, Manteuffel, repeatedly demanded that the Cologne Public Prosecutor's office and legal authorities bring an action against its editors. By that time, the number of charges against them had grown to 23 (some were later used as a pretext for instituting legal proceedings against Marx and Engels by default, see this volume, p. 516). However, Marx's and Engels' acquittal by the jury in February 1849 and fear of the people's unrest compelled the Public Prosecutor's office to refrain from making the legal proceedings against the paper public. Only after the main uprisings in the Rhine Province had, on the whole, been suppressed, was a long-prepared measure applied against Marx—expulsion from Prussia. He was refused Prussian citizenship in due time, despite the Cologne magistrate's favourable reply to his application for this on his arrival in Cologne on April 11, 1848. After four months' delay, the Royal Government refused to confirm the magistrate's decision, and Minister Kühlwetter, to whom Marx sent a complaint, turned it down (see present edition, Vol. 7, p. 581). Marx continued to remain "a foreigner" who could at any moment be accused of abusing hospitality and be subject to expulsion. The Royal Government's note to this effect followed on May 11, 1849 (see below) and was handed to Marx on May 16. Other editors were also persecuted. Weerth and Dronke, who did not enjoy Prussian citizenship either, were likewise ordered to leave Cologne. Legal proceedings were instituted against Engels for his part in the Elberfeld uprising. The democratic press still surviving in Germany protested against the police measures towards the newspaper's editors (see this volume, pp. 509-13). Forced to cease publication of the *Neue Rheinische Zeitung*, Marx and Engels cherished hopes of resuming it shortly in some other place (see this volume, p. 473), but the situation in the country did not allow them to carry out these intentions. The entire issue No. 301 of the *Neue Rheinische Zeitung* which carried this and other articles by Marx and Engels, together with the editors' address to the Cologne workers, was printed in red ink.

This article was first published in English in the collection: Karl Marx and Frederick Engels, *Articles from the "Neue Rheinische Zeitung". 1848-49*, Progress Publishers, Moscow, 1972. p. 451

[366] This refers to the verdicts of the Cologne jury court pronounced on February 7 and 8, 1849. On February 7, Karl Marx, editor-in-chief of the *Neue Rheinische Zeitung*, Frederick Engels, co-editor, and Hermann Korff, responsible publisher, were brought before the court on a charge of having insulted the Chief Public Prosecutor Zweiffel and having libelled the policemen who arrested workers' leaders, in the article "Arrests" published in the *Neue Rheinische Zeitung* No. 35, July 5, 1848 (see present edition, Vol. 7).

On February 8, 1849 the second trial—against the Rhenish District Committee of Democrats—was held. For details see Note 289.

At both trials, the jury returned a verdict of not guilty. For the speeches made by Marx and Engels at the trial, see present edition, Vol. 8, pp. 304-22.
p. 451

367 In English this article was first published in the collection: Karl Marx and Frederick Engels, *Articles from the "Neue Rheinische Zeitung". 1848-49*, Progress Publishers, Moscow, 1972.
p. 455

368 The delegates of the opposition headed by Kossuth submitted a whole programme of progressive reforms to the National Assembly (Diet) of the Hungarian Kingdom convened in November 1847 in Pressburg. However, the demands of the opposition came up against stubborn resistance on the part of the Right aristocratic wing of the Assembly, especially its Upper Chamber, and were implemented only under pressure of the revolutionary masses after the popular uprising in Pest and Buda on March 15, 1848. Even at this stage, the reforms carried out were of a narrow nature (see notes 193 and 263) because the Assembly was dominated by moderate liberal aristocrats inclined to compromise with the Austrian Court and conservative circles. Equality and autonomy were not granted to the oppressed nationalities and this allowed the Habsburg reaction to use their national movements in the struggle against the Hungarian revolution.   p. 455

369 See Note 232.
p. 456

370 The reference is to the appointment of Kossuth as head of the Defence Council, the actual government of revolutionary Hungary (see Note 70).   p. 456

371 Engels is evidently referring to the rescript issued by the Austrian Emperor Ferdinand on October 3, 1848 when he ordered that the Hungarian Assembly be dissolved and its resolutions not sanctioned by the Crown (including that on the formation of the Defence Council) be regarded as invalid. According to this rescript, the Croatian Ban Jellachich was appointed commander-in-chief of all troops and extraordinary government commissioner in Hungary, and martial law was introduced throughout the country. The rescript was published in the *Wiener Zeitung* No. 275, October 5, 1848.   p. 456

372 The *battle of Schwechat* (near Vienna), in which the Hungarian army was defeated by Austrian troops under Windischgrätz, took place on October 30, 1848, on the eve of the fall of revolutionary Vienna.   p. 457

373 See Note 55.
p. 457

374 See Note 9.
p. 459

375 The reference is to the *Declaration of Hungary's Independence* adopted by the National Assembly on April 14, 1849 (see Note 313).   p. 461

376 See Note 40.
p. 462

377 The reference is to the Polish national liberation insurrection of 1830-31.
p. 463

378 The reference is to the elections to the French Legislative Assembly held on May 13, 1849. The monarchist groups—legitimists, Orleanists and Bonapartists who formed a joint "party of order"—got the majority. Though the elections were held in an atmosphere of administrative pressure and accompanied by ballot-rigging on the part of the conservative authorities, a major success was scored by a bloc of democrats and petty-bourgeois socialists called the Mountain

party. About two million electors voted for their candidates, who received 180 seats in the Assembly.                                        p. 463

379 The expectation of a new upsurge of the European revolution, which is expressed in Engels' article closing his series about the revolutionary war in Hungary, as well as in other items by Marx and Engels in the last issues of the *Neue Rheinische Zeitung*, was fostered by the brilliant victories scored by the Hungarian army, the uprisings in South-West Germany and the maturing conflict between the democratic and counter-revolutionary forces in the French Republic. Hopes of a more extensive and wider revolution did not come true, however. The uprisings in Baden and the Palatinate did not extend beyond local limits and the activities of petty-bourgeois democrats in France in June 1849 failed (see this volume, pp. 477-79). In the Hungarian campaign, a change shortly took place unfavourable to the revolutionary movement. Internal differences intensified between radical circles and the supporters of a compromise with the Habsburgs among the liberal landowners who were afraid that the revolution would go further. The views of the latter were also shared by Görgey, Hungarian commander-in-chief (in May also appointed War Minister), who often acted contrary to the instructions of Kossuth and other radicals. Görgey's strategic error was that he actually refused to undertake operations to capture Vienna and use the main forces for the siege of the fortress of Buda (Ofen), and this gave the Austrian command time to bring up reserves. In mid-June 1849 the Tsarist army under Paskevich entered Hungary to offer help to the Austrian counter-revolution. The Tsarist intervention was carried out according to the agreement concluded by Emperor Nicholas I and Francis Joseph in Warsaw on May 21, and was in fact approved by the ruling circles of France and England who were eager to destroy the revolution in Central Europe. The combined forces of the Habsburgs and the Tsar far outnumbered those of the Hungarians and inflicted several defeats on the latter. On August 13, Görgey, who was in command of the Hungarian main army, signed a capitulation at Világos. The Hungarian revolution was suppressed amid great terror of which many Hungarian military and political figures fell victims. Kossuth, Bem, Dembiński and the head of the last Hungarian Government Szemere who had to flee the country, were sentenced to death by default.                                         p. 463

380 See Note 19.                                          p. 464

381 After the defeat of the Prussian troops by Napoleon's army at Jena and Auerstedt (October 14, 1806), a number of Prussian fortresses capitulated to the French without a fight. The fortress of Küstrin, for instance, surrendered to a small French detachment on October 31 and Magdeburg, with its many thousand-strong garrison and artillery, was surrendered by General Kleist on November 8, after the first salvo fired by the French from light field mortars.

In the Appeal *To My People (An Mein Volk)* of March 17, 1813 Frederick William III promised to introduce a Constitution in Prussia, but this remained a dead letter.                                          p. 464

382 See Note 340.                                          p. 464

383 See Note 274.                                          p. 464

384 "*I and My house wish to serve the lord*"—words from the royal speech of Frederick William IV at the opening of the first United Diet on April 11, 1847. The words "*unweakened crown*" (see Note 46) are also from that speech.          p. 465

[385] This address was first published in English in the collection: Karl Marx and Frederick Engels, *Articles from the "Neue Rheinische Zeitung". 1848-49*, Progress Publishers, Moscow, 1972. ·                                                      p. 467

[386] This statement was written by Marx in Bingen (Hesse) during his last days in Germany. Immediately after the suppression of the *Neue Rheinische Zeitung*, Marx and Engels went to Frankfurt am Main and then to insurgent Baden and the Palatinate. However, they failed in their attempts to convince the Left deputies of the Frankfurt Assembly and members of the provisional governments of Baden and the Palatinate of the need to give the movement an all-German character, to mount a resolute offensive, to bring the Assembly openly to join the uprising, to compel it to call upon the people everywhere to take up arms, set up an energetic executive power and carry out radical agrarian and other reforms. Their bold revolutionary plan was turned down by the representatives of petty-bourgeois democrats. From Bingen, Marx decided to go to France where new revolutionary events were expected, intending to establish closer ties between the German democrats and the revolutionary circles in Paris. For his part, Engels thought it expedient to return to the Palatinate and join personally the forthcoming struggle against the counter-revolutionary troops that were then concentrating.

This statement in the press was in reply to the claims of the democratic *Westdeutsche Zeitung* (which first came out in Cologne on May 25, 1849) to be the successor of the *Neue Rheinische Zeitung*. Its editorial board announced that the subscribers to the *Neue Rheinische Zeitung* would receive the *Westdeutsche Zeitung* instead. The covering letter addressed to the editorial board of the liberal *Frankfurter Journal* has survived in manuscript form. There are no data about the statement being published in this newspaper, but it was printed in the democratic newspapers of Frankfurt and Cologne.                                        p. 473

[387] This article was written by Engels in early June 1849, immediately after his return to Kaiserslautern—the capital of the Palatinate which he and Marx visited in the last ten days of May after the *Neue Rheinische Zeitung* ceased to appear. In the Palatinate, Engels refused to accept the civil and military posts offered him by the provisional government, because he did not want to take responsibility for the policy of the petty-bourgeois democratic members of the government, a policy which he, a proletarian revolutionary, did not support. He agreed, however, to write a few articles for the government newspaper, *Der Bote für Stadt und Land*, in defence of the democratic movement against attacks from conservative and moderately liberal papers.

Engels' second article was not published because of objections that it was too "inflammatory" (see Engels' article "The Campaign for the German Imperial Constitution", present edition, Vol. 10). This induced Engels to cease contributing to the newspaper. On June 13, Engels left Kaiserslautern for Offenbach in order to join the ranks of the Baden-Palatinate army—Willich's volunteer corps. As Willich's aide, he took part in drafting the plan for military operations and supervised the implementation of the most important assignments. He fought in four big battles, in particular at Rastatt. On July 12, 1849, Engels was one of the last fighters to cross the Swiss border.                                        p. 474

[388] See Note 40.                                                          p. 474

[389] An allusion to Marx who, in view of the decisive revolutionary events expected in France, went to Paris about June 2, 1849. He was issued with the mandate of the Central Committee of German Democrats signed by d'Ester, the most active member of the provisional government in the Palatinate, and this empowered him

to represent the German revolutionary party before the French democrats and socialists in Paris.                                                          p. 475

390  See Note 244.                                                          p. 475

391  The reference is to the Prussian General Peucker who, from July 15, 1848 to May 10, 1849, held the post of Minister of War in the so-called Central Authority (see Note 41) and was then in command of the imperial troops sent to the Palatinate and Baden to suppress the movement for the imperial Constitution there.
                                                          p. 475

392  See Note 335.                                                          p. 475

393  See Note 136.                                                          p. 476

394  On June 13, 1849, in Paris the petty-bourgeois *Mountain* party (see Note 378) came out against the Government, on account of the bombardment of Rome by French troops sent to Italy to suppress the Roman Republic. That was done in violation of Article 5 of the French Constitution, which forbade the use of armed forces against the freedom of other nations. The representatives of the Mountain in the Legislative Assembly declared that they would use all possible means to defend the Constitution. At the decisive moment, however, the leaders of the Mountain were frightened of a new armed uprising by the Paris proletariat and called upon Parisians to confine themselves to a peaceful protest demonstration against intervention in Italy. The demonstration took place on June 13 and was dispersed by troops and bourgeois detachments of the National Guard prepared in advance. A state of siege was declared in Paris, massive repressions began against democratic and proletarian organisations, some representatives of the Mountain emigrated, others were arrested and put on trial. The Legislative Assembly was overwhelmed by the conservative "party of order", a union of monarchist factions, which started a campaign against the democratic freedoms and rights that still survived. The events of June 13 testified to the bankruptcy of the tactics used by petty-bourgeois democrats and inflicted a severe blow to the revolutionary movement in Europe.                                                          p. 477

395  The reference is to the revolutionary group within the Commission of the Twenty-Five, the agency of the Paris Democratic-Socialist Electoral Committee. The group included members of workers' clubs and secret societies. The Democratic-Socialist Committee headed the campaign carried on in Paris by the Mountain for the elections to the French Legislative Assembly held on May 13, 1849 (see Note 378).                                                          p. 477

396  *Conservatoire des Arts*—an educational establishment in Paris.                                                          p. 478

397  The reference is to the *Democratic Association of the Friends of the Constitution,* an organisation of moderate bourgeois republicans set up by the members of the *National* party (see Note 71) during the campaign for the elections to the French Legislative Assembly held on May 13, 1849.                                                          p. 478

398  Ledru-Rollin stated in the Legislative Assembly on June 11, 1849, that the Mountain intended to defend the Constitution by force of arms if necessary.
                                                          p. 478

399  During the proletarian uprising in Paris on May 15, 1848 (see Note 77), Ledru-Rollin persuaded demonstrators who had burst into the premises of the Constituent Assembly to cease from decisive action, clear the premises and allow the Assembly to discuss their demands calmly.

During the uprising of the French proletariat on June 23-26, 1848, Ledru-Rollin supported the measures taken by the Government and the Constituent Assembly to suppress the insurgents and was one of the first to send a telegraph request for military reinforcements to be dispatched from the provinces to Paris.                                                                                          p. 478

400 The reference is to the brutal suppression of the workers' uprising in Lyons which broke out on June 15, 1849 under the impact of the June 13 events in Paris.
p. 479

401 In view of the great financial and organisational difficulties which arose after the introduction of the state of siege in Cologne on September 26, 1848 and the suspension of the *Neue Rheinische Zeitung* (see Note 307), Marx was compelled to take financial responsibility for the newspaper's publication upon himself; he invested in it all the cash he had and thus, in fact, became its owner.          p. 480

402 Marx began to study political economy at the end of 1843 and, in the spring of 1844, set himself the task of giving critical examination of bourgeois political economy from the standpoint of materialism and communism. The draft written in this connection— *Economic and Philosophic Manuscripts of 1844* (see present edition, Vol. 3)—has reached us in an incomplete form. In February 1845, just before his first expulsion from France, Marx concluded a contract with the Leske publishers in Darmstadt for the publication of a two-volume *Kritik der Politik und Nationalökonomie,* which he continued to work on in Brussels (see present edition, Vol. 4, p. 675). In September 1846, however, Leske informed Marx that, in view of rigorous censorship and police persecution, he would not be able to publish the work. The contract was soon cancelled. Nevertheless Marx did not cease his economic studies and added new material to his notebooks containing extracts on political economy. He set out the results of his economic research in a book directed against Proudhon, *The Poverty of Philosophy,* in his Speech on the Question of Free Trade, in his *Wage Labour and Capital* and other works (see present edition, Vol. 6 and this volume, pp. 197-228). Marx did not give up his intention of writing . a big treatise on political economy, but during the intensive revolutionary activities of 1848-49, he had to postpone it. Marx managed to resume his economic research on a regular basis only after he moved to London in August 1849.                                                                                    p. 480

403 On July 19, 1849 in an atmosphere of repression against democrats and socialists following the events of June 13 in Paris, the French authorities informed Marx that an order had been issued for his expulsion from Paris to Morbihan, a swampy and unhealthy place in Brittany. Marx protested and the expulsion was delayed, but on August 23 he again received a police order to leave Paris within 24 hours. At the end of August, Marx set off for London where he spent the rest of his life.
p. 481

404 This is a rough version of the Repudiation drawn up by Engels on behalf of a group of men who had served in the volunteer corps under Willich (Engels was his aide) and had taken part in the military operations of the Baden-Palatinate army. Willich's corps consisted of eight companies numbering 700-800 people, partly students but mostly workers—German emigrants in Besançon (France), members of workers' associations and gymnastics societies, etc. Two companies were formed from the workers of Rhenish Prussia, participants in the May uprising in Elberfeld and other towns. Engels described them as the most steady and reliable in the insurgent army. At the closing stage of the military campaign, when the insurgents were defeated at the battle at Rastatt, Willich's corps covered the retreat of other

insurgent units and on July 12, 1849 was the last to leave German territory. During their stay in Switzerland, the men and officers of the corps were criticised and abused by petty-bourgeois emigrants, leaders of the uprising in the Palatinate and Baden. This compelled Engels, who happened to be in the town of Vevey, in the Swiss Canton of Waad (Vaud), to write this Repudiation.

On Marx's advice (see his letter to Engels dated August 1, 1849), Engels soon began to write "The Campaign for the German Imperial Constitution" directed against the petty-bourgeois democrats. He finished it in February 1850 in London, where he had moved from Switzerland (it took him October and November 1849 to travel to England). The facts given in the rough copy of the Repudiation and pertaining to the moment when the Baden-Palatinate army was retreating towards the Swiss border are found in the concluding part of that work (see present edition, Vol. 10). Engels' manuscript was discovered in the Berne Federal Archives by Rolf Dlubek, an historian from the German Democratic Republic, who published it in 1967. There are many deletions. Judging from the first lines, the document was intended to be signed by several participants in the campaign. At the end of the rough copy, there is the pencilled signature of Captain Koehler.                                                   p. 482

405  The reference is to one of the units in the insurgent army, the Baden *Landsturm* under Becker. During the revolution of 1848-49, Becker played an important role in the republican uprisings in South Germany. At that time he took a revolutionary-democratic stand, but his views on programme and tactics were confined to petty-bourgeois socialism.                                 p. 482

406  The commanders of the Baden-Palatinate army that was retreating before the enemy's superior forces held a council of war in Jestetten on July 10, 1849, on the eve of the crossing on to Swiss territory. At the council, most of the commanders spoke for ending the struggle. Among them was the commander-in-chief Franz Siegel, who was reinstated in this post when on July 1, 1849, the Polish general, Mieroslawski, who had commanded the insurgent army for some time, resigned.
                                                              p. 483

407  The reference is to the acquittals of the *Neue Rheinische Zeitung* (the accused were Marx, Engels and Korff) and of the Rhenish District Committee of Democrats (the accused were Marx, Schapper and the lawyer Schneider II) at the trials held on February 7 and 8, 1849 (see notes 289 and 366).                         p. 487

408  What is meant here is evidently the order issued by the Prussian Minister of the Interior Kühlwetter to the effect that the decision of the Cologne royal government authorities not to grant Prussian citizenship to Marx remained in force (see Note 365, and also the article "The Conflict between Marx and Prussian Citizenship" and the letter from the Minister of the Interior Kühlwetter to Marx dated September 12, 1848, present edition, Vol. 7).                     p. 488

409  In February and March 1849, a number of democratic banquets were organised in the Rhine Province to mark the anniversaries of the revolutions in France and Germany. Marx and Engels regarded these banquets as a form of revolutionary education for the masses, and gave them their general support. They themselves, however, attended only those that were held under genuinely revolutionary slogans and did not approve the attempts of petty-bourgeois democrats to exaggerate the significance of those revolutionary events that were half-hearted and incomplete in character and thereby sowed constitutional illusions among the masses. Among these events, they believed, was the March revolution in Prussia (see this volume, p. 108). Therefore, having published in the *Neue Rheinische*

*Zeitung* (No. 245, May 14, 1849) an announcement of the banquet in Solingen in compliance with its organisers' request, they did not accept an invitation to attend in person. Their refusal to accept this and other invitations was tactfully explained in the editorial note published in the *Neue Rheinische Zeitung* No. 249, second edition, March 18, 1849 which read: "The editorial board of the *Neue Rheinische Zeitung* has received from many neighbouring towns, both on the left and the right bank of the Rhine, invitations to attend banquets to be held on March 18. We are very grateful to our democratic friends for these kind invitations, but unfortunately having plenty of work to do we could not accept a single one of them." Nevertheless, Marx, Engels and other newspaper editors took an active part in the banquet organised in Cologne at the Gürzenich hall, on March 19, not to celebrate the March revolution but in honour of those who fought on the barricades in Berlin on March 18 and 19, 1848 (see next document, pp. 490-91).

p. 489

[410] On the trial of Barbès, Blanqui, Raspail and other revolutionary leaders held in Bourges between March 7 and April 3, 1849, see Note 78.                                  p. 490

[411] The reference is to the banquet organised by liberals and moderate democrats in Cologne to mark the anniversary of the revolution of March 18, 1848.
*Wailers*— see Note 136.                                                           p. 491

[412] This refers to the attempt by the Minister of the Interior, Manteuffel, to implicate Marx, Engels and their associates in the case against cobbler Hätzel, a member of the Communist League, at whose house in Berlin the Rules of the League, weapons and hand grenades had been found. On March 30, 1848, Manteuffel sent a secret police agent to Cologne to carry out house searches, seize papers and, using the evidence thus obtained, arrest the Cologne leaders of the Communist League. However, this police action misfired owing to lack of evidence. p. 493

[413] These decisions by the general meeting of the Cologne Workers' Association were connected with the policy of strengthening the class independence of the workers' organisations and with practical steps to form a mass political party in Germany. Marx, Engels and their associates in the Communist League and the *Neue Rheinische Zeitung* adopted this policy in view of the changes that had taken place in the country's political situation by the spring of 1849 (see Note 225). Marx and Engels attached great importance to the Cologne Workers' Association in their plans for founding the party. By that time, the Association had become the bulwark of their ideological influence on the workers' movement and one of the initiators of the union of workers' associations in the Rhine Province and throughout Germany.

The *Cologne Workers' Association*—a workers' organisation founded on April 13, 1848 by Andreas Gottschalk. By the beginning of May it had up to 5,000 members, most of whom were workers and artisans. The Association was headed by a President and a committee, which included representatives of various trades, and had several branches.

Most of the leading figures in the Workers' Association (Gottschalk, Anneke, Schapper, Moll, Lessner, Jansen, Röser, Nothjung, Bedorf) were members of the Communist League. After Gottschalk's arrest on July 6, Moll was elected President of the Association, and on October 16, on request of the Association's members, the presidency was temporarily assumed by Marx. From February to May 1849 the post was held by Schapper.

In the initial period of its existence, the Workers' Association was influenced by Gottschalk who ignored the tasks of the proletariat in the democratic revolution, pursued a policy of boycotting elections to representative institutions and came out against a union with democracy. Gottschalk combined ultra-Left phrases with quite moderate methods of struggle (e.g. petitions) and support for the demands advanced by workers affected by craft prejudices. From the very outset, Gottschalk's sectarian position was opposed by the supporters of Marx and Engels. Under their impact, a change took place at the end of June 1848 in the activities of the Workers' Association, which became a centre of revolutionary agitation among the workers, and from the autumn of 1848 among the peasants as well. Propaganda of scientific communism and study of Marx's works were carried on within the Association. It maintained contacts with other workers' and democratic organisations.

With the aim of strengthening the Association, Marx, Schapper and its other leaders reorganised it in January and February 1849. On February 25, new Rules were adopted declaring a higher class consciousness on the part of the workers to be the main task of the Association.

The mounting counter-revolution and intensified police persecution frustrated the Association's activities aimed at unity and organisation of the working masses. After the *Neue Rheinische Zeitung* was suppressed and Marx, Schapper and other leaders left Cologne, the Association gradually turned into an ordinary workers' educational society.                                                                 p. 494

414  The reference is to the *Central Committee of German Workers* that was elected at the Workers' Congress held in Berlin from August 23 to September 3, 1848. At this congress the Workers' Fraternity, a union of many workers' associations, was founded. The programme of the congress was drawn up under the influence of Stephan Born and set the workers the task of implementing narrow craft-union demands, thereby diverting them from the revolutionary struggle. The Central Committee, which included Stephan Born, Schwenniger and Kick, had its headquarters in Leipzig.

At the end of 1848, under the impact of the revolutionary events and experience drawn from them, the leaders of the Workers' Fraternity began to display certain revolutionary tendencies. They recognised the need to arm the workers and for them to take an active part in the political struggle. There was a great desire to set up an all-German workers' organisation. In the spring of 1849, the Workers' Fraternity and a number of regional congresses of workers' associations proposed that a national workers' congress be convened in Leipzig to found a general workers' union. These plans, however, were frustrated by the developing counter-revolution.                                                                 p. 494

415  See Note 412.                                                                 p. 497

416  This resolution criticises the sectarian stand taken by Gottschalk. From the very start of the revolution, it was evident that he did not agree with the tactics pursued by Marx and Engels (see Note 413) and, for that reason, he withdrew from the Communist League at the beginning of May 1848.

In July 1848, Gottschalk, together with Anneke and Esser, was arrested and put on trial on a charge of "inciting to an armed uprising against royal power". The trial was held on December 21-23. Under public pressure, the jury returned a verdict of not guilty. After his release, Gottschalk first went to Bonn and later to Paris and Brussels, but through his associates attempted to cause a split in the ranks of the Cologne Workers' Association and impose sectarian organisational principles and tactics upon it.                                                                 p. 498

417  The reference is to the participation of Gottschalk, prior to his arrest, in the *First Democratic Congress*. It was held in Frankfurt am Main from June 14 to 17, 1848

and attended by delegates of 89 democratic and workers' associations from different towns in Germany. The congress decided to unite all democratic associations and to set up district committees under the Central Committee of German Democrats. However, due to the weakness and vacillations of the petty-bourgeois leaders, even after the congress the democratic movement in Germany still lacked unity and organisation, and remained ideologically heterogeneous.

p. 498

[418] When the *Zeitung des Arbeiter-Vereines zu Köln* ceased to appear because of police reprisals against the owner of its printing-press, the newspaper *Freiheit, Brüderlichkeit, Arbeit*, which began publication on October 26, 1848, became the organ of the Cologne Workers' Association. At the end of December, as a result of Gottschalk's interference in the paper's affairs, its publication was interrupted. From January 14, 1849, the newspaper *Freiheit, Arbeit* began to appear. Its responsible editor was Prinz, who supported Gottschalk and pursued the latter's policy of splitting the Cologne Workers' Association. Prinz refused to submit to the editorial commission which had been appointed at the committee meeting of the Cologne Workers' Association on January 15 and included Schapper, Röser and Reiff; the committee meeting of January 29 resolved, therefore, that the *Freiheit, Arbeit* could not be regarded as the Association's newspaper and that the *Freiheit, Brüderlichkeit, Arbeit* should resume publication with Esser as its editor. The *Freiheit, Brüderlichkeit, Arbeit* reappeared on February 8 and continued publication up to the middle of 1849. The *Freiheit, Arbeit* continued to appear until June 17, 1849, carrying a variety of insinuations against Marx and Engels.

p. 499

[419] In a declaration written in Brussels on January 9, 1849 and published in the *Freiheit, Arbeit* on January 18, Gottschalk explained his "voluntary banishment" by the fact that, despite his acquittal, many of his fellow-citizens remained convinced of his guilt. He declared that he would come back only if he was called by "the hitherto supreme arbiter in the country" (an allusion to the King, Frederick William IV), or by "his fellow-citizens", by "the voice of the people".

p. 499

[420] The reference is to the *Workers' Fraternity* (see Note 414).

p. 504

[421] This receipt was made at the time of Marx's trip to North-West Germany and Westphalia in mid-April 1849 with the aim of drawing local workers' associations into the preparations for organising a proletarian party, of establishing closer contacts with the members of the Communist League and democrats and of collecting funds to continue the publication of the *Neue Rheinische Zeitung*.

p. 505

[422] Simultaneously with the Congress of Workers' Associations of the Rhine Province and Westphalia (about the preparations for which see this volume, p. 392) on May 6, 1849 in Cologne a congress of the democratic organisations of these provinces, and then a joint sitting were held. Both congresses took place at a time when the authorities were preparing reprisals against those who engaged in revolutionary disturbances. It was expected that a state of siege would be declared in Cologne. The sittings of the congresses were therefore short and reports on their resolutions were not published in the newspapers. These resolutions evidently concerned urgent measures to combat the counter-revolution. The joint sitting of the congresses showed that, despite the organisational break with the petty-bourgeois democrats, the workers' organisations led by Marx and Engels did not reject combined actions with them in the struggle against the counter-revolution.

Marx and Engels planned that the congress of the workers' associations of Rhenish Prussia, which, as the newspaper report indicates, was attended by a considerable number of delegates, would be a new step towards the convocation of an all-German workers' congress and a union of workers' associations on a country-wide scale. The mounting reaction, however, upset this plan to create a mass political party of the German proletariat.                                    p. 506

423 As the report of May 18 from Cologne published in the *Trier'sche Zeitung* indicates, the news of reprisals against the *Neue Rheinische Zeitung* was circulating among journalists before May 19, when the last issue of the newspaper appeared. A Cologne correspondent of the constitutional monarchist *Deutsche Zeitung* put out in Frankfurt am Main wrote as follows about this in a report also dated May 18: "The editor-in-chief of the *Neue Rheinische Zeitung*, Herr Karl Marx, has received orders from our *Regierungspräsident* to leave Cologne within 24 hours, failing which the authorities will be obliged to resort to force. The reason given in the letter from the *Regierungspräsident* is that by the unbridled language predominating in recent numbers of his newspaper, by deriding and insulting the Royal Government and the authorities, as well as by openly working for the Social Republic, Herr Marx has shamelessly abused the hospitality extended to him. Since orders for the arrest of his other colleagues as well are to be implemented and the latter therefore intend to escape, the last number of the *Neue Rheinische Zeitung* will appear tomorrow morning, and it will be printed in red. Furthermore, this number will contain a remarkable valedictory poem by Freiligrath. The editors and the workers are said to be intending to proceed to the Palatinate without delay" (*Deutsche Zeitung* No. 138, May 20, 1849).                      p. 509

424 The reference is to a number of Marx's items and his speech for the defence at the trial against the Rhenish District Committee of Democrats on February 8, 1849. These were published in the *Neue Rheinische Zeitung* and proved that by effecting the coup d'état and dispersing the Prussian National Assembly on December 5, 1848, the Government of Frederick William IV had grossly violated the edicts sanctioned by the King after the March revolution introducing a constitutional system in the country. In his speech for the defence Marx pointed to the "Decision on Some Principles of the Future Prussian Constitution" adopted on April 6, 1848 and the electoral law for the convocation of the National Assembly adopted on April 8, 1848 (see Note 86).                                                     p. 512

425 This is an excerpt from the section "Continental Europe" in "The Political and Historical Survey" published in several issues of the *Democratic Review*. The author of the "Survey" was obviously George Julian Harney, editor of the journal.
                                                                           p. 512

426 On the stay of Marx and Engels in South-West Germany (Baden and the Palatinate) after being compelled to leave Cologne, see Note 386.       p. 515

427 In September 1848 Marx, Korff and others were accused by the imperial Ministry of having libelled the deputies of the Frankfurt National Assembly in: 1) Georg Weerth's series of feuilletons *Leben und Taten des berühmten Ritters Schnapphahnski* directed against Lichnowski, a Right-wing representative, and published anonymously in the *Neue Rheinische Zeitung* in August, September and December 1848 and January 1849; 2) a report from Breslau in the *Neue Rheinische Zeitung* No. 95 for September 6, 1848 about Prince Lichnowski's machinations in the electoral campaign; 3) a report from Frankfurt am Main in the *Neue Rheinische Zeitung* No. 102 for September 14, 1848 exposing false information in the report by Stedtmann, deputy to the Frankfurt National Assembly, concerning the vote on

the armistice with Denmark; 4) a resolution of the public meeting in Cologne published in the *Neue Rheinische Zeitung* No. 110, September 23, 1848, in which the deputies of the Frankfurt National Assembly who had voted for the armistice with Denmark were accused of having betrayed the nation (see present edition, Vol. 7, pp. 588-89). For more details on the trial, see this volume, pp. 517-20.  p. 516

428  See Note 92.
                                                                         p. 518

429  The reference is to the *Democratic Society* in Cologne which was set up in April 1848 and included small businessmen, as well as workers and artisans. Marx, Engels and other editors of the *Neue Rheinische Zeitung* who formed the leadership of the Society strove to direct its activities towards a resolute struggle against the counter-revolutionary policy of the Prussian ruling circles and exposure of the liberal bourgeoisie's "agreement" policy. In April 1849 Marx and his supporters, who had in fact begun to organise an independent mass proletarian party, found it necessary to separate from the petty-bourgeois democrats and so withdrew from the Democratic Society. At the same time, they continued to support the revolutionary actions of all the democratic forces in Germany.
                                                                         p. 519

430  This was the third time that the authorities instituted legal proceedings against the *Neue Rheinische Zeitung*. At the first trial of Marx, Engels and Korff, held on February 7, 1849, the jury returned a verdict of not guilty (see present edition, Vol. 8, pp. 304-22). At the second trial on May 29, 1849 the Public Prosecutor's office and the police authorities failed to sentence Marx and other newspaper editors in their absence and only Korff, the former responsible manager, was sentenced to a one-month term of imprisonment and to pay one-seventh of the costs (see this volume, pp. 519-20), so the third time it was decided to put only Korff on trial. It was thought that, by condemning him, other leading editors of the newspaper would likewise be morally discredited, above all Marx as editor-in-chief. But the reactionaries miscalculated: Korff was acquitted. p. 521

431  See Note 307.
                                                                         p. 521

432  The news of Marx's arrival in Paris was evidently somewhat delayed in reaching Cologne. Judging from Marx's letter to Engels of July 7, 1849 sent from Paris to Kaiserslautern (the Palatinate), he arrived in the French capital in the first days of June.
                                                                         p. 525

433  On Marx's expulsion from Paris, see Note 403.
                                                                         p. 526

# NAME INDEX

chief of the 1st Infantry Regiment, took part in suppressing the 1848-49 revolution in Italy.—161, 175

Auersperg, Maximilian, Count (1771-1850)—Austrian lieutenant-field marshal, commander of the Austrian troops in the Banat (1836), fought against revolutionary Hungary in 1848 and 1849, chief of the 5th Cuirassier Regiment.—269, 274

Auerswald, Rudolf von (1795-1866)—Prussian statesman, liberal aristocrat; Prime Minister and Minister of Foreign Affairs (June-September 1848), Oberpräsident of Western Prussia (from September 1848 to 1850).—69

Aulich, Lajos (1792-1849)—Hungarian revolutionary general (from March 1849), executed after the revolution was suppressed.—11, 100, 408

Aumale, Henri Eugène Philippe Louis d'Orléans, duc de (1822-1897)—son of Louis Philippe, King of the French, took part in the conquest of Algeria in the 1840s, one of the French troops' commanders.—83

B

Barbès, Armand (1809-1870)—French revolutionary, a leader of secret societies during the July monarchy; deputy to the Constituent Assembly in 1848; sentenced to life imprisonment for his participation in the popular insurrection of May 15, 1848; after amnesty in 1854 emigrated to Belgium.—81

Barco, Joseph, Baron von (1798-1861)—Austrian major-general, later lieutenant-field marshal; took part in the war against revolutionary Hungary (1848-49) and in the siege of Komorn (July 1849).—365

Barrot, Camille Hyacinthe Odilon (1791-1873)—French politician, before February 1848 leader of the liberal dynastic opposition; from December 1848 to October 1849 headed the Ministry that relied on a monarchist coalition.—85, 170, 191, 192, 323, 414

Bassermann, Friedrich Daniel (1811-1855)—German politician, represented the Baden Government in the Federal Diet during the 1848-49 revolution; deputy to the Frankfurt National Assembly (Right Centre).—48, 377, 417

Batthyány—participant in the revolution of 1848-49 in Hungary, commandant of Peterwardein.—278, 286, 293

Batthyány, Kazimir (Kázmér), Count von (1807-1854)—Hungarian statesman, liberal aristocrat, Minister of Foreign Affairs in the Hungarian revolutionary Government of Szemere (1849); after the suppression of the revolution emigrated to Turkey and then to France.—97

Batthyány, Lajos, Count von (1806-1849)—Hungarian politician, Prime Minister of Hungary (from March 17 to September 15, 1848), a moderate liberal leader; after the victory of the counter-revolution he was shot by decision of the Austrian court martial.—100, 239-40

Beaumarchais, Pierre Augustin Caron de (1732-1799)—French dramatist.—340

Bechtold, Arnold—typesetter in the Cologne printing works where the Neue Rheinische Zeitung was published.—516-19

Becker, Hermann Heinrich (1820-1885)—German lawyer and journalist, a leader of the Cologne Association for Workers and Employers, member of the Rhenish District Committee of Democrats, editor of the Westdeutsche Zeitung (from May 1849 to July 1850); member of the Communist League from 1850.—282, 490, 506, 516-19

Becker, Johann Philipp (1809-1886)—German revolutionary, participant in the democratic movement of the 1830s-40s in Germany and Switzerland and in the war against the Sonderbund; took an active part in the revolution of 1848-49; was in command of the Baden people's militia during the Baden-Palatinate uprising of 1849; prominent figure in the First International in the 1860s, and delegate to all its congresses; friend and associate of Marx and Engels.—482-83

*Bekk, Johann Baptist* (1797-1855)—Baden statesman, moderate liberal; Minister of the Interior from 1846 but he lost this post as a result of the spring 1849 revolutionary uprising in Baden.—55

*Bem, Józef* (1795-1850)—Polish general and prominent figure in the national liberation movement, participant in the Polish insurrection of 1830-31 and in the revolutionary struggle in Vienna in 1848. One of the commanders of the Hungarian revolutionary army (1848-49), he emigrated to Turkey after the defeat of the revolution.—9, 13, 17, 25, 26, 39, 59, 61, 94, 112, 113-14, 122, 124, 134, 146, 158-59, 168, 179, 182, 187, 188-90, 230, 232, 235, 236, 237, 238, 242, 243, 248, 252, 253, 256, 257, 270, 279-80, 287-89, 294, 304, 318-19, 331, 337, 344, 356, 367

*Benedek, Ludwig, von* (1804-1881)—Austrian general, took part in the suppression of the peasant uprising in Galicia in 1846 and of the national liberation movements in Italy and Hungary in 1848 and 1849; commander-in-chief of the Austrian army during the Austro-Prussian war of 1866.—253, 293, 303, 344, 365.

*Berends, Julius* (b. 1817)—owner of a printing works in Berlin, petty-bourgeois democrat, deputy to the Prussian National Assembly (Left wing) in 1848, deputy to the Second Chamber (extreme Left wing) in 1849; emigrated to America in 1853.—329

*Berg, Fyodor Fyodorovich, Count* (1790-1874)—Russian general, later field marshal; in 1849 carried out diplomatic missions at the Prussian and Austrian courts in connection with Russian participation in the war against revolutionary Hungary; Governor-General of Finland (1855-63); Deputy Governor of the Kingdom of Poland (1863-73).—398

*Berg, Philipp Karl Peter von* (1815-1866)—Prussian Catholic priest; in 1848 deputy to the Prussian National Assembly (Left Centre); in 1849 deputy to the Second Chamber.—137-38, 139

*Berger von der Pleisse, Georg, Baron*—Austrian lieutenant-colonel, staff officer of the 34th Infantry Regiment.—237

*Berger von der Pleisse, Johann, Baron* (1768-1864)—Austrian lieutenant field-marshal, later Master of Ordnance, took part in the wars against revolutionary and Napoleonic France (1793-1815); commandant of the Arad fortress (1844-49); after defending it for nine months, he surrendered the fortress to the Hungarian troops.—238

*Bernicki*—Polish army officer, took part in the revolution of 1848-49 in Hungary.—304

*Bès, Michelle Giuseppe* (1794-1855)—Piedmontese general, participated in the war against Austria in 1848 and 1849.—175, 176

*Bias*—45

*Bibesco, George Demetrius* (1804-1873)—ruler of Wallachia (1843-48), during the revolution of 1848 was obliged to resign and emigrate.—278

*Bilski*—Polish army officer, took part in the revolution of 1848-49 in Hungary. He was executed by the Austrians in 1849.—235

*Birck*—official of the Royal Government in Cologne.—496, 497

*Bischoffswerder, Johann Rudolf von* (1741-1803)—Prussian general and conservative statesman, exerted considerable influence on Prussia's home and foreign policy under Frederick William II.—419

*Bloudek, Bedřich* (d. 1875)—participant in the Slovak national movement of 1848-49 in the region of Dukla.—409

*Blum, Robert* (1807-1848)—German democrat, journalist, leader of the Left in the Frankfurt National Assembly; in October 1848 he participated in the defence of Vienna; was executed by court martial decision.—47, 48, 257

Czartoryski—son of Adam Czartoryski.—
78
Czartoryski, Adam Jerzy, Prince (1770-
1861)—Polish magnate; Russian
Foreign Minister (1804-06); head of
the Provisional Government during
the Polish insurrection of 1830-31,
later leader of Polish monarchist
émigrés in France.—78

D

Dahlen von Orlaburg, Franz, Baron
(b. 1779)—Austrian lieutenant-field
marshal, second chief of the 59th
Infantry Regiment.—284, 457, 458
Damjanich, János (1804-1849)—
Hungarian general, participant in the
1848-49 revolution in Hungary, supporter of Kossuth; after the revolution
was defeated, he was executed together with twelve other Hungarian
generals by the Austrian authorities on
October 6, 1849.—26, 123, 179, 233,
262, 282, 408
Deák, Ferencz (1803-1876)—Hungarian
politician, liberal aristocrat, supporter
of compromise with the Austrian
monarchy; Minister of Justice in the
Batthyány Government (March-
September 1848) and an initiator of
the Austro-Hungarian agreement of
1867 to transform the Empire into a
dual monarchy—Austria-Hungary;
leader of the Hungarian ruling
party.—240
Dembiński, Henryk (1791-1864)—Polish
general and prominent figure in the
national liberation movement, participant in the Polish insurrection of
1830-31, commander-in-chief of the
Hungarian revolutionary army (end of
January and February 1849) and then
of the Northern Theiss army; after the
defeat of the révolution emigrated
first to Turkey and then to
France.—11, 16, 58, 76, 78, 112, 144,
149, 181, 187, 188, 232-34, 245, 268,
269, 270, 272, 275, 286, 292, 300, 314,
401, 460
Deym, Moritz, Count (1805-1872)—
Austrian major-general, took part in

the war against revolutionary Hun-
gary in 1848 and 1849.—28, 110
Dietz, Johann Wilhelm—owner of the
Cologne printing press where the Neue
Rheinische Zeitung was published from
August 30, 1848.—516-18
Diez, Friedrich Christian (1794-1876)—
German philologist, founder of com-
parative study of the Romance lan-
guages, author of Grammatik der
romanischen Sprachen.—325
Dourlens—police commissioner in the
Faubourg St. Germain (Paris) in
1849.—526, 529
Dragich—Serbian army officer.—183
Drigalski, von—Prussian general, com-
mander of a division in Düsseldorf in
1848.—70, 432, 443
Dronke, Ernst (1822-1891)—German
journalist, at first "true socialist", later
a member of the Communist League
and an editor of the Neue Rheinische
Zeitung.—473, 490, 514, 516-19
Druey, Henri (1799-1855)—Swiss radical
statesman, took part in drafting the
1848 Constitution; member of the
Federal Council, President of the Swiss
Confederation in 1850.—45
Duchâtel—participant in the 1848-49
revolution in Hungary, general
in the Hungarian revolutionary
army, French by birth.—78, 124,
181, 187
Dufaure, Jules Armand Stanislas (1798-
1881)—French statesman, Orleanist;
Minister of the Interior (October-
December 1848, June-October 1849),
Minister of Justice (February 1871-
May 1873, March 1875-August 1876)
and Prime Minister (March-December
1876, September 1877-February
1879).—481, 526, 529
Duhamel, Alexander Osipovich (1801-
1880)—Russian general and diplomat, took part in suppressing the
Polish insurrection of 1830-31, carried
out special diplomatic missions in Moldavia and Wallachia in 1842 and
1849.—78, 305
Dumanski—Polish army officer, took
part in the 1848-49 revolution in
Hungary; executed by the Austrians in
1849.—235

Gustavus II Adolphus (1594-1632)—King of Sweden (1611-32) and general; headed the alliance of Protestant states during the Thirty Years' War; one of the Protestant unions founded in Germany in the 1830s was named after him.—321

Guyon, Richard Debaufre (1803-1856)— participant in the 1848-49 revolution in Hungary, general in the Hungarian revolutionary army, English by birth; after the defeat of the revolution emigrated to Turkey; in 1852 became a Turkish general known as Khourschid Pasha; fought in the 1853-56 Crimean war.—78, 285, 406

Gyurkovics—Austrian army officer, fought against revolutionary Hungary in 1848 and 1849.—273

## H

Habsburgs—dynasty of emperors of the Holy Roman Empire from 1273 to 1806 (with intervals), of Austria (from 1804) and of Austria-Hungary (1867-1918).—148, 397, 425

Hagen—Prussian lawyer, defended Korff at the trial held in Cologne on May 30, 1849.—522

Hám, Johann von (1781-1857)—Hungarian Cardinal, Lord Primate, in 1849 the Hungarian Government deposed him for high treason.—92

Hammerstein-Ecquord, Wilhelm, Baron von (1785-1861)—Austrian general, took part in suppressing the national liberation movement in Galicia and the Bukovina in 1848 and 1849.—152-53, 160, 186, 253, 262, 275, 280, 287, 293, 365

Hansemann, David Justus (1790-1864)— German capitalist, a leader of the Rhenish liberal bourgeoisie; Prussian Minister of Finance (from March to September 1848).—56, 69, 138

Harkort, Friedrich Wilhelm (1793-1880) —Prussian industrialist and liberal politician, deputy to the Prussian National Assembly in 1848 and 1849, then deputy to the Second Chamber (Centre), later Progressist.—88

Harney, George Julian (1817-1897) —prominent figure in the English labour movement, a Chartist leader (Left wing); editor of The Northern Star and Democratic Review, associate of Marx and Engels.—490

Hartmann—Düsseldorf forwarding agent.—429

Haschka, Lorenz Leopold (1749-1827)— Austrian poet, author of the Austrian state anthem.—107

Havas, Joseph—in 1849 imperial commissioner in Pest.—364

Hayde—Austrian major, took part in the war against revolutionary Hungary in 1848 and 1849.—279

Haydn, Franz Joseph (1732-1809)—Austrian composer.—107

Haynau, Julius Jakob, Baron von (1786-1853)—Austrian Master of Ordnance, took part in suppressing the 1848-49 revolution in Italy, commander of the Austrian troops in Hungary (1849 and 1850), initiated butchery of Hungarian revolutionaries.—280, 293, 317

Hecker—Prussian officer of justice, Public Prosecutor in Cologne (1848).—339, 340

Hegel, Georg Wilhelm Friedrich (1770-1831)—German philosopher.—421

Heine, Heinrich (1797-1856)—German revolutionary poet.—418, 446

Heinrich von Bordeaux (Henry V)—see Chambord, Henri Charles Ferdinand Marie Dieudonné d'Artois, duc de Bordeaux, comte de

Henry V—see Chambord, Henri Charles Ferdinand Marie Dieudonné d'Artois, duc de Bordeaux, comte de

Hess, Heinrich, Baron von (1788-1870) —Austrian lieutenant-field marshal, later field marshal; took part in suppressing the 1848-49 revolution in Italy; in 1854 and 1855 commander-in-chief of troops in Hungary, Galicia and the Danube principalities.—175, 253, 286, 401

Hexamer, Adolf (1801-1874)—editor of Die Reforme (Berlin), physician; attended the first and the second democratic congresses (Frankfurt am Main and Berlin), member of the Central

*Sophia* (1805-1872)—Archduchess of Austria, mother of Emperor Francis Joseph I.—49, 457

*Sossay, Anton, Baron von* (1790-1874)— Austrian major-general, later lieutenant-field marshal; commanded a brigade during the war against revolutionary Hungary in 1848 and 1849.—30, 245

*Stadion, Franz, Count von* (1806-1853)— Austrian statesman; an organiser of the struggle against the national liberation movement in Galicia and Bohemia; Minister of the Interior (1848-49).—147, 161, 308, 351, 397

*Stangier, Johann*—farmer in the Altenkirchen district, participant in the democratic movement in the Rhine Province.—339, 373, 375

*Stankovich, Johann*—prominent figure in the Serbian national movement, became a member of the local administration of the Voivodina in February 1849.—40

*Stanojevich, Milija*—commander of an auxiliary corps sent by the Principality of Serbia to support the Voivodina Serbs during the war against revolutionary Hungary in 1848 and 1849. —183

*Stedtmann, Karl* (1804-1882)—Prussian moderate liberal politician; deputy to the Frankfurt National Assembly (Centre); member of the commission for signing an armistice in Malmö (1848) and imperial commissioner in Schleswig-Holstein (September 1848 to March 1849).—516, 518, 520

*Stein*—member of the local administration in the Voivodina (1849).—40

*Stein*—a commander of the Voivodina Serbian troops that fought against revolutionary Hungary (1848-49).— 183

*Stephan* (1817-1867)—Austrian Archduke, Palatine in Hungary (1847-48); in September 1848 was appointed commander of the Hungarian army; sabotaged the struggle against Jellachich's counter-revolutionary troops; fled from Hungary.—239-41, 456

*Stephen Dushan* (c. 1308-1355)—King of Serbia (from 1331), recaptured a number of Greek and Slav lands from Byzantium, in 1346 was proclaimed "Tsar of the Serbs and the Greeks".— 31

*Stminger*—member of the local administration in the Voivodina (1849).—40

*Stojacković, Alex* (b. 1822)—Serbian writer and historian; official of the local administration in the Voivodina (February 1849).—40

*Stojakovich, Georg*—participant in the Serbian national movement in 1848 and 1849.—190

*Stratimirovich, Georg (Džordže)* (1822-1908)—leader of the Serbian national movement in the Voivodina, moderate liberal; commanded the Serbian units in the Austrian army, participated in the war against revolutionary Hungary (1848-49).—12, 78, 98, 116, 117, 332, 334, 344

*Strobach, Antonín* (1814-1856).—Czech lawyer and prominent figure in the national movement, held pro-Austrian views; President of the Austrian Imperial Diet (1848).—106

*Strotha, Karl Adolf von* (1786-1870)— Prussian general, conservative, deputy to the First Chamber, War Minister (November 1848 to February 1850).— 296-98, 320, 439

*Štúr, L'udovìt* (1815-1856)—Slovak philologist, literary critic and journalist, a representative of Slovak Renaissance and a leader of the national movement; opposing the Hungarian aristocracy's great-power policy, he fought against the Hungarian revolution of 1848-49 in alliance with the Austrians; later advocated pan-Slavism.—11, 62, 101, 119, 120

*Stürmer, Bartolomäus, Count von* (1787-1863)—Austrian diplomat, internuncio in Constantinople (February 1849).—41

*Stutterheim, Johann, Baron* (1803-1870)— Austrian colonel, later major-general, fought against revolutionary Hungary in 1848 and 1849.—113

*Stüve, Johann Karl Bertram* (1798-1872)—German politician, liberal; Minister of the Interior of Hanover (1848-50).—56

## INDEX OF LITERARY AND MYTHOLOGICAL NAMES

621

# INDEX OF QUOTED
# AND MENTIONED LITERATURE

WORKS BY KARL MARX AND FREDERICK ENGELS

Marx, Karl

*The Bourgeoisie and the Counter-Revolution* (present edition, Vol. 8)
— Die Bourgeoisie und die Kontrerevolution. In: *Neue Rheinische Zeitung* Nr. 165, 169, 170, 183; 10., 15., 16., 31. Dezember 1848.—453

*The Deeds of the Hohenzollern Dynasty* (this volume)
— Die Taten des Hauses Hohenzollern. In: *Neue Rheinische Zeitung* Nr. 294, 10. Mai 1849; *Deutsche Londoner Zeitung* Nr. 218, 1. Juni 1849.—437, 511-12

*Drigalski—Legislator, Citizen and Communist* (present edition, Vol. 8)
— Drigalski der Gesetzgeber, Bürger und Kommunist. In: *Neue Rheinische Zeitung* Nr. 153, 26. November 1848.—70, 432

*Further Contribution on the Old-Prussian Financial Administration* (present edition, Vol. 8)
— Weiterer Beitrag zur altpreußischen Finanzwirtschaft. In: *Neue Rheinische Zeitung* Nr. 229, 23. Februar 1849.—510

*The Hohenzollern General Plan of Reform* (this volume)
— Der Hohenzollern'sche Gesamtreformplan. In: *Neue Rheinische Zeitung* Nr. 246, 15. März 1849.—88, 125

*The Hohenzollern Press Bill* (this volume)
— Der Hohenzollern'sche Preßgesetzentwurf. In: *Neue Rheinische Zeitung* Nr. 252, 22. März 1849; Nr. 253, 23. März 1849.—69

*Lassalle* (present edition, Vol. 8)
— Lassalle. In: *Neue Rheinische Zeitung* Nr. 219, 237; 11. Februar, 4. März 1849.—339, 372

*The "Model State" of Belgium* (present edition, Vol. 7)
— Der "Musterstaat" Belgien. In: *Neue Rheinische Zeitung* Nr. 68, 7. August 1848.—42

*The Proceedings against Lassalle* (present edition, Vol. 8)
— Lassalle's Prozess. In: *Neue Rheinische Zeitung* Nr. 238, 6. März 1849.—339, 372

*Prussian Financial Administration under Bodelschwingh and Co.* (present edition, Vol. 8)
— Preußische Finanzwirtschaft unter Bodelschwingh und Konsorten. In: *Neue Rheinische Zeitung* Nr. 224, 17. Februar 1849.—510

*Public Prosecutor "Hecker" and the "Neue Rheinische Zeitung"* (present edition, Vol. 7)
— Der Staatsprokurator "Hecker" und die *Neue Rheinische Zeitung*. In: *Neue Rheinische Zeitung* Nr. 129, 29. Oktober 1848.—453

*Reply of the King of Prussia to the Delegation of the National Assembly* (present edition, Vol. 7)
— Antwort des Königs von Preußen an die Deputation der National-Versammlung. In: *Neue Rheinische Zeitung* Nr. 120, 19. Oktober 1848.—452

*The Revolutionary Movement* (present edition, Vol. 8)
— Die revolutionäre Bewegung. In: *Neue Rheinische Zeitung* Nr. 184, 1. Januar 1849.—454

*Speech on the Question of Free Trade* (present edition, Vol. 6)
— Discours sur la question du libre échange. Bruxelles, 1848.—4

*The Victory of the Counter-Revolution in Vienna* (present edition, Vol. 7)
— Sieg der Kontrerevolution zu Wien. In: *Neue Rheinische Zeitung* Nr. 136, 7. November 1848.—452-53

*Wage Labour and Capital* (this volume)
— Lohnarbeit und Kapital. In: *Neue Rheinische Zeitung* Nr. 264, 265, 266, 267, 269; 5., 6., 7., 8., 11. April 1849.—504, 510

Engels, Frederick

*The Economic Congress* (present edition, Vol. 6)
— Der ökonomische Kongreß. In: *Deutsche-Brüsseler-Zeitung* Nr. 76, 23. September 1847.—4

*The Frankfurt Assembly Debates the Polish Question* (present edition, Vol. 7)
— Die Polendebatte in Frankfurt. In: *Neue Rheinische Zeitung* Nr. 70, 73, 81, 82, 86, 90, 91, 93, 96; 9., 12., 20., 22., 26., 31. August, 1., 3., 7. September 1848.—359

*The Free Trade Congress at Brussels* (present edition, Vol. 6)
— The Free Trade Congress at Brussels. In: *The Northern Star* No. 520, October 9, 1847.—4

[*From the Hungarian Theatre of War*] (present edition, Vol. 8)
— [Vom ungarischen Kriegsschauplatz.] In: *Neue Rheinische Zeitung* Nr. 237, 4. März 1849, Zweite Ausgabe.—31

[*From the Theatre of War*] (this volume)
— [Vom Kriegsschauplatz.] In: *Neue Rheinische Zeitung* Nr. 247, 16. März 1849, Außerordentliche Beilage.—91

*Hüser* (present edition, Vol. 7)
— Hüser. In: *Neue Rheinische Zeitung* Nr. 1, 1. Juni 1848.—452

*A Magyar Victory* (present edition, Vol. 8)
— Sieg der Magyaren. In: *Neue Rheinische Zeitung* Nr. 238, 6. März 1849.—9, 31

[*A Magyar Victory*] (this volume)
— [Sieg der Magyaren.] In: *Neue Rheinische Zeitung* Nr. 271, 13. April 1849.—271

*The Struggle in Hungary* (present edition, Vol. 8)
— Der Kampf in Ungarn. In: *Neue Rheinische Zeitung* Nr. 212, 3. Februar 1849.—15

Marx, Karl and Engels, Frederick
*The First Trial of the "Neue Rheinische Zeitung"* (present edition, Vol. 8)
— Der erste Preßprozeß der *Neuen Rheinischen Zeitung*. In: *Neue Rheinische Zeitung* Nr. 221, 14. Februar 1849.—340, 452

Marx, Karl or Engels, Frederick
*The Agreement Assembly of June 15* (present edition, Vol. 7)
— Die Vereinbarungsversammlung vom 15. Juni. In: *Neue Rheinische Zeitung* Nr. 18, 18. Juni 1848.—313

*The Russian Note* (present edition, Vol. 7)
— Die russische Note. In: *Neue Rheinische Zeitung* Nr. 64, 3. August 1848.—311

*Speech from the Throne* (present edition, Vol. 8)
— Die Thronrede. In: *Neue Rheinische Zeitung* Nr. 234, 235; 1., 2. März 1849.—65, 86


WORKS BY DIFFERENT AUTHORS


Arndt, E. M. *Des Teutschen Vaterland*. In: Arndt, E. M. *Lieder für Teutsche im Jahr der Freiheit 1813*, Leipzig, 1813.—106, 251, 305

[*Bassermann an Brandenburg. Vom 2. Mai 1849.*] In: *Preußischer Staats-Anzeiger* Nr. 125, 8. Mai 1849.—417

Beaumarchais, P. A. C. *La folle journée, ou le mariage de Figaro.*—340

*Bible*
    *The Old Testament*
        Exodus.—67
    *The New Testament*
        The Revelations of St. John.—66

Bowring, J. [Speech at the Congress of Economists in Brussels, September 18, 1847.] Summary in: *Journal des économistes*, t. XVIII, Paris, 1847.—4

Brandenburg, F. W. [Speech at the sitting of the Second Chamber, April 2, 1849.] In: *Stenographische Berichte über die Verhandlungen der durch das Allerhöchste Patent vom 5. Dezember 1848 einberufenen Kammern. Zweite Kammer*. Berlin, 1849.—193

[*Brandenburg an Bassermann. Vom 3. Mai 1849.*] In: *Preußischer Staats-Anzeiger* Nr. 125, 8. Mai 1849.—417

Bürger, G. A. *Lenore*. Ballade.—87

*Ça ira* (French revolutionary song, end of the 18th century).—446

Cervantes Saavedra, Miguel de. *Coloquio de los perros* (from *Novelas ejemplares*).—443

Schumacher, B. G. *Heil Dir im Siegerkranz* (Prussian anthem).—322

Schwanbeck, A. *Erklärung.* In: *Kölnische Zeitung* Nr. 117, 17. Mai 1849.—450


*Vaticinium Lehninense* (Latin poem, end of the 17th century).—421

Virgil. *Bucolica.* Ecloga III. Palaemon.—66


Weerth, G. *Leben und Taten des berühmten Ritters Schnapphahnski.* In: *Neue Rheinische Zeitung*, August, September u. Dezember 1848, und Januar 1849.—517

Wolff, W. *Die Schlesische Milliarde.* In: *Neue Rheinische Zeitung*, März-April 1849.—510

## DOCUMENTS

*Allerhöchste Cabinetsorder vom 13. März 1833 betreffend den Ankauf subhastirter größerer Besitzungen polnischer Gutsbesitzer in der Provinz Posen für Rechnung des Staats und deren Wiederveräußerung an Erwerber deutscher Abkunft.* In: *Stenographischer Bericht über die Verhandlungen der deutschen constituirenden Nationalversammlung zu Frankfurt am Main.* Bd. 1-9. Frankfurt a. M. und Leipzig, 1848-1849, Bd. 2.—360

*Allerhöchste Kabinetsorder vom 6ten März 1821, betreffend die Strafgesetze und das Verfahren in den Rheinprovinzen bei Verbrechen und Vergehungen gegen den Staat und dessen Oberhaupt und bei Dienstvergehen der Verwaltungsbeamten.* In: *Gesetz-Sammlung für die Königlichen Preußischen Staaten.* Jg. 1821, Nr. 3.—128-29, 131

*Allgemeines Landrecht für die Preußischen Staaten.* Th. 1-2. Berlin, 1794.—52, 53, 54, 65, 126-29, 131

*An die Königl. Ober-Präsidenten.* Vom 7. Mai 1849. In: *Preußischer Staats-Anzeiger* Nr. 125, 8. Mai 1849.—417

*19. Armee-Bulletin.* Vom 30. Januar 1849. In: *Wiener Zeitung* Nr. 27, 1. Februar 1849; *Die Presse* Nr. 27, 1. Februar 1849.—160

*26. Armee-Bulletin.* Vom 3. März 1849. In: *Der Lloyd* Nr. 107, 3. März 1849, Abend-Ausgabe; *Die Presse* Nr. 54, 4. März 1849; *Wiener Zeitung* Nr. 54, 4. März 1849; *Kölnische Zeitung* Nr. 56, 7. März 1849, Zweite Ausgabe.—19-21, 24, 25

*27. Armee-Bulletin.* Vom 5. März 1849. In: *Der Lloyd* Nr. 110, 6. März 1849, Morgen-Ausgabe; *Die Presse* Nr. 55, 6. März 1849; *Wiener Zeitung* Nr. 55, 6. März 1849; *Kölnische Zeitung* Nr. 59, 10. März 1849, Beilage.—28-30, 115

*28. Armee-Bulletin.* Vom 14. März 1849. In: *Der Lloyd* Nr. 125, 15. März 1849, Morgen-Ausgabe; *Die Presse* Nr. 63, 15. März 1849; *Wiener Zeitung* Nr. 63, 15. März 1849.—113-14, 115, 117, 121

*33. Armee-Bulletin.* Vom 7. April 1849. In: *Der Lloyd* Nr. 169, 9. April 1849, Abend-Ausgabe; *Österreichischer Correspondent* Nr. 82, 11. April 1849, Beilage; *Die Presse* Nr. 85, 10. April 1849; *Wiener Zeitung* Nr. 84, 9. April 1849.—271-75, 284

*34. Armee-Bulletin.* Vom 9. April 1849. In: *Der Lloyd* Nr. 169, 9. April 1849, Abend-Ausgabe; *Österreichischer Correspondent* Nr. 82, 11. April 1849, Beilage; *Die Presse* Nr. 85, 10. April 1849; *Wiener Zeitung* Nr. 85, 9. April 1849, Abend-Beilage; *Wiener Zeitung* Nr. 85, 10. April 1849.—268-75, 284

35. *Armee-Bulletin.* Vom 24. April 1849. In: *Der Lloyd* Nr. 195, 24. April 1849, Abend-Ausgabe; *Österreichischer Correspondent* Nr. 94, 25. April 1849; *Die Presse* Nr. 98, 25. April 1849; *Wiener Zeitung* Nr. 97, 24. April 1849; *Wiener Zeitung* Nr. 98, 24. April 1849, Abend-Beilage.—352-54

*Bericht über die Verhältnisse vor Comorn.* In: *Wiener Zeitung* Nr. 79, 3. April 1849; *Die Presse* Nr. 80, 4. April 1849.—245-46

Böhm. *Kundmachung.* Vom 18. April 1849. In: *Wiener Zeitung* Nr. 93, 19. April 1849; *Der Lloyd* Nr. 187, 19. April 1849, Abend-Ausgabe (summary).—331
— *Kundmachung.* Wien, 24. April 1849. In: *Die Presse* Nr. 98, 25. April 1849; *Wiener Zeitung* Nr. 98, 25. April 1849.—363-64

*Censur-Edict vom 19. December 1788.* In: *Sammlung Preußischer Gesetze und Verordnungen....* Bd. 1, Abt. 7, Halle, 1823.—419

*Code civil*—see *Code Napoléon*

*Code d'instruction criminelle.* Paris, 1809.—372

*Code Napoléon.* Édition originale et seule officielle. Paris, 1808.—52-53

*Code pénal, ou code des delits et des peines.* Cologne, 1810.— 125, 126, 128, 129-31, 368, 383-85, 387

*Collection complète des lois, décrets, ordonnances, réglemens et avis du Conseil d'Etat,* par J. B. Duvergier, t. 35, année 1835. Paris, 1836.—50, 52, 65, 127

*Edict vom 9. Juli* [1788] *die Religions-Verfassung in den Preußischen Staaten betr.* In: *Sammlung Preußischer Gesetze und Verordnungen....* Bd. 1, Abt. 7, Halle, 1823.—419

*Entwurf der Constitutionsurkunde nach den Beschlüssen des Verfassungsausschusses.* Later published in: *Protokolle des Verfassungs-Ausschusses im Oesterreichischen Reichstage 1848-1849.* Leipzig, 1885.—47

*Entwurf des Strafgesetzbuchs für die preußischen Staaten, nebst dem Entwurf des Gesetzes über die Einführung des Strafgesetzbuches und dem Entwurf des Gesetzes über die Kompetenz und das Verfahren in dem Bezirke des Appellationsgerichtshofes zu Köln,* Berlin, 1847.—125, 126-31

*Der Erste Vereinigte Landtag in Berlin 1847.* Th. 1-4. Berlin, 1847, Th. 4.—50, 125-27, 128, 129-32

Ferdinand I. [Rescript of October 3, 1848.] In: *Wiener Zeitung* Nr. 275, 5. Oktober 1848; *Journal des Oesterreichischen Lloyd* Nr. 232, 6. Oktober 1848; *Sammlung der für Ungarn erlassenen Allerhöchsten Manifeste und Proklamationen, dann der Kundmachungen der Oberbefehlshaber der Kaiserlichen Armee in Ungarn,* 1. Heft. Ofen, 1849.—456

Franz Joseph I. [Manifesto attached to *Reichsverfassung für das Kaiserthum Oesterreich,* March 4, 1849.] In: *Reichsverfassung für das Kaiserthum Oesterreich sammt den Manifesten.* Wien, 1849.—263

*Freudige Nachricht.* In: *Agramer Zeitung,* 31. März 1849; *Der Lloyd* Nr. 157, 2. April 1849; *Österreichischer Correspondent* Nr. 77, 4. April 1849.—246, 249

— 1820.—420
— 1821.—127-29, 131
— 1848.—47, 52, 53-54, 86, 87, 129, 131, 140-42, 295, 321-22, 357, 370, 377, 385, 387, 430-32, 438, 440, 441, 445, 518
— 1849.—430-31, 438, 440-46, 465

Havas, J. *Proclamation* vom 22. April 1849. In: *Der Lloyd* Nr. 197, 25. April 1849; *Die Presse* Nr. 99, 26. April 1849.—364

[*Karlsbader Beschlüsse*. 1819.] In: Welcker, K. *Wichtige Urkunden für den Rechtszustand der deutschen Nation...*, Mannheim, 1844.—420

Kossuth, L. [*Proclamation* vom 7. April 1849.] In: *Pester Zeitung* Nr. 961, 25. April 1849; *Neue Oder-Zeitung*, beginning of May 1849.—407

*Landwehr-Ordnung*. Vom 21sten November 1815. In: *Gesetz-Sammlung für die Königlichen Preußischen Staaten*. Jg. 1816, Nr. 4.—195, 295-96, 412, 434, 466

*Motive zu dem Entwurfe eines Gesetzes, betreffend das Anheften von Anschlagezetteln und Plakaten in Städten und Ortschaften, sowie den Verkauf und das Vertheilen von Druckschriften oder bildlichen Darstellungen in öffentlichen Straßen* vom 2. März 1849. In: *Stenographische Berichte über die Verhandlungen der durch das Allerhöchste Patent vom 5. Dezember 1848 einberufenen Kammern. Zweite Kammer*. Beilage zum *Preußischen Staats-Anzeiger*. Bd. 1-2. Berlin, 1849.—50, 51, 65, 295

*Motive zu dem Entwurfe eines Gesetzes, betreffend das Recht, durch Wort, Schrift, Druck und bildliche Darstellung seine Gedanken frei zu äußern* vom 2. März 1849. In: *Stenographische Berichte über die Verhandlungen der durch das Allerhöchste Patent vom 5. Dezember 1848 einberufenen Kammern. Zweite Kammer*. Beilage zum *Preußischen Staats-Anzeiger*. Bd. 1-2. Berlin, 1849.—51, 65, 125-32, 295

*Motive zu dem Entwurfe eines Gesetzes zur Verhütung eines die gesetzliche Freiheit und Ordnung gefährdenden Mißbrauchs des Versammlungs- und Vereinigungs-Rechts* vom 2. März 1849. In: *Stenographische Berichte über die Verhandlungen der durch das Allerhöchste Patent vom 5. Dezember 1848 einberufenen Kammern. Zweite Kammer*. Beilage zum *Preußischen Staats-Anzeiger*. Bd. 1-2. Berlin, 1849.—50, 65, 125, 295

[Prussian Note of Brandenburg, April 28, 1849.] In: *Preußischer Staats-Anzeiger* Nr. 117, 30. April 1849.—377, 378

[Przyluski, L.] *Korrespondenz des Erzbischofs von Posen Przyluski mit dem Berliner Kabinet*. In: *Neue Rheinische Zeitung* Nr. 5, 7, 10, 14, 38, 39; 5., 7., 10., 14. Juni, 8., 9. Juli 1848. Also in: [Brodowski J., Kraszewski J., Potworowski G.] *Zur Beurtheilung der polnischen Frage im Großherzogthum Posen im Jahre 1848*, Berlin [1848].—359

*Reichsverfassung für das Kaiserthum Österreich*. Wien, 1849.—12, 47, 48, 105, 149, 261, 263

Ruge, A. *Wahl-Manifest der radicalen Reformpartei für Deutschland*. In: *Die Reform* Nr. 16, 16. April 1848.—34

*Sammlung Preußischer Gesetze und Verordnungen*, welche auf die allgemeine Deposital-, Hypotheken-, Gerichts-, Criminal- und Städte-Ordnung, auf das allgemeine Landrecht, auf den Anhang zum allgemeinen Landrechte und zur allgemeinen Gerichtsordnung, auf die landschaftlichen Credit-Reglements und auf Provinzial-

und Statutar-Rechte Bezug haben, nach der Zeitfolge geordnet von Carl Ludwig Heinrich Rabe, Bd. 1, Abt. 7, Enthaltend die Jahre 1782 bis 1789, Halle, 1823.—419

*Schluß Acte des wiener Congresses, vom 9. Juni 1815, und Bundes Acte oder Grundvertrag des teutschen Bundes, vom 8. Juni 1815. Beide...* vollst. hrsg. von D. Johann Ludwig Klüber. 2. Aufl., Erlangen, 1818.—420

*Stenographische Berichte über die Verhandlungen der durch das Allerhöchste Patent vom 5. Dezember 1848 einberufenen Kammern. Zweite Kammer.* Beilage zum *Preußischen Staats-Anzeiger.* Bd. 1-2. Berlin, 1849.—50-54, 65, 86-89, 125-43, 193, 295-98, 320-28, 330, 357, 358

*Stenographischer Bericht über die Verhandlungen der deutschen constituirenden Nationalversammlung zu Frankfurt am Main.* Bd. 1-9. Frankfurt a. M. und Leipzig, 1848-1849.—360, 377

*Verfassung des deutschen Reiches vom 28. März 1849. In: Verhandlungen der deutschen verfassunggebenden Reichsversammlung zu Frankfurt am Main.* Bd. 4. Frankfurt, 1849.—377, 378, 465

*Verfassungsurkunde für den Preußischen Staat.* Vom 5. Dezember 1848. In: *Gesetz-Sammlung für die Königlichen Preußischen Staaten.* Jg. 1848, Nr. 55.—47, 52, 86, 131, 135-38, 139-43, 295, 321-22, 357, 370, 387, 430-32, 440-46, 518

*Verhandlungen der constituirenden Versammlung für Preußen, 1848.* Bd. 1-8. Berlin, Bd. 9 (Suppl.-Bd.). Leipzig, 1849.—135, 138

*Verordnung, betreffend die Abberufung der preußischen Abgeordneten von der National-Versammlung zu Frankfurt a. M. Vom 14. Mai 1849.* In: *Neue Preußische Zeitung* Nr. 112, 16. Mai 1849.—438-39

*Verordnung, betreffend die Auflösung der zweiten und die Vertagung der ersten Kammer. Vom 27. April 1849.* In: *Gesetz-Sammlung für die Königlichen Preußischen Staaten.* Jg. 1849, Nr. 13.—430

*Verordnung, betreffend das Verfahren bei politischen und Pressvergehen in der Rheinprovinz und die Wiederherstellung des Rheinischen Strafrechts und Strafverfahrens bei politischen und Amtsverbrechen. Vom 15. April 1848.* In: *Gesetz-Sammlung für die Königlichen Preußischen Staaten.* Jg. 1848, Nr. 15.—54, 129

*Verordnung über den Belagerungszustand. Vom 10. Mai 1849.* In: *Gesetz-Sammlung für die Königlichen Preußischen Staaten.* Jg. 1849, Nr. 15.—431-32, 438, 440-45, 465

*Verordnung über die zu bildende Repräsentation des Volks. Vom 22ten Mai 1815.* In: *Gesetz-Sammlung für die Königlichen Preußischen Staaten.* Jg. 1815, Nr. 9.—420

*Verordnung über einige Grundlagen der künftigen Preußischen Verfassung. Vom 6. April 1848.* In: *Gesetz-Sammlung für die Königlichen Preußischen Staaten.* Jg. 1848, Nr. 11.—86, 385

*Verordnung über die Herstellung des Rheinischen Zivilgesetzbuchs in Betreff der Schließung der Ehe für die zum Bezirke des Rheinischen Appellations-Gerichtshofes gehörigen Landestheile des ehemaligen Großherzogthums Berg. Vom 15. April 1848.* In: *Gesetz-Sammlung für die Königlichen Preußischen Staaten.* Jg. 1848, Nr. 15.—129

*Verordnung über die Wahl der Preußischen Abgeordneten zur deutschen Nationalversammlung. Vom 11. April 1848.* In: *Gesetz-Sammlung für die Königlichen Preußischen Staaten.* Jg. 1848, Nr. 13.—438

*Verordnung wegen der künftigen Behandlung des gesammten Staatsschulden-Wesens. Vom 17ten Januar 1820.* In: *Gesetz-Sammlung für die Königlichen Preußischen Staaten.* Jg. 1820, Nr. 2.—420

*Wahlgesetz für die zur Vereinbarung der Preußischen Staats-Verfassung zu berufende Versammlung. Vom 8. April 1848.* In: *Gesetz-Sammlung für die Königlichen Preußischen Staaten.* Jg. 1848, Nr. 12.—86

Welden, F. *An die K. K. Armee in Ungarn.* Vom 17. April 1849. In: *Kölnische Zeitung* Nr. 95, 21. April 1849, Außerordentliche Beilage; *Der Lloyd* Nr. 183, 17. April 1849, Abend-Ausgabe; *Österreichischer Correspondent* Nr. 88, 18. April 1849; *Wiener Zeitung* Nr. 91, 17. April 1849.—316, 331, 349
— *Proclamation.* Vor Comorn, 30. März 1849. In: *Der Lloyd* Nr. 157, 2. April 1849, Abend-Ausgabe.—238-39

Windischgrätz, A. *An die Bewohner Ungarns.* Ofen, 11. März. In: *Wiener Zeitung* Nr. 64, 15. März 1849, Abend-Beilage.—120

— *Kundmachung.* Ofen, 21. März 1849. In: *Wiener Zeitung* Nr. 74, 27. März 1849, Abend-Beilage.—178
— *Proclamation.* Ofen, am 23. Februar 1849. In: *Pester Zeitung,* between February 24 and 27, 1849; *Wiener Zeitung* Nr. 51, 28. Februar 1849, Abend-Beilage; *Der Lloyd* Nr. 101, 28. Februar 1849, Abendblatt.—10
— *Proclamation.* Ofen, 8. März 1849. In: *Der Lloyd* Nr. 121, 12. März 1849, Abend-Ausgabe; *Wiener Zeitung* Nr. 61, 13. März 1849.—92
— *Verordnung.* Ofen, 8. März 1849. In: *Der Lloyd* Nr. 121, 12. März 1849, Abend-Ausgabe; *Wiener Zeitung* Nr. 61, 13. März 1849.—94
— *Verordnung.* Ofen, 10. März 1849. In: *Kölnische Zeitung* Nr. 66, 18. März 1849, Zweite Ausgabe.—118-19

Wrbna, L. *Bulletin.* Ofen, 5. April 1849. In: *Der Lloyd* Nr. 165, 7. April 1849, Abend-Ausgabe.—265
— *Kundmachung.* Vom 7. April 1849. In: *Allgemeine Zeitung* (Augsburg) Nr. 103, 13. April 1849; *Kölnische Zeitung* Nr. 90, 15. April 1849, Zweite Ausgabe; *Der Lloyd* Nr. 171, 10. April 1849, Abend-Ausgabe.—283

## ANONYMOUS ARTICLES AND REPORTS PUBLISHED IN PERIODIC EDITIONS

*Allgemeine Zeitung* (Augsburg) Nr. 65, 6. März 1849: *Oesterreich.*—27
— Nr. 65, 6. März 1849: *Wien, 3. März.*—24-25
— Nr. 65, 6. März 1849: *Pesth, 26. Febr.*—31
— Nr. 66, 7. März 1849: *Wien* (näheres über die Schlacht bei Kapolna).—38-39
— Nr. 68, 9. März 1849: *Wien, 5. März.*—58-60
— Nr. 72, 13. März 1849: *Abony bei Szolnok, 6. März.*—95
— Nr. 72, 13. März 1849: *Pesth, 8. März.*—95, 96
— Nr. 76, 17. März 1849: *Wien, 14. März.*—110
— Nr. 84, 25. März 1849: *Wien, 21. März.*—161
— Nr. 85, 26. März 1849: *Pesth, 21. März.*—167
— Nr. 88, 29. März 1849, Beilage: *Drei Monate des ungarischen Kriegs.*—187
— Nr. 91, 1. April 1849: *Prag, 25. März.*—229
— Nr. 92, 2. April 1849: *Pesth, 27. März.*—188, 233

— Nr. 166, 7. April 1849, Morgen-Ausgabe: *Wien, 6. April.*—262
— Nr. 171, 10. April 1849, Abend-Ausgabe: *Pesth, 8. April.*—284
— Nr. 173, 11. April 1849, Abend-Ausgabe: *Neuestes.*—287
— Nr. 181, 16. April 1849, Abend-Ausgabe: *Pest, 14. April.*—315
— Nr. 183, 17. April 1849, Abend-Ausgabe: *Semlin, 13. April.*—332
— Nr. 191, 21. April 1849, Abend-Ausgabe: *Neuestes.*—343
— Nr. 194, 24. April 1849, Morgen-Ausgabe: [Editorial.]—343

*Le Moniteur universel* No. 91, 1 avril 1849: [Assemblée Nationale. Séance du samedi 31 mars.]—192

*National-Zeitung* Nr. 116, 2. Mai 1849, Beiblatt: *Berlin, 1. Mai.*—394-95

*Neue Preußische Zeitung* Nr. 54, 6. März 1849: [Report in the section "Berliner Zuschauer".]—22
— Nr. 59, 11. März 1849, Beilage: *Votum über die wesentlichen Aufgaben der jetzt versammelten sogenannten Volksvertretung.*—66-68
— Nr. 64, 17. März 1849: *Jede Revolution.*—109
— Nr. 107, 10. Mai 1849: [Report in the section "Berliner Zuschauer".]—437

*Neue Rheinische Zeitung* Nr. 95, 6. September 1848: *Breslau, 29. August.*—517-18, 519
— Nr. 102, 14. September 1848: *Frankfurt, 12. September.*—518, 519
— Nr. 110, 23. September 1848: *Um Nachdruck wird gebeten! Proklamation!*—518-19
— Nr. 214, 6. Februar 1849: [Comments on Army Bulletin No. 19.]—160
— Nr. 221, 14. Februar 1849: *Der erste Preßprozeß der "Neuen Rheinischen Zeitung".*—340, 452
— Nr. 269, 11. April 1849: *Lemberg, im April.*—253, 262
— Nr. 277, 20. April 1849, Zweite Ausgabe: *Köln, 19. April.*—375
— Nr. 284, 28. April 1849, Außerordentliche Beilage: *Köln, 27. April.*—353
— Nr. 285, 29. April 1849, Zweite Ausgabe: *Berlin, 28. April.*—357
— Nr. 292, 8. Mai 1849: *Breslau, 4. Mai.*—410

*Oberschlesische Lokomotive*, between April 5 and 12, 1849: [Report from Ratibor, April 4, 1849.]—257-58

*Ost-Deutsche Post* Nr. 45, 13. März 1849: *Wien, 12. März.*—112
— Nr. 54, 23. März 1849: *Pesth, 20. März.*—152, 154
— Nr. 59, 29. März 1849: *Wien, 28. März.*—190
— Nr. 72, 13. April 1849: *Bukowina. Czernowitz, 4. April.*—289
— Nr. 73, 14. April 1849: *Pest, 11. April.*—293
— Nr. 74, 15. April 1849: *Mitrovic, 5. April.*—294
— Nr. 81, 24. April 1849: *Pesth, 21. April.*—355

*Die Presse* Nr. 83, 7. April 1849: *Pesth, 4. April.*—263-64
— Nr. 98, 25. April 1849: *Wien, 24. April.*—364

*La Presse*, 26 juillet 1849: [Item on Marx's stay in Paris.]—480

*Rosenberg-Kreuzburger Telegraph* Nr. 19, 1849: [Editorial Statement.]—70

*Schlesische Zeitung* Nr. 53, 4. März 1849, Erste Beilage: *Wien, 2. März.*—14

*Der Siebenbürger Bote* Nr. 22, 19. Februar 1849: *Nachrichten vom Kriegsschauplatz.*—26
— Nr. 24, 23. Februar 1849: *Hermannstadt, 22. Februar.*—62
— Nr. 30, 9. März 1849: *Mediasch, 7. März.*—146

*Wiener Zeitung* Nr. 62, 14. März 1849: *Agram.*—117
— Nr. 71, 24. März 1849: *Pesth.*—163
— Nr. 81, 5. April 1849: [Report from Vienna of April 4, 1849.]—252
— Nr. 82, 5. April 1849, Abend-Beilage: [Report in the section "Tagesbericht".]—254
— Nr. 82, 5. April 1849, Abend-Beilage: [Report from Transylvania.]—252
— Nr. 86, 10. April 1849, Abend-Beilage: *Siebenbürgen, 9. Apr.*—279
— Nr. 91, 16. April 1849, Abend-Beilage: [Report in the section "Ungarn".]—314
— Nr. 97, 23. April 1849, Abend-Beilage: [Report in the section "Wien".]—350
— Nr. 103, 30. April 1849, Abend-Beilage: *Wien, 29. April.*—397

*Zeitung des Osten,* after April 13, 1849: [Report from Posen of April 13, 1849.]—312

# INDEX OF PERIODICALS

heading contained a cross bearing the slogan "Forward with God for King and Fatherland!"—22-23, 65-69, 87-88, 109, 129, 193, 281, 437, 454, 466

*Neue Rheinische Zeitung. Organ der Demokratie*—a daily published in Cologne under the editorship of Marx from June 1, 1848, to May 19, 1849 (with an interval between September 27 and October 12, 1848); organ of the revolutionary-proletarian wing among the democrats during the 1848-49 revolution in Germany. Engels was among its editors.—13, 36-37, 65, 84-85, 108, 160, 262, 281, 295, 311, 340, 353, 357, 359, 372, 375, 410, 431-32, 437, 447, 449-50, 451, 454, 467, 473, 480, 489-90, 498, 503, 505, 509-12, 514-19, 521, 523-24

*Neue Zürcher-Zeitung*—a Swiss liberal newspaper published in German under this title in Zurich from July 1, 1821; from 1780 to 1821 came out under the title *Zürcher-Zeitung*.—44-45

*Oberschlesische Lokomotive*—a German newspaper published in 1849 in Rátibor (Racibórz).—257

*Ost-Deutsche Post*—an Austrian daily of the moderate liberals published in Vienna from 1848 to 1866.—112, 152, 154, 158, 190, 255, 265, 289, 293, 304, 307, 315, 355

*Österreichischer Correspondent*—a daily newspaper of the Austrian Government published in Vienna in 1848 and 1849 (from November 1848 to April 1849 in Olmütz).—9, 186, 246, 304

*Ostsee-Zeitung und Börsennachrichten der Ostsee*—a German daily published in Stettin (Szczecin) from 1835.—311

*La Patrie. Journal du commerce, de l'agriculture, de l'industrie, de la littérature, des sciences et des arts*—a daily published in Paris from 1841 to 1871; during the 1848 revolution voiced the views of the counter-revolutionary monarchist bourgeoisie (the so-called party of order) and later of the Bonapartists.—157

*Pester Zeitung*—a pro-Austrian daily published in German in Pest during the 1840s and the early 1850s.—10, 264

*Die Presse*—a liberal daily published in Vienna from July 1848 to 1896. In 1861 and 1862, when the newspaper held anti-Bonapartist views, it printed a number of articles and items by Marx.—246, 263, 364

*La Presse*—a daily published in Paris from 1836; in the 1840s, mouthpiece for the opposition to the July monarchy; in 1848 and 1849, organ of the moderate republicans, later a Bonapartist paper. From 1836 to 1857 it was edited by Émile Girardin.—480

*Preussischer Staats-Anzeiger*—a German newspaper founded in Berlin in 1819; from 1819 to April 1848 it was a semi-official organ of the Prussian Government; its title was changed several times.—69, 417, 464

*Die Reform. Organ der demokratischen Partei*—a newspaper of the German petty-bourgeois democrats published by Arnold Ruge and H. B. Oppenheim under the editorship of Eduard Meyen from April 1848 in Leipzig, from the summer of 1848 to the early 1850s in Berlin.—33-35

*Rheinische Zeitung für Politik, Handel und Gewerbe*—a German daily founded on January 1, 1842, as an organ of the Rhenish bourgeois opposition and published in Cologne till March 31, 1843. While edited by Marx (from October 15, 1842, to

March 17, 1843), the paper became a mouthpiece for revolutionary-democratic ideas, which led to its suppression. Engels was one of its contributors.—108

*Rosenberg-Kreuzburger Telegraph*—a German newspaper published in Rosenberg-Kreuzburg (Silesia) in 1849.—70

*Schlesische Zeitung*—a German daily published in Breslau (Wrocław) from 1742; the newspaper of the constitutional monarchists on the eve of and during the revolution of 1848-49.—14, 162

*Serbske Novine (Србске Новине)*—an official organ of the Serbian Government published in Belgrade from 1835.—41, 425

*Der Siebenbürger Bote*—a newspaper published in German in Hermannstadt (Sibiu), Transylvania, in 1848 and 1849.—62, 146

*Slavenski jug*—a Croatian pro-Austrian newspaper published in Agram (Zagreb) from 1848 to 1850.—116

*Slovenski pozornik*—a Slovak newspaper published in 1849.—300

*Der Spiegel. Zeitschrift für die elegante Welt, Mode, Literatur, Kunst, Theater*—an Austrian newspaper published in Pest from 1828.—315

*Staats-Anzeiger*—see *Preussischer Staats-Anzeiger*

*Südslavische Zeitung*—a weekly of the Croatian liberal monarchists published in German in Agram (Zagreb) from 1849 to 1852.—116, 184, 229

*Teutsches Volksblatt*—a German newspaper of moderate democrats published in Würzburg in the 1840s.—36, 37

*Trier'sche Zeitung*—a daily founded in Trier in 1757, appeared under this title from 1815; in the early 1840s voiced radical views, and later came under the influence of "true socialists"; during the 1848-49 revolution a democratic newspaper.—509, 514

*Triester Freihafen*—an Austrian newspaper published in Trieste.—462

*Vjestnik (Вѣстникъ)*—a Serbian newspaper published in Pest in 1848 and 1849, and later in Neusatz and Karlowitz.—425

*Der Volksfreund*—a German democratic weekly published in 1849 in Lemgo (Principality of Lippe-Detmold).—479

*Der Wächter*—a Swiss radical newspaper published in Murten (canton of Freiburg) from January 1849 and edited by Johann Kaspar Sieber.—43

*Der Wächter am Rhein*—a democratic newspaper published in Cologne in 1848 and 1849, edited by Carl Cramer.—450

*Der Wanderer*—a daily of the Austrian constitutional monarchists, published in Vienna from 1809 to 1866.—302, 335-36

*Westdeutsche Zeitung*—a democratic newspaper published in Cologne from May 25, 1849, to July 21, 1850, by Hermann Becker.—473

*Wiener Zeitung*—a daily organ of the Austrian Government published in Vienna from 1780 to 1931; had the subtitle *Kaiserlich-königlich privilegirte* (1800-06) or *Österreichisch kaiserliche privilegirte* (1807-47 and certain issues of 1848). There were a few supplements, among them *Abend-Beilage zur Wiener Zeitung.*—10, 92,

# 641

# SUBJECT INDEX

## A

*Absolutism*—68, 371, 453, 498
  See also *Monarchy, absolute*
*Agitation and propaganda*—50, 188, 326,
  365, 372-73, 386
*America*—217
*Aristocracy (nobility), French*—80
*Aristocracy (nobility), Hungarian*—40,
  186, 229-30, 299
*Army*
  — *Landsturm*—172, 182, 334, 416
  — revolutionary—181-82, 346, 349
*Army, Austrian*—148, 175-76, 231-33,
  304, 349, 411
*Army, English*—22-23
*Army, French*—170, 426, 463
*Army, German revolutionary* (in 1849)—
  463
*Army, Hungarian revolutionary* (in 1848
  and 1849)—181-82, 231-33, 319, 344-
  45, 346, 406, 459-61, 463
*Army, Piedmontese*—150-51, 175
*Army, Prussian*—22
  — as tool of reaction—69, 87-88, 195,
    402, 411-12, 416, 432, 464-65
  — civic militia (*Bürgerwehr*)—416,
    423
  — army reserve (*Landwehr*)—195-96,
    297-300, 411, 412, 414-16, 423,
    426, 434, 466
*Artillery*—234, 245, 284, 316, 423, 435
*Austria*
  — political system—47, 102, 105,
    116, 148

  — Constitution, constitutional ques-
    tion—47-49, 105, 107, 149, 246
  — finances, financial policy—94, 107,
    275, 303, 315, 345, 355, 364
  — national question—12, 105-07, 116
  — during the 1848-49 revolution—9,
    12, 31, 47, 102-07, 368, 378, 456,
    458
  — peasant movement—117, 123-24,
    289-90
  — and England—351, 463
  — and France—170
  — and Germany—47-49, 461-62
  — and Hungary, Hungarian national
    liberation movement—9-11, 14,
    15-16, 107, 133, 178, 254, 352, 353,
    368-69, 391, 397-98, 411, 424-25,
    455-62
  — and Italy—107, 247, 461-62
  — and Poland—461
  — and Prussia—257, 382, 394-95,
    419, 421
  — and Russia—17, 90, 94, 106, 113,
    134, 154, 158, 162, 182, 188-90,
    235-36, 237, 253, 279-80, 305,
    319, 331, 345, 365, 369, 382, 391,
    394, 398, 409, 414, 418
  — and Slavs, Slav question—12, 107,
    116-17, 124, 149, 246, 253, 307-09,
    456
  — and Turkey—73
  See also *Army, Austrian; Austro-
  Italian war of 1848-49; Revolution of
  1848-49 in Austrian Empire*

### Q

### R

Tsarism, Tsarist autocracy (as bulwark of
reaction in Europe)—391, 394-95, 398,
414-15, 419, 421, 440, 441, 462-63
Turkey—52, 73, 162
— and Austria—74
— and Hungary—162
— and Russia—162, 253, 262


U

United Diet in Prussia—87, 125, 143,
358, 387, 421
United States of America—4, 6-7
— and England—4
— Oregon conflict—4
See also America
Uprising, armed—49, 57, 140, 151, 157,
170, 171, 173, 175, 198, 234-35, 370
See also Campaign for Imperial Con-
stitution in Germany; June uprising of
Paris proletariat in 1848; Revolution,
proletarian


V

Value—218
— and productivity of labour—219-
20
— and cost of production—208
See also Exchange value
Vienna Congress of 1814-15 and Vienna
Treaties of 1815—127, 191, 192, 360,
395, 525
Voivodina, the—40, 98, 116, 147, 161,
244, 289, 307, 319, 332, 410
See also Serbs of the Voivodina


W

Wage labour—203
— as basis, condition and result of
development of capital—198, 203,
213-16, 218-20, 226, 228
— conditions for its existence—203
— distinction from previous forms of
labour—203
— as formally free labour—203
— antagonism between capital and
wage labour—198, 203, 213-15,
220-21

See also Exploitation; Labour
Wages
— as form of value (price) of labour
power—202-04, 209-10, 217, 227
— and reproduction of labour
power—209-10, 227
— laws of—209-10, 219-22
— minimum—210, 227
— as component of cost of production—209-10, 218
— as income of worker—220-21
— nominal and real—217-18, 220
— absolute and relative—216-21
— pay for compound, skilled labour
—227
— and price of commodity—209, 217
— and money—217
— and profit—217-18, 228
— and demand and supply of
labour—209, 216
— and employment of machinery—
217, 225-27
— and capitalist competition—225
— and competition among workers—
225-26
— and means of subsistence—217-18
Wallachia, Wallachians—189, 229, 237-
38, 242, 252-53, 263, 287, 311, 346
War, wars—173
— and bourgeoisie—191-92
— and revolution, revolutionary
movement—151, 170, 171, 172,
197, 198, 454, 461-63
— revolutionary—162, 171, 173, 455,
476
— people's, national—171-73, 175,
475
— national liberation—151, 171, 172,
197, 461-62
— guerilla—117, 151, 155, 159, 162,
171, 176, 241, 458
— civil—191-92
— colonial—4, 155
— world—198
See also Austro-Italian war of 1848-49;
Danish-Prussian war of 1848-50;
Napoleonic wars; National liberation war
of 1848-49 in Hungary; Wars of First
French Republic
Wars of First French Republic (end of
18th-beginning of 19th centuries)—
80, 139, 173, 419, 441

# GLOSSARY OF GEOGRAPHICAL NAMES [a]

| | | | |
|---|---|---|---|
| Acs | Asc | Esseg | Osijek |
| Agram | Zagreb | Felegyhaza | Kiskunfelegyháza |
| Altenburg | | Földvar | Dunaföldvár |
| (Wieselburg) | Mosonmagyaróvar | Friedek | Frýdek-Mistek |
| Alt-Orsova | Orşova | Friedland | Frydlant na |
| Aluta (Alt) | Olt or Oltul | | Ostravice |
| Andrichau | Andrychów | Fünfkirchen | Pécs |
| Arbegin | Egerbegy | Galatz | Galaţi |
| Bartfeld | Bardejov | Gnesen | Gniezno |
| Becse (Base) | Bečej | Gönyö | Gonyü |
| Becskerek | | Gran | Esztergom |
| (Nagy-Becskerek) | Zrenjanin | Gran (river) | Hron |
| Besenyö | Besenyötelek | Gross-Kikinda | Kikinda |
| Bielitz | Bielsko-Biala | Grosswardein | Oradea |
| Blasendorf | Blaj | Güns | Köszeg |
| Breslau | Wrocław | Hadersleben | Haderslev |
| Brody (Radziwilow) | Brody and | Hatzfeld | Timbolia |
| | Chervonoarmeisk | Hermannstadt | Sibiu |
| | (two towns) | Ibrail | Brăila |
| Budweis | České Budějovice | Ipolyság | Šahy |
| Cerevich | Čerević | Karánsebes | Caranşebeş |
| Crnja | Srpska Crnja | Karlowitz | Sremski Karlovci |
| Csacze | Čadca | Karlsburg | Tepenec |
| Czernowitz | Chernovtsy | Karlstadt | Karlovac |
| Dalja | Dalj | Karwin | Karvina |
| Debreczin | Debrecen | Kaschau (Kassa) | Košice |
| Demblin | Deblin | Klausenburg | Cluj |
| Dioszeg | Diosig | Kokel (Küküllö) | Tîrnava |
| Eipel | Ipoly or Ipel | Kokel (Küküllo) | |
| Eperies | Prešov | 1. Grosse Kokel | 1. Târnava Mare |
| Erlau | Eger | 2. Kleine Kokel | 2. Târnava Mică |

---

[a] This glossary includes geographical names occurring in Marx's and Engels' articles in the form customary in the German press of the time but differing from the national names or from those given on modern maps. The left column gives geographical names as used in the German original (when they differ from the national names of the time, the latter are given in brackets); the right column gives corresponding names as used on modern maps and in modern literature.— *Ed.*

| | |
|---|---|
| Kómlos | Sintana |
| Komorn | Komárom and Komárno (two towns) |
| Kosel | Koźle |
| Kremsier | Kroméřiž |
| Kronstadt | Braşov |
| Laczhaza | Kiskunlacháza |
| Lemberg | Lvov |
| Leopoldstadt | Leopoldov |
| Leutschau | Levoča |
| Leva | Levice |
| Loslau | Wodzisław-Sleynski |
| Losoncz | Lučenec |
| Lugos | Lugoj |
| Lundenburg | Břeclaw |
| Magyaros | Šieu-Magheruş |
| March | March or Morava |
| Margitfalva | Margecany |
| Mark-Schelken | Seica-Mare |
| Maros | Marosz or Mureş |
| Maros-Vásárhely | Tîrgu-Mureş |
| Masdorf | Tószeg |
| Mediasch | Mediaş |
| Mitrowitz | Mitrovica |
| Munkács | Mukačevo |
| Myslowitz | Mysłowice |
| Neograd | Nograd |
| Neudorf (Iglo) | Spišska Nova Ves |
| Neuhäusel | Nove Zámky |
| Neumarkt | Nowy Targ |
| Neusatz (Ujvidek) | Novi Sad |
| Neutitschein | Nový Tičin |
| Neutra | Nitra |
| Oedenburg | Sopron |
| Oderberg | Starý Bohumin |
| Ofen | Buda |
| Olmütz | Olomouc |
| O-Szöny | Szöny |
| Palotta | Varpalota |
| Pancsova | Pančevo |
| Pataj | Dunapataj |
| Peterwardein | Petrovaradin |
| Petrowian | Petrovany |
| Pettau | Ptuj |
| Plattensee | Balaton |
| Posen | Poznań |
| Prerau | Přerov |
| Pressburg (Pozsony) | Bratislava |
| Raab | Györ |

| | |
|---|---|
| Raab (river) | Rába |
| Radziwilow—see Brody | |
| Rátibor | Racibórz |
| Raycza | Rajcza |
| Reichenberg | Liberec |
| Rimaszombat | Rimavská Sobota |
| Rosenau | Rožnăva |
| Roterturm | Turnu Roşu |
| Sankt Thomas (Szent Tamas) | Srbobran |
| Schässburg (Segesvar) | Sighişoara |
| Schemnitz | Banska Štiavnica |
| Semlin | Zemun |
| Sillein | Žilina |
| Sissek | Sisak |
| Stettin | Szczecin |
| Stuhlweissenburg | Székesfehérvar |
| Sundewitt | Sundeved |
| Syrmien | Szerem |
| Szegedin | Szeged |
| Szegléd | Cegléd |
| Szent Peter | Dolnýpeter |
| Szerdahely | Mercurea |
| Temesvar | Timişoara |
| Teplitz | Teplice |
| Teschen | Česky Tešin (Czech) and Cieszyn (Polish), two towns |
| Theiss | Tisza |
| Theresiopel (Maria-Theresiopel) | Subotica |
| Tömös (Pass) | Predeal (Pass) |
| Törzburg | Bran |
| Törzburg (Pass) | Pasal Bran |
| Tot-Almas | Töalmás |
| Troppau | Opava |
| Turany | Turany nad Vahom |
| Tyrnau | Trnava |
| Verbasz | Vrbas |
| Verebély | Vráble |
| Vesprim | Veszprém |
| Waag (Vag) | Váh |
| Waitzen (Vacs) | Vác |
| Wallendorf | Spišske Vlachy |
| Werschetz (Versecz) | Vršac |
| Wieselburg—see Altenburg | |
| Zenta | Senta |
| Zombor | Sombor |